# ADVANCED MACROECONOMICS

## Fourth Edition

# The McGraw-Hill Series in Economics

# ADVANCED MACROECONOMICS

Fourth Edition

## David Romer

University of California, Berkeley

McGraw-Hill
Irwin

# McGraw-Hill
# Irwin

ADVANCED MACROECONOMICS, FOURTH EDITION

Published by McGraw-Hill, a business unit of The McGraw-Hill Companies, Inc.,
1221 Avenue of the Americas, New York, NY, 10020. Copyright © 2012 by
The McGraw-Hill Companies, Inc. All rights reserved. Previous editions © 2006, 2001,
and 1996. No part of this publication may be reproduced or distributed in any form or
by any means, or stored in a database or retrieval system, without the prior written
consent of The McGraw-Hill Companies, Inc., including, but not limited to, in any
network or other electronic storage or transmission, or broadcast for distance
learning.

Some ancillaries, including electronic and print components, may not be available to
customers outside the United States.

This book is printed on acid-free paper.

7 8 9  DOC 21 20 19 18 17 16

ISBN 978-0-07-351137-5
MHID 0-07-351137-4

Vice President & Editor-in-Chief: *Brent Gordon*
Vice President EDP/Central Publishing Services: *Kimberly Meriwether David*
Publisher: *Douglas Reiner*
Marketing Manager: *Dean Karampelas*
Managing Developmental Editor: *Christina Kouvelis*
Editorial Coordinator: *Alyssa Otterness*
Project Manager: *Robin A. Reed*
Design Coordinator: *Margarite Reynolds*
Cover Designer: *Studio Montage, St. Louis, Missouri*
Buyer: *Nicole Baumgartner*
Media Project Manager: *Balaji Sundararaman*
Compositor: *MPS Limited, a Macmillan Company*
Typeface: *9.25/12 Lucida Bright*
Printer: *R. R. Donnelley*

**Library of Congress Cataloging-in-Publication Data**

Romer, David.
   Advanced macroeconomics / David Romer. — 4th ed.
      p. cm.
   ISBN 978-0-07-351137-5
   1. Macroeconomics. I. Title.
HB172.5.R66 2012
339—dc22

2010040893

www.mhhe.com

To Christy

# ABOUT THE AUTHOR

**David Romer** is the Royer Professor in Political Economy at the University of California, Berkeley, where he has been on the faculty since 1988. He is also co-director of the program in Monetary Economics at the National Bureau of Economic Research. He received his A.B. from Princeton University and his Ph.D. from the Massachusetts Institute of Technology. He has been on the faculty at Princeton and has been a visiting faculty member at M.I.T. and Stanford University. At Berkeley, he is a three-time recipient of the Graduate Economic Association's distinguished teaching and advising awards. He is a fellow of the American Academy of Arts and Sciences, a former member of the Executive Committee of the American Economic Association, and co-editor of the *Brookings Papers on Economic Activity*. Most of his recent research focuses on monetary and fiscal policy; this work considers both the effects of policy on the economy and the determinants of policy. His other research interests include the foundations of price stickiness, empirical evidence on economic growth, and asset-price volatility. He is married to Christina Romer, with whom he frequently collaborates. They have three children, Katherine, Paul, and Matthew.

# CONTENTS IN BRIEF

# CONTENTS

# Chapter 3    ENDOGENOUS GROWTH                              101

# Chapter 4    CROSS-COUNTRY INCOME
             DIFFERENCES                                    150

# Chapter 5    REAL-BUSINESS-CYCLE THEORY                    189

# Chapter 6    NOMINAL RIGIDITY    238

# Chapter 7    DYNAMIC STOCHASTIC GENERAL-EQUILIBRIUM MODELS OF FLUCTUATIONS    312

# EMPIRICAL APPLICATIONS

# PREFACE TO THE FOURTH EDITION

Keeping a book on macroeconomics up to date is a challenging and never-ending task. The field is continually evolving, as new events and research lead to doubts about old views and the emergence of new ideas, models, and tests. The result is that each edition of this book is very different from the one before. This is truer of this revision than any previous one.

The largest changes are to the material on economic growth and on short-run fluctuations with incomplete price flexibility. I have split the old chapter on new growth theory in two. The first chapter (Chapter 3) covers models of endogenous growth, and has been updated to include Paul Romer's now-classic model of endogenous technological progress. The second chapter (Chapter 4) focuses on the enormous income differences across countries. This material includes a much more extensive consideration of the challenges confronting empirical work on cross-country income differences and of recent work on the underlying determinants of those differences.

Chapters 6 and 7 on short-run fluctuations when prices are not fully flexible have been completely recast. This material is now grounded in microeconomic foundations from the outset. It proceeds from simple models with exogenously fixed prices to the microeconomic foundations of price stickiness in static and dynamic settings, to the canonical three-equation new Keynesian model (the new Keynesian IS curve, the new Keynesian Phillips curve, and an interest-rate rule), to the ingredients of modern dynamic stochastic general-equilibrium models of fluctuations. These revisions carry over to the analysis of monetary policy in Chapter 11. This chapter has been entirely reorganized and is now much more closely tied to the earlier analyses of short-run fluctuations, and it includes a careful treatment of optimal policy in forward-looking models.

The two other chapters where I have made major changes are Chapter 5 on real-business-cycle models of fluctuations and Chapter 10 on the labor market and unemployment. In Chapter 5, the empirical applications and the analysis of the relation between real-business-cycle theory and other models of fluctuations have been overhauled. In Chapter 10, the presentation of search-and-matching models of the labor market has been revamped and greatly expanded, and the material on contracting models has been substantially compressed.

Keeping the book up to date has been made even more challenging by the financial and macroeconomic crisis that began in 2008. I have deliberately chosen not to change the book fundamentally in response to the crisis: although I believe that the crisis will lead to major changes in macroeconomics, I also believe that it is too soon to know what those changes will be. I have therefore taken the approach of bringing in the crisis where it is relevant and of including an epilogue that describes some of the main issues that the crisis raises for macroeconomics. But I believe that it will be years before we have a clear picture of how the crisis is changing the field.

For additional reference and general information, please refer to the book's website at **www.mhhe.com/romer4e.** Also available on the website, under the password-protected Instructor Edition, is the *Solutions Manual.* Print versions of the manual are available by request only—if interested, please contact your McGraw-Hill/Irwin representative.

This book owes a great deal to many people. The book is an outgrowth of courses I have taught at Princeton University, the Massachusetts Institute of Technology, Stanford University, and especially the University of California, Berkeley. I want to thank the many students in these courses for their feedback, their patience, and their encouragement.

Four people have provided detailed, thoughtful, and constructive comments on almost every aspect of the book over multiple editions: Laurence Ball, A. Andrew John, N. Gregory Mankiw, and Christina Romer. Each has significantly improved the book, and I am deeply grateful to them for their efforts. In addition to those four, Susanto Basu, Robert Hall, and Ricardo Reis provided extremely valuable guidance that helped shape the revisions in this edition.

Many other people have made valuable comments and suggestions concerning some or all of the book. I would particularly like to thank James Butkiewicz, Robert Chirinko, Matthew Cushing, Charles Engel, Mark Gertler, Robert Gordon, Mary Gregory, Tahereh Alavi Hojjat, A. Stephen Holland, Hiroo Iwanari, Frederick Joutz, Pok-sang Lam, Gregory Linden, Maurice Obtsfeld, Jeffrey Parker, Stephen Perez, Kerk Phillips, Carlos Ramirez, Robert Rasche, Joseph Santos, Peter Skott, Peter Temin, Henry Thompson, Matias Vernengo, and Steven Yamarik. Jeffrey Rohaly prepared the superb *Solutions Manual.* Salifou Issoufou updated the tables and figures. Tyler Arant, Zachary Breig, Chen Li, and Melina Mattos helped draft solutions to the new problems and assisted with proofreading. Finally, the editorial and production staff at McGraw-Hill did an excellent job of turning the manuscript into a finished product. I thank all these people for their help.

# INTRODUCTION

Macroeconomics is the study of the economy as a whole. It is therefore concerned with some of the most important questions in economics. Why are some countries rich and others poor? Why do countries grow? What are the sources of recessions and booms? Why is there unemployment, and what determines its extent? What are the sources of inflation? How do government policies affect output, unemployment, inflation, and growth? These and related questions are the subject of macroeconomics.

This book is an introduction to the study of macroeconomics at an advanced level. It presents the major theories concerning the central questions of macroeconomics. Its goal is to provide both an overview of the field for students who will not continue in macroeconomics and a starting point for students who will go on to more advanced courses and research in macroeconomics and monetary economics.

The book takes a broad view of the subject matter of macroeconomics. A substantial portion of the book is devoted to economic growth, and separate chapters are devoted to the natural rate of unemployment, inflation, and budget deficits. Within each part, the major issues and competing theories are presented and discussed. Throughout, the presentation is motivated by substantive questions about the world. Models and techniques are used extensively, but they are treated as tools for gaining insight into important issues, not as ends in themselves.

The first four chapters are concerned with growth. The analysis focuses on two fundamental questions: Why are some economies so much richer than others, and what accounts for the huge increases in real incomes over time? Chapter 1 is devoted to the Solow growth model, which is the basic reference point for almost all analyses of growth. The Solow model takes technological progress as given and investigates the effects of the division of output between consumption and investment on capital accumulation and growth. The chapter presents and analyzes the model and assesses its ability to answer the central questions concerning growth.

Chapter 2 relaxes the Solow model's assumption that the saving rate is exogenous and fixed. It covers both a model where the set of households in

1

the economy is fixed (the Ramsey model) and one where there is turnover (the Diamond model).

Chapter 3 presents the new growth theory. It begins with models where technological progress arises from resources being devoted to the development of new ideas, but where the division of resources between the production of ideas and the production of conventional goods is taken as given. It then considers the determinants of that division.

Chapter 4 focuses specifically on the sources of the enormous differences in average incomes across countries. This material, which is heavily empirical, emphasizes two issues. The first is the contribution of variations in the accumulation of physical and human capital and in output for given quantities of capital to cross-country income differences. The other is the determinants of those variations.

Chapters 5 through 7 are devoted to short-run fluctuations—the year-to-year and quarter-to-quarter ups and downs of employment, unemployment, and output. Chapter 5 investigates models of fluctuations where there are no imperfections, externalities, or missing markets and where the economy is subject only to real disturbances. This presentation of real-business-cycle theory considers both a baseline model whose mechanics are fairly transparent and a more sophisticated model that incorporates additional important features of fluctuations.

Chapters 6 and 7 then turn to Keynesian models of fluctuations. These models are based on sluggish adjustment of nominal prices and wages, and emphasize monetary as well as real disturbances. Chapter 6 focuses on basic features of price stickiness. It investigates baseline models where price stickiness is exogenous and the microeconomic foundations of price stickiness in static settings. Chapter 7 turns to dynamics. It first examines the implications of alternative assumptions about price adjustment in dynamic settings. It then turns to dynamic stochastic general-equilibrium models of fluctuations with price stickiness—that is, fully specified general-equilibrium models of fluctuations that incorporate incomplete nominal price adjustment.

The analysis in the first seven chapters suggests that the behavior of consumption and investment is central to both growth and fluctuations. Chapters 8 and 9 therefore examine the determinants of consumption and investment in more detail. In each case, the analysis begins with a baseline model and then considers alternative views. For consumption, the baseline is the permanent-income hypothesis; for investment, it is $q$ theory.

Chapter 10 turns to the labor market. It focuses on the determinants of an economy's natural rate of unemployment. The chapter also investigates the impact of fluctuations in labor demand on real wages and employment. The main theories considered are efficiency-wage theories, contracting theories, and search and matching models.

The final two chapters are devoted to macroeconomic policy. Chapter 11 investigates monetary policy and inflation. It starts by explaining the central role of money growth in causing inflation and by investigating the effects of money growth. It then considers optimal monetary policy. This analysis begins with the microeconomic foundations of the appropriate objective for policy, proceeds to the analysis of optimal policy in backward-looking and forward-looking models, and concludes with a discussion of a range of issues in the conduct of policy. The final sections of the chapter examine how excessive inflation can arise either from a short-run output-inflation tradeoff or from governments' need for revenue from money creation.

Chapter 12 is concerned with fiscal policy and budget deficits. The first part of the chapter describes the government's budget constraint and investigates two baseline views of deficits: Ricardian equivalence and tax-smoothing. Most of the remainder of the chapter investigates theories of the sources of deficits. In doing so, it provides an introduction to the use of economic tools to study politics.

Finally, a brief epilogue discusses the macroeconomic and financial crisis that began in 2007 and worsened dramatically in the fall of 2008. The focus is on the major issues that the crisis is likely to raise for the field of macroeconomics.[1]

Macroeconomics is both a theoretical and an empirical subject. Because of this, the presentation of the theories is supplemented with examples of relevant empirical work. Even more so than with the theoretical sections, the purpose of the empirical material is not to provide a survey of the literature; nor is it to teach econometric techniques. Instead, the goal is to illustrate some of the ways that macroeconomic theories can be applied and tested. The presentation of this material is for the most part fairly intuitive and presumes no more knowledge of econometrics than a general familiarity with regressions. In a few places where it can be done naturally, the empirical material includes discussions of the ideas underlying more advanced econometric techniques.

Each chapter concludes with a set of problems. The problems range from relatively straightforward variations on the ideas in the text to extensions that tackle important issues. The problems thus serve both as a way for readers to strengthen their understanding of the material and as a compact way of presenting significant extensions of the ideas in the text.

The fact that the book is an *advanced* introduction to macroeconomics has two main consequences. The first is that the book uses a series of formal models to present and analyze the theories. Models identify particular

---

[1] The chapters are largely independent. The growth and fluctuations sections are almost entirely self-contained (although Chapter 5 builds moderately on Part A of Chapter 2). There is also considerable independence among the chapters in each section. Chapters 2, 3, and 4 can be covered in any order, and models of price stickiness (Chapters 6 and 7) can be covered either before or after real-business-cycle theory (Chapter 5). Finally, the last five chapters are largely self-contained. The main exception is that Chapter 11 on monetary policy builds on the analysis of models of fluctuations in Chapter 7. In addition, Chapter 8 relies moderately on Chapter 2 and Chapter 10 relies moderately on Chapter 6.

features of reality and study their consequences in isolation. They thereby allow us to see clearly how different elements of the economy interact and what their implications are. As a result, they provide a rigorous way of investigating whether a proposed theory can answer a particular question and whether it generates additional predictions.

The book contains literally dozens of models. The main reason for this multiplicity is that we are interested in many issues. Features of the economy that are crucial to one issue may be unimportant to others. Money, for example, is almost surely central to inflation but not to long-run growth. Incorporating money into models of growth would only obscure the analysis. Thus instead of trying to build a single model to analyze all the issues we are interested in, the book develops a series of models.

An additional reason for the multiplicity of models is that there is considerable disagreement about the answers to many of the questions we will be examining. When there is disagreement, the book presents the leading views and discusses their strengths and weaknesses. Because different theories emphasize different features of the economy, again it is more enlightening to investigate distinct models than to build one model incorporating all the features emphasized by the different views.

The second consequence of the book's advanced level is that it presumes some background in mathematics and economics. Mathematics provides compact ways of expressing ideas and powerful tools for analyzing them. The models are therefore mainly presented and analyzed mathematically. The key mathematical requirements are a thorough understanding of single-variable calculus and an introductory knowledge of multivariable calculus. Tools such as functions, logarithms, derivatives and partial derivatives, maximization subject to constraint, and Taylor-series approximations are used relatively freely. Knowledge of the basic ideas of probability—random variables, means, variances, covariances, and independence—is also assumed.

No mathematical background beyond this level is needed. More advanced tools (such as simple differential equations, the calculus of variations, and dynamic programming) are used sparingly, and they are explained as they are used. Indeed, since mathematical techniques are essential to further study and research in macroeconomics, models are sometimes analyzed in greater detail than is otherwise needed in order to illustrate the use of a particular method.

In terms of economics, the book assumes an understanding of microeconomics through the intermediate level. Familiarity with such ideas as profit maximization and utility maximization, supply and demand, equilibrium, efficiency, and the welfare properties of competitive equilibria is presumed. Little background in macroeconomics itself is absolutely necessary. Readers with no prior exposure to macroeconomics, however, are likely to find some of the concepts and terminology difficult, and to find that the pace is rapid. These readers may wish to review an intermediate macroeconomics text before beginning the book, or to study such a book in conjunction with this one.

The book was designed for first-year graduate courses in macroeconomics. But it can be used (either on its own or in conjunction with an intermediate text) for students with strong backgrounds in mathematics and economics in professional schools and advanced undergraduate programs. It can also provide a tour of the field for economists and others working in areas outside macroeconomics.

# Chapter 1
# THE SOLOW GROWTH MODEL

## 1.1 Some Basic Facts about Economic Growth

Over the past few centuries, standards of living in industrialized countries have reached levels almost unimaginable to our ancestors. Although comparisons are difficult, the best available evidence suggests that average real incomes today in the United States and Western Europe are between 10 and 30 times larger than a century ago, and between 50 and 300 times larger than two centuries ago.[1]

Moreover, worldwide growth is far from constant. Growth has been rising over most of modern history. Average growth rates in the industrialized countries were higher in the twentieth century than in the nineteenth, and higher in the nineteenth than in the eighteenth. Further, average incomes on the eve of the Industrial Revolution even in the wealthiest countries were not dramatically above subsistence levels; this tells us that average growth over the millennia before the Industrial Revolution must have been very, very low.

One important exception to this general pattern of increasing growth is the *productivity growth slowdown*. Average annual growth in output per person in the United States and other industrialized countries from the early 1970s to the mid-1990s was about a percentage point below its earlier level. The data since then suggest a rebound in productivity growth, at least in the United States. How long the rebound will last and how widespread it will be are not yet clear.

---

[1] Maddison (2006) reports and discusses basic data on average real incomes over modern history. Most of the uncertainty about the extent of long-term growth concerns the behavior not of nominal income, but of the price indexes needed to convert those figures into estimates of real income. Adjusting for quality changes and for the introduction of new goods is conceptually and practically difficult, and conventional price indexes do not make these adjustments well. See Nordhaus (1997) and Boskin, Dulberger, Gordon, Griliches, and Jorgenson (1998) for discussions of the issues involved and analyses of the biases in conventional price indexes.

There are also enormous differences in standards of living across parts of the world. Average real incomes in such countries as the United States, Germany, and Japan appear to exceed those in such countries as Bangladesh and Kenya by a factor of about 20.[2] As with worldwide growth, cross-country income differences are not immutable. Growth in individual countries often differs considerably from average worldwide growth; that is, there are often large changes in countries' relative incomes.

The most striking examples of large changes in relative incomes are *growth miracles* and *growth disasters*. Growth miracles are episodes where growth in a country far exceeds the world average over an extended period, with the result that the country moves rapidly up the world income distribution. Some prominent growth miracles are Japan from the end of World War II to around 1990, the newly industrializing countries (NICs) of East Asia (South Korea, Taiwan, Singapore, and Hong Kong) starting around 1960, and China starting around 1980. Average incomes in the NICs, for example, have grown at an average annual rate of over 5 percent since 1960. As a result, their average incomes relative to that of the United States have more than tripled.

Growth disasters are episodes where a country's growth falls far short of the world average. Two very different examples of growth disasters are Argentina and many of the countries of sub-Saharan Africa. In 1900, Argentina's average income was only slightly behind those of the world's leaders, and it appeared poised to become a major industrialized country. But its growth performance since then has been dismal, and it is now near the middle of the world income distribution. Sub-Saharan African countries such as Chad, Ghana, and Mozambique have been extremely poor throughout their histories and have been unable to obtain any sustained growth in average incomes. As a result, their average incomes have remained close to subsistence levels while average world income has been rising steadily.

Other countries exhibit more complicated growth patterns. Côte d'Ivoire was held up as the growth model for Africa through the 1970s. From 1960 to 1978, real income per person grew at an average annual rate of 3.2 percent. But in the three decades since then, its average income has not increased at all, and it is now lower relative to that of the United States than it was in 1960. To take another example, average growth in Mexico was very high in the 1950s, 1960s, and 1970s, negative in most of the 1980s, and moderate— with a brief but severe interruption in the mid-1990s—since then.

Over the whole of the modern era, cross-country income differences have widened on average. The fact that average incomes in the richest countries at the beginning of the Industrial Revolution were not far above subsistence

---

[2] Comparisons of real incomes across countries are far from straightforward, but are much easier than comparisons over extended periods of time. The basic source for cross-country data on real income is the Penn World Tables. Documentation of these data and the most recent figures are available at http://pwt.econ.upenn.edu/.

means that the overall dispersion of average incomes across different parts of the world must have been much smaller than it is today (Pritchett, 1997). Over the past few decades, however, there has been no strong tendency either toward continued divergence or toward convergence.

The implications of the vast differences in standards of living over time and across countries for human welfare are enormous. The differences are associated with large differences in nutrition, literacy, infant mortality, life expectancy, and other direct measures of well-being. And the welfare consequences of long-run growth swamp any possible effects of the short-run fluctuations that macroeconomics traditionally focuses on. During an average recession in the United States, for example, real income per person falls by a few percent relative to its usual path. In contrast, the productivity growth slowdown reduced real income per person in the United States by about 25 percent relative to what it otherwise would have been. Other examples are even more startling. If real income per person in the Philippines continues to grow at its average rate for the period 1960–2001 of 1.5 percent, it will take 150 years for it to reach the current U.S. level. If it achieves 3 percent growth, the time will be reduced to 75 years. And if it achieves 5 percent growth, as the NICs have done, the process will take only 45 years. To quote Robert Lucas (1988), "Once one starts to think about [economic growth], it is hard to think about anything else."

The first four chapters of this book are therefore devoted to economic growth. We will investigate several models of growth. Although we will examine the models' mechanics in considerable detail, our goal is to learn what insights they offer concerning worldwide growth and income differences across countries. Indeed, the ultimate objective of research on economic growth is to determine whether there are possibilities for raising overall growth or bringing standards of living in poor countries closer to those in the world leaders.

This chapter focuses on the model that economists have traditionally used to study these issues, the Solow growth model.[3] The Solow model is the starting point for almost all analyses of growth. Even models that depart fundamentally from Solow's are often best understood through comparison with the Solow model. Thus understanding the model is essential to understanding theories of growth.

The principal conclusion of the Solow model is that the accumulation of physical capital cannot account for either the vast growth over time in output per person or the vast geographic differences in output per person. Specifically, suppose that capital accumulation affects output through the conventional channel that capital makes a direct contribution to production, for which it is paid its marginal product. Then the Solow model

---

[3] The Solow model (which is sometimes known as the Solow–Swan model) was developed by Robert Solow (Solow, 1956) and T. W. Swan (Swan, 1956).

implies that the differences in real incomes that we are trying to understand are far too large to be accounted for by differences in capital inputs.
The model treats other potential sources of differences in real incomes as
either exogenous and thus not explained by the model (in the case of technological progress, for example) or absent altogether (in the case of positive
externalities from capital, for example). Thus to address the central questions of growth theory, we must move beyond the Solow model.

Chapters 2 through 4 therefore extend and modify the Solow model.
Chapter 2 investigates the determinants of saving and investment. The
Solow model has no optimization in it; it takes the saving rate as exogenous
and constant. Chapter 2 presents two models that make saving endogenous
and potentially time-varying. In the first, saving and consumption decisions
are made by a fixed set of infinitely lived households; in the second, the
decisions are made by overlapping generations of households with finite
horizons.

Relaxing the Solow model's assumption of a constant saving rate has
three advantages. First, and most important for studying growth, it demonstrates that the Solow model's conclusions about the central questions of
growth theory do not hinge on its assumption of a fixed saving rate. Second,
it allows us to consider welfare issues. A model that directly specifies relations among aggregate variables provides no way of judging whether some
outcomes are better or worse than others: without individuals in the model,
we cannot say whether different outcomes make individuals better or worse
off. The infinite-horizon and overlapping-generations models are built up
from the behavior of individuals, and can therefore be used to discuss welfare issues. Third, infinite-horizon and overlapping-generations models are
used to study many issues in economics other than economic growth; thus
they are valuable tools.

Chapters 3 and 4 investigate more fundamental departures from the
Solow model. Their models, in contrast to Chapter 2's, provide different
answers than the Solow model to the central questions of growth theory.
Chapter 3 departs from the Solow model's treatment of technological progress as exogenous; it assumes instead that it is the result of the allocation of resources to the creation of new technologies. We will investigate
the implications of such *endogenous technological progress* for economic
growth and the determinants of the allocation of resources to innovative
activities.

The main conclusion of this analysis is that endogenous technological
progress is almost surely central to worldwide growth but probably has little to do with cross-country income differences. Chapter 4 therefore focuses
specifically on those differences. We will find that understanding them requires considering two new factors: variation in human as well as physical
capital, and variation in productivity not stemming from variation in technology. Chapter 4 explores both how those factors can help us understand

the enormous differences in average incomes across countries and potential sources of variation in those factors.

We now turn to the Solow model.

# 1.2   Assumptions

## Inputs and Output

The Solow model focuses on four variables: output ($Y$), capital ($K$), labor ($L$), and "knowledge" or the "effectiveness of labor" ($A$). At any time, the economy has some amounts of capital, labor, and knowledge, and these are combined to produce output. The production function takes the form

$$Y(t) = F(K(t), A(t)L(t)), \tag{1.1}$$

where $t$ denotes time.

Notice that time does not enter the production function directly, but only through $K$, $L$, and $A$. That is, output changes over time only if the inputs to production change. In particular, the amount of output obtained from given quantities of capital and labor rises over time—there is technological progress—only if the amount of knowledge increases.

Notice also that $A$ and $L$ enter multiplicatively. $AL$ is referred to as *effective labor,* and technological progress that enters in this fashion is known as *labor-augmenting* or *Harrod-neutral.*[4] This way of specifying how $A$ enters, together with the other assumptions of the model, will imply that the ratio of capital to output, $K/Y$, eventually settles down. In practice, capital-output ratios do not show any clear upward or downward trend over extended periods. In addition, building the model so that the ratio is eventually constant makes the analysis much simpler. Assuming that $A$ multiplies $L$ is therefore very convenient.

The central assumptions of the Solow model concern the properties of the production function and the evolution of the three inputs into production (capital, labor, and knowledge) over time. We discuss each in turn.

## Assumptions Concerning the Production Function

The model's critical assumption concerning the production function is that it has constant returns to scale in its two arguments, capital and effective labor. That is, doubling the quantities of capital and effective labor (for example, by doubling $K$ and $L$ with $A$ held fixed) doubles the amount produced.

---

[4] If knowledge enters in the form $Y = F(AK, L)$, technological progress is *capital-augmenting.* If it enters in the form $Y = AF(K, L)$, technological progress is *Hicks-neutral.*

More generally, multiplying both arguments by any nonnegative constant $c$ causes output to change by the same factor:

$$F(cK,cAL) = cF(K,AL) \qquad \text{for all } c \geq 0. \tag{1.2}$$

The assumption of constant returns can be thought of as a combination of two separate assumptions. The first is that the economy is big enough that the gains from specialization have been exhausted. In a very small economy, there are likely to be enough possibilities for further specialization that doubling the amounts of capital and labor more than doubles output. The Solow model assumes, however, that the economy is sufficiently large that, if capital and labor double, the new inputs are used in essentially the same way as the existing inputs, and so output doubles.

The second assumption is that inputs other than capital, labor, and knowledge are relatively unimportant. In particular, the model neglects land and other natural resources. If natural resources are important, doubling capital and labor could less than double output. In practice, however, as Section 1.8 describes, the availability of natural resources does not appear to be a major constraint on growth. Assuming constant returns to capital and labor alone therefore appears to be a reasonable approximation.

The assumption of constant returns allows us to work with the production function in *intensive form*. Setting $c = 1/AL$ in equation (1.2) yields

$$F\left(\frac{K}{AL},1\right) = \frac{1}{AL}F(K,AL). \tag{1.3}$$

Here $K/AL$ is the amount of capital per unit of effective labor, and $F(K,AL)/AL$ is $Y/AL$, output per unit of effective labor. Define $k = K/AL$, $y = Y/AL$, and $f(k) = F(k,1)$. Then we can rewrite (1.3) as

$$y = f(k). \tag{1.4}$$

That is, we can write output per unit of effective labor as a function of capital per unit of effective labor.

These new variables, $k$ and $y$, are not of interest in their own right. Rather, they are tools for learning about the variables we are interested in. As we will see, the easiest way to analyze the model is to focus on the behavior of $k$ rather than to directly consider the behavior of the two arguments of the production function, $K$ and $AL$. For example, we will determine the behavior of output per worker, $Y/L$, by writing it as $A(Y/AL)$, or $Af(k)$, and determining the behavior of $A$ and $k$.

To see the intuition behind (1.4), think of dividing the economy into $AL$ small economies, each with 1 unit of effective labor and $K/AL$ units of capital. Since the production function has constant returns, each of these small economies produces $1/AL$ as much as is produced in the large, undivided economy. Thus the amount of output per unit of effective labor depends only on the quantity of capital per unit of effective labor, and not on the overall size of the economy. This is expressed mathematically in equation (1.4).

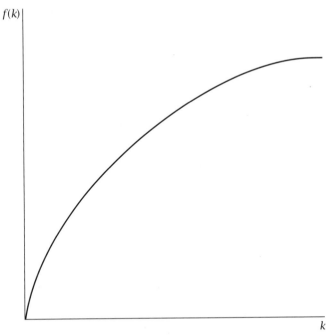

**FIGURE 1.1   An example of a production function**

The intensive-form production function, $f(k)$, is assumed to satisfy $f(0) = 0$, $f'(k) > 0$, $f''(k) < 0$.[5] Since $F(K,AL)$ equals $ALf(K/AL)$, it follows that the marginal product of capital, $\partial F(K,AL)/\partial K$, equals $ALf'(K/AL)(1/AL)$, which is just $f'(k)$. Thus the assumptions that $f'(k)$ is positive and $f''(k)$ is negative imply that the marginal product of capital is positive, but that it declines as capital (per unit of effective labor) rises. In addition, $f(\bullet)$ is assumed to satisfy the *Inada conditions* (Inada, 1964): $\lim_{k \to 0} f'(k) = \infty$, $\lim_{k \to \infty} f'(k) = 0$. These conditions (which are stronger than needed for the model's central results) state that the marginal product of capital is very large when the capital stock is sufficiently small and that it becomes very small as the capital stock becomes large; their role is to ensure that the path of the economy does not diverge. A production function satisfying $f'(\bullet) > 0$, $f''(\bullet) < 0$, and the Inada conditions is shown in Figure 1.1.

A specific example of a production function is the Cobb–Douglas function,

$$F(K,AL) = K^{\alpha}(AL)^{1-\alpha}, \qquad 0 < \alpha < 1. \tag{1.5}$$

This production function is easy to analyze, and it appears to be a good first approximation to actual production functions. As a result, it is very useful.

---

[5] The notation $f'(\bullet)$ denotes the first derivative of $f(\bullet)$, and $f''(\bullet)$ the second derivative.

It is easy to check that the Cobb–Douglas function has constant returns. Multiplying both inputs by $c$ gives us

$$F(cK, cAL) = (cK)^{\alpha}(cAL)^{1-\alpha}$$
$$= c^{\alpha}c^{1-\alpha}K^{\alpha}(AL)^{1-\alpha} \qquad (1.6)$$
$$= cF(K, AL).$$

To find the intensive form of the production function, divide both inputs by $AL$; this yields

$$f(k) \equiv F\left(\frac{K}{AL}, 1\right)$$
$$= \left(\frac{K}{AL}\right)^{\alpha} \qquad (1.7)$$
$$= k^{\alpha}.$$

Equation (1.7) implies that $f'(k) = \alpha k^{\alpha-1}$. It is straightforward to check that this expression is positive, that it approaches infinity as $k$ approaches zero, and that it approaches zero as $k$ approaches infinity. Finally, $f''(k) = -(1 - \alpha)\alpha k^{\alpha-2}$, which is negative.[6]

## The Evolution of the Inputs into Production

The remaining assumptions of the model concern how the stocks of labor, knowledge, and capital change over time. The model is set in continuous time; that is, the variables of the model are defined at every point in time.[7]

The initial levels of capital, labor, and knowledge are taken as given, and are assumed to be strictly positive. Labor and knowledge grow at constant rates:

$$\dot{L}(t) = nL(t), \qquad (1.8)$$
$$\dot{A}(t) = gA(t), \qquad (1.9)$$

where $n$ and $g$ are exogenous parameters and where a dot over a variable denotes a derivative with respect to time (that is, $\dot{X}(t)$ is shorthand for $dX(t)/dt$).

---

[6] Note that with Cobb–Douglas production, labor-augmenting, capital-augmenting, and Hicks-neutral technological progress (see n. 4) are all essentially the same. For example, to rewrite (1.5) so that technological progress is Hicks-neutral, simply define $\tilde{A} = A^{1-\alpha}$; then $Y = \tilde{A}(K^{\alpha}L^{1-\alpha})$.

[7] The alternative is discrete time, where the variables are defined only at specific dates (usually $t = 0,1,2,\ldots$). The choice between continuous and discrete time is usually based on convenience. For example, the Solow model has essentially the same implications in discrete as in continuous time, but is easier to analyze in continuous time.

The *growth rate* of a variable refers to its proportional rate of change. That is, *the growth rate of X* refers to the quantity $\dot{X}(t)/X(t)$. Thus equation (1.8) implies that the growth rate of $L$ is constant and equal to $n$, and (1.9) implies that $A$'s growth rate is constant and equal to $g$.

A key fact about growth rates is that the growth rate of a variable equals the rate of change of its natural log. That is, $\dot{X}(t)/X(t)$ equals $d \ln X(t)/dt$. To see this, note that since $\ln X$ is a function of $X$ and $X$ is a function of $t$, we can use the chain rule to write

$$\frac{d \ln X(t)}{dt} = \frac{d \ln X(t)}{dX(t)} \frac{dX(t)}{dt}$$

$$= \frac{1}{X(t)} \dot{X}(t). \tag{1.10}$$

Applying the result that a variable's growth rate equals the rate of change of its log to (1.8) and (1.9) tells us that the rates of change of the logs of $L$ and $A$ are constant and that they equal $n$ and $g$, respectively. Thus,

$$\ln L(t) = [\ln L(0)] + nt, \tag{1.11}$$

$$\ln A(t) = [\ln A(0)] + gt, \tag{1.12}$$

where $L(0)$ and $A(0)$ are the values of $L$ and $A$ at time 0. Exponentiating both sides of these equations gives us

$$L(t) = L(0)e^{nt}, \tag{1.13}$$

$$A(t) = A(0)e^{gt}. \tag{1.14}$$

Thus, our assumption is that $L$ and $A$ each grow exponentially.[8]

Output is divided between consumption and investment. The fraction of output devoted to investment, $s$, is exogenous and constant. One unit of output devoted to investment yields one unit of new capital. In addition, existing capital depreciates at rate $\delta$. Thus

$$\dot{K}(t) = sY(t) - \delta K(t). \tag{1.15}$$

Although no restrictions are placed on $n$, $g$, and $\delta$ individually, their sum is assumed to be positive. This completes the description of the model.

Since this is the first model (of many!) we will encounter, this is a good place for a general comment about modeling. The Solow model is grossly simplified in a host of ways. To give just a few examples, there is only a single good; government is absent; fluctuations in employment are ignored; production is described by an aggregate production function with just three inputs; and the rates of saving, depreciation, population growth, and technological progress are constant. It is natural to think of these features of the model as defects: the model omits many obvious features of the world,

---

[8] See Problems 1.1 and 1.2 for more on basic properties of growth rates.

and surely some of those features are important to growth. But the purpose of a model is not to be realistic. After all, we already possess a model that is completely realistic—the world itself. The problem with that "model" is that it is too complicated to understand. A model's purpose is to provide insights about particular features of the world. If a simplifying assumption causes a model to give incorrect answers *to the questions it is being used to address,* then that lack of realism may be a defect. (Even then, the simplification—by showing clearly the consequences of those features of the world in an idealized setting—may be a useful reference point.) If the simplification does not cause the model to provide incorrect answers to the questions it is being used to address, however, then the lack of realism is a virtue: by isolating the effect of interest more clearly, the simplification makes it easier to understand.

## 1.3 The Dynamics of the Model

We want to determine the behavior of the economy we have just described. The evolution of two of the three inputs into production, labor and knowledge, is exogenous. Thus to characterize the behavior of the economy, we must analyze the behavior of the third input, capital.

### The Dynamics of *k*

Because the economy may be growing over time, it turns out to be much easier to focus on the capital stock per unit of effective labor, $k$, than on the unadjusted capital stock, $K$. Since $k = K/AL$, we can use the chain rule to find

$$
\begin{aligned}
\dot{k}(t) &= \frac{\dot{K}(t)}{A(t)L(t)} - \frac{K(t)}{[A(t)L(t)]^2}[A(t)\dot{L}(t) + L(t)\dot{A}(t)] \\[2mm]
&= \frac{\dot{K}(t)}{A(t)L(t)} - \frac{K(t)}{A(t)L(t)}\frac{\dot{L}(t)}{L(t)} - \frac{K(t)}{A(t)L(t)}\frac{\dot{A}(t)}{A(t)}.
\end{aligned}
\tag{1.16}
$$

$K/AL$ is simply $k$. From (1.8) and (1.9), $\dot{L}/L$ and $\dot{A}/A$ are $n$ and $g$, respectively. $\dot{K}$ is given by (1.15). Substituting these facts into (1.16) yields

$$
\begin{aligned}
\dot{k}(t) &= \frac{sY(t) - \delta K(t)}{A(t)L(t)} - k(t)n - k(t)g \\[2mm]
&= s\frac{Y(t)}{A(t)L(t)} - \delta k(t) - nk(t) - gk(t).
\end{aligned}
\tag{1.17}
$$

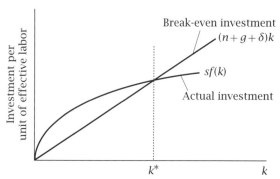

**FIGURE 1.2   Actual and break-even investment**

Finally, using the fact that $Y/AL$ is given by $f(k)$, we have

$$\dot{k}(t) = sf(k(t)) - (n + g + \delta)k(t). \tag{1.18}$$

Equation (1.18) is the key equation of the Solow model. It states that the rate of change of the capital stock per unit of effective labor is the difference between two terms. The first, $sf(k)$, is actual investment per unit of effective labor: output per unit of effective labor is $f(k)$, and the fraction of that output that is invested is $s$. The second term, $(n + g + \delta)k$, is *break-even investment,* the amount of investment that must be done just to keep $k$ at its existing level. There are two reasons that some investment is needed to prevent $k$ from falling. First, existing capital is depreciating; this capital must be replaced to keep the capital stock from falling. This is the $\delta k$ term in (1.18). Second, the quantity of effective labor is growing. Thus doing enough investment to keep the capital stock ($K$) constant is not enough to keep the capital stock per unit of effective labor ($k$) constant. Instead, since the quantity of effective labor is growing at rate $n + g$, the capital stock must grow at rate $n + g$ to hold $k$ steady.[9] This is the $(n + g)k$ term in (1.18).

When actual investment per unit of effective labor exceeds the investment needed to break even, $k$ is rising. When actual investment falls short of break-even investment, $k$ is falling. And when the two are equal, $k$ is constant.

Figure 1.2 plots the two terms of the expression for $\dot{k}$ as functions of $k$. Break-even investment, $(n + g + \delta)k$, is proportional to $k$. Actual investment, $sf(k)$, is a constant times output per unit of effective labor.

Since $f(0) = 0$, actual investment and break-even investment are equal at $k = 0$. The Inada conditions imply that at $k = 0$, $f'(k)$ is large, and thus that the $sf(k)$ line is steeper than the $(n + g + \delta)k$ line. Thus for small values of

---

[9] The fact that the growth rate of the quantity of effective labor, $AL$, equals $n + g$ is an instance of the fact that the growth rate of the product of two variables equals the sum of their growth rates. See Problem 1.1.

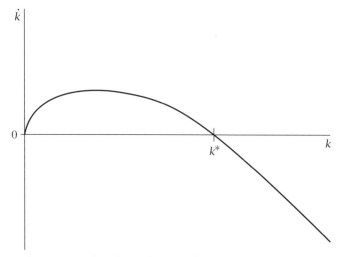

**FIGURE 1.3    The phase diagram for *k* in the Solow model**

*k*, actual investment is larger than break-even investment. The Inada conditions also imply that $f'(k)$ falls toward zero as *k* becomes large. At some point, the slope of the actual investment line falls below the slope of the break-even investment line. With the $sf(k)$ line flatter than the $(n + g + \delta)k$ line, the two must eventually cross. Finally, the fact that $f''(k) < 0$ implies that the two lines intersect only once for $k > 0$. We let $k^*$ denote the value of *k* where actual investment and break-even investment are equal.

Figure 1.3 summarizes this information in the form of a *phase diagram*, which shows $\dot{k}$ as a function of *k*. If *k* is initially less than $k^*$, actual investment exceeds break-even investment, and so $\dot{k}$ is positive—that is, *k* is rising. If *k* exceeds $k^*$, $\dot{k}$ is negative. Finally, if *k* equals $k^*$, then $\dot{k}$ is zero. Thus, regardless of where *k* starts, it converges to $k^*$ and remains there.[10]

## The Balanced Growth Path

Since *k* converges to $k^*$, it is natural to ask how the variables of the model behave when *k* equals $k^*$. By assumption, labor and knowledge are growing at rates *n* and *g*, respectively. The capital stock, *K*, equals *ALk*; since *k* is constant at $k^*$, *K* is growing at rate $n + g$ (that is, $\dot{K}/K$ equals $n + g$). With both capital and effective labor growing at rate $n + g$, the assumption of constant returns implies that output, *Y*, is also growing at that rate. Finally, capital per worker, $K/L$, and output per worker, $Y/L$, are growing at rate *g*.

---

[10] If *k* is initially zero, it remains there. However, this possibility is ruled out by our assumption that initial levels of *K*, *L*, and *A* are strictly positive.

Thus the Solow model implies that, regardless of its starting point, the economy converges to a *balanced growth path*—a situation where each variable of the model is growing at a constant rate. On the balanced growth path, the growth rate of output per worker is determined solely by the rate of technological progress.[11]

# 1.4   The Impact of a Change in the Saving Rate

The parameter of the Solow model that policy is most likely to affect is the saving rate. The division of the government's purchases between consumption and investment goods, the division of its revenues between taxes and borrowing, and its tax treatments of saving and investment are all likely to affect the fraction of output that is invested. Thus it is natural to investigate the effects of a change in the saving rate.

For concreteness, we will consider a Solow economy that is on a balanced growth path, and suppose that there is a permanent increase in $s$. In addition to demonstrating the model's implications concerning the role of saving, this experiment will illustrate the model's properties when the economy is not on a balanced growth path.

## The Impact on Output

The increase in $s$ shifts the actual investment line upward, and so $k^*$ rises. This is shown in Figure 1.4. But $k$ does not immediately jump to the new value of $k^*$. Initially, $k$ is equal to the old value of $k^*$. At this level, actual investment now exceeds break-even investment—more resources are being devoted to investment than are needed to hold $k$ constant—and so $\dot{k}$ is positive. Thus $k$ begins to rise. It continues to rise until it reaches the new value of $k^*$, at which point it remains constant.

These results are summarized in the first three panels of Figure 1.5. $t_0$ denotes the time of the increase in the saving rate. By assumption, $s$ jumps up

---

[11] The broad behavior of the U.S. economy and many other major industrialized economies over the last century or more is described reasonably well by the balanced growth path of the Solow model. The growth rates of labor, capital, and output have each been roughly constant. The growth rates of output and capital have been about equal (so that the capital-output ratio has been approximately constant) and have been larger than the growth rate of labor (so that output per worker and capital per worker have been rising). This is often taken as evidence that it is reasonable to think of these economies as Solow-model economies on their balanced growth paths. Jones (2002a) shows, however, that the underlying determinants of the level of income on the balanced growth path have in fact been far from constant in these economies, and thus that the resemblance between these economies and the balanced growth path of the Solow model is misleading. We return to this issue in Section 3.3.

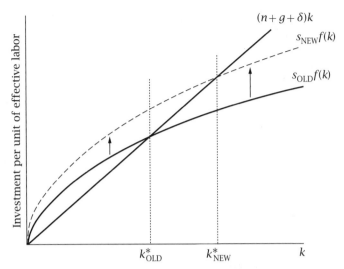

**FIGURE 1.4   The effects of an increase in the saving rate on investment**

at time $t_0$ and remains constant thereafter. Since the jump in $s$ causes actual investment to exceed break-even investment by a strictly positive amount, $\dot{k}$ jumps from zero to a strictly positive amount. $k$ rises gradually from the old value of $k^*$ to the new value, and $\dot{k}$ falls gradually back to zero.[12]

We are likely to be particularly interested in the behavior of output per worker, $Y/L$. $Y/L$ equals $Af(k)$. When $k$ is constant, $Y/L$ grows at rate $g$, the growth rate of $A$. When $k$ is increasing, $Y/L$ grows both because $A$ is increasing and because $k$ is increasing. Thus its growth rate exceeds $g$. When $k$ reaches the new value of $k^*$, however, again only the growth of $A$ contributes to the growth of $Y/L$, and so the growth rate of $Y/L$ returns to $g$. Thus a *permanent* increase in the saving rate produces a *temporary* increase in the growth rate of output per worker: $k$ is rising for a time, but eventually it increases to the point where the additional saving is devoted entirely to maintaining the higher level of $k$.

The fourth and fifth panels of Figure 1.5 show how output per worker responds to the rise in the saving rate. The *growth rate* of output per worker, which is initially $g$, jumps upward at $t_0$ and then gradually returns to its initial level. Thus output per worker begins to rise above the path it was on and gradually settles into a higher path parallel to the first.[13]

---

[12] For a sufficiently large rise in the saving rate, $\dot{k}$ can rise for a while after $t_0$ before starting to fall back to zero.

[13] Because the growth rate of a variable equals the derivative with respect to time of its log, graphs in logs are often much easier to interpret than graphs in levels. For example, if a variable's growth rate is constant, the graph of its log as a function of time is a straight line. This is why Figure 1.5 shows the log of output per worker rather than its level.

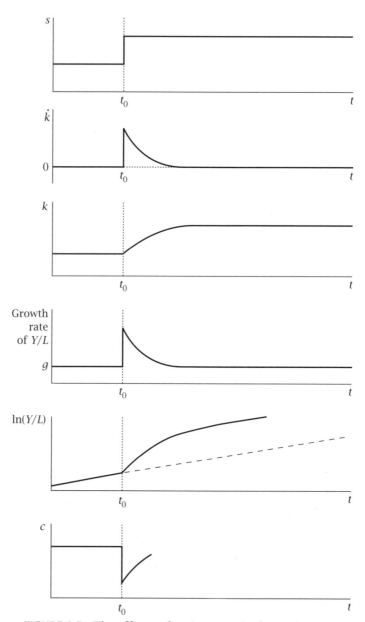

**FIGURE 1.5   The effects of an increase in the saving rate**

In sum, a change in the saving rate has a *level effect* but not a *growth effect*: it changes the economy's balanced growth path, and thus the level of output per worker at any point in time, but it does not affect the growth rate of output per worker on the balanced growth path. Indeed, in the

Solow model only changes in the rate of technological progress have growth effects; all other changes have only level effects.

## The Impact on Consumption

If we were to introduce households into the model, their welfare would depend not on output but on consumption: investment is simply an input into production in the future. Thus for many purposes we are likely to be more interested in the behavior of consumption than in the behavior of output.

Consumption per unit of effective labor equals output per unit of effective labor, $f(k)$, times the fraction of that output that is consumed, $1 - s$. Thus, since $s$ changes discontinuously at $t_0$ and $k$ does not, initially consumption per unit of effective labor jumps downward. Consumption then rises gradually as $k$ rises and $s$ remains at its higher level. This is shown in the last panel of Figure 1.5.

Whether consumption eventually exceeds its level before the rise in $s$ is not immediately clear. Let $c^*$ denote consumption per unit of effective labor on the balanced growth path. $c^*$ equals output per unit of effective labor, $f(k^*)$, minus investment per unit of effective labor, $sf(k^*)$. On the balanced growth path, actual investment equals break-even investment, $(n+g+\delta)k^*$. Thus,

$$c^* = f(k^*) - (n+g+\delta)k^*. \tag{1.19}$$

$k^*$ is determined by $s$ and the other parameters of the model, $n$, $g$, and $\delta$; we can therefore write $k^* = k^*(s,n,g,\delta)$. Thus (1.19) implies

$$\frac{\partial c^*}{\partial s} = [f'(k^*(s,n,g,\delta)) - (n+g+\delta)]\frac{\partial k^*(s,n,g,\delta)}{\partial s}. \tag{1.20}$$

We know that the increase in $s$ raises $k^*$; that is, we know that $\partial k^*/\partial s$ is positive. Thus whether the increase raises or lowers consumption in the long run depends on whether $f'(k^*)$—the marginal product of capital—is more or less than $n+g+\delta$. Intuitively, when $k$ rises, investment (per unit of effective labor) must rise by $n+g+\delta$ times the change in $k$ for the increase to be sustained. If $f'(k^*)$ is less than $n+g+\delta$, then the additional output from the increased capital is not enough to maintain the capital stock at its higher level. In this case, consumption must fall to maintain the higher capital stock. If $f'(k^*)$ exceeds $n+g+\delta$, on the other hand, there is more than enough additional output to maintain $k$ at its higher level, and so consumption rises.

$f'(k^*)$ can be either smaller or larger than $n+g+\delta$. This is shown in Figure 1.6. The figure shows not only $(n+g+\delta)k$ and $sf(k)$, but also $f(k)$. Since consumption on the balanced growth path equals output less break-even investment (see [1.19]), $c^*$ is the distance between $f(k)$ and $(n+g+\delta)k$ at $k = k^*$. The figure shows the determinants of $c^*$ for three different values

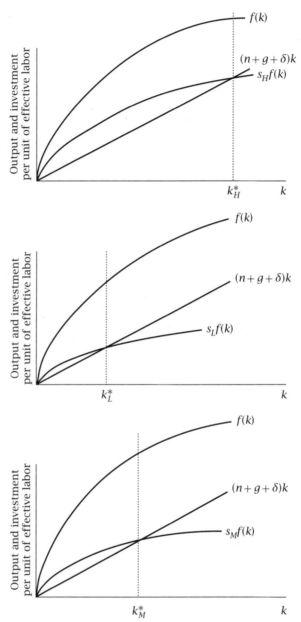

FIGURE 1.6   Output, investment, and consumption on the balanced growth path

of $s$ (and hence three different values of $k^*$). In the top panel, $s$ is high, and so $k^*$ is high and $f'(k^*)$ is less than $n + g + \delta$. As a result, an increase in the saving rate lowers consumption even when the economy has reached its new balanced growth path. In the middle panel, $s$ is low, $k^*$ is low, $f'(k^*)$ is greater than $n + g + \delta$, and an increase in $s$ raises consumption in the long run.

Finally, in the bottom panel, $s$ is at the level that causes $f'(k^*)$ to just equal $n + g + \delta$—that is, the $f(k)$ and $(n + g + \delta)k$ loci are parallel at $k = k^*$. In this case, a marginal change in $s$ has no effect on consumption in the long run, and consumption is at its maximum possible level among balanced growth paths. This value of $k^*$ is known as the *golden-rule* level of the capital stock. We will discuss the golden-rule capital stock further in Chapter 2. Among the questions we will address are whether the golden-rule capital stock is in fact desirable and whether there are situations in which a decentralized economy with endogenous saving converges to that capital stock. Of course, in the Solow model, where saving is exogenous, there is no more reason to expect the capital stock on the balanced growth path to equal the golden-rule level than there is to expect it to equal any other possible value.

# 1.5  Quantitative Implications

We are usually interested not just in a model's qualitative implications, but in its quantitative predictions. If, for example, the impact of a moderate increase in saving on growth remains large after several centuries, the result that the impact is temporary is of limited interest.

For most models, including this one, obtaining exact quantitative results requires specifying functional forms and values of the parameters; it often also requires analyzing the model numerically. But in many cases, it is possible to learn a great deal by considering approximations around the long-run equilibrium. That is the approach we take here.

## The Effect on Output in the Long Run

The long-run effect of a rise in saving on output is given by

$$\frac{\partial y^*}{\partial s} = f'(k^*)\frac{\partial k^*(s, n, g, \delta)}{\partial s}, \tag{1.21}$$

where $y^* = f(k^*)$ is the level of output per unit of effective labor on the balanced growth path. Thus to find $\partial y^*/\partial s$, we need to find $\partial k^*/\partial s$. To do this, note that $k^*$ is defined by the condition that $\dot{k} = 0$. Thus $k^*$ satisfies

$$sf(k^*(s, n, g, \delta)) = (n + g + \delta)k^*(s, n, g, \delta). \tag{1.22}$$

Equation (1.22) holds for all values of $s$ (and of $n$, $g$, and $\delta$). Thus the derivatives of the two sides with respect to $s$ are equal:[14]

$$sf'(k^*)\frac{\partial k^*}{\partial s} + f(k^*) = (n+g+\delta)\frac{\partial k^*}{\partial s}, \tag{1.23}$$

where the arguments of $k^*$ are omitted for simplicity. This can be rearranged to obtain[15]

$$\frac{\partial k^*}{\partial s} = \frac{f(k^*)}{(n+g+\delta)-sf'(k^*)}. \tag{1.24}$$

Substituting (1.24) into (1.21) yields

$$\frac{\partial y^*}{\partial s} = \frac{f'(k^*)f(k^*)}{(n+g+\delta)-sf'(k^*)}. \tag{1.25}$$

Two changes help in interpreting this expression. The first is to convert it to an elasticity by multiplying both sides by $s/y^*$. The second is to use the fact that $sf(k^*) = (n+g+\delta)k^*$ to substitute for $s$. Making these changes gives us

$$\begin{aligned}
\frac{s}{y^*}\frac{\partial y^*}{\partial s} &= \frac{s}{f(k^*)}\frac{f'(k^*)f(k^*)}{(n+g+\delta)-sf'(k^*)} \\
&= \frac{(n+g+\delta)k^*f'(k^*)}{f(k^*)[(n+g+\delta)-(n+g+\delta)k^*f'(k^*)/f(k^*)]} \\
&= \frac{k^*f'(k^*)/f(k^*)}{1-[k^*f'(k^*)/f(k^*)]}.
\end{aligned} \tag{1.26}$$

$k^*f'(k^*)/f(k^*)$ is the elasticity of output with respect to capital at $k=k^*$. Denoting this by $\alpha_K(k^*)$, we have

$$\frac{s}{y^*}\frac{\partial y^*}{\partial s} = \frac{\alpha_K(k^*)}{1-\alpha_K(k^*)}. \tag{1.27}$$

Thus we have found a relatively simple expression for the elasticity of the balanced-growth-path level of output with respect to the saving rate.

To think about the quantitative implications of (1.27), note that if markets are competitive and there are no externalities, capital earns its marginal

---

[14] This technique is known as *implicit differentiation*. Even though (1.22) does not explicitly give $k^*$ as a function of $s$, $n$, $g$, and $\delta$, it still determines how $k^*$ depends on those variables. We can therefore differentiate the equation with respect to $s$ and solve for $\partial k^*/\partial s$.

[15] We saw in the previous section that an increase in $s$ raises $k^*$. To check that this is also implied by equation (1.24), note that $n+g+\delta$ is the slope of the break-even investment line and that $sf'(k^*)$ is the slope of the actual investment line at $k^*$. Since the break-even investment line is steeper than the actual investment line at $k^*$ (see Figure 1.2), it follows that the denominator of (1.24) is positive, and thus that $\partial k^*/\partial s > 0$.

product. Since output equals $ALf(k)$ and $k$ equals $K/AL$, the marginal product of capital, $\partial Y/\partial K$, is $ALf'(k)[1/(AL)]$, or just $f'(k)$. Thus if capital earns its marginal product, the total amount earned by capital (per unit of effective labor) on the balanced growth path is $k^*f'(k^*)$. The share of total income that goes to capital on the balanced growth path is then $k^*f'(k^*)/f(k^*)$, or $\alpha_K(k^*)$. In other words, if the assumption that capital earns its marginal product is a good approximation, we can use data on the share of income going to capital to estimate the elasticity of output with respect to capital, $\alpha_K(k^*)$.

In most countries, the share of income paid to capital is about one-third. If we use this as an estimate of $\alpha_K(k^*)$, it follows that the elasticity of output with respect to the saving rate in the long run is about one-half. Thus, for example, a 10 percent increase in the saving rate (from 20 percent of output to 22 percent, for instance) raises output per worker in the long run by about 5 percent relative to the path it would have followed. Even a 50 percent increase in $s$ raises $y^*$ only by about 22 percent. Thus significant changes in saving have only moderate effects on the level of output on the balanced growth path.

Intuitively, a small value of $\alpha_K(k^*)$ makes the impact of saving on output low for two reasons. First, it implies that the actual investment curve, $sf(k)$, bends fairly sharply. As a result, an upward shift of the curve moves its intersection with the break-even investment line relatively little. Thus the impact of a change in $s$ on $k^*$ is small. Second, a low value of $\alpha_K(k^*)$ means that the impact of a change in $k^*$ on $y^*$ is small.

## The Speed of Convergence

In practice, we are interested not only in the eventual effects of some change (such as a change in the saving rate), but also in how rapidly those effects occur. Again, we can use approximations around the long-run equilibrium to address this issue.

For simplicity, we focus on the behavior of $k$ rather than $y$. Our goal is thus to determine how rapidly $k$ approaches $k^*$. We know that $\dot{k}$ is determined by $k$: recall that the key equation of the model is $\dot{k} = sf(k) - (n + g + \delta)k$ (see [1.18]). Thus we can write $\dot{k} = \dot{k}(k)$. When $k$ equals $k^*$, $\dot{k}$ is zero. A first-order Taylor-series approximation of $\dot{k}(k)$ around $k = k^*$ therefore yields

$$\dot{k} \simeq \left[ \left. \frac{\partial \dot{k}(k)}{\partial k} \right|_{k=k^*} \right] (k - k^*). \tag{1.28}$$

That is, $\dot{k}$ is approximately equal to the product of the difference between $k$ and $k^*$ and the derivative of $\dot{k}$ with respect to $k$ at $k = k^*$.

Let $\lambda$ denote $-\partial \dot{k}(k)/\partial k|_{k=k^*}$. With this definition, (1.28) becomes

$$\dot{k}(t) \simeq -\lambda[k(t) - k^*]. \tag{1.29}$$

Since $\dot{k}$ is positive when $k$ is slightly below $k^*$ and negative when it is slightly above, $\partial\dot{k}(k)/\partial k|_{k=k^*}$ is negative. Equivalently, $\lambda$ is positive.

Equation (1.29) implies that in the vicinity of the balanced growth path, $k$ moves toward $k^*$ at a speed approximately proportional to its distance from $k^*$. That is, the growth rate of $k(t) - k^*$ is approximately constant and equal to $-\lambda$. This implies

$$k(t) \simeq k^* + e^{-\lambda t}[k(0) - k^*], \tag{1.30}$$

where $k(0)$ is the initial value of $k$. Note that (1.30) follows just from the facts that the system is stable (that is, that $k$ converges to $k^*$) and that we are linearizing the equation for $\dot{k}$ around $k = k^*$.

It remains to find $\lambda$; this is where the specifics of the model enter the analysis. Differentiating expression (1.18) for $\dot{k}$ with respect to $k$ and evaluating the resulting expression at $k = k^*$ yields

$$
\begin{aligned}
\lambda \equiv -\left.\frac{\partial\dot{k}(k)}{\partial k}\right|_{k=k^*} &= -[sf'(k^*) - (n+g+\delta)] \\
&= (n+g+\delta) - sf'(k^*) \\
&= (n+g+\delta) - \frac{(n+g+\delta)k^*f'(k^*)}{f(k^*)} \\
&= [1 - \alpha_K(k^*)](n+g+\delta).
\end{aligned}
\tag{1.31}
$$

Here the third line again uses the fact that $sf(k^*) = (n+g+\delta)k^*$ to substitute for $s$, and the last line uses the definition of $\alpha_K$. Thus, $k$ converges to its balanced-growth-path value at rate $[1 - \alpha_K(k^*)](n+g+\delta)$. In addition, one can show that $y$ approaches $y^*$ at the same rate that $k$ approaches $k^*$. That is, $y(t) - y^* \simeq e^{-\lambda t}[y(0) - y^*]$.[16]

We can calibrate (1.31) to see how quickly actual economies are likely to approach their balanced growth paths. Typically, $n+g+\delta$ is about 6 percent per year. This arises, for example, with 1 to 2 percent population growth, 1 to 2 percent growth in output per worker, and 3 to 4 percent depreciation. If capital's share is roughly one-third, $(1 - \alpha_K)(n+g+\delta)$ is thus roughly 4 percent. Therefore $k$ and $y$ move 4 percent of the remaining distance toward $k^*$ and $y^*$ each year, and take approximately 17 years to get halfway to their balanced-growth-path values.[17] Thus in our example of a 10 percent

---

[16] See Problem 1.11.

[17] The time it takes for a variable (in this case, $y - y^*$) with a constant negative growth rate to fall in half is approximately equal to 70 divided by its growth rate in percent. (Similarly, the doubling time of a variable with positive growth is 70 divided by the growth rate.) Thus in this case the *half-life* is roughly 70/(4%/year), or about 17 years. More exactly, the half-life, $t^*$, is the solution to $e^{-\lambda t^*} = 0.5$, where $\lambda$ is the rate of decrease. Taking logs of both sides, $t^* = -\ln(0.5)/\lambda \simeq 0.69/\lambda$.

increase in the saving rate, output is 0.04(5%) = 0.2% above its previous path after 1 year; is 0.5(5%) = 2.5% above after 17 years; and asymptotically approaches 5 percent above the previous path. Thus not only is the overall impact of a substantial change in the saving rate modest, but it does not occur very quickly.[18]

## 1.6  The Solow Model and the Central Questions of Growth Theory

The Solow model identifies two possible sources of variation—either over time or across parts of the world—in output per worker: differences in capital per worker ($K/L$) and differences in the effectiveness of labor ($A$). We have seen, however, that only growth in the effectiveness of labor can lead to permanent growth in output per worker, and that for reasonable cases the impact of changes in capital per worker on output per worker is modest. As a result, only differences in the effectiveness of labor have any reasonable hope of accounting for the vast differences in wealth across time and space. Specifically, the central conclusion of the Solow model is that if the returns that capital commands in the market are a rough guide to its contributions to output, then variations in the accumulation of physical capital do not account for a significant part of either worldwide economic growth or cross-country income differences.

There are two ways to see that the Solow model implies that differences in capital accumulation cannot account for large differences in incomes, one direct and the other indirect. The direct approach is to consider the required differences in capital per worker. Suppose we want to account for a difference of a factor of $X$ in output per worker between two economies on the basis of differences in capital per worker. If output per worker differs by a factor of $X$, the difference in log output per worker between the two economies is $\ln X$. Since the elasticity of output per worker with respect to capital per worker is $\alpha_K$, log capital per worker must differ by $(\ln X)/\alpha_K$. That is, capital per worker differs by a factor of $e^{(\ln X)/\alpha_K}$, or $X^{1/\alpha_K}$.

Output per worker in the major industrialized countries today is on the order of 10 times larger than it was 100 years ago, and 10 times larger than it is in poor countries today. Thus we would like to account for values of

---

[18] These results are derived from a Taylor-series approximation around the balanced growth path. Thus, formally, we can rely on them only in an arbitrarily small neighborhood around the balanced growth path. The question of whether Taylor-series approximations provide good guides for finite changes does not have a general answer. For the Solow model with conventional production functions, and for moderate changes in parameter values (such as those we have been considering), the Taylor-series approximations are generally quite reliable.

$X$ in the vicinity of 10. Our analysis implies that doing this on the basis of differences in capital requires a difference of a factor of $10^{1/\alpha_K}$ in capital per worker. For $\alpha_K = \frac{1}{3}$, this is a factor of 1000. Even if capital's share is one-half, which is well above what data on capital income suggest, one still needs a difference of a factor of 100.

There is no evidence of such differences in capital stocks. Capital-output ratios are roughly constant over time. Thus the capital stock per worker in industrialized countries is roughly 10 times larger than it was 100 years ago, not 100 or 1000 times larger. Similarly, although capital-output ratios vary somewhat across countries, the variation is not great. For example, the capital-output ratio appears to be 2 to 3 times larger in industrialized countries than in poor countries; thus capital per worker is "only" about 20 to 30 times larger. In sum, differences in capital per worker are far smaller than those needed to account for the differences in output per worker that we are trying to understand.

The indirect way of seeing that the model cannot account for large variations in output per worker on the basis of differences in capital per worker is to notice that the required differences in capital imply enormous differences in the rate of return on capital (Lucas, 1990). If markets are competitive, the rate of return on capital equals its marginal product, $f'(k)$, minus depreciation, $\delta$. Suppose that the production function is Cobb–Douglas, which in intensive form is $f(k) = k^\alpha$ (see equation [1.7]). With this production function, the elasticity of output with respect to capital is simply $\alpha$. The marginal product of capital is

$$
\begin{aligned}
f'(k) &= \alpha k^{\alpha-1} \\
&= \alpha y^{(\alpha-1)/\alpha}.
\end{aligned}
\tag{1.32}
$$

Equation (1.32) implies that the elasticity of the marginal product of capital with respect to output is $-(1-\alpha)/\alpha$. If $\alpha = \frac{1}{3}$, a tenfold difference in output per worker arising from differences in capital per worker thus implies a hundredfold difference in the marginal product of capital. And since the return to capital is $f'(k) - \delta$, the difference in rates of return is even larger.

Again, there is no evidence of such differences in rates of return. Direct measurement of returns on financial assets, for example, suggests only moderate variation over time and across countries. More tellingly, we can learn much about cross-country differences simply by examining where the holders of capital want to invest. If rates of return were larger by a factor of 10 or 100 in poor countries than in rich countries, there would be immense incentives to invest in poor countries. Such differences in rates of return would swamp such considerations as capital-market imperfections, government tax policies, fear of expropriation, and so on, and we would observe immense flows of capital from rich to poor countries. We do not see such flows.[19]

Thus differences in physical capital per worker cannot account for the differences in output per worker that we observe, at least if capital's contribution to output is roughly reflected by its private returns.

The other potential source of variation in output per worker in the Solow model is the effectiveness of labor. Attributing differences in standards of living to differences in the effectiveness of labor does not require huge differences in capital or in rates of return. Along a balanced growth path, for example, capital is growing at the same rate as output; and the marginal product of capital, $f'(k)$, is constant.

Unfortunately, however, the Solow model has little to say about the effectiveness of labor. Most obviously, the growth of the effectiveness of labor is exogenous: the model takes as given the behavior of the variable that it identifies as the driving force of growth. Thus it is only a small exaggeration to say that we have been modeling growth by assuming it.

More fundamentally, the model does not identify what the "effectiveness of labor" is; it is just a catchall for factors other than labor and capital that affect output. Thus saying that differences in income are due to differences in the effectiveness of labor is no different than saying that they are not due to differences in capital per worker. To proceed, we must take a stand concerning what we mean by the effectiveness of labor and what causes it to vary. One natural possibility is that the effectiveness of labor corresponds to abstract knowledge. To understand worldwide growth, it would then be necessary to analyze the determinants of the stock of knowledge over time. To understand cross-country differences in real incomes, one would have to explain why firms in some countries have access to more knowledge than firms in other countries, and why that greater knowledge is not rapidly transmitted to poorer countries.

There are other possible interpretations of $A$: the education and skills of the labor force, the strength of property rights, the quality of infrastructure, cultural attitudes toward entrepreneurship and work, and so on. Or $A$ may reflect a combination of forces. For any proposed view of what $A$ represents, one would again have to address the questions of how it affects output, how it evolves over time, and why it differs across parts of the world.

The other possible way to proceed is to consider the possibility that capital is more important than the Solow model implies. If capital encompasses

---

[19] One can try to avoid this conclusion by considering production functions where capital's marginal product falls less rapidly as $k$ rises than it does in the Cobb–Douglas case. This approach encounters two major difficulties. First, since it implies that the marginal product of capital is similar in rich and poor countries, it implies that capital's share is much larger in rich countries. Second, and similarly, it implies that real wages are only slightly larger in rich than in poor countries. These implications appear grossly inconsistent with the facts.

more than just physical capital, or if physical capital has positive externalities, then the private return on physical capital is not an accurate guide to capital's importance in production. In this case, the calculations we have done may be misleading, and it may be possible to resuscitate the view that differences in capital are central to differences in incomes.

These possibilities for addressing the fundamental questions of growth theory are the subject of Chapters 3 and 4.

## 1.7   Empirical Applications

### Growth Accounting

In many situations, we are interested in the proximate determinants of growth. That is, we often want to know how much of growth over some period is due to increases in various factors of production, and how much stems from other forces. *Growth accounting,* which was pioneered by Abramovitz (1956) and Solow (1957), provides a way of tackling this subject.

To see how growth accounting works, consider again the production function $Y(t) = F(K(t), A(t)L(t))$. This implies

$$\dot{Y}(t) = \frac{\partial Y(t)}{\partial K(t)}\dot{K}(t) + \frac{\partial Y(t)}{\partial L(t)}\dot{L}(t) + \frac{\partial Y(t)}{\partial A(t)}\dot{A}(t), \tag{1.33}$$

where $\partial Y/\partial L$ and $\partial Y/\partial A$ denote $[\partial Y/\partial (AL)]A$ and $[\partial Y/\partial(AL)]L$, respectively. Dividing both sides by $Y(t)$ and rewriting the terms on the right-hand side yields

$$\frac{\dot{Y}(t)}{Y(t)} = \frac{K(t)}{Y(t)}\frac{\partial Y(t)}{\partial K(t)}\frac{\dot{K}(t)}{K(t)} + \frac{L(t)}{Y(t)}\frac{\partial Y(t)}{\partial L(t)}\frac{\dot{L}(t)}{L(t)} + \frac{A(t)}{Y(t)}\frac{\partial Y(t)}{\partial A(t)}\frac{\dot{A}(t)}{A(t)}$$

$$\equiv \alpha_K(t)\frac{\dot{K}(t)}{K(t)} + \alpha_L(t)\frac{\dot{L}(t)}{L(t)} + R(t). \tag{1.34}$$

Here $\alpha_L(t)$ is the elasticity of output with respect to labor at time $t$, $\alpha_K(t)$ is again the elasticity of output with respect to capital, and $R(t) \equiv [A(t)/Y(t)][\partial Y(t)/\partial A(t)][\dot{A}(t)/A(t)]$. Subtracting $\dot{L}(t)/L(t)$ from both sides and using the fact that $\alpha_L(t) + \alpha_K(t) = 1$ (see Problem 1.9) gives an expression for the growth rate of output per worker:

$$\frac{\dot{Y}(t)}{Y(t)} - \frac{\dot{L}(t)}{L(t)} = \alpha_K(t)\left[\frac{\dot{K}(t)}{K(t)} - \frac{\dot{L}(t)}{L(t)}\right] + R(t). \tag{1.35}$$

The growth rates of $Y$, $K$, and $L$ are straightforward to measure. And we know that if capital earns its marginal product, $\alpha_K$ can be measured using data on the share of income that goes to capital. $R(t)$ can then be measured as the residual in (1.35). Thus (1.35) provides a way of decomposing the growth of output per worker into the contribution of growth of capital per worker and a remaining term, the *Solow residual*. The Solow residual is sometimes interpreted as a measure of the contribution of technological progress. As the derivation shows, however, it reflects all sources of growth other than the contribution of capital accumulation via its private return.

This basic framework can be extended in many ways. The most common extensions are to consider different types of capital and labor and to adjust for changes in the quality of inputs. But more complicated adjustments are also possible. For example, if there is evidence of imperfect competition, one can try to adjust the data on income shares to obtain a better estimate of the elasticity of output with respect to the different inputs.

Growth accounting only examines the immediate determinants of growth: it asks how much factor accumulation, improvements in the quality of inputs, and so on contribute to growth while ignoring the deeper issue of what causes the changes in those determinants. One way to see that growth accounting does not get at the underlying sources of growth is to consider what happens if it is applied to an economy described by the Solow model that is on its balanced growth path. We know that in this case growth is coming entirely from growth in $A$. But, as Problem 1.13 asks you to show and explain, growth accounting in this case attributes only fraction $1 - \alpha_K(k^*)$ of growth to the residual, and fraction $\alpha_K(k^*)$ to capital accumulation.

Even though growth accounting provides evidence only about the immediate sources of growth, it has been fruitfully applied to many issues. For example, it has played a major role in a recent debate concerning the exceptionally rapid growth of the newly industrializing countries of East Asia. Young (1995) uses detailed growth accounting to argue that the higher growth in these countries than in the rest of the world is almost entirely due to rising investment, increasing labor force participation, and improving labor quality (in terms of education), and not to rapid technological progress and other forces affecting the Solow residual. This suggests that for other countries to replicate the NICs' successes, it is enough for them to promote accumulation of physical and human capital and greater use of resources, and that they need not tackle the even more difficult task of finding ways of obtaining greater output for a given set of inputs. In this view, the NICs' policies concerning trade, regulation, and so on have been important largely only to the extent they have influenced factor accumulation and factor use.

Hsieh (2002), however, observes that one can do growth accounting by examining the behavior of factor returns rather than quantities. If rapid growth comes solely from capital accumulation, for example, we will see either a large fall in the return to capital or a large rise in capital's share (or a combination). Doing the growth accounting this way, Hsieh finds a much larger role for the residual. Young (1998) and Fernald and Neiman (2008) extend the analysis further, and identify reasons that Hsieh's analysis may have underestimated the role of factor accumulation.

Growth accounting has also been used extensively to study both the productivity growth slowdown (the reduced growth rate of output per worker-hour in the United States and other industrialized countries that began in the early 1970s) and the productivity growth rebound (the return of U.S. productivity growth starting in the mid-1990s to close to its level before the slowdown). Growth-accounting studies of the rebound suggest that computers and other types of information technology are the main source of the rebound (see, for example, Oliner and Sichel, 2002, and Oliner, Sichel, and Stiroh, 2007). Until the mid-1990s, the rapid technological progress in computers and their introduction in many sectors of the economy appear to have had little impact on aggregate productivity. In part, this was simply because computers, although spreading rapidly, were still only a small fraction of the overall capital stock. And in part, it was because the adoption of the new technologies involved substantial adjustment costs. The growth-accounting studies find, however, that since the mid-1990s, computers and other forms of information technology have had a large impact on aggregate productivity.[20]

## Convergence

An issue that has attracted considerable attention in empirical work on growth is whether poor countries tend to grow faster than rich countries. There are at least three reasons that one might expect such convergence. First, the Solow model predicts that countries converge to their balanced growth paths. Thus to the extent that differences in output per worker arise from countries being at different points relative to their balanced growth paths, one would expect poor countries to catch up to rich ones. Second, the Solow model implies that the rate of return on capital is lower in countries with more capital per worker. Thus there are incentives for capital to flow from rich to poor countries; this will also tend to cause convergence. And third, if there are lags in the diffusion of knowledge, income differences can arise because some countries are not yet employing the best available technologies. These differences might tend to shrink as poorer countries gain access to state-of-the-art methods.

Baumol (1986) examines convergence from 1870 to 1979 among the 16 industrialized countries for which Maddison (1982) provides data. Baumol regresses output growth over this period on a constant and initial income.

---

[20] The simple information-technology explanation of the productivity growth rebound faces an important challenge, however: other industrialized countries have for the most part not shared in the rebound. The leading candidate explanation of this puzzle is closely related to the observation that there are large adjustments costs in adopting the new technologies. In this view, the adoption of computers and information technology raises productivity substantially only if it is accompanied by major changes in worker training, the composition of the firm's workforce, and the organization of the firm. Thus in countries where firms lack the ability to make these changes (because of either government regulation or business culture), the information-technology revolution is, as yet, having little impact on overall economic performance (see, for example, Breshnahan, Brynjolfsson, and Hitt, 2002; Basu, Fernald, Oulton, and Srinivasan, 2003; and Bloom, Sadun, and Van Reenan, 2008).

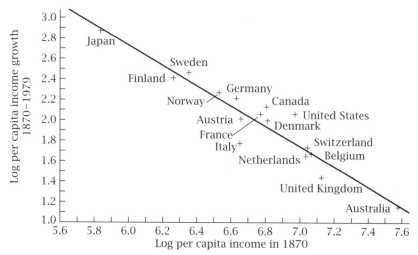

**FIGURE 1.7  Initial income and subsequent growth in Baumol's sample (from DeLong, 1988; used with permission)**

That is, he estimates

$$\ln\left[\left(\frac{Y}{N}\right)_{i,1979}\right] - \ln\left[\left(\frac{Y}{N}\right)_{i,1870}\right] = a + b\ln\left[\left(\frac{Y}{N}\right)_{i,1870}\right] + \varepsilon_i. \tag{1.36}$$

Here $\ln(Y/N)$ is log income per person, $\varepsilon$ is an error term, and $i$ indexes countries.[21] If there is convergence, $b$ will be negative: countries with higher initial incomes have lower growth. A value for $b$ of $-1$ corresponds to perfect convergence: higher initial income on average lowers subsequent growth one-for-one, and so output per person in 1979 is uncorrelated with its value in 1870. A value for $b$ of 0, on the other hand, implies that growth is uncorrelated with initial income and thus that there is no convergence.

The results are

$$\ln\left[\left(\frac{Y}{N}\right)_{i,1979}\right] - \ln\left[\left(\frac{Y}{N}\right)_{i,1870}\right] = 8.457 - \underset{(0.094)}{0.995}\ \ln\left[\left(\frac{Y}{N}\right)_{i,1870}\right],$$

$$R^2 = 0.87, \qquad \text{s.e.e.} = 0.15, \tag{1.37}$$

where the number in parentheses, 0.094, is the standard error of the regression coefficient. Figure 1.7 shows the scatterplot corresponding to this regression.

The regression suggests almost perfect convergence. The estimate of $b$ is almost exactly equal to $-1$, and it is estimated fairly precisely; the

---

[21] Baumol considers output per worker rather than output per person. This choice has little effect on the results.

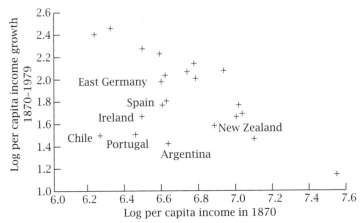

**FIGURE 1.8    Initial income and subsequent growth in the expanded sample (from DeLong, 1988; used with permission)**

two-standard-error confidence interval is $(0.81, 1.18)$. In this sample, per capita income today is essentially unrelated to its level 100 years ago.

DeLong (1988) demonstrates, however, that Baumol's finding is largely spurious. There are two problems. The first is *sample selection*. Since historical data are constructed retrospectively, the countries that have long data series are generally those that are the most industrialized today. Thus countries that were not rich 100 years ago are typically in the sample only if they grew rapidly over the next 100 years. Countries that were rich 100 years ago, in contrast, are generally included even if their subsequent growth was only moderate. Because of this, we are likely to see poorer countries growing faster than richer ones in the sample of countries we consider, even if there is no tendency for this to occur on average.

The natural way to eliminate this bias is to use a rule for choosing the sample that is not based on the variable we are trying to explain, which is growth over the period 1870–1979. Lack of data makes it impossible to include the entire world. DeLong therefore considers the richest countries as of 1870; specifically, his sample consists of all countries at least as rich as the second poorest country in Baumol's sample in 1870, Finland. This causes him to add seven countries to Baumol's list (Argentina, Chile, East Germany, Ireland, New Zealand, Portugal, and Spain) and to drop one (Japan).[22]

Figure 1.8 shows the scatterplot for the unbiased sample. The inclusion of the new countries weakens the case for convergence considerably. The

---

[22] Since a large fraction of the world was richer than Japan in 1870, it is not possible to consider all countries at least as rich as Japan. In addition, one has to deal with the fact that countries' borders are not fixed. DeLong chooses to use 1979 borders. Thus his 1870 income estimates are estimates of average incomes in 1870 in the geographic regions defined by 1979 borders.

regression now produces an estimate of $b$ of $-0.566$, with a standard error of $0.144$. Thus accounting for the selection bias in Baumol's procedure eliminates about half of the convergence that he finds.

The second problem that DeLong identifies is *measurement error*. Estimates of real income per capita in 1870 are imprecise. Measurement error again creates bias toward finding convergence. When 1870 income is overstated, growth over the period 1870-1979 is understated by an equal amount; when 1870 income is understated, the reverse occurs. Thus measured growth tends to be lower in countries with higher measured initial income even if there is no relation between actual growth and actual initial income.

DeLong therefore considers the following model:

$$
\ln\left[\left(\frac{Y}{N}\right)_{i,1979}\right] - \ln\left[\left(\frac{Y}{N}\right)_{i,1870}\right]^* = a + b\ln\left[\left(\frac{Y}{N}\right)_{i,1870}\right]^* + \varepsilon_i, \qquad (1.38)
$$

$$
\ln\left[\left(\frac{Y}{N}\right)_{i,1870}\right] = \ln\left[\left(\frac{Y}{N}\right)_{i,1870}\right]^* + u_i. \qquad (1.39)
$$

Here $\ln[(Y/N)_{1870}]^*$ is the true value of log income per capita in 1870 and $\ln[(Y/N)_{1870}]$ is the measured value. $\varepsilon$ and $u$ are assumed to be uncorrelated with each other and with $\ln[(Y/N)_{1870}]^*$.

Unfortunately, it is not possible to estimate this model using only data on $\ln[(Y/N)_{1870}]$ and $\ln[(Y/N)_{1979}]$. The problem is that there are different hypotheses that make identical predictions about the data. For example, suppose we find that measured growth is negatively related to measured initial income. This is exactly what one would expect either if measurement error is unimportant and there is true convergence or if measurement error is important and there is no true convergence. Technically, the model is *not identified*.

DeLong argues, however, that we have at least a rough idea of how good the 1870 data are, and thus have a sense of what is a reasonable value for the standard deviation of the measurement error. For example, $\sigma_u = 0.01$ implies that we have measured initial income to within an average of 1 percent; this is implausibly low. Similarly, $\sigma_u = 0.50$—an average error of 50 percent—seems implausibly high. DeLong shows that if we fix a value of $\sigma_u$, we can estimate the remaining parameters.

Even moderate measurement error has a substantial impact on the results. For the unbiased sample, the estimate of $b$ reaches 0 (no tendency toward convergence) for $\sigma_u \simeq 0.15$, and is 1 (tremendous divergence) for $\sigma_u \simeq 0.20$. Thus plausible amounts of measurement error eliminate most or all of the remainder of Baumol's estimate of convergence.

It is also possible to investigate convergence for different samples of countries and different time periods. Figure 1.9 is a *convergence scatterplot* analogous to Figures 1.7 and 1.8 for virtually the entire non-Communist

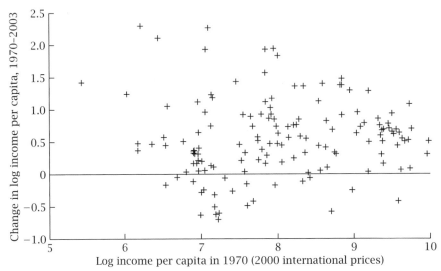

**FIGURE 1.9   Initial income and subsequent growth in a large sample**

world for the period 1970–2003. As the figure shows, there is little evidence of convergence. We return to the issue of convergence in Section 3.12.

## Saving and Investment

Consider a world where every country is described by the Solow model and where all countries have the same amount of capital per unit of effective labor. Now suppose that the saving rate in one country rises. If all the additional saving is invested domestically, the marginal product of capital in that country falls below that in other countries. The country's residents therefore have incentives to invest abroad. Thus if there are no impediments to capital flows, not all the additional saving is invested domestically. Instead, the investment resulting from the increased saving is spread uniformly over the whole world; the fact that the rise in saving occurred in one country has no special effect on investment there. Thus in the absence of barriers to capital movements, there is no reason to expect countries with high saving to also have high investment.

Feldstein and Horioka (1980) examine the association between saving and investment rates. They find that, contrary to this simple view, saving and investment rates are strongly correlated. Specifically, Feldstein and Horioka run a cross-country regression for 21 industrialized countries of the average share of investment in GDP during the period 1960–1974 on a constant and the average share of saving in GDP over the same period. The results are

$$\left(\frac{I}{Y}\right)_i = \underset{(0.018)}{0.035} + \underset{(0.074)}{0.887} \left(\frac{S}{Y}\right)_i, \qquad R^2 = 0.91, \qquad (1.40)$$

where again the numbers in parentheses are standard errors. Thus, rather than there being no relation between saving and investment, there is an almost one-to-one relation.

There are various possible explanations for Feldstein and Horioka's finding. One possibility, suggested by Feldstein and Horioka, is that there are significant barriers to capital mobility. In this case, differences in saving and investment across countries would be associated with rate-of-return differences. There is little evidence of such rate-of-return differences, however.

Another possibility is that there are underlying variables that affect both saving and investment. For example, high tax rates can reduce both saving and investment (Barro, Mankiw, and Sala-i-Martin, 1995). Similarly, countries whose citizens have low discount rates, and thus high saving rates, may provide favorable investment climates in ways other than the high saving; for example, they may limit workers' ability to form strong unions or adopt low tax rates on capital income.

Finally, the strong association between saving and investment can arise from government policies that offset forces that would otherwise make saving and investment differ. Governments may be averse to large gaps between saving and investment—after all, a large gap must be associated with a large trade deficit (if investment exceeds saving) or a large trade surplus (if saving exceeds investment). If economic forces would otherwise give rise to a large imbalance between saving and investment, the government may choose to adjust its own saving behavior or its tax treatment of saving or investment to bring them into rough balance. Helliwell (1998) finds that the saving-investment correlation is much weaker if we look across regions within a country rather than across countries. This is certainly consistent with the hypothesis that national governments take steps to prevent large imbalances between aggregate saving and investment, but that such imbalances can develop in the absence of government intervention.

In sum, the strong relationship between saving and investment differs dramatically from the predictions of a natural baseline model. Most likely, however, this difference reflects not major departures from the baseline (such as large barriers to capital mobility), but something less fundamental (such as underlying forces affecting both saving and investment).

# 1.8   The Environment and Economic Growth

Natural resources, pollution, and other environmental considerations are absent from the Solow model. But at least since Malthus (1798) made his classic argument, many people have believed that these considerations are critical to the possibilities for long-run economic growth. For example, the amounts of oil and other natural resources on earth are fixed. This could mean that any attempt to embark on a path of perpetually rising output will eventually deplete those resources, and must therefore fail. Similarly, the fixed supply of land may become a binding constraint on our ability to produce. Or ever-increasing output may generate an ever-increasing stock of pollution that will bring growth to a halt.

This section addresses the issue of how environmental limitations affect long-run growth. In thinking about this issue, it is important to distinguish between environmental factors for which there are well-defined property rights—notably natural resources and land—and those for which there are not—notably pollution-free air and water.

The existence of property rights for an environmental good has two important implications. The first is that markets provide valuable signals concerning how the good should be used. Suppose, for example, that the best available evidence indicates that the limited supply of oil will be an important limitation on our ability to produce in the future. This means that oil will command a high price in the future. But this in turn implies that the owners of oil do not want to sell their oil cheaply today. Thus oil commands a high price today, and so current users have an incentive to conserve. In short, evidence that the fixed amount of oil is likely to limit our ability to produce in the future would not be grounds for government intervention. Such a situation, though unfortunate, would be addressed by the market.

The second implication of the existence of property rights for an environmental good is that we can use the good's price to obtain evidence about its importance in production. For example, since evidence that oil will be an important constraint on future production would cause it to have a high price today, economists can use the current price to infer what the best available evidence suggests about oil's importance; they do not need to assess that evidence independently.

With environmental goods for which there are no property rights, the use of a good has externalities. For example, firms can pollute without compensating the people they harm. Thus the case for government intervention is much stronger. And there is no market price to provide a handy summary of the evidence concerning the good's importance. As a result, economists interested in environmental issues must attempt to assess that evidence themselves.

We will begin by considering environmental goods that are traded in markets. We will analyze both a simple baseline case and an important complication to the baseline. We will then turn to environmental goods for which there is no well-functioning market.

## Natural Resources and Land: A Baseline Case

We want to extend our analysis to include natural resources and land. To keep the analysis manageable, we start with the case of Cobb–Douglas production. Thus the production function, (1.1), becomes

$$Y(t) = K(t)^\alpha R(t)^\beta T(t)^\gamma [A(t)L(t)]^{1-\alpha-\beta-\gamma},$$

$$\alpha > 0, \qquad \beta > 0, \qquad \gamma > 0, \qquad \alpha + \beta + \gamma < 1. \tag{1.41}$$

Here $R$ denotes resources used in production, and $T$ denotes the amount of land.

The dynamics of capital, labor, and the effectiveness of labor are the same as before: $\dot{K}(t) = sY(t) - \delta K(t)$, $\dot{L}(t) = nL(t)$, and $\dot{A}(t) = gA(t)$. The new assumptions concern resources and land. Since the amount of land on earth is fixed, in the long run the quantity used in production cannot be growing. Thus we assume

$$\dot{T}(t) = 0. \tag{1.42}$$

Similarly, the facts that resource endowments are fixed and that resources are used in production imply that resource use must eventually decline. Thus, even though resource use has been rising historically, we assume

$$\dot{R}(t) = -bR(t), \qquad b > 0. \tag{1.43}$$

The presence of resources and land in the production function means that $K/AL$ no longer converges to some value. As a result, we cannot use our previous approach of focusing on $K/AL$ to analyze the behavior of this economy. A useful strategy in such situations is to ask whether there can be a balanced growth path and, if so, what the growth rates of the economy's variables are on that path.

By assumption, $A$, $L$, $R$, and $T$ are each growing at a constant rate. Thus what is needed for a balanced growth path is that $K$ and $Y$ each grow at a constant rate. The equation of motion for capital, $\dot{K}(t) = sY(t) - \delta K(t)$, implies that the growth rate of $K$ is

$$\frac{\dot{K}(t)}{K(t)} = s\frac{Y(t)}{K(t)} - \delta. \tag{1.44}$$

Thus for the growth rate of $K$ to be constant, $Y/K$ must be constant. That is, the growth rates of $Y$ and $K$ must be equal.

We can use the production function, (1.41), to find when this can occur. Taking logs of both sides of (1.41) gives us

$$\ln Y(t) = \alpha \ln K(t) + \beta \ln R(t) + \gamma \ln T(t)$$

$$+ (1 - \alpha - \beta - \gamma)[\ln A(t) + \ln L(t)]. \tag{1.45}$$

We can now differentiate both sides of this expression with respect to time. Using the fact that the time derivative of the log of a variable equals the variable's growth rate, we obtain

$$g_Y(t) = \alpha g_K(t) + \beta g_R(t) + \gamma g_T(t) + (1 - \alpha - \beta - \gamma)[g_A(t) + g_L(t)], \tag{1.46}$$

where $g_X$ denotes the growth rate of $X$. The growth rates of $R$, $T$, $A$, and $L$ are $-b$, $0$, $g$, and $n$, respectively. Thus (1.46) simplifies to

$$g_Y(t) = \alpha g_K(t) - \beta b + (1 - \alpha - \beta - \gamma)(n + g). \tag{1.47}$$

We can now use our finding that $g_Y$ and $g_K$ must be equal if the economy is on a balanced growth path. Imposing $g_K = g_Y$ on (1.47) and solving for $g_Y$ gives us

$$g_Y^{bgp} = \frac{(1 - \alpha - \beta - \gamma)(n + g) - \beta b}{1 - \alpha}, \tag{1.48}$$

where $g_Y^{bgp}$ denotes the growth rate of $Y$ on the balanced growth path.

This analysis leaves out a step: we have not determined whether the economy in fact converges to this balanced growth path. From (1.47), we know that if $g_K$ exceeds its balanced-growth-path value, $g_Y$ does as well, but by less than $g_K$ does. Thus if $g_K$ exceeds its balanced-growth-path value, $Y/K$ is falling. Equation (1.44) tells us that $g_K$ equals $s(Y/K) - \delta$. Thus if $Y/K$ is falling, $g_K$ is falling as well. That is, if $g_K$ exceeds its balanced-growth-path value, it is falling. Similarly, if it is less than its balanced-growth-path value, it is rising. Thus $g_K$ converges to its balanced-growth-path value, and so the economy converges to its balanced growth path.[23]

Equation (1.48) implies that the growth rate of output per worker on the balanced growth path is

$$
\begin{aligned}
g_{Y/L}^{bgp} &= g_Y^{bgp} - g_L^{bgp} \\
&= \frac{(1 - \alpha - \beta - \gamma)(n + g) - \beta b}{1 - \alpha} - n \\
&= \frac{(1 - \alpha - \beta - \gamma)g - \beta b - (\beta + \gamma)n}{1 - \alpha}.
\end{aligned}
\tag{1.49}
$$

Equation (1.49) shows that growth in income per worker on the balanced growth path, $g_{Y/L}^{bgp}$, can be either positive or negative. That is, resource and land limitations can cause output per worker to eventually be falling, but they need not. The declining quantities of resources and land per worker are drags on growth. But technological progress is a spur to growth. If the spur is larger than the drags, then there is sustained growth in output per worker. This is precisely what has happened over the past few centuries.

---

[23] This analysis overlooks one subtlety. If $(1 - \alpha - \beta - \gamma)(n + g) + (1 - \alpha)\delta - \beta b$ is negative, the condition $g_K = g_K^{bgp}$ holds only for a negative value of $Y/K$. And the statement that $Y/K$ is falling when $g_Y$ is less than $g_K$ is not true if $Y/K$ is zero or negative. As a result, if $(1 - \alpha - \beta - \gamma)(n + g) + (1 - \alpha)\delta - \beta b$ is negative, the economy does not converge to the balanced growth path described in the text, but to a situation where $Y/K = 0$ and $g_K = -\delta$. But for any reasonable parameter values, $(1 - \alpha - \beta - \gamma)(n + g) + (1 - \alpha)\delta - \beta b$ is positive. Thus this complication is not important.

## An Illustrative Calculation

In recent history, the advantages of technological progress have outweighed the disadvantages of resource and land limitations. But this does not tell us how large those disadvantages are. For example, they might be large enough that only a moderate slowing of technological progress would make overall growth in income per worker negative.

Resource and land limitations reduce growth by causing resource use per worker and land per worker to be falling. Thus, as Nordhaus (1992) observes, to gauge how much these limitations are reducing growth, we need to ask how much greater growth would be if resources and land per worker were constant. Concretely, consider an economy identical to the one we have just considered except that the assumptions $\dot{T}(t) = 0$ and $\dot{R}(t) = -bR(t)$ are replaced with the assumptions $\dot{T}(t) = nT(t)$ and $\dot{R}(t) = nR(t)$. In this hypothetical economy, there are no resource and land limitations; both grow as population grows. Analysis parallel to that used to derive equation (1.49) shows that growth of output per worker on the balanced growth path of this economy is[24]

$$\tilde{g}_{Y/L}^{bgp} = \frac{1}{1-\alpha}(1 - \alpha - \beta - \gamma)g. \tag{1.50}$$

The "growth drag" from resource and land limitations is the difference between growth in this hypothetical case and growth in the case of resource and land limitations:

$$
\begin{aligned}
\text{Drag} &= \tilde{g}_{Y/L}^{bgp} - g_{Y/L}^{bgp} \\
&= \frac{(1 - \alpha - \beta - \gamma)g - [(1 - \alpha - \beta - \gamma)g - \beta b - (\beta + \gamma)n]}{1 - \alpha} \\
&= \frac{\beta b + (\beta + \gamma)n}{1 - \alpha}.
\end{aligned}
\tag{1.51}
$$

Thus, the growth drag is increasing in resources' share ($\beta$), land's share ($\gamma$), the rate that resource use is falling ($b$), the rate of population growth ($n$), and capital's share ($\alpha$).

It is possible to quantify the size of the drag. Because resources and land are traded in markets, we can use income data to estimate their importance in production—that is, to estimate $\beta$ and $\gamma$. As Nordhaus (1992) describes, these data suggest a combined value of $\beta + \gamma$ of about 0.2. Nordhaus goes on to use a somewhat more complicated version of the framework presented here to estimate the growth drag. His point estimate is a drag of 0.0024—that is, about a quarter of a percentage point per year. He finds that only about a quarter of the drag is due to the limited supply of land. Of

---

[24] See Problem 1.15.

the remainder, he estimates that the vast majority is due to limited energy resources.

Thus this evidence suggests that the reduction in growth caused by environmental limitations, while not trivial, is not large. In addition, since growth in income per worker has been far more than a quarter of a percentage point per year, the evidence suggests that there would have to be very large changes for resource and land limitations to cause income per worker to start falling.

## A Complication

The stock of land is fixed, and resource use must eventually fall. Thus even though technology has been able to keep ahead of resource and land limitations over the past few centuries, it may still appear that those limitations must eventually become a binding constraint on our ability to produce.

The reason that this does not occur in our model is that production is Cobb-Douglas. With Cobb-Douglas production, a given percentage change in $A$ always produces the same percentage change in output, regardless of how large $A$ is relative to $R$ and $T$. As a result, technological progress can always counterbalance declines in $R/L$ and $T/L$.

This is not a general property of production functions, however. With Cobb-Douglas production, the elasticity of substitution between inputs is 1. If this elasticity is less than 1, the share of income going to the inputs that are becoming scarcer rises over time. Intuitively, as the production function becomes more like the Leontief case, the inputs that are becoming scarcer become increasingly important. Conversely, if the elasticity of substitution is greater than 1, the share of income going to the inputs that are becoming scarcer is falling. This, too, is intuitive: as the production function becomes closer to linear, the abundant factors benefit.

In terms of our earlier analysis, what this means is that if we do not restrict our attention to Cobb-Douglas production, the shares in expression (1.51) for the growth drag are no longer constant, but are functions of factor proportions. And if the elasticity of substitution is less than 1, the share of income going to resources and land is rising over time—and thus the growth drag is as well. Indeed, in this case the share of income going to the slowest-growing input—resources—approaches 1. Thus the growth drag approaches $b + n$. That is, asymptotically income per worker declines at rate $b + n$, the rate at which resource use per worker is falling. This case supports our apocalyptic intuition: in the long run, the fixed supply of resources leads to steadily declining incomes.

In fact, however, recognizing that production may not be Cobb–Douglas should not raise our estimate of the importance of resource and land limitations, but reduce it. The reason is that the shares of income going to resources and land are falling rather than rising. We can write land's share as the real rental price of land multiplied by the ratio of land to output. The real rental price shows little trend, while the land-to-GDP ratio has been falling steadily. Thus land's share has been declining. Similarly, real resource prices have had a moderate downward trend, and the ratio of resource use to GDP has also been falling. Thus resources' share has also been declining. And declining resource and land shares imply a falling growth drag.

The fact that land's and resources' shares have been declining despite the fact that these factors have been becoming relatively scarcer means that the elasticity of substitution between these inputs and the others must be greater than 1. At first glance, this may seem surprising. If we think in terms of narrowly defined goods—books, for example—possibilities for substitution among inputs may not seem particularly large. But if we recognize that what people value is not particular goods but the ultimate services they provide—information storage, for example—the idea that there are often large possibilities for substitution becomes more plausible. Information can be stored not only through books, but through oral tradition, stone tablets, microfilm, videotape, DVDs, hard drives, and more. These different means of storage use capital, resources, land, and labor in very different proportions. As a result, the economy can respond to the increasing scarcity of resources and land by moving to means of information storage that use those inputs less intensively.

## Pollution

Declining quantities of resources and land per worker are not the only ways that environmental problems can limit growth. Production creates pollution. This pollution reduces properly measured output. That is, if our data on real output accounted for all the outputs of production at prices that reflect their impacts on utility, pollution would enter with a negative price. In addition, pollution could rise to the point where it reduces conventionally measured output. For example, global warming could reduce output through its impact on sea levels and weather patterns.

Economic theory does not give us reason to be sanguine about pollution. Because those who pollute do not bear the costs of their pollution, an unregulated market leads to excessive pollution. Similarly, there is nothing to prevent an environmental catastrophe in an unregulated market. For example, suppose there is some critical level of pollution that would result in a sudden and drastic change in climate. Because pollution's effects are external, there is no market mechanism to prevent pollution from rising to such a level, or even a market price of a pollution-free environment to warn us that well-informed individuals believe a catastrophe is imminent.

Conceptually, the correct policy to deal with pollution is straightforward. We should estimate the dollar value of the negative externality and tax pollution by this amount. This would bring private and social costs in line, and thus would result in the socially optimal level of pollution.[25]

Although describing the optimal policy is easy, it is still useful to know how severe the problems posed by pollution are. In terms of understanding economic growth, we would like to know by how much pollution is likely to retard growth if no corrective measures are taken. In terms of policy, we would like to know how large a pollution tax is appropriate. We would also like to know whether, if pollution taxes are politically infeasible, the benefits of cruder regulatory approaches are likely to outweigh their costs. Finally, in terms of our own behavior, we would like to know how much effort individuals who care about others' well-being should make to curtail their activities that cause pollution.

Since there are no market prices to use as guides, economists interested in pollution must begin by looking at the scientific evidence. In the case of global warming, for example, a reasonable point estimate is that in the absence of major intervention, the average temperature will rise by 3 degrees centigrade over the next century, with various effects on climate (Nordhaus, 2008). Economists can help estimate the welfare consequences of these changes. To give just one example, experts on farming had estimated the likely impact of global warming on U.S. farmers' ability to continue growing their current crops. These studies concluded that global warming would have a significant negative impact. Mendelsohn, Nordhaus, and Shaw (1994), however, note that farmers can respond to changing weather patterns by moving into different crops, or even switching their land use out of crops altogether. They find that once these possibilities for substitution are taken into account, the overall effect of global warming on U.S. farmers is small and may be positive (see also Deschenes and Greenstone, 2007).

After considering the various channels through which global warming is likely to affect welfare, Nordhaus (2008) concludes that a reasonable estimate is that the overall welfare effect as of 2100 is likely to be slightly negative—the equivalent of a reduction in GDP of 2 to 3 percent. This corresponds to a reduction in average annual growth of only about 0.03 percentage points. Not surprisingly, Nordhaus finds that drastic measures to combat global warming, such as policies that would largely halt further warming by cutting emissions of greenhouse gases to less than half their 1990 levels, would be much more harmful than simply doing nothing.

Using a similar approach, Nordhaus (1992) concludes that the welfare costs of other types of pollution are larger, but still limited. His point estimate is that they will lower appropriately measured annual growth by roughly 0.04 percentage points.

---

[25] Alternatively, we could find the socially optimal level of pollution and auction off a quantity of tradable permits that allow that level of pollution. Weitzman (1974) provides the classic analysis of the choice between controlling prices or quantities.

Of course, it is possible that this reading of the scientific evidence or this effort to estimate welfare effects is far from the mark. It is also possible that considering horizons longer than the 50 to 100 years usually examined in such studies would change the conclusions substantially. But the fact remains that most economists who have studied environmental issues seriously, even ones whose initial positions were sympathetic to environmental concerns, have concluded that the likely impact of environmental problems on growth is at most moderate.[26]

# Problems

**1.1. Basic properties of growth rates.** Use the fact that the growth rate of a variable equals the time derivative of its log to show:

(a) The growth rate of the product of two variables equals the sum of their growth rates. That is, if $Z(t) = X(t)Y(t)$, then $\dot{Z}(t)/Z(t) = [\dot{X}(t)/X(t)] + [\dot{Y}(t)/Y(t)]$.

(b) The growth rate of the ratio of two variables equals the difference of their growth rates. That is, if $Z(t) = X(t)/Y(t)$, then $\dot{Z}(t)/Z(t) = [\dot{X}(t)/X(t)] - [\dot{Y}(t)/Y(t)]$.

(c) If $Z(t) = X(t)^\alpha$, then $\dot{Z}(t)/Z(t) = \alpha\dot{X}(t)/X(t)$.

**1.2.** Suppose that the growth rate of some variable, $X$, is constant and equal to $a > 0$ from time 0 to time $t_1$; drops to 0 at time $t_1$; rises gradually from 0 to $a$ from time $t_1$ to time $t_2$; and is constant and equal to $a$ after time $t_2$.

(a) Sketch a graph of the growth rate of $X$ as a function of time.

(b) Sketch a graph of $\ln X$ as a function of time.

**1.3.** Describe how, if at all, each of the following developments affects the break-even and actual investment lines in our basic diagram for the Solow model:

(a) The rate of depreciation falls.

(b) The rate of technological progress rises.

(c) The production function is Cobb–Douglas, $f(k) = k^\alpha$, and capital's share, $\alpha$, rises.

(d) Workers exert more effort, so that output per unit of effective labor for a given value of capital per unit of effective labor is higher than before.

---

[26] This does not imply that environmental factors are always unimportant to long-run growth. Brander and Taylor (1998) make a strong case that Easter Island suffered an environmental disaster of the type envisioned by Malthusians sometime between its settlement around 400 and the arrival of Europeans in the 1700s. And they argue that other primitive societies may have also suffered such disasters.

**1.4.** Consider an economy with technological progress but without population growth that is on its balanced growth path. Now suppose there is a one-time jump in the number of workers.

(a) At the time of the jump, does output per unit of effective labor rise, fall, or stay the same? Why?

(b) After the initial change (if any) in output per unit of effective labor when the new workers appear, is there any further change in output per unit of effective labor? If so, does it rise or fall? Why?

(c) Once the economy has again reached a balanced growth path, is output per unit of effective labor higher, lower, or the same as it was before the new workers appeared? Why?

**1.5.** Suppose that the production function is Cobb–Douglas.

(a) Find expressions for $k^*$, $y^*$, and $c^*$ as functions of the parameters of the model, $s$, $n$, $\delta$, $g$, and $\alpha$.

(b) What is the golden-rule value of $k$?

(c) What saving rate is needed to yield the golden-rule capital stock?

**1.6.** Consider a Solow economy that is on its balanced growth path. Assume for simplicity that there is no technological progress. Now suppose that the rate of population growth falls.

(a) What happens to the balanced-growth-path values of capital per worker, output per worker, and consumption per worker? Sketch the paths of these variables as the economy moves to its new balanced growth path.

(b) Describe the effect of the fall in population growth on the path of output (that is, total output, not output per worker).

**1.7.** Find the elasticity of output per unit of effective labor on the balanced growth path, $y^*$, with respect to the rate of population growth, $n$. If $\alpha_K(k^*) = \frac{1}{3}$, $g = 2\%$, and $\delta = 3\%$, by about how much does a fall in $n$ from 2 percent to 1 percent raise $y^*$?

**1.8.** Suppose that investment as a fraction of output in the United States rises permanently from 0.15 to 0.18. Assume that capital's share is $\frac{1}{3}$.

(a) By about how much does output eventually rise relative to what it would have been without the rise in investment?

(b) By about how much does consumption rise relative to what it would have been without the rise in investment?

(c) What is the immediate effect of the rise in investment on consumption? About how long does it take for consumption to return to what it would have been without the rise in investment?

**1.9. Factor payments in the Solow model.** Assume that both labor and capital are paid their marginal products. Let $w$ denote $\partial F(K, AL)/\partial L$ and $r$ denote $[\partial F(K, AL)/\partial K] - \delta$.

(a) Show that the marginal product of labor, $w$, is $A[f(k) - kf'(k)]$.

(*b*) Show that if both capital and labor are paid their marginal products, constant returns to scale imply that the total amount paid to the factors of production equals total net output. That is, show that under constant returns, $wL + rK = F(K,AL) - \delta K$.

(*c*) The return to capital ($r$) is roughly constant over time, as are the shares of output going to capital and to labor. Does a Solow economy on a balanced growth path exhibit these properties? What are the growth rates of $w$ and $r$ on a balanced growth path?

(*d*) Suppose the economy begins with a level of $k$ less than $k^*$. As $k$ moves toward $k^*$, is $w$ growing at a rate greater than, less than, or equal to its growth rate on the balanced growth path? What about $r$?

**1.10.** Suppose that, as in Problem 1.9, capital and labor are paid their marginal products. In addition, suppose that all capital income is saved and all labor income is consumed. Thus $\dot{K} = [\partial F(K,AL)/\partial K]K - \delta K$.

(*a*) Show that this economy converges to a balanced growth path.

(*b*) Is $k$ on the balanced growth path greater than, less than, or equal to the golden-rule level of $k$? What is the intuition for this result?

**1.11.** Go through steps analogous to those in equations (1.28)–(1.31) to find how quickly $y$ converges to $y^*$ in the vicinity of the balanced growth path. (Hint: Since $y = f(k)$, we can write $k = g(y)$, where $g(\bullet) = f^{-1}(\bullet)$.)

**1.12. Embodied technological progress.** (This follows Solow, 1960, and Sato, 1966.) One view of technological progress is that the productivity of capital goods built at $t$ depends on the state of technology at $t$ and is unaffected by subsequent technological progress. This is known as *embodied technological progress* (technological progress must be "embodied" in new capital before it can raise output). This problem asks you to investigate its effects.

(*a*) As a preliminary, let us modify the basic Solow model to make technological progress capital-augmenting rather than labor-augmenting. So that a balanced growth path exists, assume that the production function is Cobb–Douglas: $Y(t) = [A(t)K(t)]^\alpha L(t)^{1-\alpha}$. Assume that $A$ grows at rate $\mu$: $\dot{A}(t) = \mu A(t)$.

Show that the economy converges to a balanced growth path, and find the growth rates of $Y$ and $K$ on the balanced growth path. (Hint: Show that we can write $Y/(A^\phi L)$ as a function of $K/(A^\phi L)$, where $\phi = \alpha/(1-\alpha)$. Then analyze the dynamics of $K/(A^\phi L)$.)

(*b*) Now consider embodied technological progress. Specifically, let the production function be $Y(t) = J(t)^\alpha L(t)^{1-\alpha}$, where $J(t)$ is the effective capital stock. The dynamics of $J(t)$ are given by $\dot{J}(t) = sA(t)Y(t) - \delta J(t)$. The presence of the $A(t)$ term in this expression means that the productivity of investment at $t$ depends on the technology at $t$.

Show that the economy converges to a balanced growth path. What are the growth rates of $Y$ and $J$ on the balanced growth path? (Hint: Let $\bar{J}(t) = J(t)/A(t)$. Then use the same approach as in (*a*), focusing on $\bar{J}/(A^\phi L)$ instead of $K/(A^\phi L)$.)

(c) What is the elasticity of output on the balanced growth path with respect to $s$?

(d) In the vicinity of the balanced growth path, how rapidly does the economy converge to the balanced growth path?

(e) Compare your results for (c) and (d) with the corresponding results in the text for the basic Solow model.

**1.13.** Consider a Solow economy on its balanced growth path. Suppose the growth-accounting techniques described in Section 1.7 are applied to this economy.

(a) What fraction of growth in output per worker does growth accounting attribute to growth in capital per worker? What fraction does it attribute to technological progress?

(b) How can you reconcile your results in (a) with the fact that the Solow model implies that the growth rate of output per worker on the balanced growth path is determined solely by the rate of technological progress?

**1.14.** (a) In the model of convergence and measurement error in equations (1.38) and (1.39), suppose the true value of $b$ is $-1$. Does a regression of $\ln(Y/N)_{1979} - \ln(Y/N)_{1870}$ on a constant and $\ln(Y/N)_{1870}$ yield a biased estimate of $b$? Explain.

(b) Suppose there is measurement error in measured 1979 income per capita but not in 1870 income per capita. Does a regression of $\ln(Y/N)_{1979} - \ln(Y/N)_{1870}$ on a constant and $\ln(Y/N)_{1870}$ yield a biased estimate of $b$? Explain.

**1.15.** Derive equation (1.50). (Hint: Follow steps analogous to those in equations [1.47] and [1.48].)

# Chapter **2**
# INFINITE-HORIZON AND OVERLAPPING-GENERATIONS MODELS

This chapter investigates two models that resemble the Solow model but in which the dynamics of economic aggregates are determined by decisions at the microeconomic level. Both models continue to take the growth rates of labor and knowledge as given. But the models derive the evolution of the capital stock from the interaction of maximizing households and firms in competitive markets. As a result, the saving rate is no longer exogenous, and it need not be constant.

The first model is conceptually the simplest. Competitive firms rent capital and hire labor to produce and sell output, and a fixed number of infinitely lived households supply labor, hold capital, consume, and save. This model, which was developed by Ramsey (1928), Cass (1965), and Koopmans (1965), avoids all market imperfections and all issues raised by heterogeneous households and links among generations. It therefore provides a natural benchmark case.

The second model is the overlapping-generations model developed by Diamond (1965). The key difference between the Diamond model and the Ramsey–Cass–Koopmans model is that the Diamond model assumes continual entry of new households into the economy. As we will see, this seemingly small difference has important consequences.

# Part A   The Ramsey–Cass–Koopmans Model

## 2.1   Assumptions

### Firms

There are a large number of identical firms. Each has access to the production function $Y = F(K, AL)$, which satisfies the same assumptions as

49

in Chapter 1. The firms hire workers and rent capital in competitive factor markets, and sell their output in a competitive output market. Firms take $A$ as given; as in the Solow model, $A$ grows exogenously at rate $g$. The firms maximize profits. They are owned by the households, so any profits they earn accrue to the households.

## Households

There are also a large number of identical households. The size of each household grows at rate $n$. Each member of the household supplies 1 unit of labor at every point in time. In addition, the household rents whatever capital it owns to firms. It has initial capital holdings of $K(0)/H$, where $K(0)$ is the initial amount of capital in the economy and $H$ is the number of households. As in the Solow model, the initial capital stock is assumed to be strictly positive. For simplicity, here we assume there is no depreciation. The household divides its income (from the labor and capital it supplies and, potentially, from the profits it receives from firms) at each point in time between consumption and saving so as to maximize its lifetime utility.

The household's utility function takes the form

$$U = \int_{t=0}^{\infty} e^{-\rho t} u(C(t)) \frac{L(t)}{H} \, dt. \tag{2.1}$$

$C(t)$ is the consumption of each member of the household at time $t$. $u(\bullet)$ is the *instantaneous utility function*, which gives each member's utility at a given date. $L(t)$ is the total population of the economy; $L(t)/H$ is therefore the number of members of the household. Thus $u(C(t))L(t)/H$ is the household's total instantaneous utility at $t$. Finally, $\rho$ is the discount rate; the greater is $\rho$, the less the household values future consumption relative to current consumption.[1]

The instantaneous utility function takes the form

$$u(C(t)) = \frac{C(t)^{1-\theta}}{1-\theta}, \qquad \theta > 0, \qquad \rho - n - (1-\theta)g > 0. \tag{2.2}$$

This functional form is needed for the economy to converge to a balanced growth path. It is known as *constant-relative-risk-aversion* (or *CRRA*) utility. The reason for the name is that the coefficient of relative risk aversion (which is defined as $-Cu''(C)/u'(C)$) for this utility function is $\theta$, and thus is independent of $C$.

Since there is no uncertainty in this model, the household's attitude toward risk is not directly relevant. But $\theta$ also determines the household's

---

[1] One can also write utility as $\int_{t=0}^{\infty} e^{-\rho' t} u(C(t)) \, dt$, where $\rho' \equiv \rho - n$. Since $L(t) = L(0)e^{nt}$, this expression equals the expression in equation (2.1) divided by $L(0)/H$, and thus has the same implications for behavior.

willingness to shift consumption between different periods. When $\theta$ is smaller, marginal utility falls more slowly as consumption rises, and so the household is more willing to allow its consumption to vary over time. If $\theta$ is close to zero, for example, utility is almost linear in $C$, and so the household is willing to accept large swings in consumption to take advantage of small differences between the discount rate and the rate of return on saving. Specifically, one can show that the elasticity of substitution between consumption at any two points in time is $1/\theta$.[2]

Three additional features of the instantaneous utility function are worth mentioning. First, $C^{1-\theta}$ is increasing in $C$ if $\theta < 1$ but decreasing if $\theta > 1$; dividing $C^{1-\theta}$ by $1 - \theta$ thus ensures that the marginal utility of consumption is positive regardless of the value of $\theta$. Second, in the special case of $\theta \to 1$, the instantaneous utility function simplifies to $\ln C$; this is often a useful case to consider.[3] And third, the assumption that $\rho - n - (1 - \theta)g > 0$ ensures that lifetime utility does not diverge: if this condition does not hold, the household can attain infinite lifetime utility, and its maximization problem does not have a well-defined solution.[4]

# 2.2 The Behavior of Households and Firms

## Firms

Firms' behavior is relatively simple. At each point in time they employ the stocks of labor and capital, pay them their marginal products, and sell the resulting output. Because the production function has constant returns and the economy is competitive, firms earn zero profits.

As described in Chapter 1, the marginal product of capital, $\partial F(K, AL)/\partial K$, is $f'(k)$, where $f(\bullet)$ is the intensive form of the production function. Because markets are competitive, capital earns its marginal product. And because there is no depreciation, the real rate of return on capital equals its earnings per unit time. Thus the real interest rate at time $t$ is

$$r(t) = f'(k(t)). \tag{2.3}$$

Labor's marginal product is $\partial F(K, AL)/\partial L$, which equals $A\partial F(K, AL)/\partial AL$. In terms of $f(\bullet)$, this is $A[f(k) - kf'(k)]$.[5] Thus the real wage

---

[2] See Problem 2.2.

[3] To see this, first subtract $1/(1-\theta)$ from the utility function; since this changes utility by a constant, it does not affect behavior. Then take the limit as $\theta$ approaches 1; this requires using l'Hôpital's rule. The result is $\ln C$.

[4] Phelps (1966a) discusses how growth models can be analyzed when households can obtain infinite utility.

[5] See Problem 1.9.

at $t$ is

$$W(t) = A(t)[f(k(t)) - k(t)f'(k(t))]. \tag{2.4}$$

The wage per unit of *effective* labor is therefore

$$w(t) = f(k(t)) - k(t)f'(k(t)). \tag{2.5}$$

## Households' Budget Constraint

The representative household takes the paths of $r$ and $w$ as given. Its budget constraint is that the present value of its lifetime consumption cannot exceed its initial wealth plus the present value of its lifetime labor income. To write the budget constraint formally, we need to account for the fact that $r$ may vary over time. To do this, define $R(t)$ as $\int_{\tau=0}^{t} r(\tau)\, d\tau$. One unit of the output good invested at time 0 yields $e^{R(t)}$ units of the good at $t$; equivalently, the value of 1 unit of output at time $t$ in terms of output at time 0 is $e^{-R(t)}$. For example, if $r$ is constant at some level $\bar{r}$, $R(t)$ is simply $\bar{r}t$ and the present value of 1 unit of output at $t$ is $e^{-\bar{r}t}$. More generally, $e^{R(t)}$ shows the effects of continuously compounding interest over the period $[0,t]$.

Since the household has $L(t)/H$ members, its labor income at $t$ is $W(t)L(t)/H$, and its consumption expenditures are $C(t)L(t)/H$. Its initial wealth is $1/H$ of total wealth at time 0, or $K(0)/H$. The household's budget constraint is therefore

$$\int_{t=0}^{\infty} e^{-R(t)}C(t)\frac{L(t)}{H}\, dt \leq \frac{K(0)}{H} + \int_{t=0}^{\infty} e^{-R(t)}W(t)\frac{L(t)}{H}\, dt. \tag{2.6}$$

In general, it is not possible to find the integrals in this expression. Fortunately, we can express the budget constraint in terms of the limiting behavior of the household's capital holdings; and it is usually possible to describe the limiting behavior of the economy. To see how the budget constraint can be rewritten in this way, first bring all the terms of (2.6) over to the same side and combine the two integrals; this gives us

$$\frac{K(0)}{H} + \int_{t=0}^{\infty} e^{-R(t)}[W(t) - C(t)]\frac{L(t)}{H}\, dt \geq 0. \tag{2.7}$$

We can write the integral from $t = 0$ to $t = \infty$ as a limit. Thus (2.7) is equivalent to

$$\lim_{s\to\infty}\left[\frac{K(0)}{H} + \int_{t=0}^{s} e^{-R(t)}[W(t) - C(t)]\frac{L(t)}{H}\, dt\right] \geq 0. \tag{2.8}$$

Now note that the household's capital holdings at time $s$ are

$$\frac{K(s)}{H} = e^{R(s)}\frac{K(0)}{H} + \int_{t=0}^{s} e^{R(s)-R(t)}[W(t) - C(t)]\frac{L(t)}{H}\,dt. \qquad (2.9)$$

To understand (2.9), observe that $e^{R(s)}K(0)/H$ is the contribution of the household's initial wealth to its wealth at $s$. The household's saving at $t$ is $[W(t) - C(t)]L(t)/H$ (which may be negative); $e^{R(s)-R(t)}$ shows how the value of that saving changes from $t$ to $s$.

The expression in (2.9) is $e^{R(s)}$ times the expression in brackets in (2.8). Thus we can write the budget constraint as simply

$$\lim_{s\to\infty} e^{-R(s)}\frac{K(s)}{H} \geq 0. \qquad (2.10)$$

Expressed in this form, the budget constraint states that the present value of the household's asset holdings cannot be negative in the limit.

Equation (2.10) is known as the *no-Ponzi-game condition*. A Ponzi game is a scheme in which someone issues debt and rolls it over forever. That is, the issuer always obtains the funds to pay off debt when it comes due by issuing new debt. Such a scheme allows the issuer to have a present value of lifetime consumption that exceeds the present value of his or her lifetime resources. By imposing the budget constraint (2.6) or (2.10), we are ruling out such schemes.[6]

## Households' Maximization Problem

The representative household wants to maximize its lifetime utility subject to its budget constraint. As in the Solow model, it is easier to work with variables normalized by the quantity of effective labor. To do this, we need to express both the objective function and the budget constraint in terms of consumption and labor income per unit of effective labor.

---

[6] This analysis sweeps a subtlety under the rug: we have assumed rather than shown that households must satisfy the no-Ponzi-game condition. Because there are a finite number of households in the model, the assumption that Ponzi games are not feasible is correct. A household can run a Ponzi game only if at least one other household has a present value of lifetime consumption that is strictly less than the present value of its lifetime wealth. Since the marginal utility of consumption is always positive, no household will accept this. But in models with infinitely many households, such as the overlapping-generations model of Part B of this chapter, Ponzi games are possible in some situations. We return to this point in Section 12.1.

We start with the objective function. Define $c(t)$ to be consumption per unit of effective labor. Thus $C(t)$, consumption per worker, equals $A(t)c(t)$. The household's instantaneous utility, (2.2), is therefore

$$\frac{C(t)^{1-\theta}}{1-\theta} = \frac{[A(t)c(t)]^{1-\theta}}{1-\theta}$$

$$= \frac{[A(0)e^{gt}]^{1-\theta}c(t)^{1-\theta}}{1-\theta} \tag{2.11}$$

$$= A(0)^{1-\theta}e^{(1-\theta)gt}\frac{c(t)^{1-\theta}}{1-\theta}.$$

Substituting (2.11) and the fact that $L(t) = L(0)e^{nt}$ into the household's objective function, (2.1)–(2.2), yields

$$U = \int_{t=0}^{\infty} e^{-\rho t}\frac{C(t)^{1-\theta}}{1-\theta}\frac{L(t)}{H}\,dt$$

$$= \int_{t=0}^{\infty} e^{-\rho t}\left[A(0)^{1-\theta}e^{(1-\theta)gt}\frac{c(t)^{1-\theta}}{1-\theta}\right]\frac{L(0)e^{nt}}{H}\,dt \tag{2.12}$$

$$= A(0)^{1-\theta}\frac{L(0)}{H}\int_{t=0}^{\infty} e^{-\rho t}e^{(1-\theta)gt}e^{nt}\frac{c(t)^{1-\theta}}{1-\theta}\,dt$$

$$\equiv B\int_{t=0}^{\infty} e^{-\beta t}\frac{c(t)^{1-\theta}}{1-\theta}\,dt,$$

where $B \equiv A(0)^{1-\theta}L(0)/H$ and $\beta \equiv \rho - n - (1-\theta)g$. From (2.2), $\beta$ is assumed to be positive.

Now consider the budget constraint, (2.6). The household's total consumption at $t$, $C(t)L(t)/H$, equals consumption per unit of effective labor, $c(t)$, times the household's quantity of effective labor, $A(t)L(t)/H$. Similarly, its total labor income at $t$ equals the wage per unit of effective labor, $w(t)$, times $A(t)L(t)/H$. And its initial capital holdings are capital per unit of effective labor at time 0, $k(0)$, times $A(0)L(0)/H$. Thus we can rewrite (2.6) as

$$\int_{t=0}^{\infty} e^{-R(t)}c(t)\frac{A(t)L(t)}{H}\,dt$$

$$\leq k(0)\frac{A(0)L(0)}{H} + \int_{t=0}^{\infty} e^{-R(t)}w(t)\frac{A(t)L(t)}{H}\,dt. \tag{2.13}$$

$A(t)L(t)$ equals $A(0)L(0)e^{(n+g)t}$. Substituting this fact into (2.13) and dividing both sides by $A(0)L(0)/H$ yields

$$\int_{t=0}^{\infty} e^{-R(t)}c(t)e^{(n+g)t}\,dt \leq k(0) + \int_{t=0}^{\infty} e^{-R(t)}w(t)e^{(n+g)t}\,dt. \tag{2.14}$$

Finally, because $K(s)$ is proportional to $k(s)e^{(n+g)s}$, we can rewrite the no-Ponzi-game version of the budget constraint, (2.10), as

$$\lim_{s \to \infty} e^{-R(s)} e^{(n+g)s} k(s) \ge 0. \tag{2.15}$$

## Household Behavior

The household's problem is to choose the path of $c(t)$ to maximize lifetime utility, (2.12), subject to the budget constraint, (2.14). Although this involves choosing $c$ at each instant of time (rather than choosing a finite set of variables, as in standard maximization problems), conventional maximization techniques can be used. Since the marginal utility of consumption is always positive, the household satisfies its budget constraint with equality. We can therefore use the objective function, (2.12), and the budget constraint, (2.14), to set up the Lagrangian:

$$\mathcal{L} = B \int_{t=0}^{\infty} e^{-\beta t} \frac{c(t)^{1-\theta}}{1-\theta} \, dt$$

$$+ \lambda \left[ k(0) + \int_{t=0}^{\infty} e^{-R(t)} e^{(n+g)t} w(t) \, dt - \int_{t=0}^{\infty} e^{-R(t)} e^{(n+g)t} c(t) \, dt \right]. \tag{2.16}$$

The household chooses $c$ at each point in time; that is, it chooses infinitely many $c(t)$'s. The first-order condition for an individual $c(t)$ is[7]

$$B e^{-\beta t} c(t)^{-\theta} = \lambda e^{-R(t)} e^{(n+g)t}. \tag{2.17}$$

The household's behavior is characterized by (2.17) and the budget constraint, (2.14).

---

[7] This step is slightly informal; the difficulty is that the terms in (2.17) are of order $dt$ in (2.16); that is, they make an infinitesimal contribution to the Lagrangian. There are various ways of addressing this issue more formally than simply "canceling" the $dt$'s (which is what we do in [2.17]). For example, we can model the household as choosing consumption over the finite intervals $[0,\Delta t)$, $[\Delta t, 2\Delta t)$, $[2\Delta t, 3\Delta t)$, ..., with its consumption required to be constant within each interval, and then take the limit as $\Delta t$ approaches zero. This also yields (2.17). Another possibility is to use the *calculus of variations* (see n. 13, at the end of Section 2.4). In this particular application, however, the calculus-of-variations approach simplifies to the approach we have used here. That is, here the calculus-of-variations approach is no more rigorous than the approach we have used. To put it differently, the methods used to derive the calculus of variations provide a formal justification for canceling the $dt$'s in (2.17).

To see what (2.17) implies for the behavior of consumption, first take logs of both sides:

$$\ln B - \beta t - \theta \ln c(t) = \ln \lambda - R(t) + (n + g)t$$

$$= \ln \lambda - \int_{\tau=0}^{t} r(\tau)\, d\tau + (n + g)t, \tag{2.18}$$

where the second line uses the definition of $R(t)$ as $\int_{\tau=0}^{t} r(\tau)\, d\tau$. Now note that since the two sides of (2.18) are equal for every $t$, the derivatives of the two sides with respect to $t$ must be the same. This condition is

$$-\beta - \theta\frac{\dot{c}(t)}{c(t)} = -r(t) + (n + g), \tag{2.19}$$

where we have once again used the fact that the time derivative of the log of a variable equals its growth rate. Solving (2.19) for $\dot{c}(t)/c(t)$ yields

$$\frac{\dot{c}(t)}{c(t)} = \frac{r(t) - n - g - \beta}{\theta}$$

$$= \frac{r(t) - \rho - \theta g}{\theta}, \tag{2.20}$$

where the second line uses the definition of $\beta$ as $\rho - n - (1 - \theta)g$.

To interpret (2.20), note that since $C(t)$ (consumption per worker) equals $c(t)A(t)$, the growth rate of $C$ is given by

$$\frac{\dot{C}(t)}{C(t)} = \frac{\dot{A}(t)}{A(t)} + \frac{\dot{c}(t)}{c(t)}$$

$$= g + \frac{r(t) - \rho - \theta g}{\theta} \tag{2.21}$$

$$= \frac{r(t) - \rho}{\theta},$$

where the second line uses (2.20). This condition states that consumption per worker is rising if the real return exceeds the rate at which the household discounts future consumption, and is falling if the reverse holds. The smaller is $\theta$—the less marginal utility changes as consumption changes—the larger are the changes in consumption in response to differences between the real interest rate and the discount rate.

Equation (2.20) is known as the *Euler equation* for this maximization problem. A more intuitive way of deriving (2.20) is to think of the household's consumption at two consecutive moments in time.[8] Specifically, imagine the household reducing $c$ at some date $t$ by a small (formally, infinitesimal) amount $\Delta c$, investing this additional saving for a short (again,

---

[8] The intuition for the Euler equation is considerably easier if time is discrete rather than continuous. See Section 2.9.

infinitesimal) period of time $\Delta t$, and then consuming the proceeds at time $t + \Delta t$; assume that when it does this, the household leaves consumption and capital holdings at all times other than $t$ and $t + \Delta t$ unchanged. If the household is optimizing, the marginal impact of this change on lifetime utility must be zero. If the impact is strictly positive, the household can marginally raise its lifetime utility by making the change. And if the impact is strictly negative, the household can raise its lifetime utility by making the opposite change.

From (2.12), the marginal utility of $c(t)$ is $Be^{-\beta t}c(t)^{-\theta}$. Thus the change has a utility cost of $Be^{-\beta t}c(t)^{-\theta}\Delta c$. Since the instantaneous rate of return is $r(t)$, $c$ at time $t + \Delta t$ can be increased by $e^{[r(t) - n - g]\Delta t}\Delta c$. Similarly, since $c$ is growing at rate $\dot{c}(t)/c(t)$, we can write $c(t + \Delta t)$ as $c(t)e^{[\dot{c}(t)/c(t)]\Delta t}$. Thus the marginal utility of $c(t + \Delta t)$ is $Be^{-\beta(t+\Delta t)}c(t + \Delta t)^{-\theta}$, or $Be^{-\beta(t+\Delta t)}[c(t)e^{[\dot{c}(t)/c(t)]\Delta t}]^{-\theta}$. For the path of consumption to be utility-maximizing, it must therefore satisfy

$$Be^{-\beta t}c(t)^{-\theta}\Delta c = Be^{-\beta(t+\Delta t)}[c(t)e^{[\dot{c}(t)/c(t)]\Delta t}]^{-\theta}e^{[r(t)-n-g]\Delta t}\Delta c. \quad (2.22)$$

Dividing by $Be^{-\beta t}c(t)^{-\theta}\Delta c$ and taking logs yields

$$-\beta\,\Delta t - \theta\frac{\dot{c}(t)}{c(t)}\,\Delta t + [r(t) - n - g]\,\Delta t = 0. \quad (2.23)$$

Finally, dividing by $\Delta t$ and rearranging yields the Euler equation in (2.20).

Intuitively, the Euler equation describes how $c$ must behave over time given $c(0)$: if $c$ does not evolve according to (2.20), the household can re-arrange its consumption in a way that raises its lifetime utility without changing the present value of its lifetime spending. The choice of $c(0)$ is then determined by the requirement that the present value of lifetime consumption over the resulting path equals initial wealth plus the present value of future earnings. When $c(0)$ is chosen too low, consumption spending along the path satisfying (2.20) does not exhaust lifetime wealth, and so a higher path is possible; when $c(0)$ is set too high, consumption spending more than uses up lifetime wealth, and so the path is not feasible.[9]

# 2.3   The Dynamics of the Economy

The most convenient way to describe the behavior of the economy is in terms of the evolution of $c$ and $k$.

---

[9] Formally, equation (2.20) implies that $c(t) = c(0)e^{[R(t) - (\rho + \theta g)t]/\theta}$, which implies that $e^{-R(t)}e^{(n+g)t}c(t) = c(0)e^{[(1-\theta)R(t) + (\theta n - \rho)t]/\theta}$. Thus $c(0)$ is determined by the fact that $c(0)\int_{t=0}^{\infty} e^{[(1-\theta)R(t) + (\theta n - \rho)t]/\theta}\,dt$ must equal the right-hand side of the budget constraint, (2.14).

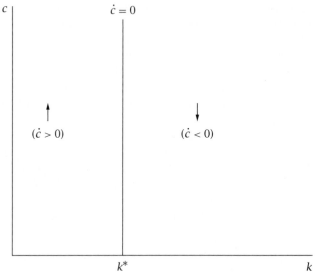

**FIGURE 2.1   The dynamics of c**

## The Dynamics of $c$

Since all households are the same, equation (2.20) describes the evolution of $c$ not just for a single household but for the economy as a whole. Since $r(t) = f'(k(t))$, we can rewrite (2.20) as

$$\frac{\dot{c}(t)}{c(t)} = \frac{f'(k(t)) - \rho - \theta g}{\theta}. \tag{2.24}$$

Thus $\dot{c}$ is zero when $f'(k)$ equals $\rho + \theta g$. Let $k^*$ denote this level of $k$. When $k$ exceeds $k^*$, $f'(k)$ is less than $\rho + \theta g$, and so $\dot{c}$ is negative; when $k$ is less than $k^*$, $\dot{c}$ is positive.

This information is summarized in Figure 2.1. The arrows show the direction of motion of $c$. Thus $c$ is rising if $k < k^*$ and falling if $k > k^*$. The $\dot{c} = 0$ line at $k = k^*$ indicates that $c$ is constant for this value of $k$.[10]

## The Dynamics of $k$

As in the Solow model, $\dot{k}$ equals actual investment minus break-even investment. Since we are assuming that there is no depreciation, break-even

---

[10] Note that (2.24) implies that $\dot{c}$ also equals zero when $c$ is zero. That is, $\dot{c}$ is also zero along the horizontal axis of the diagram. But since, as we will see below, in equilibrium $c$ is never zero, this is not relevant to the analysis of the model.

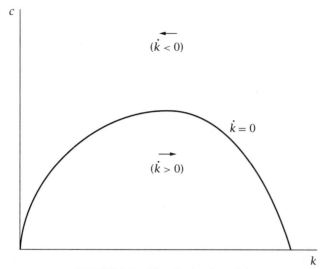

**FIGURE 2.2   The dynamics of k**

investment is $(n + g)k$. Actual investment is output minus consumption, $f(k) - c$. Thus,

$$\dot{k}(t) = f(k(t)) - c(t) - (n + g)k(t). \tag{2.25}$$

For a given $k$, the level of $c$ that implies $\dot{k} = 0$ is given by $f(k) - (n + g)k$; in terms of Figure 1.6 (in Chapter 1), $\dot{k}$ is zero when consumption equals the difference between the actual output and break-even investment lines. This value of $c$ is increasing in $k$ until $f'(k) = n + g$ (the golden-rule level of $k$) and is then decreasing. When $c$ exceeds the level that yields $\dot{k} = 0$, $k$ is falling; when $c$ is less than this level, $k$ is rising. For $k$ sufficiently large, break-even investment exceeds total output, and so $\dot{k}$ is negative for all positive values of $c$. This information is summarized in Figure 2.2; the arrows show the direction of motion of $k$.

## The Phase Diagram

Figure 2.3 combines the information in Figures 2.1 and 2.2. The arrows now show the directions of motion of both $c$ and $k$. To the left of the $\dot{c} = 0$ locus and above the $\dot{k} = 0$ locus, for example, $\dot{c}$ is positive and $\dot{k}$ negative. Thus $c$ is rising and $k$ falling, and so the arrows point up and to the left. The arrows in the other sections of the diagram are based on similar reasoning. On the $\dot{c} = 0$ and $\dot{k} = 0$ curves, only one of $c$ and $k$ is changing. On the $\dot{c} = 0$ line above the $\dot{k} = 0$ locus, for example, $c$ is constant and $k$ is falling; thus

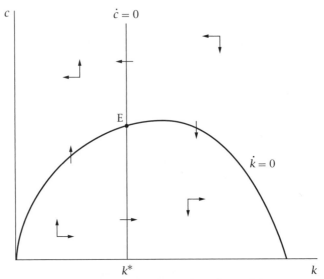

**FIGURE 2.3   The dynamics of $c$ and $k$**

the arrow points to the left. Finally, at Point E both $\dot{c}$ and $\dot{k}$ are zero; thus there is no movement from this point.[11]

Figure 2.3 is drawn with $k^*$ (the level of $k$ that implies $\dot{c} = 0$) less than the golden-rule level of $k$ (the value of $k$ associated with the peak of the $\dot{k} = 0$ locus). To see that this must be the case, recall that $k^*$ is defined by $f'(k^*) = \rho + \theta g$, and that the golden-rule $k$ is defined by $f'(k_{GR}) = n + g$. Since $f''(k)$ is negative, $k^*$ is less than $k_{GR}$ if and only if $\rho + \theta g$ is greater than $n + g$. This is equivalent to $\rho - n - (1 - \theta)g > 0$, which we have assumed to hold so that lifetime utility does not diverge (see [2.2]). Thus $k^*$ is to the left of the peak of the $\dot{k} = 0$ curve.

## The Initial Value of $c$

Figure 2.3 shows how $c$ and $k$ must evolve over time to satisfy households' intertemporal optimization condition (equation [2.24]) and the equation

---

[11] Recall from n. 10 that $\dot{c}$ is also zero along the horizontal axis of the phase diagram. As a result, there are two other points where $c$ and $k$ are constant. The first is the origin: if the economy has no capital and no consumption, it remains there. The second is the point where the $\dot{k} = 0$ curve crosses the horizontal axis. Here all of output is being used to hold $k$ constant, so $c = 0$ and $f(k) = (n + g)k$. Since having consumption change from zero to any positive amount violates households' intertemporal optimization condition, (2.24), if the economy is at this point it must remain there to satisfy (2.24) and (2.25). We will see shortly, however, that the economy is never at either of these points.

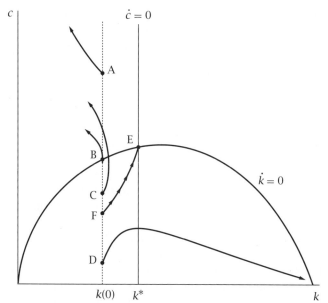

**FIGURE 2.4**   The behavior of *c* and *k* for various initial values of *c*

relating the change in *k* to output and consumption (equation [2.25]) *given initial values of c and k.* The initial value of *k* is given; but the initial value of *c* must be determined.

This issue is addressed in Figure 2.4. For concreteness, $k(0)$ is assumed to be less than $k^*$. The figure shows the trajectory of *c* and *k* for various assumptions concerning the initial level of *c*. If $c(0)$ is above the $\dot{k} = 0$ curve, at a point like A, then $\dot{c}$ is positive and $\dot{k}$ negative; thus the economy moves continually up and to the left in the diagram. If $c(0)$ is such that $\dot{k}$ is initially zero (Point B), the economy begins by moving directly up in $(k,c)$ space; thereafter $\dot{c}$ is positive and $\dot{k}$ negative, and so the economy again moves up and to the left. If the economy begins slightly below the $\dot{k} = 0$ locus (Point C), $\dot{k}$ is initially positive but small (since $\dot{k}$ is a continuous function of *c*), and $\dot{c}$ is again positive. Thus in this case the economy initially moves up and slightly to the right; after it crosses the $\dot{k} = 0$ locus, however, $\dot{k}$ becomes negative and once again the economy is on a path of rising *c* and falling *k*.

Point D shows a case of very low initial consumption. Here $\dot{c}$ and $\dot{k}$ are both initially positive. From (2.24), $\dot{c}$ is proportional to *c*; when *c* is small, $\dot{c}$ is therefore small. Thus *c* remains low, and so the economy eventually crosses the $\dot{c} = 0$ line. After this point, $\dot{c}$ becomes negative, and $\dot{k}$ remains positive. Thus the economy moves down and to the right.

$\dot{c}$ and $\dot{k}$ are continuous functions of *c* and *k*. Thus there is some critical point between Points C and D—Point F in the diagram—such that at that level of initial $c$, the economy converges to the stable point, Point E. For any level of consumption above this critical level, the $\dot{k} = 0$ curve is crossed before the $\dot{c} = 0$ line is reached, and so the economy ends up on a path of perpetually rising consumption and falling capital. And if consumption is less than the critical level, the $\dot{c} = 0$ locus is reached first, and so the economy embarks on a path of falling consumption and rising capital. But if consumption is just equal to the critical level, the economy converges to the point where both $c$ and $k$ are constant.

All these various trajectories satisfy equations (2.24) and (2.25). Does this mean that they are all possible? The answer is no, because we have not yet imposed the requirements that households must satisfy their budget constraint and that the economy's capital stock cannot be negative. These conditions determine which of the trajectories in fact describes the behavior of the economy.

If the economy starts at some point above F, $c$ is high and rising. As a result, the equation of motion for $k$, (2.25), implies that $k$ eventually reaches zero. For (2.24) and (2.25) to continue to be satisfied, $c$ must continue to rise and $k$ must become negative. But this cannot occur. Since output is zero when $k$ is zero, $c$ must drop to zero. This means that households are not satisfying their intertemporal optimization condition, (2.24). We can therefore rule out such paths.

To rule out paths starting below F, we use the budget constraint expressed in terms of the limiting behavior of capital holdings, equation (2.15): $\lim_{s \to \infty} e^{-R(s)} e^{(n+g)s} k(s) \geq 0$. If the economy starts at a point like D, eventually $k$ exceeds the golden-rule capital stock. After that time, the real interest rate, $f'(k)$, is less than $n + g$, so $e^{-R(s)} e^{(n+g)s}$ is rising. Since $k$ is also rising, $e^{-R(s)} e^{(n+g)s} k(s)$ diverges. Thus $\lim_{s \to \infty} e^{-R(s)} e^{(n+g)s} k(s)$ is infinity. From the derivation of (2.15), we know that this is equivalent to the statement that the present value of households' lifetime income is infinitely larger than the present value of their lifetime consumption. Thus each household can afford to raise its consumption at each point in time, and so can attain higher utility. That is, households are not maximizing their utility. Hence, such a path cannot be an equilibrium.

Finally, if the economy begins at Point F, $k$ converges to $k^*$, and so $r$ converges to $f'(k^*) = \rho + \theta g$. Thus eventually $e^{-R(s)} e^{(n+g)s}$ is falling at rate $\rho - n - (1 - \theta)g = \beta > 0$, and so $\lim_{s \to \infty} e^{-R(s)} e^{(n+g)s} k(s)$ is zero. Thus the path beginning at F, and only this path, is possible.

## The Saddle Path

Although this discussion has been in terms of a single value of $k$, the idea is general. For any positive initial level of $k$, there is a unique initial level of $c$ that is consistent with households' intertemporal optimization, the dynamics of the capital stock, households' budget constraint, and the requirement

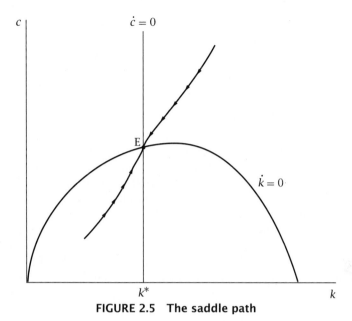

**FIGURE 2.5 The saddle path**

that $k$ not be negative. The function giving this initial $c$ as a function of $k$ is known as the *saddle path;* it is shown in Figure 2.5. For any starting value for $k$, the initial $c$ must be the value on the saddle path. The economy then moves along the saddle path to Point E.

## 2.4 Welfare

A natural question is whether the equilibrium of this economy represents a desirable outcome. The answer to this question is simple. The *first welfare theorem* from microeconomics tells us that if markets are competitive and complete and there are no externalities (and if the number of agents is finite), then the decentralized equilibrium is Pareto-efficient—that is, it is impossible to make anyone better off without making someone else worse off. Since the conditions of the first welfare theorem hold in our model, the equilibrium must be Pareto-efficient. And since all households have the same utility, this means that the decentralized equilibrium produces the highest possible utility among allocations that treat all households in the same way.

To see this more clearly, consider the problem facing a social planner who can dictate the division of output between consumption and investment at each date and who wants to maximize the lifetime utility of a representative household. This problem is identical to that of an individual household except that, rather than taking the paths of $w$ and $r$ as given, the planner takes into account the fact that these are determined by the path of $k$, which is in turn determined by (2.25).

The intuitive argument involving consumption at consecutive moments used to derive (2.20) or (2.24) applies to the social planner as well: reducing $c$ by $\Delta c$ at time $t$ and investing the proceeds allows the planner to increase $c$ at time $t + \Delta t$ by $e^{f'(k(t))\Delta t}e^{-(n+g)\Delta t}\Delta c$.[12] Thus $c(t)$ along the path chosen by the planner must satisfy (2.24). And since equation (2.25) giving the evolution of $k$ reflects technology, not preferences, the social planner must obey it as well. Finally, as with households' optimization problem, paths that require that the capital stock becomes negative can be ruled out on the grounds that they are not feasible, and paths that cause consumption to approach zero can be ruled out on the grounds that they do not maximize households' utility.

In short, the solution to the social planner's problem is for the initial value of $c$ to be given by the value on the saddle path, and for $c$ and $k$ to then move along the saddle path. That is, the competitive equilibrium maximizes the welfare of the representative household.[13]

# 2.5   The Balanced Growth Path

## Properties of the Balanced Growth Path

The behavior of the economy once it has converged to Point E is identical to that of the Solow economy on the balanced growth path. Capital, output, and consumption per unit of effective labor are constant. Since $y$ and $c$ are constant, the saving rate, $(y - c)/y$, is also constant. The total capital stock, total output, and total consumption grow at rate $n + g$. And capital per worker, output per worker, and consumption per worker grow at rate $g$.

Thus the central implications of the Solow model concerning the driving forces of economic growth do not hinge on its assumption of a constant saving rate. Even when saving is endogenous, growth in the effectiveness of

---

[12] Note that this change does affect $r$ and $w$ over the (brief) interval from $t$ to $t + \Delta t$. $r$ falls by $f''(k)$ times the change in $k$, while $w$ rises by $-f''(k)k$ times the change in $k$. But the effect of these changes on total income (per unit of effective labor), which is given by the change in $w$ plus $k$ times the change in $r$, is zero. That is, since capital is paid its marginal product, total payments to labor and to previously existing capital remain equal to the previous level of output (again per unit of effective labor). This is just a specific instance of the general result that the *pecuniary externalities*—externalities operating through prices—balance in the aggregate under competition.

[13] A formal solution to the planner's problem involves the use of the calculus of variations. For a formal statement and solution of the problem, see Blanchard and Fischer (1989, pp. 38–43). For an introduction to the calculus of variations, see Section 9.2; Barro and Sala-i-Martin, 2003, Appendix A.3; Kamien and Schwartz (1991); or Obstfeld (1992).

labor remains the only source of persistent growth in output per worker. And since the production function is the same as in the Solow model, one can repeat the calculations of Section 1.6 demonstrating that significant differences in output per worker can arise from differences in capital per worker only if the differences in capital per worker, and in rates of return to capital, are enormous.

## The Social Optimum and the Golden-Rule Level of Capital

The only notable difference between the balanced growth paths of the Solow and Ramsey–Cass–Koopmans models is that a balanced growth path with a capital stock above the golden-rule level is not possible in the Ramsey–Cass–Koopmans model. In the Solow model, a sufficiently high saving rate causes the economy to reach a balanced growth path with the property that there are feasible alternatives that involve higher consumption at every moment. In the Ramsey–Cass–Koopmans model, in contrast, saving is derived from the behavior of households whose utility depends on their consumption, and there are no externalities. As a result, it cannot be an equilibrium for the economy to follow a path where higher consumption can be attained in every period; if the economy were on such a path, households would reduce their saving and take advantage of this opportunity.

This can be seen in the phase diagram. Consider again Figure 2.5. If the initial capital stock exceeds the golden-rule level (that is, if $k(0)$ is greater than the $k$ associated with the peak of the $\dot{k} = 0$ locus), initial consumption is above the level needed to keep $k$ constant; thus $\dot{k}$ is negative. $k$ gradually approaches $k^*$, which is below the golden-rule level.

Finally, the fact that $k^*$ is less than the golden-rule capital stock implies that the economy does not converge to the balanced growth path that yields the maximum sustainable level of $c$. The intuition for this result is clearest in the case of $g$ equal to zero, so that there is no long-run growth of consumption and output per worker. In this case, $k^*$ is defined by $f'(k^*) = \rho$ (see [2.24]) and $k_{GR}$ is defined by $f'(k_{GR}) = n$, and our assumption that $\rho - n - (1 - \theta)g > 0$ simplifies to $\rho > n$. Since $k^*$ is less than $k_{GR}$, an increase in saving starting at $k = k^*$ would cause consumption per worker to eventually rise above its previous level and remain there (see Section 1.4). But because households value present consumption more than future consumption, the benefit of the eventual permanent increase in consumption is bounded. At some point—specifically, when $k$ exceeds $k^*$—the tradeoff between the temporary short-term sacrifice and the permanent long-term gain is sufficiently unfavorable that accepting it reduces rather than raises lifetime utility. Thus $k$ converges to a value below the golden-rule level. Because $k^*$ is the optimal level of $k$ for the economy to converge to, it is known as the *modified golden-rule* capital stock.

# 2.6 The Effects of a Fall in the Discount Rate

Consider a Ramsey–Cass–Koopmans economy that is on its balanced growth path, and suppose that there is a fall in $\rho$, the discount rate. Because $\rho$ is the parameter governing households' preferences between current and future consumption, this change is the closest analogue in this model to a rise in the saving rate in the Solow model.

Since the division of output between consumption and investment is determined by forward-looking households, we must specify whether the change is expected or unexpected. If a change is expected, households may alter their behavior before the change occurs. We therefore focus on the simple case where the change is unexpected. That is, households are optimizing given their belief that their discount rate will not change, and the economy is on the resulting balanced growth path. At some date households suddenly discover that their preferences have changed, and that they now discount future utility at a lower rate than before.[14]

## Qualitative Effects

Since the evolution of $k$ is determined by technology rather than preferences, $\rho$ enters the equation for $\dot{c}$ but not the one for $\dot{k}$. Thus only the $\dot{c} = 0$ locus is affected. Recall equation (2.24): $\dot{c}(t)/c(t) = [f'(k(t)) - \rho - \theta g]/\theta$. Thus the value of $k$ where $\dot{c}$ equals zero is defined by $f'(k^*) = \rho + \theta g$. Since $f''(\bullet)$ is negative, this means that the fall in $\rho$ raises $k^*$. Thus the $\dot{c} = 0$ line shifts to the right. This is shown in Figure 2.6.

At the time of the change in $\rho$, the value of $k$—the *stock* of capital per unit of effective labor—is given by the history of the economy, and it cannot change discontinuously. In particular, $k$ at the time of the change equals the value of $k^*$ on the old balanced growth path. In contrast, $c$—the *rate* at which households are consuming—can jump at the time of the shock.

Given our analysis of the dynamics of the economy, it is clear what occurs: at the instant of the change, $c$ jumps down so that the economy is on the new saddle path (Point A in Figure 2.6).[15] Thereafter, $c$ and $k$ rise gradually to their new balanced-growth-path values; these are higher than their values on the original balanced growth path.

Thus the effects of a fall in the discount rate are similar to the effects of a rise in the saving rate in the Solow model with a capital stock below the

---

[14] See Section 2.7 and Problems 2.11 and 2.12 for examples of how to analyze anticipated changes.

[15] Since we are assuming that the change is unexpected, the discontinuous change in $c$ does not imply that households are not optimizing. Their original behavior is optimal given their beliefs; the fall in $c$ is the optimal response to the new information that $\rho$ is lower.

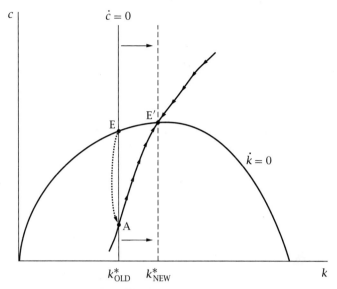

**FIGURE 2.6   The effects of a fall in the discount rate**

golden-rule level. In both cases, $k$ rises gradually to a new higher level, and in both $c$ initially falls but then rises to a level above the one it started at. Thus, just as with a permanent rise in the saving rate in the Solow model, the permanent fall in the discount rate produces temporary increases in the growth rates of capital per worker and output per worker. The only difference between the two experiments is that, in the case of the fall in $\rho$, in general the fraction of output that is saved is not constant during the adjustment process.

## The Rate of Adjustment and the Slope of the Saddle Path

Equations (2.24) and (2.25) describe $\dot{c}(t)$ and $\dot{k}(t)$ as functions of $k(t)$ and $c(t)$. A fruitful way to analyze their quantitative implications for the dynamics of the economy is to replace these nonlinear equations with linear approximations around the balanced growth path. Thus we begin by taking first-order Taylor approximations to (2.24) and (2.25) around $k = k^*$, $c = c^*$. That is, we write

$$\dot{c} \simeq \frac{\partial \dot{c}}{\partial k}[k - k^*] + \frac{\partial \dot{c}}{\partial c}[c - c^*], \tag{2.26}$$

$$\dot{k} \simeq \frac{\partial \dot{k}}{\partial k}[k - k^*] + \frac{\partial \dot{k}}{\partial c}[c - c^*], \tag{2.27}$$

where $\partial\dot{c}/\partial k$, $\partial\dot{c}/\partial c$, $\partial\dot{k}/\partial k$, and $\partial\dot{k}/\partial c$ are all evaluated at $k = k^*$, $c = c^*$. Our strategy will be to treat (2.26) and (2.27) as exact and analyze the dynamics of the resulting system.[16]

It helps to define $\tilde{c} = c - c^*$ and $\tilde{k} = k - k^*$. Since $c^*$ and $k^*$ are both constant, $\dot{\tilde{c}}$ equals $\dot{c}$, and $\dot{\tilde{k}}$ equals $\dot{k}$. We can therefore rewrite (2.26) and (2.27) as

$$\dot{\tilde{c}} \simeq \frac{\partial\dot{c}}{\partial k}\tilde{k} + \frac{\partial\dot{c}}{\partial c}\tilde{c}, \tag{2.28}$$

$$\dot{\tilde{k}} \simeq \frac{\partial\dot{k}}{\partial k}\tilde{k} + \frac{\partial\dot{k}}{\partial c}\tilde{c}. \tag{2.29}$$

(Again, the derivatives are all evaluated at $k = k^*$, $c = c^*$.) Recall that $\dot{c} = \{[f'(k) - \rho - \theta g]/\theta\}c$ (equation [2.24]). Using this expression to compute the derivatives in (2.28) and evaluating them at $k = k^*$, $c = c^*$ gives us

$$\dot{\tilde{c}} \simeq \frac{f''(k^*)c^*}{\theta}\tilde{k}. \tag{2.30}$$

Similarly, (2.25) states that $\dot{k} = f(k) - c - (n + g)k$. We can use this to find the derivatives in (2.29); this yields

$$\dot{\tilde{k}} \simeq [f'(k^*) - (n + g)]\tilde{k} - \tilde{c}$$

$$= [(\rho + \theta g) - (n + g)]\tilde{k} - \tilde{c} \tag{2.31}$$

$$= \beta\tilde{k} - \tilde{c},$$

where the second line uses the fact that (2.24) implies that $f'(k^*) = \rho + \theta g$ and the third line uses the definition of $\beta$ as $\rho - n - (1 - \theta)g$. Dividing both sides of (2.30) by $\tilde{c}$ and both sides of (2.31) by $\tilde{k}$ yields expressions for the growth rates of $\tilde{c}$ and $\tilde{k}$:

$$\frac{\dot{\tilde{c}}}{\tilde{c}} \simeq \frac{f''(k^*)c^*}{\theta}\frac{\tilde{k}}{\tilde{c}}, \tag{2.32}$$

$$\frac{\dot{\tilde{k}}}{\tilde{k}} \simeq \beta - \frac{\tilde{c}}{\tilde{k}}. \tag{2.33}$$

Equations (2.32) and (2.33) imply that the growth rates of $\tilde{c}$ and $\tilde{k}$ depend only on the ratio of $\tilde{c}$ and $\tilde{k}$. Given this, consider what happens if the values of $\tilde{c}$ and $\tilde{k}$ are such that $\tilde{c}$ and $\tilde{k}$ are falling at the same rate (that is, if they imply $\dot{\tilde{c}}/\tilde{c} = \dot{\tilde{k}}/\tilde{k}$). This implies that the ratio of $\tilde{c}$ to $\tilde{k}$ is not changing, and thus that their growth rates are also not changing. That is, if $c - c^*$ and

---

[16] For a more formal introduction to the analysis of systems of differential equations (such as [2.26]-[2.27]), see Simon and Blume (1994, Chapter 25).

$k - k^*$ are initially falling at the same rate, they continue to fall at that rate. In terms of the diagram, from a point where $\tilde{c}$ and $\tilde{k}$ are falling at equal rates, the economy moves along a straight line to $(k^*,c^*)$, with the distance from $(k^*,c^*)$ falling at a constant rate.

Let $\mu$ denote $\dot{\tilde{c}}/\tilde{c}$. Equation (2.32) implies

$$\frac{\tilde{c}}{\tilde{k}} = \frac{f''(k^*)c^*}{\theta}\frac{1}{\mu}. \tag{2.34}$$

From (2.33), the condition that $\dot{\tilde{k}}/\tilde{k}$ equals $\dot{\tilde{c}}/\tilde{c}$ is thus

$$\mu = \beta - \frac{f''(k^*)c^*}{\theta}\frac{1}{\mu}, \tag{2.35}$$

or

$$\mu^2 - \beta\mu + \frac{f''(k^*)c^*}{\theta} = 0. \tag{2.36}$$

This is a quadratic equation in $\mu$. The solutions are

$$\mu = \frac{\beta \pm [\beta^2 - 4f''(k^*)c^*/\theta]^{1/2}}{2}. \tag{2.37}$$

Let $\mu_1$ and $\mu_2$ denote these two values of $\mu$.

If $\mu$ is positive, then $\tilde{c}$ and $\tilde{k}$ are growing; that is, instead of moving along a straight line toward $(k^*,c^*)$, the economy is moving on a straight line away from $(k^*,c^*)$. Thus if the economy is to converge to $(k^*,c^*)$, then $\mu$ must be negative. Inspection of (2.37) shows that only one of the $\mu$'s, namely $\{\beta - [\beta^2 - 4f''(k^*)c^*/\theta]^{1/2}\}/2$, is negative. Let $\mu_1$ denote this value of $\mu$. Equation (2.34) (with $\mu = \mu_1$) then tells us how $\tilde{c}$ must be related to $\tilde{k}$ for both to be falling at rate $\mu_1$.

Figure 2.7 shows the line along which the economy converges smoothly to $(k^*,c^*)$; it is labeled AA. This is the saddle path of the linearized system. The figure also shows the line along which the economy moves directly away from $(k^*,c^*)$; it is labeled BB. If the initial values of $c(0)$ and $k(0)$ lay along this line, (2.32) and (2.33) would imply that $\tilde{c}$ and $\tilde{k}$ would grow steadily at rate $\mu_2$.[17] Since $f''(\bullet)$ is negative, (2.34) implies that the relation between $\tilde{c}$ and $\tilde{k}$ has the opposite sign from $\mu$. Thus the saddle path AA is positively sloped, and the BB line is negatively sloped.

Thus if we linearize the equations for $\dot{c}$ and $\dot{k}$, we can characterize the dynamics of the economy in terms of the model's parameters. At time 0, $c$ must equal $c^* + [f''(k^*)c^*/(\theta\mu_1)](k-k^*)$. Thereafter, $c$ and $k$ converge to their balanced-growth-path values at rate $\mu_1$. That is, $k(t) = k^* + e^{\mu_1 t}[k(0) - k^*]$ and $c(t) = c^* + e^{\mu_1 t}[c(0) - c^*]$.

---

[17] Of course, it is not possible for the initial value of $(k,c)$ to lie along the BB line. As we saw in Section 2.3, if it did, either $k$ would eventually become negative or households would accumulate infinite wealth.

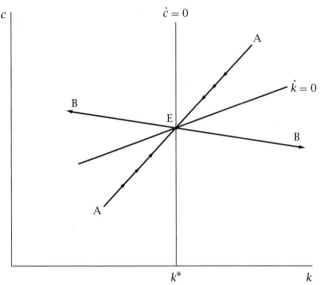

**FIGURE 2.7   The linearized phase diagram**

## The Speed of Adjustment

To understand the implications of (2.37) for the speed of convergence to the balanced growth path, consider our usual example of Cobb–Douglas production, $f(k) = k^\alpha$. This implies $f''(k^*) = \alpha(\alpha - 1)k^{*\alpha-2}$. Since consumption on the balanced growth path equals output minus break-even investment, consumption per unit of effective labor, $c^*$, equals $k^{*\alpha} - (n + g)k^*$. Thus in this case we can write the expression for $\mu_1$ as

$$\mu_1 = \frac{1}{2}\left(\beta - \left\{\beta^2 - \frac{4}{\theta}\alpha(\alpha - 1)k^{*\alpha-2}[k^{*\alpha} - (n + g)k^*]\right\}^{1/2}\right). \quad (2.38)$$

Recall that on the balanced growth path, $f'(k)$ equals $\rho + \theta g$ (see [2.24]). For the Cobb–Douglas case, this is equivalent to $\alpha k^{*\alpha-1} = \rho + \theta g$, or $k^* = [(\rho + \theta g)/\alpha]^{1/(\alpha-1)}$. Substituting this into (2.38) and doing some uninteresting algebraic manipulations yields

$$\mu_1 = \frac{1}{2}\left(\beta - \left\{\beta^2 + \frac{4}{\theta}\frac{1-\alpha}{\alpha}(\rho + \theta g)[\rho + \theta g - \alpha(n + g)]\right\}^{1/2}\right). \quad (2.39)$$

Equation (2.39) expresses the rate of adjustment in terms of the underlying parameters of the model.

To get a feel for the magnitudes involved, suppose $\alpha = \frac{1}{3}$, $\rho = 4\%$, $n = 2\%$, $g = 1\%$, and $\theta = 1$. One can show that these parameter values imply that on the balanced growth path, the real interest rate is 5 percent and the saving rate 20 percent. And since $\beta$ is defined as $\rho - n - (1 - \theta)g$, they imply $\beta = 2\%$. Equation (2.38) or (2.39) then implies $\mu_1 \simeq -5.4\%$. Thus adjustment is quite rapid in this case; for comparison, the Solow model with the same values of $\alpha$, $n$, and $g$ (and as here, no depreciation) implies an adjustment speed of 2 percent per year (see equation [1.31]). The reason for the difference is that in this example, the saving rate is greater than $s^*$ when $k$ is less than $k^*$ and less than $s^*$ when $k$ is greater than $k^*$. In the Solow model, in contrast, $s$ is constant by assumption.

# 2.7 The Effects of Government Purchases

Thus far, we have left government out of our model. Yet modern economies devote their resources not just to investment and private consumption but also to public uses. In the United States, for example, about 20 percent of total output is purchased by the government; in many other countries the figure is considerably higher. It is thus natural to extend our model to include a government sector.

## Adding Government to the Model

Assume that the government buys output at rate $G(t)$ per unit of effective labor per unit time. Government purchases are assumed not to affect utility from private consumption; this can occur if the government devotes the goods to some activity that does not affect utility at all, or if utility equals the sum of utility from private consumption and utility from government-provided goods. Similarly, the purchases are assumed not to affect future output; that is, they are devoted to public consumption rather than public investment. The purchases are financed by lump-sum taxes of amount $G(t)$ per unit of effective labor per unit time; thus the government always runs a balanced budget. Consideration of deficit finance is postponed to Chapter 11. We will see there, however, that in this model the government's choice between tax and deficit finance has no impact on any important variables. Thus the assumption that the purchases are financed with current taxes only serves to simplify the presentation.

Investment is now the difference between output and the sum of private consumption and government purchases. Thus the equation of motion for $k$, (2.25), becomes

$$\dot{k}(t) = f(k(t)) - c(t) - G(t) - (n + g)k(t). \tag{2.40}$$

A higher value of $G$ shifts the $\dot{k} = 0$ locus down: the more goods that are purchased by the government, the fewer that can be purchased privately if $k$ is to be held constant.

By assumption, households' preferences ([2.1]–[2.2] or [2.12]) are unchanged. Since the Euler equation ([2.20] or [2.24]) is derived from households' preferences without imposing their lifetime budget constraint, this condition continues to hold as before. The taxes that finance the government's purchases affect households' budget constraint, however. Specifically, (2.14) becomes

$$\int_{t=0}^{\infty} e^{-R(t)} c(t) e^{(n+g)t} \, dt \leq k(0) + \int_{t=0}^{\infty} e^{-R(t)} [w(t) - G(t)] e^{(n+g)t} \, dt. \quad (2.41)$$

Reasoning parallel to that used before shows that this implies the same expression as before for the limiting behavior of $k$ (equation [2.15]).

## The Effects of Permanent and Temporary Changes in Government Purchases

To see the implications of the model, suppose that the economy is on a balanced growth path with $G(t)$ constant at some level $G_L$, and that there is an unexpected, permanent increase in $G$ to $G_H$. From (2.40), the $\dot{k} = 0$ locus shifts down by the amount of the increase in $G$. Since government purchases do not affect the Euler equation, the $\dot{c} = 0$ locus is unaffected. This is shown in Figure 2.8.[18]

We know that in response to such a change, $c$ must jump so that the economy is on its new saddle path. If not, then as before, either capital would become negative at some point or households would accumulate infinite wealth. In this case, the adjustment takes a simple form: $c$ falls by the amount of the increase in $G$, and the economy is immediately on its new balanced growth path. Intuitively, the permanent increases in government purchases and taxes reduce households' lifetime wealth. And because the increases in purchases and taxes are permanent, there is no scope for households to raise their utility by adjusting the time pattern of their consumption. Thus the size of the immediate fall in consumption is equal to the full amount of the increase in government purchases, and the capital stock and the real interest rate are unaffected.

An older approach to modeling consumption behavior assumes that consumption depends only on current disposable income and that it moves less than one-for-one with disposable income. Recall, for example, that the Solow model assumes that consumption is simply fraction $1 - s$ of current income. With that approach, consumption falls by less than the amount of the increase in government purchases. As a result, the rise in government

---

[18] We assume that $G_H$ is not so large that $\dot{k}$ is negative when $c = 0$. That is, the intersection of the new $\dot{k} = 0$ locus with the $\dot{c} = 0$ line is assumed to occur at a positive level of $c$. If it does not, the government's policy is not feasible. Even if $c$ is always zero, $\dot{k}$ is negative, and eventually the economy's output per unit of effective labor is less than $G_H$.

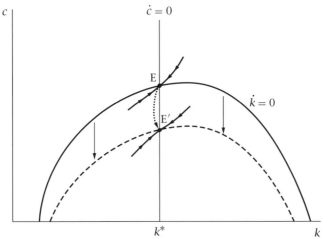

**FIGURE 2.8   The effects of a permanent increase in government purchases**

purchases crowds out investment, and so the capital stock starts to fall and the real interest rate starts to rise. Our analysis shows that those results rest critically on the assumption that households follow mechanical rules: with intertemporal optimization, a permanent increase in government purchases does not cause crowding out.

A more complicated case is provided by an unanticipated increase in $G$ that is expected to be temporary. For simplicity, assume that the terminal date is known with certainty. In this case, $c$ does not fall by the full amount of the increase in $G$, $G_H - G_L$. To see this, note that if it did, consumption would jump up discontinuously at the time that government purchases returned to $G_L$; thus marginal utility would fall discontinuously. But since the return of $G$ to $G_L$ is anticipated, the discontinuity in marginal utility would also be anticipated, which cannot be optimal for households.

During the period of time that government purchases are high, $\dot{k}$ is governed by the capital-accumulation equation, (2.40), with $G = G_H$; after $G$ returns to $G_L$, it is governed by (2.40) with $G = G_L$. The Euler equation, (2.24), determines the dynamics of $c$ throughout, and $c$ cannot change discontinuously at the time that $G$ returns to $G_L$. These facts determine what happens at the time of the increase in $G$: $c$ must jump to the value such that the dynamics implied by (2.40) with $G = G_H$ (and by [2.24]) bring the economy to the old saddle path at the time that $G$ returns to its initial level. Thereafter, the economy moves along that saddle path to the old balanced growth path.[19]

---

[19] As in the previous example, because the initial change in $G$ is unexpected, the discontinuities in consumption and marginal utility at that point do not mean that households are not behaving optimally. See n. 15.

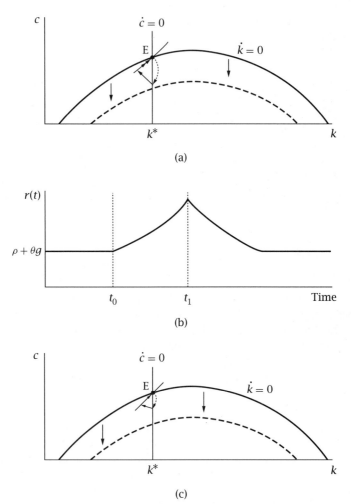

**FIGURE 2.9   The effects of a temporary increase in government purchases**

   This is depicted in Figure 2.9. Panel (a) shows a case where the increase in $G$ is relatively long-lasting. In this case $c$ falls by most of the amount of the increase in $G$. Because the increase is not permanent, however, households decrease their capital holdings somewhat. $c$ rises as the economy approaches the time that $G$ returns to $G_L$.
   Since $r = f'(k)$, we can deduce the behavior of $r$ from the behavior of $k$. Thus $r$ rises gradually during the period that government spending is high and then gradually returns to its initial level. This is shown in Panel (b); $t_0$ denotes the time of the increase in $G$, and $t_1$ the time of its return to its initial value.
   Finally, Panel (c) shows the case of a short-lived rise in $G$. Here households change their consumption relatively little, choosing instead to pay for most

of the temporarily higher taxes out of their savings. Because government purchases are high for only a short period, the effects on the capital stock and the real interest rate are small.

Note that once again allowing for forward-looking behavior yields insights we would not get from the older approach of assuming that consumption depends only on current disposable income. With that approach, the duration of the change in government purchases is irrelevant to the impact of the change during the time that $G$ is high. But the idea that households do not look ahead and put some weight on the likely future path of government purchases and taxes is implausible.

## Empirical Application: Wars and Real Interest Rates

This analysis suggests that temporarily high government purchases cause real interest rates to rise, whereas permanently high purchases do not. Intuitively, when the government's purchases are high only temporarily, households expect their consumption to be greater in the future than it is in the present. To make them willing to accept this, the real interest rate must be high. When the government's purchases are permanently high, on the other hand, households' current consumption is low, and they expect it to remain low. Thus in this case, no movement in real interest rates is needed for households to accept their current low consumption.

A natural example of a period of temporarily high government purchases is a war. Thus our analysis predicts that real interest rates are high during wars. Barro (1987) tests this prediction by examining military spending and interest rates in the United Kingdom from 1729 to 1918. The most significant complication he faces is that, instead of having data on short-term real interest rates, he has data only on long-term nominal interest rates. Long-term interest rates should be, loosely speaking, a weighted average of expected short-term interest rates.[20] Thus, since our analysis implies that temporary increases in government purchases raise the short-term rate over an extended period, it implies that they raise the long-term rate. Similarly, since the analysis implies that permanent increases never change the short-term rate, it predicts that they do not affect the long-term rate. In addition, the real interest rate equals the nominal rate minus expected inflation; thus the nominal rate should be corrected for changes in expected inflation. Barro does not find any evidence, however, of systematic changes in expected inflation in his sample period; thus the data are at least consistent with the view that movements in nominal rates represent changes in real rates.[21]

---

[20] See Section 11.2.

[21] Two further complications are that wars increase the probability that the bonds will be defaulted on and that there is some chance that a war, rather than leading to a return of consumption to normal, will lead to a catastrophic fall in consumption. Barro (2006) argues that both complications may be important.

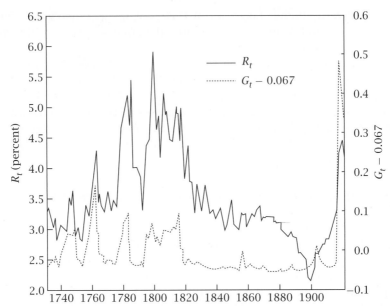

**FIGURE 2.10   Temporary military spending and the long-term interest rate in the United Kingdom (from Barro, 1987; used with permission)**

Figure 2.10 plots British military spending as a share of GNP (relative to the mean of this series for the full sample) and the long-term interest rate. The spikes in the military spending series correspond to wars; for example, the spike around 1760 reflects the Seven Years' War, and the spike around 1780 corresponds to the American Revolution. The figure suggests that the interest rate is indeed higher during periods of temporarily high government purchases.

To test this formally, Barro estimates a process for the military purchases series and uses it to construct estimates of the temporary component of military spending. Not surprisingly in light of the figure, the estimated temporary component differs little from the raw series.[22] Barro then regresses the long-term interest rate on this estimate of temporary military spending. Because the residuals are serially correlated, he includes a first-order serial correlation correction. The results are

$$R_t = 3.54 + 2.6\ \tilde{G}_t, \qquad \lambda = 0.91$$
$$\phantom{R_t = }(0.27)\ \ (0.7) \qquad\qquad (0.03) \qquad\qquad (2.42)$$

$$R^2 = 0.89, \qquad \text{s.e.e.} = 0.248, \qquad \text{D.W.} = 2.1.$$

---

[22] Since there is little permanent variation in military spending, the data cannot be used to investigate the effects of permanent changes in government purchases on interest rates.

Here $R_t$ is the long-term nominal interest rate, $\tilde{G}_t$ is the estimated value of temporary military spending as a fraction of GNP, $\lambda$ is the first-order autoregressive parameter of the residual, and the numbers in parentheses are standard errors. Thus there is a statistically significant link between temporary military spending and interest rates. The results are even stronger when World War I is excluded: stopping the sample period in 1914 raises the coefficient on $\tilde{G}_t$ to 6.1 (and the standard error to 1.3). Barro argues that the comparatively small rise in the interest rate given the tremendous rise in military spending in World War I may have occurred because the government imposed price controls and used a variety of nonmarket means of allocating resources. If this is right, the results for the shorter sample may provide a better estimate of the impact of government purchases on interest rates in a market economy.

Thus the evidence from the United Kingdom supports the predictions of the theory. The success of the theory is not universal, however. In particular, for the United States real interest rates appear to have been, if anything, generally lower during wars than in other periods (see, for example, Weber, 2008). The reasons for this anomalous behavior are not well understood. Thus the theory does not provide a full account of how real interest rates respond to changes in government purchases.

# Part B   The Diamond Model
# 2.8   Assumptions

We now turn to the Diamond overlapping-generations model. The central difference between the Diamond model and the Ramsey–Cass–Koopmans model is that there is turnover in the population: new individuals are continually being born, and old individuals are continually dying.

With turnover, it turns out to be simpler to assume that time is discrete rather than continuous. That is, the variables of the model are defined for $t = 0, 1, 2, \ldots$ rather than for all values of $t \geq 0$. To further simplify the analysis, the model assumes that each individual lives for only two periods. It is the general assumption of turnover in the population, however, and not the specific assumptions of discrete time and two-period lifetimes, that is crucial to the model's results.[23]

---

[23] See Problem 2.15 for a discrete-time version of the Solow model. Blanchard (1985) develops a tractable continuous-time model in which the extent of the departure from the infinite-horizon benchmark is governed by a continuous parameter. Weil (1989a) considers a variant of Blanchard's model where new households enter the economy but existing households do not leave. He shows that the arrival of new households is sufficient to generate most of the main results of the Diamond and Blanchard models. Finally, Auerbach and Kotlikoff (1987) use simulations to investigate a much more realistic overlapping-generations model.

$L_t$ individuals are born in period $t$. As before, population grows at rate $n$; thus $L_t = (1 + n)L_{t-1}$. Since individuals live for two periods, at time $t$ there are $L_t$ individuals in the first period of their lives and $L_{t-1} = L_t/(1+n)$ individuals in their second periods. Each individual supplies 1 unit of labor when he or she is young and divides the resulting labor income between first-period consumption and saving. In the second period, the individual simply consumes the saving and any interest he or she earns.

Let $C_{1t}$ and $C_{2t}$ denote the consumption in period $t$ of young and old individuals. Thus the utility of an individual born at $t$, denoted $U_t$, depends on $C_{1t}$ and $C_{2t+1}$. We again assume constant-relative-risk-aversion utility:

$$U_t = \frac{C_{1t}^{1-\theta}}{1-\theta} + \frac{1}{1+\rho}\frac{C_{2t+1}^{1-\theta}}{1-\theta}, \qquad \theta > 0, \qquad \rho > -1. \tag{2.43}$$

As before, this functional form is needed for balanced growth. Because lifetimes are finite, we no longer have to assume $\rho > n + (1 - \theta)g$ to ensure that lifetime utility does not diverge. If $\rho > 0$, individuals place greater weight on first-period than second-period consumption; if $\rho < 0$, the situation is reversed. The assumption $\rho > -1$ ensures that the weight on second-period consumption is positive.

Production is described by the same assumptions as before. There are many firms, each with the production function $Y_t = F(K_t, A_t L_t)$. $F(\bullet)$ again has constant returns to scale and satisfies the Inada conditions, and $A$ again grows at exogenous rate $g$ (so $A_t = [1 + g]A_{t-1}$). Markets are competitive; thus labor and capital earn their marginal products, and firms earn zero profits. As in the first part of the chapter, there is no depreciation. The real interest rate and the wage per unit of effective labor are therefore given as before by $r_t = f'(k_t)$ and $w_t = f(k_t) - k_t f'(k_t)$. Finally, there is some strictly positive initial capital stock, $K_0$, that is owned equally by all old individuals.

Thus, in period 0 the capital owned by the old and the labor supplied by the young are combined to produce output. Capital and labor are paid their marginal products. The old consume both their capital income and their existing wealth; they then die and exit the model. The young divide their labor income, $w_t A_t$, between consumption and saving. They carry their saving forward to the next period; thus the capital stock in period $t+1$, $K_{t+1}$, equals the number of young individuals in period $t$, $L_t$, times each of these individuals' saving, $w_t A_t - C_{1t}$. This capital is combined with the labor supplied by the next generation of young individuals, and the process continues.

## 2.9   Household Behavior

The second-period consumption of an individual born at $t$ is

$$C_{2t+1} = (1 + r_{t+1})(w_t A_t - C_{1t}). \tag{2.44}$$

Dividing both sides of this expression by $1 + r_{t+1}$ and bringing $C_{1t}$ over to the left-hand side yields the individual's budget constraint:

$$C_{1t} + \frac{1}{1 + r_{t+1}} C_{2t+1} = A_t w_t. \tag{2.45}$$

This condition states that the present value of lifetime consumption equals initial wealth (which is zero) plus the present value of lifetime labor income (which is $A_t w_t$).

The individual maximizes utility, (2.43), subject to the budget constraint, (2.45). We will consider two ways of solving this maximization problem. The first is to proceed along the lines of the intuitive derivation of the Euler equation for the Ramsey model in (2.22)–(2.23). Because the Diamond model is in discrete time, the intuitive derivation of the Euler equation is much easier here than in the Ramsey model. Specifically, imagine the individual decreasing $C_{1t}$ by a small (formally, infinitesimal) amount $\Delta C$ and then using the additional saving and capital income to raise $C_{2t+1}$ by $(1 + r_{t+1})\Delta C$. This change does not affect the present value of the individual's lifetime consumption stream. Thus if the individual is optimizing, the utility cost and benefit of the change must be equal. If the cost is less than the benefit, the individual can increase lifetime utility by making the change. And if the cost exceeds the benefit, the individual can increase utility by making the reverse change.

The marginal contributions of $C_{1t}$ and $C_{2t+1}$ to lifetime utility are $C_{1t}^{-\theta}$ and $[1/(1 + \rho)]C_{2t+1}^{-\theta}$, respectively. Thus as we let $\Delta C$ approach 0, the utility cost of the change approaches $C_{1t}^{-\theta}\Delta C$ and the utility benefit approaches $[1/(1 + \rho)]C_{2t+1}^{-\theta}(1 + r_{t+1})\Delta C$. As just described, these are equal when the individual is optimizing. Thus optimization requires

$$C_{1t}^{-\theta}\Delta C = \frac{1}{1 + \rho} C_{2t+1}^{-\theta}(1 + r_{t+1})\Delta C. \tag{2.46}$$

Canceling the $\Delta C$'s and multiplying both sides by $C_{2t+1}^{\theta}$ gives us

$$\frac{C_{2t+1}^{\theta}}{C_{1t}^{\theta}} = \frac{1 + r_{t+1}}{1 + \rho}, \tag{2.47}$$

or

$$\frac{C_{2t+1}}{C_{1t}} = \left( \frac{1 + r_{t+1}}{1 + \rho} \right)^{1/\theta}. \tag{2.48}$$

This condition and the budget constraint describe the individual's behavior.

Expression (2.48) is analogous to equation (2.21) in the Ramsey model. It implies that whether an individual's consumption is increasing or decreasing over time depends on whether the real rate of return is greater or less than the discount rate. $\theta$ again determines how much individuals' consumption varies in response to differences between $r$ and $\rho$.

The second way to solve the individual's maximization problem is to set up the Lagrangian:

$$
\mathcal{L} = \frac{C_{1t}^{1-\theta}}{1-\theta} + \frac{1}{1+\rho}\frac{C_{2t+1}^{1-\theta}}{1-\theta} + \lambda\left[A_t w_t - \left(C_{1t} + \frac{1}{1+r_{t+1}}C_{2t+1}\right)\right]. \qquad (2.49)
$$

The first-order conditions for $C_{1t}$ and $C_{2t+1}$ are

$$
C_{1t}^{-\theta} = \lambda, \qquad (2.50)
$$

$$
\frac{1}{1+\rho}C_{2t+1}^{-\theta} = \frac{1}{1+r_{t+1}}\lambda. \qquad (2.51)
$$

Substituting the first equation into the second yields

$$
\frac{1}{1+\rho}C_{2t+1}^{-\theta} = \frac{1}{1+r_{t+1}}C_{1t}^{-\theta}. \qquad (2.52)
$$

This can be rearranged to obtain (2.48). As before, this condition and the budget constraint characterize utility-maximizing behavior.

We can use the Euler equation, (2.48), and the budget constraint, (2.45), to express $C_{1t}$ in terms of labor income and the real interest rate. Specifically, multiplying both sides of (2.48) by $C_{1t}$ and substituting into (2.45) gives

$$
C_{1t} + \frac{(1+r_{t+1})^{(1-\theta)/\theta}}{(1+\rho)^{1/\theta}}C_{1t} = A_t w_t. \qquad (2.53)
$$

This implies

$$
C_{1t} = \frac{(1+\rho)^{1/\theta}}{(1+\rho)^{1/\theta} + (1+r_{t+1})^{(1-\theta)/\theta}}A_t w_t. \qquad (2.54)
$$

Equation (2.54) shows that the interest rate determines the fraction of income the individual consumes in the first period. If we let $s(r)$ denote the fraction of income saved, (2.54) implies

$$
s(r) = \frac{(1+r)^{(1-\theta)/\theta}}{(1+\rho)^{1/\theta} + (1+r)^{(1-\theta)/\theta}}. \qquad (2.55)
$$

We can therefore rewrite (2.54) as

$$
C_{1t} = [1 - s(r_{t+1})]A_t w_t. \qquad (2.56)
$$

Equation (2.55) implies that young individuals' saving is increasing in $r$ if and only if $(1+r)^{(1-\theta)/\theta}$ is increasing in $r$. The derivative of $(1+r)^{(1-\theta)/\theta}$ with respect to $r$ is $[(1-\theta)/\theta](1+r)^{(1-2\theta)/\theta}$. Thus $s$ is increasing in $r$ if $\theta$ is less than 1, and decreasing if $\theta$ is greater than 1. Intuitively, a rise in $r$ has both an income and a substitution effect. The fact that the tradeoff between consumption in the two periods has become more favorable for second-period consumption tends to increase saving (the substitution effect), but the fact that a given amount of saving yields more second-period consumption tends to decrease saving (the income effect). When individuals are very willing to substitute consumption between the two periods to take advantage of rate-of-return incentives (that is, when $\theta$ is low), the substitution effect dominates. When individuals have strong preferences for similar levels of consumption in the two periods (that is, when $\theta$ is high), the income effect dominates. And in the special case of $\theta = 1$ (logarithmic utility), the two effects balance, and young individuals' saving rate is independent of $r$.

## 2.10   The Dynamics of the Economy

### The Equation of Motion of $k$

As in the infinite-horizon model, we can aggregate individuals' behavior to characterize the dynamics of the economy. As described above, the capital stock in period $t + 1$ is the amount saved by young individuals in period $t$. Thus,

$$K_{t+1} = s(r_{t+1})L_t A_t w_t. \tag{2.57}$$

Note that because saving in period $t$ depends on labor income that period and on the return on capital that savers expect the next period, it is $w$ in period $t$ and $r$ in period $t + 1$ that enter the expression for the capital stock in period $t + 1$.

Dividing both sides of (2.57) by $L_{t+1}A_{t+1}$ gives us an expression for $K_{t+1}/(A_{t+1}L_{t+1})$, capital per unit of effective labor:

$$k_{t+1} = \frac{1}{(1 + n)(1 + g)} s(r_{t+1})w_t. \tag{2.58}$$

We can then substitute for $r_{t+1}$ and $w_t$ to obtain

$$k_{t+1} = \frac{1}{(1 + n)(1 + g)} s(f'(k_{t+1}))[f(k_t) - k_t f'(k_t)]. \tag{2.59}$$

### The Evolution of $k$

Equation (2.59) implicitly defines $k_{t+1}$ as a function of $k_t$. (It defines $k_{t+1}$ only implicitly because $k_{t+1}$ appears on the right-hand side as well as the left-hand side.) It therefore determines how $k$ evolves over time given its initial value. A value of $k_t$ such that $k_{t+1} = k_t$ satisfies (2.59) is a balanced-growth-path value of $k$: once $k$ reaches that value, it remains there. We therefore want to know whether there is a balanced-growth-path value (or values) of $k$, and whether $k$ converges to such a value if it does not begin at one.

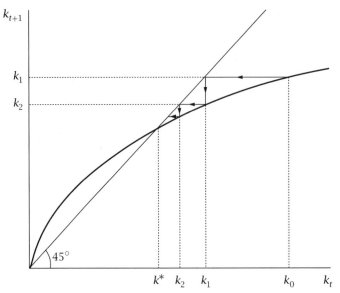

**FIGURE 2.11   The dynamics of $k$**

To answer these questions, we need to describe how $k_{t+1}$ depends on $k_t$. Unfortunately, we can say relatively little about this for the general case. We therefore begin by considering the case of logarithmic utility and Cobb–Douglas production. With these assumptions, (2.59) takes a particularly simple form. We then briefly discuss what occurs when these assumptions are relaxed.

## Logarithmic Utility and Cobb–Douglas Production

When $\theta$ is 1, the fraction of labor income saved is $1/(2 + \rho)$ (see equation [2.55]). And when production is Cobb–Douglas, $f(k)$ is $k^\alpha$ and $f'(k)$ is $\alpha k^{\alpha-1}$. Equation (2.59) therefore becomes

$$k_{t+1} = \frac{1}{(1 + n)(1 + g)} \frac{1}{2 + \rho}(1 - \alpha)k_t^\alpha. \tag{2.60}$$

Figure 2.11 shows $k_{t+1}$ as a function of $k_t$. A point where the $k_{t+1}$ function intersects the 45-degree line is a point where $k_{t+1}$ equals $k_t$. In the case we are considering, $k_{t+1}$ equals $k_t$ at $k_t = 0$; it rises above $k_t$ when $k_t$ is small; and it then crosses the 45-degree line and remains below. There is thus a unique balanced-growth-path level of $k$ (aside from $k = 0$), which is denoted $k^*$.

$k^*$ is globally stable: wherever $k$ starts (other than at 0, which is ruled out by the assumption that the initial capital stock is strictly positive), it

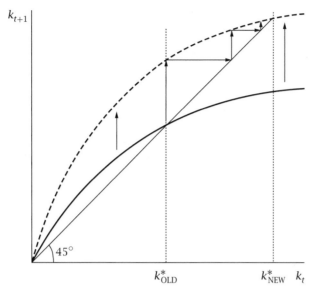

**FIGURE 2.12   The effects of a fall in the discount rate**

converges to $k^*$. Suppose, for example, that the initial value of $k$, $k_0$, is greater than $k^*$. Because $k_{t+1}$ is less than $k_t$ when $k_t$ exceeds $k^*$, $k_1$ is less than $k_0$. And because $k_0$ exceeds $k^*$ and $k_{t+1}$ is increasing in $k_t$, $k_1$ is larger than $k^*$. Thus $k_1$ is between $k^*$ and $k_0$: $k$ moves partway toward $k^*$. This process is repeated each period, and so $k$ converges smoothly to $k^*$. A similar analysis applies when $k_0$ is less than $k^*$.

These dynamics are shown by the arrows in Figure 2.11. Given $k_0$, the height of the $k_{t+1}$ function shows $k_1$ on the vertical axis. To find $k_2$, we first need to find $k_1$ on the horizontal axis; to do this, we move across to the 45-degree line. The height of the $k_{t+1}$ function at this point then shows $k_2$, and so on.

The properties of the economy once it has converged to its balanced growth path are the same as those of the Solow and Ramsey economies on their balanced growth paths: the saving rate is constant, output per worker is growing at rate $g$, the capital-output ratio is constant, and so on.

To see how the economy responds to shocks, consider our usual example of a fall in the discount rate, $\rho$, when the economy is initially on its balanced growth path. The fall in the discount rate causes the young to save a greater fraction of their labor income. Thus the $k_{t+1}$ function shifts up. This is depicted in Figure 2.12. The upward shift of the $k_{t+1}$ function increases $k^*$, the value of $k$ on the balanced growth path. As the figure shows, $k$ rises monotonically from the old value of $k^*$ to the new one.

Thus the effects of a fall in the discount rate in the Diamond model in the case we are considering are similar to its effects in the Ramsey-Cass–Koopmans model, and to the effects of a rise in the saving rate in the Solow model. The change shifts the paths over time of output and capital per worker permanently up, but it leads only to temporary increases in the growth rates of these variables.

## The Speed of Convergence

Once again, we may be interested in the model's quantitative as well as qualitative implications. In the special case we are considering, we can solve for the balanced-growth-path values of $k$ and $y$. Equation (2.60) gives $k_{t+1}$ as a function of $k_t$. The economy is on its balanced growth path when these two are equal. That is, $k^*$ is defined by

$$k^* = \frac{1}{(1+n)(1+g)}\frac{1}{2+\rho}(1-\alpha)k^{*\alpha}. \tag{2.61}$$

Solving this expression for $k^*$ yields

$$k^* = \left[\frac{1-\alpha}{(1+n)(1+g)(2+\rho)}\right]^{1/(1-\alpha)}. \tag{2.62}$$

Since $y$ equals $k^\alpha$, this implies

$$y^* = \left[\frac{1-\alpha}{(1+n)(1+g)(2+\rho)}\right]^{\alpha/(1-\alpha)}. \tag{2.63}$$

This expression shows how the model's parameters affect output per unit of effective labor on the balanced growth path. If we want to, we can choose values for the parameters and obtain quantitative predictions about the long-run effects of various developments.[24]

We can also find how quickly the economy converges to the balanced growth path. To do this, we again linearize around the balanced growth path. That is, we replace the equation of motion for $k$, (2.60), with a first-order approximation around $k = k^*$. We know that when $k_t$ equals $k^*$, $k_{t+1}$ also equals $k^*$. Thus,

$$k_{t+1} \simeq k^* + \left(\left.\frac{dk_{t+1}}{dk_t}\right|_{k_t=k^*}\right)(k_t - k^*). \tag{2.64}$$

Let $\lambda$ denote $dk_{t+1}/dk_t$ evaluated at $k_t = k^*$. With this definition, we can rewrite (2.64) as $k_{t+1} - k^* \simeq \lambda(k_t - k^*)$. This implies

$$k_t - k^* \simeq \lambda^t(k_0 - k^*), \tag{2.65}$$

where $k_0$ is the initial value of $k$.

---

[24] In choosing parameter values, it is important to keep in mind that individuals are assumed to live for only two periods. Thus, for example, $n$ should be thought of as population growth not over a year, but over half a lifetime.

The convergence to the balanced growth path is determined by $\lambda$. If $\lambda$ is between 0 and 1, the system converges smoothly. If $\lambda$ is between $-1$ and 0, there are damped oscillations toward $k^*$: $k$ alternates between being greater and less than $k^*$, but each period it gets closer. If $\lambda$ is greater than 1, the system explodes. Finally, if $\lambda$ is less than $-1$, there are explosive oscillations.

To find $\lambda$, we return to (2.60): $k_{t+1} = (1 - \alpha)k_t^\alpha/[(1 + n)(1 + g)(2 + \rho)]$. Thus,

$$
\begin{aligned}
\lambda \equiv \left. \frac{dk_{t+1}}{dk_t} \right|_{k_t=k^*} &= \alpha \frac{1 - \alpha}{(1 + n)(1 + g)(2 + \rho)} k^{*\alpha-1} \\
&= \alpha \frac{1 - \alpha}{(1 + n)(1 + g)(2 + \rho)} \left[ \frac{1 - \alpha}{(1 + n)(1 + g)(2 + \rho)} \right]^{(\alpha-1)/(1-\alpha)} \qquad (2.66) \\
&= \alpha,
\end{aligned}
$$

where the second line uses equation (2.62) to substitute for $k^*$. That is, $\lambda$ is simply $\alpha$, capital's share.

Since $\alpha$ is between 0 and 1, this analysis implies that $k$ converges smoothly to $k^*$. If $\alpha$ is one-third, for example, $k$ moves two-thirds of the way toward $k^*$ each period.[25]

The rate of convergence in the Diamond model differs from that in the Solow model (and in a discrete-time version of the Solow model—see Problem 2.15). The reason is that although the saving of the young is a constant fraction of their income and their income is a constant fraction of total income, the dissaving of the old is not a constant fraction of total income. The dissaving of the old as a fraction of output is $K_t/F(K_t, A_t L_t)$, or $k_t/f(k_t)$. The fact that there are diminishing returns to capital implies that this ratio is increasing in $k$. Since this term enters negatively into saving, it follows that total saving as a fraction of output is a decreasing function of $k$. Thus total saving as a fraction of output is above its balanced-growth-path value when $k < k^*$, and is below when $k > k^*$. As a result, convergence is more rapid than in the Solow model.

## The General Case

Let us now relax the assumptions of logarithmic utility and Cobb–Douglas production. It turns out that, despite the simplicity of the model, a wide range of behaviors of the economy are possible. Rather than attempting a comprehensive analysis, we merely discuss some of the more interesting cases.

---

[25] Recall, however, that each period in the model corresponds to half of a person's lifetime.

To understand the possibilities intuitively, it is helpful to rewrite the equation of motion, (2.59), as

$$k_{t+1} = \frac{1}{(1+n)(1+g)} s(f'(k_{t+1})) \frac{f(k_t) - k_t f'(k_t)}{f(k_t)} f(k_t). \qquad (2.67)$$

Equation (2.67) expresses capital per unit of effective labor in period $t+1$ as the product of four terms. From right to left, those four terms are the following: output per unit of effective labor at $t$, the fraction of that output that is paid to labor, the fraction of that labor income that is saved, and the ratio of the amount of effective labor in period $t$ to the amount in period $t+1$.

Figure 2.13 shows some possible forms for the relation between $k_{t+1}$ and $k_t$ other than the well-behaved case shown in Figure 2.11. Panel (a) shows a case with multiple values of $k^*$. In the case shown, $k_1^*$ and $k_3^*$ are stable: if $k$ starts slightly away from one of these points, it converges to that level. $k_2^*$ is unstable (as is $k = 0$). If $k$ starts slightly below $k_2^*$, then $k_{t+1}$ is less than $k_t$ each period, and so $k$ converges to $k_1^*$. If $k$ begins slightly above $k_2^*$, it converges to $k_3^*$.

To understand the possibility of multiple values of $k^*$, note that since output per unit of capital is lower when $k$ is higher (capital has a diminishing marginal product), for there to be two $k^*$'s the saving of the young as a fraction of total output must be higher at the higher $k^*$. When the fraction of output going to labor and the fraction of labor income saved are constant, the saving of the young is a constant fraction of total output, and so multiple $k^*$'s are not possible. This is what occurs with Cobb–Douglas production and logarithmic utility. But if labor's share is greater at higher levels of $k$ (which occurs if $f(\bullet)$ is more sharply curved than in the Cobb–Douglas case) or if workers save a greater fraction of their income when the rate of return is lower (which occurs if $\theta > 1$), or both, there may be more than one level of $k$ at which saving reproduces the existing capital stock.

Panel (b) shows a case in which $k_{t+1}$ is always less than $k_t$, and in which $k$ therefore converges to zero regardless of its initial value. What is needed for this to occur is for either labor's share or the fraction of labor income saved (or both) to approach zero as $k$ approaches zero.

Panel (c) shows a case in which $k$ converges to zero if its initial value is sufficiently low, but to a strictly positive level if its initial value is sufficiently high. Specifically, if $k_0 < k_1^*$, then $k$ approaches zero; if $k_0 > k_1^*$, then $k$ converges to $k_2^*$.

Finally, Panel (d) shows a case in which $k_{t+1}$ is not uniquely determined by $k_t$: when $k_t$ is between $k_a$ and $k_b$, there are three possible values of $k_{t+1}$. This can happen if saving is a decreasing function of the interest rate. When saving is decreasing in $r$, saving is high if individuals expect a high value of $k_{t+1}$ and therefore expect $r$ to be low, and is low when individuals expect

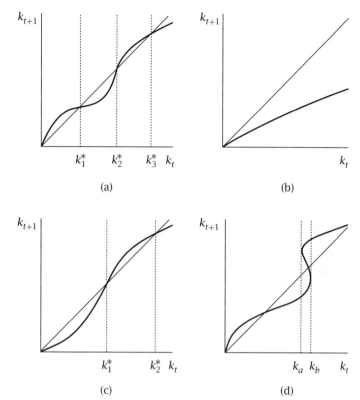

**FIGURE 2.13   Various possibilities for the relationship between $k_t$ and $k_{t+1}$**

a low value of $k_{t+1}$. If saving is sufficiently responsive to $r$, and if $r$ is sufficiently responsive to $k$, there can be more than one value of $k_{t+1}$ that is consistent with a given $k_t$. Thus the path of the economy is indeterminate: equation (2.59) (or [2.67]) does not fully determine how $k$ evolves over time given its initial value. This raises the possibility that *self-fulfilling prophecies* and *sunspots* can affect the behavior of the economy and that the economy can exhibit fluctuations even though there are no exogenous disturbances. Depending on precisely what is assumed, various dynamics are possible.[26]

Thus assuming that there are overlapping generations rather than infinitely lived households has potentially important implications for the dynamics of the economy: for example, sustained growth may not be possible, or it may depend on initial conditions.

At the same time, the model does no better than the Solow and Ramsey models at answering our basic questions about growth. Because of the Inada

---

[26] These issues are briefly discussed further in Section 6.8.

conditions, $k_{t+1}$ must be less than $k_t$ for $k_t$ sufficiently large. Specifically, since the saving of the young cannot exceed the economy's total output, $k_{t+1}$ cannot be greater than $f(k_t)/[(1 + n)(1 + g)]$. And because the marginal product of capital approaches zero as $k$ becomes large, this must eventually be less than $k_t$. The fact that $k_{t+1}$ is eventually less than $k_t$ implies that unbounded growth of $k$ is not possible. Thus, once again, growth in the effectiveness of labor is the only potential source of long-run growth in output per worker. Because of the possibility of multiple $k^*$'s, the model does imply that otherwise identical economies can converge to different balanced growth paths simply because of differences in their initial conditions. But, as in the Solow and Ramsey models, we can account for quantitatively large differences in output per worker in this way only by positing immense differences in capital per worker and in rates of return.

## 2.11   The Possibility of Dynamic Inefficiency

The one major difference between the balanced growth paths of the Diamond and Ramsey–Cass–Koopmans models involves welfare. We saw that the equilibrium of the Ramsey–Cass–Koopmans model maximizes the welfare of the representative household. In the Diamond model, individuals born at different times attain different levels of utility, and so the appropriate way to evaluate social welfare is not clear. If we specify welfare as some weighted sum of the utilities of different generations, there is no reason to expect the decentralized equilibrium to maximize welfare, since the weights we assign to the different generations are arbitrary.

A minimal criterion for efficiency, however, is that the equilibrium be Pareto-efficient. It turns out that the equilibrium of the Diamond model need not satisfy even this standard. In particular, the capital stock on the balanced growth path of the Diamond model may exceed the golden-rule level, so that a permanent increase in consumption is possible.

To see this possibility as simply as possible, assume that utility is logarithmic, production is Cobb–Douglas, and $g$ is zero. With $g = 0$, equation (2.62) for the value of $k$ on the balanced growth path simplifies to

$$k^* = \left[ \frac{1}{1+n} \frac{1}{2+\rho} (1 - \alpha) \right]^{1/(1-\alpha)}. \tag{2.68}$$

Thus the marginal product of capital on the balanced growth path, $\alpha k^{*\alpha-1}$, is

$$f'(k^*) = \frac{\alpha}{1-\alpha}(1 + n)(2 + \rho). \tag{2.69}$$

The golden-rule capital stock is the capital stock that yields the highest balanced-growth-path value of the economy's total consumption per unit of

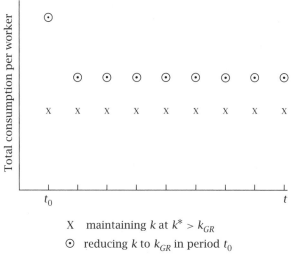

X   maintaining $k$ at $k^* > k_{GR}$

⊙   reducing $k$ to $k_{GR}$ in period $t_0$

FIGURE 2.14   How reducing $k$ to the golden-rule level affects the path of consumption per worker

effective labor. On a balanced growth path with $g = 0$, total consumption per unit of effective labor is output per unit of effective labor, $f(k)$, minus break-even investment per unit of effective labor, $nf(k)$. The golden-rule capital stock therefore satisfies $f'(k_{GR}) = n$. $f'(k^*)$ can be either more or less than $f'(k_{GR})$. In particular, for $\alpha$ sufficiently small, $f'(k^*)$ is less than $f'(k_{GR})$—the capital stock on the balanced growth path exceeds the golden-rule level.

To see why it is inefficient for $k^*$ to exceed $k_{GR}$, imagine introducing a social planner into a Diamond economy that is on its balanced growth path with $k^* > k_{GR}$. If the planner does nothing to alter $k$, the amount of output per worker available each period for consumption is output, $f(k^*)$, minus the new investment needed to maintain $k$ at $k^*$, $nk^*$. This is shown by the crosses in Figure 2.14. Suppose instead, however, that in some period, period $t_0$, the planner allocates more resources to consumption and fewer to saving than usual, so that capital per worker the next period is $k_{GR}$, and that thereafter he or she maintains $k$ at $k_{GR}$. Under this plan, the resources per worker available for consumption in period $t_0$ are $f(k^*) + (k^* - k_{GR}) - nk_{GR}$. In each subsequent period, the output per worker available for consumption is $f(k_{GR}) - nk_{GR}$. Since $k_{GR}$ maximizes $f(k) - nk$, $f(k_{GR}) - nk_{GR}$ exceeds $f(k^*) - nk^*$. And since $k^*$ is greater than $k_{GR}$, $f(k^*) + (k^* - k_{GR}) - nk_{GR}$ is even larger than $f(k_{GR}) - nk_{GR}$. The path of total consumption under this policy is shown by the circles in Figure 2.14. As the figure shows, this policy makes more resources available for consumption in every period than the policy of maintaining $k$ at $k^*$. The planner can therefore allocate consumption between the young and the old each period to make every generation better off.

Thus the equilibrium of the Diamond model can be Pareto-inefficient. This may seem puzzling: given that markets are competitive and there are no externalities, how can the usual result that equilibria are Pareto-efficient fail? The reason is that the standard result assumes not only competition and an absence of externalities, but also a finite number of agents. Specifically, the possibility of inefficiency in the Diamond model stems from the fact that the infinity of generations gives the planner a means of providing for the consumption of the old that is not available to the market. If individuals in the market economy want to consume in old age, their only choice is to hold capital, even if its rate of return is low. The planner, however, need not have the consumption of the old determined by the capital stock and its rate of return. Instead, he or she can divide the resources available for consumption between the young and old in any manner. The planner can take, for example, 1 unit of labor income from each young person and transfer it to the old. Since there are $1 + n$ young people for each old person, this increases the consumption of each old person by $1 + n$ units. The planner can prevent this change from making anyone worse off by requiring the next generation of young to do the same thing in the following period, and then continuing this process every period. If the marginal product of capital is less than $n$—that is, if the capital stock exceeds the golden-rule level—this way of transferring resources between youth and old age is more efficient than saving, and so the planner can improve on the decentralized allocation.

Because this type of inefficiency differs from conventional sources of inefficiency, and because it stems from the intertemporal structure of the economy, it is known as *dynamic inefficiency*.[27]

## Empirical Application: Are Modern Economies Dynamically Efficient?

The Diamond model shows that it is possible for a decentralized economy to accumulate capital beyond the golden-rule level, and thus to produce an allocation that is Pareto-inefficient. Given that capital accumulation in actual economies is not dictated by social planners, this raises the issue of whether actual economies might be dynamically inefficient. If they were, there would be important implications for public policy: the great concern about low rates of saving would be entirely misplaced, and it would be possible to increase both present and future consumption.

This issue is addressed by Abel, Mankiw, Summers, and Zeckhauser (1989). They start by observing that at first glance, dynamic inefficiency appears to be a possibility for the United States and other major economies. A balanced growth path is dynamically inefficient if the real rate of return, $f'(k^*) - \delta$, is less than the growth rate of the economy. A straightforward measure of the real rate of return is the real interest rate on short-term government debt. Abel et al. report that in the United States over the

---

[27] Problem 2.20 investigates the sources of dynamic inefficiency further.

period 1926–1986, this interest rate averaged only a few tenths of a percent, much less than the average growth rate of the economy. Similar findings hold for other major industrialized countries. Thus the real interest rate is less than the golden-rule level, suggesting that these economies have overaccumulated capital.

As Abel et al. point out, however, there is a problem with this argument. In a world of certainty, all interest rates must be equal; thus there is no ambiguity in what is meant by "the" rate of return. But if there is uncertainty, different assets can have different expected returns. Suppose, for example, we assess dynamic efficiency by examining the marginal product of capital net of depreciation instead of the return on a fairly safe asset. If capital earns its marginal product, the net marginal product can be estimated as the ratio of overall capital income minus total depreciation to the value of the capital stock. For the United States, this ratio is about 10 percent, which is much greater than the economy's growth rate. Thus using this approach, we would conclude that the U.S. economy is dynamically efficient. Our simple theoretical model, in which the marginal product of capital and the safe interest rate are the same, provides no guidance concerning which of these contradictory conclusions is correct.

Abel et al. therefore tackle the issue of how to assess dynamic efficiency in a world of uncertainty. Their principal theoretical result is that under uncertainty, a sufficient condition for dynamic efficiency is that net capital income exceed investment. For the balanced growth path of an economy with certainty, this condition is the same as the usual comparison of the real interest rate with the economy's growth rate. In this case, net capital income is the real interest rate times the stock of capital, and investment is the growth rate of the economy times the stock of capital. Thus capital income exceeds investment if and only if the real interest rate exceeds the economy's growth rate. But Abel et al. show that under uncertainty these two conditions are not equivalent, and that it is the comparison of capital income and investment that provides the correct way of judging whether there is dynamic efficiency. Intuitively, a capital sector that is on net making resources available by producing more output than it is using for new investment is contributing to consumption, whereas one that is using more in resources than it is producing is not.

Abel et al.'s principal empirical result is that the condition for dynamic efficiency seems to be satisfied in practice. They measure capital income as national income minus employees' compensation and the part of the income of the self-employed that appears to represent labor income;[28] investment is taken directly from the national income accounts. They find that for the period 1929–1985, capital income consistently exceeds investment in the United States and in the six other major industrialized countries they

---

[28] They argue that adjusting these figures to account for land income and monopoly rents does not change the basic results.

consider. Even in Japan, where investment has been remarkably high, the profit rate is so great that the returns to capital comfortably exceed investment. Thus, although decentralized economies can produce dynamically inefficient outcomes in principle, they do not appear to in practice.

# 2.12   Government in the Diamond Model

As in the infinite-horizon model, it is natural to ask what happens in the Diamond model if we introduce a government that makes purchases and levies taxes. For simplicity, we focus on the case of logarithmic utility and Cobb–Douglas production.

Let $G_t$ denote the government's purchases of goods per unit of effective labor in period $t$. Assume that it finances those purchases by lump-sum taxes on the young.

When the government finances its purchases entirely with taxes, workers' after-tax income in period $t$ is $(1 - \alpha)k_t^\alpha - G_t$ rather than $(1 - \alpha)k_t^\alpha$. The equation of motion for $k$, equation (2.60), therefore becomes

$$k_{t+1} = \frac{1}{(1 + n)(1 + g)} \frac{1}{2 + \rho}[(1 - \alpha)k_t^\alpha - G_t]. \qquad (2.70)$$

A higher $G_t$ therefore reduces $k_{t+1}$ for a given $k_t$.

To see the effects of government purchases, suppose that the economy is on a balanced growth path with $G$ constant, and that $G$ increases permanently. From (2.70), this shifts the $k_{t+1}$ function down; this is shown in Figure 2.15. The downward shift of the $k_{t+1}$ function reduces $k^*$. Thus—in contrast to what occurs in the infinite-horizon model—higher government purchases lead to a lower capital stock and a higher real interest rate. Intuitively, since individuals live for two periods, they reduce their first-period consumption less than one-for-one with the increase in $G$. But since taxes are levied only in the first period of life, this means that their saving falls. As usual, the economy moves smoothly from the initial balanced growth path to the new one.

As a second example, consider a temporary increase in government purchases from $G_L$ to $G_H$, again with the economy initially on its balanced growth path. The dynamics of $k$ are thus described by (2.70) with $G = G_H$ during the period that government purchases are high and by (2.70) with $G = G_L$ before and after. That is, the fact that individuals know that government purchases will return to $G_L$ does not affect the behavior of the economy during the time that purchases are high. The saving of the young— and hence next period's capital stock—is determined by their after-tax labor income, which is determined by the current capital stock and by the government's current purchases. Thus during the time that government purchases

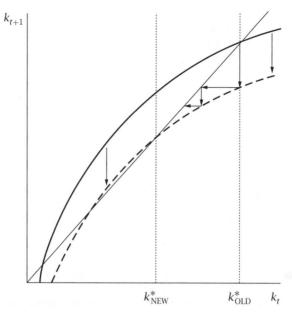

**FIGURE 2.15   The effects of a permanent increase in government purchases**

are high, $k$ gradually falls and $r$ gradually increases. Once $G$ returns to $G_L$, $k$ rises gradually back to its initial level.[29]

# Problems

**2.1.** Consider $N$ firms each with the constant-returns-to-scale production function $Y = F(K, AL)$, or (using the intensive form) $Y = ALf(k)$. Assume $f'(\bullet) > 0$, $f''(\bullet) < 0$. Assume that all firms can hire labor at wage $wA$ and rent capital at cost $r$, and that all firms have the same value of $A$.

(a) Consider the problem of a firm trying to produce $Y$ units of output at minimum cost. Show that the cost-minimizing level of $k$ is uniquely defined and is independent of $Y$, and that all firms therefore choose the same value of $k$.

(b) Show that the total output of the $N$ cost-minimizing firms equals the output that a single firm with the same production function has if it uses all the labor and capital used by the $N$ firms.

---

[29] The result that future values of $G$ do not affect the current behavior of the economy does not depend on the assumption of logarithmic utility. Without logarithmic utility, the saving of the current period's young depends on the rate of return as well as on after-tax labor income. But the rate of return is determined by the next period's capital-labor ratio, which is not affected by government purchases in that period.

**2.2. The elasticity of substitution with constant-relative-risk-aversion utility.**
Consider an individual who lives for two periods and whose utility is given
by equation (2.43). Let $P_1$ and $P_2$ denote the prices of consumption in the two
periods, and let $W$ denote the value of the individual's lifetime income; thus
the budget constraint is $P_1 C_1 + P_2 C_2 = W$.

(a) What are the individual's utility-maximizing choices of $C_1$ and $C_2$, given
$P_1$, $P_2$, and $W$?

(b) The elasticity of substitution between consumption in the two periods
is $-[(P_1/P_2)/(C_1/C_2)][\partial(C_1/C_2)/\partial(P_1/P_2)]$, or $-\partial \ln(C_1/C_2)/\partial \ln(P_1/P_2)$. Show
that with the utility function (2.43), the elasticity of substitution between
$C_1$ and $C_2$ is $1/\theta$.

**2.3.** (a) Suppose it is known in advance that at some time $t_0$ the government will
confiscate half of whatever wealth each household holds at that time. Does
consumption change discontinuously at time $t_0$? If so, why (and what is
the condition relating consumption immediately before $t_0$ to consumption
immediately after)? If not, why not?

(b) Suppose it is known in advance that at $t_0$ the government will confiscate
from each household an amount of wealth equal to half of the wealth of
the average household at that time. Does consumption change discontinuously at time $t_0$? If so, why (and what is the condition relating consumption
immediately before $t_0$ to consumption immediately after)? If not, why not?

**2.4.** Assume that the instantaneous utility function $u(C)$ in equation (2.1) is
$\ln C$. Consider the problem of a household maximizing (2.1) subject to (2.6).
Find an expression for $C$ at each time as a function of initial wealth plus the
present value of labor income, the path of $r(t)$, and the parameters of the utility
function.

**2.5.** Consider a household with utility given by (2.1)–(2.2). Assume that the real
interest rate is constant, and let $W$ denote the household's initial wealth plus
the present value of its lifetime labor income (the right-hand side of [2.6]). Find
the utility-maximizing path of $C$, given $r$, $W$, and the parameters of the utility
function.

**2.6. The productivity slowdown and saving.** Consider a Ramsey–Cass–Koopmans
economy that is on its balanced growth path, and suppose there is a permanent
fall in $g$.

(a) How, if at all, does this affect the $\dot{k} = 0$ curve?

(b) How, if at all, does this affect the $\dot{c} = 0$ curve?

(c) What happens to $c$ at the time of the change?

(d) Find an expression for the impact of a marginal change in $g$ on the fraction
of output that is saved on the balanced growth path. Can one tell whether
this expression is positive or negative?

(e) For the case where the production function is Cobb–Douglas, $f(k) = k^\alpha$,
rewrite your answer to part (d) in terms of $\rho$, $n$, $g$, $\theta$, and $\alpha$. (Hint: Use the
fact that $f'(k^*) = \rho + \theta g$.)

**2.7.** Describe how each of the following affects the $\dot{c} = 0$ and $\dot{k} = 0$ curves in Figure 2.5, and thus how they affect the balanced-growth-path values of $c$ and $k$:

(*a*) A rise in $\theta$.

(*b*) A downward shift of the production function.

(*c*) A change in the rate of depreciation from the value of zero assumed in the text to some positive level.

**2.8.** Derive an expression analogous to (2.39) for the case of a positive depreciation rate.

**2.9. A closed-form solution of the Ramsey model.** (This follows Smith, 2006.) Consider the Ramsey model with Cobb–Douglas production, $y(t) = k(t)^{\alpha}$, and with the coefficient of relative risk aversion ($\theta$) and capital's share ($\alpha$) assumed to be equal.

(*a*) What is $k$ on the balanced growth path ($k^*$)?

(*b*) What is $c$ on the balanced growth path ($c^*$)?

(*c*) Let $z(t)$ denote the capital-output ratio, $k(t)/y(t)$, and $x(t)$ denote the consumption-capital ratio, $c(t)/k(t)$. Find expressions for $\dot{z}(t)$ and $\dot{x}(t)/x(t)$ in terms of $z$, $x$, and the parameters of the model.

(*d*) Tentatively conjecture that $x$ is constant along the saddle path. Given this conjecture:

   (*i*) Find the path of $z$ given its initial value, $z(0)$.

   (*ii*) Find the path of $y$ given the initial value of $k$, $k(0)$. Is the speed of convergence to the balanced growth path, $d \ln[y(t) - y^*]/dt$, constant as the economy moves along the saddle path?

(*e*) In the conjectured solution, are the equations of motion for $c$ and $k$, (2.24) and (2.25), satisfied?

**2.10. Capital taxation in the Ramsey–Cass–Koopmans model.** Consider a Ramsey–Cass–Koopmans economy that is on its balanced growth path. Suppose that at some time, which we will call time 0, the government switches to a policy of taxing investment income at rate $\tau$. Thus the real interest rate that households face is now given by $r(t) = (1 - \tau)f'(k(t))$. Assume that the government returns the revenue it collects from this tax through lump-sum transfers. Finally, assume that this change in tax policy is unanticipated.

(*a*) How, if at all, does the tax affect the $\dot{c} = 0$ locus? The $\dot{k} = 0$ locus?

(*b*) How does the economy respond to the adoption of the tax at time 0? What are the dynamics after time 0?

(*c*) How do the values of $c$ and $k$ on the new balanced growth path compare with their values on the old balanced growth path?

(*d*) (This is based on Barro, Mankiw, and Sala-i-Martin, 1995.) Suppose there are many economies like this one. Workers' preferences are the same in each country, but the tax rates on investment income may vary across countries. Assume that each country is on its balanced growth path.

   (*i*) Show that the saving rate on the balanced growth path, $(y^* - c^*)/y^*$, is decreasing in $\tau$.

   (*ii*) Do citizens in low-$\tau$, high-$k^*$, high-saving countries have any incentive to invest in low-saving countries? Why or why not?

(*e*) Does your answer to part (*c*) imply that a policy of *subsidizing* investment (that is, making $\tau < 0$), and raising the revenue for this subsidy through lump-sum taxes, increases welfare? Why or why not?

(*f*) How, if at all, do the answers to parts (*a*) and (*b*) change if the government does not rebate the revenue from the tax but instead uses it to make government purchases?

**2.11. Using the phase diagram to analyze the impact of an anticipated change.** Consider the policy described in Problem 2.10, but suppose that instead of announcing and implementing the tax at time 0, the government announces at time 0 that at some later time, time $t_1$, investment income will begin to be taxed at rate $\tau$.

   (*a*) Draw the phase diagram showing the dynamics of $c$ and $k$ after time $t_1$.

   (*b*) Can $c$ change discontinuously at time $t_1$? Why or why not?

   (*c*) Draw the phase diagram showing the dynamics of $c$ and $k$ before $t_1$.

   (*d*) In light of your answers to parts (*a*), (*b*), and (*c*), what must $c$ do at time 0?

   (*e*) Summarize your results by sketching the paths of $c$ and $k$ as functions of time.

**2.12. Using the phase diagram to analyze the impact of unanticipated and anticipated temporary changes.** Analyze the following two variations on Problem 2.11:

   (*a*) At time 0, the government announces that it will tax investment income at rate $\tau$ from time 0 until some later date $t_1$; thereafter investment income will again be untaxed.

   (*b*) At time 0, the government announces that from time $t_1$ to some later time $t_2$, it will tax investment income at rate $\tau$; before $t_1$ and after $t_2$, investment income will not be taxed.

**2.13.** The analysis of government policies in the Ramsey-Cass-Koopmans model in the text assumes that government purchases do not affect utility from private consumption. The opposite extreme is that government purchases and private consumption are perfect substitutes. Specifically, suppose that the utility function (2.12) is modified to be

$$U = B \int_{t=0}^{\infty} e^{-\beta t} \frac{[c(t) + G(t)]^{1-\theta}}{1 - \theta} \, dt.$$

If the economy is initially on its balanced growth path and if households' preferences are given by $U$, what are the effects of a temporary increase in government purchases on the paths of consumption, capital, and the interest rate?

**2.14.** Consider the Diamond model with logarithmic utility and Cobb–Douglas production. Describe how each of the following affects $k_{t+1}$ as a function of $k_t$:

(*a*) A rise in $n$.

(*b*) A downward shift of the production function (that is, $f(k)$ takes the form $Bk^\alpha$, and $B$ falls).

(*c*) A rise in $\alpha$.

**2.15.** **A discrete-time version of the Solow model.** Suppose $Y_t = F(K_t, A_t L_t)$, with $F(\bullet)$ having constant returns to scale and the intensive form of the production function satisfying the Inada conditions. Suppose also that $A_{t+1} = (1 + g)A_t$, $L_{t+1} = (1 + n)L_t$, and $K_{t+1} = K_t + sY_t - \delta K_t$.

(*a*) Find an expression for $k_{t+1}$ as a function of $k_t$.

(*b*) Sketch $k_{t+1}$ as a function of $k_t$. Does the economy have a balanced growth path? If the initial level of $k$ differs from the value on the balanced growth path, does the economy converge to the balanced growth path?

(*c*) Find an expression for consumption per unit of effective labor on the balanced growth path as a function of the balanced-growth-path value of $k$. What is the marginal product of capital, $f'(k)$, when $k$ maximizes consumption per unit of effective labor on the balanced growth path?

(*d*) Assume that the production function is Cobb–Douglas.

(*i*) What is $k_{t+1}$ as a function of $k_t$?

(*ii*) What is $k^*$, the value of $k$ on the balanced growth path?

(*iii*) Along the lines of equations (2.64)–(2.66), in the text, linearize the expression in subpart (*i*) around $k_t = k^*$, and find the rate of convergence of $k$ to $k^*$.

**2.16.** **Depreciation in the Diamond model and microeconomic foundations for the Solow model.** Suppose that in the Diamond model capital depreciates at rate $\delta$, so that $r_t = f'(k_t) - \delta$.

(*a*) How, if at all, does this change in the model affect equation (2.59) giving $k_{t+1}$ as a function of $k_t$?

(*b*) In the special case of logarithmic utility, Cobb–Douglas production, and $\delta = 1$, what is the equation for $k_{t+1}$ as a function of $k_t$? Compare this with the analogous expression for the discrete-time version of the Solow model with $\delta = 1$ from part (*a*) of Problem 2.15.

**2.17.** **Social security in the Diamond model.** Consider a Diamond economy where $g$ is zero, production is Cobb–Douglas, and utility is logarithmic.

(*a*) **Pay-as-you-go social security.** Suppose the government taxes each young individual an amount $T$ and uses the proceeds to pay benefits to old individuals; thus each old person receives $(1 + n)T$.

    (*i*) How, if at all, does this change affect equation (2.60) giving $k_{t+1}$ as a function of $k_t$?

    (*ii*) How, if at all, does this change affect the balanced-growth-path value of $k$?

    (*iii*) If the economy is initially on a balanced growth path that is dynamically efficient, how does a marginal increase in $T$ affect the welfare of current and future generations? What happens if the initial balanced growth path is dynamically inefficient?

(*b*) **Fully funded social security.** Suppose the government taxes each young person an amount $T$ and uses the proceeds to purchase capital. Individuals born at $t$ therefore receive $(1 + r_{t+1})T$ when they are old.

    (*i*) How, if at all, does this change affect equation (2.60) giving $k_{t+1}$ as a function of $k_t$?

    (*ii*) How, if at all, does this change affect the balanced-growth-path value of $k$?

**2.18.** **The basic overlapping-generations model.** (This follows Samuelson, 1958, and Allais, 1947.) Suppose, as in the Diamond model, that $L_t$ two-period-lived individuals are born in period $t$ and that $L_t = (1 + n)L_{t-1}$. For simplicity, let utility be logarithmic with no discounting: $U_t = \ln(C_{1t}) + \ln(C_{2t+1})$.

The production side of the economy is simpler than in the Diamond model. Each individual born at time $t$ is endowed with $A$ units of the economy's single good. The good can be either consumed or stored. Each unit stored yields $x > 0$ units of the good in the following period.[30]

Finally, assume that in the initial period, period 0, in addition to the $L_0$ young individuals each endowed with $A$ units of the good, there are $[1/(1 + n)]L_0$ individuals who are alive only in period 0. Each of these "old" individuals is endowed with some amount $Z$ of the good; their utility is simply their consumption in the initial period, $C_{20}$.

(*a*) Describe the decentralized equilibrium of this economy. (Hint: Given the overlapping-generations structure, will the members of any generation engage in transactions with members of another generation?)

(*b*) Consider paths where the fraction of agents' endowments that is stored, $f_t$, is constant over time. What is total consumption (that is, consumption of all the young plus consumption of all the old) per person on such a path as a function of $f$? If $x < 1 + n$, what value of $f$ satisfying $0 \leq f \leq 1$ maximizes consumption per person? Is the decentralized equilibrium Pareto-efficient in this case? If not, how can a social planner raise welfare?

**2.19.** **Stationary monetary equilibria in the Samuelson overlapping-generations model.** (Again this follows Samuelson, 1958.) Consider the setup described

---

[30] Note that this is the same as the Diamond economy with $g = 0$, $F(K_t, AL_t) = AL_t + xK_t$, and $\delta = 1$. With this production function, since individuals supply 1 unit of labor when they are young, an individual born in $t$ obtains $A$ units of the good. And each unit saved yields $1 + r = 1 + \partial F(K, AL)/\partial K - \delta = 1 + x - 1 = x$ units of second-period consumption.

in Problem 2.18. Assume that $x < 1 + n$. Suppose that the old individuals in period 0, in addition to being endowed with $Z$ units of the good, are each endowed with $M$ units of a storable, divisible commodity, which we will call money. Money is not a source of utility.

(a) Consider an individual born at $t$. Suppose the price of the good in units of money is $P_t$ in $t$ and $P_{t+1}$ in $t+1$. Thus the individual can sell units of endowment for $P_t$ units of money and then use that money to buy $P_t/P_{t+1}$ units of the next generation's endowment the following period. What is the individual's behavior as a function of $P_t/P_{t+1}$?

(b) Show that there is an equilibrium with $P_{t+1} = P_t/(1 + n)$ for all $t \geq 0$ and no storage, and thus that the presence of "money" allows the economy to reach the golden-rule level of storage.

(c) Show that there are also equilibria with $P_{t+1} = P_t/x$ for all $t \geq 0$.

(d) Finally, explain why $P_t = \infty$ for all $t$ (that is, money is worthless) is also an equilibrium. Explain why this is the *only* equilibrium if the economy ends at some date, as in Problem 2.20(b) below. (Hint: Reason backward from the last period.)

**2.20. The source of dynamic inefficiency.** (Shell, 1971.) There are two ways in which the Diamond and Samuelson models differ from textbook models. First, markets are incomplete: because individuals cannot trade with individuals who have not been born, some possible transactions are ruled out. Second, because time goes on forever, there are an infinite number of agents. This problem asks you to investigate which of these is the source of the possibility of dynamic inefficiency. For simplicity, it focuses on the Samuelson overlapping-generations model (see the previous two problems), again with log utility and no discounting. To simplify further, it assumes $n = 0$ and $0 < x < 1$.

(a) **Incomplete markets.** Suppose we eliminate incomplete markets from the model by allowing all agents to trade in a competitive market "before" the beginning of time. That is, a Walrasian auctioneer calls out prices $Q_0, Q_1, Q_2, \ldots$ for the good at each date. Individuals can then make sales and purchases at these prices given their endowments and their ability to store. The budget constraint of an individual born at $t$ is thus $Q_t C_{1t} + Q_{t+1} C_{2t+1} = Q_t(A - S_t) + Q_{t+1} x S_t$, where $S_t$ (which must satisfy $0 \leq S_t \leq A$) is the amount the individual stores.

(i) Suppose the auctioneer announces $Q_{t+1} = Q_t/x$ for all $t > 0$. Show that in this case individuals are indifferent concerning how much to store, that there is a set of storage decisions such that markets clear at every date, and that this equilibrium is the same as the equilibrium described in part (a) of Problem 2.18.

(ii) Suppose the auctioneer announces prices that fail to satisfy $Q_{t+1} = Q_t/x$ at some date. Show that at the first date that does not satisfy this condition the market for the good cannot clear, and thus that the proposed price path cannot be an equilibrium.

(*b*) **Infinite duration.** Suppose that the economy ends at some date $T$. That is, suppose the individuals born at $T$ live only one period (and hence seek to maximize $C_{1T}$), and that thereafter no individuals are born. Show that the decentralized equilibrium is Pareto-efficient.

(*c*) In light of these answers, is it incomplete markets or infinite duration that is the source of dynamic inefficiency?

**2.21. Explosive paths in the Samuelson overlapping-generations model.** (Black, 1974; Brock, 1975; Calvo, 1978a.) Consider the setup described in Problem 2.19. Assume that $x$ is zero, and assume that utility is constant-relative-risk-aversion with $\theta < 1$ rather than logarithmic. Finally, assume for simplicity that $n = 0$.

(*a*) What is the behavior of an individual born at $t$ as a function of $P_t/P_{t+1}$? Show that the amount of his or her endowment that the individual sells for money is an increasing function of $P_t/P_{t+1}$ and approaches zero as this ratio approaches zero.

(*b*) Suppose $P_0/P_1 < 1$. How much of the good are the individuals born in period 0 planning to buy in period 1 from the individuals born then? What must $P_1/P_2$ be for the individuals born in period 1 to want to supply this amount?

(*c*) Iterating this reasoning forward, what is the qualitative behavior of $P_t/P_{t+1}$ over time? Does this represent an equilibrium path for the economy?

(*d*) Can there be an equilibrium path with $P_0/P_1 > 1$?

# Chapter **3**
# ENDOGENOUS GROWTH

The models we have seen so far do not provide satisfying answers to our central questions about economic growth. The models' principal result is a negative one: if capital's earnings reflect its contribution to output, then capital accumulation does not account for a large part of either long-run growth or cross-country income differences. And the only determinant of income in the models other than capital is a mystery variable, the "effectiveness of labor" (*A*), whose exact meaning is not specified and whose behavior is taken as exogenous.

Thus if we are to make progress in understanding economic growth, we need to go further. The view of growth that is most in keeping with the models of Chapters 1 and 2 is that the effectiveness of labor represents knowledge or technology. Certainly it is plausible that technological progress is the reason that more output can be produced today from a given quantity of capital and labor than could be produced a century or two ago. This chapter therefore focuses on the accumulation of knowledge.

One can think of the models we will consider in this chapter as elaborations of the Solow model and the models of Chapter 2. They treat capital accumulation and its role in production in ways that are similar to those earlier models. But they differ from the earlier models in explicitly interpreting the effectiveness of labor as knowledge and in modeling the determinants of its evolution over time.

Sections 3.1 through 3.3 present and analyze a model where, paralleling the treatment of saving in the Solow model, the division of the economy's factors of production between knowledge accumulation and other activities is exogenous. We will investigate the dynamics of the economy and the determinants of long-run growth under various assumptions about how inputs combine to produce additions to knowledge. Section 3.4 then discusses different views about what determines the allocation of resources to knowledge production. Section 3.5 considers one specific model of that allocation in a model where growth is exogenous—the classic model of endogenous technological change of P. Romer (1990). Sections 3.6 and 3.7 then turn to empirical work: Section 3.6 examines the evidence about one key dimension

101

on which different models of endogenous growth make sharply different predictions, and Section 3.7 considers an application of the models to the grand sweep of human history.

Section 3.8 concludes by asking what we have learned about the central questions of growth theory. We will see that the conclusions are mixed. Models of knowledge accumulation provide a plausible and appealing explanation of worldwide growth. But, as we will discuss, they are of little help in understanding cross-country income differences. Chapter 4 is therefore devoted specifically to those differences.

# 3.1    Framework and Assumptions

## Overview

To model the accumulation of knowledge, we need to introduce a separate sector of the economy where new ideas are developed. We then need to model both how resources are divided between the sector where conventional output is produced and this new *research and development* (or *R&D*) sector, and how inputs into R&D produce new ideas.

In our formal modeling, we will take a fairly mechanical view of the production of new technologies. Specifically, we will assume a largely standard production function in which labor, capital, and technology are combined to produce improvements in technology in a deterministic way. Of course, this is not a complete description of technological progress. But it is reasonable to think that, all else equal, devoting more resources to research yields more discoveries; this is what the production function captures. Since we are interested in growth over extended periods, modeling the randomness in technological progress would give little additional insight. And if we want to analyze the consequences of changes in other determinants of the success of R&D, we can introduce a shift parameter in the knowledge production function and examine the effects of changes in that parameter. The model provides no insight, however, concerning what those other determinants of the success of research activity are.

We make two other major simplifications. First, both the R&D and goods production functions are assumed to be generalized Cobb–Douglas functions; that is, they are power functions, but the sum of the exponents on the inputs is not necessarily restricted to 1. Second, in the spirit of the Solow model, the model of Sections 3.1–3.3 takes the fraction of output saved and the fractions of the labor force and the capital stock used in the R&D sector as exogenous and constant. These assumptions do not change the model's main implications.

## Specifics

The model is a simplified version of the models of R&D and growth developed by P. Romer (1990), Grossman and Helpman (1991a), and Aghion and Howitt (1992).[1] The model, like the others we have studied, involves four variables: labor ($L$), capital ($K$), technology ($A$), and output ($Y$). The model is set in continuous time. There are two sectors, a goods-producing sector where output is produced and an R&D sector where additions to the stock of knowledge are made. Fraction $a_L$ of the labor force is used in the R&D sector and fraction $1 - a_L$ in the goods-producing sector. Similarly, fraction $a_K$ of the capital stock is used in R&D and the rest in goods production. Both $a_L$ and $a_K$ are exogenous and constant. Because the use of an idea or a piece of knowledge in one place does not prevent it from being used elsewhere, both sectors use the full stock of knowledge, $A$.

The quantity of output produced at time $t$ is thus

$$Y(t) = [(1 - a_K)K(t)]^{\alpha}[A(t)(1 - a_L)L(t)]^{1-\alpha}, \qquad 0 < \alpha < 1. \qquad (3.1)$$

Aside from the $1 - a_K$ and $1 - a_L$ terms and the restriction to the Cobb–Douglas functional form, this production function is identical to those of our earlier models. Note that equation (3.1) implies constant returns to capital and labor: with a given technology, doubling the inputs doubles the amount that can be produced.

The production of new ideas depends on the quantities of capital and labor engaged in research and on the level of technology. Given our assumption of generalized Cobb–Douglas production, we therefore write

$$\dot{A}(t) = B[a_K K(t)]^{\beta}[a_L L(t)]^{\gamma} A(t)^{\theta}, \qquad B > 0, \qquad \beta \geq 0, \qquad \gamma \geq 0, \qquad (3.2)$$

where $B$ is a shift parameter.

Notice that the production function for knowledge is not assumed to have constant returns to scale to capital and labor. The standard argument that there must be at least constant returns is a replication one: if the inputs double, the new inputs can do exactly what the old ones were doing, thereby doubling the amount produced. But in the case of knowledge production, exactly replicating what the existing inputs were doing would cause the same set of discoveries to be made twice, thereby leaving $\dot{A}$ unchanged. Thus it is possible that there are diminishing returns in R&D. At the same time, interactions among researchers, fixed setup costs, and so on may be important enough in R&D that doubling capital and labor more than doubles output. We therefore also allow for the possibility of increasing returns.

The parameter $\theta$ reflects the effect of the existing stock of knowledge on the success of R&D. This effect can operate in either direction. On the one hand, past discoveries may provide ideas and tools that make future

---

[1] See also Uzawa (1965), Shell (1966, 1967), and Phelps (1966b).

discoveries easier. In this case, $\theta$ is positive. On the other hand, the easiest discoveries may be made first. In this case, it is harder to make new discoveries when the stock of knowledge is greater, and so $\theta$ is negative. Because of these conflicting effects, no restriction is placed on $\theta$ in (3.2).

As in the Solow model, the saving rate is exogenous and constant. In addition, depreciation is set to zero for simplicity. Thus,

$$\dot{K}(t) = sY(t). \tag{3.3}$$

Likewise, we continue to treat population growth as exogenous and constant. For simplicity, we do not consider the possibility that it is negative. This implies

$$\dot{L}(t) = nL(t), \qquad n \geq 0. \tag{3.4}$$

Finally, as in our earlier models, the initial levels of $A$, $K$, and $L$ are given and strictly positive. This completes the description of the model.[2]

Because the model has two state variables whose behavior is endogenous, $K$ and $A$, it is more complicated to analyze than the Solow model. We therefore begin by considering the model without capital; that is, we set $\alpha$ and $\beta$ to zero. This case shows most of the model's central messages. We then turn to the general case.

# 3.2   The Model without Capital

## The Dynamics of Knowledge Accumulation

When there is no capital in the model, the production function for output (equation [3.1]) becomes

$$Y(t) = A(t)(1 - a_L)L(t). \tag{3.5}$$

Similarly, the production function for new knowledge (equation [3.2]) is now

$$\dot{A}(t) = B[a_L L(t)]^\gamma A(t)^\theta. \tag{3.6}$$

Population growth continues to be described by equation (3.4).

Equation (3.5) implies that output per worker is proportional to $A$, and thus that the growth rate of output per worker equals the growth rate of $A$. We therefore focus on the dynamics of $A$, which are given by (3.6). This equation implies that the growth rate of $A$, denoted $g_A$, is

$$g_A(t) \equiv \frac{\dot{A}(t)}{A(t)} \tag{3.7}$$

$$= Ba_L^\gamma L(t)^\gamma A(t)^{\theta-1}.$$

---

[2] The model contains the Solow model with Cobb–Douglas production as a special case: if $\beta$, $\gamma$, $a_K$, and $a_L$ are all 0 and $\theta$ is 1, the production function for knowledge becomes $\dot{A} = BA$ (which implies that $A$ grows at a constant rate), and the other equations of the model simplify to the corresponding equations of the Solow model.

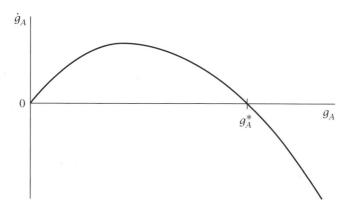

**FIGURE 3.1    The dynamics of the growth rate of knowledge when $\theta < 1$**

Taking logs of both sides of (3.7) and differentiating the two sides with respect to time gives us an expression for the *growth rate* of $g_A$ (that is, for the growth rate of the growth rate of $A$):

$$\frac{\dot{g}_A(t)}{g_A(t)} = \gamma n + (\theta - 1)g_A(t). \tag{3.8}$$

Multiplying both sides of this expression by $g_A(t)$ yields

$$\dot{g}_A(t) = \gamma n g_A(t) + (\theta - 1)[g_A(t)]^2. \tag{3.9}$$

The initial values of $L$ and $A$ and the parameters of the model determine the initial value of $g_A$ (by [3.7]). Equation (3.9) then determines the subsequent behavior of $g_A$.

To describe further how the growth rate of $A$ behaves (and thus to characterize the behavior of output per worker), we must distinguish among the cases $\theta < 1$, $\theta > 1$, and $\theta = 1$. We discuss each in turn.

## Case 1: $\theta < 1$

Figure 3.1 shows the phase diagram for $g_A$ when $\theta$ is less than 1. That is, it plots $\dot{g}_A$ as a function of $A$ for this case. Because the production function for knowledge, (3.6), implies that $g_A$ is always positive, the diagram considers only positive values of $g_A$. As the diagram shows, equation (3.9) implies that for the case of $\theta$ less than 1, $\dot{g}_A$ is positive for small positive values of $g_A$ and negative for large values. We will use $g_A^*$ to denote the unique positive value of $g_A$ that implies that $\dot{g}_A$ is zero. From (3.9), $g_A^*$ is defined by $\gamma n + (\theta - 1)g_A^* = 0$. Solving this for $g_A^*$ yields

$$g_A^* = \frac{\gamma}{1 - \theta}n. \tag{3.10}$$

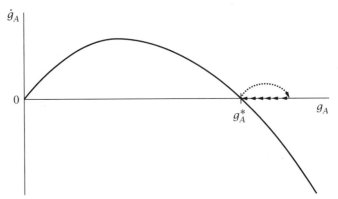

**FIGURE 3.2   The effects of an increase in $a_L$ when $\theta < 1$**

This analysis implies that regardless of the economy's initial conditions, $g_A$ converges to $g_A^*$. If the parameter values and the initial values of $L$ and $A$ imply $g_A(0) < g_A^*$, for example, $\dot{g}_A$ is positive; that is, $g_A$ is rising. It continues to rise until it reaches $g_A^*$. Similarly, if $g_A(0) > g_A^*$, then $g_A$ falls until it reaches $g_A^*$. Once $g_A$ reaches $g_A^*$, both $A$ and $Y/L$ grow steadily at rate $g_A^*$. Thus the economy is on a balanced growth path.

This model is our first example of a model of *endogenous growth.* In this model, in contrast to the Solow, Ramsey, and Diamond models, the long-run growth rate of output per worker is determined within the model rather than by an exogenous rate of technological progress.

The model implies that the long-run growth rate of output per worker, $g_A^*$, is an increasing function of the rate of population growth, $n$. Indeed, positive population growth is necessary for sustained growth of output per worker. This may seem troubling; for example, the growth rate of output per worker is not on average higher in countries with faster population growth. We will return to this issue after we consider the other cases of the model.

Equation (3.10) also implies that the fraction of the labor force engaged in R&D does not affect long-run growth. This too may seem surprising: since growth is driven by technological progress and technological progress is endogenous, it is natural to expect an increase in the fraction of the economy's resources devoted to technological progress to increase long-run growth. To see why it does not, suppose there is a permanent increase in $a_L$ starting from a situation where $A$ is growing at rate $g_A^*$. This change is analyzed in Figure 3.2. $a_L$ does not enter expression (3.9) for $\dot{g}_A$: $\dot{g}_A(t) = \gamma n g_A(t) + (\theta - 1)[\dot{g}_A(t)]^2$. Thus the rise in $a_L$ does not affect the curve showing $\dot{g}_A$ as a function of $g_A$. But $a_L$ does enter expression (3.7) for $g_A$: $g_A(t) = B a_L^\gamma L(t)^\gamma A(t)^{\theta-1}$. The increase in $a_L$ therefore causes an immediate increase

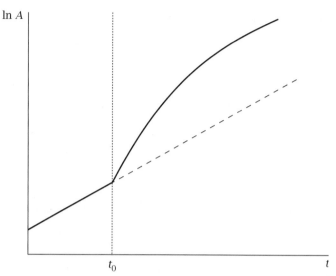

**FIGURE 3.3** The impact of an increase in $a_L$ on the path of A when $\theta < 1$

in $g_A$ but no change in $\dot{g}_A$ as a function of $g_A$. This is shown by the dotted arrow in Figure 3.2.

As the phase diagram shows, the increase in the growth rate of knowledge is not sustained. When $g_A$ is above $g_A^*$, $\dot{g}_A$ is negative. $g_A$ therefore returns gradually to $g_A^*$ and then remains there. This is shown by the solid arrows in the figure. Intuitively, the fact that $\theta$ is less than 1 means that the contribution of additional knowledge to the production of new knowledge is not strong enough to be self-sustaining.

This analysis implies that, paralleling the impact of a rise in the saving rate on the path of output in the Solow model, the increase in $a_L$ results in a rise in $g_A$ followed by a gradual return to its initial level. That is, it has a level effect but not a growth effect on the path of $A$. This information is summarized in Figure 3.3.[3]

## Case 2: $\theta > 1$

The second case to consider is $\theta$ greater than 1. This corresponds to the case where the production of new knowledge rises more than proportionally with the existing stock. Recall from equation (3.9) that $\dot{g}_A = \gamma n g_A + (\theta - 1)g_A^2$. When $\theta$ exceeds 1, this equation implies that $\dot{g}_A$ is positive for all possible

---

[3] See Problem 3.1 for an analysis of how the change in $a_L$ affects the path of output.

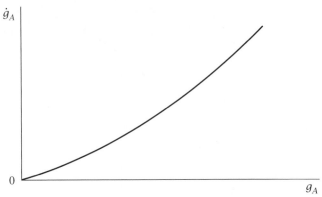

**FIGURE 3.4   The dynamics of the growth rate of knowledge when $\theta > 1$**

values of $g_A$. Further, it implies that $\dot{g}_A$ is increasing in $g_A$ (since $g_A$ must be positive). The phase diagram is shown in Figure 3.4.

The implications of this case for long-run growth are very different from those of the previous case. As the phase diagram shows, the economy exhibits ever-increasing growth rather than convergence to a balanced growth path. Intuitively, here knowledge is so useful in the production of new knowledge that each marginal increase in its level results in so much more new knowledge that the growth rate of knowledge rises rather than falls. Thus once the accumulation of knowledge begins—which it necessarily does in the model—the economy embarks on a path of ever-increasing growth.

The impact of an increase in the fraction of the labor force engaged in R&D is now dramatic. From Equation (3.7), an increase in $a_L$ causes an immediate increase in $g_A$, as before. But $\dot{g}_A$ is an increasing function of $g_A$; thus $\dot{g}_A$ rises as well. And the more rapidly $g_A$ rises, the more rapidly its growth rate rises. Thus the increase in $a_L$ causes the growth rate of $A$ to exceed what it would have been otherwise by an ever-increasing amount.

## Case 3: $\theta = 1$

When $\theta$ is exactly equal to 1, existing knowledge is just productive enough in generating new knowledge that the production of new knowledge is proportional to the stock. In this case, expressions (3.7) and (3.9) for $g_A$ and $\dot{g}_A$ simplify to

$$g_A(t) = Ba_L^{\gamma} L(t)^{\gamma}, \tag{3.11}$$

$$\dot{g}_A(t) = \gamma n g_A(t). \tag{3.12}$$

If population growth is positive, $g_A$ is growing over time; in this case the dynamics of the model are similar to those when $\theta > 1$.[4] If population growth is zero, on the other hand, $g_A$ is constant regardless of the initial situation. Thus there is no adjustment toward a balanced growth path: no matter where it begins, the economy immediately exhibits steady growth. As equations (3.5) and (3.11) show, the growth rates of knowledge, output, and output per worker are all equal to $Ba_L^\gamma L^\gamma$ in this case. Thus changes in $a_L$ affect the long-run growth rate of the economy.

Since the output good in this economy has no use other than in consumption, it is natural to think of it as being entirely consumed. Thus $1 - a_L$ is the fraction of society's resources devoted to producing goods for current consumption, and $a_L$ is the fraction devoted to producing a good (namely, knowledge) that is useful for producing output in the future. Thus one can think of $a_L$ as a measure of the saving rate in this economy.

With this interpretation, the case of $\theta = 1$ and $n = 0$ provides a simple example of a model where the saving rate affects long-run growth. Models of this form are known as *linear growth models;* for reasons that will become clear in Section 3.4, they are also known as $Y = AK$ *models.* Because of their simplicity, linear growth models have received a great deal of attention in work on endogenous growth.

## The Importance of Returns to Scale to Produced Factors

The reason that the three cases have such different implications is that whether $\theta$ is less than, greater than, or equal to 1 determines whether there are decreasing, increasing, or constant returns to scale to *produced* factors of production. The growth of labor is exogenous, and we have eliminated capital from the model; thus knowledge is the only produced factor. There are constant returns to knowledge in goods production. Thus whether there are on the whole increasing, decreasing, or constant returns to knowledge in this economy is determined by the returns to scale to knowledge in knowledge production—that is, by $\theta$.

---

[4] In the cases of $\theta > 1$ and of $\theta = 1$ and $n > 0$, the model implies not merely that growth is increasing, but that it rises so fast that output reaches infinity in a finite amount of time. Consider, for example, the case of $\theta > 1$ with $n = 0$. One can check that $A(t) = c_1/(c_2-t)^{1/(\theta-1)}$, with $c_1 = 1/[(\theta-1)Ba_L^\gamma L^\gamma]^{1/(\theta-1)}$ and $c_2$ chosen so that $A(0)$ equals the initial value of $A$, satisfies (3.6). Thus $A$ explodes at time $c_2$. Since output cannot reach infinity in a finite time, this implies that the model must break down at some point. But it does not mean that it cannot provide a good description over the relevant range. Indeed, Section 3.7 presents evidence that a model similar to this one provides a good approximation to historical data over many thousands of years.

To see why the returns to the produced input are critical to the behavior of the economy, suppose that the economy is on some path, and suppose there is an exogenous increase in $A$ of 1 percent. If $\theta$ is exactly equal to 1, $\dot{A}$ grows by 1 percent as well: knowledge is just productive enough in the production of new knowledge that the increase in $A$ is self-sustaining. Thus the jump in $A$ has no effect on its growth rate. If $\theta$ exceeds 1, the 1 percent increase in $A$ causes more than a 1 percent increase in $\dot{A}$. Thus in this case the increase in $A$ raises the growth rate of $A$. Finally, if $\theta$ is less than 1, the 1 percent increase in $A$ results in an increase of less than 1 percent in $\dot{A}$, and so the growth rate of knowledge falls.

## The Importance of Population Growth

Recall that when $\theta < 1$, the model has the surprising implication that positive population growth is necessary for long-run growth in income per person, and that the economy's long-run growth rate is increasing in population growth. The other cases have similar implications. When $\theta = 1$ and $n = 0$, long-run growth is an increasing function of the *level* of population. And when $\theta > 1$ (or $\theta = 1$ and $n > 0$), one can show that an increase in population growth causes income per person to be higher than it otherwise would have been by an ever-increasing amount.

To understand these results, consider equation (3.7) for knowledge accumulation: $g_A(t) = Ba_L^\gamma L(t)^\gamma A(t)^{\theta-1}$. Built into this expression is the completely natural idea that when there are more people to make discoveries, more discoveries are made. And when more discoveries are made, the stock of knowledge grows faster, and so (all else equal) output per person grows faster. In the particular case of $\theta = 1$ and $n = 0$, this effect operates in a special way: long-run growth is increasing in the level of population. When $\theta$ is greater than 1, the effect is even more powerful, as increases in the level or growth rate of population lead to ever-rising increases in growth. When $\theta$ is less than 1, there are decreasing returns to scale to produced factors, and so the implication is slightly different. In this case, although knowledge may be helpful in generating new knowledge, the generation of new knowledge rises less than proportionally with the existing stock. Thus without something else making an increasing contribution to knowledge production, growth would taper off. Because people contribute to knowledge production, population growth provides that something else: positive population growth is needed for long-run growth, and the rate of long-run growth is increasing in the rate of population growth.

A natural interpretation of the model (which we will return to at the end of the chapter) is that $A$ represents knowledge that can be used anywhere in the world. With this interpretation, the model does not imply that countries with larger populations, or countries with greater population growth, enjoy greater income growth; it only implies that higher worldwide population growth raises worldwide income growth. This implication is plausible: because people are an essential input into producing knowledge, it makes sense that, at least up to the point where resource limitations (which are omitted from the model) become important, higher population growth is beneficial to the growth of worldwide knowledge.

## 3.3 The General Case

We now want to reintroduce capital into the model and determine how this modifies the earlier analysis. Thus the model is now described by equations (3.1)–(3.4) rather than by (3.4)–(3.6).

### The Dynamics of Knowledge and Capital

As mentioned above, when the model includes capital, there are two endogenous state variables, $A$ and $K$. Paralleling our analysis of the simple model, we focus on the dynamics of the growth rates of $A$ and $K$. Substituting the production function, (3.1), into the expression for capital accumulation, (3.3), yields

$$\dot{K}(t) = s(1 - a_K)^\alpha (1 - a_L)^{1-\alpha} K(t)^\alpha A(t)^{1-\alpha} L(t)^{1-\alpha}. \tag{3.13}$$

Dividing both sides by $K(t)$ and defining $c_K = s(1 - a_K)^\alpha (1 - a_L)^{1-\alpha}$ gives us

$$g_K(t) \equiv \frac{\dot{K}(t)}{K(t)}$$
$$= c_K \left[ \frac{A(t)L(t)}{K(t)} \right]^{1-\alpha}. \tag{3.14}$$

Taking logs of both sides and differentiating with respect to time yields

$$\frac{\dot{g}_K(t)}{g_K(t)} = (1 - \alpha)[g_A(t) + n - g_K(t)]. \tag{3.15}$$

From (3.13), $g_K$ is always positive. Thus $g_K$ is rising if $g_A + n - g_K$ is positive, falling if this expression is negative, and constant if it is zero. This information is summarized in Figure 3.5. In $(g_A, g_K)$ space, the locus of points where $g_K$ is constant has an intercept of $n$ and a slope of 1. Above the locus, $g_K$ is falling; below the locus, it is rising.

Similarly, dividing both sides of equation (3.2), $\dot{A} = B(a_K K)^\beta (a_L L)^\gamma A^\theta$, by $A$ yields an expression for the growth rate of $A$:

$$g_A(t) = c_A K(t)^\beta L(t)^\gamma A(t)^{\theta-1}, \tag{3.16}$$

where $c_A \equiv Ba_K^\beta a_L^\gamma$. Aside from the presence of the $K^\beta$ term, this is essentially the same as equation (3.7) in the simple version of the model. Taking

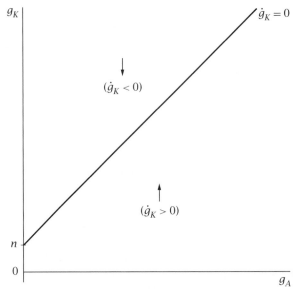

**FIGURE 3.5   The dynamics of the growth rate of capital in the general version of the model**

logs and differentiating with respect to time gives

$$\frac{\dot{g}_A(t)}{g_A(t)} = \beta g_K(t) + \gamma n + (\theta - 1)g_A(t). \tag{3.17}$$

Thus $g_A$ is rising if $\beta g_K + \gamma n + (\theta - 1)g_A$ is positive, falling if it is negative, and constant if it is zero. This is shown in Figure 3.6. The set of points where $g_A$ is constant has an intercept of $-\gamma n/\beta$ and a slope of $(1 - \theta)/\beta$.[5] Above this locus, $g_A$ is rising; and below the locus, it is falling.

The production function for output (equation [3.1]) exhibits constant returns to scale in the two produced factors of production, capital and knowledge. Thus whether there are on net increasing, decreasing, or constant returns to scale to the produced factors depends on their returns to scale in the production function for knowledge, equation (3.2). As that equation shows, the degree of returns to scale to $K$ and $A$ in knowledge production is $\beta + \theta$: increasing both $K$ and $A$ by a factor of $X$ increases $\dot{A}$ by a factor of $X^{\beta+\theta}$. Thus the key determinant of the economy's behavior is now not how $\theta$ compares with 1, but how $\beta + \theta$ compares with 1. We will limit our attention to the cases of $\beta + \theta < 1$ and of $\beta + \theta = 1$ with $n = 0$. The remaining cases ($\beta + \theta > 1$ and $\beta + \theta = 1$ with $n > 0$) have implications similar to those of $\theta > 1$ in the simple model; they are considered in Problem 3.6.

---

[5] The figure is drawn for the case of $\theta < 1$, so the slope is shown as positive.

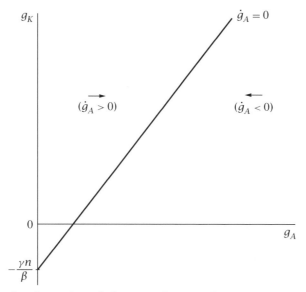

**FIGURE 3.6** **The dynamics of the growth rate of knowledge in the general version of the model**

## Case 1: $\beta + \theta < 1$

If $\beta + \theta$ is less than 1, $(1 - \theta)/\beta$ is greater than 1. Thus the locus of points where $\dot{g}_A = 0$ is steeper than the locus where $\dot{g}_K = 0$. This case is shown in Figure 3.7. The initial values of $g_A$ and $g_K$ are determined by the parameters of the model and by the initial values of $A$, $K$, and $L$. Their dynamics are then as shown in the figure.

Figure 3.7 shows that regardless of where $g_A$ and $g_K$ begin, they converge to Point E in the diagram. Both $\dot{g}_A$ and $\dot{g}_K$ are zero at this point. Thus the values of $g_A$ and $g_K$ at Point E, which we denote $g_A^*$ and $g_K^*$, must satisfy

$$g_A^* + n - g_K^* = 0 \tag{3.18}$$

and

$$\beta g_K^* + \gamma n + (\theta - 1)g_A^* = 0. \tag{3.19}$$

Rewriting (3.18) as $g_K^* = g_A^* + n$ and substituting into (3.19) yields

$$\beta g_A^* + (\beta + \gamma)n + (\theta - 1)g_A^* = 0, \tag{3.20}$$

or

$$g_A^* = \frac{\beta + \gamma}{1 - (\theta + \beta)}n. \tag{3.21}$$

From above, $g_K^*$ is simply $g_A^* + n$. Equation (3.1) then implies that when $A$ and $K$ are growing at these rates, output is growing at rate $g_K^*$. Output per worker is therefore growing at rate $g_A^*$.

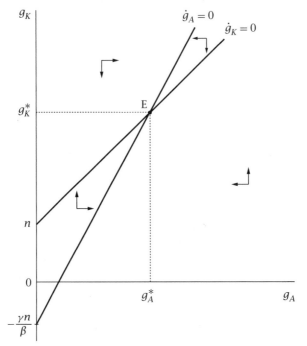

**FIGURE 3.7   The dynamics of the growth rates of capital and knowledge when $\beta + \theta < 1$**

This case is similar to the case when $\theta$ is less than 1 in the version of the model without capital. Here, as in that case, the long-run growth rate of the economy is endogenous, and again long-run growth is an increasing function of population growth and is zero if population growth is zero. The fractions of the labor force and the capital stock engaged in R&D, $a_L$ and $a_K$, do not affect long-run growth; nor does the saving rate, $s$. The reason that these parameters do not affect long-run growth is essentially the same as the reason that $a_L$ does not affect long-run growth in the simple version of the model.[6]

Models like this one and like the model without capital in the case of $\theta < 1$ are often referred to as *semi-endogenous growth models*. On the one hand, long-run growth arises endogenously in the model. On the other, it depends only on population growth and parameters of the knowledge production function, and is unaffected by any other parameters of the model. Thus, as the name implies, growth seems only somewhat endogenous.

---

[6] See Problem 3.4 for a more detailed analysis of the impact of a change in the saving rate in this model.

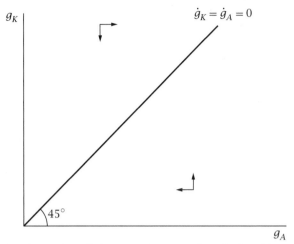

**FIGURE 3.8** The dynamics of the growth rates of capital and knowledge when $\beta + \theta = 1$ and $n = 0$

## Case 2: $\beta + \theta = 1$ and $n = 0$

We have seen that the locus of points where $\dot{g}_K = 0$ is given by $g_K = g_A + n$, and that the locus of points where $\dot{g}_A = 0$ is given by $g_K = -(\gamma n/\beta) + [(1 - \theta)/\beta]g_A$. When $\beta + \theta$ is 1 and $n$ is 0, both expressions simplify to $g_K = g_A$. That is, in this case the two loci lie directly on top of each other: both are given by the 45-degree line. Figure 3.8 shows the dynamics of the economy in this case.

As the figure shows, regardless of where the economy begins, the dynamics of $g_A$ and $g_K$ carry them to the 45-degree line. Once that happens, $g_A$ and $g_K$ are constant, and the economy is on a balanced growth path. As in the case of $\theta = 1$ and $n = 0$ in the model without capital, the phase diagram does not tell us what balanced growth path the economy converges to. One can show, however, that the economy has a unique balanced growth path for a given set of parameter values, and that the economy's growth rate on that path is a complicated function of the parameters. Increases in the saving rate and in the size of the population increase this long-run growth rate; the intuition is essentially the same as the intuition for why increases in $a_L$ and $L$ increase long-run growth when there is no capital. And because changes in $a_L$ and $a_K$ involve shifts of resources between goods production (and hence investment) and R&D, they have ambiguous effects on long-run growth. Unfortunately, the derivation of the long-run growth rate is tedious and not particularly insightful. Thus we will not work through the details.[7] Because

---

[7] See Problem 3.5.

long-run growth depends on a wide range of parameters, models like this one, as well as the model of the previous section when $\theta \geq 1$ and the model of this section when $\beta + \theta > 1$ or $\beta + \theta = 1$ and $n > 0$, are known as *fully endogenous growth models*.

# 3.4   The Nature of Knowledge and the Determinants of the Allocation of Resources to R&D

## Overview

The previous analysis takes the saving rate, $s$, and the fractions of inputs devoted to R&D, $a_L$ and $a_K$, as given. The models of Chapter 2 (and of Chapter 8 as well) show the ingredients needed to make $s$ endogenous. This leaves the question of what determines $a_L$ and $a_K$. This section is devoted to that issue.

So far we have simply described the "$A$" variable produced by R&D as knowledge. But knowledge comes in many forms. It is useful to think of there being a continuum of types of knowledge, ranging from the highly abstract to the highly applied. At one extreme is basic scientific knowledge with broad applicability, such as the Pythagorean theorem and the germ theory of disease. At the other extreme is knowledge about specific goods, such as how to start a particular lawn mower on a cold morning. There are a wide range of ideas in between, from the design of the transistor or the invention of the record player to an improved layout for the kitchen of a fast-food restaurant or a recipe for a better-tasting soft drink.

Many of these different types of knowledge play important roles in economic growth. Imagine, for example, that 100 years ago there had been a halt to basic scientific progress, or to the invention of applied technologies useful in broad classes of goods, or to the invention of new products, or to improvements in the design and use of products after their invention. These changes would have had different effects on growth, and those effects would have occurred with different lags, but it seems likely that all of them would have led to substantial reductions in growth.

There is no reason to expect the determinants of the accumulation of these different types of knowledge to be the same: the forces underlying, for example, the advancement of basic mathematics differ from those behind improvements in the design of fast-food restaurants. There is thus no reason to expect a unified theory of the growth of knowledge. Rather, we should expect to find various factors underlying the accumulation of knowledge.

At the same time, all types of knowledge share one essential feature: they are *nonrival.* That is, the use of an item of knowledge, whether it is the Pythagorean theorem or a soft-drink recipe, in one application makes its use by someone else no more difficult. Conventional private economic goods, in contrast, are *rival:* the use of, say, an item of clothing by one individual precludes its simultaneous use by someone else.

An immediate implication of this fundamental property of knowledge is that the production and allocation of knowledge cannot be completely governed by competitive market forces. The marginal cost of supplying an item of knowledge to an additional user, once the knowledge has been discovered, is zero. Thus the rental price of knowledge in a competitive market is zero. But then the creation of knowledge could not be motivated by the desire for private economic gain. It follows that either knowledge is sold at above its marginal cost or its development is not motivated by market forces.

Although all knowledge is nonrival, it is heterogeneous along a second dimension: *excludability.* A good is excludable if it is possible to prevent others from using it. Thus conventional private goods are excludable: the owner of a piece of clothing can prevent others from using it.

In the case of knowledge, excludability depends both on the nature of the knowledge itself and on economic institutions governing property rights. Patent laws, for example, give inventors rights over the use of their designs and discoveries. Under a different set of laws, inventors' ability to prevent the use of their discoveries by others might be smaller. To give another example, copyright laws give an author who finds a better organization for a textbook little ability to prevent other authors from adopting that organization. Thus the excludability of the superior organization is limited. (Because, however, the copyright laws prevent other authors from simply copying the entire textbook, adoption of the improved organization requires some effort; as a result there is some degree of excludability, and thus some potential to earn a return from the superior organization.) But it would be possible to alter the law to give authors stronger rights concerning the use of similar organizations by others.

In some cases, excludability is more dependent on the nature of the knowledge and less dependent on the legal system. The recipe for Coca-Cola is sufficiently complex that it can be kept secret without copyright or patent protection. The technology for recording television programs onto videocassette is sufficiently simple that the makers of the programs were unable to prevent viewers from recording the programs (and the "knowledge" they contained) even before courts ruled that such recording for personal use is legal.

The degree of excludability is likely to have a strong influence on how the development and allocation of knowledge depart from perfect competition. If a type of knowledge is entirely nonexcludable, there can be no private gain in its development; thus R&D in these areas must come from elsewhere. But when knowledge is excludable, the producers of new knowledge can license the right to use the knowledge at positive prices, and hence hope to earn positive returns on their R&D efforts.

With these broad remarks, we can now turn to a discussion of some of the major forces governing the allocation of resources to the development of knowledge. Four forces have received the most attention: support for basic scientific research, private incentives for R&D and innovation, alternative opportunities for talented individuals, and learning-by-doing.

## Support for Basic Scientific Research

Basic scientific knowledge has traditionally been made available relatively freely; the same is true of the results of much of the research undertaken in such institutions as modern universities and medieval monasteries. Thus this research is not motivated by the desire to earn private returns in the market. Instead it is supported by governments, charities, and wealthy individuals and is pursued by individuals motivated by this support, by desire for fame, and perhaps even by love of knowledge.

The economics of this type of knowledge are relatively straightforward. Since it is useful in production and is given away at zero cost, it has a positive externality. Thus its production should be subsidized.[8] If one added, for example, the infinitely lived households of the Ramsey model to a model of growth based on this view of knowledge accumulation, one could compute the optimal research subsidy. Phelps (1966b) and Shell (1966) provide examples of this type of analysis.

## Private Incentives for R&D and Innovation

Many innovations, ranging from the introductions of entirely new products to small improvements in existing goods, receive little or no external support and are motivated almost entirely by the desire for private gain. The modeling of these private R&D activities and of their implications for economic growth has been the subject of considerable research; important examples include P. Romer (1990), Grossman and Helpman (1991a), and Aghion and Howitt (1992).

As described above, for R&D to result from economic incentives, the knowledge that is created must be at least somewhat excludable. Thus the developer of a new idea has some degree of market power. Typically, the developer is modeled as having exclusive control over the use of the

---

[8] This implication makes academics sympathetic to this view of knowledge.

idea and as licensing its use to the producers of final goods. The fee that the innovator can charge for the use of the idea is limited by the usefulness of the idea in production, or by the possibility that others, motivated by the prospect of high returns, will devote resources to learning the idea. The quantities of the factors of production engaged in R&D are modeled in turn as resulting from factor movements that equate the private factor payments in R&D with the factor payments in the production of final goods.

Since economies like these are not perfectly competitive, their equilibria are not in general optimal. In particular, the decentralized equilibria may have inefficient divisions of resources between R&D and conventional goods production. There are in fact three distinct externalities from R&D: the *consumer-surplus* effect, the *business-stealing* effect, and the *R&D* effect.

The consumer-surplus effect is that the individuals or firms licensing ideas from innovators obtain some surplus, since innovators cannot engage in perfect price discrimination. Thus this is a positive externality from R&D.

The business-stealing effect is that the introduction of a superior technology typically makes existing technologies less attractive, and therefore harms the owners of those technologies. This externality is negative.[9]

Finally, the R&D effect is that innovators are generally assumed not to control the use of their knowledge in the production of additional knowledge. In terms of the model of the previous section, innovators are assumed to earn returns on the use of their knowledge in goods production (equation [3.1]) but not in knowledge production (equation [3.2]). Thus the development of new knowledge has a positive externality on others engaged in R&D.

The net effect of these three externalities is ambiguous. It is possible to construct examples where the business-stealing externality outweighs both the consumer-surplus and R&D externalities. In this case the incentives to capture the profits being earned by other innovators cause too many resources to be devoted to R&D. The result is that the economy's equilibrium growth rate may be inefficiently high (Aghion and Howitt, 1992). It is generally believed, however, that the normal situation is for the overall externality from R&D to be positive. In this case the equilibrium level of R&D is inefficiently low, and R&D subsidies can increase welfare.

There can be additional externalities as well. For example, if innovators have only incomplete control over the use of their ideas in goods production (that is, if there is only partial excludability), there is an additional reason that the private return to R&D is below the social return. On the other hand,

---

[9] Both the consumer-surplus and business-stealing effects are pecuniary externalities: they operate through markets rather than outside them. As described in Section 2.4, such externalities do not cause inefficiency in a competitive market. For example, the fact that an individual's love of carrots drives up the price of carrots harms other carrot buyers, but benefits carrot producers. In the competitive case, these harms and benefits balance, and so the competitive equilibrium is Pareto-efficient. But when there are departures from perfect competition, pecuniary externalities can cause inefficiency.

the fact that the first individual to create an invention is awarded exclusive rights to the invention can create excessive incentives for some kinds of R&D; for example, the private returns to activities that cause one inventor to complete an invention just ahead of a competitor can exceed the social returns.

In Section 3.5, we will investigate a specific model where R&D is motivated by the private returns from innovation. This investigation serves several purposes. First, and probably most important, it shows the inner workings of a model of this type and illustrates some of the tools used in constructing and analyzing the models. Second, it allows us to see how various forces can affect the division of the economy's resources between R&D and other activities. And third, it shows how equilibrium and optimal R&D differ in a particular setting.

## Alternative Opportunities for Talented Individuals

Baumol (1990) and Murphy, Shleifer, and Vishny (1991) observe that major innovations and advances in knowledge are often the result of the work of extremely talented individuals. They also observe that such individuals typically have choices other than just pursuing innovations and producing goods. These observations suggest that the economic incentives and social forces influencing the activities of highly talented individuals may be important to the accumulation of knowledge.

Baumol takes a historical view of this issue. He argues that, in various places and times, military conquest, political and religious leadership, tax collection, criminal activity, philosophical contemplation, financial dealings, and manipulation of the legal system have been attractive to the most talented members of society. He also argues that these activities often have negligible (or even negative) social returns. That is, his argument is that these activities are often forms of *rent-seeking*—attempts to capture existing wealth rather than to create new wealth. Finally, he argues that there has been a strong link between how societies direct the energies of their most able members and whether the societies flourish over the long term.

Murphy, Shleifer, and Vishny provide a general discussion of the forces that influence talented individuals' decisions whether to pursue activities that are socially productive. They emphasize three factors in particular. The first is the size of the relevant market: the larger is the market from which a talented individual can reap returns, the greater are the incentives to enter a given activity. Thus, for example, low transportation costs and an absence of barriers to trade encourage entrepreneurship; poorly defined property rights that make much of an economy's wealth vulnerable to expropriation encourage rent-seeking. The second factor is the degree of diminishing returns. Activities whose scale is limited by the entrepreneur's time (performing surgeries, for example) do not offer the same potential returns as activities whose returns are limited only by the scale of the market (creating inventions, for instance). Thus, for example, well-functioning capital markets that permit firms to expand rapidly tend to promote entrepreneurship over rent-seeking. The final factor is the ability to keep the returns from one's activities. Thus, clear property rights tend to encourage entrepreneurship, whereas legally sanctioned rent-seeking (through government or religion, for example) tends to encourage socially unproductive activities.

## Learning-by-Doing

The final determinant of knowledge accumulation is somewhat different in character. The central idea is that, as individuals produce goods, they inevitably think of ways of improving the production process. For example, Arrow (1962) cites the empirical regularity that after a new airplane design is introduced, the time required to build the frame of the marginal aircraft is inversely proportional to the cube root of the number of aircraft of that model that have already been produced; this improvement in productivity occurs without any evident innovations in the production process. Thus the accumulation of knowledge occurs in part not as a result of deliberate efforts, but as a side effect of conventional economic activity. This type of knowledge accumulation is known as *learning-by-doing.*

When learning-by-doing is the source of technological progress, the rate of knowledge accumulation depends not on the fraction of the economy's resources engaged in R&D, but on how much new knowledge is generated by conventional economic activity. Analyzing learning-by-doing therefore requires some changes to our model. All inputs are now engaged in goods production; thus the production function becomes

$$Y(t) = K(t)^{\alpha}[A(t)L(t)]^{1-\alpha}. \tag{3.22}$$

The simplest case of learning-by-doing is when learning occurs as a side effect of the production of new capital. With this formulation, since the increase in knowledge is a function of the increase in capital, the stock of knowledge is a function of the stock of capital. Thus there is only one state variable.[10] Making our usual choice of a power function, we have

$$A(t) = BK(t)^{\phi}, \qquad B > 0, \qquad \phi > 0. \tag{3.23}$$

Equations (3.22)–(3.23), together with (3.3)–(3.4) describing the accumulation of capital and labor, characterize the economy.

---

[10] See Problem 3.7 for the case in which knowledge accumulation occurs as a side effect of goods production rather than of capital accumulation.

To analyze this economy, begin by substituting (3.23) into (3.22). This yields

$$Y(t) = K(t)^\alpha B^{1-\alpha} K(t)^{\phi(1-\alpha)} L(t)^{1-\alpha}. \tag{3.24}$$

Since $\dot{K}(t) = sY(t)$, the dynamics of $K$ are given by

$$\dot{K}(t) = sB^{1-\alpha} K(t)^\alpha K(t)^{\phi(1-\alpha)} L(t)^{1-\alpha}. \tag{3.25}$$

In our model of knowledge accumulation without capital in Section 3.2, the dynamics of $A$ are given by $\dot{A}(t) = B[a_L L(t)]^\gamma A(t)^\theta$ (equation [3.6]). Comparing equation (3.25) of the learning-by-doing model with this equation shows that the structures of the two models are similar. In the model of Section 3.2, there is a single productive input, knowledge. Here, we can think of there also being only one productive input, capital. As equations (3.6) and (3.25) show, the dynamics of the two models are essentially the same. Thus we can use the results of our analysis of the earlier model to analyze this one. There, the key determinant of the economy's dynamics is how $\theta$ compares with 1. Here, by analogy, it is how $\alpha + \phi(1 - \alpha)$ compares with 1, which is equivalent to how $\phi$ compares with 1.

If $\phi$ is less than 1, the long-run growth rate of the economy is a function of the rate of population growth, $n$. If $\phi$ is greater than 1, there is explosive growth. And if $\phi$ equals 1, there is explosive growth if $n$ is positive and steady growth if $n$ equals 0.

Once again, a case that has received particular attention is $\phi = 1$ and $n = 0$. In this case, the production function (equation [3.24]) becomes

$$Y(t) = bK(t), \qquad b \equiv B^{1-\alpha} L^{1-\alpha}. \tag{3.26}$$

Capital accumulation is therefore given by

$$\dot{K}(t) = sbK(t). \tag{3.27}$$

As in the similar cases we have already considered, the dynamics of this economy are straightforward. Equation (3.27) immediately implies that $K$ grows steadily at rate $sb$. And since output is proportional to $K$, it also grows at this rate. Thus we have another example of a model in which long-run growth is endogenous and depends on the saving rate. Moreover, since $b$ is the inverse of the capital-output ratio, which is easy to measure, the model makes predictions about the *size* of the saving rate's impact on growth—an issue we will return to in Section 3.6.

In this model, the saving rate affects long-run growth because the contribution of capital is larger than its conventional contribution: increased capital raises output not only through its direct role in production (the $K^\alpha$ term in [3.24]), but also by indirectly contributing to the development of new ideas and thereby making all other capital more productive (the $K^{\phi(1-\alpha)}$ term in [3.24]). Because the production function in these models is often written using the symbol "$A$" rather than the "$b$" used in (3.26), these models are often referred to as "$Y = AK$" models.[11]

# 3.5  The Romer Model

## Overview

In this section we consider a specific model where the allocation of resources to R&D is built up from microeconomic foundations: the model of P. Romer (1990) of endogenous technological change. In this model, R&D is undertaken by profit-maximizing economic factors. That R&D fuels growth, which in turn affects the incentives for devoting resources to R&D.

As we know from the previous section, any model where the creation of knowledge is motivated by the returns that the knowledge commands in the market must involve departures from perfect competition: if knowledge is sold at marginal cost, the creators of knowledge earn negative profits. Romer deals with this issue by assuming that knowledge consists of distinct ideas and that inputs into production that embody different ideas are imperfect substitutes. He also assumes that the developer of an idea has monopoly rights to the use of the idea. These assumptions imply that the developer can charge a price above marginal cost for the use of his or her idea. The resulting profits provide the incentives for R&D.

The assumptions of imperfect substitutability and monopoly power add complexity to the model. To keep things as simple as possible, the variant of Romer's model we will consider is constructed so that its aggregate behavior is similar to the model in Section 3.2 in the special case of $\theta = 1$ and $n = 0$. The reason for constructing the model this way is not any evidence that this is a particularly realistic case. Rather, it is that it simplifies the analysis dramatically. Models of this type exhibit no *transition dynamics*. In response to a shock, the economy jumps immediately to its new balanced growth path. This feature makes it easier to characterize exactly how various changes affect the economy and to explicitly compute both the equilibrium and optimal allocations of resources to R&D.

Two types of simplifications are needed to give the model these aggregate properties. The first are assumptions about functional forms and parameter values, analogous to the assumptions of $\theta = 1$ and $n = 0$ in our earlier model.

---

[11] The model in P. Romer (1986) that launched new growth theory is closely related to our learning-by-doing model with $\phi = 1$ and $n = 0$. There are two main differences. First, the role played by physical capital here is played by knowledge in Romer's model: privately controlled knowledge both contributes directly to production at a particular firm and adds to aggregate knowledge, which contributes to production at all firms. Second, knowledge accumulation occurs through a separate production function rather than through forgone output; there are increasing returns to knowledge in goods production and (asymptotically) constant returns in knowledge accumulation. As a result, the economy converges to a constant growth rate.

The other is the elimination of all types of physical and human capital. In versions of Romer's model that include capital, there is generally some long-run equilibrium ratio of capital to the stock of ideas. Any disturbance that causes the actual ratio to differ from the long-run equilibrium ratio then sets off transition dynamics.

## The Ethier Production Function and the Returns to Knowledge Creation

The first step in presenting the model is to describe how knowledge creators have market power. Thus for the moment, we take the level of knowledge as given and describe how inputs embodying different ideas combine to produce final output.

There is an infinity of potential specialized inputs into production. For concreteness, one can think of each input as a chemical compound and each idea as the formula for a particular compound. When more ideas are used, more output is produced from a given quantity of inputs. For example, if output is initially produced with a single compound, adding an equal amount of a second compound yields more output than just doubling the amount of the first compound. Thus there is a benefit to new ideas.

Specifically, assume that there is a range of ideas that are currently available that extends from 0 to $A$, where $A > 0$. (In a moment, $A$ will be a function of time. But here we are looking at the economy at a point in time, and so it is simplest to leave out the time argument.) When an idea is available, the input into production embodying the idea can be produced using a technology that transforms labor one-for-one into the input. Thus we will use $L(i)$ to denote both the quantity of labor devoted to producing input $i$ and the quantity of input $i$ that goes into final-goods production. For ideas that have not yet been discovered (that is, for $i > A$), inputs embodying the ideas cannot be produced at any cost.

The specific assumption about how the inputs combine to produce final output uses the production function proposed by Ethier (1982):

$$Y = \left[ \int_{i=0}^{A} L(i)^{\phi} di \right]^{1/\phi}, \quad 0 < \phi < 1. \tag{3.28}$$

To see the implications of this function, let $L_Y$ denote the total number of workers producing inputs, and suppose the number producing each available input is the same. Then $L(i) = L_Y/A$ for all $i$, and so

$$Y = \left[ A \left( \frac{L_Y}{A} \right)^{\phi} \right]^{1/\phi} \tag{3.29}$$

$$= A^{(1-\phi)/\phi} L_Y.$$

This expression has two critical implications. First, there are constant returns to $L_Y$: holding the stock of knowledge constant, doubling the inputs into production doubles output. Second, output is increasing in $A$: holding the total quantity of inputs constant, raising the stock of knowledge raises output. This creates a value to a new idea.

To say more about the implications of the production function, it helps to introduce the model's assumptions about market structure. The exclusive rights to the use of a given idea are held by a monopolist; we can think of the monopolist as holding a patent on the idea. The patent–holder hires workers in a competitive labor market to produce the input associated with his or her idea, and then sells the input to producers of final output. The monopolist charges a constant price for each unit of the input; that is, price discrimination and other complicated contracts are ruled out. Output is produced by competitive firms that take the prices of inputs as given. Competition causes these firms to sell output at marginal cost. We will see shortly that this causes them to earn zero profits.

Consider the cost-minimization problem of a representative output producer. Let $p(i)$ denote the price charged by the holder of the patent on idea $i$ for each unit of the input embodying that idea. The Lagrangian for the problem of producing one unit of output at minimum cost is

$$\mathcal{L} = \int_{i=0}^{A} p(i)L(i)di - \lambda \left\{ \left[ \int_{i=0}^{A} L(i)^{\phi} di \right]^{1/\phi} - 1 \right\}. \tag{3.30}$$

The firm's choice variables are the $L(i)$'s for all values of $i$ from 0 to $A$. The first-order condition for an individual $L(i)$ is

$$p(i) = \lambda L(i)^{\phi-1}, \tag{3.31}$$

where we have used the fact that $\int_{i=0}^{A} L(i)^{\phi} di$ must equal 1.[12]

Equation (3.31) implies $L(i)^{\phi-1} = p(i)/\lambda$, which in turn implies

$$L(i) = \left[ \frac{p(i)}{\lambda} \right]^{\frac{1}{\phi-1}}$$

$$= \left[ \frac{\lambda}{p(i)} \right]^{\frac{1}{1-\phi}}. \tag{3.32}$$

Equation (3.32) shows that the holder of the patent on an idea faces a downward-sloping demand curve for the input embodying the idea: $L(i)$ is a smoothly decreasing function of $p(i)$. When $\phi$ is closer to 1, the marginal

---

[12] Because the terms in (3.31) are of order $di$ in the Lagrangian, this step—like the analysis of household optimization in continuous time in Section 2.2—is slightly informal. Assuming that the number of inputs is finite, so $Y = \left[ \sum_{i=1}^{N} \left( \frac{A}{N} \right) \left( \frac{NL_i}{A} \right)^{\phi} \right]^{1/\phi}$, and then letting that number ($N$) approach infinity, yields the same results. Note that this approach is analogous to the approach sketched in n. 7 of Chapter 2 to analyzing household optimization there.

product of an input declines more slowly as the quantity of the input rises. As a result, the inputs are closer substitutes, and so the elasticity of demand for each input is greater.

Because firms producing final output face constant costs for each input and the production function exhibits constant returns, marginal cost equals average cost. As a result, these firms earn zero profits.[13]

## The Rest of the Model

We now turn to the remainder of the model, which involves four sets of assumptions. The first set concern economic aggregates. Population is fixed and equal to $\bar{L} > 0$. Workers can be employed either in producing intermediate inputs or in R&D. If we let $L_A(t)$ denote the number of workers engaged in R&D at time $t$, then equilibrium in the labor market at $t$ requires

$$L_A(t) + L_Y(t) = \bar{L}, \qquad (3.33)$$

where, as before, $L_Y(t) = \int_{i=0}^{A(t)} L(i,t)di$ is the total number of workers producing inputs. Note that we have now made the time arguments explicit, since we will be considering the evolution of the economy over time.

The production function for new ideas is linear in the number of workers employed in R&D and proportional to the existing stock of knowledge:

$$\dot{A}(t) = BL_A(t)A(t), \qquad B > 0. \qquad (3.34)$$

Finally, the initial level of $A$, $A(0)$, is assumed to be strictly positive.

These assumptions are chosen to give the model the aggregate dynamics of a linear growth model. Equation (3.34) and the assumption of no population growth imply that if the fraction of the population engaged in R&D is constant, the stock of knowledge grows at a constant rate, and that this rate is an increasing function of the fraction of the population engaged in R&D.

The second group of assumptions concern the microeconomics of household behavior. Individuals are infinitely lived and maximize a conventional utility function like the one we saw in Section 2.1. Individuals' discount rate is $\rho$ and, for simplicity, their instantaneous utility function is logarithmic.[14] Thus the representative individual's lifetime utility is

$$U = \int_{t=0}^{\infty} e^{-\rho t} \ln C(t)dt, \qquad \rho > 0, \qquad (3.35)$$

where $C(t)$ is the individual's consumption at $t$.

---

[13] One could use the condition that $\left[ \int_{i=0}^{A} L(i)^\phi di \right]^{1/\phi} = 1$ to solve for $\lambda$, and then solve for the cost-minimizing levels of the $L(i)$'s and the level of marginal cost. These steps are not needed for what follows, however.

[14] Assuming constant-relative-risk-aversion utility leads to very similar results. See Problem 3.8.

As in the Ramsey-Cass-Koopmans model, the individual's budget constraint is that the present value of lifetime consumption cannot exceed his or her initial wealth plus the present value of lifetime labor income. If individuals all have the same initial wealth (which we assume) and if the interest rate is constant (which will prove to be the case in equilibrium), this constraint is

$$\int_{t=0}^{\infty} e^{-rt} C(t)dt \leq X(0) + \int_{t=0}^{\infty} e^{-rt} w(t)dt, \tag{3.36}$$

where $r$ is the interest rate, $X(0)$ is initial wealth per person, and $w(t)$ is the wage at $t$. The individual takes all of these as given.

The third set of assumptions concern the microeconomics of R&D. There is free entry into idea creation: anyone can hire $1/[BA(t)]$ units of labor at the prevailing wage $w(t)$ and produce a new idea (see [3.34]). Even though an increase in $A$ raises productivity in R&D, R&D firms are not required to compensate the inventors of past ideas. Thus the model assumes the R&D externality discussed in Section 3.4.

The creator of an idea is granted permanent patent rights to the use of the idea in producing the corresponding input into output production (but, as just described, not in R&D). The patent-holder chooses how much of the input that embodies his or her idea to produce, and the price to charge for the input, at each point in time. In making this decision, the patent-holder takes as given the wage, the prices charged for other inputs, and the total amount of labor used in goods production, $L_Y$.[15]

The free-entry condition in R&D requires that the present value of the profits earned from selling the input embodying an idea equals the cost of creating it. Suppose idea $i$ is created at time $t$, and let $\pi(i,\tau)$ denote the profits earned by the creator of the idea at time $\tau$. Then this condition is

$$\int_{\tau=t}^{\infty} e^{-r(\tau-t)} \pi(i,\tau)d\tau = \frac{w(t)}{BA(t)}. \tag{3.37}$$

The final assumptions of the model concern general equilibrium. First, the assumption that the labor market is competitive implies that the wage paid in R&D and the wages paid by all input producers are equal. Second, the only asset in the economy is the patents. Thus initial wealth is the present value of the future profits from the ideas that have already been invented. Finally, the only use of the output good is for consumption. Because all

---

[15] It might seem natural to assume that the patent-holder takes the price charged by producers of final goods rather than $L_Y$ as given. However, this approach implies that no equilibrium exists. Consider a situation where the price charged by goods producers equals their marginal cost. If one patent-holder cuts his or her price infinitesimally with the prices of other inputs and of final output unchanged, goods producers' marginal cost is less than price, and so their input demands are infinite. Assuming that patent-holders take $L_Y$ as given avoids this problem.

individuals are the same, they all choose the same consumption path. Thus equilibrium in the goods market at time $t$ requires

$$C(t)\overline{L} = Y(t). \tag{3.38}$$

This completes the description of the model.

## Solving the Model

The fact that at the aggregate level the economy resembles a linear growth model suggests that in equilibrium, the allocation of labor between R&D and the production of intermediate inputs is likely not to change over time. Thus, rather than taking a general approach to find the equilibrium, we will look for an equilibrium where $L_A$ and $L_Y$ are constant. Specifically, we will investigate the implications of a given (and constant) value of $L_A$ to the point where we can find what it implies about both the present value of the profits from the creation of an idea and the cost of creating the idea. The condition that these two quantities must be equal will then pin down the equilibrium value of $L_A$. We will then verify that this equilibrium value is constant over time.

Of course, this approach will not rule out the possibility that there are also equilibria where $L_A$ varies over time. It turns out, however, that there are no such equilibria, and thus that the equilibrium we will find is the model's only one. We will not demonstrate this formally, however.

The first step in solving the model is to consider the problem of a patent-holder choosing the price to charge for his or her input at a point in time. A standard result from microeconomics is that the profit-maximizing price of a monopolist is $\eta/(\eta-1)$ times marginal cost, where $\eta$ is the elasticity of demand. In our case, we know from equation (3.32) for cost-minimization by the producers of final goods that the elasticity of demand is constant and equal to $1/(1 - \phi)$. And since one unit of the input can be produced from one unit of labor, the marginal cost of supplying the input at time $t$ is $w(t)$. Each monopolist therefore charges $[1/(1 - \phi)]/\{[1/(1 - \phi)] - 1\}$ times $w(t)$, or $w(t)/\phi$.[16]

Knowing the price each monopolist charges allows us to determine his or her profits at a point in time. Because the prices of all inputs are the same, the quantity of each input used at time $t$ is the same. Given our assumption that $L_A$ is constant and the requirement that $L_A(t) + L_Y(t) = \overline{L}$, this quantity

---

[16] This neglects the potential complication that the analysis in equations (3.30)–(3.32) shows the elasticity of input demand *conditional* on producing a given amount of output. Thus we might need to consider possible effects through changes in the quantity of output produced. However, because each input accounts for an infinitesimal fraction of total costs, the impact of a change in the price of a single input on the total amount produced from a given $L_Y$ is negligible. Thus allowing for the possibility that a change in $p(i)$ could change the quantity produced does not change the elasticity of demand each monopolist faces.

is $(\bar{L} - L_A)/A(t)$. Each patent-holder's profits are thus

$$\pi(t) = \frac{\bar{L} - L_A}{A(t)} \left[ \frac{w(t)}{\phi} - w(t) \right]$$

$$= \frac{1 - \phi}{\phi} \frac{\bar{L} - L_A}{A(t)} w(t).$$

$\qquad\qquad\qquad(3.39)$

To determine the present value of profits from an invention, and hence the incentive to innovate, we need to determine the economy's growth rate and the interest rate. Equation (3.34) for knowledge creation, $\dot{A}(t) = BL_A(t)A(t)$, implies that if $L_A$ is constant, $\dot{A}(t)/A(t)$ is just $BL_A$. We know that all input suppliers charge the same price at a point in time, and thus that all available inputs are used in the same quantity. Equation (3.29) tells us that in this case, $Y(t) = A(t)^{[(1-\phi)/\phi]}L_Y(t)$. Since $L_Y(t)$ is constant, the growth rate of $Y$ is $(1 - \phi)/\phi$ times the growth rate of $A$, or $[(1 - \phi)/\phi]BL_A$.

Both consumption and the wage grow at the same rate as output. In the case of consumption, we know this because all output is consumed. In the case of the wage, one way to see this is to note that because of constant returns and competition, all the revenues of final goods producers are paid to the intermediate goods suppliers. Because their markup is constant, their payments to workers are a constant fraction of their revenues. Since the number of workers producing intermediate inputs is constant, it follows that the growth rate of the wage equals the growth rate of output.

We can use this analysis, together with equation (3.39), to find the growth rate of profits from an invention. $\bar{L} - L_A$ is constant; $w$ is growing at rate $[(1 - \phi)/\phi]BL_A$; and $A$ is growing at rate $BL_A$. Equation (3.39) then implies that profits from a given invention are growing at rate $[(1 - \phi)/\phi]BL_A - BL_A$, or $[(1 - 2\phi)/\phi]BL_A$.

Once we know the growth rate of consumption, finding the real interest rate is straightforward. Recall from Section 2.2 that consumption growth for a household with constant-relative-risk-aversion utility is $\dot{C}(t)/C(t) = [r(t) - \rho]/\theta$, where $\theta$ is the coefficient of relative risk aversion. With logarithmic utility, $\theta$ is 1. Thus equilibrium requires

$$r(t) = \rho + \frac{\dot{C}(t)}{C(t)}$$

$$= \rho + \frac{1 - \phi}{\phi}BL_A.$$

$\qquad\qquad\qquad(3.40)$

Thus if $L_A$ is constant, the real interest rate is constant, as we have been assuming.

The profits from an invention grow at rate $[(1 - 2\phi)/\phi]BL_A$, and are discounted at the interest rate, $\rho + [(1 - \phi)/\phi]BL_A$. Equation (3.39) tells us that the profits at $t$ are $[(1 - \phi)/\phi][(\bar{L} - L_A)w(t)/A(t)]$. The present value of the profits earned from the discovery of a new idea at time $t$ is therefore

$$\pi(t) = \frac{\frac{1 - \phi}{\phi}(\bar{L} - L_A)\frac{w(t)}{A(t)}}{\rho + \frac{1 - \phi}{\phi}BL_A - \frac{1 - 2\phi}{\phi}BL_A}$$

$$= \frac{1 - \phi}{\phi}\frac{\bar{L} - L_A}{\rho + BL_A}\frac{w(t)}{A(t)}.$$

(3.41)

We are now in a position to find the equilibrium value of $L_A$. If the amount of R&D is strictly positive, the present value of profits from an invention must equal the costs of the invention. Since one worker can produce $BA(t)$ ideas per unit time, the cost of an invention is $w(t)/[BA(t)]$. The equilibrium condition is therefore

$$\frac{1 - \phi}{\phi}\frac{\bar{L} - L_A}{\rho + BL_A}\frac{w(t)}{A(t)} = \frac{w(t)}{BA(t)}.$$

(3.42)

Solving this equation for $L_A$ yields

$$L_A = (1 - \phi)\bar{L} - \frac{\phi\rho}{B}.$$

(3.43)

The amount of R&D need not be strictly positive, however. In particular, when (3.43) implies $L_A < 0$, the discounted profits from the first invention starting from $L_A = 0$ are less than its costs. As a result, R&D is 0. Thus we need to modify equation (3.43) to

$$L_A = \max\left\{(1 - \phi)\bar{L} - \frac{\phi\rho}{B}, 0\right\}.$$

(3.44)

Finally, since the growth rate of output is $[(1 - \phi)/\phi]BL_A$, we have

$$\frac{\dot{Y}(t)}{Y(t)} = \max\left\{\frac{(1 - \phi)^2}{\phi}B\bar{L} - (1 - \phi)\rho, 0\right\}.$$

(3.45)

Thus we have succeeded in describing how long-run growth is determined by the underlying microeconomic environment. And note that since none of the terms on the right-hand side of (3.40) are time-varying, the equilibrium value of $L_A$ is constant.[17]

---

[17] To verify that individuals are satisfying their budget constraint, recall from Section 2.2 that the lifetime budget constraint can be expressed in terms of the behavior of wealth as $t$ approaches infinity. When the interest rate is constant, this version of the budget constraint simplifies to $\lim_{t\to\infty} e^{-rt}[X(t)/\bar{L}] \geq 0$. $X(t)$, the economy's wealth at $t$, is the present value of future profits from ideas already invented, and is growing at the growth rate of the economy. From (3.40), the interest rate exceeds the economy's growth rate. Thus $\lim_{t\to\infty} e^{-rt}[X(t)/\bar{L}] = 0$, and so individuals are satisfying their budget constraint with equality.

## Implications

The model has two major sets of implications. The first concern the determinants of long-run growth. Four parameters affect the economy's growth rate.[18] First, when individuals are less patient (that is, when $\rho$ is higher), fewer workers engage in R&D (equation [3.44]), and so growth is lower (equation [3.45]). Since R&D is a form of investment, this makes sense.

Second, an increase in substitutability among inputs ($\phi$) also reduces growth. There are two reasons. First, fewer workers engage in R&D (again, equation [3.44]). Second, although a given amount of R&D translates into the same growth rate of $A$ (equation [3.34]), a given growth rate of $A$ translates into slower output growth (equation [3.29]). This finding is also intuitive: when the inputs embodying different ideas are better substitutes, patent-holders' market power is lower, and each additional idea contributes less to output. Both effects make R&D less attractive.

Third, an increase in productivity in the R&D sector ($B$) increases growth. There are again two effects at work. The first is the straightforward one that a rise in $B$ raises growth for a given number of workers engaged in R&D. The other is that increased productivity in R&D draws more workers into that sector.

Finally, an increase in the size of the population ($\overline{L}$) raises long-run growth. Paralleling the effects of an increase in $B$, there are two effects: growth increases for a given fraction of workers engaged in R&D, and the fraction of workers engaged in R&D increases. The second effect is another consequence of the nonrivalry of knowledge: an increase in the size of the economy expands the market an inventor can reach, and so increases the returns to R&D.

All four parameters affect growth at least in part by changing the fraction of workers who are engaged in R&D. None of these effects are present in the simple model of R&D and growth in Sections 3.1–3.3, since that model takes the allocation of workers between activities as given. Thus the Romer model identifies a rich set of determinants of long-run growth.

The model's second major set of implications concern the gap between equilibrium and optimal growth. Since the economy is not perfectly competitive, there is no reason to expect the decentralized equilibrium to be socially optimal. Paralleling our analysis of the equilibrium, let us look for the constant level of $L_A$ that yields the highest level of lifetime utility for the representative individual.[19]

Because all output is consumed, the representative individual's consumption is $1/\overline{L}$ times output. Equation (3.29) for output therefore implies that

---

[18] The discussion that follows assumes that the parameter values are in the range where $L_A$ is strictly positive.

[19] One can show that a social planner would in fact choose to have $L_A$ be constant, so the restriction to paths where $L_A$ is constant is not a binding constraint.

the representative individual's consumption at time 0 is

$$C(0) = \frac{(\overline{L} - L_A)A(0)^{(1-\phi)/\phi}}{\overline{L}}.$$
(3.46)

Output and consumption grow at rate $[(1 - \phi)/\phi]BL_A$. The representative individual's lifetime utility is therefore

$$U = \int_{t=0}^{\infty} e^{-\rho t} \ln \left[ \frac{\overline{L} - L_A}{\overline{L}} A(0)^{(1-\phi)/\phi} e^{[(1-\phi)/\phi]BL_A t} \right] dt.$$
(3.47)

One can show that the solution to this integral is[20]

$$U = \frac{1}{\rho} \left( \ln \frac{\overline{L} - L_A}{\overline{L}} + \frac{1 - \phi}{\phi} \ln A(0) + \frac{1 - \phi}{\phi} \frac{BL_A}{\rho} \right).$$
(3.48)

Maximizing this expression with respect to $L_A$ shows that the socially optimal level of $L_A$ is given by[21]

$$L_A^{OPT} = \max \left\{ \overline{L} - \frac{\phi}{1 - \phi} \frac{\rho}{B}, 0 \right\}.$$
(3.49)

Comparing this expression with equation (3.44) for the equilibrium level of $L_A$ shows a simple relation between the two:

$$L_A^{EQ} = (1 - \phi)L_A^{OPT},$$
(3.50)

where $L_A^{EQ}$ is the equilibrium level of $L_A$.

The model potentially has all three externalities described in Section 3.4. There is a consumer-surplus effect (or, in this case, a goods-producer-surplus effect): because a patent-holder charges a fixed price per unit of the input embodying his or her idea, the firms producing final output obtain surplus from buying the intermediate input. There can be either a business-stealing or a business-creating effect. Equation (3.39) shows that the profits of each supplier of intermediate goods are proportional to $w(t)/A(t)$. $w(t)$ is proportional to $Y(t)$, which is proportional to $A(t)^{(1-\phi)/\phi}$. Thus profits are proportional to $A(t)^{(1-2\phi)/\phi}$. It follows that the profits of existing patent-holders are reduced by an increase in $A$ if $\phi > 1/2$, but increased if $\phi < 1/2$. Finally, there is an R&D effect: an increase in $A$ makes the R&D sector more productive, but innovators do not have to compensate existing patent-holders for this benefit.

Despite the three externalities, the relation between the equilibrium and optimal allocation of workers to R&D takes a simple form. The equilibrium number of workers engaged in R&D is always less than the optimal number (unless both are at the corner solution of zero). Thus growth is always inefficiently low. Moreover, the proportional gap between the equilibrium

---

[20] See Problem 3.10.

[21] Again, see Problem 3.10.

and optimal numbers (and hence between equilibrium and optimal growth) depends only on a single parameter. The smaller the degree of differentiation among inputs embodying different ideas (that is, the greater is $\phi$), the greater the gap.

## Extensions

Romer's model has proven seminal. As a result, there are almost innumerable extensions, variations, and alternatives. Here, we discuss three of the most significant.

First, the key difference between Romer's original model and the version we have been considering is that Romer's model includes physical capital. In his version, ideas are embodied in specialized capital goods rather than intermediate inputs. The capital goods are used together with labor to produce final output.

Introducing physical capital does not change the model's central messages. And as described above, by introducing another state variable, it complicates the analysis considerably. But it does allow one to examine policies that affect the division of output between consumption and investment. In Romer's model, where physical capital is not an input into R&D, policies that increase physical-capital investment have only level effects, not growth effects. In variants where capital enters the production function for ideas, such policies generally have growth effects.

Second, as we have stressed repeatedly, for reasons of simplicity the macroeconomics of the version of the model we have been considering correspond to a linear growth model. In the next section, we will encounter important evidence against the predictions of linear growth models and other models with fully endogenous growth. Jones (1995a) therefore extends the Romer model to the case where the exponent on $A$ in the production function for ideas is less than 1. This creates transition dynamics, and so complicates the analysis. More importantly, it changes the model's messages concerning the determinants of long-run growth. The macroeconomics of Jones's model correspond to those of a semi-endogenous growth model. As a result, long-run growth depends only on the rate of population growth. Forces that affect the allocation of inputs between R&D and goods production, and forces that affect the division of output between investment and consumption, have only level effects.

Third, in Romer's model, technological progress takes the form of expansion of the number of inputs into production. An alternative is that it takes the form of improvements in existing inputs. This leads to the "quality-ladder" models of Grossman and Helpman (1991a) and Aghion and Howitt (1992). In those models, there is a fixed number of inputs, and innovations take the form of discrete improvements in the inputs. One implication is that the price a patent-holder charges is limited not just by downward-sloping demand for a given input, but also by the possibility of output-producers switching to an older, lower-quality version of the patent-holder's input.

Quality-ladder models do not produce sharply different answers than expanding-variety models concerning the long-run growth and level of income. But they identify additional microeconomic determinants of incentives for innovation, and so show other factors that affect long-run economic performance.

## 3.6   Empirical Application: Time-Series Tests of Endogenous Growth Models

A central motivation for work on new growth theory is the desire to understand variations in long-run growth. As a result, the initial work in this area focused on fully endogenous growth models—that is, models with constant or increasing returns to produced factors, where changes in saving rates and resources devoted to R&D can permanently change growth. Jones (1995b) raises a critical issue about these models: Does growth in fact vary with the factors identified by the models in the way the models predict?

### Are Growth Rates Stationary?

Jones considers two approaches to testing the predictions of fully endogenous growth models about changes in growth. The first starts with the observation that the models predict that changes in the models' parameters permanently affect growth. For example, in the model of Section 3.3 with $\beta + \theta = 1$ and $n = 0$, changes in $s$, $a_L$, and $a_K$ change the economy's long-run growth rate. He therefore asks whether the actual growth rate of income per person is *stationary* or *nonstationary*. Loosely speaking, a variable is stationary if its distribution is constant over time. To take a simple example, consider a variable that follows the process

$$X_t = \alpha + \rho X_{t-1} + \varepsilon_t, \tag{3.51}$$

where the $\varepsilon$'s are *white-noise* disturbances—that is, a series of independent mean-zero shocks with the same distribution. If $|\rho| < 1$, $X$ is stationary: the effects of a shock gradually fade, and the mean of $X_t$ is $\alpha/(1 - \rho)$ for all $t$. If $|\rho| > 1$, $X$ is nonstationary: the effects of a shock increase over time, and the entire distribution of $X_t$ is different for different values of $t$.

Jones argues that because models of fully endogenous growth imply that long-run growth is easily changed, they predict that growth rates are nonstationary. He therefore considers several tests of stationarity versus nonstationarity. A simple one is to regress the growth rate of income per person on a constant and a trend,

$$g_t = a + bt + e_t, \tag{3.52}$$

and then test the null hypothesis that $b = 0$. A second test is an *augmented Dickey-Fuller test.* Consider a regression of the form

$$\Delta g_t = \mu + \rho g_{t-1} + \alpha_1 \Delta g_{t-1} + \alpha_2 \Delta g_{t-2} + \cdots + \alpha_n \Delta g_{t-n} + \varepsilon_t. \tag{3.53}$$

If growth has some normal level that it reverts to when it is pushed away, $\rho$ is negative. If it does not, $\rho$ is 0.[22]

Unfortunately, although trying to look at the issue of stationarity versus nonstationarity is intuitively appealing, it is not in fact an appropriate way to test endogenous growth models. There are two difficulties, both related to the fact that stationarity and nonstationarity concern characteristics of the data at infinite horizons. First, no finite amount of data can shed *any* light on how series behave at infinite horizons. Suppose, for example, we see highly persistent changes in growth in some sample. Although this is consistent with the presence of permanent changes in growth, it is equally consistent with the view that growth reverts very slowly to some value. Alternatively, suppose we observe that growth returns rapidly to some value over a sample. Such a finding is completely consistent not only with stationarity, but with the view that a small portion of changes in growth are permanent, or even explosive.[23]

Second, it is hard to think of any substantive economic question that hinges on the stationarity or nonstationarity of a series. In the case of growth theory, growth could be nonstationary even if fully endogenous growth models do not describe the world. For example, the correct model could be a semi-endogenous growth model and $n$ could be nonstationary. Likewise, growth could be stationary even if a fully endogenous growth model is correct; all that is required is that the parameters that determine long-run growth are stationary. No important question depends on whether movements in some series are extremely long-lasting or literally permanent.

The results of Jones's tests illustrate the dangers of conducting tests of stationarity versus nonstationarity to try to address substantive questions. Jones examines data on U.S. income per person over the period 1880–1987. His statistical results seem to provide powerful evidence that growth is stationary. The augmented Dickey-Fuller test overwhelmingly rejects the null hypothesis that $\rho = 0$, thus appearing to indicate stationarity. And the $t$-statistic on $b$ in equation (3.52) is just 0.1, suggesting an almost complete lack of evidence against the hypothesis of no trend in growth.

But, as Jones points out, the results are in fact essentially uninformative about whether there have been economically important changes in growth.

---

[22] It is the presence of the lagged $\Delta g_t$ terms that makes this test an "augmented" Dickey-Fuller test. A simple Dickey-Fuller test would focus on $g_t = \mu + \rho g_{t-1} + \varepsilon_t$.

[23] See Blough (1992) and Campbell and Perron (1991).

The two-standard-error confidence interval for $b$ in (3.52) is $(-0.026, 0.028)$. A value of 0.02, which is comfortably within the confidence interval, implies that annual growth is rising by 0.2 percentage points per decade, and thus that average growth was more than two percentage points higher at the end of Jones's sample than at the beginning. That is, while the results do not reject the null of no trend in growth, they also fail to reject the null of an enormous trend in growth.

Intuitively, what the statistical results are telling us is not whether growth is stationary or nonstationary—which, as just described, is both impossible and uninteresting. Rather, they are telling us that there are highly transitory movements in growth that are large relative to any long-lasting movements that may be present. But this does not tell us whether such long-lasting movements are economically important.

## The Magnitudes and Correlates of Changes in Long-Run Growth

Jones's second approach is to examine the relationships between the determinants of growth identified by endogenous growth models and actual growth rates. He begins by considering learning-by-doing models like the one discussed in Section 3.4 with $\phi = 1$. Recall that that model yields a relationship of the form

$$\frac{Y(t)}{L(t)} = b \frac{K(t)}{L(t)} \tag{3.54}$$

(see equation [3.26]). This implies that the growth rate of income per person is

$$g_{Y/L}(t) = g_K(t) - g_L(t), \tag{3.55}$$

where $g_x$ denotes the growth rate of $x$. $g_K$ is given by

$$\frac{\dot{K}(t)}{K(t)} = \frac{sY(t)}{K(t)} - \delta, \tag{3.56}$$

where $s$ is the fraction of output that is invested and $\delta$ is the depreciation rate.

Jones observes that $Y/K$, $\delta$, and $g_L$ all both appear to be fairly steady, while investment rates have been trending up. Thus the model predicts an upward trend in growth. More importantly, it makes predictions about the *magnitude* of the trend. Jones reports that in most major industrialized countries, $Y/K$ is about 0.4 and the ratio of investment to GDP has been rising by about one percentage point per decade. The model therefore predicts an increase in growth of about 0.4 percentage points per decade. This figure is far outside the confidence interval noted above for the estimated trend in growth in the United States. Jones reports similar findings for other major countries.

Jones then turns to endogenous growth models that emphasize R&D. The simplest version of such a model is the model of Section 3.2 with $\gamma = 1$ (constant returns to the number of workers engaged in R&D) and $\theta = 1$ (the production of new knowledge is proportional to the stock of knowledge). In this case, growth in income per person is proportional to the number of workers engaged in R&D. Reasonable variants of the model, as long as they imply fully endogenous growth, have similar implications.

Over the postwar period, the number of scientists and engineers engaged in R&D and real R&D spending have both increased by roughly a factor of five. Thus R&D models of fully endogenous growth predict roughly a quintupling of the growth rate of income per person. Needless to say, this prediction is grossly contradicted by the data.

Finally, Jones observes that other variables that fully endogenous growth models plausibly identify as potential determinants of growth also have strong upward trends. Examples include the resources devoted to human-capital accumulation, the number of highly educated workers, the extent of interactions among countries, and world population. But again, we do not observe large increases in growth.

Thus Jones's second approach delivers clear results. Models of fully endogenous growth predict that growth should have been rising rapidly. Yet the data reveal no trend at all in growth over the past century, and are grossly inconsistent with a trend of the magnitude predicted by the models.

## Discussion

The simplest interpretation of Jones's results, and the one that he proposes, is that there are decreasing returns to produced factors. That is, Jones's results support semi-endogenous growth models over models of fully endogenous growth.

Several subsequent papers suggest another possibility, however. These papers continue to assume constant or increasing returns to produced factors, but add a channel through which the overall expansion of the economy does not lead to faster growth. Specifically, they assume that it is the amount of R&D activity per sector that determines growth, and that the number of sectors grows with the economy. As a result, growth is steady despite the fact that population is rising. But because of the returns to produced factors, increases in the fraction of resources devoted to R&D permanently raise growth. Thus the models maintain the ability of early new growth models to potentially explain variations in long-run growth, but do not imply that worldwide population growth leads to ever-increasing growth (see, for example, Peretto, 1998; Dinopoulos and Thompson, 1998; and Howitt, 1999).

There are two difficulties with this line of argument. First, it is not just population that has been trending up. The basic fact emphasized by Jones is that R&D's share and rates of investment in physical and human capital have also been rising. Thus the failure of growth to rise is puzzling for these second-generation models of fully endogenous growth as well. Second, as Jones (1999) and Li (2000) show, the parameter restrictions needed in these models to eliminate scale effects on growth are strong and appear arbitrary.

With decreasing returns, the lack of a trend in growth is not puzzling. In this case, a rise in, say, the saving rate or R&D's share leads to a temporary period of above-normal growth. As a result, repeated rises in these variables lead not to increasing growth, but to an extended period of above-normal growth. This suggests that despite the relative steadiness of growth, one should not think of the United States and other major economies as being on conventional balanced growth paths (Jones, 2002a).

Saving rates and R&D's share cannot continue rising indefinitely (though in the case of the R&D share, the current share is sufficiently low that it can continue to rise at a rapid rate for a substantial period). Thus one corollary of this analysis is that in the absence of countervailing forces, growth must slow at some point. Moreover, the calculations in Jones (2002a) suggest that the slowdown would be considerable.

# 3.7  Empirical Application: Population Growth and Technological Change since 1 Million B.C.

Our goal in developing models of endogenous knowledge accumulation has been to learn about the sources of modern economic growth and of the vast differences in incomes across countries today. Kremer (1993), however, applies the models in a very different setting: he argues that they provide insights into the dynamics of population, technology, and income over the broad sweep of human history.

Kremer begins his analysis by noting that essentially all models of the endogenous growth of knowledge predict that technological progress is an increasing function of population size. The reasoning is simple: the larger the population, the more people there are to make discoveries, and thus the more rapidly knowledge accumulates.

He then argues that over almost all of human history, technological progress has led mainly to increases in population rather than increases in output per person. Population grew by several orders of magnitude between prehistoric times and the Industrial Revolution. But since incomes at the beginning of the Industrial Revolution were not far above subsistence levels, output per person could not have risen by anything close to the same amount as population. Only in the past few centuries has the impact of technological progress fallen to any substantial degree on output per person. Putting these observations together, Kremer concludes that models of endogenous technological progress predict that over most of human history, the rate of population growth should have been rising.

## A Simple Model

Kremer's formal model is a straightforward variation on the models we have been considering. The simplest version consists of three equations. First, output depends on technology, labor, and land:

$$Y(t) = T^{\alpha}[A(t)L(t)]^{1-\alpha}, \tag{3.57}$$

where $T$ denotes the fixed stock of land. (Capital is neglected for simplicity, and land is included to keep population finite.) Second, additions to knowledge are proportional to population, and also depend on the stock of knowledge:

$$\dot{A}(t) = BL(t)A(t)^{\theta}. \tag{3.58}$$

And third, population adjusts so that output per person equals the subsistence level, denoted $\bar{y}$:

$$\frac{Y(t)}{L(t)} = \bar{y}. \tag{3.59}$$

Aside from this Malthusian assumption about the determination of population, this model is similar to the model of Section 3.2 with $\gamma = 1$.

We solve the model in two steps. The first is to find the size of the population that can be supported on the fixed stock of land at a given time. Substituting expression (3.57) for output into the Malthusian population condition, (3.59), yields

$$\frac{T^{\alpha}[A(t)L(t)]^{1-\alpha}}{L(t)} = \bar{y}. \tag{3.60}$$

Solving this condition for $L(t)$ gives us

$$L(t) = \left(\frac{1}{\bar{y}}\right)^{1/\alpha} A(t)^{(1-\alpha)/\alpha} T. \tag{3.61}$$

This equation states that the population that can be supported is decreasing in the subsistence level of output, increasing in technology, and proportional to the amount of land.

The second step is to find the dynamics of technology and population. Since both $\bar{y}$ and $T$ are constant, (3.61) implies that the growth rate of $L$ is $(1 - \alpha)/\alpha$ times the growth rate of $A$:

$$\frac{\dot{L}(t)}{L(t)} = \frac{1 - \alpha}{\alpha} \frac{\dot{A}(t)}{A(t)}. \tag{3.62}$$

In the special case of $\theta = 1$, equation (3.58) for knowledge accumulation implies that $\dot{A}(t)/A(t)$ is just $BL(t)$. Thus in this case, (3.62) implies that the growth rate of population is proportional to the level of population. In the general case, one can show that the model implies that the rate of population growth is proportional to $L(t)^{\psi}$, where $\psi = 1 - [(1 - \theta)\alpha/(1 - \alpha)]$.[24] Thus population growth is increasing in the size of the population unless $\alpha$ is large or $\theta$ is much less than 1 (or a combination of the two). Intuitively, Kremer's model implies increasing growth even with diminishing returns to knowledge in the production of new knowledge (that is, even with $\theta < 1$) because labor is now a produced factor: improvements in technology lead to higher population, which in turn leads to further improvements in technology. Further, the effect is likely to be substantial. For example, even if $\alpha$ is one-third and $\theta$ is one-half rather than 1, $1 - [(1 - \theta)\alpha/(1 - \alpha)]$ is 0.75.

## Results

Kremer tests the model's predictions using population estimates extending back to 1 million B.C. that have been constructed by archaeologists and anthropologists. Figure 3.9 shows the resulting scatter plot of population growth against population. Each observation shows the level of population at the beginning of some period and the average annual growth rate of population over that period. The length of the periods considered falls gradually from many thousand years early in the sample to 10 years at the end. Because the periods considered for the early part of the sample are so long, even substantial errors in the early population estimates would have little impact on the estimated growth rates.

The figure shows a strongly positive, and approximately linear, relationship between population growth and the level of population. A regression of growth on a constant and population (in billions) yields

$$n_t = -0.0023 + 0.524\, L_t, \qquad R^2 = 0.92, \qquad D.W. = 1.10, \qquad (3.63)$$
$$\phantom{n_t = } (0.0355) \quad (0.026)$$

where $n$ is population growth and $L$ is population, and where the numbers in parentheses are standard errors. Thus there is an overwhelmingly statistically significant association between the level of population and its growth rate.

The argument that technological progress is a worldwide phenomenon fails if there are regions that are completely cut off from one another. Kremer uses this observation to propose a second test of theories of

---

[24] To see this, divide both sides of (3.58) by $A$ to obtain an expression for $\dot{A}/A$. Then use (3.60) to express $A$ in terms of $L$, and substitute the result into the expression for $\dot{A}/A$. Expression (3.62) then implies that $\dot{L}/L$ equals a constant times $L(t)^{\psi}$.

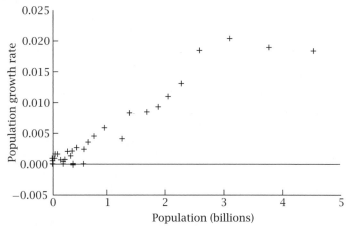

**FIGURE 3.9** **The level and growth rate of population, 1 million B.C. to 1990 (from Kremer, 1993; used with permission)**

endogenous knowledge accumulation. From the disappearance of the intercontinental land bridges at the end of the last ice age to the voyages of the European explorers, Eurasia-Africa, the Americas, Australia, and Tasmania were almost completely isolated from one another. The model implies that at the time of the separation, the populations of each region had the same technology. Thus the initial populations should have been approximately proportional to the land areas of the regions (see equation [3.61]). The model predicts that during the period that the regions were separate, technological progress was faster in the regions with larger populations. The theory thus predicts that, when contact between the regions was reestablished around 1500, population density was highest in the largest regions. Intuitively, inventions that would allow a given area to support more people, such as the domestication of animals and the development of agriculture, were much more likely in Eurasia-Africa, with its population of millions, than in Tasmania, with its population of a few thousand.

The data confirm this prediction. The land areas of the four regions are 84 million square kilometers for Eurasia-Africa, 38 million for the Americas, 8 million for Australia, and 0.1 million for Tasmania. Population estimates for the four regions in 1500 imply densities of approximately 4.9 people per square kilometer for Eurasia-Africa, 0.4 for the Americas, and 0.03 for both Australia and Tasmania.[25]

---

[25] Kremer argues that, since Australia is largely desert, these figures understate Australia's effective population density. He also argues that direct evidence suggests that Australia was more technologically advanced than Tasmania. Finally, he notes that there was in fact a fifth separate region, Flinders Island, a 680-square-kilometer island between Tasmania and Australia. Humans died out entirely on Flinders Island around 3000 B.C.

## Discussion

What do we learn from the confirmation of the model's time-series and cross-section predictions? The basic source of Kremer's predictions is the idea that the rate of increase in the stock of knowledge is increasing in population: innovations do not arrive exogenously, but are made by people. Although this idea is assumed away in the Solow, Ramsey, and Diamond models, it is hardly controversial. Thus Kremer's main qualitative findings for the most part confirm predictions that are not at all surprising.

Any tractable model of technological progress and population growth over many millennia must inevitably be so simplified that it would closely match the quantitative features of the data only by luck. For example, it would be foolish to attach much importance to the finding that population growth appears to be roughly proportional to the level of population rather than to $L^{0.75}$ or $L^{0.9}$. Thus, Kremer's evidence tells us little about, say, the exact value of $\theta$ in equation (3.58).

The value of Kremer's evidence, then, lies not in discriminating among alternative theories of growth, but in using growth theory to help understand major features of human history. The dynamics of human population over the very long run and the relative technological performance of different regions in the era before 1500 are important issues. Kremer's evidence shows that the ideas of new growth theory shed significant light on them.

## Population Growth versus Growth in Income per Person over the Very Long Run

As described above, over nearly all of history technological progress has led almost entirely to higher population rather than to higher average income. But this has not been true over the past few centuries: the enormous technological progress of the modern era has led not only to vast population growth, but also to vast increases in average income.

It may appear that explaining this change requires appealing to some demographic change, such as the development of contraceptive techniques or preferences for fewer children when technological progress is rapid. In fact, however, Kremer shows that the explanation is much simpler. Malthusian population dynamics are not instantaneous. Rather, at low levels of income, population growth is an increasing function of income. That is, Kremer argues that instead of assuming that $Y/L$ always equals $\bar{y}$ (equation [3.59]), it is more realistic to assume $n = n(y)$, with $n(\bar{y}) = 0$ and $n'(\bullet) > 0$ in the vicinity of $\bar{y}$.

This formulation implies that when income rises, population growth rises, tending to push income back down. When technological progress is slow, the fact that the adjustment is not immediate is of little importance. With slow technological progress, population adjusts rapidly enough to keep income per person very close to $\bar{y}$. Income and population growth rise very slowly, but almost all of technological progress is reflected in higher population rather than higher average income. But when population becomes large enough that technological progress is relatively rapid, this no longer occurs; instead, a large fraction of the effect of technological progress falls on average income rather than on population. Thus, a small and natural variation on Kremer's basic model explains another important feature of human history.[26]

A further extension of the demographic assumptions leads to additional implications. The evidence suggests that preferences are such that once average income is sufficiently high, population growth is decreasing in income. That is, $n(y)$ appears to be decreasing in $y$ when $y$ exceeds some $y^*$. With this modification, the model predicts that population growth peaks at some point and then declines.[27] This reinforces the tendency for an increasing fraction of the effect of technological progress to fall on average income rather than on population. And if $n(y)$ is negative for $y$ sufficiently large, population itself peaks at some point. In this case, assuming that $\theta$ is less than or equal to 1, the economy converges to a path where both the rate of technological progress and the level of the population are converging to 0.[28]

# 3.8   Models of Knowledge Accumulation and the Central Questions of Growth Theory

Our analysis of economic growth is motivated by two issues: the growth over time in standards of living, and their disparities across different parts of the world. It is therefore natural to ask what the models of R&D and knowledge accumulation have to say about these issues.

Researchers' original hope was that models of knowledge accumulation would provide a unified explanation of worldwide growth and cross-country income differences. After all, the models provided candidate theories of the determinants of growth rates and levels of income, which is what we are trying to understand.

---

[26] Section III of Kremer's paper provides a formal analysis of these points.

[27] The facts that the population does not adjust immediately and that beyond some point population growth is decreasing in income can explain why the relationship between the level of population and its growth rate shown in Figure 3.9 breaks down somewhat for the last two observations in the figure, which correspond to the period after 1970.

[28] Of course, we should not expect any single model to capture the major features of all of history. For example, it seems likely that sometime over the next few centuries, genetic engineering will progress to the point where the concept of a "person" is no longer well defined. When that occurs, a different type of model will be needed.

Explaining cross-country income differences on the basis of differences in knowledge accumulation faces a fundamental problem, however: the non-rivalry of knowledge. As emphasized in Section 3.4, the use of knowledge by one producer does not prevent its use by others. Thus there is no inherent reason that producers in poor countries cannot use the same knowledge as producers in rich countries. If the relevant knowledge is publicly available, poor countries can become rich by having their workers or managers read the appropriate literature. And if the relevant knowledge is proprietary knowledge produced by private R&D, poor countries can become rich by instituting a credible program for respecting foreign firms' property rights. With such a program, the firms in developed countries with proprietary knowledge would open factories in poor countries, hire their inexpensive labor, and produce output using the proprietary technology. The result would be that the marginal product of labor in poor countries, and hence wages, would rapidly rise to the level of developed countries.

Although lack of confidence on the part of foreign firms in the security of their property rights is surely an important problem in many poor countries, it is difficult to believe that this alone is the cause of the countries' poverty. There are numerous examples of poor regions or countries, ranging from European colonies over the past few centuries to many countries today, where foreign investors can establish plants and use their know-how with a high degree of confidence that the political environment will be relatively stable, their plants will not be nationalized, and their profits will not be taxed at exorbitant rates. Yet we do not see incomes in those areas jumping to the levels of industrialized countries.

One might object to this argument on the grounds that in practice the flow of knowledge is not instantaneous. In fact, however, this does not resolve the difficulties with attributing cross-country income differences to differences in knowledge. As Problem 3.14 asks you to demonstrate, if one believes that economies are described by something like the Solow model but do not all have access to the same technology, the lags in the diffusion of knowledge from rich to poor countries that are needed to account for observed differences in incomes are extremely long—on the order of a century or more. It is hard to believe that the reason that some countries are so poor is that they do not have access to the improvements in technology that have occurred over the past century.

One may also object on the grounds that the difficulty countries face is not lack of access to advanced technology, but lack of ability to use the technology. But this objection implies that the main source of differences in standards of living is not different levels of knowledge or technology, but differences in whatever factors allow richer countries to take better advantage of technology. Understanding differences in incomes therefore requires understanding the reasons for the differences in these factors. This task is taken up in the next chapter.

With regard to worldwide growth, the case for the relevance of models of knowledge accumulation is much stronger. At an informal level, the growth of knowledge appears to be the central reason that output and standards of living are so much higher today than in previous centuries. And formal growth-accounting studies attribute large portions of the increases in output per worker over extended periods to the unexplained residual component, which may reflect technological progress.[29] Work on endogenous growth has identified many determinants of knowledge accumulation, provided tools and insights for studying the externalities involved, and analyzed ways that knowledge accumulation affects the level and growth of income.

It would of course be desirable to refine these ideas by improving our understanding of what types of knowledge are most important for growth, their quantitative importance, and the forces determining how knowledge is accumulated. For example, suppose we want to address a concrete policy intervention, such as doubling government support for basic scientific research or eliminating the R&D tax credit. Models of endogenous knowledge accumulation are far from the point where they can deliver reliable quantitative predictions about how such interventions would affect the path of growth. But they identify many relevant considerations and channels. Thus, although the analysis is not as far along as we would like, it appears to be headed in the right direction.

# Problems

**3.1.** Consider the model of Section 3.2 with $\theta < 1$.

(a) On the balanced growth path, $\dot{A} = g_A^* A(t)$, where $g_A^*$ is the balanced-growth-path value of $g_A$. Use this fact and equation (3.6) to derive an expression for $A(t)$ on the balanced growth path in terms of $B$, $a_L$, $\gamma$, $\theta$, and $L(t)$.

(b) Use your answer to part (a) and the production function, (3.5), to obtain an expression for $Y(t)$ on the balanced growth path. Find the value of $a_L$ that maximizes output on the balanced growth path.

**3.2.** Consider two economies (indexed by $i = 1,2$) described by $Y_i(t) = K_i(t)^\theta$ and $\dot{K}_i(t) = s_i Y_i(t)$, where $\theta > 1$. Suppose that the two economies have the same initial value of $K$, but that $s_1 > s_2$. Show that $Y_1/Y_2$ is continually rising.

**3.3.** Consider the economy analyzed in Section 3.3. Assume that $\theta + \beta < 1$ and $n > 0$, and that the economy is on its balanced growth path. Describe how

---

[29] Moreover, as noted in Section 1.7 and Problem 1.13, by considering only the proximate determinants of growth, growth accounting understates the underlying importance of the residual component.

each of the following changes affects the $\dot{g}_A = 0$ and $\dot{g}_K = 0$ lines and the position of the economy in $(g_A, g_K)$ space at the moment of the change:

(a) An increase in $n$.

(b) An increase in $a_K$.

(c) An increase in $\theta$.

**3.4.** Consider the economy described in Section 3.3, and assume $\beta + \theta < 1$ and $n > 0$. Suppose the economy is initially on its balanced growth path, and that there is a permanent increase in $s$.

(a) How, if at all, does the change affect the $\dot{g}_A = 0$ and $\dot{g}_K = 0$ lines? How, if at all, does it affect the location of the economy in $(g_A, g_K)$ space at the time of the change?

(b) What are the dynamics of $g_A$ and $g_K$ after the increase in $s$? Sketch the path of log output per worker.

(c) Intuitively, how does the effect of the increase in $s$ compare with its effect in the Solow model?

**3.5.** Consider the model of Section 3.3 with $\beta + \theta = 1$ and $n = 0$.

(a) Using (3.14) and (3.16), find the value that $A/K$ must have for $g_K$ and $g_A$ to be equal.

(b) Using your result in part (a), find the growth rate of $A$ and $K$ when $g_K = g_A$.

(c) How does an increase in $s$ affect the long-run growth rate of the economy?

(d) What value of $a_K$ maximizes the long-run growth rate of the economy? Intuitively, why is this value not increasing in $\beta$, the importance of capital in the R&D sector?

**3.6.** Consider the model of Section 3.3 with $\beta + \theta > 1$ and $n > 0$.

(a) Draw the phase diagram for this case.

(b) Show that regardless of the economy's initial conditions, eventually the growth rates of $A$ and $K$ (and hence the growth rate of $Y$) are increasing continually.

(c) Repeat parts (a) and (b) for the case of $\beta + \theta = 1$, $n > 0$.

**3.7. Learning-by-doing.** Suppose that output is given by equation (3.22), $Y(t) = K(t)^\alpha [A(t)L(t)]^{1-\alpha}$; that $L$ is constant and equal to 1; that $\dot{K}(t) = sY(t)$; and that knowledge accumulation occurs as a side effect of goods production: $\dot{A}(t) = BY(t)$.

(a) Find expressions for $g_A(t)$ and $g_K(t)$ in terms of $A(t)$, $K(t)$, and the parameters.

(b) Sketch the $\dot{g}_A = 0$ and $\dot{g}_K = 0$ lines in $(g_A, g_K)$ space.

(c) Does the economy converge to a balanced growth path? If so, what are the growth rates of $K$, $A$, and $Y$ on the balanced growth path?

(d) How does an increase in $s$ affect long-run growth?

**3.8.** Consider the model of Section 3.5. Suppose, however, that households have constant-relative-risk-aversion utility with a coefficient of relative risk aversion of $\theta$. Find the equilibrium level of labor in the R&D sector, $L_A$.

**3.9.** Suppose that policymakers, realizing that monopoly power creates distortions, put controls on the prices that patent-holders in the Romer model can charge for the inputs embodying their ideas. Specifically, suppose they require patent-holders to charge $\delta w(t)/\phi$, where $\delta$ satisfies $\phi \leq \delta \leq 1$.

    (*a*) What is the equilibrium growth rate of the economy as a function of $\delta$ and the other parameters of the model? Does a reduction in $\delta$ increase, decrease, or have no effect on the equilibrium growth rate, or is it not possible to tell?

    (*b*) Explain intuitively why setting $\delta = \phi$, thereby requiring patent-holders to charge marginal cost and so eliminating the monopoly distortion, does not maximize social welfare.

**3.10.** (*a*) Show that (3.48) follows from (3.47).

    (*b*) Derive (3.49).

**3.11. Learning-by-doing with microeconomic foundations.** Consider a variant of the model in equations (3.22)–(3.25). Suppose firm $i$'s output is $Y_i(t) = K_i(t)^{\alpha}[A(t)L_i(t)]^{1-\alpha}$, and that $A(t) = BK(t)$. Here $K_i$ and $L_i$ are the amounts of capital and labor used by firm $i$ and $K$ is the aggregate capital stock. Capital and labor earn their *private* marginal products. As in the model of Section 3.5, the economy is populated by infinitely lived households that own the economy's initial capital stock. The utility of the representative household takes the constant-relative-risk-aversion form in equations (2.1)–(2.2). Population growth is zero.

    (*a*)   (*i*) What are the private marginal products of capital and labor at firm $i$ as functions of $K_i(t)$, $L_i(t)$, $K(t)$, and the parameters of the model?

        (*ii*) Explain why the capital-labor ratio must be the same at all firms, so $K_i(t)/L_i(t) = K(t)/L(t)$ for all $i$.

        (*iii*) What are $w(t)$ and $r(t)$ as functions of $K(t)$, $L$, and the parameters of the model?

    (*b*) What must the growth rate of consumption be in equilibrium? (Hint: Consider equation [2.21].) Assume for simplicity that the parameter values are such that the growth rate is strictly positive and less than the interest rate. Sketch an explanation of why the equilibrium growth rate of output equals the equilibrium growth rate of consumption.

    (*c*) Describe how long-run growth is affected by:

        (*i*) A rise in $B$.

        (*ii*) A rise in $\rho$.

        (*iii*) A rise in $L$.

    (*d*) Is the equilibrium growth rate more than, less than, or equal to the socially optimal rate, or is it not possible to tell?

**3.12.** (This follows Rebelo, 1991.) Assume that there are two sectors, one producing consumption goods and one producing capital goods, and two factors of
production: capital and land. Capital is used in both sectors, but land is used
only in producing consumption goods. Specifically, the production functions
are $C(t) = K_C(t)^{\alpha} T^{1-\alpha}$ and $\dot{K}(t) = BK_K(t)$, where $K_C$ and $K_K$ are the amounts of
capital used in the two sectors (so $K_C(t) + K_K(t) = K(t)$) and $T$ is the amount
of land, and $0 < \alpha < 1$ and $B > 0$. Factors are paid their marginal products,
and capital can move freely between the two sectors. $T$ is normalized to 1 for
simplicity.

(a) Let $P_K(t)$ denote the price of capital goods relative to consumption goods
at time $t$. Use the fact that the earnings of capital in units of consumption
goods in the two sectors must be equal to derive a condition relating $P_K(t)$,
$K_C(t)$, and the parameters $\alpha$ and $B$. If $K_C$ is growing at rate $g_K(t)$, at what
rate must $P_K$ be growing (or falling)? Let $g_P(t)$ denote this growth rate.

(b) The real interest rate in terms of consumption is $B + g_P(t)$.[30] Thus, assuming that households have our standard utility function, (2.21-2.22), the
growth rate of consumption must be $(B + g_P - \rho)/\theta \equiv g_C$. Assume $\rho < B$.

  (i) Use your results in part (a) to express $g_C(t)$ in terms of $g_K(t)$ rather
  than $g_P(t)$.

  (ii) Given the production function for consumption goods, at what rate
  must $K_C$ be growing for $C$ to be growing at rate $g_C(t)$?

  (iii) Combine your answers to (i) and (ii) to solve for $g_K(t)$ and $g_C(t)$ in
  terms of the underlying parameters.

(c) Suppose that investment income is taxed at rate $\tau$, so that the real interest rate households face is $(1 - \tau)(B + g_P)$. How, if at all, does $\tau$ affect the
equilibrium growth rate of consumption?

**3.13.** (This follows Krugman, 1979; see also Grossman and Helpman, 1991b.) Suppose the world consists of two regions, the "North" and the "South." Output
and capital accumulation in region $i$ ($i = N,S$) are given by $Y_i(t) = K_i(t)^{\alpha}[A_i(t)$
$(1 - a_{Li})L_i]^{1-\alpha}$ and $\dot{K}_i(t) = s_i Y_i(t)$. New technologies are developed in the
North. Specifically, $\dot{A}_N(t) = Ba_{LN}L_N A_N(t)$. Improvements in Southern technology, on the other hand, are made by learning from Northern technology:
$\dot{A}_S(t) = \mu a_{LS}L_S[A_N(t) - A_S(t)]$ if $A_N(t) > A_S(t)$; otherwise $\dot{A}_S(t) = 0$. Here $a_{LN}$
is the fraction of the Northern labor force engaged in R&D, and $a_{LS}$ is the frac-
tion of the Southern labor force engaged in learning Northern technology; the
rest of the notation is standard. Note that $L_N$ and $L_S$ are assumed constant.

(a) What is the long-run growth rate of Northern output per worker?

(b) Define $Z(t) = A_S(t)/A_N(t)$. Find an expression for $\dot{Z}$ as a function of $Z$ and
the parameters of the model. Is $Z$ stable? If so, what value does it converge
to? What is the long-run growth rate of Southern output per worker?

---

[30] To see this, note that capital in the investment sector produces new capital at rate $B$
and changes in value relative to the consumption good at rate $g_P$. (Because the return to
capital is the same in the two sectors, the same must be true of capital in the consumption
sector.)

(c) Assume $a_{LN} = a_{LS}$ and $s_N = s_S$. What is the ratio of output per worker in the South to output per worker in the North when both economies have converged to their balanced growth paths?

**3.14. Delays in the transmission of knowledge to poor countries.**

(a) Assume that the world consists of two regions, the North and the South. The North is described by $Y_N(t) = A_N(t)(1-a_L)L_N$ and $\dot{A}_N(t) = a_L L_N A_N(t)$. The South does not do R&D but simply uses the technology developed in the North; however, the technology used in the South lags the North's by $\tau$ years. Thus $Y_S(t) = A_S(t)L_S$ and $A_S(t) = A_N(t-\tau)$. If the growth rate of output per worker in the North is 3 percent per year, and if $a_L$ is close to 0, what must $\tau$ be for output per worker in the North to exceed that in the South by a factor of 10?

(b) Suppose instead that both the North and the South are described by the Solow model: $y_i(t) = f(k_i(t))$, where $y_i(t) \equiv Y_i(t)/[A_i(t)L_i(t)]$ and $k_i(t) \equiv K_i(t)/[A_i(t)L_i(t)]$ ($i = N,S$). As in the Solow model, assume $\dot{K}_i(t) = sY_i(t) - \delta K_i(t)$ and $\dot{L}_i(t) = nL_i(t)$; the two countries are assumed to have the same saving rates and rates of population growth. Finally, $\dot{A}_N(t) = gA_N(t)$ and $A_S(t) = A_N(t-\tau)$.

(i) Show that the value of $k$ on the balanced growth path, $k^*$, is the same for the two countries.

(ii) Does introducing capital change the answer to part (a)? Explain. (Continue to assume $g = 3\%$.)

# Chapter 4
# CROSS-COUNTRY INCOME DIFFERENCES

One of our central goals over the past three chapters has been to understand the vast variation in average income per person around the world. So far, however, our progress has been very limited. A key conclusion of the Solow model is that if physical capital's share in income is a reasonable measure of capital's importance in production, differences in capital account for little of cross-country income differences. The Ramsey–Cass–Koopmans and Diamond models have the same implication. And a key implication of models of endogenous growth is that since technology is nonrival, differences in technology are unlikely to be important to differences in income among countries.

This chapter attempts to move beyond these negative conclusions. Work on cross-country income differences is extremely active, and has a much greater empirical focus than the work discussed in the previous chapters. It has two main branches. The first focuses on the proximate determinants of income. That is, it considers factors whose influence on income is clear and direct, such as the quantities of physical and human capital. It generally employs techniques like those of growth accounting, which we discussed in Section 1.7. Factors' marginal products are measured using the prices they command in the market; these estimates of marginal products are then combined with estimates of differences in the quantities of factors to obtain estimates of the factors' contributions to income differences.

This work has the strength that one can often have a fair amount of confidence in its conclusions, but the weakness that it considers only immediate determinants of income. The second branch of work on cross-country income differences therefore tries to go deeper. Among the potential underlying determinants of income that researchers have considered are political institutions, geography, and religion. Unfortunately, accounting-style approaches can rarely be used to measure these forces' effects on incomes. Researchers instead use various statistical techniques to attempt to estimate their effects. As a result, the effort to go deeper comes at the cost of reduced certainty about the results.

One obvious proximate determinant of countries' incomes other than physical capital is human capital. Section 4.1 therefore sets the stage for the accounting approach by extending our modeling of growth to include human capital. Section 4.2 then develops the accounting approach. Its main focus is on decomposing income differences into the contributions of physical capital, human capital, and output for given amounts of capital. We will see that variations in both physical and human capital contribute to income differences, but that variations in output for given capital stocks are considerably more important.

Sections 4.3 through 4.5 consider attempts to go deeper and investigate the sources of differences in these determinants of average incomes. Section 4.3 introduces *social infrastructure*: institutions and policies that determine the allocation of resources between activities that raise overall output and ones that redistribute it. Section 4.4 examines the evidence about the importance of social infrastructure. Section 4.5, which takes us very much to the frontier of current research, extends the analysis of social infrastructure in three directions. First, what specific factors within social infrastructure might be particularly important? Second, can we go even further and say anything about the determinants of social infrastructure? And third, are there factors that are not part of social infrastructure that are important to cross-country income differences?

Finally, Section 4.6 asks what insights our analysis provides about cross-country differences in income growth rather than in income levels.

# 4.1 Extending the Solow Model to Include Human Capital

This section develops a model of growth that includes human as well as physical capital.[1] Because the model is not intended to explain growth in overall world income, it follows the Solow, Ramsey, and Diamond models in taking worldwide technological progress as exogenous. Further, our eventual goal is to make quantitative statements about cross-country income differences. The model therefore assumes Cobb–Douglas production; this makes the model tractable and leads easily to quantitative analysis. Our desire to do quantitative analysis also means that it is easiest to consider a model that, in the spirit of the Solow model, takes the saving rate and the allocation of resources to human-capital accumulation as exogenous. This will allow us to relate the model to measures of capital accumulation, which we can observe, rather than to preferences, which we cannot.

---

[1] Jones (2002b, Chapter 3) presents a similar model.

## Assumptions

The model is set in continuous time. Output at time $t$ is

$$Y(t) = K(t)^{\alpha}[A(t)H(t)]^{1-\alpha}. \tag{4.1}$$

$Y$, $K$, and $A$ are the same as in the Solow model: $Y$ is output, $K$ is capital, and $A$ is the effectiveness of labor. $H$ is the total amount of productive services supplied by workers. That is, it is the total contribution of workers of different skill levels to production. It therefore includes the contributions of both raw labor (that is, skills that individuals are endowed with) and human capital (that is, acquired skills).

The dynamics of $K$ and $A$ are the same as in the Solow model. An exogenous fraction $s$ of output is saved, and capital depreciates at an exogenous rate $\delta$. Thus,

$$\dot{K}(t) = sY(t) - \delta K(t). \tag{4.2}$$

The effectiveness of labor grows at an exogenous rate $g$:

$$\dot{A}(t) = gA(t). \tag{4.3}$$

The model revolves around its assumptions about how the quantity of human capital is determined. The accumulation of human capital depends both on the amount of human capital created by a given amount of resources devoted to human-capital accumulation (that is, on the production function for human capital), and on the quantity of resources devoted to human-capital accumulation. With regard to the amount of human capital created from a given set of inputs, the model assumes that each worker's human capital depends only on his or her years of education. This is equivalent to assuming that the only input into the production function for human capital is students' time. The next section briefly discusses what happens if physical capital and existing workers' human capital are also inputs to human-capital production. With regard to the quantity of resources devoted to human-capital accumulation, the model, paralleling the treatment of physical capital, takes the allocation of resources to human-capital accumulation as exogenous. To simplify further, it assumes that each worker obtains the same amount of education, and for the most part we focus on the case where that amount is constant over time.

Thus, our assumption is that the quantity of human capital, $H$, is given by

$$H(t) = L(t)G(E), \tag{4.4}$$

where $L$ is the number of workers and $G(\bullet)$ is a function giving human capital per worker as a function of years of education per worker.[2] As usual,

---

[2] Expression (4.4) implies that of total labor services, $LG(0)$ is raw labor and $L[G(E)-G(0)]$ is human capital. If $G(0)$ is much smaller than $G(E)$, almost all of labor services are human capital.

the number of workers grows at an exogenous rate $n$:

$$\dot{L}(t) = nL(t). \tag{4.5}$$

It is reasonable to assume that the more education a worker has, the more human capital he or she has. That is, we assume $G'(\bullet) > 0$. But there is no reason to impose $G''(\bullet) < 0$. As individuals acquire human capital, their ability to acquire additional human capital may improve. To put it differently, the first few years of education may provide individuals mainly with basic tools, such as the ability to read, count, and follow directions, that by themselves do not allow the individuals to contribute much to output but that are essential for acquiring additional human capital.

The microeconomic evidence suggests that each additional year of education increases an individual's wage by approximately the same *percentage* amount. If wages reflect the labor services that individuals supply, this implies that $G'(\bullet)$ is indeed increasing. Specifically, it implies that $G(\bullet)$ takes the form

$$G(E) = e^{\phi E}, \qquad \phi > 0, \tag{4.6}$$

where we have normalized $G(0)$ to 1. For the most part, however, we will not impose this functional form in our analysis.

## Analyzing the Model

The dynamics of the model are exactly like those of the Solow model. The easiest way to see this is to define $k$ as physical capital per unit of effective labor services: $k = K/[AG(E)L]$. Analysis like that in Section 1.3 shows that the dynamics of $k$ are identical to those in the Solow model. That is,

$$\dot{k}(t) = sf(k(t)) - (n + g + \delta)k(t)$$
$$= sk(t)^{\alpha} - (n + g + \delta)k(t). \tag{4.7}$$

In the first line, $f(\bullet)$ is the intensive form of the production function (see Section 1.2). The second line uses the fact that the production function is Cobb–Douglas.

As in the Solow model, $k$ converges to the point where $\dot{k} = 0$. From (4.7), this value of $k$ is $[s/(n + g + \delta)]^{1/(1-\alpha)}$, which we will denote $k^*$. We know that once $k$ reaches $k^*$, the economy is on a balanced growth path with output per worker growing at rate $g$.

This analysis implies that the qualitative and quantitative effects of a change in the saving rate are the same as in the Solow model. To see this, note that since the equation of motion for $k$ is identical to that in the Solow model, the effects of a change in $s$ on the path of $k$ are identical to those in the Solow model. And since output per unit of effective labor services, $y$, is determined by $k$, it follows that the impact on the path of $y$ is identical.

Finally, output per worker equals output per unit of effective labor services, $y$, times effective labor services per worker, $AG(E)$: $Y/L = AG(E)y$. The path of $AG(E)$ is not affected by the change in the saving rate: $A$ grows at exogenous rate $g$, and $G(E)$ is constant. Thus the impact of the change on the path of output per worker is determined entirely by its impact on the path of $y$.

We can also describe the long-run effects of a rise in the number of years of schooling per worker, $E$. Since $E$ does not enter the equation for $\dot{K}$, the balanced-growth-path value of $k$ is unchanged, and so the balanced-growth-path value of $y$ is unchanged. And since $Y/L$ equals $AG(E)y$, it follows that the rise in $E$ increases output per worker on the balanced growth path by the same proportion that it increases $G(E)$.

This model has two implications for cross-country income differences. First, it identifies an additional potential source of these differences: they can stem from differences in human capital as well as physical capital. Second, it implies that recognizing the existence of human capital does not change the Solow model's implications about the effects of physical-capital accumulation. That is, the effects of a change in the saving rate are no different in this model than they are in the Solow model.

## Students and Workers

Our analysis thus far focuses on output per *worker*. In the case of a change in the saving rate, output per person behaves the same way as output per worker. But a change in the amount of time individuals spend in school changes the proportion of the population that is working. Thus in this case, output per person and output per worker behave differently.

To say more about this point, we need some additional demographic assumptions. The most natural ones are that each individual has some fixed lifespan, $T$, and spends the first $E$ years of life in school and the remaining $T - E$ years working. Further, for the overall population to be growing at rate $n$ and the age distribution to be well behaved, the number of people born per unit time must be growing at rate $n$.

With these assumptions, the total population at $t$ equals the number of people born from $t - T$ to $t$. Thus if we use $N(t)$ to denote the population at $t$ and $B(t)$ to denote the number of people born at $t$,

$$
\begin{aligned}
N(t) &= \int_{\tau=0}^{T} B(t - \tau)\,d\tau \\
&= \int_{\tau=0}^{T} B(t)e^{-n\tau}d\tau \\
&= \frac{1 - e^{-nT}}{n} B(t),
\end{aligned}
\tag{4.8}
$$

where the second line uses the fact that the number of people born per unit time grows at rate $n$.

Similarly, the number of workers at time $t$ equals the number of individuals who are alive and no longer in school. Thus it equals the number of people born from $t - T$ to $t - E$:

$$L(t) = \int_{\tau=E}^{T} B(t - \tau)\,d\tau$$

$$= \int_{\tau=E}^{T} B(t)e^{-n\tau}\,d\tau \qquad (4.9)$$

$$= \frac{e^{-nE} - e^{-nT}}{n}\,B(t).$$

Combining expressions (4.8) and (4.9) gives the ratio of the number of workers to the total population:

$$\frac{L(t)}{N(t)} = \frac{e^{-nE} - e^{-nT}}{1 - e^{-nT}}. \qquad (4.10)$$

We can now find output per person (as opposed to output per worker) on the balanced growth path. Output per person equals output per unit of effective labor services, $y$, times the amount of effective labor services supplied by the average person. And the amount of labor services supplied by the average person equals the amount supplied by the average worker, $A(t)G(E)$, times the fraction of the population that is working, $(e^{-nE} - e^{-nT})/(1 - e^{-nT})$. Thus,

$$\left(\frac{Y}{N}\right)^* = y^* A(t)G(E)\frac{e^{-nE} - e^{-nT}}{1 - e^{-nT}}, \qquad (4.11)$$

where $y^*$ equals $f(k^*)$, output per unit of effective labor services on the balanced growth path.

We saw above that a change in $E$ does not affect $y^*$. In addition, the path of $A$ is exogenous. Thus our analysis implies that a change in the amount of education each person receives, $E$, alters output per person on the balanced growth path by the same proportion that it changes $G(E)[(e^{-nE} - e^{-nT})/(1 - e^{-nT})]$. A rise in education therefore has two effects on output per person. Each worker has more human capital; that is, the $G(E)$ term rises. But a smaller fraction of the population is working; that is, the $(e^{-nE} - e^{-nT})/(1 - e^{-nT})$ term falls. Thus a rise in $E$ can either raise or lower output per person in the long run.[3]

The specifics of how the economy converges to its new balanced growth path in response to a rise in $E$ are somewhat complicated. In the short run, the rise reduces output relative to what it otherwise would have been. In

---

[3] See Problem 4.1 for an analysis of the "golden-rule" level of $E$ in this model.

addition, the adjustment to the new balanced growth path is very gradual. To see these points, suppose the economy is on a balanced growth path with $E = E_0$. Now suppose that everyone born after some time, $t_0$, obtains $E_1 > E_0$ years of education. This change first affects the economy at date $t_0 + E_0$. From this date until $t_0 + E_1$, everyone who is working still has $E_0$ years of education, and some individuals who would have been working if $E$ had not risen are still in school. The highly educated individuals start to enter the labor force at date $t_0 + E_1$. The average level of education in the labor force does not reach its new balanced-growth-path value until date $t_0 + T$, however. And even then, the stock of physical capital is still adjusting to the changed path of effective labor services, and so the adjustment to the new balanced growth path is not complete.

These results about the effects of an increase in education on the path of output per person are similar to the Solow model's implications about the effects of an increase in the saving rate on the path of consumption per person. In both cases, the shift in resources leads to a short-run fall in the variable of interest (output per person in this model, consumption per person in the Solow model). And in both cases, the long-run effect on the variable of interest is ambiguous.

# 4.2 Empirical Application: Accounting for Cross-Country Income Differences

A central goal of accounting-style studies of income differences is to decompose those differences into the contributions of physical-capital accumulation, human-capital accumulation, and other factors. Such a decomposition has the potential to offer significant insights into cross-country income differences. For example, if we were to find that differences in human-capital accumulation account for most of income differences, this would suggest that to understand income differences, we should focus on factors that affect human-capital accumulation.

Two leading examples accounting-style income decompositions are those performed by Hall and Jones (1999) and Klenow and Rodríguez-Clare (1997). These authors measure differences in the accumulation of physical and human capital, and then use a framework like the previous section's to estimate the quantitative importance of those differences to income differences. They then measure the role of other forces as a residual.

## Procedure

Hall and Jones and Klenow and Rodríguez-Clare begin by assuming, as we did in the previous section, that output in a given country is a Cobb–Douglas combination of physical capital and effective labor services:

$$Y_i = K_i^\alpha (A_i H_i)^{1-\alpha}, \tag{4.12}$$

where $i$ indexes countries. Since $A$'s contribution will be measured as a residual, it reflects not just technology or knowledge, but all forces that determine output for given amounts of physical capital and labor services.

Dividing both sides of (4.12) by the number of workers, $L_i$, and taking logs yields

$$\ln \frac{Y_i}{L_i} = \alpha \ln \frac{K_i}{L_i} + (1-\alpha) \ln \frac{H_i}{L_i} + (1-\alpha) \ln A_i. \tag{4.13}$$

The basic idea in these papers, as in growth accounting over time, is to measure directly all the ingredients of this equation other than $A_i$ and then compute $A_i$ as a residual. Thus (4.13) can be used to decompose differences in output per worker into the contributions of physical capital per worker, labor services per worker, and other factors.

Klenow and Rodríguez-Clare and Hall and Jones observe, however, that this decomposition may not be the most interesting one. Suppose, for example, that the level of $A$ rises with no change in the saving rate or in education per worker. The resulting higher output increases the amount of physical capital (since the premise of the example is that the saving *rate* is unchanged). When the country reaches its new balanced growth path, physical capital and output are both higher by the same proportion as the increase in $A$. The decomposition in (4.13) therefore attributes fraction $\alpha$ of the long-run increase in output per worker in response to the increase in $A$ to physical capital per worker. It would be more useful to have a decomposition that attributes all the increase to the residual, since the rise in $A$ was the underlying source of the increase in output per worker.

To address this issue, Klenow and Rodríguez-Clare and Hall and Jones subtract $\alpha \ln(Y_i/L_i)$ from both sides of (4.13). This yields

$$(1-\alpha) \ln \frac{Y_i}{L_i} = \left( \alpha \ln \frac{K_i}{L_i} - \alpha \ln \frac{Y_i}{L_i} \right) + (1-\alpha) \ln \frac{H_i}{L_i} + (1-\alpha) \ln A_i$$
$$\tag{4.14}$$
$$= \alpha \ln \frac{K_i}{Y_i} + (1-\alpha) \ln \frac{H_i}{L_i} + (1-\alpha) \ln A_i.$$

Dividing both sides by $1-\alpha$ gives us

$$\ln \frac{Y_i}{L_i} = \frac{\alpha}{1-\alpha} \ln \frac{K_i}{Y_i} + \ln \frac{H_i}{L_i} + \ln A_i. \tag{4.15}$$

Equation (4.15) expresses output per worker in terms of physical-capital intensity (that is, the capital-output ratio, $K/Y$), labor services per worker, and a residual. It is no more correct than equation (4.13): both result from manipulating the production function, (4.12). But (4.15) is more insightful for our purposes: it assigns the long-run effects of changes in labor services per worker and the residual entirely to those variables.

## Data and Basic Results

Data on output and the number of workers are available from the Penn World Tables. Hall and Jones and Klenow and Rodríguez-Clare estimate physical-capital stocks using data on investment from the Penn World Tables and reasonable assumptions about the initial stocks and depreciation. Data on income shares suggest that $\alpha$, physical capital's share in the production function, is around one-third for almost all countries (Gollin, 2002).

The hardest part of the analysis is to estimate the stock of labor services, $H$. Hall and Jones take the simplest approach. They consider only years of schooling. Specifically, they assume that $H_i$ takes the form $e^{\phi(E_i)}L_i$, where $E_i$ is the average number of years of education of workers in country $i$ and $\phi(\bullet)$ is an increasing function. In the previous section, we considered the possibility of a linear $\phi(\bullet)$ function: $\phi(E) = \phi E$. Hall and Jones argue, however, that the microeconomic evidence suggests that the percentage increase in earnings from an additional year of schooling falls as the amount of schooling rises. On the basis of this evidence, they assume that $\phi(E)$ is a piecewise linear function with a slope of 0.134 for $E$ below 4 years, 0.101 for $E$ between 4 and 8 years, and 0.068 for $E$ above 8 years.

Armed with these data and assumptions, Hall and Jones use expression (4.15) to estimate the contributions of physical-capital intensity, schooling, and the residual to output per worker in each country. They summarize their results by comparing the five richest countries in their sample with the five poorest. Average output per worker in the rich group exceeds the average in the poor group by a stunning factor of 31.7. On a log scale, this is a difference of 3.5. The difference in the average $[\alpha/(1 - \alpha)]\ln(K/Y)$ between the two groups is 0.6; in $\ln(H/L)$, 0.8; and in $\ln A$, 2.1. That is, they find that only about a sixth of the gap between the richest and poorest countries is due to differences in physical-capital intensity, and that less than a quarter is due to differences in schooling. Klenow and Rodríguez-Clare, using slightly different assumptions, reach similar conclusions.

An additional finding from Hall and Jones's and Klenow and Rodríguez-Clare's decompositions is that the contributions of physical capital, schooling, and the residual are not independent. Hall and Jones, for example, find a substantial correlation across countries between their estimates of $\ln(H_i/L_i)$ and $\ln A_i$ ($\rho = 0.52$), and a modest correlation between their estimates of $[\alpha/(1 - \alpha)]\ln(K_i/L_i)$ and $\ln A_i$ ($\rho = 0.25$); they also find a substantial correlation between the two capital terms ($\rho = 0.60$).

## More Detailed Examinations of Human Capital

Hall and Jones's and Klenow and Rodríguez-Clare's decompositions have been extended in numerous ways. For the most part, the extensions suggest an even larger role for the residual.

Many of the extensions concern the role of human capital. Hall and Jones's calculations ignore all differences in human capital other than differences in years of education. But there are many other sources of variation in human capital. School quality, on-the-job training, informal human-capital acquisition, child-rearing, and even prenatal care vary significantly across countries. The resulting differences in human capital may be large.

One way to incorporate differences in human-capital quality into the analysis is to continue to use the decomposition in equation (4.15), but to obtain a more comprehensive measure of human capital. A natural approach to comparing the overall human capital of workers in different countries is to compare the wages they would earn in the same labor market. Since the United States has immigrants from many countries, this can be done by examining the wages of immigrants from different countries in the United States. Of course, there are complications. For example, immigrants are not chosen randomly from the workers in their home countries, and they may have characteristics that affect their earnings in the United States that would not affect their earnings in their home countries. Nonetheless, looking at immigrants' wages provides important information about whether there are large differences in human-capital quality.

This idea is implemented by Klenow and Rodríguez-Clare and by Hendricks (2002). These authors find that immigrants to the United States with a given amount of education typically earn less when they come from lower-income countries. This suggests that cross-country differences in human capital are larger than suggested solely by differences in years of schooling, and that the role of the residual is therefore smaller. Crucially, however, the magnitudes involved are small.[4]

Hendricks extends the analysis of human capital in two other ways. First, he estimates the returns to different amounts of education rather than imposing the piecewise linear form assumed by Hall and Jones. His results suggest somewhat smaller differences in human capital across countries, and hence somewhat larger differences in the residual.

Second, he examines the possibility that low-skill and high-skill workers are complements in production. In this case, the typical worker in a

---

[4] The approach of using the decomposition in equation (4.15) with a broader measure of human capital has a disadvantage like that of our preliminary decomposition, (4.13). Physical capital is likely to affect human-capital quality. For example, differences in the amount of physical capital in schools are likely to lead to differences in school quality. When physical capital affects human-capital quality, a rise in the saving rate or the residual raises income per worker partly by raising human-capital quality via a higher stock of physical capital. With a comprehensive measure of human capital, the decomposition in (4.15) assigns that portion of the rise in income to human-capital quality. Ideally, however, we would assign it to the underlying change in the saving rate or in the residual.

The alternative is to specify a production function for human capital and then use this to create a decomposition that is more informative. Klenow and Rodríguez-Clare consider this approach. It turns out, however, that the results are quite sensitive to the details of how the production function for human capital is specified.

low-income country (who has low skills) may have low wages in part not be-cause output for a given set of inputs is low, but because he or she has few high-skill workers to work with. And indeed, the premium to having high skills is larger in poor countries. Hendricks finds that when he chooses an elasticity of substitution between low-skill and high-skill workers to fit the cross-country pattern of skill premia, he is able to explain a moderate addi-tional part of cross-country income differences.

The combined effect of these more careful analyses of the role of human capital is not large. For example, Hendricks finds an overall role for human-capital differences in income differences that is slightly smaller than what Hall and Jones estimate.

## More Detailed Examinations of Physical Capital

Hall and Jones's and Klenow and Rodríguez-Clare's decomposition has also been extended on the physical-capital side. The most thorough extension is that of Hsieh and Klenow (2007). Hsieh and Klenow begin by observ-ing that a lower capital-output ratio presumably reflects a lower average investment-output ratio. They then note that, as a matter of accounting, there are three possible sources of a lower investment-output ratio. First, and most obviously, it can arise because the fraction of nominal income devoted to investment is smaller. Second, it can arise because investment goods are more costly (for example, because of distortionary policies or transportation costs), so that a given amount of investment spending yields a smaller quantity of investment (Jones, 1994). And third, it can arise be-cause noninvestment goods have lower prices, which again has the effect that devoting a given fraction of nominal income to investment yields a smaller quantity of investment goods.

It has long been known that nontradable consumption goods, such as haircuts and taxi rides, are generally cheaper in poorer countries; this is the *Balassa-Samuelson effect*. The reasons for the effect are uncertain. One possibility is that it arises because these goods use unskilled labor, which is comparatively cheap in poor countries, more intensively. Another is that it occurs because these goods are of lower quality in poor countries.

If lower income leads to lower prices of nontradable consumption goods, this implies that a fall in $H$ or $A$ with the saving rate and the price of in-vestment goods held fixed tends to lower the capital-output ratio. Thus, al-though the decomposition in (4.15) (like the decomposition in [4.13]) is not incorrect, it is probably more insightful to assign the differences in income per worker that result from income's impact on the price of nontradables, and hence on investment for a given saving rate, to the underlying differ-ences in $H$ and $A$ rather than to physical capital.

To see how Hsieh and Klenow decompose differences in the investment-output ratio into the contributions of the three determinants they identify, consider for simplicity a country that produces nontradable and tradable consumption goods and that purchases all its investment goods abroad. Let $Q_N$ and $Q_T$ denote the quantities of the two types of consumption goods that are produced in the country, and let $I$ denote the quantity of investment goods purchased from abroad. Similarly, let $P_N$, $P_T$, and $P_I$ denote the domestic prices of the three types of goods, and let $P_N^*$, $P_T^*$, and $P_I^*$ denote their prices in a typical country in the world. Finally, assume that $P_T$ and $P_T^*$ are equal.[5]

With these assumptions, the value of the country's output at "world" prices is $P_N^* Q_N + P_T^* Q_T$, and the value of its investment at world prices is $P_I^* I$. Thus its investment-output ratio is $P_I^* I / (P_N^* Q_N + P_T^* Q_T)$. We can write this ratio as the product of three terms:

$$
\frac{P_I^* I}{P_N^* Q_N + P_T^* Q_T} = \frac{P_I I}{P_N Q_N + P_T Q_T} \frac{P_I^*}{P_I} \frac{\dfrac{P_N}{P_T} Q_N + Q_T}{\dfrac{P_N^*}{P_T^*} Q_N + Q_T}. \tag{4.16}
$$

The three terms correspond to the three determinants of the investment-output ratio described above. The first is the fraction of nominal income devoted to investment; that is, loosely speaking, it is the economy's saving rate. The second is the world price relative to the domestic price of investment goods. The third reflects differences between the domestic and world prices of nontradable consumption goods (recall that $P_T = P_T^*$ by assumption).

Hsieh and Klenow find that as we move from rich to poor countries, only about a quarter of the decline in the investment-output ratio comes from a fall in the saving rate; almost none comes from increases in the price of investment goods (as would occur, for example, if poor countries imposed tariffs and other barriers to the purchase of investment goods); and three-quarters comes from the lower price of nontradable consumption goods. Because only a small fraction of cross-country income differences is due to variation in the capital-output ratio to begin with, this implies that only a very small part is due to variation in the saving rate.

As we have discussed, the reasons that nontradable consumption goods are cheaper in poorer countries are not fully understood. But if lower income from any source tends to reduce the price of nontradables, this would magnify the importance of variation in human capital and the residual. Thus a revised decomposition would assign the large majority of variations in income across countries to the residual, and almost all of the remainder to human capital.

---

[5] It is straightforward to extend the analysis to allow for the possibilities that $P_T \neq P_T^*$ and that some investment goods are produced domestically.

# 4.3   Social Infrastructure

The analysis in the previous section tells us about the roles of physical-capital accumulation, human-capital accumulation, and output for given quantities of capital in cross-country income differences. But we would like to go deeper and investigate the determinants of these sources of income differences.

A leading candidate hypothesis is that differences in these determinants of income stem largely from differences in what Hall and Jones call *social infrastructure*. By social infrastructure, Hall and Jones mean institutions and policies that align private and social returns to activities.[6]

There is a tremendous range of activities where private and social returns may differ. They fall into two main categories. The first consists of various types of investment. If an individual engages in conventional saving, acquires education, or devotes resources to R&D, his or her private returns are likely to fall short of the social returns because of taxation, expropriation, crime, externalities, and so on.

The second category consists of activities intended for the individual's current benefit. An individual can attempt to increase his or her current income through either production or diversion. Production refers to activities that increase the economy's total output at a point in time. Diversion, which we encountered in Section 3.4 under the name *rent-seeking*, refers to activities that merely reallocate that output. The social return to rent-seeking activities is zero by definition, and the social return to productive activities is the amount they contribute to output. As with investment, there are many reasons the private returns to rent-seeking and to production may differ from their social returns.

Discussions of diversion or rent-seeking often focus on its most obvious forms, such as crime, lobbying for tax benefits, and frivolous lawsuits. Since these activities use only small fractions of resources in advanced economies, it is natural to think that rent-seeking is not of great importance in those countries. But rent-seeking consists of much more than these pure forms. Such commonplace activities as firms engaging in price discrimination, workers providing documentation for performance evaluations, and consumers clipping coupons have large elements of rent-seeking. Indeed, such everyday actions as locking one's car or going to a concert early to try to get a ticket involve rent-seeking. Thus substantial fractions of resources are probably devoted to rent-seeking even in advanced countries. And it seems plausible that the fraction is considerably higher in less developed

---

[6] This specific definition of social infrastructure is due to Jones.

countries. If this is correct, differences in rent-seeking may be an important source of cross-country income differences. Likewise, as described in Section 3.4, the extent of rent-seeking in the world as a whole may be an important determinant of worldwide growth.[7]

There are many different aspects of social infrastructure. It is useful to divide them into three groups. The first group consists of features of the government's fiscal policy. For example, the tax treatment of investment and marginal tax rates on labor income directly affect relationships between private and social returns. Only slightly more subtly, high tax rates induce such forms of rent-seeking as devoting resources to tax evasion and working in the underground economy despite its relative inefficiency.

The second group of institutions and policies that make up social infrastructure consists of factors that determine the environment that private decisions are made in. If crime is unchecked or there is civil war or foreign invasion, private rewards to investment and to activities that raise overall output are low. At a more mundane level, if contracts are not enforced or the courts' interpretation of them is unpredictable, long-term investment projects are unattractive. Similarly, competition, with its rewards for activities that increase overall output, is more likely when the government allows free trade and limits monopoly power.

The final group of institutions and policies that constitute social infrastructure are ones that affect the extent of rent-seeking activities by the government itself. As Hall and Jones stress, although well-designed government policies can be an important source of beneficial social infrastructure, the government can be a major rent-seeker. Government expropriation, the solicitation of bribes, and the doling out of benefits in response to lobbying or to actions that benefit government officials can be important forms of rent-seeking.

Because social infrastructure has many dimensions, poor social infrastructure takes many forms. There can be Stalinist central planning where property rights and economic incentives are minimal. There can be "kleptocracy"—an economy run by an oligarchy or a dictatorship whose main interest is personal enrichment and preservation of power, and which relies on expropriation and corruption. There can be near-anarchy, where property and lives are extremely insecure. And so on.

---

[7] The seminal paper on rent-seeking is Tullock (1967). Rent-seeking is important to many phenomena other than cross-country income differences. For example, Krueger (1974) shows its importance for understanding the effects of tariffs and other government interventions, and Posner (1975) argues that it is essential to understanding the welfare effects of monopoly.

# 4.4   Empirical Application: Social Infrastructure and Cross-Country Income Differences

The idea that institutions and policies that affect the relationship between private returns and social benefits are crucial to economic performance dates back at least to Adam Smith. But it has recently received renewed attention. One distinguishing feature of this recent work is that it attempts to provide empirical evidence about the importance of social infrastructure.

## A Regression Framework

In thinking about the evidence concerning the importance of social infrastructure, it is natural to consider a simple regression framework. Suppose income in country $i$ is determined by social infrastructure and other forces. We can express this as

$$\ln\left(\frac{Y_i}{L_i}\right) = a + bSI_i + e_i. \tag{4.17}$$

Here $Y/L$ is output per worker, $SI$ is social infrastructure, and $e$ reflects other influences on income. Examples of papers that try to find measures of social infrastructure and then estimate regressions in the spirit of (4.17) include Sachs and Warner (1995); Knack and Keefer (1995); Mauro (1995); Acemoglu, Johnson, and Robinson (2001, 2002); and Hall and Jones. These papers investigate both the magnitude of social infrastructure's effect on income and the fraction of the cross-country variation in income that is due to variations in social infrastructure. The hypothesis that social infrastructure is critical to income differences predicts that it is the source of a large fraction of those differences.

Attempts to estimate relationships like (4.17) must confront two major problems. The first is the practical one of how to measure social infrastructure. The second is the conceptual one of how to obtain accurate estimates of the parameters in (4.17) given a measure of social infrastructure.

For the moment, assume that we have a perfect measure of social infrastructure, and focus on the second problem. Equation (4.17) looks like a regression. Thus it is natural to consider estimating it by ordinary least squares (OLS). And indeed, many papers estimating the effects of social infrastructure use OLS regressions.

For OLS to produce unbiased estimates, the right-hand-side variable (here, social infrastructure) must be uncorrelated with the residual (here, other influences on income per worker). So to address the question of whether OLS is likely to yield reliable estimates of social infrastructure's impact on income, we must think about whether social infrastructure is likely to be correlated with other influences on income.

Unfortunately, the answer to that question appears to be yes. Suppose, for example, that cultural factors, such as religion, have important effects on income that operate through channels other than social infrastructure. Some religions may instill values that promote thrift and education and that discourage rent-seeking. It seems likely that countries where such religions are prevalent would tend to adopt institutions and policies that do a relatively good job of aligning private and social returns. Thus there would be positive correlation between social infrastructure and the residual.

To give another example, suppose geography has an important direct impact on income. Some climates may be unfavorable to agriculture and favorable to disease, for example. The fact that countries with worse climates are poorer means they have fewer resources with which to create good social infrastructure. Thus again there will be correlation between social infrastructure and the residual.[8]

In short, OLS estimates of (4.17) are likely to suffer from *omitted-variable bias*. Omitted-variable bias is a pervasive problem in empirical work in economics.

The solution to omitted-variable bias is to use *instrumental variables* (IV) rather than OLS. The intuition behind IV estimation is easiest to see using the two-stage least squares interpretation of instrumental variables. What one needs are variables correlated with the right-hand-side variables but not systematically correlated with the residual. Once one has such *instruments*, the first-stage regression is a regression of the right-hand-side variable, $SI$, on the instruments. The second-stage regression is then a regression of the left-hand-side variable, $\ln(Y/L)$, on the fitted value of $SI$ from the first-stage regression, $\widehat{SI}$. That is, think of rewriting (4.17) as

$$\ln \frac{Y_i}{L_i} = a + b\widehat{SI}_l + b(SI_i - \widehat{SI}_l) + e_i$$
$$\equiv a + b\widehat{SI}_l + u_i,$$

(4.18)

and then estimating the equation by OLS. $u$ consists of two terms, $e$ and $b(SI - \widehat{SI})$. By assumption, the instruments used to construct $\widehat{SI}$ are not systematically correlated with $e$. And since $\widehat{SI}$ is the fitted value from a regression, by construction it is not correlated with the residual from that

---

[8] We will return to the subject of geography and cross-country income differences in Section 4.5. There, we will encounter another potential source of correlation between direct geographic influences on income and social infrastructure.

regression, $SI - \widehat{SI}$. Thus regressing $\ln(Y/L)$ on $\widehat{SI}$ yields a valid estimate of $b$.[9]

Thus, the key to addressing the second problem—how to estimate (4.17)—is to find valid instruments. Before discussing that issue, let us return to the first problem—how to measure social infrastructure. It is clear that any measure of social infrastructure will be imperfect. Let $SI^*$ denote "true" social infrastructure, and let $\widetilde{SI}$ denote measured social infrastructure. The underlying relationship of interest is that between true social infrastructure and income:

$$\ln\left(\frac{Y_i}{L_i}\right) = a + bSI_i^* + e_i. \tag{4.19}$$

True social infrastructure equals measured social infrastructure plus the difference between true and measured social infrastructure: $SI_i^* = \widetilde{SI}_i + (SI_i^* - \widetilde{SI}_i)$. This allows us to rewrite (4.19) in terms of observables and other factors:

$$\ln \frac{Y_i}{L_i} = a + b\widetilde{SI}_i + b(SI_i^* - \widehat{SI}_i) + e_i$$

$$\equiv a + b\widetilde{SI}_i + v_i. \tag{4.20}$$

To consider what happens if we estimate (4.20) by OLS, consider the case of *classical measurement error*: $\widetilde{SI}_i = SI_i^* + w_i$, where $w$ is uncorrelated with $SI^*$. In this case, the right-hand-side variable in the regression is $SI^* + w$, and one component of the composite residual, $v$, is $-bw$. Thus if $b$ is positive, the measurement error causes negative correlation between the right-hand-side variable and the residual. Thus again there is omitted-variable bias, but now it biases the estimate of $b$ down rather than up.

Since measurement error leads to omitted-variable bias, the solution is again instrumental variables. That is, to obtain valid estimates of the impact of social infrastructure on income, we need to find variables that are not systematically correlated both with the measurement error in social infrastructure (the $b(SI^* - \widehat{SI})$ component of the composite residual in [4.20], $v$) and with forces other than social infrastructure that affect income (the $e$ component).

---

[9] The fact that $\widehat{SI}$ is based on estimated coefficients causes two complications. First, the uncertainty about the estimated coefficients must be accounted for in finding the standard error in the estimate of $b$; this is done in the usual formulas for the standard errors of instrumental-variables estimates. Second, the fact that the first-stage coefficients are estimated introduces some correlation between $\widehat{SI}$ and $e$ in the same direction as the correlation between $SI$ and $e$. This correlation disappears as the sample size becomes large; thus IV is consistent but not unbiased. If the instruments are only moderately correlated with the right-hand-side variable, however, the bias in finite samples can be large. See, for example, Staiger and Stock (1997).

## Implementation and Results

One of the most serious attempts to use a regression approach to examine social infrastructure's effect on income is Hall and Jones's. As their measure of social infrastructure, $\widetilde{SI}$, Hall and Jones use an index based on two variables. First, companies interested in doing business in foreign countries often want to know about the quality of countries' institutions. As a result, there are consulting firms that construct measures of institutional quality based on a mix of objective data and subjective assessments. Following earlier work by Knack and Keefer (1995) and Mauro (1995), Hall and Jones use one such measure, an index of "government anti-diversion policies" based on assessments by the company Political Risk Services. The second variable that enters Hall and Jones's measure is an index of openness or market-orientation constructed by Sachs and Warner (1995).

In selecting instruments, Hall and Jones argue that the main channel through which Western European, and especially British, influence affected incomes in the rest of the world was social infrastructure. They therefore propose four instruments: the fraction of a country's population who are native speakers of English; the fraction who are native speakers of a major European language (English, French, German, Portuguese, or Spanish); the country's distance from the equator; and a measure of geographic influences on openness to trade constructed by Frankel and D. Romer (1999).

Unfortunately, as Hall and Jones recognize, the case for the validity of these instruments is far from compelling. For example, distance from the equator is correlated with climate, which may directly affect income. Geographic proximity to other countries may affect income through channels other than social infrastructure. And Western European influence may operate through channels other than social infrastructure, such as culture.

Nonetheless, it is interesting to examine Hall and Jones's results, which are generally representative of the findings of regression-based efforts to estimate the role of social infrastructure in cross-country income differences. There are three main findings. First, the estimated impact of social infrastructure on income is quantitatively large and highly statistically significant. Second, variations in social infrastructure appear to account for a large fraction of cross-country income differences.[10] And third, the IV estimates are substantially larger than the OLS estimates. This could arise because measurement error in social infrastructure is a larger problem with the OLS regression than correlation between omitted influences on growth and true social infrastructure. Or, more troublingly, it could occur because

---

[10] When there is important measurement error in the right-hand-side variable, interpreting the magnitudes of the coefficient estimate and estimating the fraction of the variation in the left-hand-side variable that is due to variation in the true right-hand-side variable are not straightforward. Hall and Jones provide a careful discussion of these issues.

the instruments are positively correlated with omitted influences on growth, so that the IV estimates are biased upward.

## Natural Experiments

In light of the limitations of the regression-based tests, Olson (1996) argues for a different approach.[11] Specifically, he argues that the experiences of divided countries provide powerful evidence concerning the importance of social infrastructure. For most of the post-World War II period, both Germany and Korea were divided into two countries. Similarly, Hong Kong and Taiwan were separated from China. Many variables that might affect income, such as climate, natural resources, initial levels of physical and human capital, and cultural attitudes toward work, thrift, and entrepreneurship, were similar in the different parts of these divided areas. Their social infrastructures, however, were very different: East Germany, North Korea, and China were communist, while West Germany, South Korea, Hong Kong, and Taiwan had relatively free-market economies.

In effect, these cases provide *natural experiments* for determining the effects of social infrastructure. If economies were laboratories, economists could take relatively homogeneous countries and divide them in half; they could then randomly assign one type of social infrastructure to one half and another type to the other, and examine the halves' subsequent economic performances. Since the social infrastructures would be assigned randomly, the possibility that there were other factors causing both the differences in social infrastructure and the differences in economic performance could be ruled out. And since the countries would be fairly homogeneous before their divisions, the possibility that the different halves would have large differences on dimensions other than social infrastructure simply by chance would be minimal.

Unfortunately for economic science (though fortunately for other reasons), economies are not laboratories. The closest we can come to a laboratory experiment is when historical developments happen to bring about situations similar to those of an experiment. The cases of the divided regions fit this description almost perfectly. The regions that were divided (particularly Germany and Korea) were fairly homogeneous initially, and the enormous differences in social infrastructure between the different parts were the result of minor details of geography.

The results of these natural experiments are clear-cut: social infrastructure matters. In every case, the market-oriented regimes were dramatically more successful economically than the communist ones. When China began

---

[11] See also the historical evidence in Baumol (1990); Olson (1982); North (1981); and DeLong and Shleifer (1993).

its move away from communism around 1980, Hong Kong had achieved a level of income per person between 15 and 20 times larger than China, and Taiwan had achieved a level between 5 and 10 times larger. When Germany was reunited in 1990, income per person was about $2^1/_2$ times larger in the West than in the East. And although we have no reliable data on output in North Korea, the available evidence suggests that the income gap between South and North Korea is even larger than the others. Thus in the cases of these very large cross-country income differences, differences in social infrastructure appear to have been crucial. More importantly, the evidence provided by these historical accidents strongly suggests that social infrastructure has a large effect on income.

Although the natural-experiment and regression approaches appear very different, the natural-experiment approach can in fact be thought of as a type of instrumental-variables estimation. Consider an instrument that equals plus one for the capitalist halves of divided countries, minus one for the communist halves, and zero for all other countries.[12] Running an IV regression of income on measured social infrastructure using this instrument uses only the information from the differences in social infrastructure and income in the divided countries, and so is equivalent to focusing on the natural experiment. Thus one can think of a natural experiment as an instrumental-variables approach using an instrument that captures only a very small, but carefully chosen, portion of the variation in the right-hand-side variable. And at least in this case, this approach appears to provide more compelling evidence than approaches that try to use much larger amounts of the variation in the right-hand-side variable.

# 4.5   Beyond Social Infrastructure

Social infrastructure is an extremely broad concept, encompassing aspects of economies ranging from the choice between capitalism and communism to the details of the tax code. This breadth is unsatisfying both scientifically and normatively. Scientifically, it makes the hypothesis that social infrastructure is important to cross-country income differences very hard to test. For example, persuasive evidence that one specific component of social infrastructure had no impact on income would leave many other components that could be important. Normatively, it means that the hypothesis that social infrastructure is crucial to income does not have clear implications about what specific institutions or policies policymakers should focus on in their efforts to raise incomes in poor countries.

---

[12] For simplicity, this discussion neglects the fact that China is paired with both Hong Kong and Taiwan in Olson's natural experiment.

Thus, we would like to move beyond the general statement that social infrastructure is important. This section discusses three ways that current research is trying to do this.

## Looking within Social Infrastructure

One way to move beyond the view that social infrastructure is important is to be more specific about what features of it matter. Ideally, we could identify a specific subset of institutions and policies that are critical to cross-country income differences, or provide a list of different elements of social infrastructure with weights attached to each one.

Our current knowledge does not come close to this ideal. Rather, research is actively considering a range of features of social infrastructure. For example, Glaeser, La Porta, Lopez-de-Silanes, and Shleifer (2004) and, especially, Jones and Olken (2005) ask whether "policies"—defined as features of social infrastructure that can be changed by a country's leaders, with no change in the institutions that determine how leaders are chosen or how they exercise their power—are important to growth. Another line of work examines whether institutional constraints on executive power are important to economic performance. North (1981) argues that they are critical, while Glaeser, La Porta, Lopez-de-Silanes, and Shleifer argue that they are of little importance.

Many other papers (and many informal arguments) single out specific features of social infrastructure and argue that they are particularly important. Examples include the security of property rights, political stability, market orientation, and lack of corruption. Unfortunately, obtaining persuasive evidence about the effects of a specific aspect of social infrastructure is very hard. Countries that perform well on one measure of social infrastructure tend to do well on others. Thus a cross-country regression of income on a specific feature of social infrastructure is subject to potentially severe omitted-variable bias: the right-hand-side variable is likely to be correlated not just with determinants of income other than social infrastructure, but also with other elements of social infrastructure. And because social infrastructure is multifaceted and hard to measure, we cannot simply control for those other elements.

In the absence of a way to comprehensively analyze the effects of each component of social infrastructure, researchers search for tools that provide insights into the roles of particular components. The work of Jones and Olken on policies is an excellent example of this approach. Their strategy is to look at what happens to growth in the wake of essentially random deaths of leaders from accident or disease. One would expect such deaths to result in changes in policies, but generally not in institutions. Thus asking whether growth rates change unusually (in either direction) provides a test of whether policies are important. Jones and Olken find strong evidence of such changes. Thus their strategy allows them to learn about whether a subset of social infrastructure is important. It does not, however, allow them to address more precise questions, such as the relative importances of policies and deep institutions to income differences or what specific policies are important.

## The Determinants of Social Infrastructure

The second way that current research is attempting to look more deeply into social infrastructure is by examining its determinants. Unfortunately, there has been relatively little work on this issue. Our knowledge consists of little more than speculation and scraps of evidence.

One set of speculations focuses on incentives, particularly those of individuals with power under the existing system. The clearest example of the importance of incentives to social infrastructure is provided by absolute dictators. An absolute dictator can expropriate any wealth that individuals accumulate; but the knowledge that dictators can do this discourages individuals from accumulating wealth in the first place. Thus for the dictator to encourage saving and entrepreneurship, he or she may need to give up some power. Doing so might make it possible to make everyone, including the dictator, much better off. But in practice, for reasons that are not well understood, it is difficult for a dictator to do this in a way that does not involve some risk of losing power (and perhaps much more) entirely. Further, the dictator is likely to have little difficulty in amassing large amounts of wealth even in a poor economy. Thus he or she is unlikely to accept even a small chance of being overthrown in return for a large increase in expected wealth. The result may be that an absolute dictator prefers a social infrastructure that leads to low average income (DeLong and Shleifer, 1993; North, 1981; Jones, 2002b, pp. 148–149).

Similar considerations may be relevant for others who benefit from an existing system, such as bribe-taking government officials and workers earning above-market wages in industries where production occurs using labor-intensive, inefficient technologies. If the existing system is highly inefficient, it should be possible to compensate these individuals generously for agreeing to move to a more efficient system. But again, in practice we rarely observe such arrangements, and as a result these individuals have a large stake in the continuation of the existing system.[13]

A second set of speculations focuses on factors that fall under the heading of culture. Societies have fairly persistent characteristics arising from religion, family structure, and so on that can have important effects on social

---

[13] See Shleifer and Vishny (1993) and Parente and Prescott (1999). Acemoglu and Robinson (2000, 2002) argue that it is individuals who benefit economically under the current system and would lose politically if there were reform (and who therefore ex post cannot protect any compensation they had been given to accept the reform) who prevent moves to more efficient systems.

infrastructure. For example, different religions suggest different views about the relative importance of tradition, authority, and individual initiative. The implicit or explicit messages of the prevailing religion about these factors may influence individuals' views, and may in turn affect society's choice of social infrastructure. To give another example, there seems to be considerable variation across countries in norms of civic responsibility and in the extent to which people generally view one another as trustworthy (Knack and Keefer, 1997; La Porta, Lopez-de-Silanes, Shleifer, and Vishny, 1997). Again, these difference are likely to affect social infrastructure. As a final example, countries differ greatly in their ethnic diversity, and countries with greater ethnic diversity appear to have less favorable social infrastructure (Easterly and Levine, 1997, and Alesina, Devleeschauwer, Easterly, Kurlat, and Wacziarg, 2003).

A third set of ideas focuses on geography. For example, recall that in their analysis of social infrastructure and income, Hall and Jones's instruments include geographic variables. Their argument is that geography has been an important determinant of exposure to Western European ideas and institutions, and hence of social infrastructure. We will return to this issue shortly, when we discuss the large income differences between temperate and tropical countries.

A final set of speculations focuses on individuals' beliefs about what types of policies and institutions are best for economic development. For example, Sachs and Warner (1995) emphasize that in the early postwar period, the relative merits of state planning and markets were not at all clear. The major market economies had just been through the Great Depression, while the Soviet Union had gone from a backward economy to one of the world's leading industrial countries in just a few decades. Reasonable people disagreed about the merits of alternative forms of social infrastructure. As a result, one important source of differences in social infrastructure was differences in leaders' judgments.

The combination of beliefs and incentives in the determination of social infrastructure creates the possibility of "vicious circles" in social infrastructure. A country may initially adopt a relatively centralized, interventionist system because its leaders sincerely believe that this system is best for the majority of the population. But the adoption of such a system creates groups with interests in its continuation. Thus even as the evidence accumulates that other types of social infrastructure are preferable, the system is very difficult to change. This may capture important elements of the determination of social infrastructure in many sub-Saharan African countries after they became independent (Krueger, 1993).

## Other Sources of Cross-Country Income Differences

The third way that current research is trying to go beyond the general hypothesis that social infrastructure is important to income differences is by investigating other potential sources of those differences. To the extent that this work is just trying to identify additional determinants, it complements the social-infrastructure view. But to the extent that it argues that those other determinants are in fact crucial, it challenges the social-infrastructure view.

Like work on the determinants of social infrastructure, work on other sources of income differences is at an early and speculative stage. There is another important parallel between the two lines of work: they emphasize many of the same possibilities. In particular, both culture and geography have the potential to affect income not just via social infrastructure, but directly.

In the case of culture, it seems clear that views and norms about such matters as thrift, education, trust, and the merits of material success could directly affect economic performance. Clark (1987) and Landes (1998) argue that these direct effects are important, but the evidence on this issue is very limited.

In the case of geography, one line of work argues that the lower incomes of tropical countries are largely the direct result of their geographies. We will discuss this work below. Another line of work focuses on geographic determinants of economic interactions: geographic barriers can reduce incomes not just by decreasing exposure to beneficial institutions and policies, but also by decreasing trade and specialization and reducing exposure to new ideas (see, for example, Nunn and Puga, 2007).

A very different alternative to social infrastructure stresses externalities from capital. In this view, human and physical capital earn less than their marginal products. High-skill workers create innovations, which benefit all workers, and increase other workers' human capital in ways for which they are not compensated. The accumulation of physical capital causes workers to acquire human capital and promotes the development of new techniques of production; again, the owners of the capital are not fully compensated for these contributions. We encountered such possibilities in the learning-by-doing model of Section 3.4.[14] If this view is correct, Klenow and Rodríguez-Clare's and Hall and Jones's accounting exercises are largely uninformative: when capital has positive externalities, a decomposition that uses its private returns to measure its marginal product understates its importance.

This view implies that focusing on social infrastructure in general is misplaced, and that the key determinants of income differences are whatever forces give rise to differences in capital accumulation. This would mean that only aspects of social infrastructure that affect capital accumulation are important, and that factors other than social infrastructure that

---

[14] For such externalities to contribute to cross-country income differences, they must be somewhat localized. If the externalities are global (as would be the case if capital accumulation produces additional knowledge, as in the learning-by-doing models), they raise world income but do not produce differences among countries.

affect capital accumulation, such as cultural attitudes toward thrift and education, are important as well.

Although externalities from capital attracted considerable attention in early work on new growth theory, several types of evidence suggest that they are not crucial to cross-country income differences. First, the hypothesis of large positive externalities from physical capital predicts that an increase in the saving rate raises income by even more than conventional growth-accounting calculations imply. Thus the absence of a noticeable correlation between the saving rate and income is consistent with this view only if there are negative influences on income that are correlated with the saving rate.

Second, there is no compelling microeconomic evidence of local externalities from capital large enough to account for the enormous income differences we observe. Third, highly statist economies have often been very successful at the accumulation of physical and human capital, and at achieving higher capital-output ratios than their market-oriented counterparts. But these countries' economic performance has been generally dismal.

Finally, Bils and Klenow (2000) observe that we can use the simple fact that there is not technological regress to place an upper bound on the externalities from human capital. In the United States and other industrialized countries, the average education of the labor force has been rising at an average rate of about 0.1 years each year. An additional year of education typically raises an individual's earnings by about 10 percent. If the social return to education were double this, increases in education would be raising average output per worker by about 2 percent per year (see equation [4.15], for example). But this would account for essentially all growth of output per worker. Since technology cannot be regressing, we can conclude that the social return to education cannot be greater than this. And if we are confident that technology is improving, we can conclude that the social return to education is less than this.

For these reasons, recent work on cross-country income differences for the most part does not emphasize externalities from capital.[15]

## Empirical Application: Geography, Colonialism, and Economic Development

A striking fact about cross-country income differences is that average incomes are much lower closer to the equator. Figure 4.1, from Bloom and Sachs (1998), shows this pattern dramatically. Average incomes in countries

---

[15] Early theoretical models of externalities from capital include P. Romer (1986), Lucas (1988), and Rebelo (1991). When applied naively to the issue of cross-country income differences, these models tend to have the counterfactual implication that countries with higher saving rates have permanently higher growth rates. Later models of capital externalities that focus explicitly on the issue of income differences among countries generally avoid this implication. See, for example, Basu and Weil (1999).

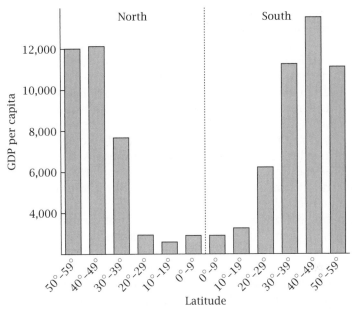

**FIGURE 4.1** **Geography and income (from Bloom and Sachs, 1998; used with permission)**

within 20 degrees of the equator, for example, are less than a sixth of those in countries at more than 40 degrees of latitude.

As we have discussed, one possible reason for this pattern is that the tropics have characteristics that directly reduce income. This idea has a long history, and has been advocated more recently by Diamond (1997), Bloom and Sachs (1998), and others. These authors identify numerous geographic disadvantages of the tropics. Some, such as environments more conducive to disease and climates less favorable to agriculture, are direct consequences of tropical locations. Others, such as the fact that relatively little of the world's land is in the tropics (which reduces opportunities for trade and incentives for innovations that benefit the tropics) are not inherently tied to tropical locations, but are nonetheless geographic disadvantages.

The hypothesis that the tropics' poverty is a direct consequence of geography has a serious problem, however: social infrastructure is dramatically worse in the tropics. The measures of social infrastructure employed by Sachs and Warner (1995), Mauro (1995), and Knack and Keefer (1995) all show much lower levels of social infrastructure in the tropics. The countries' poor social infrastructure is almost surely not a consequence of their poverty. For example, social infrastructure in much of Europe a century ago was much more favorable than social infrastructure in most of Africa today.

Examining why tropical countries are poor therefore has the potential to shed light on two of the three issues that are the focus of this section. The first is the determinants of social infrastructure: what is it about tropical countries that causes them to have poor social infrastructure? The second is the determinants of income other than social infrastructure: does geography have important direct effects on income, or does its impact operate largely through social infrastructure?

With regard to the first question, Acemoglu, Johnson, and Robinson (2001, 2002) and Engerman and Sokoloff (2002) argue that what links geography and poor social infrastructure is colonialism. In their view, differences between tropical and temperate areas at the time of colonization (which were largely the result of geography) caused the Europeans to colonize them differently. These different strategies of colonization affected subsequent institutional development, and so are a crucial source of differences in social infrastructure today.

The specific determinants of colonization strategy that these papers focus on differ. In their 2001 paper, Acemoglu, Johnson, and Robinson emphasize the disease environment. They argue that Europeans faced extremely high mortality risks in tropical areas, particularly from malaria and yellow fever, and that their death rates in temperate regions were similar to (and in some cases less than) those in Europe. They then argue that in the high-disease environments, European colonizers established "extractive states"—authoritarian institutions designed to exploit the areas' population and resources with little settlement, and with minimal property rights or incentives to invest for the vast majority of the population. In the low-disease environments, they established "settler colonies" with institutions broadly similar to those in Europe.

In their 2002 paper, Acemoglu, Johnson, and Robinson focus on the existing level of development in the colonized areas. In regions that were more densely populated and had more developed institutions, establishing extractive states was more attractive (because there was a larger population to exploit and an existing institutional structure that could be used in that effort) and establishing settler colonies more difficult. The result, Acemoglu, Johnson, and Robinson argue, was a "great reversal": among the areas that were colonized, those that were the most developed on the eve of colonization are the least developed today.

Engerman and Sokoloff argue that another geographic characteristic had a large effect on colonization strategies: conduciveness to slavery. A majority of the people who came to the Americas between 1500 and 1800 came as slaves, and the extent of slavery varied greatly across different regions. Engerman and Sokoloff argue that geography was key: although all the colonizing powers accepted slavery, slavery flourished mainly in areas suitable to crops that could be grown effectively on large plantations with heavy use of manual labor. These initial differences in colonization strategy, Engerman and Sokoloff argue, had long-lasting effects on the areas' political and institutional development.

Acemoglu, Johnson, and Robinson and Engerman and Sokoloff present compelling evidence that there were large differences in colonization strategies. And these differences are almost surely an important source of differences in social infrastructure today. However, both the reasons for the differences in colonization strategies and the channels through which the different strategies led to differences in institutions are not clear.

With regard to the reasons for the differences in colonization strategies, researchers have made little progress in determining the relative importance of the different reasons the three papers propose for the differences. Moreover, the evidence in Acemoglu, Johnson, and Robinson's 2001 paper is the subject of considerable debate. Albouy (2008) reexamines the data on settler mortality and finds that in many cases the best available data suggest that mortality was lower in the tropics and higher in temperate regions than in the figures used by Acemoglu, Johnson, and Robinson. He finds that as a result, the statistical relationship between modern social infrastructure and settler mortality is much weaker than found by Acemoglu, Johnson, and Robinson.[16]

With regard to the channels through which the differences in colonization strategies affected institutional development, Acemoglu, Johnson, and Robinson stress the distinction between extractive states and settler colonies and the resulting effects on the strength of property rights. Engerman and Sokoloff, in contrast, stress the impact of colonization strategies on political and economic inequality, and the resulting effects on the development of democracy, public schooling, and other institutions. Another possibility is that there was greater penetration of European ideas, and hence European institutions, in regions more heavily settled by Europeans.

Now turn to the second issue that the poverty of tropical countries may be able to shed light on—whether geography has important direct effects on income. Here Acemoglu, Johnson, and Robinson take a strong view (particularly in their 2001 paper). They argue that it is *only* through their past impact on institutional development that the geographic factors have important effects on income today. For example, yellow fever, which they argue had important effects on colonization strategies and subsequent institutional development, has been largely eradicated throughout the world. Thus it cannot be a direct source of income differences today.

Unfortunately, however, the evidence on this issue is inconclusive. Consider the negative correlation between the prevalence of yellow fever a century or two ago and income today. Clearly, this cannot reflect any effects of current risk of yellow fever, since that risk is minimal everywhere. But it does not follow that it reflects long-lasting effects (through institutions or other channels) of past risk of yellow fever. It could equally well reflect the effects of other variables that are correlated with past risk of yellow fever

---

[16] See Acemoglu, Johnson, and Robinson (2006) for their response to Albouy's analysis.

and that directly affect income today, such as risk of other tropical diseases, climates poorly suited to agriculture, and so on. Thus the issue of whether the direct effects of geography are important remains unsettled.[17]

## Conclusion: "Five Papers in Fifteen Minutes"

The state of our understanding of the enormous differences in standards of living across the world is mixed. On the one hand, we are far from having a clear quantitative understanding of the ultimate determinants of those differences. And we are even farther from being able to quantitatively assess the contributions that different policies would make to the incomes of poor countries. On the other hand, our knowledge is advancing rapidly. Our understanding of the proximate determinants of income has been revolutionized over the past 15 years and is continuing to advance impressively. And work on deeper determinants is a cauldron of new ideas and new evidence.

When I teach this material to my students, to illustrate the ferment and excitement of current research, I conclude with a short section I call "Five Papers in Fifteen Minutes." The idea is that there is so much current work that is of high quality and potentially important that it is not possible to do more than give a flavor of it. Some of the papers are accounting-based, some are statistical, and some are theoretical. What unites them is that they all provide important insights into cross-country income differences and the low incomes of poor countries. The current list is Acemoglu and Robinson (2000); Pritchett (2000); Jones and Olken (2005); Schmitz (2005); Caselli and Feyrer (2007); Hsieh and Klenow (2008); Albouy (2008); and Lagakos (2009).[18]

# 4.6  Differences in Growth Rates

Our discussion so far has focused on differences in countries' average levels of income per person. But recall from Section 1.1 that relative incomes are not fixed; they often change by large amounts, sometimes in just a few decades. It is therefore natural to ask what insights our discussion of differences in income levels provides about differences in income growth.

---

[17] Other recent papers that address the issue of geography versus institutions include Easterly and Levine (2003); Sachs (2003); Rodrik, Subramanian, and Trebbi (2004); and Glaeser, La Porta, Lopez-de-Silanes, and Shleifer (2004).

[18] The careful reader will notice that there are more than five papers on this list. This reflects the fact that so much important research is being done that it is hard to limit the list to five. The even more careful reader will notice that one of the papers is about changes in productivity in a specific industry in the United States and Canada. This reflects the fact that one can obtain insights into the sources of low incomes in many ways.

## Convergence to Balanced Growth Paths

We begin with the case where the underlying determinants of long-run relative income per person across countries are constant over time. That is, we begin by ignoring changes in relative saving rates, years of education, and long-run determinants of output for a given set of inputs.

Countries' incomes do not jump immediately to their long-run paths. For example, if part of a country's capital stock is destroyed in a war, capital returns to its long-run path only gradually. During the return, capital per worker is growing more rapidly than normal, and so output per worker is growing more rapidly than normal. More generally, one source of differences in growth rates across countries is differences in the countries' initial positions relative to their long-run paths. Countries that begin below their long-run paths grow more rapidly than countries that begin above.

To see this more formally, assume for simplicity that differences in output per worker across countries stem only from differences in physical capital per worker. That is, human capital per worker and output for given inputs are the same in all countries. Assume that output is determined by a standard production function, $Y_i(t) = F(K_i(t), A(t)L_i(t))$, with constant returns. Because of the constant-returns assumption, we can write output per worker in country $i$ as

$$\frac{Y_i(t)}{L_i(t)} = A(t)f(k_i(t)). \tag{4.21}$$

(As in our earlier models, $k \equiv K/(AL)$ and $f(k) \equiv F(k, 1)$.) By assumption, the path of $A$ is the same in all countries. Thus (4.21) implies that differences in growth come only from differences in the behavior of $k$.

In the Solow and Ramsey models, each economy has a balanced-growth-path value of $k$, and the rate of change of $k$ is approximately proportional to its departure from its balanced-growth-path value (see Sections 1.5 and 2.6). If we assume that the same is true here, we have

$$\dot{k}_i(t) = \lambda[k_i^* - k_i(t)], \tag{4.22}$$

where $k_i^*$ is the balanced-growth-path value of $k$ in country $i$ and $\lambda > 0$ is the rate of convergence. Equation (4.22) implies that when a country is farther below its balanced growth path, its capital per unit of effective labor rises more rapidly, and so its growth in income per worker is greater.

There are two possibilities concerning the values of $k_i^*$. The first is that they are the same in all countries. In this case, all countries have the same income per worker on their balanced growth paths. Differences in average income stem only from differences in where countries stand relative to the common balanced growth path. Thus in this case, the model predicts that the lower a country's income per person, the faster its growth. This is known as *unconditional convergence*.

Unconditional convergence provides a reasonably good description of differences in growth among the industrialized countries in the postwar period. Long-run fundamentals—saving rates, levels of education, and incentives for production rather than diversion—are broadly similar in these countries. Yet, because World War II affected the countries very differently, they had very different average incomes at the beginning of the postwar period. For example, average incomes in Japan and Germany were far below those in the United States and Canada. Thus the bulk of the variation in initial income came from differences in where countries stood relative to their long-run paths rather than from differences in those paths. As a result, the industrialized countries that were the poorest at the start of the postwar period grew the fastest over the next several decades (Dowrick and Nguyen, 1989; Mankiw, D. Romer, and Weil, 1992).

The other possibility is that the $k_i^*$'s vary across countries. In this case, there is a persistent component of cross-country income differences. Countries that are poor because their saving rates are low, for example, will have no tendency to grow faster than other countries. But differences that stem from countries being at different points relative to their balanced growth paths gradually disappear as the countries converge to those balanced growth paths. That is, the model predicts *conditional convergence:* countries that are poorer after controlling for the determinants of income on the balanced growth path grow faster (Barro and Sala-i-Martin, 1991, 1992; Mankiw, Romer, and Weil, 1992).

These ideas extend to situations where initial income differences do not arise just from differences in physical capital. With human capital, as with physical capital, capital per worker does not move immediately to its long-run level. For example, if the young spend more years in school than previous generations, average human capital per worker rises gradually as new workers enter the labor force and old workers leave. Similarly, workers and capital cannot switch immediately and costlessly between rent-seeking and productive activities. Thus the allocation of resources between these activities does not jump immediately to its long-run level. Again, countries that begin with incomes below their long-run paths experience periods of temporarily high growth as they move to their long-run paths.

## Changes in Fundamentals

So far we have assumed that the underlying determinants of countries' relative long-run levels of income per worker are fixed. The fact that those underlying determinants can change creates another source of differences in growth among countries.

To see this, begin again with the case where incomes per worker differ only because of differences in physical capital per worker. As before, assume that economies have balanced growth paths they would converge to in the absence of shocks. Recall equation (4.22): $\dot{k}_i(t) = \lambda[k_i^* - k_i(t)]$. We want to consider growth over some interval of time where $k_i^*$ need not be constant. To see the issues involved, it is easiest to assume that time is discrete and to consider growth over just two periods. Assume that the change in $k_i$ from period $t$ to period $t+1$, denoted, $\Delta k_{it+1}$, depends on the period-$t$ values of $k_i^*$ and $k_i$. The equation analogous to (4.22) is thus

$$\Delta k_{it+1} = \lambda(k_{it}^* - k_{it}), \tag{4.23}$$

with $\lambda$ assumed to be between 0 and 1. The change in $k_i$ from $t$ to $t+2$ is therefore

$$\Delta k_{it+1} + \Delta k_{it+2} = \lambda(k_{it}^* - k_{it}) + \lambda(k_{it+1}^* - k_{it+1}). \tag{4.24}$$

To interpret this expression, rewrite $k_{it+1}^*$ as $k_{it}^* + \Delta k_{it+1}^*$ and $k_{it+1}$ as $k_{it} + \Delta k_{it+1}$. Thus (4.24) becomes

$$\Delta k_{it+1} + \Delta k_{it+2} = \lambda(k_{it}^* - k_{it}) + \lambda(k_{it}^* + \Delta k_{it+1}^* - k_{it} - \Delta k_{it+1})$$

$$= \lambda(k_{it}^* - k_{it}) + \lambda[k_{it}^* + \Delta k_{it+1}^* - k_{it} - \lambda(k_{it}^* - k_{it})] \tag{4.25}$$

$$= [\lambda + \lambda(1 - \lambda)](k_{it}^* - k_{it}) + \lambda \Delta k_{it+1}^*,$$

where the second line uses (4.23) to substitute for $\Delta k_{it+1}$.

It is also useful to consider the continuous-time case. One can show that if $k_i^*$ does not change discretely, then (4.22) implies that the change in $k$ over some interval, say from 0 to $T$, is

$$k_i(T) - k_i(0) = (1 - e^{-\lambda T})[k_i^*(0) - k_i(0)]$$

$$+ \int_{\tau=0}^{T} (1 - e^{-\lambda(T-\tau)}) \dot{k}_i^*(\tau) \, d\tau. \tag{4.26}$$

Expressions (4.25) and (4.26) show that we can decompose that change in $k$ over an interval into two terms. The first depends on the country's initial position relative to its balanced growth path. This is the conditional-convergence effect we discussed above. The second term depends on changes in the balanced growth path during the interval. A rise in the balanced-growth-path value of $k$, for example, raises growth. Further, as the expression for the continuous-time case shows (and as one would expect), such a rise has a larger effect if it occurs earlier in the interval.

For simplicity, we have focused on physical capital. But analogous results apply to human capital and efficiency: growth depends on countries' starting points relative to their balanced growth paths and on changes in their balanced growth paths.

This analysis shows that the issue of convergence is more complicated than our earlier discussion suggests. Overall convergence depends not only on the distribution of countries' initial positions relative to their long-run paths and on the dispersion of those long-run paths, but also on the distribution of changes in the underlying determinants of countries' long-run paths. For example, there can be overall convergence as a result of convergence of fundamentals.

It is tempting to infer from this that there are strong forces promoting convergence. A country's average income can be far below the world average either because it is far below its long-run path or because its long-run path has unusually low income. In the first case, the country is likely to grow rapidly as it converges to its long-run path. In the second case, the country can grow rapidly by improving its fundamentals. For example, it can adopt policies and institutions that have proved successful in wealthier countries.

Unfortunately, the evidence does not support this conclusion. Over the postwar period, poorer countries have shown no tendency to grow faster than rich ones. This appears to reflect two factors. First, little of the initial gap between poor and rich countries was due to poor countries being below their long-run paths and rich countries being above. In fact, there is some evidence that it was rich countries that tended to begin farther below their long-run paths (Cho and Graham, 1996). This could reflect the fact that World War II disproportionately affected those countries. Second, although there are many cases where fundamentals improved in poor countries, there are also many cases where they worsened.

Further, recall from Section 1.1 that if we look over the past several centuries, the overall pattern has been one of strong divergence. Countries that were slightly industrialized in 1800—mainly the countries of Western Europe plus the United States and Canada—are now overwhelmingly richer than the poorer countries of the world. What appears to have happened is that these countries improved their fundamentals dramatically while many poor countries did not.

## Growth Miracles and Disasters

This analysis provides us with a framework for understanding the most extreme cases of changes in countries' relative incomes: growth miracles and disasters. A period of very rapid or very slow growth relative to the rest of the world can occur as a result of either a shock that pushes an economy very far from its long-run path or a large change in fundamentals. Shocks large enough to move an economy very far from its long-run path are rare, however. The best example might be the impact of World War II on West Germany. On the eve of the war, average income per person in the region that became West Germany was about three-quarters of that of the United States. In 1946, after the end of the war, it was about one-quarter the level in the United States. West German output grew rapidly over the next two decades as the country returned toward its long-run trajectory: in the 20 years after 1946, growth of income per person in

West Germany averaged more than 7 percent per year. As a result, its average income in 1966 was again about three-quarters of that of the United States (Maddison, 1995).[19]

Such large disturbances are rare, however. As a result, growth miracles and disasters are usually the result of large changes in fundamentals. Further, since social infrastructure is central to fundamentals, most growth miracles and disasters are the result of large, rapid changes in social infrastructure.

Not surprisingly, growth miracles and disasters appear to be more common under strong dictators; large, rapid changes in institutions are difficult in democracies. More surprisingly, there is not a clear correlation between the dictators' motives and the nature of the changes in social infrastructure. Large favorable shifts in social infrastructure can occur under dictators who are far from benevolent (to put it mildly), and large unfavorable shifts can occur under dictators whose main objective is to improve the well-being of the average citizen of their countries. Some apparent examples of major shifts toward favorable social infrastructure, followed by periods of miraculous growth, are Singapore and South Korea around 1960, Chile in the early 1970s, and China around 1980. Some examples of the opposite pattern include Argentina after World War II, many newly independent African countries in the early 1960s, China's "cultural revolution" of the mid-1960s, and Uganda in the early 1970s.

It is possible that the evidence about what types of social infrastructure are most conducive to high levels of average income is becoming increasingly clear, and that as a result many of the world's poorer countries are beginning, or are about to begin, growth miracles. Unfortunately, it is too soon to know whether this optimistic view is correct.

# Problems

**4.1. The golden-rule level of education.** Consider the model of Section 4.1 with the assumption that $G(E)$ takes the form $G(E) = e^{\phi E}$.

  (a) Find an expression that characterizes the value of $E$ that maximizes the level of output per person on the balanced growth path. Are there cases where this value equals 0? Are there cases where it equals $T$?

  (b) Assuming an interior solution, describe how, if at all, the golden-rule level of $E$ (that is, the level of $E$ you characterized in part (a)) is affected by each of the following changes:

   (i) A rise in $T$.

   (ii) A fall in $n$.

---

[19] East Germany, in contrast, suffered an unfavorable change in fundamentals in the form of the imposition of communism. Thus its recovery was much weaker.

**4.2. Endogenizing the choice of $E$.** (This follows Bils and Klenow, 2000.) Suppose that the wage of a worker with education $E$ at time $t$ is $be^{gt}e^{\phi E}$. Consider a worker born at time 0 who will be in school for the first $E$ years of life and will work for the remaining $T - E$ years. Assume that the interest rate is constant and equal to $\bar{r}$.

(a) What is the present discounted value of the worker's lifetime earnings as a function of $E$, $T$, $b$, $\bar{r}$, $\phi$, and $g$?

(b) Find the first-order condition for the value of $E$ that maximizes the expression you found in part (a). Let $E^*$ denote this value of $E$. (Assume an interior solution.)

(c) Describe how each of the following developments affects $E^*$:

   (i) A rise in $T$.

   (ii) A rise in $\bar{r}$.

   (iii) A rise in $g$.

**4.3.** Suppose output in country $i$ is given by $Y_i = A_i Q_i e^{\phi E_i} L_i$. Here $E_i$ is each worker's years of education, $Q_i$ is the quality of education, and the rest of the notation is standard. Higher output per worker raises the quality of education. Specifically, $Q_i$ is given by $B_i(Y_i/L_i)^\gamma$, $0 < \gamma < 1$, $B_i > 0$.

Our goal is to decompose the difference in log output per worker between two countries, 1 and 2, into the contributions of education and all other forces. We have data on $Y$, $L$, and $E$ in the two countries, and we know the values of the parameters $\phi$ and $\gamma$.

(a) Explain in what way attributing amount $\phi(E_2 - E_1)$ of $\ln(Y_2/L_2) - \ln(Y_1/L_1)$ to education and the remainder to other forces would understate the contribution of education to the difference in log output per worker between the two countries.

(b) What would be a better measure of the contribution of education to the difference in log output per worker?

**4.4.** Suppose the production function is $Y = K^\alpha (e^{\phi E} L)^{1-\alpha}$, $0 < \alpha < 1$. $E$ is the amount of education workers receive; the rest of the notation is standard. Assume that there is perfect capital mobility. In particular, $K$ always adjusts so that the marginal product of capital equals the world rate of return, $r^*$.

(a) Find an expression for the marginal product of capital as a function of $K$, $E$, $L$, and the parameters of the production function.

(b) Use the equation you derived in (a) to find $K$ as a function of $r^*$, $E$, $L$, and the parameters of the production function.

(c) Use your answer in (b) to find an expression for $d(\ln Y)/dE$, incorporating the effect of $E$ on $Y$ via $K$.

(d) Explain intuitively how capital mobility affects the impact of the change in $E$ on output.

**4.5.** (This follows Mankiw, D. Romer, and Weil, 1992.) Suppose output is given by $Y(t) = K(t)^\alpha H(t)^\beta [A(t)L(t)]^{1-\alpha-\beta}$, $\alpha > 0$, $\beta > 0$, $\alpha + \beta < 1$. Here $L$ is the number of workers and $H$ is their total amount of skills. The remainder of the notation is standard. The dynamics of the inputs are $\dot{L}(t) = nL(t)$, $\dot{A}(t) = gA(t)$, $\dot{K}(t) = s_k Y(t) - \delta K(t)$, $\dot{H}(t) = s_h Y(t) - \delta H(t)$, where $0 < s_k < 1$, $0 < s_h < 1$, and $n + g + \delta > 0$. $L(0)$, $A(0)$, $K(0)$, and $H(0)$ are given, and are all strictly positive. Finally, define $y(t) \equiv Y(t)/[A(t)L(t)]$, $k(t) \equiv K(t)/[A(t)L(t)]$, and $h(t) \equiv H(t)/[A(t)L(t)]$.

(a) Derive an expression for $y(t)$ in terms of $k(t)$ and $h(t)$ and the parameters of the model.

(b) Derive an expression for $\dot{k}(t)$ in terms of $k(t)$ and $h(t)$ and the parameters of the model. In $(k,h)$ space, sketch the set of points where $\dot{k} = 0$.

(c) Derive an expression for $\dot{h}(t)$ in terms of $k(t)$ and $h(t)$ and the parameters of the model. In $(k,h)$ space, sketch the set of points where $\dot{h} = 0$.

(d) Does the economy converge to a balanced growth path? Why or why not? If so, what is the growth rate of output per worker on the balanced growth path? If not, in general terms what is the behavior of output per worker over time?

**4.6.** Consider the model in Problem 4.5.

(a) What are the balanced-growth-path values of $k$ and $h$ in terms of $s_k$, $s_h$, and the other parameters of the model?

(b) Suppose $\alpha = 1/3$ and $\beta = 1/2$. Consider two countries, $A$ and $B$, and suppose that both $s_k$ and $s_h$ are twice as large in Country A as in Country B and that the countries are otherwise identical. What is the ratio of the balanced-growth-path value of income per worker in Country A to its value in Country B implied by the model?

(c) Consider the same assumptions as in part (b). What is the ratio of the balanced-growth-path value of skills per worker in Country A to its value in Country B implied by the model?

**4.7.** (This follows Jones, 2002a.) Consider the model of Section 4.1 with the assumption that $G(E) = e^{\phi E}$. Suppose, however, that $E$, rather than being constant, is increasing steadily: $\dot{E}(t) = m$, where $m > 0$. Assume that, despite the steady increase in the amount of education people are getting, the growth rate of the number of workers is constant and equal to $n$, as in the basic model.

(a) With this change in the model, what is the long-run growth rate of output per worker?

(b) In the United States over the past century, if we measure $E$ as years of schooling, $\phi \approx 0.1$ and $m \approx 1/15$. Overall growth of output per worker has been about 2 percent per year. In light of your answer to (a), approximately what fraction of this overall growth has been due to increasing education?

(c) Can $\dot{E}(t)$ continue to equal $m > 0$ forever? Explain.

**4.8.** Consider the following model with physical and human capital:

$$Y(t) = [(1 - a_K)K(t)]^\alpha[(1 - a_H)H(t)]^{1-\alpha}, \quad 0 < \alpha < 1, \quad 0 < a_K < 1, \quad 0 < a_H < 1,$$

$$\dot{K}(t) = sY(t) - \delta_K K(t),$$

$$\dot{H}(t) = B[a_K K(t)]^\gamma[a_H H(t)]^\phi[A(t)L(t)]^{1-\gamma-\phi} - \delta_H H(t), \quad \gamma > 0, \quad \phi > 0, \quad \gamma + \phi < 1,$$

$$\dot{L}(t) = nL(t),$$

$$\dot{A}(t) = gA(t),$$

where $a_K$ and $a_H$ are the fractions of the stocks of physical and human capital used in the education sector.

This model assumes that human capital is produced in its own sector with its own production function. Bodies ($L$) are useful only as something to be educated, not as an input into the production of final goods. Similarly, knowledge ($A$) is useful only as something that can be conveyed to students, not as a direct input to goods production.

(a) Define $k = K/(AL)$ and $h = H/(AL)$. Derive equations for $\dot{k}$ and $\dot{h}$.

(b) Find an equation describing the set of combinations of $h$ and $k$ such that $\dot{k} = 0$. Sketch in $(h,k)$ space. Do the same for $\dot{h} = 0$.

(c) Does this economy have a balanced growth path? If so, is it unique? Is it stable? What are the growth rates of output per person, physical capital per person, and human capital per person on the balanced growth path?

(d) Suppose the economy is initially on a balanced growth path, and that there is a permanent increase in $s$. How does this change affect the path of output per person over time?

**4.9. Increasing returns in a model with human capital.** (This follows Lucas, 1988.) Suppose that $Y(t) = K(t)^\alpha[(1 - a_H)H(t)]^\beta$, $\dot{H}(t) = Ba_H H(t)$, and $\dot{K}(t) = sY(t)$. Assume $0 < \alpha < 1, 0 < \beta < 1$, and $\alpha + \beta > 1$.[20]

(a) What is the growth rate of $H$?

(b) Does the economy converge to a balanced growth path? If so, what are the growth rates of $K$ and $Y$ on the balanced growth path?

**4.10.** (A different form of measurement error.) Suppose the true relationship between social infrastructure ($SI$) and log income per person ($y$) is $y_i = a + bSI_i + e_i$. There are two components of social infrastructure, $SI^A$ and $SI^B$ (with $SI_i = SI_i^A + SI_i^B$), and we only have data on one of the components, $SI^A$. Both $SI^A$ and $SI^B$ are uncorrelated with $e$. We are considering running an OLS regression of $y$ on a constant and $SI^A$.

(a) Derive an expression of the form, $y_i = a + bSI_i^A + $ other terms.

---

[20] Lucas's model differs from this formulation by letting $a_H$ and $s$ be endogenous and potentially time-varying, and by assuming that the social and private returns to human capital differ.

(b) Use your answer to part (a) to determine whether an OLS regression of $y$ on a constant and $SI^A$ will produce an unbiased estimate of the impact of social infrastructure on income if:

(i) $SI^A$ and $SI^B$ are uncorrelated.

(ii) $SI^A$ and $SI^B$ are positively correlated.

**4.11.** Briefly explain whether each of the following statements concerning a cross-country regression of income per person on a measure of social infrastructure is true or false:

(a) "If the regression is estimated by ordinary least squares, it shows the effect of social infrastructure on output per person."

(b) "If the regression is estimated by instrumental variables using variables that are not affected by social infrastructure as instruments, it shows the effect of social infrastructure on output per person."

(c) "If the regression is estimated by ordinary least squares and has a high $R^2$, this means that there are no important influences on output per person that are omitted from the regression; thus in this case, the coefficient estimate from the regression is likely to be close to the true effect of social infrastructure on output per person."

**4.12. Convergence regressions.**

(a) **Convergence.** Let $y_i$ denote log output per worker in country $i$. Suppose all countries have the same balanced-growth-path level of log income per worker, $y^*$. Suppose also that $y_i$ evolves according to $dy_i(t)/dt = -\lambda[y_i(t) - y^*]$.

(i) What is $y_i(t)$ as a function of $y_i(0)$, $y^*$, $\lambda$, and $t$?

(ii) Suppose that $y_i(t)$ in fact equals the expression you derived in part (i) plus a mean-zero random disturbance that is uncorrelated with $y_i(0)$. Consider a cross-country growth regression of the form $y_i(t) - y_i(0) = \alpha + \beta y_i(0) + \varepsilon_i$. What is the relation between $\beta$, the coefficient on $y_i(0)$ in the regression, and $\lambda$, the speed of convergence? (Hint: For a univariate OLS regression, the coefficient on the right-hand-side variable equals the covariance between the right-hand-side and left-hand-side variables divided by the variance of the right-hand-side variable.) Given this, how could you estimate $\lambda$ from an estimate of $\beta$?

(iii) If $\beta$ in part (ii) is negative (so that rich countries on average grow less than poor countries), is Var($y_i(t)$) necessarily less than Var($y_i(0)$), so that the cross-country variance of income is falling? Explain. If $\beta$ is positive, is Var($y_i(t)$) necessarily more than Var($y_i(0)$)? Explain.

(b) **Conditional convergence.** Suppose $y_i^* = a + bX_i$, and that $dy_i(t)/dt = -\lambda[y_i(t) - y_i^*]$.

(i) What is $y_i(t)$ as a function of $y_i(0)$, $X_i$, $\lambda$, and $t$?

(ii) Suppose that $y_i(0) = y_i^* + u_i$ and that $y_i(t)$ equals the expression you derived in part (i) plus a mean-zero random disturbance, $e_i$, where

$X_i$, $u_i$, and $e_i$ are uncorrelated with one another. Consider a cross-country growth regression of the form $y_i(t) - y_i(0) = \alpha + \beta y_i(0) + \varepsilon_i$. Suppose one attempts to infer $\lambda$ from the estimate of $\beta$ using the formula in part $(a)(ii)$. Will this lead to a correct estimate of $\lambda$, an overestimate, or an underestimate?

(iii) Consider a cross-country growth regression of the form $y_i(t) - y_i(0) = \alpha + \beta y_i(0) + \gamma X_i + \varepsilon_i$. Under the same assumptions as in part $(ii)$, how could one estimate $b$, the effect of $X$ on the balanced-growth-path value of $y$, from estimates of $\beta$ and $\gamma$?

# Chapter **5**
# REAL-BUSINESS-CYCLE THEORY

## 5.1 Introduction: Some Facts about Economic Fluctuations

Modern economies undergo significant short-run variations in aggregate output and employment. At some times, output and employment are falling and unemployment is rising; at others, output and employment are rising rapidly and unemployment is falling. For example, the U.S. economy underwent a severe contraction in 2007–2009. From the fourth quarter of 2007 to the second quarter of 2009, real GDP fell 3.8 percent, the fraction of the adult population employed fell by 3.1 percentage points, and the unemployment rate rose from 4.8 to 9.3 percent. In contrast, over the previous 5 years (that is, from the fourth quarter of 2002 to the fourth quarter of 2007), real GDP rose at an average annual rate of 2.9 percent, the fraction of the adult population employed rose by 0.3 percentage points, and the unemployment rate fell from 5.9 to 4.8 percent.

Understanding the causes of aggregate fluctuations is a central goal of macroeconomics. This chapter and the two that follow present the leading theories concerning the sources and nature of macroeconomic fluctuations. Before we turn to the theories, this section presents a brief overview of some major facts about short-run fluctuations. For concreteness, and because of the central role of the U.S. experience in shaping macroeconomic thought, the focus is on the United States.

A first important fact about fluctuations is that they do not exhibit any simple regular or cyclical pattern. Figure 5.1 plots seasonally adjusted real GDP per person since 1947, and Table 5.1 summarizes the behavior of real GDP in the eleven postwar recessions.[1] The figure and table show that output declines vary considerably in size and spacing. The falls in real GDP range from 0.3 percent in 2000–2001 to 3.8 percent in the recent recession.

---

[1] The formal dating of recessions for the United States is not based solely on the behavior of real GDP. Instead, recessions are identified judgmentally by the National Bureau of Economic Research (NBER) on the basis of various indicators. For that reason, the dates of the official NBER peaks and troughs differ somewhat from the dates shown in Table 5.1.

TABLE 5.1    Recessions in the United States since World War II

| Year and quarter of peak in real GDP | Number of quarters until trough in real GDP | Change in real GDP, peak to trough |
|---|---|---|
| 1948:4 | 2 | −1.7% |
| 1953:2 | 3 | −2.6 |
| 1957:3 | 2 | −3.7 |
| 1960:1 | 3 | −1.6 |
| 1970:3 | 1 | −1.1 |
| 1973:4 | 5 | −3.2 |
| 1980:1 | 2 | −2.2 |
| 1981:3 | 2 | −2.9 |
| 1990:2 | 3 | −1.4 |
| 2000:4 | 1 | −0.3 |
| 2008:2 | 4 | −3.8 |

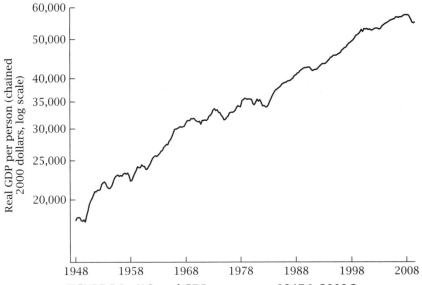

FIGURE 5.1    U.S. real GDP per person, 1947:1–2009:3

The times between the end of one recession and the beginning of the next range from 4 quarters in 1980–1981 to almost 10 years in 1991–2000. The patterns of the output declines also vary greatly. In the 1980 recession, over 90 percent of the overall decline of 2.2 percent took place in a single quarter; in the 1960 recession, output fell for a quarter, then rose slightly, and then fell again; and in the 1957–1958 and 1981–1982 recessions, output fell sharply for two consecutive quarters.

Because output movements are not regular, the prevailing view is that the economy is perturbed by disturbances of various types and sizes at more or less random intervals, and that those disturbances then propagate through

TABLE 5.2   Behavior of the components of output in recessions

| Component of GDP | Average share in GDP | Average share in fall in GDP in recessions relative to normal growth |
|---|---|---|
| Consumption | | |
| Durables | 8.9% | 14.6% |
| Nondurables | 20.6 | 9.7 |
| Services | 35.2 | 10.9 |
| Investment | | |
| Residential | 4.7 | 10.5 |
| Fixed nonresidential | 10.7 | 21.0 |
| Inventories | 0.6 | 44.8 |
| Net exports | −1.0 | −12.7 |
| Government purchases | 20.2 | 1.3 |

the economy. Where the major macroeconomic schools of thought differ is in their hypotheses concerning these shocks and propagation mechanisms.[2]

A second important fact is that fluctuations are distributed very unevenly over the components of output. Table 5.2 shows both the average shares of each of the components in total output and their average shares in the declines in output (relative to its normal growth) in recessions. As the table shows, even though inventory investment on average accounts for only a trivial fraction of GDP, its fluctuations account for close to half of the shortfall in growth relative to normal in recessions: inventory accumulation is on average large and positive at peaks, and large and negative at troughs. Consumer purchases of durable goods, residential investment (that is, housing), and fixed nonresidential investment (that is, business investment other than inventories) also account for disproportionate shares of output fluctuations. Consumer purchases of nondurables and services, government purchases, and net exports are relatively stable.[3] Although there is some variation across recessions, the general pattern shown in Table 5.2 holds in most. And the same components that decline disproportionately when aggregate output is falling also rise disproportionately when output is growing at above-normal rates.

A third set of facts involves asymmetries in output movements. There are no large asymmetries between rises and falls in output; that is, output growth is distributed roughly symmetrically around its mean. There does, however, appear to be asymmetry of a second type: output seems to be

---

[2] There is an important exception to the claim that fluctuations are irregular: there are large seasonal fluctuations that are similar in many ways to conventional business-cycle fluctuations. See Barsky and Miron (1989) and Miron (1996).

[3] The entries for net exports indicate that they are on average negative over the postwar period, and that they typically grow—that is, become less negative—during recessions.

characterized by relatively long periods when it is slightly above its usual path, interrupted by brief periods when it is relatively far below.[4]

A fourth set of facts concerns changes in the magnitude of fluctuations over time. One can think of the macroeconomic history of the United States since the late 1800s as consisting of four broad periods: the period before the Great Depression; the Depression and World War II; the period from the end of World War II to about the mid-1980s; and the mid-1980s to the present. Although our data for the first period are highly imperfect, it appears that fluctuations before the Depression were only moderately larger than in the period from World War II to the mid-1980s. Output movements in the era before the Depression appear slightly larger, and slightly less persistent, than in the period following World War II; but there was no sharp change in the character of fluctuations. Since such features of the economy as the sectoral composition of output and role of government were very different in the two eras, this suggests either that the character of fluctuations is determined by forces that changed much less over time, or that there was a set of changes to the economy that had roughly offsetting effects on overall fluctuations.[5]

The remaining two periods are the extremes. The collapse of the economy in the Depression and the rebound of the 1930s and World War II dwarf any fluctuations before or since. Real GDP in the United States fell by 27 percent between 1929 and 1933, with estimated unemployment reaching 25 percent in 1933. Over the next 11 years, real GDP rose at an average annual rate of 10 percent; as a result, unemployment in 1944 was 1.2 percent. Finally, real GDP declined by 13 percent between 1944 and 1947, and unemployment rose to 3.9 percent.

In contrast, the period following the recovery from the 1981–1982 recession was one of unprecedented macroeconomic stability (McConnell and Perez-Quiros, 2000). Indeed, this period has come to be known as the "Great Moderation." From 1982 to 2007, the United States underwent only two mild recessions, separated by the longest expansion on record.

The crisis that began in 2007 represents a sharp change from the economic stability of recent decades. But one severe recession is not enough to bring average volatility since the mid-1980s even close to its average in the early postwar decades. And it is obviously too soon to know whether the recent events represent the end of the Great Moderation or a one-time aberration.

Finally, Table 5.3 summarizes the behavior of some important macroeconomic variables during recessions. Not surprisingly, employment falls and

---

[4] More precisely, periods of extremely low growth quickly followed by extremely high growth are much more common than periods exhibiting the reverse pattern. See, for example, Sichel (1993).

[5] For more on fluctuations before the Great Depression, see C. Romer (1986, 1989, 1999) and Davis (2004).

**TABLE 5.3    Behavior of some important macroeconomic variables in recessions**

| Variable | Average change in recessions | Number of recessions in which variable falls |
|---|---|---|
| Real GDP* | −4.1% | 11/11 |
| Employment* | −3.1% | 11/11 |
| Unemployment rate (percentage points) | +1.8 | 0/11 |
| Average weekly hours, production workers, manufacturing | −2.3% | 11/11 |
| Output per hour, nonfarm business* | −1.7% | 10/11 |
| Inflation (GDP deflator; percentage points) | −0.3 | 5/11 |
| Real compensation per hour, nonfarm business* | −0.5% | 7/11 |
| Nominal interest rate on 3-month Treasury bills (percentage points) | −1.6 | 10/11 |
| Ex post real interest rate on 3-month Treasury bills (percentage points) | −1.4 | 9/11 |
| Real money stock (M-2/GDP deflator)*† | −0.5% | 3/8 |

*Change in recessions is computed relative to the variable's average growth over the full postwar period, 1947:1–2009:3.
†Available only beginning in 1959.

unemployment rises during recessions. The table shows that, in addition, the length of the average workweek falls. The declines in employment and the declines in hours in the economy as a whole (though not in the man-ufacturing sector) are generally small relative to the falls in output. Thus productivity—output per worker-hour—almost always declines during re-cessions. The conjunction of the declines in productivity and hours implies that the movements in the unemployment rate are smaller than the move-ments in output. The relationship between changes in output and the un-employment rate is known as *Okun's law*. As originally formulated by Okun (1962), the "law" stated that a shortfall in GDP of 3 percent relative to nor-mal growth produces a 1 percentage-point rise in the unemployment rate; a more accurate description of the current relationship is 2 to 1.

The remaining lines of Table 5.3 summarize the behavior of various price and financial variables. Inflation shows no clear pattern. The real wage, at least as measured in aggregate data, tends to fall slightly in recessions. Nominal and real interest rates generally decline, while the real money stock shows no clear pattern.

# 5.2    An Overview of Business-Cycle Research

It is natural to begin our study of aggregate fluctuations by asking whether they can be understood using a Walrasian model—that is, a competitive model without any externalities, asymmetric information, missing markets, or other imperfections. If they can, then the analysis of fluctuations may not require any fundamental departure from conventional microeconomic analysis.

As emphasized in Chapter 2, the Ramsey model is the natural Walrasian baseline model of the aggregate economy: the model excludes not only market imperfections, but also all issues raised by heterogeneity among households. This chapter is therefore devoted to extending a variant of the Ramsey model to incorporate aggregate fluctuations. This requires modifying the model in two ways. First, there must be a source of disturbances: without shocks, a Ramsey economy converges to a balanced growth path and then grows smoothly. The initial extensions of the Ramsey model to include fluctuations emphasized shocks to the economy's technology—that is, changes in the production function from period to period.[6] Subsequent work in this area also emphasizes changes in government purchases.[7] Both types of shocks represent real—as opposed to monetary, or nominal— disturbances: technology shocks change the amount that is produced from a given quantity of inputs, and government-purchases shocks change the quantity of goods available to the private economy for a given level of production. For this reason, the models are known as *real-business-cycle* (or *RBC*) models.

The second change that is needed to the Ramsey model is to allow for variations in employment. In all the models we have seen, labor supply is exogenous and either constant or growing smoothly. Real-business-cycle theory focuses on the question of whether a Walrasian model provides a good description of the main features of observed fluctuations. Models in this literature therefore allow for changes in employment by making households' utility depend not just on their consumption but also on the amount they work; employment is then determined by the intersection of labor supply and labor demand.

Although a purely Walrasian model is the natural starting point for studying macroeconomic fluctuations, we will see that the real-business-cycle models of this chapter do a poor job of explaining actual fluctuations. Thus we will need to move beyond them. At the same time, however, what these models are trying to accomplish remains the ultimate goal of business-cycle research: building a general-equilibrium model from microeconomic foundations and a specification of the underlying shocks that explains, both qualitatively and quantitatively, the main features of macroeconomic fluctuations. Thus the models of this chapter do not just allow us to explore how far we can get in understanding fluctuations with purely Walrasian models; they also illustrate the type of analysis that is the goal of business-cycle

---

[6] The seminal papers include Kydland and Prescott (1982); Long and Plosser (1983); Prescott (1986); and Black (1982).

[7] See Aiyagari, Christiano, and Eichenbaum (1992), Baxter and King (1993), and Christiano and Eichenbaum (1992).

research. Fully specified general-equilibrium models of fluctuations are known as *dynamic stochastic general-equilibrium* (or DSGE) models. When they are quantitative and use additional evidence to choose parameter values and properties of the shocks, they are *calibrated* DSGE models.

As we will discuss in Section 5.9, one way that the RBC models of this chapter appear to fail involves the effects of monetary disturbances: there is strong evidence that contrary to the predictions of the models, such disturbances have important real effects. As a result, there is broad (though not universal) agreement that nominal imperfections or rigidities are important to macroeconomic fluctuations. Chapters 6 and 7 therefore build on the analysis of this chapter by introducing nominal rigidities into business-cycle models.

Chapter 6 drops almost all the complexities of the models of this chapter to focus on nominal rigidity alone. It begins with simple models where nominal rigidity is specified exogenously, and then moves on to consider the microeconomic foundations of nominal rigidity in simple static models. Chapter 6 illustrates an important feature of research on business cycles: although the ultimate goal is a calibrated DSGE model rich enough to match the main features of fluctuations, not all business-cycle research is done using such models. If our goal is to understand a particular issue relevant to fluctuations, we often learn more from studying much simpler models.

Chapter 7 begins to put nominal rigidity into DSGE models of fluctuations. We will see, however, that—not surprisingly—business-cycle research is still short of its ultimate goal. Much of the chapter therefore focuses on the "dynamic" part of "dynamic stochastic general-equilibrium," analyzing dynamic models of price adjustment. The concluding sections discuss some of the elements of leading models and some main outstanding challenges.

# 5.3   A Baseline Real-Business-Cycle Model

We now turn to a specific real-business-cycle model. The assumptions and functional forms are similar to those used in most such models. The model is a discrete-time variation of the Ramsey model of Chapter 2. Because our goal is to describe the quantitative behavior of the economy, we will assume specific functional forms for the production and utility functions.

The economy consists of a large number of identical, price-taking firms and a large number of identical, price-taking households. As in the Ramsey model, households are infinitely lived. The inputs to production are again capital ($K$), labor ($L$), and "technology" ($A$). The production function is Cobb-Douglas; thus output in period $t$ is

$$Y_t = K_t^{\alpha}(A_t L_t)^{1-\alpha}, \qquad 0 < \alpha < 1. \tag{5.1}$$

Output is divided among consumption ($C$), investment ($I$), and government purchases ($G$). Fraction $\delta$ of capital depreciates each period. Thus the capital stock in period $t+1$ is

$$K_{t+1} = K_t + I_t - \delta K_t$$
$$= K_t + Y_t - C_t - G_t - \delta K_t. \tag{5.2}$$

The government's purchases are financed by lump-sum taxes that are assumed to equal the purchases each period.[8]

Labor and capital are paid their marginal products. Thus the real wage and the real interest rate in period $t$ are

$$w_t = (1-\alpha)K_t^\alpha(A_tL_t)^{-\alpha}A_t$$
$$= (1-\alpha)\left(\frac{K_t}{A_tL_t}\right)^\alpha A_t, \tag{5.3}$$

$$r_t = \alpha\left(\frac{A_tL_t}{K_t}\right)^{1-\alpha} - \delta. \tag{5.4}$$

The representative household maximizes the expected value of

$$U = \sum_{t=0}^{\infty} e^{-\rho t}u(c_t, 1-\ell_t)\frac{N_t}{H}. \tag{5.5}$$

$u(\bullet)$ is the instantaneous utility function of the representative member of the household, and $\rho$ is the discount rate.[9] $N_t$ is population and $H$ is the number of households; thus $N_t/H$ is the number of members of the household. Population grows exogenously at rate $n$:

$$\ln N_t = \overline{N} + nt, \qquad n < \rho. \tag{5.6}$$

Thus the level of $N_t$ is given by $N_t = e^{\overline{N}+nt}$.

The instantaneous utility function, $u(\bullet)$, has two arguments. The first is consumption per member of the household, $c$. The second is leisure per member, which is the difference between the time endowment per member (normalized to 1 for simplicity) and the amount each member works, $\ell$.

---

[8] As in the Ramsey model, the choice between debt and tax finance in fact has no impact on outcomes in this model. Thus the assumption of tax finance is made just for expositional convenience. Section 12.2 describes why the form of finance is irrelevant in models like this one.

[9] The usual way to express discounting in a discrete-time model is as $1/(1+\rho)^t$ rather than as $e^{-\rho t}$. But because of the log-linear structure of this model, the exponential formulation is more natural here. There is no important difference between the two approaches, however. Specifically, if we define $\rho' = e^\rho - 1$, then $e^{-\rho t} = 1/(1+\rho')^t$. The log-linear structure of the model is also the reason behind the exponential formulations for population growth and for trend growth of technology and government purchases (see equations [5.6], [5.8], and [5.10]).

Since all households are the same, $c = C/N$ and $\ell = L/N$. For simplicity, $u(\bullet)$ is log-linear in the two arguments:

$$u_t = \ln c_t + b \ln(1 - \ell_t), \qquad b > 0. \tag{5.7}$$

The final assumptions of the model concern the behavior of the two driving variables, technology and government purchases. Consider technology first. To capture trend growth, the model assumes that in the absence of any shocks, $\ln A_t$ would be $\overline{A} + gt$, where $g$ is the rate of technological progress. But technology is also subject to random disturbances. Thus,

$$\ln A_t = \overline{A} + gt + \tilde{A}_t, \tag{5.8}$$

where $\tilde{A}$ reflects departures from trend. $\tilde{A}$ is assumed to follow a *first-order autoregressive process*. That is,

$$\tilde{A}_t = \rho_A \tilde{A}_{t-1} + \varepsilon_{A,t}, \qquad -1 < \rho_A < 1, \tag{5.9}$$

where the $\varepsilon_{A,t}$'s are *white-noise* disturbances—a series of mean-zero shocks that are uncorrelated with one another. Equation (5.9) states that the random component of $\ln A_t$, $\tilde{A}_t$, equals fraction $\rho_A$ of the previous period's value plus a random term. If $\rho_A$ is positive, this means that the effects of a shock to technology disappear gradually over time.

We make similar assumptions about government purchases. The trend growth rate of per capita government purchases equals the trend growth rate of technology; if this were not the case, over time government purchases would become arbitrarily large or arbitrarily small relative to the economy. Thus,

$$\ln G_t = \overline{G} + (n + g)t + \tilde{G}_t, \tag{5.10}$$

$$\tilde{G}_t = \rho_G \tilde{G}_{t-1} + \varepsilon_{G,t}, \qquad -1 < \rho_G < 1, \tag{5.11}$$

where the $\varepsilon_G$'s are white-noise disturbances that are uncorrelated with the $\varepsilon_A$'s. This completes the description of the model.

## 5.4 Household Behavior

The two most important differences between this model and the Ramsey model are the inclusion of leisure in the utility function and the introduction of randomness in technology and government purchases. Before we analyze the model's general properties, this section discusses the implications of these features for households' behavior.

### Intertemporal Substitution in Labor Supply

To see what the utility function implies for labor supply, consider first the case where the household lives only for one period and has no initial wealth. In addition, assume for simplicity that the household has only one member.

In this case, the household's objective function is just $\ln c + b \ln(1 - \ell)$, and its budget constraint is $c = w\ell$.

The Lagrangian for the household's maximization problem is

$$\mathcal{L} = \ln c + b \ln(1 - \ell) + \lambda(w\ell - c). \tag{5.12}$$

The first-order conditions for $c$ and $\ell$, respectively, are

$$\frac{1}{c} - \lambda = 0, \tag{5.13}$$

$$-\frac{b}{1 - \ell} + \lambda w = 0. \tag{5.14}$$

Since the budget constraint requires $c = w\ell$, (5.13) implies $\lambda = 1/(w\ell)$. Substituting this into (5.14) yields

$$-\frac{b}{1 - \ell} + \frac{1}{\ell} = 0. \tag{5.15}$$

The wage does not enter (5.15). Thus labor supply (the value of $\ell$ that satisfies [5.15]) is independent of the wage. Intuitively, because utility is logarithmic in consumption and the household has no initial wealth, the income and substitution effects of a change in the wage offset each other.

The fact that the level of the wage does not affect labor supply in the static case does not mean that variations in the wage do not affect labor supply when the household's horizon is more than one period. This can be seen most easily when the household lives for two periods. Continue to assume that it has no initial wealth and that it has only one member; in addition, assume that there is no uncertainty about the interest rate or the second-period wage.

The household's lifetime budget constraint is now

$$c_1 + \frac{1}{1 + r} c_2 = w_1 \ell_1 + \frac{1}{1 + r} w_2 \ell_2, \tag{5.16}$$

where $r$ is the real interest rate. The Lagrangian is

$$\mathcal{L} = \ln c_1 + b \ln(1 - \ell_1) + e^{-\rho}[\ln c_2 + b \ln(1 - \ell_2)]$$

$$+ \lambda \left[ w_1 \ell_1 + \frac{1}{1 + r} w_2 \ell_2 - c_1 - \frac{1}{1 + r} c_2 \right]. \tag{5.17}$$

The household's choice variables are $c_1$, $c_2$, $\ell_1$, and $\ell_2$. Only the first-order conditions for $\ell_1$ and $\ell_2$ are needed, however, to show the effect of the relative wage in the two periods on relative labor supply. These conditions are

$$\frac{b}{1 - \ell_1} = \lambda w_1, \tag{5.18}$$

$$\frac{e^{-\rho} b}{1 - \ell_2} = \frac{1}{1 + r} \lambda w_2. \tag{5.19}$$

To see the implications of (5.18)–(5.19), divide both sides of (5.18) by $w_1$ and both sides of (5.19) by $w_2/(1 + r)$, and equate the two resulting expressions for $\lambda$. This yields

$$\frac{e^{-\rho}b}{1 - \ell_2}\frac{1+r}{w_2} = \frac{b}{1 - \ell_1}\frac{1}{w_1}, \tag{5.20}$$

or

$$\frac{1 - \ell_1}{1 - \ell_2} = \frac{1}{e^{-\rho}(1 + r)}\frac{w_2}{w_1}. \tag{5.21}$$

Equation (5.21) implies that relative labor supply in the two periods responds to the relative wage. If, for example, $w_1$ rises relative to $w_2$, the household decreases first-period leisure relative to second-period leisure; that is, it increases first-period labor supply relative to second-period supply. Because of the logarithmic functional form, the elasticity of substitution between leisure in the two periods is 1.

Equation (5.21) also implies that a rise in $r$ raises first-period labor supply relative to second-period supply. Intuitively, a rise in $r$ increases the attractiveness of working today and saving relative to working tomorrow. As we will see, this effect of the interest rate on labor supply is crucial to employment fluctuations in real-business-cycle models. These responses of labor supply to the relative wage and the interest rate are known as *intertemporal substitution* in labor supply (Lucas and Rapping, 1969).

## Household Optimization under Uncertainty

The second way that the household's optimization problem differs from its problem in the Ramsey model is that it faces uncertainty about rates of return and future wages. Because of this uncertainty, the household does not choose deterministic paths for consumption and labor supply. Instead, its choices of $c$ and $\ell$ at any date potentially depend on all the shocks to technology and government purchases up to that date. This makes a complete description of the household's behavior quite complicated. Fortunately, we can describe key features of its behavior without fully solving its optimization problem. Recall that in the Ramsey model, we were able to derive an equation relating present consumption to the interest rate and consumption a short time later (the Euler equation) before imposing the budget constraint and determining the level of consumption. With uncertainty, the analogous equation relates consumption in the current period to *expectations* concerning interest rates and consumption in the next period. We will derive this equation using the informal approach we used in equations (2.22)–(2.23) to derive the Euler equation.[10]

Consider the household in period $t$. Suppose it reduces current consumption per member by a small amount $\Delta c$ and then uses the resulting greater wealth to increase consumption per member in the next period above what it otherwise would have been. If the household is behaving optimally, a marginal change of this type must leave expected utility unchanged.

Equations (5.5) and (5.7) imply that the marginal utility of consumption per member in period $t$, $c_t$, is $e^{-\rho t}(N_t/H)(1/c_t)$. Thus the utility cost of this change is $e^{-\rho t}(N_t/H)(\Delta c/c_t)$. Since the household has $e^n$ times as many members in period $t+1$ as in period $t$, the increase in consumption per member in period $t+1$, $c_{t+1}$, is $e^{-n}(1+r_{t+1})\Delta c$. The marginal utility of period-$t+1$ consumption per member is $e^{-\rho(t+1)}(N_{t+1}/H)(1/c_{t+1})$. Thus the expected utility benefit as of period $t$ is $E_t[e^{-\rho(t+1)}(N_{t+1}/H)e^{-n}(1+r_{t+1})/c_{t+1}]\Delta c$, where $E_t$ denotes expectations conditional on what the household knows in period $t$ (that is, conditional on the history of the economy up through period $t$). Equating the costs and expected benefits implies

$$e^{-\rho t}\frac{N_t}{H}\frac{\Delta c}{c_t} = E_t\left[e^{-\rho(t+1)}\frac{N_{t+1}}{H}e^{-n}\frac{1}{c_{t+1}}(1+r_{t+1})\right]\Delta c. \qquad (5.22)$$

Since $e^{-\rho(t+1)}(N_{t+1}/H)e^{-n}$ is not uncertain and since $N_{t+1} = N_t e^n$, this condition simplifies to

$$\frac{1}{c_t} = e^{-\rho}E_t\left[\frac{1}{c_{t+1}}(1+r_{t+1})\right]. \qquad (5.23)$$

This is the analogue of equation (2.20) in the Ramsey model.

Note that the expression on the right-hand side of (5.23) is *not* the same as $e^{-\rho}E_t[1/c_{t+1}]E_t[1+r_{t+1}]$. That is, the tradeoff between present and future consumption depends not just on the expectations of future marginal utility and of the rate of return, but also on their interaction. Specifically, the expectation of the product of two variables equals the product of their expectations plus their covariance. Thus (5.23) implies

$$\frac{1}{c_t} = e^{-\rho}\left\{E_t\left[\frac{1}{c_{t+1}}\right]E_t[1+r_{t+1}] + \text{Cov}\left(\frac{1}{c_{t+1}}, 1+r_{t+1}\right)\right\}, \qquad (5.24)$$

where $\text{Cov}(1/c_{t+1}, 1+r_{t+1})$ denotes the covariance of $1/c_{t+1}$ and $1+r_{t+1}$. Suppose, for example, that when $r_{t+1}$ is high, $c_{t+1}$ is also high. In this case, $\text{Cov}(1/c_{t+1}, 1+r_{t+1})$ is negative; that is, the return to saving is high in the times when the marginal utility of consumption is low. This makes saving less attractive than it is if $1/c_{t+1}$ and $r_{t+1}$ are uncorrelated, and thus tends to raise current consumption.

Chapter 8 discusses the impact of uncertainty on optimal consumption further.

---

[10] The household's problem can be analyzed more formally using *dynamic programming* (see Section 10.4 or Ljungqvist and Sargent, 2004). This also yields (5.23) below.

## The Tradeoff between Consumption and Labor Supply

The household chooses not only consumption at each date, but also labor supply. Thus a second first-order condition for the household's optimization problem relates its current consumption and labor supply. Specifically, imagine the household increasing its labor supply per member in period $t$ by a small amount $\Delta\ell$ and using the resulting income to increase its consumption in that period. Again if the household is behaving optimally, a marginal change of this type must leave expected utility unchanged.

From equations (5.5) and (5.7), the marginal disutility of labor supply in period $t$ is $e^{-\rho t}(N_t/H)[b/(1 - \ell_t)]$. Thus the change has a utility cost of $e^{-\rho t}(N_t/H)[b/(1 - \ell_t)]\Delta\ell$. And since the change raises consumption per member by $w_t\,\Delta\ell$, it has a utility benefit of $e^{-\rho t}(N_t/H)(1/c_t)w_t\,\Delta\ell$. Equating the cost and benefit gives us

$$e^{-\rho t}\frac{N_t}{H}\frac{b}{1 - \ell_t}\,\Delta\ell = e^{-\rho t}\frac{N_t}{H}\frac{1}{c_t}w_t\,\Delta\ell, \qquad (5.25)$$

or

$$\frac{c_t}{1 - \ell_t} = \frac{w_t}{b}. \qquad (5.26)$$

Equation (5.26) relates current leisure and consumption, given the wage. Because it involves current variables, which are known, uncertainty does not enter. Equations (5.23) and (5.26) are the key equations describing households' behavior.

# 5.5   A Special Case of the Model

## Simplifying Assumptions

The model of Section 5.3 cannot be solved analytically. The basic problem is that it contains a mixture of ingredients that are linear—such as depreciation and the division of output into consumption, investment, and government purchases—and ones that are log-linear—such as the production function and preferences. In this section, we therefore investigate a simplified version of the model.

Specifically, we make two changes to the model: we eliminate government, and we assume 100 percent depreciation each period.[11] Thus

---

[11] With these changes, the model corresponds to a one-sector version of Long and Plosser's (1983) real-business-cycle model. McCallum (1989) investigates this model. In addition, except for the assumption of $\delta = 1$, the model corresponds to the basic case considered by Prescott (1986). It is straightforward to assume that a constant fraction of output is purchased by the government instead of eliminating government altogether.

equations (5.10) and (5.11), which describe the behavior of government purchases, are dropped from the model. And equations (5.2) and (5.4), which describe the evolution of the capital stock and the determination of the real interest rate, become

$$K_{t+1} = Y_t - C_t, \tag{5.27}$$

$$1 + r_t = \alpha \left( \frac{A_t L_t}{K_t} \right)^{1-\alpha}. \tag{5.28}$$

The elimination of government can be justified on the grounds that doing so allows us to isolate the effects of technology shocks. The grounds for the assumption of complete depreciation, on the other hand, are only that it allows us to solve the model analytically.

## Solving the Model

Because markets are competitive, externalities are absent, and there are a finite number of individuals, the model's equilibrium must correspond to the Pareto optimum. Because of this, we can find the equilibrium either by ignoring markets and finding the social optimum directly, or by solving for the competitive equilibrium. We will take the second approach, on the grounds that it is easier to apply to variations of the model where Pareto efficiency fails. Finding the social optimum is sometimes easier, however; as a result, many real-business-cycle models are solved that way.[12]

There are two state variables in the model: the capital stock inherited from the previous period, and the current value of technology. That is, the economy's situation in a given period is described by these two variables. The two endogenous variables are consumption and employment.

Because the endogenous variables are growing over time, it is easier to focus on the fraction of output that is saved, $s$, and labor supply per person, $\ell$. Our basic strategy will be to rewrite the equations of the model in log-linear form, substituting $(1-s)Y$ for $C$ whenever it appears. We will then determine how $\ell$ and $s$ must depend on the current technology and on the capital stock inherited from the previous period to satisfy the equilibrium conditions. We will focus on the two conditions for household optimization, (5.23) and (5.26); the remaining equations follow mechanically from accounting and from competition.

We will find that $s$ is independent of technology and the capital stock. Intuitively, the combination of logarithmic utility, Cobb–Douglas production, and 100 percent depreciation causes movements in both technology and

---

[12] See Problem 5.11 for the solution using the social-optimum approach.

capital to have offsetting income and substitution effects on saving. It is the fact that $s$ is constant that allows the model to be solved analytically.

Consider (5.23) first; this condition is $1/c_t = e^{-\rho} E_t[(1 + r_{t+1})/c_{t+1}]$. Since $c_t = (1 - s_t)Y_t/N_t$, rewriting (5.23) along the lines just suggested gives us

$$-\ln\left[(1 - s_t)\frac{Y_t}{N_t}\right] = -\rho + \ln E_t\left[\frac{1 + r_{t+1}}{(1 - s_{t+1})Y_{t+1}/N_{t+1}}\right]. \tag{5.29}$$

Equation (5.28) implies that $1 + r_{t+1}$ equals $\alpha(A_{t+1}L_{t+1}/K_{t+1})^{1-\alpha}$, or $\alpha Y_{t+1}/K_{t+1}$. In addition, the assumption of 100 percent depreciation implies that $K_{t+1} = Y_t - C_t = s_t Y_t$. Substituting these facts into (5.29) yields

$$-\ln(1 - s_t) - \ln Y_t + \ln N_t$$

$$= -\rho + \ln E_t\left[\frac{\alpha Y_{t+1}}{K_{t+1}(1 - s_{t+1})Y_{t+1}/N_{t+1}}\right]$$

$$= -\rho + \ln E_t\left[\frac{\alpha N_{t+1}}{s_t(1 - s_{t+1})Y_t}\right] \tag{5.30}$$

$$= -\rho + \ln \alpha + \ln N_t + n - \ln s_t - \ln Y_t + \ln E_t\left[\frac{1}{1 - s_{t+1}}\right],$$

where the final line uses the facts that $\alpha$, $N_{t+1}$, $s_t$, and $Y_t$ are known at date $t$ and that $N$ is growing at rate $n$. Equation (5.30) simplifies to

$$\ln s_t - \ln(1 - s_t) = -\rho + n + \ln \alpha + \ln E_t\left[\frac{1}{1 - s_{t+1}}\right]. \tag{5.31}$$

Crucially, the two state variables, $A$ and $K$, do not enter (5.31). This implies that there is a constant value of $s$ that satisfies this condition. To see this, note that if $s$ is constant at some value $\hat{s}$, then $s_{t+1}$ is not uncertain, and so $E_t[1/(1 - s_{t+1})]$ is simply $1/(1 - \hat{s})$. Thus (5.31) becomes

$$\ln \hat{s} = \ln \alpha + n - \rho, \tag{5.32}$$

or

$$\hat{s} = \alpha e^{n-\rho}. \tag{5.33}$$

Thus the model has a solution where the saving rate is constant.

Now consider (5.26), which states $c_t/(1 - \ell_t) = w_t/b$. Since $c_t = C_t/N_t = (1 - \hat{s})Y_t/N_t$, we can rewrite this condition as

$$\ln\left[(1 - \hat{s})\frac{Y_t}{N_t}\right] - \ln(1 - \ell_t) = \ln w_t - \ln b. \tag{5.34}$$

Since the production function is Cobb–Douglas, $w_t = (1 - \alpha)Y_t/(\ell_t N_t)$. Substituting this fact into (5.34) yields

$$\ln(1 - \hat{s}) + \ln Y_t - \ln N_t - \ln(1 - \ell_t)$$
$$= \ln(1 - \alpha) + \ln Y_t - \ln \ell_t - \ln N_t - \ln b. \tag{5.35}$$

Canceling terms and rearranging gives us

$$\ln \ell_t - \ln(1 - \ell_t) = \ln(1 - \alpha) - \ln(1 - \hat{s}) - \ln b. \tag{5.36}$$

Finally, straightforward algebra yields

$$\ell_t = \frac{1 - \alpha}{(1 - \alpha) + b(1 - \hat{s})} \tag{5.37}$$

$$\equiv \hat{\ell}.$$

Thus labor supply is also constant. The reason this occurs despite households' willingness to substitute their labor supply intertemporally is that movements in either technology or capital have offsetting impacts on the relative-wage and interest-rate effects on labor supply. An improvement in technology, for example, raises current wages relative to expected future wages, and thus acts to raise labor supply. But, by raising the amount saved, it also lowers the expected interest rate, which acts to reduce labor supply. In the specific case we are considering, these two effects exactly balance.

The remaining equations of the model do not involve optimization; they follow from technology, accounting, and competition. Thus we have found a solution to the model with $s$ and $\ell$ constant.

As described above, any competitive equilibrium of this model is also a solution to the problem of maximizing the expected utility of the representative household. Standard results about optimization imply that this problem has a unique solution (see Stokey, Lucas, and Prescott, 1989, for example). Thus the equilibrium we have found must be the only one.

## Discussion

This model provides an example of an economy where real shocks drive output movements. Because the economy is Walrasian, the movements are the optimal responses to the shocks. Thus, contrary to the conventional wisdom about macroeconomic fluctuations, here fluctuations do not reflect any market failures, and government interventions to mitigate them can only reduce welfare. In short, the implication of real-business-cycle models, in their strongest form, is that observed aggregate output movements represent the time-varying Pareto optimum.

The specific form of the output fluctuations implied by the model is determined by the dynamics of technology and the behavior of the capital stock.[13] In particular, the production function, $Y_t = K_t^\alpha (A_t L_t)^{1-\alpha}$, implies

$$\ln Y_t = \alpha \ln K_t + (1 - \alpha)(\ln A_t + \ln L_t). \tag{5.38}$$

We know that $K_t = \hat{s} Y_{t-1}$ and $L_t = \hat{\ell} N_t$; thus

$$\begin{aligned}
\ln Y_t &= \alpha \ln \hat{s} + \alpha \ln Y_{t-1} + (1 - \alpha)(\ln A_t + \ln \hat{\ell} + \ln N_t) \\
&= \alpha \ln \hat{s} + \alpha \ln Y_{t-1} + (1 - \alpha)(\overline{A} + gt) \\
&\quad + (1 - \alpha)\tilde{A}_t + (1 - \alpha)(\ln \hat{\ell} + \overline{N} + nt),
\end{aligned} \tag{5.39}$$

where the last line uses the facts that $\ln A_t = \overline{A} + gt + \tilde{A}_t$ and $\ln N_t = \overline{N} + nt$ (see [5.6] and [5.8]).

The two components of the right-hand side of (5.39) that do not follow deterministic paths are $\alpha \ln Y_{t-1}$ and $(1 - \alpha)\tilde{A}_t$. It must therefore be possible to rewrite (5.39) in the form

$$\tilde{Y}_t = \alpha \tilde{Y}_{t-1} + (1 - \alpha)\tilde{A}_t, \tag{5.40}$$

where $\tilde{Y}_t$ is the difference between $\ln Y_t$ and the value it would take if $\ln A_t$ equaled $\overline{A} + gt$ each period (see Problem 5.14 for the details).

To see what (5.40) implies concerning the dynamics of output, note that since it holds each period, it implies $\tilde{Y}_{t-1} = \alpha \tilde{Y}_{t-2} + (1 - \alpha)\tilde{A}_{t-1}$, or

$$\tilde{A}_{t-1} = \frac{1}{1-\alpha}\left(\tilde{Y}_{t-1} - \alpha \tilde{Y}_{t-2}\right). \tag{5.41}$$

Recall that (5.9) states that $\tilde{A}_t = \rho_A \tilde{A}_{t-1} + \varepsilon_{A,t}$. Substituting this fact and (5.41) into (5.40), we obtain

$$\begin{aligned}
\tilde{Y}_t &= \alpha \tilde{Y}_{t-1} + (1 - \alpha)(\rho_A \tilde{A}_{t-1} + \varepsilon_{A,t}) \\
&= \alpha \tilde{Y}_{t-1} + \rho_A(\tilde{Y}_{t-1} - \alpha \tilde{Y}_{t-2}) + (1 - \alpha)\varepsilon_{A,t} \\
&= (\alpha + \rho_A)\tilde{Y}_{t-1} - \alpha \rho_A \tilde{Y}_{t-2} + (1 - \alpha)\varepsilon_{A,t}.
\end{aligned} \tag{5.42}$$

Thus, departures of log output from its normal path follow a *second-order autoregressive process;* that is, $\tilde{Y}$ can be written as a linear combination of its two previous values plus a white-noise disturbance.[14]

The combination of a positive coefficient on the first lag of $\tilde{Y}_t$ and a negative coefficient on the second lag can cause output to have a "hump-shaped"

---

[13] The discussion that follows is based on McCallum (1989).

[14] Readers who are familiar with the use of *lag operators* can derive (5.42) using that approach. In lag operator notation, $\tilde{Y}_{t-1}$ is $L\tilde{Y}_t$, where $L$ maps variables to their previous period's value. Thus (5.40) can be written as $\tilde{Y}_t = \alpha L\tilde{Y}_t + (1 - \alpha)\tilde{A}_t$, or $(1 - \alpha L)\tilde{Y}_t = (1 - \alpha)\tilde{A}_t$. Similarly, we can rewrite (5.9) as $(1 - \rho_A L)\tilde{A}_t = \varepsilon_{A,t}$, or $\tilde{A}_t = (1 - \rho_A L)^{-1}\varepsilon_{A,t}$. Thus we have $(1 - \alpha L)\tilde{Y}_t = (1 - \alpha)(1 - \rho_A L)^{-1}\varepsilon_{A,t}$. "Multiplying" through by $1 - \rho_A L$ yields $(1 - \alpha L)(1 - \rho_A L)\tilde{Y}_t = (1 - \alpha)\varepsilon_{A,t}$, or $[1 - (\alpha + \rho_A)L + \alpha \rho_A L^2]\tilde{Y}_t = (1 - \alpha)\varepsilon_{A,t}$. This is equivalent to $\tilde{Y}_t = (\alpha + \rho_A)L\tilde{Y}_t - \alpha \rho_A L^2 \tilde{Y}_t + (1 - \alpha)\varepsilon_{A,t}$, which corresponds to (5.42). (See Section 7.3 for a discussion of lag operators and of the legitimacy of manipulating them in these ways.)

response to disturbances. Suppose, for example, that $\alpha = \frac{1}{3}$ and $\rho_A = 0.9$. Consider a one-time shock of $1/(1-\alpha)$ to $\varepsilon_A$. Using (5.42) iteratively shows that the shock raises log output relative to the path it would have otherwise followed by 1 in the period of the shock ($1 - \alpha$ times the shock), 1.23 in the next period ($\alpha + \rho_A$ times 1), 1.22 in the following period ($\alpha + \rho_A$ times 1.23, minus $\alpha$ times $\rho_A$ times 1), then 1.14, 1.03, 0.94, 0.84, 0.76, 0.68,... in subsequent periods.

Because $\alpha$ is not large, the dynamics of output are determined largely by the persistence of the technology shocks, $\rho_A$. If $\rho_A = 0$, for example, (5.42) simplifies to $\tilde{Y}_t = \alpha \tilde{Y}_{t-1} + (1-\alpha)\varepsilon_{A,t}$. If $\alpha = \frac{1}{3}$, this implies that almost nine-tenths of the initial effect of a shock disappears after only two periods. Even if $\rho_A = \frac{1}{2}$, two-thirds of the initial effect is gone after three periods. Thus the model does not have any mechanism that translates transitory technology disturbances into significant long-lasting output movements. We will see that the same is true of the more general version of the model. Nonetheless, these results show that this model yields interesting output dynamics.

Despite the output dynamics, this special case of the model does not match major features of fluctuations very well. Most obviously, the saving rate is constant—so that consumption and investment are equally volatile—and labor input does not vary. In practice, as we saw in Section 5.1, investment varies much more than consumption, and employment and hours are strongly procyclical. In addition, the model predicts that the real wage is highly procyclical. Because of the Cobb–Douglas production function, the real wage is $(1-\alpha)Y/L$; since $L$ does not respond to technology shocks, this means that the real wage rises one-for-one with $Y$. But, as we saw in Section 5.1 and will see in more detail in Section 6.3, in actual fluctuations the real wage is only moderately procyclical.

Thus the model must be modified if it is to capture many of the major features of observed output movements. The next section shows that introducing depreciation of less than 100 percent and shocks to government purchases improves the model's predictions concerning movements in employment, saving, and the real wage.

To see intuitively how lower depreciation improves the fit of the model, consider the extreme case of no depreciation and no growth, so that investment is zero in the absence of shocks. In this situation, a positive technology shock, by raising the marginal product of capital in the next period, makes it optimal for households to undertake some investment. Thus the saving rate rises. The fact that saving is temporarily high means that expected consumption growth is higher than it would be with a constant saving rate; from consumers' intertemporal optimization condition, (5.23), this requires the expected interest rate to be higher. But we know that a higher interest rate increases current labor supply. Thus introducing incomplete depreciation causes investment and employment to respond more to shocks.

The reason that introducing shocks to government purchases improves the fit of the model is straightforward: it breaks the tight link between output and the real wage. Since an increase in government purchases increases households' lifetime tax liability, it reduces their lifetime wealth. This causes them to consume less leisure—that is, to work more. When labor supply rises without any change in technology, the real wage falls; thus output and the real wage move in opposite directions. It follows that with shocks to both government purchases and technology, the model can generate an overall pattern of real wage movements that is not strongly procyclical.

# 5.6  Solving the Model in the General Case

## Log-Linearization

As discussed above, the full model of Section 5.3 cannot be solved analytically. This is true of almost all real-business-cycle models, as well as many other modern models in macroeconomics. A common way of dealing with this problem is to *log-linearize* the model. That is, agents' decision rules and the equations of motion for the state variables are replaced by first-order Taylor approximations in the logs of the relevant variables around the path the economy would follow in the absence of shocks. We will take that approach here.[15]

Unfortunately, even though taking a log-linear approximation to the model allows it to be solved analytically, the analysis is complicated and somewhat tedious. For that reason, we will only describe the broad features of the derivation and results without going through the specifics in detail.

Recall that the economy has three state variables (the capital stock inherited from the previous period and the current values of technology and government purchases) and two endogenous variables (consumption and employment). If we log-linearize the model around the nonstochastic balanced growth path, the rules for consumption and employment must take the form

$$\tilde{C}_t \simeq a_{CK}\tilde{K}_t + a_{CA}\tilde{A}_t + a_{CG}\tilde{G}_t, \tag{5.43}$$

$$\tilde{L}_t \simeq a_{LK}\tilde{K}_t + a_{LA}\tilde{A}_t + a_{LG}\tilde{G}_t, \tag{5.44}$$

where the $a$'s will be functions of the underlying parameters of the model. As before, a tilde over a variable denotes the difference between the log of that variable and the log of its balanced-growth-path value.[16] Thus, for example, $\tilde{A}_t$ denotes $\ln A_t - (\overline{A} + gt)$. Equations (5.43) and (5.44) state that

---

[15] The specifics of the analysis follow Campbell (1994).

[16] See Problem 5.10 for the balanced growth path of the model in the absence of shocks.

log consumption and log employment are linear functions of the logs of $K$, $A$, and $G$, and that consumption and employment are equal to their balanced-growth-path values when $K$, $A$, and $G$ are all equal to theirs. Since we are building a version of the model that is log-linear around the balanced growth path by construction, we know that these conditions must hold. To solve the model, we must determine the values of the $a$'s.

As with the simple version of the model, we will focus on the two conditions for household optimization, (5.23) and (5.26). For a set of $a$'s to be a solution to the model, they must imply that households are satisfying these conditions. It turns out that the restrictions that this requirement puts on the $a$'s fully determine them, and thus tell us the solution to the model.

This solution method is known as the *method of undetermined coefficients*. The idea is to use theory (or, in some cases, educated guesswork) to find the general functional form of the solution, and then to determine what values the coefficients in the functional form must take to satisfy the equations of the model. This method is useful in many situations.

## The Intratemporal First-Order Condition

Begin by considering households' first-order condition for the tradeoff between current consumption and labor supply, $c_t/(1 - \ell_t) = w_t/b$ (equation [5.26]). Using equation (5.3), $w_t = (1 - \alpha)[K_t/(A_t L_t)]^\alpha A_t$, to substitute for the wage and taking logs, we can write this condition as

$$\ln c_t - \ln(1 - \ell_t) = \ln\left(\frac{1 - \alpha}{b}\right) + (1 - \alpha)\ln A_t + \alpha\ln K_t - \alpha\ln L_t. \quad (5.45)$$

We want to find a first-order Taylor-series approximation to this expression in the logs of the variables of the model around the balanced growth path the economy would follow if there were no shocks. Approximating the right-hand side is straightforward: the difference between the actual value of the right-hand side and its balanced-growth-path value is $(1 - \alpha)\tilde{A}_t + \alpha\tilde{K}_t - \alpha\tilde{L}_t$. To approximate the left-hand side, note first that since population growth is not affected by the shocks, the log of consumption per worker differs from its balanced-growth-path value only to the extent that the log of total consumption differs from its balanced-growth-path value. Thus $\tilde{c}_t = \tilde{C}_t$. Similarly, $\tilde{\ell}_t = \tilde{L}_t$. The derivative of the left-hand side of (5.45) with respect to $\ln c_t$ is simply 1. The derivative with respect to $\ln \ell_t$ at $\ell_t = \ell^*$ is $\ell^*/(1 - \ell^*)$, where $\ell^*$ is the value of $\ell$ on the balanced growth path. Thus, log-linearizing (5.45) around the balanced growth path yields

$$\tilde{C}_t + \frac{\ell^*}{1 - \ell^*}\tilde{L}_t = (1 - \alpha)\tilde{A}_t + \alpha\tilde{K}_t - \alpha\tilde{L}_t. \quad (5.46)$$

We can now use the fact that $\tilde{C}_t$ and $\tilde{L}_t$ are linear functions of $\tilde{K}_t, \tilde{A}_t$, and $\tilde{G}_t$. Substituting (5.43) and (5.44) into (5.46) yields

$$a_{CK}\tilde{K}_t + a_{CA}\tilde{A}_t + a_{CG}\tilde{G}_t + \left(\frac{\ell^*}{1 - \ell^*} + \alpha\right)(a_{LK}\tilde{K}_t + a_{LA}\tilde{A}_t + a_{LG}\tilde{G}_t)$$

$$= \alpha\tilde{K}_t + (1 - \alpha)\tilde{A}_t. \tag{5.47}$$

Equation (5.47) must hold for all values of $\tilde{K}$, $\tilde{A}$, and $\tilde{G}$. If it does not, then for some combinations of $\tilde{K}$, $\tilde{A}$, and $\tilde{G}$, households are not satisfying their intratemporal first-order condition. Thus the coefficients on $\tilde{K}$ on the two sides of (5.47) must be equal, and similarly for the coefficients on $\tilde{A}$ and on $\tilde{G}$. The $a$'s must therefore satisfy

$$a_{CK} + \left(\frac{\ell^*}{1 - \ell^*} + \alpha\right)a_{LK} = \alpha, \tag{5.48}$$

$$a_{CA} + \left(\frac{\ell^*}{1 - \ell^*} + \alpha\right)a_{LA} = 1 - \alpha, \tag{5.49}$$

$$a_{CG} + \left(\frac{\ell^*}{1 - \ell^*} + \alpha\right)a_{LG} = 0. \tag{5.50}$$

To understand these conditions, consider first (5.50), which relates the responses of consumption and employment to movements in government purchases. Government purchases do not directly enter (5.45); that is, they do not affect the wage for a given level of labor supply. If households increase their labor supply in response to an increase in government purchases, the wage falls and the marginal disutility of working rises. Thus, they will do this only if the marginal utility of consumption is higher—that is, if consumption is lower. Thus if labor supply and consumption respond to changes in government purchases, they must move in opposite directions. Equation (5.50) tells us not only this qualitative result, but also how the movements in labor supply and consumption must be related.

Now consider an increase in $A$ (equation [5.49]). An improvement in technology raises the wage for a given level of labor supply. Thus if neither labor supply nor consumption responds, households can raise their utility by working more and increasing their current consumption. Households must therefore increase either labor supply or consumption (or both); this is what is captured in (5.49).

Finally, the restrictions that (5.45) puts on the responses of labor supply and consumption to movements in capital are similar to the restrictions it puts on their responses to movements in technology. The only difference is that the elasticity of the wage with respect to capital, given $L$, is $\alpha$ rather than $1 - \alpha$. This is what is shown in (5.48).

## The Intertemporal First-Order Condition

The analysis of the first-order condition relating current consumption and next period's consumption, $1/c_t = e^{-\rho}E_t[(1 + r_{t+1})/c_{t+1}]$ (equation [5.23]), is more complicated. The basic idea is the following. Begin by defining $\tilde{Z}_{t+1}$ as the difference between the log of $(1 + r_{t+1})/c_{t+1}$ and the log of its balanced-growth-path value. Then use equation (5.4) for $r_{t+1}$ to express $1 + r_{t+1}$ in terms of $K_{t+1}$, $A_{t+1}$, and $L_{t+1}$. This allows us to approximate $\tilde{Z}_{t+1}$ in terms of $\tilde{K}_{t+1}$, $\tilde{A}_{t+1}$, $\tilde{L}_{t+1}$ and $\tilde{C}_{t+1}$. Now note that since (5.43) and (5.44) hold at each date, they imply

$$\tilde{C}_{t+1} \simeq a_{CK}\tilde{K}_{t+1} + a_{CA}\tilde{A}_{t+1} + a_{CG}\tilde{G}_{t+1}, \tag{5.51}$$

$$\tilde{L}_{t+1} = a_{LK}\tilde{K}_{t+1} + a_{LA}\tilde{A}_{t+1} + a_{LG}\tilde{G}_{t+1}. \tag{5.52}$$

These equations allow us to express $\tilde{Z}_{t+1}$ in terms of $\tilde{K}_{t+1}$, $\tilde{A}_{t+1}$, and $\tilde{G}_{t+1}$.

Since $\tilde{K}_{t+1}$ is an endogenous variable, we need to eliminate it from the expression for $\tilde{Z}_{t+1}$. Specifically, we can log-linearize the equation of motion for capital, (5.2), to write $\tilde{K}_{t+1}$ in terms of $\tilde{K}_t$, $\tilde{A}_t$, $\tilde{G}_t$, $\tilde{L}_t$, and $\tilde{C}_t$, and then use (5.43) and (5.44) to substitute for $\tilde{L}_t$ and $\tilde{C}_t$. This yields an equation of the form

$$\tilde{K}_{t+1} \simeq b_{KK}\tilde{K}_t + b_{KA}\tilde{A}_t + b_{KG}\tilde{G}_t, \tag{5.53}$$

where the $b$'s are complicated functions of the parameters of the model and of the $a$'s.[17]

Substituting (5.53) into the expression for $\tilde{Z}_{t+1}$ in terms of $\tilde{K}_{t+1}$, $\tilde{A}_{t+1}$, and $\tilde{G}_{t+1}$ then gives us an expression for $\tilde{Z}_{t+1}$ in terms of $\tilde{A}_{t+1}$, $\tilde{G}_{t+1}$, $\tilde{K}_t$, $\tilde{A}_t$, and $\tilde{G}_t$. The final step is to use this to find $E_t[\tilde{Z}_{t+1}]$ in terms of $\tilde{K}_t$, $\tilde{A}_t$, and $\tilde{G}_t$, which we can do by using the facts that $E_t[\tilde{A}_{t+1}] = \rho_A\tilde{A}_t$ and $E_t[\tilde{G}_{t+1}] = \rho_G\tilde{G}_t$ (see [5.9] and [5.11]).[18] Substituting this into (5.23) gives us three additional restrictions on the $a$'s; this is enough to determine the $a$'s in terms of the underlying parameters.

Unfortunately, the model is sufficiently complicated that solving for the $a$'s is tedious, and the resulting expressions for the $a$'s in terms of the underlying parameters of the model are complicated. Even if we wrote down

---

[17] See Problem 5.15.

[18] There is one complication here. As emphasized in Section 5.4, (5.23) involves not just the expectations of next-period values, but their entire distribution. That is, what appears in the log-linearized version of (5.23) is not $E_t[\tilde{Z}_{t+1}]$, but $\ln E_t[e^{\tilde{Z}_{t+1}}]$. Campbell (1994) addresses this difficulty by assuming that $\tilde{Z}$ is normally distributed with constant variance; that is, $e^{\tilde{Z}}$ has a *lognormal* distribution. Standard results about this distribution then imply that $\ln E_t[e^{\tilde{Z}_{t+1}}]$ equals $E_t[\tilde{Z}_{t+1}]$ plus a constant. Thus we can express the log of the right-hand side of (5.23) in terms of $E_t[\tilde{Z}_{t+1}]$ and constants. Finally, Campbell notes that given the log-linear structure of the model, if the underlying shocks—the $\varepsilon_A$'s and $\varepsilon_G$'s in (5.9) and (5.11)—are normally distributed with constant variances, his assumption about the distribution of $\tilde{Z}_{t+1}$ is correct.

those expressions, the effects of the parameters of the model on the $a$'s, and hence on the economy's response to shocks, would not be transparent.

Thus, despite the comparative simplicity of the model and our use of approximations, we must still resort to numerical methods to describe the model's properties. What we will do is choose a set of baseline parameter values and discuss their implications for the $a$'s in (5.43)–(5.44) and the $b$'s in (5.53). Once we have determined the values of the $a$'s and $b$'s, equations (5.43), (5.44), and (5.53) specify (approximately) how consumption, employment, and capital respond to shocks to technology and government purchases. The remaining equations of the model can then be used to describe the responses of the model's other variables—output, investment, the wage, and the interest rate. For example, we can substitute equation (5.44) for $\tilde{L}$ into the log-linearized version of the production function to find the model's implications for output:

$$\begin{aligned}
\tilde{Y}_t &= \alpha\tilde{K}_t + (1-\alpha)(\tilde{L}_t + \tilde{A}_t) \\
&= \alpha\tilde{K}_t + (1-\alpha)(a_{\text{LK}}\tilde{K}_t + a_{\text{LA}}\tilde{A}_t + a_{\text{LG}}\tilde{G}_t + \tilde{A}_t) \\
&= [\alpha + (1-\alpha)a_{\text{LK}}]\tilde{K}_t + (1-\alpha)(1 + a_{\text{LA}})\tilde{A}_t + (1-\alpha)a_{\text{LG}}\tilde{G}_t.
\end{aligned} \tag{5.54}$$

# 5.7   Implications

Following Campbell (1994), assume that each period corresponds to a quarter, and take for baseline parameter values $\alpha = \frac{1}{3}$, $g = 0.5\%$, $n = 0.25\%$, $\delta = 2.5\%$, $\rho_A = 0.95$, $\rho_G = 0.95$, and $\overline{G}$, $\rho$, and $b$ such that $(G/Y)^* = 0.2$, $r^* = 1.5\%$, and $\ell^* = \frac{1}{3}$.[19]

## The Effects of Technology Shocks

One can show that these parameter values imply $a_{\text{LA}} \simeq 0.35$, $a_{\text{LK}} \simeq -0.31$, $a_{\text{CA}} \simeq 0.38$, $a_{\text{CK}} \simeq 0.59$, $b_{\text{KA}} \simeq 0.08$, and $b_{\text{KK}} \simeq 0.95$. These values can be used to trace out the effects of a change in technology. Consider, for example, a positive 1 percent technology shock. In the period of the shock, capital (which is inherited from the previous period) is unchanged, labor supply rises by 0.35 percent, and consumption rises by 0.38 percent. Since the production function is $K^{1/3}(AL)^{2/3}$, output increases by 0.90 percent. In the next period, technology is 0.95 percent above normal (since $\rho_A = 0.95$), capital is higher by 0.08 percent (since $b_{\text{KA}} \simeq 0.08$), labor supply is higher by 0.31 percent (0.35 times 0.95, minus 0.31 times 0.08), and consumption is higher by 0.41 percent (0.38 times 0.95, plus 0.59 times 0.08); the

---

[19] See Problem 5.10 for the implications of these parameter values for the balanced growth path.

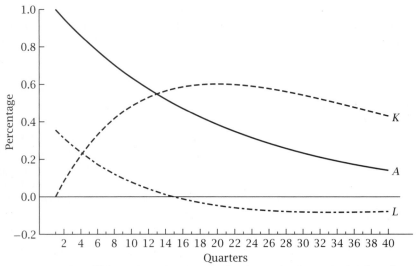

**FIGURE 5.2**   The effects of a 1 percent technology shock on the paths of technology, capital, and labor

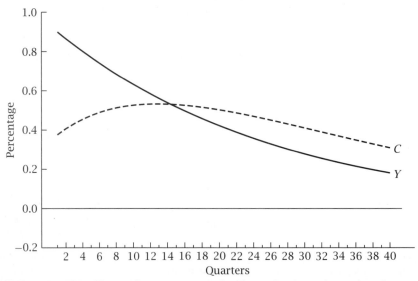

**FIGURE 5.3**   The effects of a 1 percent technology shock on the paths of output and consumption

effects on $A$, $K$, and $L$ imply that output is 0.86 percent above normal. And so on.

Figures 5.2 and 5.3 show the shock's effects on the major quantity variables of the model. By assumption, the effects on the level of technology die away slowly. Capital accumulates gradually and then slowly returns to

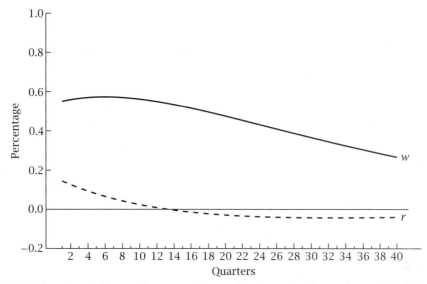

**FIGURE 5.4** **The effects of a 1 percent technology shock on the paths of the wage and the interest rate**

normal; the peak effect is an increase of 0.60 percent after 20 quarters. Labor supply jumps by 0.35 percent in the period of the shock and then declines relatively rapidly, falling below normal after 15 quarters. It reaches a low of −0.09 percent after 33 quarters and then slowly comes back to normal. The net result of the movements in $A$, $K$, and $L$ is that output increases in the period of the shock and then gradually returns to normal. Consumption responds less, and more slowly, than output; thus investment is more volatile than consumption.

Figure 5.4 shows the percentage movement in the wage and the change in percentage points in the interest rate at an annual rate. The wage rises and then returns very slowly to normal. Because the changes in the wage (after the unexpected jump at the time of the shock) are small, wage movements contribute little to the variations in labor supply. The annual interest rate increases by about one-seventh of a percentage point in the period of the shock and then returns to normal fairly quickly. Because the capital stock moves more slowly than labor supply, the interest rate dips below normal after 14 quarters. These movements in the interest rate are the main source of the movements in labor supply.

To understand the movements in the interest rate and consumption, start by considering the case where labor supply is inelastic, and recall that $r = \alpha(AL/K)^{1-\alpha} - \delta$. The immediate effect of the increase in $A$ is to raise $r$. Since the increase in $A$ dies out only slowly, $r$ must remain high unless $K$ increases rapidly. And since depreciation is low, a rapid rise in $K$ would require a large increase in the fraction of output that is invested. But if the saving rate were to rise by so much that $r$ returned immediately to its usual level, this would mean that consumption was expected to grow rapidly even though $r$ equaled its normal value; this would violate households' intertemporal first-order condition, (5.23). Thus instead, households raise the fraction of their income that they save, but not by enough to return $r$ immediately to its usual level. And since the increase in $A$ is persistent, the increase in the saving rate is also persistent. As technology returns to normal, the slow adjustment of the capital stock eventually causes $A/K$ to fall below its initial value, and thus causes $r$ to fall below its usual value. When this occurs, the saving rate falls below its balanced-growth-path level.

When we allow for variations in labor supply, some of the adjustments of the capital stock occur through changes in labor supply rather than the saving rate: households build up the capital stock during the early phase partly by increasing labor supply, and bring it back to normal in the later phase partly by decreasing labor supply.

In general, we can think of the effects of shocks as working through *wealth* and *intertemporal-substitution effects*. A positive technology shock implies that the economy will be more productive for a while. This increase in productivity means that households' lifetime wealth is greater, which acts to increase their consumption and reduce their labor supply. But there are also two reasons for them to shift labor supply from the future to the present and to save more. First, the productivity increases will dissipate over time, so that this is an especially appealing time to produce. Second, the capital stock is low relative to technology, so the marginal product of capital is especially high.

We saw in Section 5.5 that with complete depreciation, the wealth and intertemporal-substitution effects balance, so technology shocks do not affect labor supply and the saving rate. With less than complete depreciation, the intertemporal-substitution effect becomes more important, and so labor supply and the saving rate rise in the short run.

The parameter that the results are most sensitive to is $\rho_A$. When technology shocks are less persistent, the wealth effect of a shock is smaller (because its impact is shorter-lived), and its intertemporal-substitution effect is larger. As a result, $a_{CA}$ is increasing in $\rho_A$, and $a_{LA}$ and $b_{KA}$ are decreasing; $a_{CK}$, $a_{LK}$, and $b_{KK}$ are unaffected. If $\rho_A$ declines from the baseline value of 0.95 to 0.5, for example, $a_{CA}$ falls from 0.38 to 0.11, $a_{LA}$ rises from 0.35 to 0.66, and $b_{KA}$ rises from 0.08 to 0.12. The result is sharper, shorter output fluctuations. In this case, a 1 percent technology shock raises output by 1.11 percent in the period of the shock, but only by 0.30 percent two periods later. If $\rho_A = 1$, then $a_{CA}$ rises to 0.63, $a_{LA}$ falls to 0.05, and $b_{KA}$ falls to 0.04. The result is that employment fluctuations are small and output fluctuations are much more gradual. For example, a 1 percent shock causes output to increase by 0.70 percent immediately (only slightly larger than the direct effect of 0.67 percent), and then to rise very gradually to 1 percent above its initial level.[20]

In addition, suppose we generalize the way that leisure enters the instantaneous utility function, (5.7), to allow the intertemporal elasticity of substitution in labor supply to take on values other than 1.[21] With this change, this elasticity also has important effects on the economy's response to shocks: the larger the elasticity, the more responsive labor supply is to technology and capital. If the elasticity rises from 1 to 2, for example, $a_{LA}$ increases from 0.35 to 0.48 and $a_{LK}$ increases from $-0.31$ to $-0.41$ (in addition, $a_{CA}$, $a_{CK}$, $b_{KA}$, and $b_{KK}$ all change moderately). As a result, fluctuations are larger when the intertemporal elasticity of substitution is higher.[22]

## The Effects of Changes in Government Purchases

Our baseline parameter values imply $a_{CG} \simeq -0.13$, $a_{LG} \simeq 0.15$, and $b_{KG} \simeq -0.004$; $a_{CK}$, $a_{LK}$, and $b_{KK}$ are as before. Intuitively, an increase in government purchases causes consumption to fall and labor supply to rise because of its negative wealth effects. And because the rise in government purchases is not permanent, agents also respond by decreasing their capital holdings.

Since the elasticity of output with respect to $L$ is $\frac{2}{3}$, the value of $a_{LG}$ of 0.15 means that output rises by about 0.1 percent in response to a 1 percent government-purchases shock. Since output on the balanced growth path is 5 times government purchases, this means that $Y$ rises by about one-half as much as $G$. And since one can show that consumption on the balanced growth path is about $2\frac{1}{2}$ times government purchases, the value of $a_{CG}$ of $-0.13$ means that $C$ falls by about one-third as much as $G$ increases. The remaining one-sixth of the adjustment takes the form of lower investment.

Figures 5.5–5.7 trace out the effects of a positive 1 percent government-purchases shock. The capital stock is only slightly affected; the maximum impact is a decline of 0.03 percent after 20 quarters. Employment increases and then gradually returns to normal; in contrast to what occurs with technology shocks, it never falls below its normal level. Because technology is

---

[20] One might think that with a permanent shock, the intertemporal-substitution effect would be absent, and so labor supply would not rise. Recall, however, that the capital stock also creates an intertemporal-substitution effect. When technology improves, the marginal product of capital rises, creating an incentive to increase labor supply to increase investment. Equivalently, the real interest rate rises temporarily, increasing labor supply.

[21] See Campbell (1994) and Problem 5.4.

[22] In addition, Kimball (1991) shows that if we relax the assumption of a Cobb–Douglas production function, the elasticity of substitution between capital and labor has important effects on the economy's response to shocks.

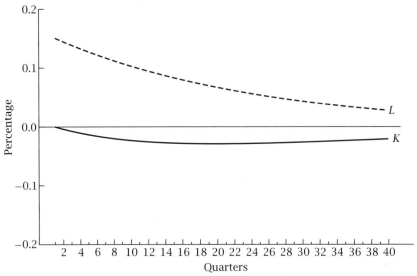

**FIGURE 5.5**   **The effects of a 1 percent government-purchases shock on the paths of capital and labor**

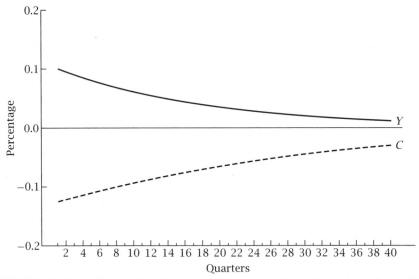

**FIGURE 5.6**   **The effects of a 1 percent government-purchases shock on the paths of output and consumption**

unchanged and the capital stock moves little, the movements in output are small and track the changes in employment fairly closely. Consumption declines at the time of the shock and then gradually returns to normal. The increase in employment and the fall in the capital stock cause the wage to fall and the interest rate to rise. The anticipated wage movements after the

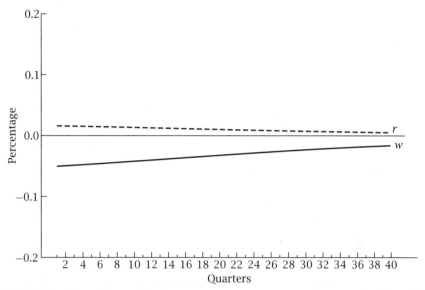

**FIGURE 5.7   The effects of a 1 percent government-purchases shock on the paths of the wage and the interest rate**

period of the shock are small and positive. Thus the increases in labor supply stem from the intertemporal-substitution effect due to the increase in the interest rate, and from the wealth effect due to the government's use of more output.

As with technology, the persistence of movements in government purchases has important effects on how the economy responds to shocks. If $\rho_G$ falls to 0.5, for example, $a_{CG}$ falls from $-0.13$ to $-0.03$, $a_{LG}$ falls from 0.15 to 0.03, and $b_{KG}$ increases from $-0.004$ to $-0.020$: because movements in purchases are much shorter-lived, much more of the response takes the form of reductions in capital holdings. These values imply that output rises by about one-tenth of the increase in government purchases, that consumption falls by about one-tenth of the increase, and that investment falls by about four-fifths of the increase. In response to a 1 percent shock, for example, output increases by just 0.02 percent in the period of the shock and then falls below normal, with a low of $-0.004$ percent after 7 quarters.

# 5.8   Empirical Application: Calibrating a Real-Business-Cycle Model

How should we judge how well a real-business-cycle model fits the data? One common approach is *calibration* (Kydland and Prescott, 1982). The basic idea of calibration is to choose parameter values on the basis of microeconomic evidence and then to compare the model's predictions concerning the variances and covariances of various series with those in the data.

Calibration has two potential advantages over estimating models econometrically. First, because parameter values are selected on the basis of microeconomic evidence, a large body of information beyond that usually employed can be brought to bear, and the models can therefore be held to a higher standard. Second, the economic importance of a statistical rejection, or lack of rejection, of a model is often hard to interpret. A model that fits the data well along every dimension except one unimportant one may be overwhelmingly rejected statistically. Or a model may fail to be rejected simply because the data are consistent with a wide range of possibilities.

To see how calibration works in practice, consider the baseline real-business-cycle model of Prescott (1986) and Hansen (1985). This model differs from the model we have been considering in two ways. First, government is absent. Second, the trend component of technology is not assumed to follow a simple linear path; instead, a smooth but nonlinear trend is removed from the data before the model's predictions and actual fluctuations are compared.[23]

We consider the parameter values proposed by Hansen and Wright (1992), which are similar to those we considered in the previous section as well as those considered by Hansen and Wright. Based on data on factor shares, the capital-output ratio, and the investment-output ratio, Hansen and Wright set $\alpha = 0.36$, $\delta = 2.5\%$ per quarter, and $\rho = 1\%$ per quarter. Based on the average division of discretionary time between work and nonwork activities, they set $b$ to 2. They choose the parameters of the process for technology on the basis of the empirical behavior of the Solow residual, $R_t \equiv \Delta \ln Y_t - [\alpha \Delta \ln K_t + (1 - \alpha)\Delta \ln L_t]$. As described in Chapter 1, the Solow residual is a measure of all influences on output growth other than the contributions of capital and labor through their private marginal products. Under the assumptions of real-business-cycle theory, the only such other influence on output is technology, and so the Solow residual is a measure of technological change. Based on the behavior of the Solow residual, Hansen and Wright set $\rho_A = 0.95$ and the standard deviation of the quarterly $\varepsilon_A$'s to 1.1 percent.[24]

Table 5.4 shows the model's implications for some key features of fluctuations. The figures in the first column are from actual U.S. data; those in

---

[23] The detrending procedure that is used is known as the *Hodrick–Prescott filter* (Hodrick and Prescott, 1997).

[24] In addition, Prescott argues that, under the assumption that technology multiplies an expression of form $F(K,L)$, the absence of a strong trend in capital's share suggests that $F(\bullet)$ is approximately Cobb–Douglas. Similarly, he argues on the basis of the lack of a trend in leisure per person and of studies of substitution between consumption in different periods that (5.7) provides a good approximation to the instantaneous utility function. Thus the choices of functional forms are not arbitrary.

TABLE 5.4   A calibrated real-business-cycle model
versus actual data

|  | U.S. data | Baseline real-business-cycle model |
|---|---|---|
| $\sigma_Y$ | 1.92 | 1.30 |
| $\sigma_C/\sigma_Y$ | 0.45 | 0.31 |
| $\sigma_I/\sigma_Y$ | 2.78 | 3.15 |
| $\sigma_L/\sigma_Y$ | 0.96 | 0.49 |
| Corr($L,Y/L$) | −0.14 | 0.93 |

*Source:* Hansen and Wright (1992).

the second column are from the model. All of the numbers are based on the deviation-from-trend components of the variables, with the trends found using the nonlinear procedure employed by Prescott and Hansen.

The first line of the table reports the standard deviation of output. The model produces output fluctuations that are only moderately smaller than those observed in practice. This finding is the basis for Prescott's (1986) famous conclusion that aggregate fluctuations are not just consistent with a competitive, neoclassical model, but are predicted by such a model. The second and third lines of the table show that both in the United States and in the model, consumption is considerably less volatile than output, and investment is considerably more volatile.

The final two lines of the table show that the baseline model is less successful in its predictions about the contributions of variations in labor input and in output per unit of labor input to aggregate fluctuations. In the U.S. economy, labor input is nearly as volatile as output; in the model it is much less so. And in the United States, labor input and productivity are essentially uncorrelated; in the model they move together closely.

Thus a simple calibration exercise can be used to identify a model's major successes and failures. In doing so, it suggests ways in which the model might be modified to improve its fit with the data. For example, additional sources of shocks would be likely to increase output fluctuations and to reduce the correlation between movements in labor input and in productivity. Indeed, Hansen and Wright show that, for their suggested parameter values, adding government-purchases shocks along the lines of the model of this chapter lowers the correlation of $L$ and $Y/L$ from 0.93 to 0.49; the change has little effect on the magnitude of output fluctuations, however.

Of course, calibration has disadvantages as well. As we will see over the next two chapters, models of business cycles have moved away from the simple, highly Walrasian models of this chapter. As a result, calibration exercises no longer rely on the original idea of using microeconomic evidence to tie down essentially all the relevant parameters and functional forms: given the models' wide variety of features, they have some flexibility in matching the data. As a result, we do not know how informative it is when they match important moments of the data relatively well. Nor, because the models are generally not tested against alternatives, do we know whether there are other, perhaps completely different, models that can match the moments just as well.

Further, given the state of economic knowledge, it is not clear that matching the major moments of the data should be viewed as a desirable feature of a model.[25] Even the most complicated models of fluctuations are grossly simplified descriptions of reality. It would be remarkable if none of the simplifications had quantitatively important effects on the models' implications. But given this, it is hard to determine how informative the fact that a model does or does not match aggregate data is about its overall usefulness.

It would be a mistake to think that the only alternative to calibration is formal estimation of fully specified models. Often, the alternative is to focus more narrowly. Researchers frequently assess models by considering the microeconomic evidence about the reasonableness of the models' central building blocks or by examining the models' consistency with a handful of "stylized facts" that the modelers view as crucial.

Unfortunately, there is little evidence concerning the relative merits of different approaches to evaluating macroeconomic models. Researchers use various mixes and types of calibration exercises, formal estimation, examination of the plausibility of the ingredients, and consideration of consistency with specific facts. At this point, choices among these approaches seem to be based more on researchers' "tastes" than on a body of knowledge about the strengths and weaknesses of the approaches. Trying to move beyond this situation by developing evidence about the merits of different approaches is an important and largely uncharted area of research.

# 5.9   Empirical Application: Money and Output

One dimension on which the real-business-cycle view of macroeconomic fluctuations departs strikingly from traditional views concerns the effects of monetary disturbances. A monetary shock, such as a change in the money supply, does not change the economy's technology, agents' preferences, or the government's purchases of goods and services. As a result, in models with completely flexible prices, including the RBC models of this chapter, its only effect is to change nominal prices; all real quantities and relative prices are unaffected. In traditional views of fluctuations, in contrast, monetary changes have substantial real effects, and they are often viewed as important sources of output movements. Moreover, as we will see in the next two chapters, the same factors that can cause monetary disturbances

---

[25] The argument that follows is due to Matthew Shapiro.

to have significant real effects have important consequences for the effects of other disturbances.

This discussion suggests that a critical test of pure real-business-cycle models is whether monetary disturbances have substantial real effects. Partly for this reason, an enormous amount of research has been devoted to trying to determine the effects of monetary changes.

## The St. Louis Equation

Since our goal is to test whether monetary changes have real effects, a seemingly obvious place to start is to just regress output on money. Such regressions have a long history. One of the earliest and most straightforward was carried out by Leonall Andersen and Jerry Jordan of the Federal Reserve Bank of St. Louis (Andersen and Jordan, 1968). For that reason, the regression of output on money is known as the *St. Louis equation.*

Here we consider an example of the St. Louis equation. The left-hand-side variable is the change in the log of real GDP. The main right-hand-side variable is the change in the log of the money stock, as measured by $M2$; since any effect of money on output may occur with a lag, the contemporaneous and four lagged values are included. The regression also includes a constant and a time trend (to account for trends in output and money growth). The data are quarterly, and the sample period is 1960Q2–2008Q4.

The results are

$$\Delta \ln Y_t = \underset{(0.0024)}{0.0046} - \underset{(0.10)}{0.09} \, \Delta \ln m_t + \underset{(0.12)}{0.18} \, \Delta \ln m_{t-1} + \underset{(0.12)}{0.16} \, \Delta \ln m_{t-2}$$

$$+ \underset{(0.12)}{0.02} \, \Delta \ln m_{t-3} - \underset{(0.10)}{0.02} \, \Delta \ln m_{t-4} - \underset{(0.000011)}{0.000010} \, t, \qquad (5.55)$$

$$\bar{R}^2 = 0.056, \qquad \text{D.W.} = 1.51, \qquad \text{s.e.e.} = 0.008,$$

where the numbers in parentheses are standard errors. The sum of the coefficients on the current and four lagged values of the money-growth variable is 0.25, with a standard error of 0.10. Thus the estimates suggest that a 1 percent increase in the money stock is associated with an increase of $\frac{1}{4}$ percent in output over the next year, and the null hypothesis of no association is rejected at high levels of significance.

Does this regression, then, provide powerful evidence in support of monetary over real theories of fluctuations? The answer is no. There are several basic problems with a regression like this one. First, causation may run from output to money rather than from money to output. A simple story, formalized by King and Plosser (1984), is that when firms plan to increase production, they may increase their money holdings because they will need to purchase more intermediate inputs. Similarly, households may increase their money holdings when they plan to increase their purchases. Aggregate measures of the money stock, such as $M2$, are not set directly by the Federal Reserve but are determined by the interaction of the supply of high-powered money with the behavior of the banking system and the public. Thus shifts in money demand stemming from changes in firms' and households' production plans can lead to changes in the money stock. As a result, we may see changes in the money stock in advance of output movements even if the changes in money are not causing the output movements.

The second major problem with the St. Louis equation involves the determinants of monetary policy. Suppose the Federal Reserve adjusts the money stock to try to offset other factors that influence aggregate output. Then if monetary changes have real effects and the Federal Reserve's efforts to stabilize the economy are successful, we will observe fluctuations in money without movements in output (Kareken and Solow, 1963). Thus, just as we cannot conclude from the positive correlation between money and output that money causes output, if we fail to observe such a correlation we cannot conclude that money does not cause output.

A more prosaic difficulty with the St. Louis equation is that there have been a series of large shifts in the demand for money over this period. At least some of the shifts are probably due to financial innovation and deregulation, but their causes are not entirely understood. Models with sticky prices predict that if the Federal Reserve does not adjust the money supply fully in response to these disturbances, there will be a negative relationship between money and output. A positive money demand shock, for example, will increase the money stock but increase the interest rate and reduce output. And even if the Federal Reserve accommodates the shifts, the fact that they are so large may cause a few observations to have a disproportionate effect on the results.

As a result of the money demand shifts, the estimated relationship between money and output is sensitive to such matters as the sample period and the measure of money. For example, if equation (5.55) is estimated using $M1$ in place of $M2$, or if it is estimated over a somewhat different sample period, the results change considerably.

Because of these difficulties, regressions like (5.55) are of little value in determining the effects of monetary changes on output.

## Other Types of Evidence

A very different approach to testing whether monetary shocks have real effects stems from the work of Friedman and Schwartz (1963). Friedman and Schwartz undertake a careful historical analysis of the sources of movements in the money stock in the United States from the end of the Civil War to 1960. On the basis of this analysis, they argue that many of the movements in money, especially the largest ones, were mainly the result of developments in the monetary sector of the economy rather than the response of the money stock to real developments. Friedman and Schwartz demonstrate that these monetary movements were followed by output movements in the same direction. Thus, Friedman and Schwartz conclude, unless the money-output relationship in these episodes is an extraordinary fluke, it must reflect causation running from money to output.[26]

C. Romer and D. Romer (1989) provide additional evidence along the same lines. They search the records of the Federal Reserve for the postwar period for evidence of policy shifts designed to lower inflation that were not motivated by developments on the real side of the economy. They identify six such shifts, and find that all of them were followed by recessions. For example, in October 1979, shortly after Paul Volcker became chairman of the Federal Reserve Board, the Federal Reserve tightened monetary policy dramatically. The change appears to have been motivated by a desire to reduce inflation, and not by the presence of other forces that would have caused output to decline in any event. Yet it was followed by one of the largest recessions in postwar U.S. history.[27]

What Friedman and Schwartz and Romer and Romer are doing is searching for natural experiments to determine the effects of monetary shocks analogous to the natural experiments described in Section 4.4 for determining the effects of social infrastructure. For example, Friedman and Schwartz argue that the death in 1928 of Benjamin Strong, the president of the Federal Reserve Bank of New York, brought about a large monetary change that was not caused by the behavior of output. Strong's death, they argue, left a power vacuum in the Federal Reserve System and therefore caused monetary policy to be conducted very differently over the next several years than it otherwise would have been.[28]

Natural experiments such as Strong's death are unlikely to be as ideal as genuine randomized experiments for determining the effects of monetary

---

[26] See especially Chapter 13 of their book—something that every macroeconomist should read.

[27] It is possible that similar studies of open economies could provide stronger evidence concerning the importance of monetary forces. For example, shifts in monetary policy to combat high rates of inflation in small, highly open economies appear to be associated with large changes in real exchange rates, real interest rates, and real output. What we observe is more complicated than anti-inflationary monetary policy being consistently followed by low output, however. In particular, when the policy attempts to reduce inflation by targeting the exchange rate, there is typically an output boom in the short run. Why this occurs is not known. Likewise, the more general question of whether the evidence from inflation stabilizations in open economies provides strong evidence of monetary nonneutrality is unresolved. Analyzing stabilizations is complicated by the fact that the policy shifts are often accompanied by fiscal reforms and by large changes in uncertainty. See, for example, Sargent (1982), Rebelo and Végh (1995), and Calvo and Végh (1999).

[28] Velde (2008) identifies and analyzes a fascinating natural monetary experiment in eighteenth-century France. The results provide strong evidence of incomplete price adjustment and real effects of monetary changes even then.

changes. There is room for disagreement concerning whether any episodes are sufficiently clear-cut to be viewed as independent monetary disturbances, and if so, what set of episodes should be considered. But since randomized experiments are not possible, the evidence provided by natural experiments may be the best we can obtain.

A related approach is to use the evidence provided by specific monetary interventions to investigate the impact of monetary changes on relative prices. For example, as described in Section 11.2, Cook and Hahn (1989) confirm formally the common observation that Federal Reserve open-market operations are associated with changes in nominal interest rates (see also Kuttner, 2001). Given the discrete nature of the open-market operations and the specifics of how their timing is determined, it is not plausible that they occur endogenously at times when interest rates would have moved in any event. And the fact that monetary expansions lower nominal rates strongly suggests that the changes in nominal rates represent changes in real rates as well. For example, monetary expansions lower nominal interest rates for terms as short as a day; it seems unlikely that they reduce expected inflation over such horizons. Since changes in real rates affect real behavior even in Walrasian models, this evidence strongly suggests that monetary changes have real effects.

Similarly, the nominal exchange-rate regime appears to affect the behavior of real exchange rates. Under a fixed exchange rate, the central bank adjusts the money supply to keep the nominal exchange rate constant; under a floating exchange rate, it does not. There is strong evidence that not just nominal but also real exchange rates are much less volatile under fixed than floating exchange rates. In addition, when a central bank switches from pegging the nominal exchange rate against one currency to pegging it against another, the volatility of the two associated real exchange rates seems to change sharply as well. (See, for example, Genberg, 1978; Stockman, 1983; Mussa, 1986; and Baxter and Stockman, 1989.) Since shifts between exchange-rate regimes are usually discrete, explaining this behavior of real exchange rates without appealing to real effects of monetary forces appears to require positing sudden large changes in the real shocks affecting economies. And again, all classes of theories predict that the behavior of real exchange rates has real effects.

The most significant limitation of this evidence is that the importance of these apparent effects of monetary changes on real interest rates and real exchange rates for quantities has not been determined. Baxter and Stockman (1989), for example, do not find any clear difference in the behavior of economic aggregates under floating and fixed exchange rates. Since real-business-cycle theories attribute fairly large changes in quantities to relatively modest movements in relative prices, however, a finding that the price changes were not important would be puzzling from the perspective of many theories, not just ones predicting real effects of monetary changes.

# More Sophisticated Statistical Evidence

The evidence involving natural experiments and monetary policy's impact on relative prices has caused the proposition that monetary disturbances have real effects to gain broad support among macroeconomists. But these kinds of evidence are of little use in determining the details of policy's effects. For example, because Friedman and Schwartz and Romer and Romer identify only a few episodes, their evidence cannot be used to obtain precise quantitative estimates of policy's impact on output or to shed much light on the exact timing of different variables' responses to monetary changes.

The desire to obtain a more detailed picture of monetary policy's effects has motivated a large amount of work reexamining the statistical relationship between monetary policy and the economy. Most of the work has been done in the context of *vector autoregressions*, or VARs. In its simplest form, a VAR is a system of equations where each variable in the system is regressed on a set of its own lagged values and lagged values of each of the other variables (for example, Sims, 1980; Hamilton, 1994, Chapter 11, provides a general introduction to VARs). Early VARs put little or no structure on the system. As a result, attempts to make inferences from them about the effects of monetary policy suffered from the same problems of omitted variables, reverse causation, and money-demand shifts that doom the St. Louis equation (Cooley and LeRoy, 1985).

Modern VARs improve on the early attempts in two ways. First, since the Federal Reserve has generally let the money stock fluctuate in response to money-demand shifts, the modern VARs choose measures of monetary policy other than the money stock. The most common choice is the Federal funds rate (Bernanke and Blinder, 1992). Second, and more important, they recognize that drawing inferences about the economy from the data requires a model. They therefore make assumptions about the conduct of policy and its effects that allow the estimates of the VAR parameters to be mapped into estimates of policy's impact on macroeconomic variables. These *structural VARs* were pioneered by Sims (1986), Bernanke (1986), and Blanchard and Watson (1986). Important contributions in the context of monetary policy include Sims (1992); Galí (1992); Christiano, Eichenbaum, and Evans (1996); Bernanke and Mihov (1998); Cochrane (1998); Barth and Ramey (2001); and Hanson (2004). The results of these studies are broadly consistent with the evidence discussed above. More importantly, these studies provide a variety of evidence about lags in policy's effects, its impact on financial markets, and other issues.

Unfortunately, it is not clear that such VARs have solved the difficulties with simpler money-output regressions (Rudebusch, 1998). In particular, these papers have not found a compelling way of addressing the problem that the Federal Reserve may be adjusting policy in response to information it has about future economic developments that the VARs do not control for. Consider, for example, the Federal Reserve's interest-rate cuts in 2007.

Since output had been growing rapidly for several years and unemployment was low (which is not a situation in which the Federal Reserve normally cuts interest rates), the typical VAR identifies the cuts as expansionary monetary-policy shocks, and as therefore appropriate to use to investigate policy's effects. In fact, however, the Federal Reserve made the cuts because it believed the declines in housing prices and disruptions to financial markets would lead to slower growth of aggregate demand; it lowered interest rates only to try to offset these contractionary forces. Thus looking at the behavior of the macroeconomy after the interest-rate cuts is not a good way of determining the impact of monetary policy. As this example shows, monetary policymaking is sufficiently complicated that it is extremely difficult to control for the full set of factors that influence policy and that may also directly influence the economy.

This discussion suggests that obtaining reliable estimates of the size and timing of the effects of monetary changes will be very difficult: we will need both the careful attention to the sources of changes in monetary policy or of other monetary disturbances that characterizes the natural-experiments literature, and the careful attention to statistical issues and estimation that characterizes the VAR literature. C. Romer and D. Romer (2004) provide one attempt in this direction. They find larger and faster impacts of monetary policy on output and prices than conventional VARs, which is consistent with the discussion above about likely biases in VARs. However, work trying to marry the natural-experiment and VAR approaches is still in its early stages.

# 5.10   Assessing the Baseline Real-Business-Cycle Model

## Difficulties

As described in Section 5.2, models like those we have been analyzing are the simplest and most natural extensions of the Ramsey model to include fluctuations. As a result, they are the natural baseline models of fluctuations. It would therefore be gratifying—and would simplify macroeconomics greatly—if they captured the key features of observed fluctuations. Unfortunately, however, the evidence is overwhelming that they do not.

We met one major problem in the previous section: there is strong evidence that monetary shocks have important real effects. This finding means more than just that baseline real-business-cycle models omit one source of output movements. As described in the next two chapters, the leading candidate explanations of real effects of monetary changes rest on incomplete adjustment of nominal prices or wages. We will see that incomplete nominal adjustment implies a new channel through which other disturbances, such as changes in government purchases, have real effects. We will also see that incomplete nominal adjustment is most likely to arise when labor, credit, and goods markets depart significantly from the competitive assumptions of pure real-business-cycle theory. Thus the existence of substantial monetary nonneutrality raises the possibility that there are significant problems with many of the central features of the basic real-business-cycle model.

A second difficulty concerns the technology shocks. The model posits technology shocks with a standard deviation of about 1 percent each quarter. It seems likely that such large technological innovations would often be readily apparent. Yet it is usually difficult to identify specific innovations associated with the large quarter-to-quarter swings in the Solow residual.

More importantly, there is significant evidence that short-run variations in the Solow residual reflect more than changes in the pace of technological innovation. For example, Bernanke and Parkinson (1991) find that the Solow residual moves just as much with output in the Great Depression as it does in the postwar period, even though the Depression was almost surely not caused by technological regress. Mankiw (1989) shows that the Solow residual behaves similarly in the World War II boom—for which technology shocks again appear an unlikely explanation—as it does during other periods. Hall (1988a) demonstrates that movements in the Solow residual are correlated with the political party of the President, changes in military purchases, and oil price movements; yet none of these variables seem likely to affect technology significantly in the short run.[29]

These findings suggest that variations in the Solow residual may be a poor measure of technology shocks. There are several reasons that a rise in output stemming from a source other than a positive technology shock can cause the measured Solow residual to rise. The leading possibilities are increasing returns, increases in the intensity of capital and labor utilization, and the reallocation of inputs toward more productive firms. The evidence suggests that the variation in utilization is important and provides less support for increasing returns. Less work has been done on reallocation.[30]

Technology shocks are central to the basic real-business-cycle model. Thus if true technology shocks are considerably smaller than the variation in the Solow residual suggests, the model's ability to account for fluctuations is much smaller than the calibration exercise of Section 5.8 implies.

A third problem with the model concerns the effects of properly identified technology shocks. A body of recent work attempts to estimate series of true technological disturbances, for example by purging the simple Solow

---

[29] As Hall explains, oil price movements should not affect productivity once oil's role in production is accounted for.

[30] Some important papers in this area are Basu (1995, 1996); Burnside, Eichenbaum, and Rebelo (1995); Caballero and Lyons (1992) and the critique by Basu and Fernald (1995); Basu and Fernald (1997); and Bils and Klenow (1998).

residual of confounding influences due to such factors as variable utilization. The papers then estimate the macroeconomic effects of those disturbances. The general finding is that following a positive technology shock, labor input falls rather than rises (see Shea, 1998; Galí and Rabanal, 2004; Francis and Ramey, 2005; Basu, Fernald, and Kimball, 2006; and Fernald, 2007). Thus in practice, the key source of fluctuations in baseline real-business-cycle models appears to cause labor and output to move in opposite directions. Moreover, this is exactly what one would expect in a sticky-price model where output is determined by demand in the short run.

A fourth difficulty concerns the microeconomic foundations of the model. As noted above, the evidence concerning the effects of monetary disturbances is suggestive of important non-Walrasian features of the economy. More importantly, there is strong direct evidence from the markets for goods, labor, and credit that those markets depart from the assumptions underlying the models of this chapter in ways that are potentially very relevant to aggregate fluctuations. To give an obvious example, the events since August 2007 appear to provide overwhelming evidence that credit markets are not Walrasian, and that this can have major consequences for the macroeconomy. To give a more prosaic example, we will see in Section 7.6 that prices of goods are not perfectly flexible, but often remain fixed for extended periods. A third example is provided by studies of the microeconomics of labor supply. These studies generally find that the intertemporal elasticity of substitution is low, casting doubt on a critical mechanism behind changes in employment in real-business-cycle models. They also often find that the prediction of the model that changes in labor demand affect the quantity of labor supplied only through their impact on wages is rejected by the data, suggesting that there is more to employment fluctuations than the forces included in the model (see, for example, MaCurdy, 1981, Altonji, 1986, and Ham and Reilly, 2002). Although we would not want or expect the microeconomics of a successful macroeconomic model to be completely realistic, such systematic departures are worrisome for real-business-cycle models.

Finally, Cogley and Nason (1995) and Rotemberg and Woodford (1996) show that the dynamics of the basic real-business-cycle model do not look at all like what one would think of as a business cycle. Cogley and Nason show that the model has no significant propagation mechanisms: the dynamics of output follow the dynamics of the shocks quite closely. That is, the model produces realistic output dynamics only to the extent that it assumes them in the driving processes. Rotemberg and Woodford, in contrast, show that there are important predictable movements in output, consumption, and hours in actual economies but not in the baseline real-business-cycle model. In the data, for example, times when hours are unusually low or the ratio of consumption to income is unusually high are typically followed by above-normal output growth. Rotemberg and Woodford demonstrate that predictable output movements in the basic real-business-cycle model are much smaller than what we observe in the data, and have very different characteristics.

## "Real" Extensions

Because of these difficulties, there is broad agreement that the models of this chapter do not provide a remotely accurate account of fluctuations. Moreover, as we have discussed, there are important features of fluctuations that appear impossible to understand without incorporating some type of nominal rigidity or imperfection. Nonetheless, much work on fluctuations is done in purely real models. One reason is to create building blocks for more complete models. As we will see, incorporating nominal rigidity into dynamic models of fluctuations is difficult. As a result, in considering some new feature, it is often easier to start with models that lack nominal rigidity. Another reason is that there may be features of fluctuations that can be understood without appeal to nominal rigidity. Thus, although a complete model will presumably incorporate it, we may be able to gain insights in models without it. Here we briefly discuss some important extensions on the real side of business-cycle research.

One extension of the models of this chapter that has attracted considerable attention is the addition of *indivisible labor*. Changes in labor input come not just from smooth changes in hours, but also from movements into and out of employment. To investigate the implications of this fact, Rogerson (1988) and Hansen (1985) consider the extreme case where $\ell$ for each individual has only two possible values, 0 (which corresponds to not being employed) and some positive value, $\ell_0$ (which corresponds to being employed). Rogerson and Hansen justify this assumption by arguing that there are fixed costs of working.

This change in the model greatly increases the responsiveness of labor input to shocks; this in turn increases both the size of output fluctuations and the share of changes in labor input in those fluctuations. From the results of the calibration exercise described in Section 5.8, we know that these changes improve the fit of the model.

To see why assuming all-or-nothing employment increases fluctuations in labor input, assume that once the number of workers employed is determined, individuals are divided between employment and unemployment randomly. The number of workers employed in period $t$, denoted by $E_t$, must satisfy $E_t \ell_0 = L_t$; thus the probability that any given individual is employed in period $t$ is $(L_t/\ell_0)/N_t$. Each individual's expected utility from leisure in period $t$ is therefore

$$\frac{L_t/\ell_0}{N_t} b \ln(1 - \ell_0) + \frac{N_t - (L_t/\ell_0)}{N_t} b \ln 1. \tag{5.56}$$

This expression is linear in $L_t$: individuals are not averse to employment fluctuations. In contrast, when all individuals work the same amount, utility from leisure in period $t$ is $b \ln [1 - (L_t/N_t)]$. This expression has a negative second derivative with respect to $L_t$: there is increasing marginal disutility of working. As a result, $L_t$ varies less in response to a given amount of variation in wages in the conventional version of the model than in the indivisible-labor version. Hansen and Wright (1992) report that introducing indivisible labor into the Prescott model discussed in Section 5.8 raises the standard deviation of output from 1.30 to 1.73 percent (versus 1.92 percent in the data), and the ratio of the standard deviation of total hours to the standard deviation of output from 0.49 to 0.76 (versus 0.96 in the data).[31]

A second major extension is to include distortionary taxes (see Greenwood and Huffman, 1991; Baxter and King, 1993; Campbell, 1994; Braun, 1994; and McGrattan, 1994). A particularly appealing case is proportional output taxation, so $T_t = \tau_t Y_t$, where $\tau_t$ is the tax rate in period $t$. Output taxation corresponds to equal tax rates on capital and labor, which is a reasonable first approximation for many countries. With output taxation, a change in $1 - \tau$ is, from the point of view of private agents, just like a change in technology, $A^{1-\alpha}$: it changes the amount of output they obtain from a given amount of capital and labor. Thus for a given process for $1 - \tau$, after-tax output behaves just as total output does in a model without taxation in which $A^{1-\alpha}$ follows that same process. This makes the analysis of distortionary taxation straightforward (Campbell, 1994).

Since tax revenues are used to finance government purchases, it is natural to analyze the effects of distortionary taxation and government purchases together. Doing this can change our earlier analysis of the effects of government purchases significantly. Most importantly, predictable changes in marginal tax rates create additional intertemporal-substitution effects that can be quantitatively important. For example, in response to a temporary increase in government purchases financed by a temporary increase in distortionary taxation, the tax-induced incentives for intertemporal substitution typically outweigh the other forces affecting output, so that aggregate output falls rather than rises (Baxter and King, 1993).

Another important extension of real models of fluctuations is the inclusion of multiple sectors and sector-specific shocks. Long and Plosser (1983) develop a multisector model similar to the model of Section 5.5 and investigate its implications for the transmission of shocks among sectors. Lilien (1982) proposes a distinct mechanism through which sectoral technology or relative-demand shocks can cause employment fluctuations. The basic idea is that if the reallocation of labor across sectors is time-consuming, employment falls more rapidly in the sectors suffering negative shocks than it rises in the sectors facing favorable shocks. As a result, sector-specific

---

[31] Because the instantaneous utility function, (5.7), is separable between consumption and leisure, expected utility is maximized when employed and unemployed workers have the same consumption. Thus the indivisible-labor model implies that the unemployed are better off than the employed. See Problem 10.6 and Rogerson and Wright (1988).

shocks cause temporary increases in unemployment. Lilien finds that a simple measure of the size of sector-specific disturbances appears to account for a large fraction of the variation in aggregate employment. Subsequent research, however, shows that Lilien's original measure is flawed and that his results are almost surely too strong. This work has not reached any firm conclusions concerning the contribution of sectoral shocks to fluctuations or to average unemployment, however.[32]

These are only a few of a large number of extensions of real-business-cycle models. Since there is nothing inherent in real-business-cycle modeling that requires that the models be Walrasian, many of the extensions incorporate non-Walrasian features.[33]

# Incorporating Nominal Rigidity into Models of Business Cycles

As we have stressed, finding some channel through which nominal disturbances have real effects appears essential to understanding some central features of business cycles. The main focus of the next two chapters is therefore on incorporating nominal rigidity into business-cycle modeling. Chapter 6 steps back from the complexities of this chapter and considers nominal rigidity in isolation. Chapter 7 begins the process of putting things back together by considering increasingly rich dynamic models of fluctuations with nominal rigidity.

One drawback of this organization is that it may give a false sense of disagreement about research on business cycles. It is wrong to think of macroeconomics as divided into two camps, one favoring rich Walrasian models along the lines of the real extensions of the models of this chapter, the other favoring relatively simple models with nominal rigidity like many

---

[32] See, for example, Abraham and Katz (1986); Murphy and Topel (1987a); Davis and Haltiwanger (1999); and Phelan and Trejos (2000).

[33] Examples of Walrasian features that have been incorporated into the models include lags in the investment process, or *time-to-build* (Kydland and Prescott, 1982); non-time-separable utility (so that instantaneous utility at $t$ does not depend just on $c_t$ and $\ell_t$) (Kydland and Prescott, 1982); home production (Benhabib, Rogerson, and Wright, 1991, and Greenwood and Hercowitz, 1991); roles for government-provided goods and capital in utility and production (for example, Christiano and Eichenbaum, 1992, and Baxter and King, 1993); multiple countries (for example, Baxter and Crucini, 1993); embodied technological change (Greenwood, Hercowitz, and Huffman, 1988, and Hornstein and Krusell, 1996); variable capital utilization and labor hoarding (Greenwood, Hercowitz, and Huffman, 1988, Burnside, Eichenbaum, and Rebelo, 1993, and Burnside and Eichenbaum, 1996); and learning-by-doing (Chang, Gomes, and Schorfheide, 2002, and Cooper and Johri, 2002). Examples of non-Walrasian features include externalities from capital (for example, Christiano and Harrison, 1999); efficiency wages (for example, Danthine and Donaldson, 1990); job search (for example, den Haan, Ramey, and Watson, 2000); and uninsurable idiosyncratic risk (for example, Krusell and Smith, 1998).

of the models of the next two chapters. The almost universally shared ideal is a fully specified quantitative model built up from microeconomic foundations, and the almost universal consensus is that such a model will need to be relatively complicated and will need to include an important role for nominal rigidity.

In terms of how to make progress toward that objective, again there is no sharp division into distinct camps with conflicting views. Instead, researchers pursue a wide range of approaches. There are at least two dimensions along which there is considerable heterogeneity in research strategies. The first is the extent to which the "default" modeling choices are Walrasian. Suppose, for example, one is interested in the business-cycle implications of efficiency wages. If one needed to model consumption decisions in analyzing that issue, one could let them be made by infinitely lived households that face no borrowing constraints, or one could take a shortcut (such as considering a static model or excluding capital) that implies that consumption equals current income.

There is no clearly "right" answer concerning which approach is likely to be more fruitful. The use of a Walrasian baseline imposes discipline: the modeler is not free to make a long list of non-Walrasian assumptions that generate the results he or she desires. It also makes clear what non-Walrasian features are essential to the results. But it makes the models more complicated, and thereby makes the sources of the results more difficult to discern. And it may cause modelers to adopt assumptions that are not good approximations for analyzing the questions at hand.

A second major dimension along which approaches vary is partial-equilibrium versus general-equilibrium. Consider, for example, the issue we will discuss in Part B of Chapter 6 of whether small costs of price adjustment can cause substantial nominal rigidity. At one extreme, one could focus on a single firm's response to a one-time monetary disturbance. At the other, one could build a dynamic model where the money supply follows a stochastic process and examine the resulting general equilibrium.

Again, there are strengths and weaknesses to both approaches. The focus on general equilibrium guards against the possibility that the effect being considered has implausible implications along some dimension the modeler would not otherwise consider. But this comes at the cost of making the analysis more complicated. As a result, the analysis must often take a simpler approach to modeling the central issue of interest, and the greater complexity again makes it harder to see the intuition for the results.

It is tempting to say that all these approaches are valuable, and that macroeconomists should therefore pursue them all. There is clearly much truth in this statement. For example, the proposition that both partial-equilibrium and general-equilibrium models are valuable is unassailable. But there are tradeoffs: simultaneously pursuing general-equilibrium and partial-equilibrium analysis, and fully specified dynamic models and simple static models, means that less attention can be paid to any one avenue. Thus saying that all approaches have merit avoids the harder question of when different approaches are more valuable and what mix is appropriate for analyzing a particular issue. Unfortunately, as with the issue of calibration versus other approaches to evaluating models' empirical performance, we have little systematic evidence on this question. As a result, macroeconomists have little choice but to make tentative judgments, based on the currently available models and evidence, about what types of inquiry are most promising. And they must remain open to the possibility that those judgments will need to be revised.

# Problems

**5.1.** Redo the calculations reported in Table 5.1, 5.2, or 5.3 for any country other than the United States.

**5.2.** Redo the calculations reported in Table 5.3 for the following:

(a) Employees' compensation as a share of national income.

(b) The labor force participation rate.

(c) The federal government budget deficit as a share of GDP.

(d) The Standard and Poor's 500 composite stock price index.

(e) The difference in yields between Moody's Baa and Aaa bonds.

(f) The difference in yields between 10-year and 3-month U.S. Treasury securities.

(g) The weighted average exchange rate of the U.S. dollar against major currencies.

**5.3.** Let $A_0$ denote the value of $A$ in period 0, and let the behavior of $\ln A$ be given by equations (5.8)-(5.9).

(a) Express $\ln A_1$, $\ln A_2$, and $\ln A_3$ in terms of $\ln A_0$, $\varepsilon_{A1}$, $\varepsilon_{A2}$, $\varepsilon_{A3}$, $\overline{A}$, and $g$.

(b) In light of the fact that the expectations of the $\varepsilon_A$'s are zero, what are the expectations of $\ln A_1$, $\ln A_2$, and $\ln A_3$ given $\ln A_0$, $\overline{A}$, and $g$?

**5.4.** Suppose the period-$t$ utility function, $u_t$, is $u_t = \ln c_t + b(1 - \ell_t)^{1-\gamma}/(1 - \gamma)$, $b > 0$, $\gamma > 0$, rather than (5.7).

(a) Consider the one-period problem analogous to that investigated in (5.12)-(5.15). How, if at all, does labor supply depend on the wage?

(b) Consider the two-period problem analogous to that investigated in (5.16)-(5.21). How does the relative demand for leisure in the two periods depend on the relative wage? How does it depend on the interest rate? Explain intuitively why $\gamma$ affects the responsiveness of labor supply to wages and the interest rate.

**5.5.** Consider the problem investigated in (5.16)–(5.21).

(a) Show that an increase in both $w_1$ and $w_2$ that leaves $w_1/w_2$ unchanged does not affect $\ell_1$ or $\ell_2$.

(b) Now assume that the household has initial wealth of amount $Z > 0$.

(i) Does (5.23) continue to hold? Why or why not?

(ii) Does the result in (a) continue to hold? Why or why not?

**5.6.** Suppose an individual lives for two periods and has utility $\ln C_1 + \ln C_2$.

(a) Suppose the individual has labor income of $Y_1$ in the first period of life and zero in the second period. Second-period consumption is thus $(1+r)(Y_1 - C_1)$; $r$, the rate of return, is potentially random.

(i) Find the first-order condition for the individual's choice of $C_1$.

(ii) Suppose $r$ changes from being certain to being uncertain, without any change in $E[r]$. How, if at all, does $C_1$ respond to this change?

(b) Suppose the individual has labor income of zero in the first period and $Y_2$ in the second. Second-period consumption is thus $Y_2 - (1+r)C_1$. $Y_2$ is certain; again, $r$ may be random.

(i) Find the first-order condition for the individual's choice of $C_1$.

(ii) Suppose $r$ changes from being certain to being uncertain, without any change in $E[r]$. How, if at all, does $C_1$ respond to this change?

**5.7.** (a) Use an argument analogous to that used to derive equation (5.23) to show that household optimization requires $b/(1 - \ell_t) = e^{-\rho}E_t[w_t(1 + r_{t+1})b/\left[w_{t+1}(1 - \ell_{t+1})\right]]$.

(b) Show that this condition is implied by (5.23) and (5.26). (Note that [5.26] must hold in every period.)

**5.8. A simplified real-business-cycle model with additive technology shocks.** (This follows Blanchard and Fischer, 1989, pp. 329–331.) Consider an economy consisting of a constant population of infinitely lived individuals. The representative individual maximizes the expected value of $\sum_{t=0}^{\infty} u(C_t)/(1+\rho)^t$, $\rho > 0$. The instantaneous utility function, $u(C_t)$, is $u(C_t) = C_t - \theta C_t^2$, $\theta > 0$. Assume that $C$ is always in the range where $u'(C)$ is positive.

Output is linear in capital, plus an additive disturbance: $Y_t = AK_t + e_t$. There is no depreciation; thus $K_{t+1} = K_t + Y_t - C_t$, and the interest rate is $A$. Assume $A = \rho$. Finally, the disturbance follows a first-order autoregressive process: $e_t = \phi e_{t-1} + \varepsilon_t$, where $-1 < \phi < 1$ and where the $\varepsilon_t$'s are mean-zero, i.i.d. shocks.

(a) Find the first-order condition (Euler equation) relating $C_t$ and expectations of $C_{t+1}$.

(b) Guess that consumption takes the form $C_t = \alpha + \beta K_t + \gamma e_t$. Given this guess, what is $K_{t+1}$ as a function of $K_t$ and $e_t$?

(c) What values must the parameters $\alpha$, $\beta$, and $\gamma$ have for the first-order condition in part (a) to be satisfied for all values of $K_t$ and $e_t$?

(*d*) What are the effects of a one-time shock to $\varepsilon$ on the paths of $Y, K$, and $C$?

**5.9. A simplified real-business-cycle model with taste shocks.** (This follows Blanchard and Fischer, 1989, p. 361.) Consider the setup in Problem 5.8. Assume, however, that the technological disturbances (the $e$'s) are absent and that the instantaneous utility function is $u(C_t) = C_t - \theta(C_t + v_t)^2$. The $v$'s are mean-zero, i.i.d. shocks.

(*a*) Find the first-order condition (Euler equation) relating $C_t$ and expectations of $C_{t+1}$.

(*b*) Guess that consumption takes the form $C_t = \alpha + \beta K_t + \gamma v_t$. Given this guess, what is $K_{t+1}$ as a function of $K_t$ and $v_t$?

(*c*) What values must the parameters $\alpha, \beta$, and $\gamma$ have for the first-order condition in (*a*) to be satisfied for all values of $K_t$ and $v_t$?

(*d*) What are the effects of a one-time shock to $v$ on the paths of $Y, K$, and $C$?

**5.10. The balanced growth path of the model of Section 5.3.** Consider the model of Section 5.3 without any shocks. Let $y^*$, $k^*$, $c^*$, and $G^*$ denote the values of $Y/(AL)$, $K/(AL)$, $C/(AL)$, and $G/(AL)$ on the balanced growth path; $w^*$ the value of $w/A$; $\ell^*$ the value of $L/N$; and $r^*$ the value of $r$.

(*a*) Use equations (5.1)–(5.4), (5.23), and (5.26) and the fact that $y^*$, $k^*$, $c^*$, $w^*$, $\ell^*$, and $r^*$ are constant on the balanced growth path to find six equations in these six variables. (Hint: The fact that $c$ in [5.23] is consumption per person, $C/N$, and $c^*$ is the balanced-growth-path value of consumption per unit of effective labor, $C/(AL)$, implies that $c = c^*\ell^*A$ on the balanced growth path.)

(*b*) Consider the parameter values assumed in Section 5.7. What are the implied shares of consumption and investment in output on the balanced growth path? What is the implied ratio of capital to annual output on the balanced growth path?

**5.11. Solving a real-business-cycle model by finding the social optimum.**[34] Consider the model of Section 5.5. Assume for simplicity that $n = g = \bar{A} = \bar{N} = 0$. Let $V(K_t, A_t)$, the *value function*, be the expected present value from the current period forward of lifetime utility of the representative individual as a function of the capital stock and technology.

(*a*) Explain intuitively why $V(\bullet)$ must satisfy

$$V(K_t, A_t) = \max_{C_t, \ell_t} \{[\ln C_t + b\ln(1 - \ell_t)] + e^{-\rho}E_t[V(K_{t+1}, A_{t+1})]\}.$$

This condition is known as the *Bellman equation.*

Given the log-linear structure of the model, let us guess that $V(\bullet)$ takes the form $V(K_t, A_t) = \beta_0 + \beta_K \ln K_t + \beta_A \ln A_t$, where the values of the $\beta$'s are to be determined. Substituting this conjectured form and the facts

---

[34] This problem uses dynamic programming and the method of undetermined coefficients. These two methods are explained in Section 10.4 and Section 5.6, respectively.

that $K_{t+1} = Y_t - C_t$ and $E_t[\ln A_{t+1}] = \rho_A \ln A_t$ into the Bellman equation yields

$$V(K_t, A_t) = \max_{C_t, \ell_t} \{[\ln C_t + b \ln(1 - \ell_t)] + e^{-\rho}[\beta_0 + \beta_K \ln(Y_t - C_t) + \beta_A \rho_A \ln A_t]\}.$$

(b) Find the first-order condition for $C_t$. Show that it implies that $C_t/Y_t$ does not depend on $K_t$ or $A_t$.

(c) Find the first-order condition for $\ell_t$. Use this condition and the result in part (b) to show that $\ell_t$ does not depend on $K_t$ or $A_t$.

(d) Substitute the production function and the results in parts (b) and (c) for the optimal $C_t$ and $\ell_t$ into the equation above for $V(\bullet)$, and show that the resulting expression has the form $V(K_t, A_t) = \beta_0' + \beta_K' \ln K_t + \beta_A' \ln A_t$.

(e) What must $\beta_K$ and $\beta_A$ be so that $\beta_K' = \beta_K$ and $\beta_A' = \beta_A$?[35]

(f) What are the implied values of $C/Y$ and $\ell$? Are they the same as those found in Section 5.5 for the case of $n = g = 0$?

**5.12.** Suppose technology follows some process other than (5.8)–(5.9). Do $s_t = \hat{s}$ and $\ell_t = \hat{\ell}$ for all $t$ continue to solve the model of Section 5.5? Why or why not?

**5.13.** Consider the model of Section 5.5. Suppose, however, that the instantaneous utility function, $u_t$, is given by $u_t = \ln c_t + b(1 - \ell_t)^{1-\gamma}/(1 - \gamma), b > 0, \gamma > 0$, rather than by (5.7) (see Problem 5.4).

(a) Find the first-order condition analogous to equation (5.26) that relates current leisure and consumption, given the wage.

(b) With this change in the model, is the saving rate ($s$) still constant?

(c) Is leisure per person $(1 - \ell)$ still constant?

**5.14.** (a) If the $\tilde{A}_t$'s are uniformly 0 and if $\ln Y_t$ evolves according to (5.39), what path does $\ln Y_t$ settle down to? (Hint: Note that we can rewrite [5.39] as $\ln Y_t - (n + g)t = Q + \alpha[\ln Y_{t-1} - (n + g)(t - 1)] + (1 - \alpha)\tilde{A}_t$, where $Q \equiv \alpha \ln \hat{s} + (1 - \alpha)(\bar{A} + \ln \hat{\ell} + \bar{N}) - \alpha(n + g)$.)

(b) Let $\tilde{Y}_t$ denote the difference between $\ln Y_t$ and the path found in (a). With this definition, derive (5.40).

**5.15.** **The derivation of the log-linearized equation of motion for capital.** Consider the equation of motion for capital, $K_{t+1} = K_t + K_t^\alpha(A_t L_t)^{1-\alpha} - C_t - G_t - \delta K_t$.

(a) (i) Show that $\partial \ln K_{t+1}/\partial \ln K_t$ (holding $A_t, L_t, C_t$, and $G_t$ fixed) equals $(1 + r_{t+1})(K_t/K_{t+1})$.

(ii) Show that this implies that $\partial \ln K_{t+1}/\partial \ln K_t$ evaluated at the balanced growth path is $(1 + r^*)/e^{n+g}$.[36]

---

[35] The calculation of $\beta_0$ is tedious and is therefore omitted.

[36] One could express $r^*$ in terms of the discount rate $\rho$. Campbell (1994) argues, however, that it is easier to discuss the model's implications in terms of $r^*$ than $\rho$.

(b) Show that

$$\tilde{K}_{t+1} \simeq \lambda_1 \tilde{K}_t + \lambda_2(\tilde{A}_t + \tilde{L}_t) + \lambda_3 \tilde{G}_t + (1 - \lambda_1 - \lambda_2 - \lambda_3)\tilde{C}_t,$$

where $\lambda_1 \equiv (1 + r^*)/e^{n+g}, \lambda_2 \equiv (1 - \alpha)(r^* + \delta)/(\alpha e^{n+g})$, and $\lambda_3 = -(r^* + \delta)$ $(G/Y)^*/(\alpha e^{n+g})$; and where $(G/Y)^*$ denotes the ratio of $G$ to $Y$ on the balanced growth path without shocks. (Hints: Since the production function is Cobb-Douglas, $Y^* = (r^* + \delta)K^*/\alpha$. On the balanced growth path, $K_{t+1} = e^{n+g}K_t$, which implies that $C^* = Y^* - G^* - \delta K^* - (e^{n+g} - 1)K^*$.)

(c) Use the result in (b) and equations (5.43)-(5.44) to derive (5.53), where $b_{KK} = \lambda_1 + \lambda_2 a_{LK} + (1 - \lambda_1 - \lambda_2 - \lambda_3)a_{CK}$, $b_{KA} = \lambda_2(1 + a_{LA}) + (1 - \lambda_1 - \lambda_2 - \lambda_3)a_{CA}$, and $b_{KG} = \lambda_2 a_{LG} + \lambda_3 + (1 - \lambda_1 - \lambda_2 - \lambda_3)a_{CG}$.

**5.16.** Redo the regression reported in equation (5.55):

(a) Incorporating more recent data.

(b) Incorporating more recent data, and using $M1$ rather than $M2$.

(c) Including eight lags of the change in log money rather than four.

# Chapter **6**
# NOMINAL RIGIDITY

As we discussed at the end of the previous chapter, a major limitation of real-business-cycle models is their omission of any role for monetary changes in driving macroeconomic fluctuations. It is therefore important to extend our analysis of fluctuations to incorporate a role for such changes.

For monetary disturbances to have real effects, there must be some type of nominal rigidity or imperfection. Otherwise, even in a model that is highly non-Walrasian, a monetary change results only in proportional changes in all prices with no impact on real prices or quantities. By far the most common nominal imperfection in modern business-cycle models is some type of barrier or limitation to the adjustment of nominal prices or wages. This chapter therefore focuses on such barriers.

Introducing incomplete nominal price adjustment does more than just add a channel through which monetary disturbances have real effects. As we will see, for realistic cases just adding plausible barriers to price adjustment to an otherwise Walrasian model is not enough to produce quantitatively important effects of monetary changes. Thus introducing an important role for nominal disturbances usually involves significant changes to the microeconomics of the model. In addition, nominal rigidity changes how disturbances other than monetary shocks affect the economy. Thus it affects our understanding of the effects of nonmonetary changes. Because nominal rigidity has such strong effects and is so central to understanding important features of fluctuations, most modern business-cycle models include some form of nominal rigidity.

This chapter begins the process of adding nominal rigidity to business-cycle models by considering the effects of nominal rigidity in relatively simple models that are either static or consider only one-time shocks. In Part A of the chapter, nominal rigidity is taken as given. The goal is to understand the effects of nominal rigidity and to analyze the effects of various assumptions about the specifics of the rigidity, such as whether it is prices or wages that are sticky and the nature of inflation dynamics. Part B then turns to the microeconomic foundations of nominal rigidity. The key question we will consider there is how barriers to nominal adjustment—which, as we will see, are almost certainly small—can lead to substantial aggregate nominal rigidity.

# Part A   Exogenous Nominal Rigidity

# 6.1   A Baseline Case: Fixed Prices

In this part of the chapter, we take nominal rigidity as given and investigate its effects. We begin with the extreme case where nominal prices are not just less than fully flexible, but completely fixed. Aside from this exogenously imposed assumption of price rigidity, the model is built up from microeconomic foundations.

## Assumptions

Time is discrete. Firms produce output using labor as their only input. Aggregate output is therefore given by

$$Y = F(L), \quad F'(\bullet) > 0, F''(\bullet) \leq 0. \tag{6.1}$$

Government and international trade are absent from the model. Together with the assumption that there is no capital, this implies that aggregate consumption and aggregate output are equal.

There is a fixed number of infinitely lived households that obtain utility from consumption and from holding real money balances, and disutility from working. For simplicity, we ignore population growth and normalize the number of households to 1. The representative household's objective function is

$$\mathcal{U} = \sum_{t=0}^{\infty} \beta^t [U(C_t) + \Gamma\left(\frac{M_t}{P_t}\right) - V(L_t)], \quad 0 < \beta < 1. \tag{6.2}$$

There is diminishing marginal utility of consumption and money holdings, and increasing marginal disutility of working: $U'(\bullet) > 0$, $U''(\bullet) < 0$, $\Gamma'(\bullet) > 0$, $\Gamma''(\bullet) < 0$, $V'(\bullet) > 0$, $V''(\bullet) > 0$. We assume that $U(\bullet)$ and $\Gamma(\bullet)$ take our usual constant-relative-risk-aversion forms:

$$U(C_t) = \frac{C_t^{1-\theta}}{1-\theta}, \quad \theta > 0, \tag{6.3}$$

$$\Gamma\left(\frac{M_t}{P_t}\right) = \frac{(M_t/P_t)^{1-\nu}}{1-\nu}, \quad \nu > 0. \tag{6.4}$$

The assumption that money is a direct source of utility is a shortcut. In truth, individuals hold cash not because it provides utility directly, but because it allows them to purchase some goods more easily. One can think of the contribution of $M_t/P_t$ to the objective function as reflecting this increased convenience rather than direct utility.[1]

There are two assets: money, which pays a nominal interest rate of zero, and bonds, which pay an interest rate of $i_t$. Let $A_t$ denote the household's wealth at the start of period $t$. Its labor income is $W_t L_t$ (where $W$ is the nominal wage), and its consumption expenditures are $P_t C_t$. The quantity of bonds it holds from $t$ to $t+1$ is therefore $A_t + W_t L_t - P_t C_t - M_t$. Thus its wealth evolves according to

$$A_{t+1} = M_t + (A_t + W_t L_t - P_t C_t - M_t)(1 + i_t). \tag{6.5}$$

The household takes the paths of $P$, $W$, and $i$ as given. It chooses the paths of $C$ and $M$ to maximize its lifetime utility subject to its flow budget constraint and a no-Ponzi-game condition (see Section 2.2). Because we want to allow for the possibility of nominal wage rigidity and of a labor market that does not clear, for now we do not take a stand concerning whether the household's labor supply, $L$, is exogenous to the household or a choice variable. Likewise, for now we make no assumption about how firms choose $L$.

The path of $M$ is set by the central bank. Thus, although households view the path of $i$ as given and the path of $M$ as something they choose, in general equilibrium the path of $M$ is exogenous and the path of $i$ is determined endogenously.

## Household Behavior

In period $t$, the household's choice variables are $C_t$ and $M_t$ (and as just described, perhaps $L_t$). Consider the experiment we used in Sections 2.2 and 5.4 to find the Euler equation relating $C_t$ and $C_{t+1}$. The household reduces $C_t$ by $dC$, and therefore increases its bond holdings by $P_t dC$. It then uses those bonds and the interest on them to increase $C_{t+1}$ by $(1 + i_t)P_t dC/P_{t+1}$. Equivalently, it increases $C_{t+1}$ by $(1 + r_t)dC$, where $r_t$ is the real interest rate, defined by $1 + r_t = (1 + i_t)P_t/P_{t+1}$.[2] Analysis paralleling that in the earlier chapters yields

$$C_t^{-\theta} = (1 + r_t)\beta C_{t+1}^{-\theta}. \tag{6.6}$$

---

[1] Feenstra (1986) demonstrates formally that this *money-in-the-utility-function* formulation and transactions benefits of money holdings are observationally equivalent. The classic model of the transactions demand for money is the Baumol-Tobin model (Baumol, 1952; Tobin, 1956). See Problem 6.2.

[2] If we define $\pi_t$ by $1 + \pi_t = P_{t+1}/P_t$, we have $1 + r_t = (1 + i_t)/(1 + \pi_t)$. For small values of $i_t$ and $\pi_t$, $r_t \approx i_t - \pi_t$.

Taking logs of both sides and solving for $\ln C_t$ gives us

$$\ln C_t = \ln C_{t+1} - \frac{1}{\theta} \ln[(1 + r_t)\beta]. \qquad (6.7)$$

To get this expression into a form that is more useful, we make three changes. First, and most importantly, recall that the only use of output is for consumption and that we have normalized the number of households to 1. Thus in equilibrium, aggregate output, $Y$, and the consumption of the representative household, $C$, must be equal. We therefore substitute $Y$ for $C$. Second, for small values of $r$, $\ln(1 + r) \approx r$. For simplicity, we treat this relationship as exact. And third, we suppress the constant term, $-(1/\theta)\ln \beta$.[3] These changes give us:

$$\ln Y_t = \ln Y_{t+1} - \frac{1}{\theta} r_t. \qquad (6.8)$$

Equation (6.8) is known as the *new Keynesian IS curve*. In contrast to the traditional *IS* curve, it is derived from microeconomic foundations. The main difference from the traditional *IS* curve is the presence of $Y_{t+1}$ on the right-hand side.[4]

For our purposes, the most important feature of the new Keynesian *IS* curve is that it implies an inverse relationship between $r_t$ and $Y_t$. More elaborate analyses of the demand for goods have the same implication. For example, we will see in Chapter 9 that increases in the real interest rate reduce the amount of investment firms want to undertake. Thus adding capital to the model would introduce another reason for a downward-sloping relationship. Similarly, suppose we introduced international trade. A rise in the country's interest rate would generally increase demand for the country's assets, and so cause its exchange rate to appreciate. This in turn would reduce exports and increase imports.

To find the first-order condition for households' money holdings, consider a balanced-budget change in $M_t/P_t$ and $C_t$. Specifically, suppose the household raises $M_t/P_t$ by $dm$ and lowers $C_t$ by $[i_t/(1 + i_t)]dm$. The household's real bond holdings therefore fall by $\{1 - [i_t/(1 + i_t)]\}dm$, or $[1/(1 + i_t)]dm$. This change has no effect on the household's wealth at the beginning of period $t + 1$. Thus if the household is optimizing, at the margin this change must not affect utility.

The utility benefit of the change is $\Gamma'(M_t/P_t)dm$, and the utility cost is $U'(C_t)[i_t/(1 + i_t)]dm$. The first-order condition for optimal money holdings

---

[3] This can be formalized by reinterpreting $r$ as the difference between the real interest rate and $-\ln \beta$.

[4] The new Keynesian *IS* curve is derived by Kerr and King (1996) and McCallum and Nelson (1999). Under uncertainty, with appropriate assumptions $\ln Y_{t+1}$ can be replaced with $E_t[\ln Y_{t+1}]$ plus a constant.

is therefore

$$\Gamma'\left(\frac{M_t}{P_t}\right) = \frac{i_t}{1+i_t}U'(C_t). \tag{6.9}$$

Since $U(\bullet)$ and $\Gamma(\bullet)$ are given by (6.3) and (6.4) and since $C_t = Y_t$, this condition implies

$$\frac{M_t}{P_t} = Y_t^{\theta/\nu}\left(\frac{1+i_t}{i_t}\right)^{1/\nu}. \tag{6.10}$$

Thus money demand is increasing in output and decreasing in the nominal interest rate.

## The Effects of Shocks with Fixed Prices

We are now in a position to describe the effects of changes in the money supply and of other disturbances. To see how price rigidity alters the behavior of the economy, it is easiest to begin with the case where prices are completely fixed, both now and in the future. Thus in this section we assume

$$P_t = \bar{P} \quad \text{for all } t. \tag{6.11}$$

This assumption allows us to depict the solutions to the two conditions for household optimization, (6.8) and (6.10), graphically. With completely rigid prices, the nominal and real interest rates are the same. Equation (6.8), the new Keynesian *IS* curve, implies an inverse relationship between the interest rate and output (for a given value of the expectation of next period's output). The set of combinations of the interest rate and output that satisfy equation (6.10) for optimal money holdings (for a given level of the money supply) is upward-sloping. The two curves are shown in Figure 6.1. They are known as the *IS* and *LM* curves.

We know that in the absence of any type of nominal rigidity or imperfection, a change in the money supply leads to a proportional change in all prices and wages, with no impact on real quantities. Thus the most important experiment to consider to investigate the effects of nominal rigidity is a change in the money supply.

For concreteness, consider an increase in the money supply in period $t$ that is fully reversed the next period, so that future output is unaffected. The increase shifts the *LM* curve down and does not affect the *IS* curve. As a result, the interest rate falls and output rises. This is shown in Figure 6.2. Thus we have a simple but crucial result: with nominal rigidity, monetary disturbances have real effects.

Nominal rigidity also has implications for the effects of other disturbances. Suppose, for example, we introduce government purchases to the model. The Euler equation for households' intertemporal optimization problem is the same as before; thus equation (6.7) continues to describe

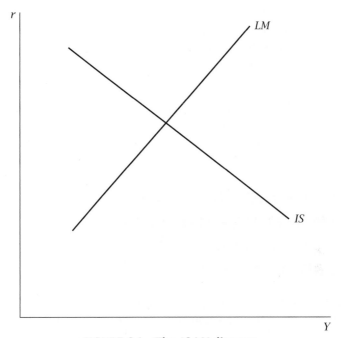

**FIGURE 6.1   The *IS-LM* diagram**

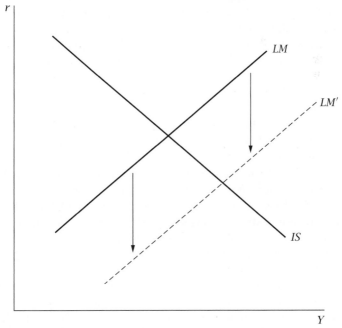

**FIGURE 6.2   The effects of a temporary increase in the money supply with completely fixed prices**

consumption demand. Now, however, the demand for goods comes from both households and the government. An increase in government purchases that is temporary (so that future output is unaffected) shifts the *IS* curve to the right, and so raises output and the real interest rate. Because of the nominal rigidity, the intertemporal-substitution and wealth effects that are central to the effects of changes in government purchases in the real-business-cycle model of Chapter 5 are irrelevant. Thus the transmission mechanism is now completely different: the government demands more goods and, because prices are fixed, firms supply them at the fixed prices.

# 6.2 Price Rigidity, Wage Rigidity, and Departures from Perfect Competition in the Goods and Labor Markets

The discussion in the previous section of the effects of increases in demand with rigid prices neglects an important question: Why do firms supply the additional output? Although by assumption they do not have the option of raising prices, they could just leave their output unchanged and choose not to meet the additional demand.

There is one important case where this is exactly what they do. Suppose the markets for goods and labor are perfectly competitive and are initially in equilibrium. Thus workers' wages equal their marginal disutility of supplying labor, and firms' prices equal their marginal cost. Workers are therefore not willing to supply more labor unless the wage rises. But the marginal product of labor declines as labor input rises, and so marginal cost rises. Thus firms are not willing to employ more labor unless the wage falls. The result is that employment and output do not change when the money supply increases. The rise in demand leads not to a rise in output, but to rationing in the goods market.

This discussion tells us that for monetary expansion to have real effects, nominal rigidity is not enough; there must also be some departure from perfect competition in either the product market or the labor market. This section therefore investigates various combinations of nominal price and wage rigidity and imperfections in the goods and labor markets that could cause nominal disturbances to have real effects.

In all of the cases we will consider, incomplete nominal adjustment is assumed rather than derived. Thus this section's purpose is not to discuss possible microeconomic foundations of nominal stickiness; that is the job of Part B of this chapter. Instead, the goal is to examine the implications that different assumptions concerning nominal wage and price rigidity and characteristics of the labor and goods markets have for unemployment, firms' pricing behavior, and the behavior of the real wage and the markup in response to demand fluctuations.

We consider four sets of assumptions. The first two are valuable baselines. Both, however, appear to fail as even remotely approximate descriptions of actual economies. The other two are more complicated and potentially more accurate. Together, the four cases illustrate the wide range of possibilities.

## Case 1: Keynes's Model

The supply side of the model in Keynes's *General Theory* (1936) has two key features. First, the nominal wage is completely unresponsive to current-period developments (at least over some range):

$$W = \overline{W}. \tag{6.12}$$

(Throughout this section, we focus on the economy in a single period. Thus we omit time subscripts for simplicity.) Second, for reasons that Keynes did not specify explicitly, the wage that prevails in the absence of nominal rigidity is above the level that equates supply and demand. Thus, implicitly, the labor market has some non-Walrasian feature that causes the equilibrium real wage to be above the market-clearing level.

Keynes's assumptions concerning the goods market, in contrast, are conventional. As in Section 6.1, output is given by $Y = F(L)$, with $F'(\bullet) > 0$ and $F''(\bullet) \leq 0$ (see equation [6.1]). Firms are competitive and their prices are flexible, and so they hire labor up to the point where the marginal product of labor equals the real wage:

$$F'(L) = \frac{W}{P}. \tag{6.13}$$

With these assumptions, an increase in demand raises output through its impact on the real wage. When the money supply or some other determinant of demand rises, goods prices rise, and so the real wage falls and employment rises. Because the real wage is initially above the market-clearing level, workers are willing to supply the additional labor.

Figure 6.3 shows the situation in the labor market. The initial level of employment is determined by labor demand and the prevailing real wage (Point E in the diagram). Thus there is involuntary unemployment: some workers would like to work at the prevailing wage but cannot. The amount of unemployment is the difference between supply and demand at the prevailing real wage (distance EA in the diagram).

Fluctuations in the demand for goods lead to movements of employment and the real wage along the downward-sloping labor demand curve. Higher demand, for example, raises the price level. Thus it leads to a lower real wage and higher employment. This is shown as Point $E'$ in the diagram. This

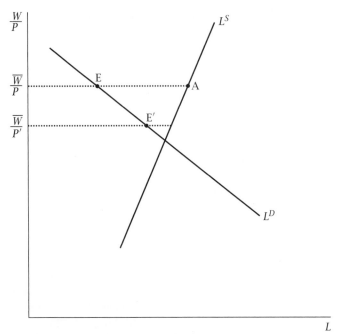

**FIGURE 6.3  The labor market with sticky wages, flexible prices, and a competitive goods market**

view of the supply side of the economy therefore implies a countercyclical real wage in response to aggregate demand shocks. This prediction has been subject to extensive testing beginning shortly after the publication of the *General Theory*. It has consistently failed to find support. As described in the next section, our current understanding suggests that real wages are moderately procyclical.[5]

## Case 2: Sticky Prices, Flexible Wages, and a Competitive Labor Market

The view of supply in the *General Theory* assumes that the goods market is competitive and goods prices are completely flexible, and that the source of nominal stickiness is entirely in the labor market. This raises the question

_____

[5] In responding to early studies of the cyclical behavior of wages, Keynes (1939) largely disavowed the specific formulation of the supply side of the economy in the *General Theory*, saying that he had chosen it to keep the model as classical as possible and to simplify the presentation. His 1939 view of supply is closer to Case 4, below.

of what occurs in the reverse case where the labor market is competitive and wages are completely flexible, and where the source of incomplete nominal adjustment is entirely in the goods market.

In the previous case, we assumed that in the absence of nominal rigidity, the wage is above the market-clearing level. This assumption was necessary for increases in demand to lead to higher employment. Likewise, when the nominal rigidity is in the goods market, we assume that the flexible-price equilibrium involves prices that exceed marginal costs. Without this assumption, if the demand for goods rose, firms would turn customers away rather than meet the additional demand at their fixed prices.

Models of nominal rigidity in the goods market almost always assume that the reason prices normally exceed marginal costs is that firms have market power, so that profit-maximizing prices are above marginal costs. Under this assumption, at the flexible-price equilibrium, firms are better off if they can sell more at the prevailing price. As a result, a rise in demand with rigid prices leads to higher output.

When prices rather than wages are assumed rigid, the assumption from Section 6.1 that $P = \bar{P}$ (equation [6.11]), which we dropped in Case 1, again applies. Wages are flexible and the labor market is competitive. Thus workers choose their labor supply to maximize utility taking the real wage as given. From the utility function, (6.2)–(6.4), the first-order condition for optimal labor supply is

$$C^{-\theta}\frac{W}{P} = V'(L). \tag{6.14}$$

In equilibrium, $C = Y = F(L)$. Thus (6.14) implies

$$\frac{W}{P} = [F(L)]^{\theta}V'(L). \tag{6.15}$$

The right-hand side of this expression is increasing in $L$. Thus (6.15) implicitly defines $L$ as an increasing function of the real wage:

$$L = L^{s}\left(\frac{W}{P}\right), \qquad L^{s\prime}(\bullet) > 0. \tag{6.16}$$

Finally, firms meet demand at the prevailing price as long as it does not exceed the level where marginal cost equals price.

With these assumptions, fluctuations in demand cause firms to change employment and output at the fixed price level. Figure 6.4 shows the model's implications for the labor market. Firms' demand for labor is determined by their desire to meet the demand for their goods. Thus, as long as the real wage is not so high that it is unprofitable to meet the full demand, the labor demand curve is a vertical line in employment-wage space. The term *effective labor demand* is used to describe a situation, such as this, where the

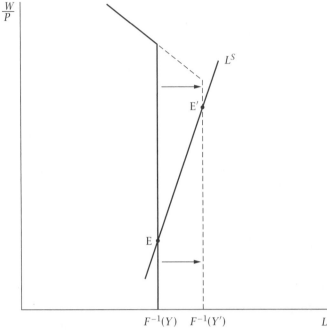

**FIGURE 6.4   A competitive labor market when prices are sticky and wages are flexible**

quantity of labor demanded depends on the amount of goods that firms are able to sell.[6] The real wage is determined by the intersection of the effective labor demand curve and the labor supply curve (Point E). Thus workers are on their labor supply curve, and there is no unemployment.

This model implies a procyclical real wage in the face of demand fluctuations. A rise in demand, for example, leads to a rise in effective labor demand, and thus to an increase in the real wage as workers move up their labor supply curve (to Point E′ in the diagram). If labor supply is relatively unresponsive to the real wage, the real wage varies greatly when demand for goods changes.

Finally, this model implies a countercyclical markup (ratio of price to marginal cost) in response to demand fluctuations. A rise in demand, for example, leads to a rise in costs, both because the wage rises and because the marginal product of labor declines as output rises. Prices, however, stay fixed, and so the ratio of price to marginal cost falls.

---

[6] If the real wage is so high that it is unprofitable for firms to meet the demand for their goods, the quantity of labor demanded is determined by the condition that the marginal product equals the real wage. Thus this portion of the labor demand curve is downward-sloping.

Because markups are harder to measure than real wages, it is harder to determine their cyclical behavior. Nonetheless, work in this area has largely reached a consensus that markups are significantly countercyclical. See, for example, Bils (1987); Warner and Barsky (1995); Chevalier and Scharfstein (1996); and Chevalier, Kashyap, and Rossi (2003).[7]

The reason that incomplete nominal adjustment causes changes in the demand for goods to affect output is quite different in this case than in the previous one. A fall in demand, for example, lowers the amount that firms are able to sell; thus they reduce their production. In the previous model, in contrast, a fall in demand, by raising the real wage, reduces the amount that firms want to sell.

This model of the supply side of the economy is important for three reasons. First, it is the natural starting point for models in which nominal stickiness involves prices rather than wages. Second, it shows that there is no necessary connection between nominal rigidity and unemployment. And third, it is easy to use; because of this, models like it often appear in the theoretical literature.

## Case 3: Sticky Prices, Flexible Wages, and Real Labor Market Imperfections

Since fluctuations in output appear to be associated with fluctuations in unemployment, it is natural to ask whether movements in the demand for goods can lead to changes in unemployment when it is nominal prices that adjust sluggishly. To see how this can occur, suppose that nominal wages are still flexible, but that there is some non-Walrasian feature of the labor market that causes the real wage to remain above the level that equates demand and supply. Chapter 10 investigates characteristics of the labor market that can cause this to occur and how the real wage may vary with the level of aggregate economic activity in such situations. For now, let us simply assume that firms have some "real-wage function." Thus we write

$$\frac{W}{P} = w(L), \qquad w'(\bullet) \geq 0. \tag{6.17}$$

For concreteness, one can think of firms paying more than market-clearing wages for *efficiency-wage* reasons (see Sections 10.2–10.4). As before, prices are fixed at $\bar{P}$, and output and employment are related by the production function, $Y = F(L)$.

---

[7] Rotemberg and Woodford (1999a) synthesize much of the evidence and discuss its implications. Nekarda and Ramey (2009) present evidence in support of procyclical markups.

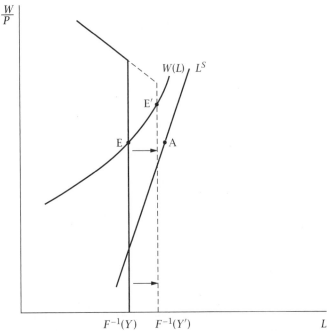

**FIGURE 6.5** A non-Walrasian labor market when prices are sticky and nominal wages are flexible

These assumptions, like the previous ones, imply that increases in demand raise output up to the point where marginal cost equals the exogenously given price level. Thus again changes in demand have real effects. This case's implications for the labor market are shown in Figure 6.5. Employment and the real wage are now determined by the intersection of the effective labor demand curve and the real-wage function. In contrast to the previous case, there is unemployment; the amount is given by distance EA in the diagram. Fluctuations in labor demand lead to movements along the real-wage function rather than along the labor supply curve. Thus the elasticity of labor supply no longer determines how the real wage responds to changes in the demand for goods. And if the real-wage function is flatter than the labor supply curve, unemployment falls when demand rises.

## Case 4: Sticky Wages, Flexible Prices, and Imperfect Competition

Just as Case 3 extends Case 2 by introducing real imperfections in the labor market, the final case extends Case 1 by introducing real imperfections in the goods market. Specifically, assume (as in Case 1) that the nominal wage is rigid at $\overline{W}$ and that nominal prices are flexible, and continue to assume that output and employment are related by the production function. Now, however, assume that the goods market is imperfectly competitive. With imperfect competition, price is a markup over marginal cost. Paralleling our assumptions about the real wage in Case 3, we do not model the determinants of the markup, but simply assume that there is a "markup function." With these assumptions, price is given by

$$P = \mu(L)\frac{W}{F'(L)};$$
(6.18)

$W/F'(L)$ is marginal cost and $\mu$ is the markup.

Equation (6.18) implies that the real wage, $W/P$, is given by $F'(L)/\mu(L)$. Without any restriction on $\mu(L)$, one cannot say how $W/P$ varies with $L$. If $\mu$ is constant, the real wage is countercyclical because of the diminishing marginal product of labor, just as in Case 1. Since the nominal wage is fixed, the price level must be higher when output is higher. And again as in Case 1, there is unemployment.

If $\mu(L)$ is sufficiently countercyclical—that is, if the markup is sufficiently lower in booms than in recoveries—the real wage can be acyclical or procyclical even though the nominal rigidity is entirely in the labor market. A particularly simple case occurs when $\mu(L)$ is precisely as countercyclical as $F'(L)$. In this situation, the real wage is not affected by changes in $L$. Since the nominal wage is unaffected by $L$ by assumption, the price level is unaffected as well. If $\mu(L)$ is more countercyclical than $F'(L)$, then $P$ must actually be lower when $L$ is higher. In all these cases, employment continues to be determined by effective labor demand.

Figure 6.6 shows this case's implications for the labor market. The real wage equals $F'(L)/\mu(L)$, which can be decreasing in $L$ (Panel (a)), constant (Panel (b)), or increasing (Panel (c)). The level of goods demand determines where on the $F'(L)/\mu(L)$ locus the economy is. Unemployment again equals the difference between labor supply and employment at the prevailing real wage.

In short, different views about the sources of incomplete nominal adjustment and the characteristics of labor and goods markets have different implications for unemployment, the real wage, and the markup. As a result, Keynesian theories do not make strong predictions about the behavior of these variables. For example, the fact that the real wage does not appear to be countercyclical is perfectly consistent with the view that nominal disturbances are a major source of aggregate fluctuations. The behavior of these variables can be used, however, to test specific Keynesian models. The absence of a countercyclical real wage, for example, appears to be strong evidence against the view that fluctuations are driven by changes in goods

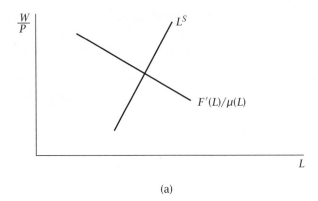

(a)

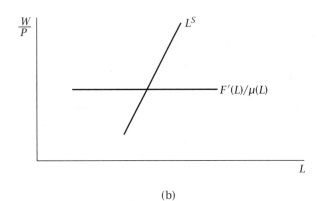

(b)

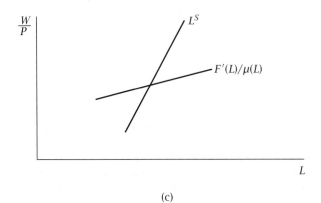

(c)

**FIGURE 6.6   The labor market with sticky wages, flexible prices, and an imperfectly competitive goods market**

demand and that Keynes's original model provides a good description of the supply side of the economy.

# 6.3 Empirical Application: The Cyclical Behavior of the Real Wage

Economists have been interested in the cyclical behavior of the real wage ever since the appearance of Keynes's *General Theory*. Early studies of this issue examined aggregate data. The general conclusion of this literature is that the real wage in the United States and other countries is approximately acyclical or moderately procyclical (see, for example, Geary and Kennan, 1982).

The set of workers who make up the aggregate is not constant over the business cycle, however. Since employment is more cyclical for lower-skill, lower-wage workers, lower-skill workers constitute a larger fraction of employed individuals in booms than in recessions. As a result, examining aggregate data is likely to understate the extent of procyclical movements in the typical individual's real wage. To put it differently, the skill-adjusted aggregate real wage is likely to be more procyclical than the unadjusted aggregate real wage.

Because of this possibility, various authors have examined the cyclical behavior of real wages using panel data. One of the most thorough and careful attempts is that of Solon, Barsky, and Parker (1994). They employ U.S. data from the Panel Study of Income Dynamics (commonly referred to as the PSID) for the period 1967–1987. As Solon, Barsky, and Parker describe, the aggregate real wage is unusually procyclical in this period. Specifically, they report that in this period a rise in the unemployment rate of 1 percentage point is associated with a fall in the aggregate real wage of 0.6 percent (with a standard error of 0.17 percent).

Solon, Barsky, and Parker consider two approaches to addressing the effects of cyclical changes in the skill mix of workers. The first is to consider only individuals who are employed throughout their sample period and to examine the cyclical behavior of the aggregate real wage for this group. The second approach uses more observations. With this approach, Solon, Barsky, and Parker in effect estimate a regression of the form

$$\Delta \ln w_{it} = a'X_{it} + b\Delta u_t + e_{it}. \tag{6.19}$$

Here $i$ indexes individuals and $t$ years, $w$ is the real wage, $u$ is the unemployment rate, and $X$ is a vector of control variables. They use all available observations; that is, observation $it$ is included if individual $i$ is employed in both year $t - 1$ and year $t$. The fact that the individual must be employed in both years to be included is what addresses the possibility of composition bias.[8]

The results of the two approaches are quite similar: the real wage is roughly twice as procyclical at the individual level as in the aggregate. A fall in the unemployment rate of 1 percentage point is associated with a rise in a typical worker's real wage of about 1.2 percent. And with both approaches, the estimates are highly statistically significant.

One concern is that these results might reflect not composition bias, but differences between the workers in the PSID and the population as a whole. To address this possibility, Solon, Barsky, and Parker construct an aggregate real wage series for the PSID in the conventional way; that is, they compute the real wage in a given year as the average real wage paid to individuals in the PSID who are employed in that year. Since the set of workers used in computing this wage varies from year to year, these estimates are subject to composition bias. Thus, comparing the estimates of wage cyclicality for this measure with those for a conventional aggregate wage measure shows the importance of the PSID sample. And comparing the estimates from this measure with the panel data estimates shows the importance of composition bias.

When they perform this exercise, Solon, Barsky, and Parker find that the cyclicality of the aggregate PSID real wage is virtually identical to that of the conventional aggregate real wage. Thus the difference between the panel-data estimates and the aggregate estimates reflects composition bias.

Solon, Barsky, and Parker are not the first authors to examine the cyclical behavior of the real wage using panel data. Yet they report much greater composition bias than earlier researchers. If we are to accept their conclusions rather than those of the earlier studies, we need to understand why they obtain different results.

Solon, Barsky, and Parker discuss this issue in the context of three earlier studies: Blank (1990), Coleman (1984), and Bils (1985). Blank's results in fact indicated considerable composition bias. She was interested in other issues, however, and so did not call attention to this finding. Coleman focused on the fact that movements in an aggregate real wage series and in a series purged of composition bias show essentially the same *correlation* with movements in the unemployment rate. He failed to note that the *magnitude* of the movements in the corrected series is much larger. This is an illustration of the general principle that in doing empirical work, it is important to consider not just statistical measures such as correlations and

---

[8] Because of the need to avoid composition bias, Solon, Barsky, and Parker do not use all PSID workers with either approach. Thus it is possible that their procedures suffer from a different type of composition bias. Suppose, for example, that wages conditional on being employed are highly countercyclical for individuals who work only sporadically. Then by excluding these workers, Solon, Barsky, and Parker are overstating the procyclicality of wages for the typical individual. This possibility seems farfetched, however.

*t*-statistics, but also the economic magnitudes of the estimates. Finally, Bils found that real wages at the individual level are substantially procyclical. But he found that an aggregate real wage series for his sample was nearly as procyclical, and thus he concluded that composition bias is not large. His sample, however, consisted only of young men. Thus a finding that there is only a small amount of composition bias within this fairly homogeneous group does not rule out the possibility that there is substantial bias in the population as a whole.

Can we conclude from Solon, Barsky, and Parker's findings that short-run fluctuations in the quantity of labor represent movements along an upward-sloping short-run labor supply curve? Solon, Barsky, and Parker argue that we cannot, for two reasons. First, they find that explaining their results in this way requires a labor supply elasticity in response to cyclical wage variation of 1.0 to 1.4. They argue that microeconomic studies suggest that this elasticity is implausibly high even in response to purely temporary changes. More importantly, they point out that short-run wage movements are far from purely temporary; this makes an explanation based on movements along the labor supply function even more problematic. Second, as described above, the aggregate real wage is unusually procyclical in Solon, Barsky, and Parker's sample period. If the same is true of individuals' wages, explaining employment movements on the basis of shifts along the labor supply function in other periods is even more difficult.

Thus, Solon, Barsky, and Parker's evidence does not eliminate the likelihood that non-Walrasian features of the labor market (or, possibly, shifts in labor supply) are important to the comovement of the quantity of labor and real wages. Nonetheless, it significantly changes our understanding of a basic fact about short-run fluctuations, and therefore about what we should demand of our models of macroeconomic fluctuations.

# 6.4 Toward a Usable Model with Exogenous Nominal Rigidity

The models of Sections 6.1 and 6.2 are extremely stylized. They all assume that nominal prices or wages are completely fixed, which is obviously not remotely accurate. They also assume that the central bank fixes the money supply. Although this assumption is not as patently counterfactual as the assumption of complete nominal rigidity, it provides a poor description of how modern central banks behave.

Our goal in Sections 6.1 and 6.2 was to address qualitative questions about nominal rigidity, such as whether monetary disturbances have real effects when there is nominal rigidity and whether nominal rigidity implies a countercyclical real wage. The models in those sections are not useful for addressing more practical questions, however. This section therefore discusses how one can modify the models to turn them into a potentially helpful framework for thinking about real-world issues. We will begin with the supply side, and then turn to the demand side.

## A Permanent Output-Inflation Tradeoff?

To build a model we would want to use in practice, we need to relax the assumption that nominal prices or wages never change. One natural way to do this is to suppose that the level at which current prices or wages are fixed is determined by what happened the previous period. Consider, for example, our first model of supply; this is the model with fixed wages, flexible prices, and a competitive goods market.[9] Suppose, however, that rather than being an exogenous parameter, $\overline{W}$ is proportional to the previous period's price level. That is, suppose that wages are adjusted to make up for the previous period's inflation:

$$W_t = AP_{t-1}, \qquad A > 0, \tag{6.20}$$

Recall that in our first model of supply, employment is determined by $F'(L_t) = W_t/P_t$ (equation [6.13]). Equation (6.20) for $W_t$ therefore implies

$$\begin{aligned} F'(L_t) &= \frac{AP_{t-1}}{P_t} \\ &= \frac{A}{1 + \pi_t}, \end{aligned} \tag{6.21}$$

where $\pi_t$ is the inflation rate. Equation (6.21) implies a stable, upward-sloping relationship between employment (and hence output) and inflation. That is, it implies that there is a permanent output-inflation tradeoff: by accepting higher inflation, policymakers can permanently raise output. And since higher output is associated with lower unemployment, it also implies a permanent unemployment-inflation tradeoff.

In a famous paper, Phillips (1958) showed that there was in fact a strong and relatively stable negative relationship between unemployment and wage inflation in the United Kingdom over the previous century. Subsequent researchers found a similar relationship between unemployment and price inflation—a relationship that became known as the *Phillips curve*. Thus there appeared to be both theoretical and empirical support for a stable unemployment-inflation tradeoff.

---

[9] The other models of Section 6.2 could be modified in similar ways, and would have similar implications.

## The Natural Rate

The case for this stable tradeoff was shattered in the late 1960s and early 1970s. On the theoretical side, the attack took the form of the *natural-rate hypothesis* of Friedman (1968) and Phelps (1968). Friedman and Phelps argued that the idea that nominal variables, such as the money supply or inflation, could permanently affect real variables, such as output or unemployment, was unreasonable. In the long run, they argued, the behavior of real variables is determined by real forces.

In the specific case of the output-inflation or unemployment-inflation tradeoff, Friedman's and Phelps's argument was that a shift by policymakers to permanently expansionary policy would, sooner or later, change the way that prices or wages are set. Consider again the example analyzed in (6.20)–(6.21). When policymakers adopt permanently more expansionary policies, they permanently increase output and employment, and (with this version of supply) they permanently reduce the real wage. Yet there is no reason for workers and firms to settle on different levels of employment and the real wage just because inflation is higher: if there are forces causing the employment and real wage that prevail in the absence of inflation to be an equilibrium, those same forces are present when there is inflation. Thus wages will not always be adjusted mechanically for the previous period's inflation. Sooner or later, they will be set to account for the expansionary policies that workers and firms know are going to be undertaken. Once this occurs, employment, output, and the real wage will return to the levels that prevailed at the original inflation rate.

In short, the natural-rate hypothesis states that there is some "normal" or "natural" rate of unemployment, and that monetary policy cannot keep unemployment below this level indefinitely. The precise determinants of the natural rate are unimportant. Friedman's and Phelps's argument was simply that it was determined by real rather than nominal forces. In Friedman's famous definition (1968, p. 8):

> "The natural rate of unemployment" ... is the level that would be ground out by the Walrasian system of general equilibrium equations, provided there is embedded in them the actual structural characteristics of the labor and commodity markets, including market imperfections, stochastic variability in demands and supplies, the cost of gathering information about job vacancies and labor availabilities, the costs of mobility, and so on.

The empirical downfall of the stable unemployment-inflation tradeoff is illustrated by Figure 6.7, which shows the combinations of unemployment and inflation in the United States during the heyday of belief in a stable tradeoff and in the quarter-century that followed. The points for the 1960s suggest a fairly stable downward-sloping relationship. The points over the subsequent 25 years do not.

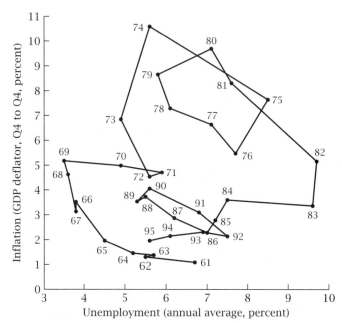

**FIGURE 6.7  Unemployment and inflation in the United States, 1961–1995**

One source of the empirical failure of the Phillips curve is mundane: if there are disturbances to supply rather than demand, then even the models of the previous section imply that high inflation and high unemployment can occur together. And there certainly are plausible candidates for significant supply shocks in the 1970s. For example, there were tremendous increases in oil prices in 1973–74 and 1978–79; such increases are likely to cause firms to charge higher prices for a given level of wages. To give another example, there were large influxes of new workers into the labor force during this period; such influxes may increase unemployment for a given level of wages.

Yet these supply shocks cannot explain all the failings of the Phillips curve in the 1970s and 1980s. In 1981 and 1982, for example, there were no identifiable large supply shocks, yet both inflation and unemployment were much higher than they were at any time in the 1960s. The reason, if Friedman and Phelps are right, is that the high inflation of the 1970s changed how prices and wages were set.

Thus, the models of price and wage behavior that imply a stable relationship between inflation and unemployment do not provide even a moderately accurate description of the dynamics of inflation and the choices facing policymakers. We must therefore go further if our models of the supply side of the economy are to be used to address these issues.

## The Expectations-Augmented Phillips Curve

Our purpose at the moment is not to build models of pricing from microeconomic foundations. Rather, our goal is to directly specify a model of pricing that is realistic enough to have some practical use. The model in equations (6.20)–(6.21), with its implication of a permanent unemployment-inflation tradeoff, does not meet that standard for most purposes.

Modern non-micro-founded formulations of pricing behavior generally differ from the simple models in equations (6.20)–(6.21) and in Section 6.2 in three ways. First, neither wages nor prices are assumed to be completely unresponsive to the current state of the economy. Instead, higher output is assumed to be associated with higher wages and prices. Second, the possibility of supply shocks is allowed for. Third, and most important, adjustment to past and expected future inflation is assumed to be more complicated than the simple formulation in (6.20).

A typical modern non-micro-founded formulation of supply is

$$\pi_t = \pi_t^* + \lambda(\ln Y_t - \ln \overline{Y}_t) + \varepsilon_t^S, \qquad \lambda > 0. \tag{6.22}$$

Here $\overline{Y}$ is the level of output that would prevail if prices were fully flexible. It is known as the *natural rate of output,* or *potential* or *full-employment* output, or *flexible-price* output. The $\lambda(\ln Y - \ln \overline{Y})$ term implies that at any time there is an upward-sloping relationship between inflation and output; the relationship is log-linear for simplicity. Equation (6.22) takes no stand concerning whether it is nominal prices or wages, or some combination of the two, that are the source of the incomplete adjustment.[10] The $\varepsilon^S$ term captures supply shocks.

The key difference between (6.22) and the earlier models of supply is the $\pi^*$ term. Tautologically, $\pi^*$ is what inflation would be if output is equal to its natural rate and there are no supply shocks. $\pi^*$ is known as *core* or *underlying* inflation. Equation (6.22) is referred to as the *expectations-augmented Phillips curve*—although, as we will see shortly, modern formulations do not necessarily interpret $\pi^*$ as expected inflation.

A simple model of $\pi^*$ that is useful for fixing ideas is that it equals the previous period's actual inflation:

$$\pi_t^* = \pi_{t-1}. \tag{6.23}$$

---

[10] Equation (6.22) can be combined with Case 2 or 3 of Section 6.2 by assuming that the nominal wage is completely flexible and using the assumption in (6.22) in place of the assumption that $P$ equals $\overline{P}$. Similarly, one can assume that wage inflation is given by an expression analogous to (6.22) and use that assumption in place of the assumption that the wage is completely unresponsive to current-period developments in Case 1 or 4. This implies somewhat more complicated behavior of price inflation, however.

With this assumption, there is a tradeoff between output and the *change in inflation*, but no permanent tradeoff between output and inflation. For inflation to be held steady at any level, output must equal the natural rate. And any level of inflation is sustainable. But for inflation to fall, there must be a period when output is below the natural rate. The formulation in (6.22)–(6.23) is known as the *accelerationist* Phillips curve.[11]

This model is much more successful than models with a permanent output-inflation tradeoff at fitting the macroeconomic history of the United States over the past quarter-century. Consider, for example, the behavior of unemployment and inflation from 1980 to 1995. The model attributes the combination of high inflation and high unemployment in the early 1980s to contractionary shifts in demand with inflation starting from a high level. The high unemployment was associated with falls in inflation (and with larger falls when unemployment was higher), just as the model predicts. Once unemployment fell below the 6 to 7 percent range in the mid-1980s, inflation began to creep up. When unemployment returned to this range at the end of the decade, inflation held steady. Inflation again declined when unemployment rose above 7 percent in 1992, and it again held steady when unemployment fell below 7 percent in 1993 and 1994. All these movements are consistent with the model.

Although the model of core inflation in (6.23) is often useful, it has important limitations. For example, if we interpret a period as being fairly short (such as a quarter), core inflation is likely to take more than one period to respond fully to changes in actual inflation. In this case, it is reasonable to replace the right-hand side of (6.23) with a weighted average of inflation over the previous several periods.

Perhaps the most important drawback of the model of supply in (6.22)–(6.23) is that it assumes that the behavior of core inflation is independent of the economic environment. For example, if the formulation in (6.23) always held, there would be a permanent tradeoff between output and the change in inflation. That is, equations (6.22) and (6.23) imply that if policymakers are willing to accept ever-increasing inflation, they can push output permanently above its natural rate. But the same arguments that Friedman and Phelps make against a permanent output-inflation tradeoff imply that if policymakers attempt to pursue this strategy, workers and firms will eventually stop following (6.22)–(6.23) and will adjust their behavior to account for the increases in inflation they know are going to occur; as a result, output will return to its natural rate.

In his original presentation of the natural-rate hypothesis, Friedman discussed another, more realistic, example of how the behavior of core inflation

---

[11] The standard rule of thumb is that for each percentage point that the unemployment rate exceeds the natural rate, inflation falls by one-half percentage point per year. And, as we saw in Section 5.1, for each percentage point that $u$ exceeds $\bar{u}$, $Y$ is roughly 2 percent less than $\bar{Y}$. Thus if each period corresponds to a year, $\lambda$ in equation (6.22) is about $\frac{1}{4}$.

may depend on the environment: how rapidly core inflation adjusts to changes in inflation is likely to depend on how long-lasting actual movements in inflation typically are. If this is right, then in a situation like the one that Phillips studied, where there are many transitory movements in inflation, core inflation will vary little; the data will therefore suggest a stable relationship between output and inflation. But in a setting like the United States in the 1970s and 1980s, where there are sustained periods of high and of low inflation, core inflation will vary more, and thus there will be no consistent link between output and the level of inflation.

Carrying these criticisms of (6.22)-(6.23) to their logical extreme would suggest that we replace core inflation in (6.22) with expected inflation:

$$\pi_t = \pi_t^e + \lambda(\ln Y_t - \ln \overline{Y}_t) + \varepsilon_t^S, \tag{6.24}$$

where $\pi_t^e$ is expected inflation. This formulation captures the ideas in the previous examples. For example, (6.24) implies that unless expectations are grossly irrational, no policy can permanently raise output above its natural rate, since that requires that workers' and firms' forecasts of inflation are always too low. Similarly, since expectations of future inflation respond less to current inflation when movements in inflation tend to be shorter-lived, (6.24) is consistent with Friedman's example of how the output-inflation relationship is likely to vary with the behavior of actual inflation.

Nonetheless, practical modern formulations of pricing behavior generally do not use the model of supply in (6.24). The central reason is that, as we will see in Section 6.9, if one assumes that price- and wage-setters are rational in forming their expectations, then (6.24) has strong implications—implications that do not appear to be supported by the data. Alternatively, if one assumes that workers and firms do not form their expectations rationally, one is resting the theory on irrationality.

A natural compromise between the models of core inflation in (6.23) and in (6.24) is to assume that core inflation is a weighted average of past inflation and expected inflation. With this assumption, we have a *hybrid* Phillips curve:

$$\pi_t = \phi\pi_t^e + (1 - \phi)\pi_{t-1} + \lambda(\ln Y_t - \ln \overline{Y}_t) + \varepsilon_t^S, \qquad 0 \le \phi \le 1. \tag{6.25}$$

As long as $\phi$ is strictly less than 1, there is some *inertia* in wage and price inflation. That is, there is some link between past and future inflation beyond effects operating through expectations. We will return to this issue in the next chapter.

## Aggregate Demand, Aggregate Supply, and the AS-AD Diagram

Our simple formulation of the demand side of the economy in Section 6.1 had two elements: the new Keynesian *IS* curve, $\ln Y_t = E[\ln Y_{t+1}] - \frac{1}{\theta}r_t$

(equation [6.8]), and the *LM* curve, $M_t/P_t = Y_t^{\theta/\nu}[(1+i_t)/i_t]^{1/\nu}$ (equation [6.10]). Coupled with the assumption that $M_t$ was set exogenously by the central bank, these equations led to the *IS-LM* diagram in $(Y,r)$ space (Figure 6.1).

The ideas captured by the new Keynesian *IS* curve are appealing and useful: increases in the real interest rate reduce the current demand for goods relative to future demand, and increases in expected future income raise current demand. The *LM* curve, in contrast, is quite problematic in practical applications. One difficulty is that the model becomes much more complicated once we relax Section 6.1's assumption that prices are permanently fixed; changes in either $P_t$ or $\pi_t^e$ shift the *LM* curve in $(Y,r)$ space. A second difficulty is that modern central banks do not focus on the money supply.

An alternative approach that avoids the difficulties with the LM curve is to assume that the central bank conducts policy in terms of a rule for the interest rate (Taylor, 1993; Bryant, Hooper, and Mann, 1993). We will discuss such *interest-rate rules* extensively in our examination of monetary policy in Chapter 11. For now, however, we simply assume that the central bank conducts policy so as to make the real interest rate an increasing function of the gap between actual and potential output and of inflation:

$$r_t = r(\ln Y_t - \ln \overline{Y}_t, \pi_t), \qquad r_1(\bullet) > 0, r_2(\bullet) > 0. \tag{6.26}$$

The way the central bank carries out this policy is by adjusting the money supply to make (6.26) hold. That is, it sets the money supply at $t$ so that the money market equilibrium condition, which we can write as $\frac{M_t}{P_t} = Y_t^{\theta/\nu}[(1+r_t+\pi_t^e)/(r_t+\pi_t^e)]^{1/\nu}$ yields the value of $r_t$ that satisfies (6.26). For most purposes, however, we can neglect the money market and work directly with (6.26).

The central bank's interest-rate rule, (6.26), directly implies an upward-sloping relationship between $Y_t$ and $r_t$ (for a given value of $\pi_t$). This relationship is known as the *MP* curve. It is shown together with the *IS* curve in Figure 6.8.

The determination of output and inflation can then be described by two curves in output-inflation space, an upward-sloping aggregate supply (*AS*) curve and a downward-sloping aggregate demand (*AD*) curve. The *AS* curve follows directly from (6.22), $\pi_t = \pi_t^* + \lambda(\ln Y_t - \ln \overline{Y}_t) + \varepsilon_t^S$. The *AD* curve comes from the *IS* and *MP* curves. To see this, consider a rise in inflation. Since $\pi$ does not enter households' intertemporal first-order condition, (6.7), the *IS* curve is unaffected. But since the monetary-policy rule, $r = r(\ln Y - \ln \overline{Y}, \pi)$, is increasing in $\pi$, the rise in inflation increases the real interest rate the central bank sets at a given level of output. That is, the *MP* curve shifts up. As a result, $r$ rises and $Y$ falls. Thus the level of output at the intersection of the *IS* and *MP* curves is a decreasing function of inflation. The *AS* and *AD* curves are shown in Figure 6.9.

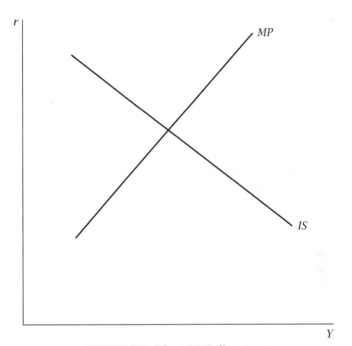

**FIGURE 6.8 The *IS-MP* diagram**

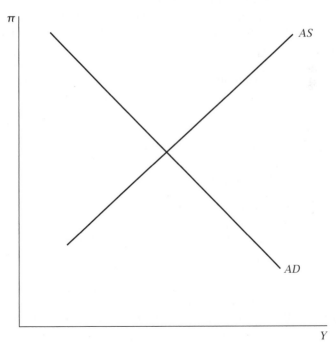

**FIGURE 6.9 The *AS-AD* diagram**

## Example: IS Shocks

We now have a three-equation model: the new Keynesian *IS* curve, the *MP* curve, and the *AS* curve. A common approach to obtaining a model one can work with is to assume that core inflation, $\pi_t^*$, is given by lagged inflation, $\pi_{t-1}$, as in (6.23), and that the *MP* curve is linear. Even then, however, the conjunction of forward-looking elements (from the $E_t[\ln Y_{t+1}]$ term in the *IS* curve) and backward-looking ones (from the $\pi_{t-1}$ term in the *AS* curve) makes solving the model complicated.

A solution to this difficulty that is somewhat arbitrary but nonetheless often useful is to simply drop the $E_t[\ln Y_{t+1}]$ term from the *IS* curve. The result is the traditional *IS* curve, where output depends negatively on the real interest rate and is not affected by any other endogenous variables. The attractiveness of this approach is that it makes the model very easy to solve. There is no need to assume linear functional forms; shocks to any of the equations can be considered without making assumptions about the processes followed by the shocks; and the analysis can be done graphically. For these reasons, this approach is often useful and is the standard approach in undergraduate teaching.

At the same time, however, the logic of the model implies that the expected output term belongs in the *IS* equation, and thus that it is desirable to understand the implications of the full model. To get a feel for this, here we consider a very stripped-down version. Crucially, we assume that the monetary-policy rule depends only on output and not on inflation; this assumption eliminates the backward-looking element of output behavior. Second, we assume that the only shocks are to the *IS* curve, and that the shocks follow a first-order autoregressive process. Finally, we make several minor assumptions to simplify the notation and presentation: $\ln \overline{Y}_t$ is zero for all $t$, the *MP* equation is linear, the constant term in the *MP* equation is zero, and $y_t$ denotes $\ln Y_t$.

These assumptions give us the system:

$$\pi_t = \pi_{t-1} + \lambda y_t, \qquad \lambda > 0, \tag{6.27}$$

$$r_t = b y_t, \qquad b > 0, \tag{6.28}$$

$$y_t = E_t[y_{t+1}] - \frac{1}{\theta} r_t + u_t^{IS}, \qquad \theta > 0, \tag{6.29}$$

$$u_t^{IS} = \rho_{IS} u_{t-1}^{IS} + e_t^{IS}, \qquad -1 < \rho_{IS} < 1, \tag{6.30}$$

where $e^{IS}$ is white noise. Equation (6.27) is the *AS* curve, (6.28) is the *MP* curve, (6.29) is the *IS* curve, and (6.30) describes the behavior of the *IS* shocks.

We can combine (6.28) and (6.29) and use straightforward algebra to solve for $y_t$ in terms of $u_t^{IS}$ and $E_t[y_{t+1}]$:

$$y_t = \frac{\theta}{\theta + b} E_t[y_{t+1}] + \frac{\theta}{\theta + b} u_t^{IS}$$

$$\equiv \phi E_t[y_{t+1}] + \phi u_t^{IS},$$

(6.31)

where $\phi = \theta/(\theta + b)$. Note that our assumptions imply $0 < \phi < 1$.

Equation (6.31) poses a challenge: it expresses $y$ in terms of not just the disturbance, $u_t^{IS}$, but the expectation of the future value of an endogenous variable, $E_t[y_{t+1}]$. Thus it is not immediately clear how to trace out the effect of a shock. To address this problem, note that (6.31) holds in all future periods:

$$y_{t+j} = \phi E_{t+j}[y_{t+j+1}] + \phi u_{t+j}^{IS} \qquad \text{for } j = 1, 2, 3, \ldots$$

(6.32)

Taking expectations of both sides of (6.32) as of time $t$ implies

$$E_t[y_{t+j}] = \phi E_t[y_{t+j+1}] + \phi \rho_{IS}^j u_t^{IS}.$$

(6.33)

Equation (6.33) uses the fact that $E_t[E_{t+j}[y_{t+j+1}]]$ is simply $E_t[y_{t+j+1}]$; otherwise agents would be expecting to revise their estimate of $y_{t+j+1}$ either up or down, which would imply that their original estimate was not rational. The fact that the current expectation of a future expectation of a variable equals the current expectation of the variable is known as *the law of iterated projections*.

We can now iterate (6.31) forward. That is, we first express $E_t[y_{t+1}]$ in terms of $E_t[y_{t+2}]$ and $E_t[u_{t+1}^{IS}]$; we then express $E_t[y_{t+2}]$ in terms of $E_t[y_{t+3}]$ and $E_t[u_{t+2}^{IS}]$; and so on. Doing this gives us:

$$y_t = \phi u_t^{IS} + \phi\big(\phi E_t[y_{t+2}] + \phi \rho_{IS} u_t^{IS}\big)$$

$$= \phi u_t^{IS} + \phi^2 \rho_{IS} u_t^{IS} + \phi^2\big(\phi E_t[y_{t+3}] + \phi \rho_{IS}^2 u_t^{IS}\big)$$

$$= \cdots$$

(6.34)

$$= \big(\phi + \phi^2 \rho_{IS} + \phi^3 \rho_{IS}^2 + \cdots\big) u_t^{IS} + \lim_{n \to \infty} \phi^n E_t[y_{t+n}]$$

$$= \frac{\phi}{1 - \phi \rho_{IS}} u_t^{IS} + \lim_{n \to \infty} \phi^n E_t[y_{t+n}].$$

If we assume that $\lim_{n \to \infty} \phi^n E_t[y_{t+n}]$ converges to zero (an issue we will return to in a moment) and substitute back in for $\phi$, we obtain

$$y_t = \frac{\theta}{\theta + b - \theta \rho_{IS}} u_t^{IS}.$$

(6.35)

This expression shows how various forces influence how shocks to demand affect output. For example, a more aggressive monetary-policy response to output movements (that is, a higher value of $b$) dampens the effects of shocks to the $IS$ curve.

Observe that in the absence of the forward-looking aspect of the $IS$ curve (that is, if the $IS$ equation is just $y_t = -(1/\theta)r_t + u_t^{IS}$), output is $[\theta/(\theta + b)]u_t^{IS}$. Equation (6.35) shows that accounting for forward-looking behavior raises the coefficient on $u_t^{IS}$ as long as $\rho_{IS} > 0$. That is, forward-looking consumption behavior magnifies the effects of persistent shocks to demand.

Equation (6.35) for output and the $AS$ equation, (6.27), imply that inflation is given by

$$\pi_t = \pi_{t-1} + \frac{\theta\lambda}{\theta + b - \theta\rho_{IS}}u_t^{IS}. \tag{6.36}$$

Because there is no feedback from inflation to the real interest rate, there is no force acting to stabilize inflation. Indeed, if the shocks to the $IS$ curve are positively serially correlated, the change in inflation is positively serially correlated.

The solution for $y_t$ in (6.34) includes the term $\lim_{n\to\infty} \phi^n E_t[y_{t+n}]$, which thus far we have been assuming converges to zero. Since $\phi$ is less than one, this term could fail to converge only if $E_t[y_{t+n}]$ diverged. That is, agents would have to expect $y$ to diverge, which cannot happen. Thus assuming $\lim_{n\to\infty} \phi^n E_t[y_{t+n}] = 0$ is appropriate.

One other aspect of this example is worth noting. Suppose $\phi > 1$ but $\phi\rho_{IS} < 1$. $\phi > 1$ could arise if the central bank followed the perverse policy of cutting the real interest rate in response to increases in output (so that $b$ was negative). With $\phi\rho_{IS} < 1$, the sum in equation (6.34) still converges, and so that expression is still correct. And if (6.35) holds, $\lim_{n\to\infty} \phi^n E_t[y_{t+n}]$ equals $\lim_{n\to\infty} \phi^n \rho_{IS}^n[\theta/(\theta + b - \theta\rho_{IS})]u_t^{IS}$, which is zero. That is, although one might expect $\phi > 1$ to generate instability, the conventional solution to the model still carries over to this case as long as $\phi\rho_{IS} < 1$.

Interestingly, however, this is now no longer the only solution. If $\phi$ exceeds 1, then $\lim_{n\to\infty} \phi^n E_t[y_{t+n}]$ can differ from zero without $E_t[y_{t+n}]$ diverging. As a result, there can be spontaneous, self-fulfilling changes in the path of output. To see this, suppose that $u_t^{IS} = 0$ for all $t$ and that initially $y_t = 0$ for all $t$. Now suppose that in some period, which we will call period 0, $y$ rises by some amount X—not because of a change in tastes, government purchases, or some other external influence (that is, not because of a nonzero realization of $u_0^{IS}$), but simply because a change in agents' beliefs about the equilibrium path of the economy. If agents' expectation of $y_t$ is $X/\phi^t$ for $t \geq 0$, they will act in ways that make their expectations correct. That is, this change can be self-fulfilling.

When the economy has multiple equilibria in this way, the solution without spontaneous, self-fulfilling output movements is known as the *fundamental solution*. Solutions with self-fulfilling output movements are known as *sunspot solutions*. Although here the assumption that leads to the possibility of a sunspot solution is contrived, there are many models where this possibility arises naturally. We will therefore return to the general issue of self-fulfilling equilibria in Section 6.8, and to sunspot solutions in a model similar in spirit to this one in Section 11.5.[12]

# Part B   Microeconomic Foundations of Incomplete Nominal Adjustment

Some type of incomplete nominal adjustment appears essential to understanding why monetary changes have real effects. This part of the chapter therefore examines the question of what might give rise to incomplete nominal adjustment.

The fact that what is needed is a nominal imperfection has an important implication.[13] Individuals care mainly about real prices and quantities: real wages, hours of work, real consumption levels, and the like. Nominal magnitudes matter to them only in ways that are minor and easily overcome. Prices and wages are quoted in nominal terms, but it costs little to change (or index) them. Individuals are not fully informed about the aggregate price level, but they can obtain accurate information at little cost. Debt contracts are usually specified in nominal terms, but they too could be indexed with little difficulty. And individuals hold modest amounts of currency, which is denominated in nominal terms, but they can change their holdings easily. There is no way in which nominal magnitudes are of great direct importance to individuals.

This discussion suggests that nominal frictions that are small at the microeconomic level somehow have a large effect on the macroeconomy. Much of the research on the microeconomic foundations of nominal rigidity is devoted to addressing the questions of whether this can plausibly be the case and of what conditions are needed for this to be true.[14]

Most of this part of the chapter addresses these questions for a specific view about the nominal imperfection. In particular, we focus on a static model where firms face a *menu cost* of price adjustment—a small fixed cost of changing a nominal price. (The standard example is the cost incurred by a restaurant in printing new menus—hence the name.) The goal is to characterize the microeconomic conditions that cause menu costs to lead to significant nominal stickiness in response to a one-time monetary shock. Section 6.9 considers the case where the nominal imperfection is instead lack of complete information about the aggregate price level and briefly

---

[12] For more on the model of this section, see Problems 6.8–6.9. For more on the solutions of linear models with expectations of future variables, see Blanchard and Kahn (1980).

[13] In places, the introduction to Part B and the material in Sections 6.6–6.7 draw on D. Romer (1993).

[14] The seminal papers are Mankiw (1985) and Akerlof and Yellen (1985). See also Parkin (1986), Rotemberg (1982), and Blanchard and Kiyotaki (1987).

discusses other possible sources of incomplete nominal adjustment. We will see that the same fundamental issues that arise with menu costs also arise with other nominal imperfections.

Our goal in this chapter is not to try to construct an even remotely realistic macroeconomic model. For that reason, the models we will consider are very simple. The next chapter will begin to make the models more realistic and useful in practical applications.

# 6.5   A Model of Imperfect Competition and Price-Setting

Before turning to menu costs and the effects of monetary shocks, we first examine an economy of imperfectly competitive price-setters with complete price flexibility. There are two reasons for analyzing this model. First, as we will see, imperfect competition alone has interesting macroeconomic consequences. Second, the models in the rest of the chapter are concerned with the causes and effects of barriers to price adjustment. To address these issues, we will need a model that shows us what prices firms would choose in the absence of barriers to adjustment and what happens when prices depart from those levels.

## Assumptions

There is a continuum of differentiated goods indexed by $i \in [0,1]$. Each good is produced by a single firm with monopoly rights to the production of the good. Firm $i$'s production function is just

$$Y_i = L_i, \tag{6.37}$$

where $L_i$ is the amount of labor it hires and $Y_i$ is its output. Firms hire labor in a perfectly competitive labor market and sell output in imperfectly competitive goods markets. In this section, firms can set their prices freely. They are owned by the households, and so any profits they earn accrue to the households. As in the model of Section 6.1, we normalize the number of households to 1.

The utility of the representative household depends positively on its consumption and negatively on the amount of labor it supplies. It takes the form

$$U = C - \frac{1}{\gamma} L^{\gamma}, \qquad \gamma > 1. \tag{6.38}$$

Crucially, $C$ is not the household's total consumption of all goods. If it were, goods would be perfect substitutes for one another, and so firms would not have market power. Instead, it is an index of the household's consumption of the individual goods. It takes the constant-elasticity-of-substitution form

$$C = \left[ \int_{i=0}^{1} C_i^{(\eta-1)/\eta} \right]^{\eta/(\eta-1)}, \qquad \eta > 1. \tag{6.39}$$

This formulation, which parallels the production function in the Romer model of endogenous technological change in Section 3.5, is due to Dixit and Stiglitz (1977). Note that it has the convenient feature that if all the $C_i$'s are equal, $C$ equals the common level of the $C_i$'s. The assumption that $\eta > 1$ implies that the elasticity of demand for each good is greater than 1, and thus that profit-maximizing prices are not infinite.

As in the model in Section 6.1, investment, government purchases, and international trade are absent from the model. We will therefore use $C$ as our measure of output in this economy:

$$Y \equiv C. \tag{6.40}$$

Households choose their labor supply and their purchases of the consumption goods to maximize their utility, taking as given the wage, prices of goods, and profits from firms. Firms choose their prices and the amounts of labor to hire to maximize profits, taking the wage and the demand curves for their goods as given.

Finally, to be able to analyze the effects of monetary changes and other shifts in aggregate demand, we need to add an aggregate demand side to the model. We do this in the simplest possible way by assuming

$$Y = \frac{M}{P}. \tag{6.41}$$

There are various interpretations of (6.41). The simplest, and most appropriate for our purposes, is that it is just a shortcut approach to modeling aggregate demand. Equation (6.41) implies an inverse relationship between the price level and output, which is the essential feature of aggregate demand. Since our focus is on the supply side of the economy, there is little point in modeling aggregate demand more fully. Under this interpretation, $M$ should be thought of as a generic variable affecting aggregate demand rather than as money.

It is also possible to derive (6.41) from more complete models. We could introduce real money balances to the utility function along the lines of Section 6.1. With an appropriate specification, this gives rise to (6.41). Rotemberg (1987) derives (6.41) from a *cash-in-advance constraint*. Finally, Woodford (2003) observes that (6.41) arises if the central bank conducts monetary policy to achieve a target level of nominal GDP.

Under the money-in-the-utility function and cash-in-advance-constraint interpretations of (6.41), it is natural to think of $M$ as literally money. In this case the right-hand side should be modified to $MV/P$, where $V$ captures aggregate demand disturbances other than shifts in money supply. Under Woodford's interpretation, in contrast, $M$ is the central bank's target level of nominal GDP.

## Household Behavior

In analyzing households' behavior, it is easiest to start by considering how they allocate their consumption spending among the different goods. Consider a household that spends $S$. The Lagrangian for its utility-maximization problem is

$$\mathcal{L} = \left[ \int_{i=0}^{1} C_i^{(\eta-1)/\eta} di \right]^{\eta/(\eta-1)} + \lambda \left[ S - \int_{i=0}^{1} P_i C_i di \right]. \tag{6.42}$$

The first-order condition for $C_i$ is

$$\frac{\eta}{\eta-1} \left[ \int_{j=0}^{1} C_j^{(\eta-1)/\eta} dj \right]^{1/(\eta-1)} \frac{\eta-1}{\eta} C_i^{-1/\eta} = \lambda P_i. \tag{6.43}$$

The only terms in (6.43) that depend on $i$ are $C_i^{-1/\eta}$ and $P_i$. Thus, $C_i$ must take the form

$$C_i = A P_i^{-\eta}. \tag{6.44}$$

To find $A$ in terms of the variables the household takes as given, substitute (6.44) into the budget constraint, $\int_{i=0}^{1} P_i C_i \, di = S$, and then solve for $A$. This yields

$$A = \frac{S}{\int_{j=0}^{1} P_j^{1-\eta} dj}. \tag{6.45}$$

Substituting this result into expression (6.44) for the $C_i$'s and then into the definition of $C$ in (6.39) gives us

$$C = \left[ \int_{i=0}^{1} \left( \frac{S}{\int_{j=0}^{1} P_j^{1-\eta} dj} P_i^{-\eta} \right)^{(\eta-1)/\eta} di \right]^{\eta/(\eta-1)}$$

$$= \frac{S}{\int_{j=0}^{1} P_j^{1-\eta} dj} \left( \int_{i=0}^{1} P_i^{1-\eta} di \right)^{\eta/(\eta-1)} \tag{6.46}$$

$$= \frac{S}{\left( \int_{i=0}^{1} P_i^{1-\eta} di \right)^{1/(1-\eta)}}.$$

Equation (6.46) tells us that when households allocate their spending across goods optimally, the cost of obtaining one unit of $C$ is

$\left(\int_{i=0}^{1} P_i^{1-\eta} di\right)^{1/(1-\eta)}$. That is, the price index corresponding to the utility function (6.39) is

$$P = \left(\int_{i=0}^{1} P_i^{1-\eta} di\right)^{1/(1-\eta)}. \tag{6.47}$$

Note that the index has the attractive feature that if all the $P_i$'s are equal, the index equals the common level of the $P_i$'s.

Finally, expressions (6.44), (6.45), and (6.47) imply

$$C_i = \left(\frac{P_i}{P}\right)^{-\eta} \frac{S}{P}$$

$$= \left(\frac{P_i}{P}\right)^{-\eta} C. \tag{6.48}$$

Thus the elasticity of demand for each individual good is $\eta$.

The household's only other choice variable is its labor supply. Its spending equals $WL + R$, where $W$ is the wage and $R$ is its profit income, and so its consumption is $(WL + R)/P$. Its problem for choosing $L$ is therefore

$$\max_{L} \frac{WL + R}{P} - \frac{1}{\gamma} L^{\gamma}. \tag{6.49}$$

The first-order condition for $L$ is

$$\frac{W}{P} - L^{\gamma-1} = 0, \tag{6.50}$$

which implies

$$L = \left(\frac{W}{P}\right)^{1/(\gamma-1)}. \tag{6.51}$$

Thus labor supply is an increasing function of the real wage, with an elasticity of $1/(\gamma - 1)$.

Since all households are the same and we have normalized the number of households to one, equation (6.51) describes not just $L$ for a representative household, but the aggregate value of $L$.

## Firm Behavior

The real profits of the monopolistic producer of good $i$ are its real revenues minus its real costs:

$$\frac{R_i}{P} = \frac{P_i}{P} Y_i - \frac{W}{P} L_i. \tag{6.52}$$

The production function, (6.37), implies $L_i = Y_i$, and the demand function, (6.48), implies $Y_i = (P_i/P)^{-\eta} Y$. (Recall that $Y = C$ and that the amount of good $i$ produced must equal the amount consumed.) Substituting these expressions into (6.52) implies

$$\frac{R_i}{P} = \left(\frac{P_i}{P}\right)^{1-\eta} Y - \frac{W}{P}\left(\frac{P_i}{P}\right)^{-\eta} Y. \tag{6.53}$$

The first-order condition for $P_i/P$ is

$$(1 - \eta)\left(\frac{P_i}{P}\right)^{-\eta} Y + \eta \frac{W}{P}\left(\frac{P_i}{P}\right)^{-\eta-1} Y = 0. \tag{6.54}$$

To solve this expression for $P_i/P$, divide both sides by $Y$ and by $(P_i/P)^{-\eta}$. Solving for $P_i/P$ then yields

$$\frac{P_i}{P} = \frac{\eta}{\eta - 1}\frac{W}{P}. \tag{6.55}$$

That is, we get the standard result that a producer with market power sets price as a markup over marginal cost, with the size of the markup determined by the elasticity of demand.

## Equilibrium

Because the model is symmetric, its equilibrium is also symmetric. As described above, all households supply the same amount of labor and have the same demand curves. Similarly, the fact that all firms face the same demand curve and the same real wage implies that they all charge the same amount and produce the same amount. And since the production of each good is the same, the measure of aggregate output, $Y$, is just this common level of output. Finally, since the production function is one-for-one, this in turn equals the common level of labor supply. That is, in equilibrium $Y = C = L$.

We can use (6.50) or (6.51) to express the real wage as a function of output:

$$\frac{W}{P} = Y^{\gamma-1}. \tag{6.56}$$

Substituting this expression into the price equation, (6.55), yields an expression for each producer's desired relative price as a function of aggregate output:

$$\frac{P_i^*}{P} = \frac{\eta}{\eta - 1} Y^{\gamma-1}. \tag{6.57}$$

For future reference, it is useful to write this expression in logarithms:

$$p_i^* - p = \ln\frac{\eta}{\eta - 1} + (\gamma - 1)y \tag{6.58}$$

$$\equiv c + \phi y,$$

where lowercase letters denote the logs of the corresponding uppercase variables.

We know that each producer charges the same price, and that the price index, $P$, equals this common price. Equilibrium therefore requires that each producer, taking $P$ as given, sets his or her own price equal to $P$; that is, each producer's desired relative price must equal 1. From (6.57), this condition is $[\eta/(\eta-1)]Y^{\gamma-1}=1$, or

$$Y=\left(\frac{\eta-1}{\eta}\right)^{1/(\gamma-1)}. \tag{6.59}$$

This is the equilibrium level of output.

Finally, we can use the aggregate demand equation, $Y=M/P$, to find the equilibrium price level:

$$P=\frac{M}{Y}$$

$$=\frac{M}{\left(\dfrac{\eta-1}{\eta}\right)^{1/(\gamma-1)}}. \tag{6.60}$$

## Implications

When producers have market power, they produce less than the socially optimal amount. To see this, note that in a symmetric allocation each individual supplies some amount $\bar{L}$ of labor, and production of each good and each individual's consumption equal that $\bar{L}$. Thus the problem of finding the best symmetric allocation reduces to choosing $\bar{L}$ to maximize $\bar{L}-(1/\gamma)\bar{L}^{\gamma}$. The solution is simply $\bar{L}=1$. As (6.59) shows, equilibrium output is less than this. Intuitively, the fact that producers face downward-sloping demand curves means that the marginal revenue product of labor is less than its marginal product. As a result, the real wage is less than the marginal product of labor: from (6.55) (and the fact that each $P_i$ equals $P$ in equilibrium), the real wage is $(\eta-1)/\eta$; the marginal product of labor, in contrast, is 1. This reduces the quantity of labor supplied, and thus causes equilibrium output to be less than optimal. From (6.59), equilibrium output is $[(\eta-1)/\eta]^{1/(\gamma-1)}$. Thus the gap between the equilibrium and optimal levels of output is greater when producers have more market power (that is, when $\eta$ is lower) and when labor supply is more responsive to the real wage (that is, when $\gamma$ is lower).

The fact that equilibrium output is inefficiently low under imperfect competition has important implications for fluctuations. To begin with, it implies that recessions and booms have asymmetric effects on welfare (Mankiw, 1985). In practice, periods when output is unusually high are viewed as good times, and periods when output is unusually low are viewed as bad times. But think about an economy where fluctuations arise from incomplete nominal adjustment in the face of monetary shocks. If the equilibrium in the absence of shocks is optimal, both times of high output and times of low output are departures from the optimum, and thus both are undesirable. But if equilibrium output is less than optimal, a boom brings output closer to the social optimum, whereas a recession pushes it farther away.

In addition, the gap between equilibrium and optimal output implies that pricing decisions have externalities. Suppose the economy is initially in equilibrium, and consider the effects of a marginal reduction in all prices. $M/P$ rises, and so aggregate output rises. This potentially affects welfare through two channels. First, the real wage increases (see [6.56]). Since households employ the same amount of labor in their capacity as owners of the firms as they supply to the labor market, at the margin this increase does not affect welfare. Second, because aggregate output increases, the demand curve for each good, $Y(P_i/P)^{-\eta}$, shifts out. Since firms are selling at prices that exceed marginal costs, this change raises profits, and so increases households' welfare. Thus under imperfect competition, pricing decisions have externalities, and those externalities operate through the overall demand for goods. This externality is often referred to as an *aggregate demand externality* (Blanchard and Kiyotaki, 1987).

The final implication of this analysis is that imperfect competition alone does not imply monetary nonneutrality. A change in the money stock leads to proportional changes in the nominal wage and all nominal prices; output and the real wage are unchanged (see [6.59] and [6.60]).

Finally, since a pricing equation of the form (6.58) is important in later sections, it is worth noting that the basic idea captured by the equation is much more general than the specific model of price-setters' desired prices we are considering here. Equation (6.58) states that $p_i^* - p$ takes the form $c + \phi y$. That is, it states that a price-setter's optimal relative price is increasing in aggregate output. In the particular model we are considering, this arises from increases in the prevailing real wage when output rises. But in a more general setting, it can also arise from increases in the costs of other inputs, from diminishing returns, or from costs of adjusting output.

The fact that price-setters' desired real prices are increasing in aggregate output is necessary for the flexible-price equilibrium to be stable. To see this, note that we can use the fact that $y = m - p$ to rewrite (6.58) as

$$p_i^* = c + (1 - \phi)p + \phi m. \tag{6.61}$$

If $\phi$ is negative, an increase in the price level raises each price-setter's desired price more than one-for-one. This means that if $p$ is above the level that causes individuals to charge a relative price of 1, each individual wants to charge more than the prevailing price level; and if $p$ is below its equilibrium value, each individual wants to charge less than the prevailing price level. Thus if $\phi$ is negative, the flexible-price equilibrium is unstable. We will return to this issue in Section 6.8.

# 6.6   Are Small Frictions Enough?

## General Considerations

Consider an economy, such as that of the previous section, consisting of many price-setting firms. Assume that it is initially at its flexible-price equilibrium. That is, each firm's price is such that if aggregate demand is at its expected level, marginal revenue equals marginal cost. After prices are set, aggregate demand is determined; at this point each firm can change its price by paying a menu cost. For simplicity, prices are assumed to be set afresh at the start of each period. This means that we can consider a single period in isolation. It also means that if a firm pays the menu cost, it sets its price to the new profit-maximizing level.

We want to know when firms change their prices in response to a departure of aggregate demand from its expected level. For concreteness, suppose that demand is less than expected. Since the economy is large, each firm takes other firms' actions as given. Constant nominal prices are thus an equilibrium if, when all other firms hold their prices fixed, the maximum gain to a representative firm from changing its price is less than the menu cost of price adjustment.[15]

To see the general issue involved, consider the marginal revenue–marginal cost diagram in Figure 6.10. The economy begins in equilibrium; thus the representative firm is producing at the point where marginal cost equals marginal revenue (Point A in the diagram). A fall in aggregate demand with other prices unchanged reduces aggregate output, and thus shifts the demand curve that the firm faces to the left—at a given price, demand for the firm's product is lower. Thus the marginal revenue curve shifts in. If the firm does not change its price, its output is determined by demand at the existing price (Point B). At this level of output, marginal revenue exceeds marginal cost, and so the firm has some incentive to lower its price and raise output.[16] If the firm changes its price, it produces at the point where marginal cost and marginal revenue are equal (Point C). The area of the shaded triangle in the diagram shows the additional profits to be gained from reducing price and increasing quantity produced. For the firm to be willing to hold its price fixed, the area of the triangle must be small.

The diagram reveals a crucial point: the firm's incentive to reduce its price may be small even if it is harmed greatly by the fall in demand. The firm would prefer to face the original, higher demand curve, but of course it can only choose a point on the new demand curve. This is an example of

---

[15] The condition for price adjustment by all firms to be an equilibrium is not simply the reverse of this. As a result, there can be cases when both price adjustment and unchanged prices are equilibria. See Problem 6.10.

[16] The fall in aggregate output is likely to reduce the prevailing wage, and therefore to shift the marginal cost curve down. For simplicity, this effect is not shown in the figure.

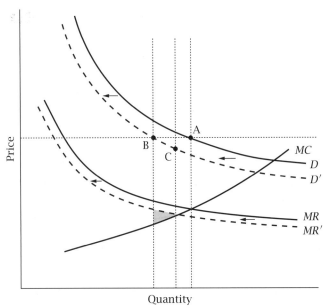

FIGURE 6.10   A representative firm's incentive to change its price in response to a fall in aggregate output (from D. Romer, 1993)

the aggregate demand externality described above: the representative firm is harmed by other firms' failure to cut their prices in the face of the fall in the money supply, just as it is harmed in the model of the previous section by a decision by all firms to raise their prices. As a result, the firm may find that the gain from reducing its price is small even if the shift in its demand curve is large. Thus there is no contradiction between the view that recessions have large costs and the hypothesis that they are caused by falls in aggregate demand and small barriers to price adjustment.

It is not possible, however, to proceed further using a purely diagrammatic analysis. To answer the question of whether the firm's incentive to change its price is likely to be more or less than the menu cost for plausible cases, we must turn to a specific model and find the incentive for price adjustment for reasonable parameter values.

## A Quantitative Example

Consider the model of imperfect competition in Section 6.5. Firm $i$'s real profits equal the quantity sold, $Y(P_i/P)^{-\eta}$, times price minus cost, $(P_i/P) - (W/P)$ (see [6.52]). In addition, labor-market equilibrium requires that the real wage equals $Y^{1/\nu}$, where $\nu \equiv 1/(\gamma - 1)$ is the elasticity of labor supply (see [6.56]). Thus,

$$
\pi_i = Y \left( \frac{P_i}{P} \right)^{-\eta} \left( \frac{P_i}{P} - Y^{1/\nu} \right)
$$

$$
= \frac{M}{P} \left( \frac{P_i}{P} \right)^{1-\eta} - \left( \frac{M}{P} \right)^{(1+\nu)/\nu} \left( \frac{P_i}{P} \right)^{-\eta},
\tag{6.62}
$$

where the second line uses the fact that $Y = M/P$. We know that the profit-maximizing real price in the absence of the menu cost is $\eta/(\eta - 1)$ times marginal cost, or $[\eta/(\eta - 1)](M/P)^{1/\nu}$ (see [6.57]). It follows that the equilibrium when prices are flexible occurs when $[\eta/(\eta - 1)](M/P)^{1/\nu} = 1$, or $M/P = [(\eta - 1)/\eta]^\nu$ (see [6.59]).

We want to find the condition for unchanged nominal prices to be a Nash equilibrium in the face of a departure of $M$ from its expected value. That is, we want to find the condition under which, if all other firms do not adjust their prices, a representative firm does not want to pay the menu cost and adjust its own price. This condition is $\pi_{ADJ} - \pi_{FIXED} < Z$, where $\pi_{ADJ}$ is the representative firm's profits if it adjusts its price to the new profit-maximizing level and other firms do not, $\pi_{FIXED}$ is its profits if no prices change, and $Z$ is the menu cost. Thus we need to find these two profit levels.

Initially all firms are charging the same price, and by assumption, other firms do not change their prices. Thus if firm $i$ does not adjust its price, we have $P_i = P$. Substituting this into (6.62) yields

$$
\pi_{FIXED} = \frac{M}{P} - \left( \frac{M}{P} \right)^{(1+\nu)/\nu}.
\tag{6.63}
$$

If the firm does adjust its price, it sets it to the profit-maximizing value, $[\eta/(\eta - 1)](M/P)^{1/\nu}$. Substituting this into (6.62) yields

$$
\pi_{ADJ} = \frac{M}{P} \left( \frac{\eta}{\eta - 1} \right)^{1-\eta} \left( \frac{M}{P} \right)^{(1-\eta)/\nu} - \left( \frac{M}{P} \right)^{(1+\nu)/\nu} \left( \frac{\eta}{\eta - 1} \right)^{-\eta} \left( \frac{M}{P} \right)^{-\eta/\nu}
$$

$$
= \frac{1}{\eta - 1} \left( \frac{\eta}{\eta - 1} \right)^{-\eta} \left( \frac{M}{P} \right)^{(1+\nu-\eta)/\nu}.
\tag{6.64}
$$

It is straightforward to check that $\pi_{ADJ}$ and $\pi_{FIXED}$ are equal when $M/P$ equals its flexible-price equilibrium value, and that otherwise $\pi_{ADJ}$ is greater than $\pi_{FIXED}$.

To find the firm's incentive to change its price, we need values for $\eta$ and $\nu$. Since labor supply appears relatively inelastic, consider $\nu = 0.1$. Suppose also that $\eta = 5$, which implies that price is 1.25 times marginal cost. These parameter values imply that the flexible-price level of output is $Y^{EQ} = [(\eta - 1)/\eta]^\nu \simeq 0.978$. Now consider a firm's incentive to adjust its price in response to a 3 percent fall in $M$ with other prices unchanged.

Substituting $v = 0.1, \eta = 5$, and $Y = 0.97Y^{\mathrm{EQ}}$ into (6.63) and (6.64) yields $\pi_{\mathrm{ADJ}} - \pi_{\mathrm{FIXED}} \simeq 0.253$.

Since $Y^{\mathrm{EQ}}$ is about 1, this calculation implies that the representative firm's incentive to pay the menu cost in response to a 3 percent change in output is about a quarter of revenue. No plausible cost of price adjustment can prevent firms from changing their prices in the face of this incentive. Thus, in this setting firms adjust their prices in the face of all but the smallest shocks, and money is virtually neutral.[17]

The source of the difficulty lies in the labor market. The labor market clears, and labor supply is relatively inelastic. Thus, as in Case 2 of Section 6.2, the real wage falls considerably when aggregate output falls. Producers' costs are therefore very low, and so they have a strong incentive to cut their prices and raise output. But this means that unchanged nominal prices cannot be an equilibrium.[18]

# 6.7   Real Rigidity

## General Considerations

Consider again a firm that is deciding whether to change its price in the face of a fall in aggregate demand with other prices held fixed. Figure 6.11 shows the firm's profits as a function of its price. The fall in aggregate output affects this function in two ways. First, it shifts the profit function vertically. The fact that the demand for the firm's good falls tends to shift the function down. The fact that the real wage falls, on the other hand, tends to shift the function up. In the case shown in the figure, the net effect is a downward shift. As described above, the firm cannot undo this change. Second, the firm's profit-maximizing price is less than before.[19] This the firm can do

---

[17] Although $\pi_{\mathrm{ADJ}} - \pi_{\mathrm{FIXED}}$ is sensitive to the values of $v$ and $\eta$, there are no remotely reasonable values that imply that the incentive for price adjustment is small. Consider, for example, $\eta = 3$ (implying a markup of 50 percent) and $v = \frac{1}{3}$. Even with these extreme values, the incentive to pay the menu cost is 0.8 percent of the flexible-price level of revenue for a 3 percent fall in output, and 2.4 percent for a 5 percent fall. Even though these incentives are much smaller than those in the baseline calculation, they are still surely larger than the barriers to price adjustment for most firms.

[18] It is not possible to avoid the problem by assuming that the cost of adjustment applies to wages rather than prices, in the spirit of Case 1 of Section 6.2. With this assumption, the incentive to cut prices would indeed be low. But the incentive to cut wages would be high: firms (which could greatly reduce their labor costs) and workers (who could greatly increase their hours of work) would bid wages down.

[19] This corresponds to the assumption that the profit-maximizing relative price is increasing in aggregate output; that is, it corresponds to the assumption that $\phi > 0$ in the pricing equation, (6.58). As described in Section 6.5, this condition is needed for the equilibrium with flexible prices to be stable.

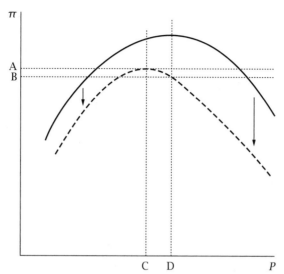

**FIGURE 6.11** The impact of a fall in aggregate output on the representative firm's profits as a function of its price

something about. If the firm does not pay the menu cost, its price remains the same, and so it is not charging the new profit-maximizing price. If the firm pays the menu cost, on the other hand, it can go to the peak of the new profit function.

The firm's incentive to adjust its price is thus given by the distance AB in the diagram. This distance depends on two factors: the difference between the old and new profit-maximizing prices, and the curvature of the profit function. We consider each in turn.

Since other firms' prices are unchanged, a change in the firm's nominal price is also a change in its real price. In addition, the fact that others' prices are unchanged means that the shift in aggregate demand changes aggregate output. Thus the difference between the firm's new and old profit-maximizing prices (distance CD in the figure) is determined by how the profit-maximizing real price depends on aggregate output: when the firm's profit-maximizing price is less responsive to aggregate output (holding the curvature of the profit function fixed), its incentive to adjust its price is smaller.

A smaller responsiveness of profit-maximizing real prices to aggregate output is referred to as greater *real rigidity* (Ball and D. Romer, 1990). In terms of equation (6.58) ($p_i^* - p = c + \phi y$), greater real rigidity corresponds to a lower value of $\phi$. Real rigidity alone does not cause monetary disturbances to have real effects: if prices can adjust fully, money is neutral regardless of the degree of real rigidity. But real rigidity magnifies the effects of nominal rigidity: the greater the degree of real rigidity, the larger the range of prices for which nonadjustment of prices is an equilibrium.

The curvature of the profit function determines the cost of a given departure of price from the profit-maximizing level. When profits are less sensitive to departures from the optimum, the incentive for price adjustment is smaller (for a given degree of real rigidity), and so the range of shocks for which nonadjustment is an equilibrium is larger. Thus, in general terms, what is needed for small costs of price adjustment to generate substantial nominal rigidity is some combination of real rigidity and of insensitivity of the profit function.

Seen in terms of real rigidity and insensitivity of the profit function, it is easy to see why the incentive for price adjustment in our baseline calculation is so large: there is immense "real flexibility" rather than real rigidity. Since the profit-maximizing real price is $[\eta/(\eta-1)]Y^{1/\nu}$, its elasticity with respect to output is $1/\nu$. If the elasticity of labor supply, $\nu$, is small, the elasticity of $(P_i/P)^*$ with respect to $Y$ is large. A value of $\nu$ of 0.1, for example, implies an elasticity of $(P_i/P)^*$ with respect to $Y$ of 10.

An analogy may help to make clear how the combination of menu costs with either real rigidity or insensitivity of the profit function (or both) can lead to considerable nominal stickiness: monetary disturbances may have real effects for the same reasons that the switch to daylight saving time does.[20] The resetting of clocks is a purely nominal change—it simply alters the labels assigned to different times of day. But the change is associated with changes in real schedules—that is, the times of various activities relative to the sun. And there is no doubt that the switch to daylight saving time is the cause of the changes in real schedules.

If there were literally no cost to changing nominal schedules and communicating this information to others, daylight saving time would just cause everyone to do this and would have no effect on real schedules. Thus for daylight saving time to change real schedules, there must be some cost to changing nominal schedules. These costs are analogous to the menu costs of changing prices; and like the menu costs, they do not appear to be large. The reason that these small costs cause the switch to have real effects is that individuals and businesses are generally much more concerned about their schedules relative to one another's than about their schedules relative to the sun. Thus, given that others do not change their scheduled hours, each individual does not wish to incur the cost of changing his or hers. This is analogous to the effects of real rigidity in the price-setting case. Finally, the less concerned that individuals are about precisely what their schedules are, the less willing they are to incur the cost of changing them; this is analogous to the insensitivity of the profit function in the price-setting case.

---

[20] This analogy is originally due to Friedman (1953, p. 173), in the context of exchange rates.

# Specific Sources of Real Rigidity

A great deal of research on macroeconomic fluctuations is concerned with factors that can give rise to real rigidity or to insensitivity of the profit function. This work is done in various ways. For example, one can focus on the partial-equilibrium question of how some feature of financial, goods, or labor markets affects either a firm's incentive to adjust its real price in response to a change in aggregate output or the sensitivity of its profits to departures from the optimum. Or one can add the candidate feature to a calibrated dynamic stochastic general equilibrium model that includes barriers to nominal adjustment, like those we will meet at the end of the next chapter, and ask how the addition affects such properties of the model as the variance of output, the covariance of money growth and output growth, and the real effects of a monetary disturbance. Or one need not focus on monetary disturbances and nominal imperfections at all. As we will see in the next section, most forces that make the real economy more responsive to monetary shocks when there are nominal frictions make it more responsive to other types of shocks. As a result, many analyses of specific sources of real rigidity and insensitivity focus on their general implications for the effects of shocks, or on their implications for some type of shock other than monetary shocks.

Here we will take the approach of considering a single firm's incentive to adjust its price in response to a change in aggregate output when other firms do not change their prices. To do this, consider again the marginal revenue–marginal cost framework of Figure 6.10. When the fall in marginal cost as a result of the fall in aggregate output is smaller, the firm's incentive to cut its price and increase its output is smaller; thus nominal rigidity is more likely to be an equilibrium. This can occur in two ways. First, a smaller downward shift of the marginal cost curve in response to a fall in aggregate output implies a smaller decline in the firm's profit-maximizing price—that is, it corresponds to greater real rigidity.[21] Second, a flatter marginal cost curve implies both greater insensitivity of the profit function and greater real rigidity.

Similarly, when the fall in marginal revenue in response to a decline in aggregate output is larger, the gap between marginal revenue and marginal cost the representative firm's initial price is smaller, and so the incentive for price adjustment is smaller. Specifically, a larger leftward shift of the marginal revenue curve corresponds to increased real rigidity, and so reduces the incentive for price adjustment. In addition, a steeper marginal revenue curve (for a given leftward shift) also increases the degree of real rigidity, and so again acts to reduce the incentive for adjustment.

---

[21] Recall that for simplicity the marginal cost curve was not shown as shifting in Figure 6.10 (see n. 16). There is no reason to expect it to stay fixed in general, however.

Since there are many potential determinants of the cyclical behavior of marginal cost and marginal revenue, the hypothesis that small frictions in price adjustment result in considerable nominal rigidity is not tied to any specific view of the structure of the economy. On the cost side, researchers have identified various factors that may make costs less procyclical than in our baseline case. A factor that has been the subject of considerable research is capital-market imperfections that raise the cost of finance in recessions. This can occur through reductions in cash flow (Bernanke and Gertler, 1989) or declines in asset values (Kiyotaki and Moore, 1997). Another factor that may be quantitatively important is input-output linkages that cause firms to face constant costs for their inputs when prices are sticky (Basu, 1995). A factor that has received a great deal of attention is thick-market exter-nalities and other external economies of scale. These externalities have the potential to make purchasing inputs and selling products easier in times of high economic activity. Although this is an appealing idea, its empirical importance is unknown.[22]

On the revenue side, any factor that makes firms' desired markups coun-tercyclical increases real rigidity. Typically, when the desired markup is more countercyclical, the marginal revenue curve shifts down more in a recession. One specific factor that might make this occur is the combina-tion of long-term relationships between customers and firms and capital-market imperfections. With long-term relationships, some of the increased revenues from cutting prices and thereby attracting new customers come in the future. And with capital-market imperfections, firms may face short-term financing difficulties in recessions that lower the present value to them of these future revenues (see, for example, Greenwald, Stiglitz, and Weiss, 1984, and Chevalier and Scharfstein, 1996). Another possibility is thick-market effects that make it easier for firms to disseminate information and for consumers to acquire it when aggregate output is high, and thus make demand more elastic (Warner and Barsky, 1995). Three other factors that tend to make desired markups lower when output is higher are shifts in the composition of demand toward goods with more elastic demand, increased competition as a result of entry, and the fact that higher sales increase the incentive for firms to deviate from patterns of implicit collusion by cut-ting their prices (Rotemberg and Woodford, 1999a, Section 4.2). Finally, an example of a factor on the revenue side that affects real rigidity by mak-ing the marginal revenue curve steeper (rather than by causing it to shift more in response to movements in aggregate output) is imperfect infor-mation that makes existing customers more responsive to price increases

---

[22] The classic reference is Diamond (1982). See also Caballero and Lyons (1992), Cooper and Haltiwanger (1996), and Basu and Fernald (1995).

than prospective new customers are to price decreases (for example, Stiglitz, 1979, Woglom, 1982, and Kimball, 1995).[23]

Although the view of fluctuations we have been considering does not depend on any specific view about the sources of real rigidity and insensitivity of the profit function, the labor market is almost certainly crucial. In the example in the previous section, the combination of relatively inelastic labor supply and a clearing labor market causes the real wage to fall sharply when output falls. As a result, firms have very large incentives to cut their prices and then hire large amounts of labor at the lower real wage to meet the resulting increase in the quantity of their goods demanded. These incentives for price adjustment will almost surely swamp the effects of any complications in the goods and credit markets.

One feature of the labor market that has an important effect on the degree of real rigidity is the extent of labor mobility. As we will discuss in more detail in Chapter 10, the enormous heterogeneity of workers and jobs means that there is not simply a prevailing wage at which firms can hire as much labor as they want. Instead, there are significant *search and matching frictions* that generate important barriers to short-run labor mobility.

Reduced labor mobility affects both the slope of firms' marginal cost curve and how it shifts in response to changes in aggregate output: it makes the marginal cost curve steeper (because incomplete mobility causes the real wage a firm faces to rise as it hires more labor), and causes it to respond less to aggregate output (because conditions in the economy as a whole have smaller effects on the availability of labor to an individual firm). The overall effect is to increase the degree of real rigidity. When the output of all firms falls together, labor mobility is unimportant to the level of marginal cost. But the steepening of the marginal cost curve from lower mobility reduces the amount an individual firm wants to cut its price and increase its production relative to others'.

Even relatively high barriers to labor mobility, however, are unlikely to be enough. Thus the view that small costs of nominal adjustment have large effects almost surely requires that the cost of labor not fall nearly as dramatically as it would if labor supply is relatively inelastic and workers are on their labor supply curves.

At a general level, real wages might not be highly procyclical for two reasons. First, short-run aggregate labor supply could be relatively elastic (as a result of intertemporal substitution, for example). But as described in

---

[23] As described in Section 6.2, markups appear to be at least moderately countercyclical. If this occurs because firms' *desired* markups are countercyclical, then there are real rigidities on the revenue side. But this is not the case if, as argued by Sbordone (2002), markups are countercyclical only because barriers to nominal price adjustment cause firms not to adjust their prices in the face of procyclical fluctuations in marginal cost.

Sections 5.10 and 6.3, this view of the labor market has had limited empirical success.

Second, imperfections in the labor market, such as those that are the subject of Chapter 10, can cause workers to be off their labor supply curves over at least part of the business cycle. The models presented there (including more complicated models of search and matching frictions) break the link between the elasticity of labor supply and the response of the cost of labor to demand disturbances. Indeed, Chapter 10 presents several models that imply relatively acyclical wages (or relatively acyclical costs of labor to firms) despite inelastic labor supply. If imperfections like these cause real wages to respond little to demand disturbances, they greatly reduce firms' incentive to vary their prices in response to these demand shifts.[24]

## A Second Quantitative Example

To see the potential importance of labor-market imperfections, consider the following variation (from Ball and Romer, 1990) on our example of firms' incentives to change prices in response to a monetary disturbance. Suppose that for some reason firms pay wages above the market-clearing level, and that the elasticity of the real wage with respect to aggregate output is $\beta$:

$$\frac{W}{P} = AY^{\beta}. \tag{6.65}$$

Thus, as in Case 3 of Section 6.2, the cyclical behavior of the real wage is determined by a "real-wage function" rather than by the elasticity of labor supply.

With the remainder of the model as before, firm $i$'s profits are given by (6.53) with the real wage equal to $AY^{\beta}$ rather than $Y^{1/\nu}$. It follows that

$$\pi_i = \frac{M}{P}\left(\frac{P_i}{P}\right)^{1-\eta} - A\left(\frac{M}{P}\right)^{1+\beta}\left(\frac{P_i}{P}\right)^{-\eta} \tag{6.66}$$

(compare [6.62]). The profit-maximizing real price is again $\eta/(\eta - 1)$ times the real wage; thus it is $[\eta/(\eta - 1)]AY^{\beta}$. It follows that equilibrium output under flexible prices is $[(\eta - 1)/(\eta A)]^{1/\beta}$. Assume that $A$ and $\beta$ are such that

---

[24] In addition, the possibility of substantial real rigidities in the labor market suggests that small barriers to nominal adjustment may cause nominal disturbances to have substantial real effects through stickiness of nominal wages rather than of nominal prices. If wages display substantial real rigidity, a demand-driven expansion leads only to small increases in optimal real wages. As a result, just as small frictions in nominal price adjustment can lead to substantial nominal price rigidity, so small frictions in nominal wage adjustment can lead to substantial nominal wage rigidity.

labor supply at the flexible-price equilibrium exceeds the amount of labor employed by firms.[25]

Now consider the representative firm's incentive to change its price in the face of a decline in aggregate demand, again assuming that other firms do not change their prices. If the firm does not change its price, then $P_i/P = 1$, and so (6.66) implies

$$\pi_{\text{FIXED}} = \frac{M}{P} - A\left(\frac{M}{P}\right)^{1+\beta}. \tag{6.67}$$

If the firm changes its price, it charges a real price of $[\eta/(\eta - 1)]AY^\beta$. Substituting this expression into (6.66) yields

$$
\begin{aligned}
\pi_{\text{ADJ}} &= \frac{M}{P}\left(\frac{\eta}{\eta - 1}\right)^{1-\eta} A^{1-\eta}\left(\frac{M}{P}\right)^{\beta(1-\eta)} \\
&\quad - A\left(\frac{M}{P}\right)^{1+\beta}\left(\frac{\eta}{\eta - 1}\right)^{-\eta} A^{-\eta}\left(\frac{M}{P}\right)^{-\beta\eta} \\
&= A^{1-\eta}\frac{1}{\eta - 1}\left(\frac{\eta}{\eta - 1}\right)^{-\eta}\left(\frac{M}{P}\right)^{1+\beta-\beta\eta}.
\end{aligned}
\tag{6.68}
$$

If $\beta$, the parameter that governs the cyclical behavior of the real wage, is small, the effect of this change in the model on the incentive for price adjustment is dramatic. Suppose, for example, that $\beta = 0.1$, that $\eta = 5$ as before, and that $A = 0.806$ (so that the flexible-price level of $Y$ is 0.928, or about 95 percent of its level with $v = 0.1$ and a clearing labor market). Substituting these parameter values into (6.67) and (6.68) implies that if the money stock falls by 3 percent and firms do not adjust their prices, the representative firm's gain from changing its price is approximately 0.0000168, or about 0.0018 percent of the revenue it gets at the flexible-price equilibrium. Even if $M$ falls by 5 percent and $\beta = 0.25$ (and $A$ is changed to 0.815, so that the flexible-price level of $Y$ continues to be 0.928), the incentive for price adjustment is only 0.03 percent of the firm's flexible-price revenue.

This example shows how real rigidity and small barriers to nominal price adjustment can produce a large amount of nominal rigidity. But the example almost surely involves an unrealistic degree of real rigidity in the labor market: the example assumes that the elasticity of the real wage with respect to output is only 0.1, while the evidence discussed in Section 6.3 suggests that the true elasticity is considerably higher. A more realistic account would probably involve less real rigidity in the labor market, but would include

---

[25] When prices are flexible, each firm sets its relative price to $[\eta/(\eta - 1)](W/P)$. Thus the real wage at the flexible-price equilibrium must be $(\eta - 1)/\eta$, and so labor supply is $[(\eta - 1)/\eta]^v$. Thus the condition that labor supply exceeds demand at the flexible-price equilibrium is $[(\eta - 1)/\eta]^v > [(\eta - 1)/(\eta A)]^{1/\beta}$.

the presence of other forces dampening fluctuations in costs and making desired markups countercyclical.

# 6.8   Coordination-Failure Models and Real Non-Walrasian Theories

## Coordination-Failure Models

Our analysis suggests that real rigidities play an important role in fluctuations. As desired real prices become less responsive to aggregate output (that is, as $\phi$ falls), the degree to which nominal frictions lead nominal disturbances to have real effects increases. Throughout, however, we have assumed that desired real prices are increasing in aggregate output (that is, that $\phi > 0$). An obvious question is what happens if real rigidities are so strong that desired real prices are decreasing in output ($\phi < 0$).

When producers reduce their relative prices, their relative output rises. Thus if they want to cut their relative prices when aggregate output rises, their desired output is rising more than one-for-one with aggregate output. This immediately raises the possibility that there could be more than one equilibrium level of output when prices are flexible.

Cooper and John (1988) present a framework for analyzing the possibility of multiple equilibria in aggregate activity under flexible prices in a framework that is considerably more general than the particular model we have been considering. The economy consists of many identical agents. Each agent chooses the value of some variable, which we call output for concreteness, taking others' choices as given. Let $U_i = V(y_i, y)$ be agent $i$'s payoff when he or she chooses output $y_i$ and all others choose $y$. (We will consider only symmetric equilibria; thus we do not need to specify what happens when others' choices are heterogeneous.) Let $y_i^*(y)$ denote the representative agent's optimal choice of $y_i$ given $y$. Assume that $V(\bullet)$ is sufficiently well behaved that $y_i^*(y)$ is uniquely defined for any $y$, continuous, and always between 0 and some upper bound $\bar{y}$. $y_i^*(y)$ is referred to as the *reaction function*.

Equilibrium occurs when $y_i^*(y) = y$. In such a situation, if each agent believes that other agents will produce $y$, each agent in fact chooses to produce $y$.

Figure 6.12 shows an economy without multiple equilibria. The figure plots the reaction function, $y_i^*(y)$. Equilibrium occurs when the reaction function crosses the 45-degree line. Since there is only one crossing, the equilibrium is unique.

Figure 6.13 shows a case with multiple equilibria. Since $y_i^*(y)$ is bounded between 0 and $\bar{y}$, it must begin above the 45-degree line and end up below. And since it is continuous, it must cross the 45-degree line an odd number

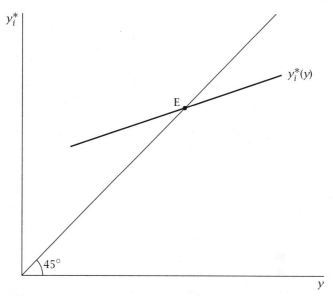

**FIGURE 6.12   A reaction function that implies a unique equilibrium**

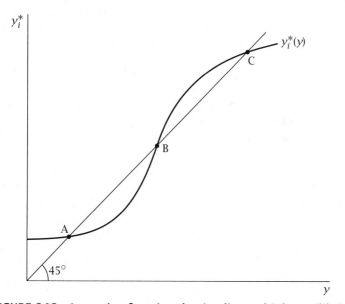

**FIGURE 6.13   A reaction function that implies multiple equilibria**

of times (if we ignore the possibility of tangencies). The figure shows a case with three crossings and thus three equilibrium levels of output. Under plausible assumptions, the equilibrium at Point B is unstable. If, for example, agents expect output to be slightly above the level at B, they produce slightly more than they expect others to produce. With natural assumptions about dynamics, this causes the economy to move away from B. The equilibria at A and C, however, are stable.

With multiple equilibria, fundamentals do not fully determine outcomes. If agents expect the economy to be at A, it ends up there; if they expect it to be at C, it ends up there instead. Thus *animal spirits, self-fulfilling prophecies,* and *sunspots* can affect aggregate outcomes.[26]

It is plausible that $V(y_i, y)$ is increasing in $y$—that is, that a typical individual is better off when aggregate output is higher. In the model of Section 6.5, for example, higher aggregate output shifts the demand curve that the representative firm faces outward, and thus increases the real price the firm obtains for a given level of its output. If $V(y_i, y)$ is increasing in $y$, equilibria with higher output involve higher welfare. To see this, consider two equilibrium levels of output, $y_1$ and $y_2$, with $y_2 > y_1$. Since $V(y_i, y)$ is increasing in $y$, $V(y_1, y_2)$ is greater than $V(y_1, y_1)$. And since $y_2$ is an equilibrium, $y_i = y_2$ maximizes $V(y_i, y)$ given $y = y_2$, and so $V(y_2, y_2)$ exceeds $V(y_1, y_2)$. Thus the representative agent is better off at the higher-output equilibrium.

Models with multiple, Pareto-ranked equilibria are known as *coordination-failure* models. The possibility of coordination failure implies that the economy can get stuck in an underemployment equilibrium. That is, output can be inefficiently low just because everyone believes that it will be. In such a situation, there is no force tending to restore output to normal. As a result, there may be scope for government policies that coordinate expectations on a high-output equilibrium. For example, a temporary stimulus might permanently move the economy to a better equilibrium.

One weakness of models with multiple equilibria is that they are inherently incomplete: they fail to tell us what outcomes will be as a function of underlying conditions. Work by Morris and Shin (1998, 2000) addresses this limitation by introducing heterogeneous information about fundamentals. Under plausible assumptions, adding heterogeneous information to coordination-failure models makes each agent's action a unique function of his or her information, and so eliminates the indeterminacy. At the same time, when the heterogeneity is small, the modified models have the feature that small changes in fundamentals (or in beliefs about fundamentals, or in beliefs about others' beliefs about fundamentals, and so on) can lead to very large changes in outcomes and welfare. Thus the basic message of coordination-failure models carries over to this more realistic and more complete case.

---

[26] A sunspot equilibrium occurs when some variable that has no inherent effect on the economy matters because agents believe that it does. Any model with multiple equilibria has the potential for sunspots: if agents believe that the economy will be at one equilibrium when the extraneous variable takes on a high value and at another when it takes on a low value, they behave in ways that validate this belief. For more on these issues, see Woodford (1990) and Benhabib and Farmer (1999).

As noted above, there is a close connection between multiple equilibria and real rigidity. The existence of multiple equilibria requires that over some range, increases in aggregate output cause the representative producer to want to lower its price and thus increase its output relative to others'. That is, coordination failure requires that real rigidity be very strong over some range. One implication of this observation is that since there are many potential sources of real rigidity, there are many potential sources of coordination failure. Thus there are many possible models that fit Cooper and John's general framework.

## Empirical Application: Experimental Evidence on Coordination-Failure Games

Coordination-failure models have more than one Nash equilibrium. Traditional game theory predicts that such economies will arrive at one of their equilibria, but does not predict which one. Various theories of equilibrium refinements make predictions about which equilibrium will be reached (as do the extensions to heterogeneous information mentioned above). For example, a common view is that Pareto-superior equilibria are focal, and that economies where there is the potential for coordination failure therefore attain the best possible equilibrium. There are other possibilities as well. For example, it may be that each agent is unsure about what rule others are using to choose among the possible outcomes, and that as a result such economies do not reach any of their equilibria.

One approach to testing theories that has been pursued extensively in recent years, especially in game theory, is the use of experiments. Experiments have the advantage that they allow researchers to control the economic environment precisely. They have the disadvantages, however, that they are often not feasible and that behavior may be different in the laboratory than in similar situations in practice.

An example of this approach in the context of coordination-failure models is the test of the game proposed by Bryant (1983) that is conducted by Van Huyck, Battalio, and Beil (1990). In Bryant's game, each of $N$ agents chooses an effort level over the range $[0, \bar{e}]$. The payoff to agent $i$ is

$$U_i = \alpha \min[e_1, e_2, \ldots, e_N] - \beta e_i, \qquad \alpha > \beta > 0. \qquad (6.69)$$

The best Nash equilibrium is for every agent to choose the maximum effort level, $\bar{e}$; this gives each agent a payoff of $(\alpha - \beta)\bar{e}$. But any common effort level in $[0, \bar{e}]$ is also a Nash equilibrium: if every agent other than agent $i$ sets his or her effort to some level $\hat{e}$, $i$ also wants to choose effort of $\hat{e}$. Since each agent's payoff is increasing in the common effort level, Bryant's game is a coordination-failure model with a continuum of equilibria.

Van Huyck, Battalio, and Beil consider a version of Bryant's game with effort restricted to the integers 1 through 7, $\alpha = \$0.20, \beta = \$0.10$, and $N$

between 14 and 16.[27] They report several main results. The first concerns the first time a group plays the game; since Bryant's model is not one of repeated play, this situation may correspond most closely to the model. Van Huyck, Battalio, and Beil find that in the first play, the players do not reach any of the equilibria. The most common levels of effort are 5 and 7, but there is a great deal of dispersion. Thus, no deterministic theory of equilibrium selection successfully describes behavior.

Second, repeated play of the game results in rapid movement toward low effort. Among five of the seven experimental groups, the minimum effort in the first period is more than 1. But in all seven groups, by the fourth play the minimum level of effort reaches 1 and remains there in every subsequent round. Thus there is strong coordination failure.

Third, the game fails to converge to any equilibrium. Each group played the game 10 times, for a total of 70 trials. Yet in none of the 70 trials do all the players choose the same effort. Even in the last several trials, which are preceded in every group by a string of trials where the minimum effort is 1, more than a quarter of players choose effort greater than 1.

Finally, even modifying the payoff function to induce "coordination successes" does not prevent reversion to inefficient outcomes. After the initial 10 trials, each group played 5 trials with the parameter $\beta$ in (6.69) set to zero. With $\beta = 0$, there is no cost to higher effort. As a result, most groups converge to the Pareto-efficient outcome of $e_i = 7$ for all players. But when $\beta$ is changed back to \$0.10, there is a rapid return to the situation where most players choose the minimum effort.

Van Huyck, Battalio, and Beil's results suggest that predictions from deductive theories of behavior should be treated with caution: even though Bryant's game is fairly simple, actual behavior does not correspond well with the predictions of any standard theory. The results also suggest that coordination-failure models can give rise to complicated behavior and dynamics.

## Real Non-Walrasian Theories

Substantial real rigidity, even if it is not strong enough to cause multiple equilibria, can make the equilibrium highly sensitive to disturbances. Consider the case where the reaction function is upward-sloping with a slope slightly less than 1. As shown in Figure 6.14, this leads to a unique equilibrium. Now let $x$ be some variable that shifts the reaction function; thus we now write the reaction function as $y_i = y_i^*(y,x)$. The equilibrium level of $y$ for a given $x$, denoted $\hat{y}(x)$, is defined by the condition $y_i^*(\hat{y}(x),x) = \hat{y}(x)$.

---

[27] In addition, they add a constant of \$0.60 to the payoff function so that no one can lose money.

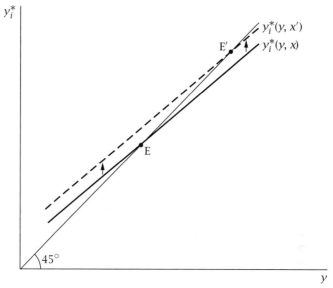

**FIGURE 6.14   A reaction function that implies a unique but fragile equilibrium**

Differentiating this condition with respect to $x$ yields

$$\frac{\partial y_i^*}{\partial y}\hat{y}'(x) + \frac{\partial y_i^*}{\partial x} = \hat{y}'(x), \tag{6.70}$$

or

$$\hat{y}'(x) = \frac{1}{1 - (\partial y_i^*/\partial y)}\frac{\partial y_i^*}{\partial x}. \tag{6.71}$$

Equation (6.71) shows that when the reaction function slopes up, there is a "multiplier" that magnifies the effect of the shift of the reaction function at a given level of $y$, $\partial y_i^*/\partial x$. In terms of the diagram, the impact on the equilibrium level of $y$ is larger than the upward shift of the reaction function. The closer the slope is to 1, the larger is the multiplier.

In a situation like this, any factor that affects the reaction function has a large impact on overall economic activity. In the terminology of Summers (1988), the equilibrium is *fragile*. Thus it is possible that there is substantial real rigidity but that fluctuations are driven by real rather than nominal shocks. When there is substantial real rigidity, technology shocks, credit-market disruptions, changes in government spending and tax rates, shifts in uncertainty about future policies, and other real disturbances can all be important sources of output movements. Since, as we have seen, there is unlikely to be substantial real rigidity in a Walrasian model, we refer to theories of fluctuations based on real rigidities and real disturbances as *real non-Walrasian theories.* Just as there are many candidate real rigidities, there are many possible theories of this type.

This discussion suggests that whether there are multiple flexible-price equilibria or merely a unique but fragile equilibrium is not crucial to fluctuations. Suppose first that (as we have been assuming throughout this section) there are no barriers to nominal adjustment. If there are multiple equilibria, fluctuations can occur without any disturbances at all as the economy moves among the different equilibria. With a unique but fragile equilibrium, on the other hand, fluctuations can occur in response to small disturbances as the equilibrium is greatly affected by the shocks.

The situation is similar with small barriers to price adjustment. Strong real rigidity (plus appropriate insensitivity of the profit function) causes firms' incentives to adjust their prices in response to a nominal disturbance to be small; whether the real rigidity is strong enough to create multiple equilibria when prices are flexible is not important.

# 6.9   The Lucas Imperfect-Information Model

The nominal imperfection we have focused on so far is a cost of changing nominal prices. Long before the modern work on menu costs, however, Lucas (1972) and Phelps (1970) suggested a different nominal imperfection: perhaps producers do not observe the aggregate price level perfectly.

If a producer does not know the price level, then it does not know whether a change in the price of its good reflects a change in the good's relative price or a change in the aggregate price level. A change in the relative price alters the optimal amount to produce. A change in the aggregate price level, on the other hand, leaves optimal production unchanged.

When the price of the producer's good increases, there is some chance that the increase reflects a rise in the price level, and some chance that it reflects a rise in the good's relative price. The rational response for the producer is to attribute part of the change to an increase in the price level and part to an increase in the relative price, and therefore to increase output somewhat. When the aggregate price level rises, all producers see increases in the prices of their goods. Thus, not knowing that the increases reflect a rise in the price level, they raise their output. As a result, an increase in aggregate demand that is not publicly observed leads to some combination of a rise in the overall price level and a rise in overall output.

This section develops these ideas in a variation of the model of Section 6.5. We now need to allow for unobserved movements in the overall price level and in relative prices. We do this by assuming that the money supply (or some other aggregate-demand variable) and the demands for individual goods are subject to random shocks that are not observed by producers. We also make two smaller changes to the earlier model. First, producers behave competitively rather than imperfectly competitively; that is, they ignore the impact of their output choices on the prices of their goods. We make this assumption both because it keeps the model closer to Lucas's original model and because it is easier to talk about producers making inferences from the prices of their goods than from the positions of their demand curves. Nothing substantive hinges on this assumption, however. Second, there is no economy-wide labor market; each firm is owned by a particular household that produces the firm's output using its own labor. If firms hired labor in a competitive labor market, their observation of the prevailing wage would allow them to deduce the aggregate price level. Assuming away an economy-wide labor market eliminates this possibility.

## The Model

As in the model of Section 6.5, each household maximizes $C - (1/\gamma)L^\gamma$, where $C$ is its consumption and $L$ is its labor supply. Each good is produced by a single household using only its own labor. For simplicity, we will refer to the household that produces good $i$ as household $i$. Household $i$'s objective function is therefore

$$U_i = C_i - \frac{1}{\gamma}L_i^\gamma$$

$$= \frac{P_i}{P}Y_i - \frac{1}{\gamma}Y_i^\gamma, \tag{6.72}$$

where $C_i$ is its consumption index. The second line of (6.72) uses the production function, $Y_i = L_i$, and the fact that $C_i$ equals the household's revenues from selling its good, $P_iY_i$, divided by the price index, $P$.

The producers takes prices as given. Thus if producer $i$ knew $P_i$ and $P$, the first-order condition for its utility-maximizing choice of $Y_i$ would be

$$\frac{P_i}{P} - Y_i^{\gamma-1} = 0, \tag{6.73}$$

or

$$Y_i = \left(\frac{P_i}{P}\right)^{1/(\gamma-1)}. \tag{6.74}$$

Letting lowercase letters denote logarithms of the corresponding uppercase variables, we can rewrite this as

$$y_i = \frac{1}{\gamma - 1}(p_i - p). \tag{6.75}$$

The model allows for both changes in the money supply (or aggregate demand) and the demands for individual goods. Specifically, the demand for good $i$ is given by

$$y_i = y + z_i - \eta(p_i - p), \qquad \eta > 0, \tag{6.76}$$

where $z_i$ is the good-specific demand shock. We assume that the aggregate demand equation (6.41), $y = m - p$, holds as before. Thus (6.76) becomes

$$y_i = (m - p) + z_i - \eta(p_i - p). \tag{6.77}$$

Note that aside from the presence of the $z_i$ term, this is the same as the demand curve in the model in Section 6.5, equation (6.48).

With heterogeneous demands arising from taste shocks, the price index corresponding to individuals' utility function takes a somewhat more complicated form than the previous price index, (6.47). For simplicity, we therefore define the log price index, $p$, to be just the average log price:

$$p = \bar{p}_i. \tag{6.78}$$

Similarly, we define

$$y = \bar{y}_i. \tag{6.79}$$

Using the more theoretically appropriate definitions of $p$ and $y$ would have no effects on the messages of the model.

The model's key assumption is that the producer cannot observe $z_i$ and $m$. Instead, it can only observe the price of its good, $p_i$. We can write $p_i$ as

$$\begin{aligned} p_i &= p + (p_i - p) \\ &\equiv p + r_i, \end{aligned} \tag{6.80}$$

where $r_i \equiv p_i - p$ is the relative price of good $i$. Thus, in logs, the variable that the producer observes—the price of its good—equals the sum of the aggregate price level and the good's relative price.

The producer would like to base its production decision on $r_i$ alone (see [6.75]). The producer does not observe $r_i$, but must estimate it given the observation of $p_i$.[28] At this point, Lucas makes two simplifying assumptions. First, he assumes that the producer finds the expectation of $r_i$ given $p_i$, and then produces as much as it would if this estimate were certain. Thus (6.75) becomes

$$y_i = \frac{1}{\gamma - 1} E[r_i \mid p_i]. \tag{6.81}$$

---

[28] Recall that the firm is owned by a single household. If the household knew others' prices as a result of making purchases, it could deduce $p$, and hence $r_i$. This can be ruled out in several ways. One approach is to assume that the household consists of two individuals, a "producer" and a "shopper," and that communication between them is limited. In his original model, Lucas avoids the problem by assuming an overlapping-generations structure where individuals produce in the first period of their lives and make purchases in the second.

As Problem 6.14 shows, this *certainty-equivalence* behavior is not identical to maximizing expected utility: in general, the utility-maximizing choice of $y_i$ depends not just on the household's point estimate of $r_i$, but also on its uncertainty. Like the assumption that $p = \bar{P_i}$, however, the assumption that households use certainty equivalence simplifies the analysis and has no effect on the central messages of the model.

Second, Lucas assumes that the monetary shock ($m$) and the shocks to the demands for the individual goods (the $z_i$'s) are normally distributed. $m$ has a mean of $E[m]$ and a variance of $V_m$. The $z_i$'s have a mean of 0 and a variance of $V_z$, and are independent of $m$. We will see that these assumptions imply that $p$ and $r_i$ are normal and independent.

Finally, one assumption of the model is so commonplace today that we passed over it without comment: in assuming that the producer chooses how much to produce based on the mathematical expectation of $r_i$, $E[r_i | p_i]$, we implicitly assumed that the producer finds expectations rationally. That is, the expectation of $r_i$ is assumed to be the true expectation of $r_i$ given $p_i$ and given the actual joint distribution of the two variables. Today, this assumption of *rational expectations* seems no more peculiar than the assumption that individuals maximize utility. But when Lucas introduced rational expectations into macroeconomics, it was highly controversial. As we will see, it is one source—but by no means the only one—of the strong implications of his model.

## The Lucas Supply Curve

We will solve the model by tentatively assuming that $p$ and $r_i$ are normal and independent, and then verifying that the equilibrium does indeed have this property.

Since $p_i$ equals $p + r_i$, the assumption that $p$ and $r_i$ are normal and independent implies that $p_i$ is also normal; its mean is the sum of the means of $p$ and $r_i$, and its variance is the sum of their variances. An important result in statistics is that when two variables are jointly normally distributed (as with $r_i$ and $p_i$ here), the expectation of one is a linear function of the observation of the other. In this particular case, where $p_i$ equals $r_i$ plus an independent variable, the expectation takes the specific form

$$E[r_i | p_i] = E[r_i] + \frac{V_r}{V_r + V_p}(p_i - E[p_i])$$
$$= \frac{V_r}{V_r + V_p}(p_i - E[p_i]),$$

(6.82)

where $V_r$ and $V_p$ are the variances of $p$ and $r_i$, and where the second line uses the fact that the symmetry of the model implies that the mean of each relative price is zero.

Equation (6.82) is intuitive. First, it implies that if $p_i$ equals its mean, the expectation of $r_i$ equals its mean (which is 0). Second, it states that the expectation of $r_i$ exceeds its mean if $p_i$ exceeds its mean, and is less than its mean if $p_i$ is less than its mean. Third, it tells us that the fraction of the departure of $p_i$ from its mean that is estimated to be due to the departure of $r_i$ from its mean is $V_r/(V_r + V_p)$; this is the fraction of the overall variance of $p_i$ (which is $V_r + V_p$) that is due to the variance of $r_i$ (which is $V_r$). If, for example, $V_p$ is 0, all the variation in $p_i$ is due to $r_i$, and so $E[r_i | p_i]$ is $p_i - E[p]$. If $V_r$ and $V_p$ are equal, half of the variance in $p_i$ is due to $r_i$, and so $E[r_i | p_i] = (p_i - E[p])/2$. And so on.

This conditional-expectations problem is referred to as *signal extraction*. The variable that the individual observes, $p_i$, equals the *signal*, $r_i$, plus *noise*, $p$. Equation (6.82) shows how the individual can best extract an estimate of the signal from the observation of $p_i$. The ratio of $V_r$ to $V_p$ is referred to as the *signal-to-noise ratio*.

Recall that the producer's output is given by $y_i = [1/(\gamma - 1)]E[r_i | p_i]$ (equation [6.81]). Substituting (6.82) into this expression yields

$$y_i = \frac{1}{\gamma - 1} \frac{V_r}{V_r + V_p}(p_i - E[p])$$

$$\equiv b(p_i - E[p]). \tag{6.83}$$

Averaging (6.83) across producers (and using the definitions of $y$ and $p$) gives us an expression for overall output:

$$y = b(p - E[p]). \tag{6.84}$$

Equation (6.84) is the *Lucas supply curve*. It states that the departure of output from its normal level (which is zero in the model) is an increasing function of the surprise in the price level.

The Lucas supply curve is essentially the same as the expectations-augmented Phillips curve of Section 6.4 with core inflation replaced by expected inflation (see equation [6.24]). Both state that if we neglect disturbances to supply, output is above normal only to the extent that inflation (and hence the price level) is greater than expected. Thus the Lucas model provides microeconomic foundations for this view of aggregate supply.

## Equilibrium

Combining the Lucas supply curve with the aggregate demand equation, $y = m - p$, and solving for $p$ and $y$ yields

$$p = \frac{1}{1 + b}m + \frac{b}{1 + b}E[p], \tag{6.85}$$

$$y = \frac{b}{1 + b}m - \frac{b}{1 + b}E[p]. \tag{6.86}$$

We can use (6.85) to find $E[p]$. Ex post, after $m$ is determined, the two sides of (6.85) are equal. Thus it must be that ex ante, before $m$ is determined, the *expectations* of the two sides are equal. Taking the expectations of both sides of (6.85), we obtain

$$E[p] = \frac{1}{1+b}E[m] + \frac{b}{1+b}E[p]. \tag{6.87}$$

Solving for $E[p]$ yields

$$E[p] = E[m]. \tag{6.88}$$

Using (6.88) and the fact that $m = E[m] + (m - E[m])$, we can rewrite (6.85) and (6.86) as

$$p = E[m] + \frac{1}{1+b}(m - E[m]), \tag{6.89}$$

$$y = \frac{b}{1+b}(m - E[m]). \tag{6.90}$$

Equations (6.89) and (6.90) show the key implications of the model: the component of aggregate demand that is observed, $E[m]$, affects only prices, but the component that is not observed, $m - E[m]$, has real effects. Consider, for concreteness, an unobserved increase in $m$—that is, a higher realization of $m$ given its distribution. This increase in the money supply raises aggregate demand, and thus produces an outward shift in the demand curve for each good. Since the increase is not observed, each supplier's best guess is that some portion of the rise in the demand for his or her product reflects a relative price shock. Thus producers increase their output.

The effects of an observed increase in $m$ are very different. Specifically, consider the effects of an upward shift in the entire distribution of $m$, with the realization of $m - E[m]$ held fixed. In this case, each supplier attributes the rise in the demand for his or her product to money, and thus does not change his or her output. Of course, the taste shocks cause variations in relative prices and in output across goods (just as they do in the case of an unobserved shock), but on average real output does not rise. Thus observed changes in aggregate demand affect only prices.

To complete the model, we must express $b$ in terms of underlying parameters rather than in terms of the variances of $p$ and $r_i$. Recall that $b = [1/(\gamma-1)][V_r/(V_r + V_p)]$ (see [6.83]). Equation (6.89) implies $V_p = V_m/(1+b)^2$. The demand curve, (6.76), and the supply curve, (6.84), can be used to find $V_r$, the variance of $p_i - p$. Specifically, we can substitute $y = b(p - E[p])$ into (6.76) to obtain $y_i = b(p - E[p]) + z_i - \eta(p_i - p)$, and we can rewrite (6.83) as $y_i = b(p_i - p) + b(p - E[p])$. Solving these two equations for $p_i - p$ then yields $p_i - p = z_i/(\eta + b)$. Thus $V_r = V_z/(\eta + b)^2$.

Substituting the expressions for $V_p$ and $V_r$ into the definition of $b$ (see [6.83]) yields

$$b = \frac{1}{\gamma - 1}\left[\frac{V_z}{V_z + \dfrac{(\eta + b)^2}{(1+b)^2}V_m}\right]. \tag{6.91}$$

Equation (6.91) implicitly defines $b$ in terms of $V_z$, $V_m$, and $\gamma$, and thus completes the model. It is straightforward to show that $b$ is increasing in $V_z$ and decreasing in $V_m$. In the special case of $\eta = 1$, we can obtain a closed-form expression for $b$:

$$b = \frac{1}{\gamma - 1}\frac{V_z}{V_z + V_m}. \tag{6.92}$$

Finally, note that the results that $p = E[m] + [1/(1+b)](m - E[m])$ and $r_i = z_i/(\eta + b)$ imply that $p$ and $r_i$ are linear functions of $m$ and $z_i$. Since $m$ and $z_i$ are independent, $p$ and $r_i$ are independent. And since linear functions of normal variables are normal, $p$ and $r_i$ are normal. This confirms the assumptions made above about these variables.

## The Phillips Curve and the Lucas Critique

Lucas's model implies that unexpectedly high realizations of aggregate demand lead to both higher output and higher-than-expected prices. As a result, for reasonable specifications of the behavior of aggregate demand, the model implies a positive association between output and inflation. Suppose, for example, that $m$ is a random walk with drift:

$$m_t = m_{t-1} + c + u_t, \tag{6.93}$$

where $u$ is white noise. This specification implies that the expectation of $m_t$ is $m_{t-1} + c$ and that the unobserved component of $m_t$ is $u_t$. Thus, from (6.89) and (6.90),

$$p_t = m_{t-1} + c + \frac{1}{1+b}u_t, \tag{6.94}$$

$$y_t = \frac{b}{1+b}u_t. \tag{6.95}$$

Equation (6.94) implies that $p_{t-1} = m_{t-2} + c + [u_{t-1}/(1+b)]$. The rate of inflation (measured as the change in the log of the price level) is thus

$$\pi_t = (m_{t-1} - m_{t-2}) + \frac{1}{1+b}u_t - \frac{1}{1+b}u_{t-1}$$

$$= c + \frac{b}{1+b}u_{t-1} + \frac{1}{1+b}u_t. \tag{6.96}$$

Note that $u_t$ appears in both (6.95) and (6.96) with a positive sign, and that $u_t$ and $u_{t-1}$ are uncorrelated. These facts imply that output and inflation are positively correlated. Intuitively, high unexpected money growth leads, through the Lucas supply curve, to increases in both prices and output. The model therefore implies a positive relationship between output and inflation—a Phillips curve.

Crucially, however, although there is a statistical output-inflation relationship in the model, there is no exploitable tradeoff between output and inflation. Suppose policymakers decide to raise average money growth (for example, by raising $c$ in equation [6.93]). If the change is not publicly known, there is an interval when unobserved money growth is typically positive, and output is therefore usually above normal. Once individuals determine that the change has occurred, however, unobserved money growth is again on average zero, and so average real output is unchanged. And if the increase in average money growth is known, expected money growth jumps immediately and there is not even a brief interval of high output. The idea that the statistical relationship between output and inflation may change if policymakers attempt to take advantage of it is not just a theoretical curiosity: as we saw in Section 6.4, when average inflation rose in the late 1960s and early 1970s, the traditional output-inflation relationship collapsed.

The central idea underlying this analysis is of wider relevance. Expectations are likely to be important to many relationships among aggregate variables, and changes in policy are likely to affect those expectations. As a result, shifts in policy can change aggregate relationships. In short, if policymakers attempt to take advantage of statistical relationships, effects operating through expectations may cause the relationships to break down. This is the famous *Lucas critique* (Lucas, 1976).

## Stabilization Policy

The result that only unobserved aggregate demand shocks have real effects has a strong implication: monetary policy can stabilize output only if policymakers have information that is not available to private agents. Any portion of policy that is a response to publicly available information—such as the unemployment rate or the index of leading indicators—is irrelevant to the real economy (Sargent and Wallace, 1975; Barro, 1976).

To see this, let aggregate demand, $m$, equal $m^* + v$, where $m^*$ is a policy variable and $v$ a disturbance outside the government's control. If the government does not pursue activist policy but simply keeps $m^*$ constant (or growing at a steady rate), the unobserved shock to aggregate demand in some period is the realization of $v$ less the expectation of $v$ given the information available to private agents. If $m^*$ is instead a function of public information, individuals can deduce $m^*$, and so the situation is unchanged. Thus systematic policy rules cannot stabilize output.

If the government observes variables correlated with $v$ that are not known to the public, it can use this information to stabilize output: it can change $m^*$ to offset the movements in $v$ that it expects on the basis of its private information. But this is not an appealing defense of stabilization policy, for two reasons. First, a central element of conventional stabilization policy involves reactions to general, publicly available information that the economy is in a boom or a recession. Second, if superior information is the basis for potential stabilization, there is a much easier way for the government to accomplish that stabilization than following a complex policy rule: it can simply announce the information that the public does not have.

## Discussion

The Lucas model is surely not a complete account of the effects of aggregate demand shifts. For example, as described in Section 5.9, there is strong evidence that publicly announced changes in monetary policy affect real interest rates and real exchange rates, contrary to the model's predictions. The more important question, however, is whether the model accounts for important elements of the effects of aggregate demand. Two major objections have been raised in this regard.

The first difficulty is that the employment fluctuations in the Lucas model, like those in real-business-cycle models, arise from changes in labor supply in response to changes in the perceived benefits of working. Thus to generate substantial employment fluctuations, the model requires a significant short-run elasticity of labor supply. But, as described in Section 5.10, there is little evidence of such a high elasticity.

The second difficulty concerns the assumption of imperfect information. In modern economies, high-quality information about changes in prices is released with only brief lags. Thus, other than in times of hyperinflation, individuals can estimate aggregate price movements with considerable accuracy at little cost. In light of this, it is difficult to see how they can be significantly confused between relative and aggregate price level movements.

In fact, however, neither of the apparently critical assumptions—a high short-run elasticity of labor supply and the difficulty of finding timely information about the price level—is essential to Lucas's central results. Suppose that price-setters choose not to acquire current information about the price level, and that the behavior of the economy is therefore described by the Lucas model. In such a situation, price-setters' incentive to obtain information about the price level, and to adjust their pricing and output decisions accordingly, is determined by the same considerations that determine their incentive to adjust their nominal prices in menu-cost models. As we have seen, there are many possible mechanisms other than highly elastic labor supply that can cause this incentive to be small. Thus neither unavailability of information about the price level nor elastic labor supply is essential to the mechanism identified by Lucas. One important friction in nominal adjustment may therefore be a small inconvenience or cost of obtaining information about the price level (or of adjusting one's pricing decisions in light of that information). We will return to this point in Section 7.7.

## Another Candidate Nominal Imperfection: Nominal Frictions in Debt Markets

Not all potential nominal frictions involve incomplete adjustment of nominal prices and wages, as they do in menu-cost models and the Lucas model. One line of research examines the consequences of the fact that debt contracts are often not indexed; that is, loan agreements and bonds generally specify streams of nominal payments the borrower must make to the lender. Nominal disturbances therefore cause redistributions. A negative nominal shock, for example, increases borrowers' real debt burdens. If capital markets are perfect, such redistributions do not have any important real effects; investments continue to be made if the risk-adjusted expected payoffs exceed the costs, regardless of whether the funds for the projects can be supplied by the entrepreneurs or have to be raised in capital markets.

But actual capital markets are not perfect. As we will discuss in Section 9.9, asymmetric information between lenders and borrowers, coupled with risk aversion or limited liability, generally makes the first-best outcome unattainable. The presence of risk aversion or limited liability means that the borrowers usually do not bear the full cost of very bad outcomes of their investment projects. But if borrowers are partially insured against bad outcomes, they have an incentive to take advantage of the asymmetric information between themselves and lenders by borrowing only if they know their projects are risky (adverse selection) or by taking risks on the projects they undertake (moral hazard). These difficulties cause lenders to charge a premium on their loans. As a result, there is generally less investment, and less efficient investment, when it is financed externally than when it is funded by the entrepreneurs' own funds.

In such settings, redistributions matter: transferring wealth from entrepreneurs to lenders makes the entrepreneurs more dependent on external finance, and thus reduces investment. Thus if debt contracts are not indexed, nominal disturbances are likely to have real effects. Indeed, price and wage flexibility can increase the distributional effects of nominal shocks, and thus potentially increase their real effects. This channel for real effects of nominal shocks is known as *debt-deflation*.[29]

This view of the nature of nominal imperfections must confront the same issues that face theories based on frictions in nominal price adjustment.

---

[29] The term is due to Irving Fisher (1933). For a modern treatment, see Bernanke and Gertler (1989).

For example, when a decline in the money stock redistributes wealth from firms to lenders because of nonindexation of debt contracts, firms' marginal cost curves shift up. For reasonable cases, this upward shift is not large. If marginal cost falls greatly when aggregate output falls (because real wages decline sharply, for example) and marginal revenue does not, the modest increase in costs caused by the fall in the money stock leads to only a small decline in aggregate output. If marginal cost changes little and marginal revenue is very responsive to aggregate output, on the other hand, the small change in costs leads to large changes in output. Thus the same kinds of forces needed to cause small barriers to price adjustment to lead to large fluctuations in aggregate output are also needed for small costs to indexing debt contracts to have this effect.

At first glance, the current financial and economic crisis, where developments in financial markets have been central, seems to provide strong evidence of the importance of nominal imperfections in debt contracts. But this inference would be mistaken. Recent events provide strong evidence that debt and financial markets affect the real economy. The bankruptcies, rises in risk spreads, drying up of credit flows, and other credit-market disruptions appear to have had enormous effects on output and employment. But essentially none of this operated through debt-deflation. Inflation has not changed sharply over the course of the crisis. Thus it appears that outcomes would have been little different if financial contracts had been written in real rather than nominal terms.

We must therefore look elsewhere to understand both the reasons for the crisis and the reasons that financial disruptions are so destructive to the real economy. We will return to this issue briefly in the Epilogue.[30]

# 6.10  Empirical Application: International Evidence on the Output-Inflation Tradeoff

The fundamental concern of the models of this chapter is the real effects of monetary changes and of other disturbances to aggregate demand. Thus a natural place to look for tests of the models is in their predictions about

---

[30] Another line of work on nominal imperfections investigates the consequences of the fact that at any given time, not all agents are adjusting their holdings of high-powered money. Thus when the monetary authority changes the quantity of high-powered money, it cannot achieve a proportionate change in everyone's holdings. As a result, a change in the money stock generally affects real money balances even if all prices and wages are perfectly flexible. Under appropriate conditions (such as an impact of real balances on consumption), this change in real balances affects the real interest rate. And if the real interest rate affects aggregate supply, the result is that aggregate output changes. See, for example, Christiano, Eichenbaum, and Evans (1997) and Williamson (2008).

the determinants of the strength of those effects. This is the approach pioneered by Lucas (1973).

## The Variability of Demand

In the Lucas model, suppliers' responses to changes in prices are determined by the relative importance of aggregate and idiosyncratic shocks. If aggregate shocks are large, for example, suppliers attribute most of the changes in the prices of their goods to changes in the price level, and so they alter their production relatively little in response to variations in prices (see [6.83]). The Lucas model therefore predicts that the real effect of a given aggregate demand shock is smaller in an economy where the variance of those shocks is larger.

To test this prediction, one must find a measure of aggregate demand shocks. Lucas (1973) uses the change in the log of nominal GDP. For this to be precisely correct, two conditions must be satisfied. First, the aggregate demand curve must be unit-elastic; that is, nominal GDP must be determined entirely by aggregate demand, so that changes in aggregate supply affect $P$ and $Y$ but not their product. Second, the change in log nominal GDP must not be predictable or observable. That is, letting $x$ denote log nominal GDP, $\Delta x$ must take the form $a + u_t$, where $u_t$ is white noise. With this process, the change in log nominal GDP (relative to its average change) is also the unobserved change. Although these conditions are surely not satisfied exactly, they may be accurate enough to be reasonable approximations.

Under these assumptions, the real effects of an aggregate demand shock in a given country can be estimated by regressing log real GDP (or the change in log real GDP) on the change in log nominal GDP and control variables. The specification Lucas employs is

$$y_t = c + \gamma t + \tau \Delta x_t + \lambda y_{t-1}, \tag{6.97}$$

where $y$ is log real GDP, $t$ is time, and $\Delta x$ is the change in log nominal GDP.

Lucas estimates (6.97) separately for various countries. He then asks whether the estimated $\tau$'s—the estimates of the responsiveness of output to aggregate demand movements—are related to the average size of countries' aggregate demand shocks. A simple way to do this is to estimate

$$\tau_i = \alpha + \beta \sigma_{\Delta x,i}, \tag{6.98}$$

where $\tau_i$ is the estimate of the real impact of an aggregate demand shift obtained by estimating (6.97) for country $i$ and $\sigma_{\Delta x,i}$ is the standard deviation of the change in log nominal GDP in country $i$. Lucas's theory predicts that nominal shocks have smaller real effects in settings where aggregate demand is more volatile, and thus that $\beta$ is negative.

Lucas employs a relatively small sample. His test has been extended to much larger samples, with various modifications in specification, in several studies. Figure 6.15, from Ball, Mankiw, and D. Romer (1988), is typical of

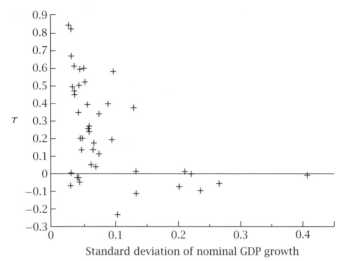

FIGURE 6.15   **The output-inflation tradeoff and the variability of aggregate demand (from Ball, Mankiw, and Romer, 1988)**

the results. It shows a scatterplot of $\tau$ versus $\sigma_{\Delta x}$ for 43 countries. The corresponding regression is

$$\tau_i = \begin{array}{cc} 0.388 & - \quad 1.639\,\sigma_{\Delta x,i}, \\ (0.057) & (0.482) \end{array} \tag{6.99}$$

$$\bar{R}^2 = 0.201, \qquad \text{s.e.e.} = 0.245,$$

where the numbers in parentheses are standard errors. Thus there is a highly statistically significant negative relationship between the variability of nominal GDP growth and the estimated effect of a given change in aggregate demand, just as the model predicts.

## The Average Inflation Rate

Ball, Mankiw, and Romer observe that menu-cost models and other models of barriers to price adjustment suggest a different determinant of the real effects of aggregate demand movements: the average rate of inflation. Their argument is straightforward. When average inflation is higher, firms must adjust their prices more often to keep up with the price level. This implies that when there is an aggregate demand disturbance, firms can pass it into prices more quickly. Thus its real effects are smaller.

Paralleling Lucas's test, Ball, Mankiw, and Romer's basic test of their prediction is to examine whether the estimated impact of aggregate demand shifts (the $\tau_i$'s) are negatively estimated to average inflation. Figure 6.16 shows a scatterplot of the estimated $\tau_i$'s versus average inflation. The figure suggests a negative relationship. The corresponding regression (with

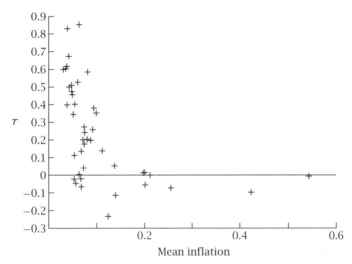

**FIGURE 6.16 The output-inflation tradeoff and average inflation (from Ball, Mankiw, and Romer, 1988)**

a quadratic term included to account for the nonlinearity apparent in the figure) is

$$\tau_i = 0.600 - 4.835 \, \overline{\pi}_i + 7.118 \, \overline{\pi}_i^2,$$
$$\quad (0.079) \quad (1.074) \quad (2.088) \tag{6.100}$$

$$\overline{R}^2 = 0.388, \quad \text{s.e.e.} = 0.215,$$

where $\overline{\pi}_i$ is average inflation in country $i$ and the numbers in parentheses are standard errors. The point estimates imply that $\partial \tau / \partial \overline{\pi} = -4.835 + 2(7.118)\overline{\pi}$, which is negative for $\overline{\pi} < 4.835/[2(7.118)] \simeq 34\%$. Thus there is a statistically significant negative relationship between average inflation and the estimated real impact of aggregate demand movements.

Countries with higher average inflation generally have more variable aggregate demand. Thus it is possible that the results in (6.100) arise not because $\overline{\pi}$ directly affects $\tau$, but because it is correlated with the standard deviation of nominal GNP growth ($\sigma_x$), which does directly affect $\tau$. Alternatively, it is possible that Lucas's results arise from the fact that $\sigma_x$ and $\overline{\pi}$ are correlated.

The appropriate way to test between these two views is to run a "horse-race" regression that includes both variables. Again quadratic terms are included to allow for nonlinearities. The results are

$$\tau_i = 0.589 - 5.729 \, \overline{\pi}_i + 8.406 \, \overline{\pi}_i^2 + 1.241 \, \sigma_x - 2.380 \, \sigma_x^2,$$
$$\quad (0.086) \quad (1.973) \quad (3.849) \quad (2.467) \quad (7.062)$$

$$\tag{6.101}$$

$$\overline{R}^2 = 0.359, \quad \text{s.e.e.} = 0.219.$$

The coefficients on the average inflation variables are essentially the same as in the previous regression, and they remain statistically significant. The variability terms, in contrast, play little role. The null hypothesis that the coefficients on both $\sigma_x$ and $\sigma_x^2$ are zero cannot be rejected at any reasonable confidence level, and the point estimates imply that reasonable changes in $\sigma_x$ have quantitatively small effect on $\tau$. For example, a change in $\sigma_x$ from 0.05 to 0.10 changes $\tau$ by only 0.04. Thus the results appear to favor the menu-cost view over the Lucas model.[31]

Kiley (2000) extends the analysis to the persistence of output movements. He first notes that menu-cost models imply that departures of output from normal are less persistent when average inflation is higher. The intuition is again that higher average inflation increases the frequency of price adjustment, and therefore causes the economy to return to its flexible-price equilibrium more rapidly after a shock. He finds that the data support this implication as well.

# Problems

**6.1.** Describe how, if at all, each of the following developments affect the curves in Figure 6.1:

(*a*) The coefficient of relative risk aversion, $\theta$, rises.

(*b*) The curvature of $\Gamma(\bullet)$, $\nu$ falls.

(*c*) We modify the utility function, (6.2), to be $\sum \beta^t[U(C_t) + B\Gamma(M_t/P_t) - V(L_t)]$, $B > 0$, and $B$ falls.

**6.2. The Baumol-Tobin model.** (Baumol, 1952; Tobin, 1956.) Consider a consumer with a steady flow of real purchases of amount $\alpha Y$, $0 < \alpha \leq 1$, that are made with money. The consumer chooses how often to convert bonds, which pay a constant interest rate of $i$, into money, which pays no interest. If the consumer chooses an interval of $\tau$, his or her money holdings decline linearly from $\alpha YP\tau$ after each conversion to zero at the moment of the next conversion (here $P$ is the price level, which is assumed constant). Each conversion has a fixed real cost of $C$. The consumer's problem is to choose $\tau$ to minimize the average cost per unit time of conversions and foregone interest.

(*a*) Find the optimal value of $\tau$.

(*b*) What are the consumer's average real money holdings? Are they decreasing in $i$ and increasing in $Y$? What is the elasticity of average money holdings with respect to $i$? With respect to $Y$?

**6.3. The multiplier-accelerator.** (Samuelson, 1939.) Consider the following model of income determination. (1) Consumption depends on the previous period's

---

[31] The lack of a discernable link between $\sigma_x$ and $\tau$, however, is a puzzle not only for the Lucas model but also for models based on barriers to price adjustment: an increase in the variability of shocks should make firms change their prices more often, and should therefore reduce the real impact of a change in aggregate demand.

income: $C_t = a + bY_{t-1}$. (2) The desired capital stock (or inventory stock) is proportional to the previous period's output: $K_t^* = cY_{t-1}$. (3) Investment equals the difference between the desired capital stock and the stock inherited from the previous period: $I_t = K_t^* - K_{t-1} = K_t^* - cY_{t-2}$. (4) Government purchases are constant: $G_t = \overline{G}$. (5) $Y_t = C_t + I_t + G_t$.

(a) Express $Y_t$ in terms of $Y_{t-1}$, $Y_{t-2}$, and the parameters of the model.

(b) Suppose $b = 0.9$ and $c = 0.5$. Suppose there is a one-time disturbance to government purchases; specifically, suppose that $G$ is equal to $\overline{G} + 1$ in period $t$ and is equal to $\overline{G}$ in all other periods. How does this shock affect output over time?

**6.4.** The analysis of Case 1 in Section 6.2 assumes that employment is determined by labor demand. Under perfect competition, however, employment at a given real wage will equal the minimum of demand and supply; this is known as the *short-side rule*. Draw diagrams showing the situation in the labor market when employment is determined by the short-side rule if:

(a) $P$ is at the level that generates the maximum possible output.

(b) $P$ is above the level that generates the maximum possible output.

**6.5. Productivity growth, the Phillips curve, and the natural rate.** (Braun, 1984, and Ball and Moffitt, 2001.) Let $g_t$ be growth of output per worker in period $t$, $\pi_t$ inflation, and $\pi_t^W$ wage inflation. Suppose that initially $g$ is constant and equal to $g^L$ and that unemployment is at the level that causes inflation to be constant. $g$ then rises permanently to $g^H > g^L$. Describe the path of $u_t$ that would keep price inflation constant for each of the following assumptions about the behavior of price and wage inflation. Assume $\phi > 0$ in all cases.

(a) (The price-price Phillips curve.) $\pi_t = \pi_{t-1} - \phi(u_t - \bar{u})$, $\pi_t^W = \pi_t + g_t$.

(b) (The wage-wage Phillips curve.) $\pi_t^W = \pi_{t-1}^W - \phi(u_t - \bar{u})$, $\pi_t = \pi_t^W - g_t$.

(c) (The pure wage-price Phillips curve.) $\pi_t^W = \pi_{t-1} - \phi(u_t - \bar{u})$, $\pi_t = \pi_t^W - g_t$.

(d) (The wage-price Phillips curve with an adjustment for normal productivity growth.) $\pi_t^W = \pi_{t-1} + \hat{g}_t - \phi(u_t - \bar{u})$, $\hat{g}_t = \rho\hat{g}_{t-1} + (1-\rho)g_t$, $\pi_t = \pi_t^W - g_t$. Assume that $0 < \rho < 1$ and that initially $\hat{g} = g^L$.

**6.6. The central bank's ability to control the real interest rate.** Suppose the economy is described by two equations. The first is the *IS* equation, which for simplicity we assume takes the traditional form, $Y_t = -r_t/\theta$. The second is the money-market equilibrium condition, which we can write as $m - p = L(r + \pi^e, Y)$, $L_{r+\pi^e} < 0$, $L_Y > 0$, where $m$ and $p$ denote $\ln M$ and $\ln P$.

(a) Suppose $P = \overline{P}$ and $\pi^e = 0$. Find an expression for $dr/dm$. Does an increase in the money supply lower the real interest rate?

(b) Suppose prices respond partially to increases in money. Specifically, assume that $dp/dm$ is exogenous, with $0 < dp/dm < 1$. Continue to assume $\pi^e = 0$. Find an expression for $dr/dm$. Does an increase in the money supply lower the real interest rate? Does achieving a given change in $r$ require a change in $m$ smaller, larger, or the same size as in part (a)?

(c) Suppose increases in money also affect expected inflation. Specifically, assume that $d\pi^e/dm$ is exogenous, with $d\pi^e/dm > 0$. Continue to assume $0 < dp/dm < 1$. Find an expression for $dr/dm$. Does an increase in the money supply lower the real interest rate? Does achieving a given change in $r$ require a change in $m$ smaller, larger, or the same size as in part (b)?

(d) Suppose there is complete and instantaneous price adjustment: $dp/dm = 1$, $d\pi^e/dm = 0$. Find an expression for $dr/dm$. Does an increase in the money supply lower the real interest rate?

6.7. **The liquidity trap.** Consider the following model. The dynamics of inflation are given by the continuous-time version of (6.22)-(6.23): $\dot\pi(t) = \lambda[y(t)-\bar y(t)]$, $\lambda > 0$. The IS curve takes the traditional form, $y(t) = -[i(t)-\pi(t)]/\theta$, $\theta > 0$. The central bank sets the interest rate according to (6.26), but subject to the constraint that the nominal interest rate cannot be negative: $i(t) = \max[0,\pi(t) + r(y(t) - \bar y(t),\pi(t))]$. For simplicity, normalize $\bar y(t) = 0$ for all $t$.

(a) Sketch the aggregate demand curve for this model—that is, the set of points in $(y,\pi)$ space that satisfy the IS equation and the rule above for the interest rate.

(b) Let $(\tilde y,\tilde\pi)$ denote the point on the aggregate demand curve where $\pi + r(y,\pi) = 0$. Sketch the paths of $y$ and $\pi$ over time if:

  (i) $\tilde y > 0$, $\pi(0) > \tilde\pi$, and $y(0) < 0$.

  (ii) $\tilde y < 0$ and $\pi(0) > \tilde\pi$.

  (iii) $\tilde y > 0$, $\pi(0) < \tilde\pi$, and $y(0) < 0$.[32]

6.8. Consider the model in equations (6.27)-(6.30). Suppose, however, that there are shocks to the MP equation but not to the IS equation. Thus $r_t = by_t + u_t^{MP}$, $u_t^{MP} = \rho_{MP}u_{t-}^{MP} + e_t^{MP}$ (where $-1 < \rho_{MP} < 1$ and $e^{MP}$ is white noise), and $y_t = E_t y_{t+1} - \frac{1}{\theta}r_t$. Find the expression analogous to (6.35).

6.9. (a) Consider the model in equations (6.27)-(6.30). Solve the model using the method of undetermined coefficients. That is, conjecture that the solution takes the form $y_t = Au_t^{IS}$, and find the value that $A$ must take for the equations of the model to hold. (Hint: The fact that $y_t = Au_t^{IS}$ for all $t$ implies $E_t y_{t+1} = AE_t u_{t+1}^{IS}$.)

(b) Now modify the MP equation to be $r_t = by_t + c\pi_t$. Conjecture that the solution takes the form $y_t = Au_t^{IS} + B\pi_{t-1}$, $\pi_t = Cu_t^{IS} + D\pi_{t-1}$. Find (but do not solve) four equations that $A$, $B$, $C$, and $D$ must satisfy for the equations of the model to hold.

6.10. **Multiple equilibria with menu costs.** (Ball and D. Romer, 1991.) Consider an economy consisting of many imperfectly competitive firms. The profits that a firm loses relative to what it obtains with $p_i = p^*$ are $K(p_i - p^*)^2$, $K > 0$. As usual, $p^* = p + \phi y$ and $y = m - p$. Each firm faces a fixed cost $Z$ of changing its nominal price.

---

[32] See Section 11.6 for more on the zero lower bound on the nominal interest rate.

Initially $m$ is 0 and the economy is at its flexible-price equilibrium, which is $y = 0$ and $p = m = 0$. Now suppose $m$ changes to $m'$.

(a) Suppose that fraction $f$ of firms change their prices. Since the firms that change their prices charge $p^*$ and the firms that do not charge 0, this implies $p = fp^*$. Use this fact to find $p$, $y$, and $p^*$ as functions of $m'$ and $f$.

(b) Plot a firm's incentive to adjust its price, $K(0 - p^*)^2 = Kp^{*2}$, as a function of $f$. Be sure to distinguish the cases $\phi < 1$ and $\phi > 1$.

(c) A firm adjusts its price if the benefit exceeds $Z$, does not adjust if the benefit is less than $Z$, and is indifferent if the benefit is exactly $Z$. Given this, can there be a situation where both adjustment by all firms and adjustment by no firms are equilibria? Can there be a situation where neither adjustment by all firms nor adjustment by no firms is an equilibrium?

**6.11.** Consider an economy consisting of many imperfectly competitive, price-setting firms. The profits of the representative firm, firm $i$, depend on aggregate output, $y$, and the firm's real price, $r_i$: $\pi_i = \pi(y, r_i)$, where $\pi_{22} < 0$ (subscripts denote partial derivatives). Let $r^*(y)$ denote the profit-maximizing price as a function of $y$; note that $r^*(y)$ is characterized by $\pi_2(y, r^*(y)) = 0$.

Assume that output is at some level $y_0$, and that firm $i$'s real price is $r^*(y_0)$. Now suppose there is a change in the money supply, and suppose that other firms do not change their prices and that aggregate output therefore changes to some new level, $y_1$.

(a) Explain why firm $i$'s incentive to adjust its price is given by $G = \pi(y_1, r^*(y_1)) - \pi(y_1, r^*(y_0))$.

(b) Use a second-order Taylor approximation of this expression in $y_1$ around $y_1 = y_0$ to show that $G \simeq -\pi_{22}(y_0, r^*(y_0))[r^{*\prime}(y_0)]^2(y_1 - y_0)^2/2$.

(c) What component of this expression corresponds to the degree of real rigidity? What component corresponds to the degree of insensitivity of the profit function?

**6.12. Indexation.** (This problem follows Ball, 1988.) Suppose production at firm $i$ is given by $Y_i = SL_i^\alpha$, where $S$ is a supply shock and $0 < \alpha \le 1$. Thus in logs, $y_i = s + \alpha\ell_i$. Prices are flexible; thus (setting the constant term to 0 for simplicity), $p_i = w_i + (1 - \alpha)\ell_i - s$. Aggregating the output and price equations yields $y = s + \alpha\ell$ and $p = w + (1 - \alpha)\ell - s$. Wages are partially indexed to prices: $w = \theta p$, where $0 \le \theta \le 1$. Finally, aggregate demand is given by $y = m - p$. $s$ and $m$ are independent, mean-zero random variables with variances $V_s$ and $V_m$.

(a) What are $p$, $y$, $\ell$, and $w$ as functions of $m$ and $s$ and the parameters $\alpha$ and $\theta$? How does indexation affect the response of employment to monetary shocks? How does it affect the response to supply shocks?

(b) What value of $\theta$ minimizes the variance of employment?

(c) Suppose the demand for a single firm's output is $y_i = y - \eta(p_i - p)$. Suppose all firms other than firm $i$ index their wages by $w = \theta p$ as before, but that firm $i$ indexes its wage by $w_i = \theta_i p$. Firm $i$ continues to set its price as $p_i = w_i + (1 - \alpha)\ell_i - s$. The production function and the pricing equation then imply that $y_i = y - \phi(w_i - w)$, where $\phi \equiv \alpha\eta/[\alpha + (1 - \alpha)\eta]$.

(i) What is employment at firm $i$, $\ell_i$, as a function of $m, s, \alpha, \eta, \theta$, and $\theta_i$?

(ii) What value of $\theta_i$ minimizes the variance of $\ell_i$?

(iii) Find the Nash equilibrium value of $\theta$. That is, find the value of $\theta$ such that if aggregate indexation is given by $\theta$, the representative firm minimizes the variance of $\ell_i$ by setting $\theta_i = \theta$. Compare this value with the value found in part (b).

**6.13. Thick-market effects and coordination failure.** (This follows Diamond, 1982.)[33] Consider an island consisting of $N$ people and many palm trees. Each person is in one of two states, not carrying a coconut and looking for palm trees (state $P$) or carrying a coconut and looking for other people with coconuts (state $C$). If a person without a coconut finds a palm tree, he or she can climb the tree and pick a coconut; this has a cost (in utility units) of $c$. If a person with a coconut meets another person with a coconut, they trade and eat each other's coconuts; this yields $\bar{u}$ units of utility for each of them. (People cannot eat coconuts that they have picked themselves.)

A person looking for coconuts finds palm trees at rate $b$ per unit time. A person carrying a coconut finds trading partners at rate $aL$ per unit time, where $L$ is the total number of people carrying coconuts. $a$ and $b$ are exogenous.

Individuals' discount rate is $r$. Focus on steady states; that is, assume that $L$ is constant.

(a) Explain why, if everyone in state $P$ climbs a palm tree whenever he or she finds one, then $rV_P = b(V_C - V_P - c)$, where $V_P$ and $V_C$ are the values of being in the two states.

(b) Find the analogous expression for $V_C$.

(c) Solve for $V_C - V_P$, $V_C$, and $V_P$ in terms of $r, b, c, \bar{u}, a$, and $L$.

(d) What is $L$, still assuming that anyone in state $P$ climbs a palm tree whenever he or she finds one? Assume for simplicity that $aN = 2b$.

(e) For what values of $c$ is it a steady-state equilibrium for anyone in state $P$ to climb a palm tree whenever he or she finds one? (Continue to assume $aN = 2b$.)

(f) For what values of $c$ is it a steady-state equilibrium for no one who finds a tree to climb it? Are there values of $c$ for which there is more than one steady-state equilibrium? If there are multiple equilibria, does one involve higher welfare than the other? Explain intuitively.

**6.14.** Consider the problem facing an individual in the Lucas model when $P_i/P$ is unknown. The individual chooses $L_i$ to maximize the expectation of $U_i$; $U_i$ continues to be given by equation (6.72).

---

[33] The solution to this problem requires dynamic programming (see Section 10.4).

(a) Find the first-order condition for $Y_i$, and rearrange it to obtain an expression for $Y_i$ in terms of $E[P_i/P]$. Take logs of this expression to obtain an expression for $y_i$.

(b) How does the amount of labor the individual supplies if he or she follows the certainty-equivalence rule in (6.81) compare with the optimal amount derived in part (a)? (Hint: How does $E[\ln(P_i/P)]$ compare with $\ln(E[P_i/P])$?)

(c) Suppose that (as in the Lucas model) $\ln(P_i/P) = E[\ln(P_i/P)|P_i] + u_i$, where $u_i$ is normal with a mean of 0 and a variance that is independent of $P_i$. Show that this implies that $\ln\{E[(P_i/P)|P_i]\} = E[\ln(P_i/P)|P_i] + C$, where $C$ is a constant whose value is independent of $P_i$. (Hint: Note that $P_i/P = \exp\{E[\ln(P_i/P)|P_i]\}\exp(u_i)$, and show that this implies that the $y_i$ that maximizes expected utility differs from the certainty-equivalence rule in (6.81) only by a constant.)

**6.15. Observational equivalence.** (Sargent, 1976.) Suppose that the money supply is determined by $m_t = c'z_{t-1} + e_t$, where $c$ and $z$ are vectors and $e_t$ is an i.i.d. disturbance uncorrelated with $z_{t-1}$. $e_t$ is unpredictable and unobservable. Thus the expected component of $m_t$ is $c'z_{t-1}$, and the unexpected component is $e_t$. In setting the money supply, the Federal Reserve responds only to variables that matter for real activity; that is, the variables in $z$ directly affect $y$.

Now consider the following two models: (i) Only unexpected money matters, so $y_t = a'z_{t-1} + be_t + v_t$; (ii) all money matters, so $y_t = \alpha'z_{t-1} + \beta m_t + v_t$. In each specification, the disturbance is i.i.d. and uncorrelated with $z_{t-1}$ and $e_t$.

(a) Is it possible to distinguish between these two theories? That is, given a candidate set of parameter values under, say, model (i), are there parameter values under model (ii) that have the same predictions? Explain.

(b) Suppose that the Federal Reserve also responds to some variables that do not directly affect output; that is, suppose $m_t = c'z_{t-1} + \gamma'w_{t-1} + e_t$ and that models (i) and (ii) are as before (with their distubances now uncorrelated with $w_{t-1}$ as well as with $z_{t-1}$ and $e_t$). In this case, is it possible to distinguish between the two theories? Explain.

**6.16.** Consider an economy consisting of some firms with flexible prices and some with rigid prices. Let $p^f$ denote the price set by a representative flexible-price firm and $p^r$ the price set by a representative rigid-price firm. Flexible-price firms set their prices after $m$ is known; rigid-price firms set their prices before $m$ is known. Thus flexible-price firms set $p^f = p_i^* = (1 - \phi)p + \phi m$, and rigid-price firms set $p^r = Ep_i^* = (1 - \phi)Ep + \phi Em$, where $E$ denotes the expectation of a variable as of when the rigid-price firms set their prices. Assume that fraction $q$ of firms have rigid prices, so that $p = qp^r + (1-q)p^f$.

(a) Find $p^f$ in terms of $p^r$, $m$, and the parameters of the model ($\phi$ and $q$).

(b) Find $p^r$ in terms of $Em$ and the parameters of the model.

(c) (i) Do anticipated changes in $m$ (that is, changes that are expected as of when rigid-price firms set their prices) affect $y$? Why or why not?

(ii) Do unanticipated changes in $m$ affect $y$? Why or why not?

# Chapter 7
# DYNAMIC STOCHASTIC GENERAL-EQUILIBRIUM MODELS OF FLUCTUATIONS

Our analysis of macroeconomic fluctuations in the previous two chapters has developed two very incomplete pieces. In Chapter 5, we considered a full intertemporal macroeconomic model built from microeconomic foundations with explicit assumptions about the behavior of the underlying shocks. The model generated quantitative predictions about fluctuations, and is therefore an example of a quantitative *dynamic stochastic general-equilibrium,* or *DSGE,* model. The problem is that, as we saw in Section 5.10, the model appears to be an empirical failure. For example, it implies that monetary disturbances do not have real effects; it rests on large aggregate technology shocks for which there is little evidence; and its predictions about the effects of technology shocks and about business-cycle dynamics appear to be far from what we observe.

To address the real effects of monetary shocks, Chapter 6 introduced nominal rigidity. It established that barriers to price adjustment and other nominal frictions can cause monetary changes to have real effects, analyzed some of the determinants of the magnitude of those effects, and showed how nominal rigidity has important implications for the impacts of other disturbances. But it did so at the cost of abandoning most of the richness of the model of Chapter 5. Its models are largely static models with one-time shocks; and to the extent their focus is on quantitative predictions at all, it is only on addressing broad questions, notably whether plausibly small barriers to price adjustment can lead to plausibly large effects of monetary disturbances.

Researchers' ultimate goal is to build a model of fluctuations that combines the strengths of the models of the previous two chapters. This chapter will not take us all the way to that goal, however. There are two reasons. First, there is no consensus about the ingredients that are critical to include in such a model. Second, the state-of-the-art models in this effort (for example, Erceg, Henderson, and Levin, 2000, Smets and Wouters, 2003, and Christiano, Eichenbaum, and Evans, 2005) are quite complicated. If there were strong evidence that one of these models captured the essence of modern macroeconomic fluctuations, it would be worth covering in detail. But in the absence of such evidence, the models are best left for more specialized treatments.

Instead, the chapter moves us partway toward constructing a realistic DSGE model of fluctuations. The bulk of the chapter extends the analysis of the microeconomic foundations of incomplete nominal flexibility to dynamic settings. This material vividly illustrates the lack of consensus about how best to build a realistic dynamic model of fluctuations: counting generously, we will consider seven distinct models of dynamic price adjustment. As we will see, the models often have sharply different implications for the macroeconomic consequences of microeconomic frictions in price adjustment. This analysis shows the main issues in moving to dynamic models of price-setting and illustrates the list of ingredients to choose from, but it does not identify a specific "best practice" model.

The main nominal friction we considered in Chapter 6 was a fixed cost of changing prices, or menu cost. In considering dynamic models of price adjustment, it is therefore tempting to assume that the only nominal imperfection is that firms must pay a fixed cost each time they change their price. There are two reasons not to make this the only case we consider, however. First, it is complicated: analyzing models of dynamic optimization with fixed adjustment costs is technically challenging and only rarely leads to closed-form solutions. Second, the vision of price-setters constantly monitoring their prices and standing ready to change them at any moment subject only to an unchanging fixed cost may be missing something important. Many prices are reviewed on a schedule and are only rarely changed at other times. For example, many wages are reviewed annually; some union contracts specify wages over a three-year period; and many companies issue catalogues with prices that are in effect for six months or a year. Thus price changes are not purely *state dependent* (that is, triggered by developments within the economy, regardless of the time over which the developments have occurred); they are partly *time dependent* (that is, triggered by the passage of time).

Because time-dependent models are easier, we will start with them. Section 7.1 presents a common framework for all the models of this part of the chapter. Sections 7.2 through 7.4 then consider three baseline models of time-dependent price adjustment: the Fischer, or Fischer-Phelps-Taylor, model (Fischer, 1977; Phelps and Taylor, 1977); the Taylor model (Taylor, 1979); and the Calvo model (Calvo, 1983). All three models posit that prices (or wages) are set by multiperiod contracts or commitments. In each period, the contracts governing some fraction of prices expire and must be renewed; expiration is determined by the passage of time, not economic developments. The central result of the models is that multiperiod contracts lead to gradual adjustment of the price level to nominal disturbances. As a result, aggregate demand disturbances have persistent real effects.

The Taylor and Calvo models differ from the Fischer model in one important respect. The Fischer model assumes that prices are *predetermined* but not *fixed*. That is, when a multiperiod contract sets prices for several periods, it can specify a different price for each period. In the Taylor and Calvo models, in contrast, prices are fixed: a contract must specify the same price each period it is in effect.

The difference between the Taylor and Calvo models is smaller. In the Taylor model, opportunities to change prices arrive deterministically, and each price is in effect for the same number of periods. In the Calvo model, opportunities to change prices arrive randomly, and so the number of periods a price is in effect is stochastic. In keeping with the assumption of time-dependence rather than state-dependence, the stochastic process governing price changes operates independently of other factors affecting the economy. The qualitative implications of the Calvo model are the same as those of the Taylor model. Its appeal is that it yields simpler inflation dynamics than the Taylor model, and so is easier to embed in larger models.

Section 7.5 then turns to two baseline models of state-dependent price adjustment, the Caplin-Spulber and Danziger-Golosov-Lucas models (Caplin and Spulber, 1987; Danziger, 1999; Golosov and Lucas, 2007). In both, the only barrier to price adjustment is a constant fixed cost. There are two differences between the models. First, money growth is always positive in the Caplin-Spulber model, while the version of the Danziger-Golosov-Lucas model we will consider assumes no trend money growth. Second, the Caplin-Spulber model assumes no firm-specific shocks, while the Danziger-Golosov-Lucas model includes them. Both models deliver strong results about the effects of monetary disturbances, but for very different reasons.

After Section 7.6 examines some empirical evidence, Section 7.7 considers two more models of dynamic price adjustment: the Calvo-with-indexation model and the Mankiw-Reis model (Christiano, Eichenbaum, and Evans, 2005; Mankiw and Reis, 2002). These models are more complicated than the models of the earlier sections, but appear to have more hope of fitting key facts about inflation dynamics.

The final two sections begin to consider how dynamic models of price adjustment can be embedded in models of the business cycle. Section 7.8 presents an example of a complete DSGE model with nominal rigidity. The model is the canonical three-equation new Keynesian model of Clarida, Galí, and Gertler (2000). Unfortunately, in many ways this model is closer to the baseline real-business-cycle model than to our ultimate objective: much of the model's appeal is tractability and elegance, not realism. Section 7.9 therefore discusses elements of other DSGE models with monetary non-neutrality. Because of the models' complexity and the lack of agreement about their key ingredients, however, it stops short of analyzing other fully specified models.

Before proceeding, it is important to emphasize that the issue we are interested in is incomplete adjustment of *nominal* prices and wages. There are many reasons—involving uncertainty, information and renegotiation costs, incentives, and so on—that prices and wages may not adjust freely to equate supply and demand, or that firms may not change their prices and wages completely and immediately in response to shocks. But simply introducing some departure from perfect markets is not enough to imply that nominal disturbances matter. All the models of unemployment in Chapter 10, for example, are real models. If one appends a monetary sector to those models without any further complications, the classical dichotomy continues to hold: monetary disturbances cause all nominal prices and wages to change, leaving the real equilibrium (with whatever non-Walrasian features it involves) unchanged. Any microeconomic basis for failure of the classical dichotomy requires some kind of *nominal* imperfection.

# 7.1   Building Blocks of Dynamic New Keynesian Models

## Overview

We will analyze the various models of dynamic price adjustment in a common framework. The framework draws heavily on the model of exogenous nominal rigidity in Section 6.1 and the model of imperfect competition in Section 6.5.

Time is discrete. Each period, imperfectly competitive firms produce output using labor as their only input. As in Section 6.5, the production function is one-for-one; thus aggregate output and aggregate labor input are equal. The model omits the government and international trade; thus, as in the models of Chapter 6, aggregate consumption and aggregate output are equal.

For simplicity, for the most part we will neglect uncertainty. Households maximize utility, taking the paths of the real wage and the real interest rate as given. Firms, which are owned by the households, maximize the present discounted value of their profits, subject to constraints on their price-setting (which vary across the models we will consider). Finally, a central bank determines the path of the real interest rate through its conduct of monetary policy.

## Households

There is a fixed number of infinitely lived households that obtain utility from consumption and disutility from working. The representative household's objective function is

$$\sum_{t=0}^{\infty} \beta^t [U(C_t) - V(L_t)], \qquad 0 < \beta < 1. \tag{7.1}$$

As in Section 6.5, $C$ is a consumption index that is a constant-elasticity-of-substitution combination of the household's consumption of the individual goods, with elasticity of substitution $\eta > 1$. We make our usual assumptions about the functional forms of $U(\bullet)$ and $V(\bullet)$:[1]

$$U(C_t) = \frac{C_t^{1-\theta}}{1-\theta}, \qquad \theta > 0, \tag{7.2}$$

$$V(L_t) = \frac{B}{\gamma} L_t^{\gamma}, \quad B > 0, \quad \gamma > 1. \tag{7.3}$$

Let $W$ denote the nominal wage and $P$ denote the price level. Formally, $P$ is the price index corresponding to the consumption index, as in Section 6.5. Throughout this chapter, however, we use the approximation we used in the Lucas model in Section 6.9 that the log of the price index, which we will denote $p$, is simply the average of firms' log prices.

An increase in labor supply in period $t$ of amount $dL$ increases the household's real income by $(W_t/P_t)\,dL$. The first-order condition for labor supply in period $t$ is therefore

$$V'(L_t) = U'(C_t)\frac{W_t}{P_t}. \tag{7.4}$$

Because the production function is one-for-one and the only possible use of output is for consumption, in equilibrium $C_t$ and $L_t$ must both equal $Y_t$. Combining this fact with (7.4) tells us what the real wage must be given the level of output:

$$\frac{W_t}{P_t} = \frac{V'(Y_t)}{U'(Y_t)}. \tag{7.5}$$

Substituting the functional forms in (7.2)–(7.3) into (7.5) and solving for the real wage yields

$$\frac{W_t}{P_t} = BY_t^{\theta+\gamma-1}. \tag{7.6}$$

Equation (7.6) is similar to equation (6.56) in the model of Section 6.5.

Since we are making the same assumptions about consumption as before, the new Keynesian *IS* curve holds in this model (see equation [6.8]):

$$\ln Y_t = \ln Y_{t+1} - \frac{1}{\theta}r_t. \tag{7.7}$$

## Firms

Firm $i$ produces output in period $t$ according to the production function $Y_{it} = L_{it}$, and, as in Section 6.5, faces demand function $Y_{it} = Y_t(P_{it}/P_t)^{-\eta}$. The

---

[1] The reason for introducing $B$ in (7.3) will be apparent below.

firm's real profits in period $t$, $R_t$, are revenues minus costs:

$$R_t = \left(\frac{P_{it}}{P_t}\right) Y_{it} - \left(\frac{W_t}{P_t}\right) Y_{it}$$

$$= Y_t \left[\left(\frac{P_{it}}{P_t}\right)^{1-\eta} - \left(\frac{W_t}{P_t}\right)\left(\frac{P_{it}}{P_t}\right)^{-\eta}\right]. \tag{7.8}$$

Consider the problem of the firm setting its price in some period, which we normalize to period 0. As emphasized above, we will consider various assumptions about price-setting, including ones that imply that the length of time a given price is in effect is random. Thus, let $q_t$ denote the probability that the price the firm sets in period zero is in effect in period $t$. Since the firm's profits accrue to the households, it values the profits according to the utility they provide to households. The marginal utility of the representative household's consumption in period $t$ relative to period 0 is $\beta^t U'(C_t)/U'(C_0)$; denote this quantity $\lambda_t$.

The firm therefore chooses its price in period 0, $P_i$, to maximize $\sum_{t=0}^{\infty} q_t \lambda_t R_t \equiv A$, where $R_t$ is the firm's profits in period $t$ if $P_i$ is still in effect. Using equation (7.8) for $R_t$, we can write $A$ as

$$A = \sum_{t=0}^{\infty} q_t \lambda_t Y_t \left[\left(\frac{P_i}{P_t}\right)^{1-\eta} - \left(\frac{W_t}{P_t}\right)\left(\frac{P_i}{P_t}\right)^{-\eta}\right]. \tag{7.9}$$

One can say relatively little about the $P_i$ that maximizes $A$ in the general case. Two assumptions allow us to make progress, however. The first, and most important, is that inflation is low and that the economy is always close to its flexible-price equilibrium. The other is that households' discount factor, $\beta$, is close to 1.

To see the usefulness of these assumptions, rewrite (7.9) as

$$A = \sum_{t=0}^{\infty} q_t \lambda_t Y_t P_t^{\eta-1} \left(P_i^{1-\eta} - W_t P_i^{-\eta}\right). \tag{7.10}$$

The production function implies that marginal cost is constant and equal to $W_t$, and the elasticity of demand for the firm's good is constant. Thus the price that maximizes profits in period $t$, which we denote $P_t^*$, is a constant times $W_t$ (see equation [6.55]). Equivalently, $W_t$ is a constant times $P_t^*$. Thus we can write the expression in parentheses in (7.10) as a function of just $P_i$ and $P_t^*$. As before, we will end up working with variables expressed in logs rather than levels. Thus, rewrite (7.10) as

$$A = \sum_{t=0}^{\infty} q_t \lambda_t Y_t P_t^{\eta-1} F(p_i, p_t^*), \tag{7.11}$$

where $p_i$ and $p_t^*$ denote the logs of $P_i$ and $P_t^*$.

Our simplifying assumptions have two important implications about (7.11). The first is that the variation in $\lambda_t Y_t P_t^{\eta-1}$ is negligible relative to the variation in $q_t$ and $p_t^*$. The second is that $F(\bullet)$ can be well approximated by a second-order approximation around $p_i = p_t^*$.[2] Period-$t$ profits are maximized at $p_i = p_t^*$; thus at $p_i = p_t^*$, $\partial F(p_i,p_t^*)/\partial p_i$ is zero and $\partial^2 F(p_i,p_t^*)/\partial p_i^2$ is negative. It follows that

$$F(p_i,p_t^*) \simeq F(p_t^*,p_t^*) - K(p_i - p_t^*)^2, \qquad K > 0. \tag{7.12}$$

This analysis implies that the problem of choosing $P_i$ to maximize $A$ can be simplified to the problem,

$$\min_{p_i} \sum_{t=0}^{\infty} q_t (p_i - p_t^*)^2. \tag{7.13}$$

Finding the first-order condition for $p_i$ and rearranging gives us

$$p_i = \sum_{t=0}^{\infty} \omega_t p_t^*, \tag{7.14}$$

where $\omega_t \equiv q_t / \sum_{\tau=0}^{\infty} q_\tau$. $\omega_t$ is the probability that the price the firm sets in period 0 will be in effect in period $t$ divided by the expected number of periods the price will be in effect. Thus it measures the importance of period $t$ to the choice of $p_i$. Equation (7.14) states that the price firm $i$ sets is a weighted average of the profit-maximizing prices during the time the price will be in effect.

Finally, paralleling our assumption of certainty equivalence in the Lucas model in Section 6.9, we assume that when there is uncertainty, firms base their prices on expectations of the $p_t^*$'s:

$$p_i = \sum_{t=0}^{\infty} \omega_t E_0[p_t^*], \tag{7.15}$$

where $E_0[\bullet]$ denotes expectations as of period 0. Again, (7.15) is a legitimate approximation under appropriate assumptions.

A firm's profit-maximizing real price, $P^*/P$, is $\eta/(\eta - 1)$ times the real wage, $W/P$. And we know from equation (7.6) that $w_t$ equals $p_t + b + (\theta + \gamma - 1)y_t$ (where $b \equiv \ln B$, $w_t \equiv \ln W_t$, and $y_t \equiv \ln Y_t$). Thus, the profit-maximizing price is

$$p^* = p + \ln[\eta/(\eta - 1)] + b + (\theta + \gamma - 1)y. \tag{7.16}$$

Note that (7.16) is of the form $p^* = p + c + \phi y, \phi > 0$, of the static model of Section 6.5 (see [6.58]). To simplify this, let $m$ denote log nominal GDP, $p + y$, define $\phi \equiv \theta + \gamma - 1$, and assume $\ln[\eta/(\eta - 1)] + b = 0$ for simplicity.[3] This yields

$$p_t^* = \phi m_t + (1 - \phi)p_t. \tag{7.17}$$

---

[2] These claims can be made precise with appropriate formalizations of the statements that inflation is small, the economy is near its flexible-price equilibrium, and $\beta$ is close to 1.

[3] It was for this reason that we introduced $B$ in (7.3).

Substituting this expression into (7.15) gives us

$$p_i = \sum_{t=0}^{\infty} \omega_t E_0[\phi m_t + (1 - \phi)p_t]. \tag{7.18}$$

## The Central Bank

Equation (7.18) is the key equation of the aggregate supply side of the model, and equation (7.7) describes aggregate demand for a given real interest rate. It remains to describe the determination of the real interest rate. To do this, we need to bring monetary policy into the model.

One approach, along the lines of Section 6.4, is to assume that the central bank follows some rule for how it sets the real interest rate as a function of macroeconomic conditions. This is the approach we will use in Section 7.8 and in much of Chapter 11. Our interest here, however, is in the aggregate supply side of the economy. Thus, along the lines of what we did in Part B of Chapter 6, we will follow the simpler approach of taking the path of nominal GDP (that is, the path of $m_t$) as given. We will then examine the behavior of the economy in response to various paths of nominal GDP, such as a one-time, permanent increase in its level or a permanent increase in its growth rate. As described in Section 6.5, a simple interpretation of the assumption that the path of nominal GDP is given is that the central bank has a target path of nominal GDP and conducts monetary policy to achieve it. This approach allows us to suppress not only the money market, but also the *IS* equation, (7.7).

# 7.2 Predetermined Prices: The Fischer Model

## Framework and Assumptions

We now turn to the Fischer model of staggered price adjustment.[4] The model follows the framework of the previous section. Price-setting is assumed to take a particular form, however: each price-setter sets prices every other period for the next two periods. And as emphasized above, the model assumes that the price-setter can set different prices for the two periods. That is, a

---

[4] The original versions of the Fischer and Taylor models focused on staggered adjustment of wages; prices were in principle flexible but were determined as markups over wages. For simplicity, we assume instead that staggered adjustment applies directly to prices. Staggered wage adjustment has qualitatively similar implications. The key difference is that the microeconomic determinants of the parameter $\phi$ in the equation for desired prices, (7.17), are different under staggered wage adjustment (Huang and Liu, 2002).

firm setting its price in period 0 sets one price for period 1 and one price for period 2. Since each price will be in effect for only one period, equation (7.15) implies that each price (in logs) equals the expectation as of period 0 of the profit-maximizing price for that period. In any given period, half of price-setters are setting their prices for the next two periods. Thus at any point, half of the prices in effect are those set the previous period, and half are those set two periods ago.

No specific assumptions are made about the process followed by aggregate demand. For example, information about $m_t$ may be revealed gradually in the periods leading up to $t$; the expectation of $m_t$ as of period $t-1$, $E_{t-1}m_t$, may therefore differ from the expectation of $m_t$ the period before, $E_{t-2}m_t$.

## Solving the Model

In any period, half of prices are ones set in the previous period, and half are ones set two periods ago. Thus the average price is

$$p_t = \tfrac{1}{2}(p_t^1 + p_t^2), \tag{7.19}$$

where $p_t^1$ denotes the price set for $t$ by firms that set their prices in $t-1$, and $p_t^2$ the price set for $t$ by firms that set their prices in $t-2$. Our assumptions about pricing from the previous section imply that $p_t^1$ equals the expectation as of period $t-1$ of $p_{it}^*$, and $p_t^2$ equals the expectation as of $t-2$ of $p_{it}^*$. Equation (7.17) therefore implies

$$
\begin{aligned}
p_t^1 &= E_{t-1}[\phi m_t + (1-\phi)p_t] \\
&= \phi E_{t-1}m_t + (1-\phi)\tfrac{1}{2}(p_t^1 + p_t^2),
\end{aligned} \tag{7.20}
$$

$$
\begin{aligned}
p_t^2 &= E_{t-2}[\phi m_t + (1-\phi)p_t] \\
&= \phi E_{t-2}m_t + (1-\phi)\tfrac{1}{2}(E_{t-2}p_t^1 + p_t^2),
\end{aligned} \tag{7.21}
$$

where $E_{t-\tau}$ denotes expectations conditional on information available through period $t-\tau$. Equation (7.20) uses the fact that $p_t^2$ is already determined when $p_t^1$ is set, and thus is not uncertain.

Our goal is to find how the price level and output evolve over time, given the behavior of $m$. To do this, we begin by solving (7.20) for $p_t^1$; this yields

$$p_t^1 = \frac{2\phi}{1+\phi}E_{t-1}m_t + \frac{1-\phi}{1+\phi}p_t^2. \tag{7.22}$$

Since the left- and right-hand sides of (7.22) are equal, the expectation as of $t-2$ of the two sides must be equal. Thus,

$$E_{t-2}p_t^1 = \frac{2\phi}{1+\phi}E_{t-2}m_t + \frac{1-\phi}{1+\phi}p_t^2, \tag{7.23}$$

where we have used the law of iterated projections to substitute $E_{t-2}m_t$ for $E_{t-2}E_{t-1}m_t$.

We can substitute (7.23) into (7.21) to obtain

$$p_t^2 = \phi E_{t-2}m_t + (1-\phi)\frac{1}{2}\left(\frac{2\phi}{1+\phi}E_{t-2}m_t + \frac{1-\phi}{1+\phi}p_t^2 + p_t^2\right). \qquad (7.24)$$

Solving this expression for $p_t^2$ yields simply

$$p_t^2 = E_{t-2}m_t. \qquad (7.25)$$

We can now combine the results and describe the equilibrium. Substituting (7.25) into (7.22) and simplifying gives

$$p_t^1 = E_{t-2}m_t + \frac{2\phi}{1+\phi}(E_{t-1}m_t - E_{t-2}m_t). \qquad (7.26)$$

Finally, substituting (7.25) and (7.26) into the expressions for the price level and output, $p_t = (p_t^1 + p_t^2)/2$ and $y_t = m_t - p_t$, implies

$$p_t = E_{t-2}m_t + \frac{\phi}{1+\phi}(E_{t-1}m_t - E_{t-2}m_t), \qquad (7.27)$$

$$y_t = \frac{1}{1+\phi}(E_{t-1}m_t - E_{t-2}m_t) + (m_t - E_{t-1}m_t). \qquad (7.28)$$

## Implications

Equation (7.28) shows the model's main implications. First, unanticipated aggregate demand shifts have real effects; this is shown by the $m_t - E_{t-1}m_t$ term. Because price-setters are assumed not to know $m_t$ when they set their prices, these shocks are passed one-for-one into output.

Second, aggregate demand shifts that become anticipated after the first prices are set affect output. Consider information about aggregate demand in $t$ that becomes available between period $t-2$ and period $t-1$. In practice, this might correspond to the release of survey results or other leading indicators of future economic activity, or to indications of likely shifts in monetary policy. As (7.27) and (7.28) show, proportion $1/(1+\phi)$ of information about $m_t$ that arrives between $t-2$ and $t-1$ is passed into output, and the remainder goes into prices. The reason that the change is not neutral is straightforward: not all prices are completely flexible in the short run.

One implication of these results is that interactions among price-setters can either increase or decrease the effects of microeconomic price stickiness. One might expect that since half of prices are already set and the other half are free to adjust, half of the information about $m_t$ that arrives between $t-2$ and $t-1$ is passed into prices and half into output. But in general this is not correct. The key parameter is $\phi$: the proportion of the shift that is passed into output is not $\frac{1}{2}$ but $1/(1+\phi)$ (see [7.28]).

Recall that $\phi$ measures the degree of real rigidity: $\phi$ is the responsiveness of price-setters' desired real prices to aggregate real output, and so a smaller value of $\phi$ corresponds to greater real rigidity. When real rigidity is large, price-setters are reluctant to allow variations in their relative prices. As a result, the price-setters that are free to adjust their prices do not allow their prices to differ greatly from the ones already set, and so the real effects of a monetary shock are large. If $\phi$ exceeds 1, in contrast, the later price-setters make large price changes, and the aggregate real effects of changes in $m$ are small.[5]

Finally, and importantly, the model implies that output does not depend on $E_{t-2}m_t$ (given the values of $E_{t-1}m_t - E_{t-2}m_t$ and $m_t - E_{t-1}m_t$). That is, any information about aggregate demand that all price-setters have had a chance to respond to has no effect on output. Thus the model does not provide an explanation of persistent effects of movements in aggregate demand. We will return to this issue in Section 7.7.

# 7.3 Fixed Prices: The Taylor Model

## The Model

We now change the model of the previous section by assuming that when a firm sets prices for two periods, it must set the same price for both periods. In the terminology introduced earlier, prices are not just predetermined, but fixed.

We make two other, less significant changes to the model. First, a firm setting a price in period $t$ now does so for periods $t$ and $t+1$ rather than for periods $t+1$ and $t+2$. This change simplifies the model without affecting the main results. Second, the model is much easier to solve if we posit a specific process for $m$. A simple assumption is that $m$ is a random walk:

$$m_t = m_{t-1} + u_t, \tag{7.29}$$

where $u$ is white noise. The key feature of this process is that an innovation to $m$ (the $u$ term) has a long-lasting effect on its level.

Let $x_t$ denote the price chosen by firms that set their prices in period $t$. Here equation (7.18) for price-setting implies

$$
\begin{aligned}
x_t &= \tfrac{1}{2}\left(p_{it}^* + E_t p_{it+1}^*\right) \\
&= \tfrac{1}{2}\{[\phi m_t + (1-\phi)p_t] + [\phi E_t m_{t+1} + (1-\phi)E_t p_{t+1}]\},
\end{aligned}
\tag{7.30}
$$

where the second line uses the fact that $p^* = \phi m + (1-\phi)p$.

Since half of prices are set each period, $p_t$ is the average of $x_t$ and $x_{t-1}$. In addition, since $m$ is a random walk, $E_t m_{t+1}$ equals $m_t$. Substituting these

---

[5] Haltiwanger and Waldman (1989) show more generally how a small fraction of agents who do not respond to shocks can have a disproportionate effect on the economy.

facts into (7.30) gives us

$$x_t = \phi m_t + \tfrac{1}{4}(1 - \phi)(x_{t-1} + 2x_t + E_t x_{t+1}). \tag{7.31}$$

Solving for $x_t$ yields

$$x_t = A(x_{t-1} + E_t x_{t+1}) + (1 - 2A)m_t, \qquad A \equiv \frac{1}{2}\frac{1 - \phi}{1 + \phi}. \tag{7.32}$$

Equation (7.32) is the key equation of the model.

Equation (7.32) expresses $x_t$ in terms of $m_t$, $x_{t-1}$, and the expectation of $x_{t+1}$. To solve the model, we need to eliminate the expectation of $x_{t+1}$ from this expression. We will solve the model in two different ways, first using the method of undetermined coefficients and then using *lag operators*. The method of undetermined coefficients is simpler. But there are cases where it is cumbersome or intractable; in those cases the use of lag operators is often fruitful.

## The Method of Undetermined Coefficients

As described in Section 5.6, the idea of the method of undetermined coefficients is to guess the general functional form of the solution and then to use the model to determine the precise coefficients. In the model we are considering, in period $t$ two variables are given: the money stock, $m_t$, and the prices set the previous period, $x_{t-1}$. In addition, the model is linear. It is therefore reasonable to guess that $x_t$ is a linear function of $x_{t-1}$ and $m_t$:

$$x_t = \mu + \lambda x_{t-1} + \nu m_t. \tag{7.33}$$

Our goal is to determine whether there are values of $\mu, \lambda$, and $\nu$ that yield a solution of the model.

Although we could now proceed to find $\mu, \lambda$, and $\nu$, it simplifies the algebra if we first use our knowledge of the model to restrict (7.33). We have normalized the constant in the expression for firms' desired prices to zero, so that $p_{it}^* = p_t + \phi y_t$. As a result, the equilibrium with flexible prices is for $y$ to equal zero and for each price to equal $m$. In light of this, consider a situation where $x_{t-1}$ and $m_t$ are equal. If period-$t$ price-setters also set their prices to $m_t$, the economy is at its flexible-price equilibrium. In addition, since $m$ follows a random walk, the period-$t$ price-setters have no reason to expect $m_{t+1}$ to be on average either more or less than $m_t$, and hence no reason to expect $x_{t+1}$ to depart on average from $m_t$. Thus in this situation $p_{it}^*$ and $E_t p_{it+1}^*$ are both equal to $m_t$, and so price-setters will choose $x_t = m_t$. In sum, it is reasonable to guess that if $x_{t-1} = m_t$, then $x_t = m_t$. In terms of (7.33), this condition is

$$\mu + \lambda m_t + \nu m_t = m_t \tag{7.34}$$

for all $m_t$.

Two conditions are needed for (7.34) to hold. The first is $\lambda + v = 1$; otherwise (7.34) cannot be satisfied for all values of $m_t$. Second, when we impose $\lambda + v = 1$, (7.34) implies $\mu = 0$. Substituting these conditions into (7.33) yields

$$x_t = \lambda x_{t-1} + (1 - \lambda)m_t. \tag{7.35}$$

Our goal is now to find a value of $\lambda$ that solves the model.

Since (7.35) holds each period, it implies $x_{t+1} = \lambda x_t + (1 - \lambda)m_{t+1}$. Thus the expectation as of period $t$ of $x_{t+1}$ is $\lambda x_t + (1 - \lambda)E_t m_{t+1}$, which equals $\lambda x_t + (1 - \lambda)m_t$. Using (7.35) to substitute for $x_t$ then gives us

$$\begin{aligned} E_t x_{t+1} &= \lambda[\lambda x_{t-1} + (1 - \lambda)m_t] + (1 - \lambda)m_t \\ &= \lambda^2 x_{t-1} + (1 - \lambda^2)m_t. \end{aligned} \tag{7.36}$$

Substituting this expression into (7.32) yields

$$\begin{aligned} x_t &= A[x_{t-1} + \lambda^2 x_{t-1} + (1 - \lambda^2)m_t] + (1 - 2A)m_t \\ &= (A + A\lambda^2)x_{t-1} + [A(1 - \lambda^2) + (1 - 2A)]m_t. \end{aligned} \tag{7.37}$$

Thus, if price-setters believe that $x_t$ is a linear function of $x_{t-1}$ and $m_t$ of the form assumed in (7.35), then, acting to maximize their profits, they will indeed set their prices as a linear function of these variables. If we have found a solution of the model, these two linear equations must be the same. Comparison of (7.35) and (7.37) shows that this requires

$$A + A\lambda^2 = \lambda \tag{7.38}$$

and

$$A(1 - \lambda^2) + (1 - 2A) = 1 - \lambda. \tag{7.39}$$

It is easy to show that (7.39) simplifies to (7.38). Thus we only need to consider (7.38). This is a quadratic in $\lambda$. The solution is

$$\lambda = \frac{1 \pm \sqrt{1 - 4A^2}}{2A}. \tag{7.40}$$

Using the definition of $A$ in equation (7.32), one can show that the two values of $\lambda$ are

$$\lambda_1 = \frac{1 - \sqrt{\phi}}{1 + \sqrt{\phi}}, \tag{7.41}$$

$$\lambda_2 = \frac{1 + \sqrt{\phi}}{1 - \sqrt{\phi}}. \tag{7.42}$$

Of the two values, only $\lambda = \lambda_1$ gives reasonable results. When $\lambda = \lambda_1$, $|\lambda| < 1$, and so the economy is stable. When $\lambda = \lambda_2$, in contrast, $|\lambda| > 1$, and thus the economy is unstable: the slightest disturbance sends output off toward plus or minus infinity. As a result, the assumptions underlying the model—for example, that sellers do not ration buyers—break down. For that reason, we focus on $\lambda = \lambda_1$.

Thus equation (7.35) with $\lambda = \lambda_1$ solves the model: if price-setters believe that others are using that rule to set their prices, they find it in their own interests to use that same rule.

We can now describe the behavior of output. $y_t$ equals $m_t - p_t$, which in turn equals $m_t - (x_{t-1} + x_t)/2$. With the behavior of $x$ given by (7.35), this implies

$$
\begin{aligned}
y_t &= m_t - \tfrac{1}{2}\{[\lambda x_{t-2} + (1-\lambda)m_{t-1}] + [\lambda x_{t-1} + (1-\lambda)m_t]\} \\
&= m_t - \left[\lambda\tfrac{1}{2}(x_{t-2} + x_{t-1}) + (1-\lambda)\tfrac{1}{2}(m_{t-1} + m_t)\right].
\end{aligned}
\tag{7.43}
$$

Using the facts that $m_t = m_{t-1} + u_t$ and $(x_{t-1} + x_{t-2})/2 = p_{t-1}$, we can simplify this to

$$
\begin{aligned}
y_t &= m_{t-1} + u_t - \left[\lambda p_{t-1} + (1-\lambda)m_{t-1} + (1-\lambda)\tfrac{1}{2}u_t\right] \\
&= \lambda(m_{t-1} - p_{t-1}) + \frac{1+\lambda}{2}u_t \\
&= \lambda y_{t-1} + \frac{1+\lambda}{2}u_t.
\end{aligned}
\tag{7.44}
$$

## Implications

Equation (7.44) is the key result of the model. As long as $\lambda_1$ is positive (which is true if $\phi < 1$), (7.44) implies that shocks to aggregate demand have long-lasting effects on output—effects that persist even after all firms have changed their prices. Suppose the economy is initially at the equilibrium with flexible prices (so $y$ is steady at 0), and consider the effects of a positive shock of size $u^0$ in some period. In the period of the shock, not all firms adjust their prices, and so not surprisingly, $y$ rises; from (7.44), $y = [(1+\lambda)/2]u^0$. In the following period, even though the remaining firms are able to adjust their prices, $y$ does not return to normal even in the absence of a further shock: from (7.44), $y$ is $\lambda[(1+\lambda)/2]u^0$. Thereafter output returns slowly to normal, with $y_t = \lambda y_{t-1}$ each period.

The response of the price level to the shock is the flip side of the response of output. The price level rises by $[1 - (1+\lambda)/2]u^0$ in the initial period, and then fraction $1 - \lambda$ of the remaining distance from $u^0$ in each subsequent period. Thus the economy exhibits price-level inertia.

The source of the long-lasting real effects of monetary shocks is again price-setters' reluctance to allow variations in their relative prices. Recall that $p^*_{it} = \phi m_t + (1 - \phi)p_t$, and that $\lambda_1 > 0$ only if $\phi < 1$. Thus there is gradual adjustment only if desired prices are an increasing function of the price level. Suppose each price-setter adjusted fully to the shock at the first opportunity. In this case, the price-setters who adjusted their prices in the period of the shock would adjust by the full amount of the shock, and the remainder would do the same in the next period. Thus $y$ would rise by $u^0/2$ in the initial period and return to normal in the next.

To see why this rapid adjustment cannot be the equilibrium if $\phi$ is less than 1, consider the firms that adjust their prices immediately. By assumption, all prices have been adjusted by the second period, and so in that period each firm is charging its profit-maximizing price. But since $\phi < 1$, the profit-maximizing price is lower when the price level is lower, and so the price that is profit-maximizing in the period of the shock, when not all prices have been adjusted, is less than the profit-maximizing price in the next period. Thus these firms should not adjust their prices fully in the period of the shock. This in turn implies that it is not optimal for the remaining firms to adjust their prices fully in the subsequent period. And the knowledge that they will not do this further dampens the initial response of the firms that adjust their prices in the period of the shock. The end result of these forward- and backward-looking interactions is the gradual adjustment shown in equation (7.35).

Thus, as in the model with prices that are predetermined but not fixed, the extent of incomplete price adjustment in the aggregate can be larger than one might expect simply from the knowledge that not all prices are adjusted every period. Indeed, the extent of aggregate price sluggishness is even larger in this case, since it persists even after every price has changed. And again a low value of $\phi$—that is, a high degree of real rigidity—is critical to this result. If $\phi$ is 1, then $\lambda$ is 0, and so each price-setter adjusts his or her price fully to changes in $m$ at the earliest opportunity. If $\phi$ exceeds 1, $\lambda$ is negative, and so $p$ moves by more than $m$ in the period after the shock, and thereafter the adjustment toward the long-run equilibrium is oscillatory.

## Lag Operators

A different, more general approach to solving the model is to use lag operators. The lag operator, which we denote by $L$, is a function that lags variables. That is, the lag operator applied to any variable gives the previous period's value of the variable: $Lz_t = z_{t-1}$.

To see the usefulness of lag operators, consider our model without the restriction that $m$ follows a random walk. Equation (7.30) continues to hold. If we proceed analogously to the derivation of (7.32), but without imposing $E_t m_{t+1} = m_t$, straightforward algebra yields

$$x_t = A(x_{t-1} + E_t x_{t+1}) + \frac{1 - 2A}{2} m_t + \frac{1 - 2A}{2} E_t m_{t+1}, \qquad (7.45)$$

where $A$ is as before. Note that (7.45) simplifies to (7.32) if $E_t m_{t+1} = m_t$.

The first step is to rewrite this expression using lag operators. $x_{t-1}$ is the lag of $x_t$: $x_{t-1} = Lx_t$. In addition, if we adopt the rule that when $L$ is applied to an expression involving expectations, it lags the date of the variables but not the date of the expectations, then $x_t$ is the lag of $E_t x_{t+1}$: $LE_t x_{t+1} = E_t x_t = x_t$.[6] Equivalently, using $L^{-1}$ to denote the inverse lag function, $E_t x_{t+1} = L^{-1} x_t$. Similarly, $E_t m_{t+1} = L^{-1} m_t$. Thus we can rewrite (7.45) as

$$x_t = A(L x_t + L^{-1} x_t) + \frac{1 - 2A}{2} m_t + \frac{1 - 2A}{2} L^{-1} m_t, \qquad (7.46)$$

or

$$(I - AL - AL^{-1}) x_t = \frac{1 - 2A}{2}(I + L^{-1}) m_t. \qquad (7.47)$$

Here $I$ is the identity operator (so $I z_t = z_t$ for any $z$). Thus $(I + L^{-1}) m_t$ is shorthand for $m_t + L^{-1} m_t$, and $(I - AL - AL^{-1}) x_t$ is shorthand for $x_t - A x_{t-1} - A E_t x_{t+1}$.

Now observe that we can "factor" $I - AL - AL^{-1}$ as $(I - \lambda L^{-1})(I - \lambda L)(A/\lambda)$, where $\lambda$ is again given by (7.40). Thus we have

$$(I - \lambda L^{-1})(I - \lambda L) x_t = \frac{\lambda}{A} \frac{1 - 2A}{2}(I + L^{-1}) m_t. \qquad (7.48)$$

This formulation of "multiplying" expressions involving the lag operator should be interpreted in the natural way: $(I - \lambda L^{-1})(I - \lambda L) x_t$ is shorthand for $(I - \lambda L) x_t$ minus $\lambda$ times the inverse lag operator applied to $(I - \lambda L) x_t$, and thus equals $(x_t - \lambda L x_t) - (\lambda L^{-1} x_t - \lambda^2 x_t)$. Simple algebra and the definition of $\lambda$ can be used to verify that (7.48) and (7.47) are equivalent.

As before, to solve the model we need to eliminate the term involving the expectation of the future value of an endogenous variable. In (7.48), $E_t x_{t+1}$ appears (implicitly) on the left-hand side because of the $I - \lambda L^{-1}$ term. It is thus natural to "divide" both sides by $I - \lambda L^{-1}$. That is, consider applying the operator $I + \lambda L^{-1} + \lambda^2 L^{-2} + \lambda^3 L^{-3} + \cdots$ to both sides of (7.48). $I + \lambda L^{-1} + \lambda^2 L^{-2} + \cdots$ times $I - \lambda L^{-1}$ is simply $I$; thus the left-hand side is $(I - \lambda L) x_t$. And $I + \lambda L^{-1} + \lambda^2 L^{-2} + \cdots$ times $I + L^{-1}$ is $I + (1 + \lambda) L^{-1} + (1 + \lambda) \lambda L^{-2} + (1 + \lambda) \lambda^2 L^{-3} + \cdots$.[7] Thus (7.48) becomes

$$(I - \lambda L) x_t$$
$$= \frac{\lambda}{A} \frac{1 - 2A}{2}[I + (1 + \lambda) L^{-1} + (1 + \lambda) \lambda L^{-2} + (1 + \lambda) \lambda^2 L^{-3} + \cdots] m_t. \qquad (7.49)$$

---

[6] Since $E_t x_{t-1} = x_{t-1}$ and $E_t m_t = m_t$, we can think of all the variables in (7.45) as being expectations as of $t$. Thus in the analysis that follows, the lag operator should always be interpreted as keeping all variables as expectations as of $t$. The *backshift operator*, $B$, lags both the date of the variable and the date of the expectations. Thus, for example, $BE_t x_{t+1} = E_{t-1} x_t$. Whether the lag operator or the backshift operator is more useful depends on the application.

[7] Since the operator $I + \lambda L^{-1} + \lambda^2 L^{-2} + \cdots$ is an infinite sum, this requires that $\lim_{n \to \infty}(I + \lambda L^{-1} + \lambda^2 L^{-2} + \cdots + \lambda^n L^{-n})(I + L^{-1}) m_t$ exists. This requires that $\lambda^n L^{-(n+1)} m_t$ (which equals $\lambda^n E_t m_{t+n+1}$) converges to 0. For the case where $\lambda = \lambda_1$ (so $|\lambda| < 1$) and where $m$ is a random walk, this condition is satisfied.

Rewriting this expression without lag operators yields

$$x_t = \lambda x_{t-1}$$
$$+ \frac{\lambda}{A} \frac{1 - 2A}{2}[m_t + (1 + \lambda)(E_t m_{t+1} + \lambda E_t m_{t+2} + \lambda^2 E_t m_{t+3} + \cdots)]. \tag{7.50}$$

Expression (7.50) characterizes the behavior of newly set prices in terms of the exogenous money supply process. To find the behavior of the aggregate price level and output, we only have to substitute this expression into the expressions for $p$ ($p_t = (x_t + x_{t-1})/2$) and $y$ ($y_t = m_t - p_t$).

In the special case when $m$ is a random walk, all the $E_t m_{t+i}$'s are equal to $m_t$. In this case, (7.50) simplifies to

$$x_t = \lambda x_{t-1} + \frac{\lambda}{A} \frac{1 - 2A}{2} \left(1 + \frac{1 + \lambda}{1 - \lambda}\right) m_t. \tag{7.51}$$

It is straightforward to show that expression (7.38), $A + A\lambda^2 = \lambda$, implies that equation (7.51) reduces to equation (7.35), $x_t = \lambda x_{t-1} + (1 - \lambda)m_t$. Thus when $m$ is a random walk, we obtain the same result as before. But we have also solved the model for a general process for $m$.

Although this use of lag operators may seem mysterious, in fact it is no more than a compact way of carrying out perfectly standard manipulations. We could have first derived (7.45) (expressed without using lag operators) by simple algebra. We could then have noted that since (7.45) holds at each date, it must be the case that

$$E_t x_{t+k} - A E_t x_{t+k-1} - A E_t x_{t+k+1} = \frac{1 - 2A}{2}(E_t m_{t+k} + E_t m_{t+k+1}) \tag{7.52}$$

for all $k \geq 0$.[8] Since the left- and right-hand sides of (7.52) are equal, it must be the case that the left-hand side for $k = 0$ plus $\lambda$ times the left-hand side for $k = 1$ plus $\lambda^2$ times the left-hand side for $k = 2$ and so on equals the right-hand side for $k = 0$ plus $\lambda$ times the right-hand side for $k = 1$ plus $\lambda^2$ times the right-hand side for $k = 2$ and so on. Computing these two expressions yields (7.50). Thus lag operators are not essential; they serve merely to simplify the notation and to suggest ways of proceeding that might otherwise be missed.[9]

---

[8] The reason that we cannot assume that (7.52) holds for $k < 0$ is that the law of iterated projections does not apply backward: the expectation today of the expectation at some date *in the past* of a variable need not equal the expectation today of the variable.

[9] For a more thorough introduction to lag operators and their uses, see Sargent (1987, Chapter 9).

# 7.4   The Calvo Model and the New Keynesian Phillips Curve

## Overview

In the Taylor model, each price is in effect for the same number of periods. One consequence is that moving beyond the two-period case quickly becomes intractable. The Calvo model (Calvo, 1983) is an elegant variation on the model that avoids this problem. Calvo assumes that price changes, rather than arriving deterministically, arrive stochastically. Specifically, he assumes that opportunities to change prices follow a *Poisson process:* the probability that a firm is able to change its price is the same each period, regardless of when it was last able to change its price. As in the Taylor model, prices are not just predetermined but fixed between the times they are adjusted.

This model's qualitative implications are similar to those of the Taylor model. Suppose, for example, the economy starts with all prices equal to the money stock, $m$, and that in period 1 there is a one-time, permanent increase in $m$. Firms that can adjust their prices will want to raise them in response to the rise in $m$. But if $\phi$ in the expression for the profit-maximizing price ($p_t^* = \phi m_t + (1 - \phi)p_t$) is less than 1, they put some weight on the overall price level, and so the fact that not all firms are able to adjust their prices mutes their adjustment. And the smaller is $\phi$, the larger is this effect. Thus, just as in the Taylor model, nominal rigidity (the fact that not all prices adjust every period) leads to gradual adjustment of the price level, and real rigidity (a low value of $\phi$) magnifies the effects of nominal rigidity.[10]

The importance of the Calvo model, then, is not in its qualitative predictions. Rather, it is twofold. First, the model can easily accommodate any degree of price stickiness; all one needs to do is change the parameter determining the probability that a firm is able to change its price each period. Second, it leads to a simple expression for the dynamics of inflation. That expression is known as the *new Keynesian Phillips curve.*

## Deriving the New Keynesian Phillips Curve

Each period, fraction $\alpha$ ($0 < \alpha \leq 1$) of firms set new prices, with the firms chosen at random. The average price in period $t$ therefore equals $\alpha$ times the price set by firms that set new prices in $t$, $x_t$, plus $1 - \alpha$ times the average price charged in $t$ by firms that do not change their prices. Because the firms that change their prices are chosen at random (and because the number of

---

[10] See Problem 7.6.

firms is large), the average price charged by the firms that do not change
their prices equals the average price charged by all firms the previous period.
Thus we have

$$p_t = \alpha x_t + (1 - \alpha) p_{t-1}, \tag{7.53}$$

where $p$ is the average price and $x$ is the price set by firms that are able to
change their prices. Subtracting $p_{t-1}$ from both sides gives us an expression
for inflation:

$$\pi_t = \alpha(x_t - p_{t-1}). \tag{7.54}$$

That is, inflation is determined by the fraction of firms that change their
prices and the relative price they set.

In deriving the rule in Section 7.1 for how a firm sets its price as a
weighted average of the expected profit-maximizing prices while the price
is in effect (equation [7.14]), we assumed the discount factor was approximately 1. For the Fischer and Taylor models, where prices are only in effect
for two periods, this assumption simplified the analysis at little cost. But
here, where firms need to look indefinitely into the future, it is not innocu-
ous. Extending expression (7.14) to the case of a general discount factor
implies

$$x_t = \sum_{j=0}^{\infty} \frac{\beta^j q_j}{\sum_{k=0}^{\infty} \beta^k q_k} E_t p_{t+j}^*, \tag{7.55}$$

where $\beta$ is the discount factor and, as before, $q_j$ is the probability the price
will still be in effect in period $t+j$. Calvo's Poisson assumption implies that
$q_j$ is $(1 - \alpha)^j$. Thus (7.55) becomes

$$x_t = [1 - \beta(1 - \alpha)] \sum_{j=0}^{\infty} \beta^j (1 - \alpha)^j E_t p_{t+j}^*. \tag{7.56}$$

Firms that can set their prices in period $t+1$ face a very similar problem.
Period $t$ is no longer relevant, and all other periods get a proportionally
higher weight. It therefore turns out to be helpful to express $x_t$ in terms of
$p_t^*$ and $E_t x_{t+1}$. To do this, rewrite (7.56) as

$$x_t = [1 - \beta(1 - \alpha)] E_t p_t^* + \beta(1 - \alpha)[1 - \beta(1 - \alpha)] \left[ \sum_{j=0}^{\infty} \beta^j (1 - \alpha)^j E_t p_{t+1+j}^* \right]$$

$$= [1 - \beta(1 - \alpha)] p_t^* + \beta(1 - \alpha) E_t x_{t+1}, \tag{7.57}$$

where the second line uses the fact that $p_t^*$ is known at time $t$ and expression (7.56) shifted forward one period. To relate (7.57) to (7.54), subtract
$p_t$ from both sides of (7.57), and rewrite $x_t - p_t$ as $(x_t - p_{t-1}) - (p_t - p_{t-1})$.

This gives us

$$(x_t - p_{t-1}) - (p_t - p_{t-1}) = [1 - \beta(1 - \alpha)](p_t^* - p_t) + \beta(1 - \alpha)(E_t x_{t+1} - p_t). \quad (7.58)$$

We can now use (7.54): $x_t - p_{t-1}$ is $\pi_t/\alpha$, and $E_t x_{t+1} - p_t$ is $E_t \pi_{t+1}/\alpha$. In addition, $p_t - p_{t-1}$ is just $\pi_t$, and $p_t^* - p_t$ is $\phi y_t$. Thus (7.58) becomes

$$(\pi_t/\alpha) - \pi_t = [1 - \beta(1 - \alpha)]\phi y_t + \beta(1 - \alpha)(E_t \pi_{t+1}/\alpha), \quad (7.59)$$

or

$$\pi_t = \frac{\alpha}{1 - \alpha}[1 - \beta(1 - \alpha)]\phi y_t + \beta E_t \pi_{t+1}$$
$$= \kappa y_t + \beta E_t \pi_{t+1}, \qquad \kappa \equiv \frac{\alpha[1 - (1 - \alpha)\beta]\phi}{1 - \alpha}. \quad (7.60)$$

## Discussion

Equation (7.60) is the new Keynesian Phillips curve.[11] Like the accelerationist Phillips curve of Section 6.4 and the Lucas supply curve of Section 6.9, it states that inflation depends on a core or expected inflation term and on output. Higher output raises inflation, as does higher core or expected inflation.

There are two features of this Phillips curve that make it "new." First, it is derived by aggregating the behavior of price-setters facing barriers to price adjustment. Second, the inflation term on the right-hand side is different from previous Phillips curves. In the accelerationist Phillips curve, it is last period's inflation. In the Lucas supply curve, it is the expectation of current inflation. Here it is the current expectation of next period's inflation. These differences are important—a point we will return to in Section 7.6.

Although the Calvo model leads to a particularly elegant expression for inflation, its broad implications stem from the general assumption of staggered price adjustment, not the specific Poisson assumption. For example, one can show that the basic equation for pricing-setting in the Taylor model, $x_t = (p_{it}^* + E_t p_{it+1}^*)/2$ (equation [7.30]) implies

$$\pi_t^x = E_t \pi_{t+1}^x + 2\phi(y_t + E_t y_{t+1}), \quad (7.61)$$

where $\pi^x$ is the growth rate of newly set prices. Although (7.61) is not as simple as (7.60), its basic message is the same: a measure of inflation depends on a measure of expected future inflation and expectations of output.

---

[11] The new Keynesian Phillips curve was originally derived by Roberts (1995).

# 7.5   State-Dependent Pricing

The Fischer, Taylor, and Calvo models assume that the timing of price changes is purely time dependent. The other extreme is that it is purely state dependent. Many retail stores, for example, can adjust the timing of their price change fairly freely in response to economic developments. This section therefore considers state-dependent pricing.

The basic message of analyses of state-dependent pricing is that it leads to more rapid adjustment of the overall price level to macroeconomic disturbances for a given average frequency of price changes. There are two distinct reasons for this result. The first is the *frequency effect:* under state-dependent pricing, the number of firms that change their prices is larger when there is a larger monetary shock. The other is the *selection effect:* the composition of the firms that adjust their prices changes in response to a shock. In this section, we consider models that illustrate each effect.

## The Frequency Effect: The Caplin-Spulber Model

Our first model is the Caplin-Spulber model. The model is set in continuous time. Nominal GDP is always growing; coupled with the assumption that there are no firm-specific shocks, this causes profit-maximizing prices to always be increasing. The specific state-dependent pricing rule that price-setters are assumed to follow is an *Ss policy*. That is, whenever a firm adjusts its price, it sets the price so that the difference between the actual price and the optimal price at that time, $p_i - p_i^*$, equals some target level, $S$. The firm then keeps its nominal price fixed until money growth has raised $p_i^*$ sufficiently that $p_i - p_i^*$ has fallen to some trigger level, $s$. Then, regardless of how much time has passed since it last changed its price, the firm resets $p_i - p_i^*$ to $S$, and the process begins anew.

Such an $Ss$ policy is optimal when inflation is steady, aggregate output is constant, and there is a fixed cost of each nominal price change (Barro, 1972; Sheshinski and Weiss, 1977). In addition, as Caplin and Spulber describe, it is also optimal in some cases where inflation or output is not constant. And even when it is not fully optimal, it provides a simple and tractable example of state-dependent pricing.

Two technical assumptions complete the model. First, to keep prices from overshooting $s$ and to prevent bunching of the distribution of prices across price-setters, $m$ changes continuously. Second, the initial distribution of $p_i - p_i^*$ across price-setters is uniform between $s$ and $S$. We continue to use the assumptions of Section 7.1 that $p_i^* = (1 - \phi)p + \phi m$, $p$ is the average of the $p_i$'s, and $y = m - p$.

Under these assumptions, shifts in aggregate demand are completely neutral in the aggregate despite the price stickiness at the level of the individual price-setters. To see this, consider an increase in $m$ of amount

$\Delta m < S - s$ over some period of time. We want to find the resulting changes in the price level and output, $\Delta p$ and $\Delta y$. Since $p_i^* = (1 - \phi)p + \phi m$, the rise in each firm's profit-maximizing price is $(1 - \phi)\Delta p + \phi \Delta m$. Firms change their prices if $p_i - p_i^*$ falls below $s$; thus firms with initial values of $p_i - p_i^*$ that are less than $s + [(1 - \phi)\Delta p + \phi \Delta m]$ change their prices. Since the initial values of $p_i - p_i^*$ are distributed uniformly between $s$ and $S$, this means that the fraction of firms that change their prices is $[(1 - \phi)\Delta p + \phi \Delta m]/(S - s)$. Each firm that changes its price does so at the moment when its value of $p_i - p_i^*$ reaches $s$; thus each price increase is of amount $S - s$. Putting all this together gives us

$$\Delta p = \frac{(1 - \phi)\Delta p + \phi \Delta m}{S - s}(S - s)$$

$$= (1 - \phi)\Delta p + \phi \Delta m. \tag{7.62}$$

Equation (7.62) implies that $\Delta p = \Delta m$, and thus that $\Delta y = 0$. Thus the change in money has no impact on aggregate output.[12]

The reason for the sharp difference between the results of this model and those of the models with time-dependent adjustment is that the number of firms changing their prices at any time is endogenous. In the Caplin–Spulber model, the number of firms changing their prices at any time is larger when aggregate demand is increasing more rapidly; given the specific assumptions that Caplin and Spulber make, this has the effect that the aggregate price level responds fully to changes in $m$. In the Fischer, Taylor, and Calvo models, in contrast, the number of firms changing their prices at any time is fixed; as a result, the price level does not respond fully to changes in $m$. Thus this model illustrates the frequency effect.

## The Selection Effect: The Danziger-Golosov-Lucas Model

A key fact about price adjustment, which we will discuss in more detail in the next section, is that it varies enormously across firms and products. For example, even in environments of moderately high inflation, a substantial fraction of price changes are price cuts.

This heterogeneity introduces a second channel through which state-dependent pricing dampens the effects of nominal disturbances. With state-dependent pricing, the composition of the firms that adjust their prices responds to shocks. When there is a positive monetary shock, for example,

---

[12] In addition, this result helps to justify the assumption that the initial distribution of $p_i - p_i^*$ is uniform between $s$ and $S$. For each firm, $p_i - p_i^*$ equals each value between $s$ and $S$ once during the interval between any two price changes; thus there is no reason to expect a concentration anywhere within the interval. Indeed, Caplin and Spulber show that under simple assumptions, a given firm's $p_i - p_i^*$ is equally likely to take on any value between $s$ and $S$.

the firms that adjust are disproportionately ones that raise their prices. As a result, it is not just the number of firms changing their prices that responds to the shock; the average change of those that adjust responds as well.

Here we illustrate these ideas using a simple example based on Danziger (1999). However, the model is similar in spirit to the richer model of Golosov and Lucas (2007).

Each firm's profit-maximizing price in period $t$ depends on aggregate demand, $m_t$, and an idiosyncratic variable, $\omega_{it}$; $\omega$ is independent across firms. For simplicity, $\phi$ in the price-setting rule is set to 1. Thus $p_{it}^* = m_t + \omega_{it}$.

To show the selection effect as starkly as possible, we make strong assumptions about the behavior of $m$ and $\omega$. Time is discrete. Initially, $m$ is constant and not subject to shocks. Each firm's $\omega$ follows a random walk. The innovation to $\omega$, denoted $\varepsilon$, can take on either positive or negative values and is distributed uniformly over a wide range (in a sense to be specified momentarily).

When profit-maximizing prices can either rise or fall, as is the case here, the analogue of an $Ss$ policy is a *two-sided Ss policy*. If a shock pushes the difference between the firm's actual and profit-maximizing prices, $p_i - p_i^*$, either above some upper bound $S$ or below some lower bound $s$, the firm resets $p_i - p_i^*$ to some target $K$. As with the one-sided $Ss$ policy in the Caplin-Spulber model, the two-sided policy is optimal in the presence of fixed costs of price adjustment under appropriate assumptions. Again, however, here we just assume that firms follow such a policy.

The sense in which the distribution of $\varepsilon$ is wide is that regardless of a firm's initial price, there is some chance the firm will raise its price and some chance that it will lower it. Concretely, let $A$ and $B$ be the lower and upper bounds of the distribution of $\varepsilon$. Then our assumptions are $S - B < s$ and $s - A > S$, or equivalently, $B > S - s$ and $A < -(S - s)$. To see the implications of these assumptions, consider a firm that is at the upper bound, $S$, and so appears to be on the verge of cutting its price. The assumption $B > S - s$ means that if it draws that largest possible realization of $\varepsilon$, its $p - p^*$ is pushed below the lower bound $s$, and so it raises its price. Thus every firm has some chance of raising its price each period. Likewise, the assumption $A < -(S - s)$ implies that every firm has some chance of cutting its price.

The steady state of the model is relatively simple. Initially, all $p_i - p_i^*$'s must be between $s$ and $S$. For any $p_i - p_i^*$ within this interval, there is a range of values of $\varepsilon$ of width $S - s$ that leaves $p_i - p_i^*$ between $s$ and $S$. Thus the probability that the firm does not adjust its price is $(S - s)/(B - A)$. Conditional on not adjusting, $p_i - p_i^*$ is distributed uniformly on $[sS]$. And with probability $1 - [(S - s)/(B - A)]$ the firm adjusts, in which case its $p_i - p_i^*$ equals the reset level, $K$.

This analysis implies that the distribution of $p_i - p_i^*$ consists of a uniform distribution over $[sS]$ with density $1/(B - A)$, plus a spike of mass $1 - [(S - s)/(B - A)]$ at $K$. This is shown in Figure 7.1. For convenience, we assume that $K = (S + s)/2$, so that the reset price is midway between $s$ and $S$.

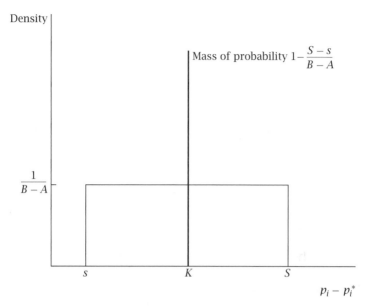

**FIGURE 7.1  The steady state of the Danziger model**

Now consider a one-time monetary shock. Specifically, suppose that at the end of some period, after firms have made price-adjustment decisions, there is an unexpected increase in $m$ of amount $\Delta m < K - s$. This raises all $p_i^*$'s by $\Delta m$. That is, the distribution in Figure 7.1 shifts to the left by $\Delta m$. Because pricing is state-dependent, firms can change their prices at any time. The firms whose $p_i - p_i^*$'s are pushed below $s$ therefore raise them to $K$. The resulting distribution is shown in Figure 7.2.

Crucially, the firms that adjust are not a random sample of firms. Instead, they are the firms whose actual prices are furthest below their optimal prices, and thus that are most inclined to make large price increases. For small values of $\Delta m$, the firms that raise their prices do so by approximately $K - s$. If instead, in the spirit of time-dependent models, we picked firms at random and allowed them to change their prices, their average price increase would be $\Delta m$.[13] Thus there is a selection effect that sharply increases the initial price response.

Now consider the next period: there is no additional monetary shock, and the firm-specific shocks behave in their usual way. But because of the initial monetary disturbance, there are now relatively few firms near $S$. Thus the firms whose idiosyncratic shocks cause them to change their prices are

---

[13] The result that the average increase is $\Delta m$ is exactly true only because of the assumption that $K = (S + s)/2$. If this condition does not hold, there is a constant term that does not depend on the sign or magnitude of $\Delta m$.

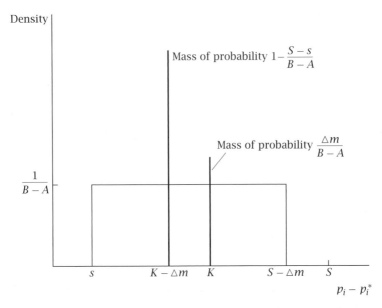

**FIGURE 7.2   The initial effects of a monetary disturbance in the Danziger model**

disproportionately toward the bottom of the [$sS$] interval, and so price changes are disproportionately price increases. Given the strong assumptions of the model, the distribution of $p_i - p_i^*$ returns to its steady state after just one period. And the distribution of $p_i - p_i^*$ being unchanged is equivalent to the distribution of $p_i$ moving one-for-one with the distribution of $p_i^*$. That is, actual prices on average adjust fully to the rise in $m$. Note that this occurs even though the fraction of firms changing their prices in this period is exactly the same as normal (all firms change their prices with probability $1 - [(S - s)/(B - A)]$, as usual), and even though all price changes in this period are the result of firm-specific shocks.

## Discussion

The assumptions of these examples are chosen to show the frequency and selection effects as starkly as possible. In the Danziger-Golosov-Lucas model, the assumption of wide, uniformly distributed firm-specific shocks is needed to deliver the strong result that a monetary shock is neutral after just one period. With a narrower distribution, for example, the effects would be more persistent. Similarly, a nonuniform distribution of the shocks generally leads to a nonuniform distribution of firms' prices, and so weakens the frequency effect. In addition, allowing for real rigidity (that is, allowing

$\phi$ in the expression for firms' desired prices to be less than 1) causes the behavior of the nonadjusters to influence the firms that change their prices, and so causes the effects of monetary shocks to be larger and longer lasting.

Similarly, if we introduced negative as well as positive monetary shocks to the Caplin-Spulber model, the result would be a two-sided *Ss* rule, and so monetary shocks would generally have real effects (see, for example, Caplin and Leahy, 1991, and Problem 7.7). In addition, the values of *S* and *s* may change in response to changes in aggregate demand. If, for example, high money growth today signals high money growth in the future, firms widen their *Ss* bands when there is a positive monetary shock; as a result, no firms adjust their prices in the short run (since no firms are now at the new, lower trigger point *s*), and so the positive shock raises output (Tsiddon, 1991).[14]

In short, the strong results of the simple cases considered in this section are not robust. What is robust is that state-dependent pricing gives rise naturally to the frequency and selection effects, and that those effects can be quantitatively important. For example, Golosov and Lucas show in the context of a much more carefully calibrated model that the effects of monetary shocks can be much smaller with state-dependent pricing than in a comparable economy with time-dependent pricing.

# 7.6  Empirical Applications

## Microeconomic Evidence on Price Adjustment

The central assumption of the models we have been analyzing is that there is some kind of barrier to complete price adjustment at the level of individual firms. It is therefore natural to investigate pricing policies at the microeconomic level. By doing so, we can hope to learn whether there are barriers to price adjustment and, if so, what form they take.

The microeconomics of price adjustment have been investigated by many authors. The broadest studies of price adjustment in the United States are the survey of firms conducted by Blinder (1998), the analysis of the data underlying the Consumer Price Index by Klenow and Kryvtsov (2008), and the analysis of the data underlying the Consumer Price Index and the Producer Price Index by Nakamura and Steinsson (2008). Blinder's and Nakamura and Steinsson's analyses show that the average interval between price changes for intermediate goods is about a year. In contrast, Klenow and Kryvtsov's and Nakamura and Steinsson's analyses find that the typical period between price changes for final goods and services is only about 4 months.

The key finding of this literature, however, is not the overall statistics concerning the frequency of adjustment. Rather, it is that price adjustment

---

[14] See Caballero and Engel (1993) for a more detailed analysis of these issues.

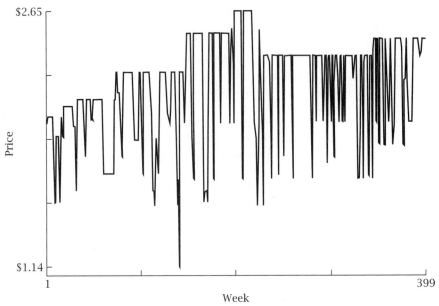

**FIGURE 7.3** Price of a 9.5 ounce box of Triscuits (from Chevalier, Kashyap, and Rossi, 2000; used with permission)

does not follow any simple pattern. Figure 7.3, from Chevalier, Kashyap, and Rossi (2000), is a plot of the price of a 9.5 ounce box of Triscuit crackers at a particular supermarket from 1989 to 1997. The behavior of this price clearly defies any simple summary. One obvious feature, which is true for many products, is that temporary "sale" prices are common. That is, the price often falls sharply and is then quickly raised again, often to its previous level. Beyond the fact that sales are common, it is hard to detect any regular patterns. Sales occur at irregular intervals and are of irregular lengths; the sizes of the reductions during sales vary; the intervals between adjustments of the "regular" price are heterogeneous; the regular price sometimes rises and sometimes falls; and the sizes of the changes in the regular price vary. Other facts that have been documented include tremendous heterogeneity across products in the frequency of adjustment; a tendency for some prices to be adjusted at fairly regular intervals, most often once a year; the presence of a substantial fraction of price decreases (of both regular and sale prices), even in environments of moderately high inflation; and the presence for many products of a second type of sale, a price reduction that is not reversed and that is followed, perhaps after further reductions, by the disappearance of the product (a "clearance" sale).

Thus the microeconomic evidence does not show clearly what assumptions about price adjustment we should use in building a macroeconomic model. Time-dependent models are grossly contradicted by the data, and purely state-dependent models fare only slightly better. The time-dependent models are contradicted by the overwhelming presence of irregular intervals between adjustments. Purely state-dependent models are most clearly contradicted by two facts: the frequent tendency for prices to be in effect for exactly a year, and the strong tendency for prices to revert to their original level after a sale.

In thinking about the aggregate implications of the evidence on price adjustment, a key issue is how to treat sales. At one extreme, they could be completely mechanical. Imagine, for example, that a store manager is instructed to discount goods representing 10 percent of the store's sales by an average of 20 percent each week. Then sale prices are unresponsive to macroeconomic conditions, and so should be ignored in thinking about macroeconomic issues. If we decide to exclude sales, we then encounter difficult issues of how to define them and how to treat missing observations and changes in products. Klenow and Kryvtsov's and Nakamura and Steinsson's analyses suggest, however, that across goods, the median frequency of changes in regular prices of final goods is about once every 7 months. For intermediate goods, sales are relatively unimportant, and so accounting for them has little impact on estimates of the average frequency of adjustment.

The other possibility is that sale prices respond to macroeconomic conditions; for example, they could be more frequent and larger when the economy is weak. At the extreme, sales should not be removed from the data at all in considering the macroeconomic implications of the microeconomics of price adjustment.

Another key issue for the aggregate implications of these data is heterogeneity. The usual summary statistic, and the one used above, is the median frequency of adjustment across goods. But the median masks an enormous range, from goods whose prices typically adjust more than once a month to ones whose prices usually change less than once a year. Carvalho (2006) poses the following question. Suppose the economy is described by a model with heterogeneity, but a researcher wants to match the economy's response to various types of monetary disturbances using a model with a single frequency of adjustment. What frequency should the researcher choose? Carvalho shows that in most cases, one would want to choose a frequency less than the median or average frequency. Moreover, the difference is magnified by real rigidity: as the degree of real rigidity rises, the importance of the firms with the stickiest prices increases. Carvalho shows that to best match the economy's response to shocks using a single-sector model, one would often want to use a frequency of price adjustment a third to a half of the median across heterogeneous firms. Thus heterogeneity has important effects.

Finally, Levy, Bergen, Dutta, and Venable (1997) look not at prices, but at the costs of price adjustment. Specifically, they report data on each step of the process of changing prices at supermarkets, such as the costs of putting on new price tags or signs on the shelves, of entering the new prices into the computer system, and of checking the prices and correcting errors. This approach does not address the possibility that there may be more sophisticated, less expensive ways of adjusting prices to aggregate disturbances. For example, a store could have a prominently displayed discount factor that it used at checkout to subtract some proportion from the amount due; it could then change the discount factor rather than the shelf prices in response to aggregate shocks. The costs of changing the discount factor would be dramatically less than the cost of changing the posted price on every item in the store.

Despite this limitation, it is still interesting to know how large the costs of changing prices are. Levy et al.'s basic finding is that the costs are surprisingly high. For the average store in their sample, expenditures on changing prices amount to between 0.5 and 1 percent of revenues. To put it differently, the average cost of a price change in their stores in 1991–1992 was about 50 cents. Thus the common statement that the physical costs of nominal price changes are extremely small is not always correct: for the stores that Levy et al. consider, these costs, while not large, are far from trivial.

In short, empirical work on the microeconomics of price adjustment and its macroeconomic implications is extremely active. A few examples of recent contributions in addition to those discussed above are Dotsey, King, and Wolman (1999), Klenow and Willis (2006), Gopinath and Rigobon (2008), and Midrigan (2009).

## Inflation Inertia

We have encountered three aggregate supply relationships that include an inflation term and an output term: the accelerationist Phillips curve of Section 6.4, the Lucas supply curve of Section 6.9, and the new Keynesian Phillips curve of Section 7.4. Although the three relationships look broadly similar, in fact they have sharply different implications. To see this, consider the experiment of an anticipated fall in inflation in an economy with no shocks. The accelerationist Phillips curve, $\pi_t = \pi_{t-1} + \lambda(y_t - \bar{y}_t)$ (see [6.22]-[6.23]), implies that disinflation requires below-normal output. The Lucas supply curve, $\pi_t = E_{t-1}\pi_t + \lambda(y_t - \bar{y}_t)$ (see [6.84]), implies that disinflation can be accomplished with no output cost. Finally, for the new Keynesian Phillips curve (equation [7.60]), it is helpful to rewrite it as

$$E_t[\pi_{t+1}] - \pi_t = \left(\frac{1-\beta}{\beta}\right)\pi_t - \frac{\kappa}{\beta}(y_t - \bar{y}_t). \qquad (7.63)$$

With $\beta$ close to 1, the $[(1-\beta)/\beta]\pi_t$ term is small. Thus the new Keynesian Phillips curve implies that anticipated disinflation is associated with an output *boom*.

The view that high inflation has a tendency to continue unless there is a period of low output is often described as the view that there is *inflation inertia*. That is, "inflation inertia" refers not to inflation being highly serially correlated, but to it being costly to reduce. Of the three Phillips curves, only the accelerationist one implies inertia. The Lucas supply curve implies that there is no inertia, while the new Keynesian Phillips curve (as well as other models of staggered price-setting) implies that there is "anti-inertia."[15]

Ball (1994b) performs a straightforward test for inflation inertia. Looking at a sample of nine industrialized countries over the period 1960–1990, he identifies 28 episodes where inflation fell substantially. He reports that in all 28 cases, observers at the time attributed the decline to monetary policy. Thus the view that there is inflation inertia predicts that output was below normal in the episodes; the Lucas supply curve suggests that it need not have departed systematically from normal; and the new Keynesian Phillips curve implies that it was above normal. Ball finds that the evidence is overwhelmingly supportive of inflation inertia: in 27 of the 28 cases, output was on average below his estimate of normal output during the disinflation.

Ball's approach of choosing episodes on the basis of ex post inflation outcomes could create bias, however. In particular, suppose the disinflations had important unanticipated components. If prices were set on the basis of expectations of higher aggregate demand than actually occurred, the low output in the episodes does not clearly contradict any of the models.

Galí and Gertler (1999) therefore take a more formal econometric approach. Their main interest is in testing between the accelerationist and new Keynesian views. They begin by positing a hybrid Phillips curve with backward-looking and forward-looking elements:

$$\pi_t = \gamma_b \pi_{t-1} + \gamma_f E_t \pi_{t+1} + \kappa(y_t - \bar{y}_t) + e_t. \tag{7.64}$$

They point out, however, that what the $\kappa(y_t - \bar{y}_t)$ term is intended to capture is the behavior of firms' real marginal costs. When output is above normal, marginal costs are high, which increases desired relative prices. In the model of Section 7.1, for example, desired relative prices rise when output rises because the real wage increases. Galí and Gertler therefore try a more direct approach to estimating marginal costs. Real marginal cost equals the real wage divided by the marginal product of labor. If the production function is Cobb-Douglas, so that $Y = K^{\alpha}(AL)^{1-\alpha}$, the marginal product of labor is $(1 - \alpha)Y/L$. Thus real marginal cost is $wL/[(1 - \alpha)Y]$, where $w$ is the real wage. That is, marginal cost is proportional to the share of income going

---

[15] The result that models of staggered price adjustment do not imply inflation inertia is due to Fuhrer and Moore (1995) and Ball (1994a).

to labor (see also Sbordone, 2002). Galí and Gertler therefore focus on the equation:

$$\pi_t = \gamma_b \pi_{t-1} + \gamma_f E_t \pi_{t+1} + \lambda S_t + e_t, \tag{7.65}$$

where $S_t$ is labor's share.[16]

Galí and Gertler estimate (7.65) using quarterly U.S. data for the period 1960–1997.[17] A typical set of estimates is

$$\pi_t = \underset{(0.020)}{0.378}\ \pi_{t-1} + \underset{(0.016)}{0.591}\ E_t\pi_{t+1} + \underset{(0.004)}{0.015}\ S_t + e_t, \tag{7.66}$$

where the numbers in parentheses are standard errors. Thus their results appear to provide strong support for the importance of forward-looking expectations.

In a series of papers, however, Rudd and Whelan show that in fact the data provide little evidence for the new Keynesian Phillips curve (see especially Rudd and Whelan, 2005, 2006). They make two key points. The first concerns labor's share. Galí and Gertler's argument for including labor's share in the Phillips curve is that under appropriate assumptions, it captures the rise in firms' marginal costs when output rises. Rudd and Whelan (2005) point out, however, that in practice labor's share is low in booms and high in recessions. In Galí and Gertler's framework, this would mean that booms are times when the economy's flexible-price level of output has risen even more than actual output, and when marginal costs are therefore unusually low. A much more plausible possibility, however, is that there are forces other than those considered by Galí and Gertler moving labor's share over the business cycle, and that labor's share is therefore a poor proxy for marginal costs.

Since labor's share is countercyclical, the finding of a large coefficient on expected future inflation and a positive coefficient on the share means that inflation tends to be above future inflation in recessions and below future inflation in booms. That is, inflation tends to fall in recessions and rise in booms, consistent with the accelerationist Phillips curve and not with the new Keynesian Phillips curve.

---

[16] How can labor's share vary if production is Cobb-Douglas? Under perfect competition (and under imperfect competition if price is a constant markup over marginal cost), it cannot. But if prices are not fully flexible, it can. For example, if a firm with a fixed price hires more labor at the prevailing wage, output rises less than proportionally than the rise in labor, and so labor's share rises.

[17] For simplicity, we omit any discussion of their estimation procedure, which, among other things, must address the fact that we do not have data on $E_t\pi_{t+1}$. Section 8.3 discusses estimation when there are expectational variables.

Rudd and Whelan's second concern has to do with the information content of current inflation. Replacing $y_t$ with a generic marginal cost variable, $mc_t$, and then iterating the new Keynesian Phillips curve, (7.60), forward implies

$$
\begin{aligned}
\pi_t &= \kappa mc_t + \beta E_t \pi_{t+1} \\
&= \kappa mc_t + \beta[\kappa E_r mc_{t+1} + \beta E_t \pi_{t+2}] \\
&= \ldots \\
&= \kappa \sum_{i=0}^{\infty} \beta^i E_t mc_{t+i}.
\end{aligned}
\tag{7.67}
$$

Thus the model implies that inflation should be a function of expectations of future marginal costs, and thus that it should help predict marginal costs. Rudd and Whelan (2005) show, however, that the evidence for this hypothesis is minimal. When marginal costs are proxied by an estimate of $y - \bar{y}$, inflation's predictive power is small and goes in the wrong direction from what the model suggests. When marginal costs are measured using labor's share (which, as Rudd and Whelan's first criticism shows, may be a poor proxy), the performance is only slightly better. In this case, inflation's predictive power for marginal costs is not robust, and almost entirely absent in Rudd and Whelan's preferred specification. They also find that the hybrid Phillips curve performs little better (Rudd and Whelan, 2006). They conclude that there is little evidence in support of the new Keynesian Phillips curve.[18]

The bottom line of this analysis is twofold. First, the evidence we have on the correct form of the Phillips curve is limited. The debate between Galí and Gertler and Rudd and Whelan, along with further analysis of the econometrics of the new Keynesian Phillips curve (for example, King and Plosser, 2005), does not lead to clear conclusions on the basis of formal econometric studies. This leaves us with the evidence from less formal analyses, such as Ball's, which is far from airtight. Second, although the evidence is not definitive, it points in the direction of inflation inertia and provides little support for the new Keynesian Phillips curve.

Because of this and other evidence, researchers attempting to match important features of business-cycle dynamics typically make modifications to models of price-setting (often along the lines of the ones we will encounter in the next section) that imply inertia. Nonetheless, because of its simplicity

---

[18] This discussion does not address the question of why Galí and Gertler's estimates suggest that the new Keynesian Phillips curve fits well. Rudd and Whelan argue that this has to do with the specifics of Galí and Gertler's estimation procedure, which we are not delving into. Loosely speaking, Rudd and Whelan's argument is that because inflation is highly serially correlated, small violations of the conditions needed for the estimation procedure to be valid can generate substantial upward bias in the coefficient on $E_t \pi_{t+1}$.

and elegance, the new Keynesian Phillips curve is still often used in theoretical models. Following that pattern, we will meet it again in Section 7.8 and in Chapter 11.

# 7.7   Models of Staggered Price Adjustment with Inflation Inertia

The evidence in the previous section suggests that a major limitation of the micro-founded models of dynamic price adjustment we have been considering is that they do not imply inflation inertia. A central focus of recent work on price adjustment is therefore bringing inflation inertia into the models. At a general level, the most common strategy is to assume that firms' prices are not fixed between the times they review them, but adjust in some way. These adjustments are assumed to give some role to past inflation, or to past beliefs about inflation. The result is inflation inertia.

The two most prominent approaches along these lines are those of Christiano, Eichenbaum, and Evans (2005) and Mankiw and Reis (2002). Christiano, Eichenbaum, and Evans assume that between reviews, prices are adjusted for past inflation. This creates a direct role for past inflation in price behavior. But whether this reasonably captures important microeconomic phenomena is not clear. Mankiw and Reis return to Fischer's assumption of prices that are predetermined but not fixed. This causes past beliefs about what inflation would be to affect price changes, and so creates behavior similar to inflation inertia. In contrast to Fischer, however, they make assumptions that imply that some intervals between reviews of prices are quite long, which has important quantitative implications. Again, however, the strength of the microeconomic case for the realism of their key assumption is not clear.

## The Christiano, Eichenbaum, and Evans Model: The New Keynesian Phillips Curve with Indexation

Christiano, Eichenbaum, and Evans begin with Calvo's assumption that opportunities for firms to review their prices follow a Poisson process. As in the basic Calvo model of Section 7.4, let $\alpha$ denote the fraction of firms that review their prices in a given period. Where Christiano, Eichenbaum, and Evans depart from Calvo is in their assumption about what happens between reviews. Rather than assuming that prices are fixed, they assume they are indexed to the previous period's inflation rate. This assumption captures the fact that even in the absence of a full-fledged reconsideration of their prices, firms can account for the overall inflationary environment. The assumption that the indexing is to lagged rather than current inflation reflects the fact that firms do not continually obtain and use all available information.

Our analysis of the model is similar to the analysis of the Calvo model in Section 7.4. Since the firms that review their prices in a given period are chosen at random, the average (log) price in period $t$ of the firms that do not review their prices is $p_{t-1} + \pi_{t-1}$. The average price in $t$ is therefore

$$p_t = (1 - \alpha)(p_{t-1} + \pi_{t-1}) + \alpha x_t, \tag{7.68}$$

where $x_t$ is the price set by firms that review their prices. Equation (7.68) implies

$$
\begin{aligned}
x_t - p_t &= x_t - [(1 - \alpha)(p_{t-1} + \pi_{t-1}) + \alpha x_t] \\
&= (1 - \alpha)x_t - (1 - \alpha)(p_{t-1} + \pi_{t-1}) \\
&= (1 - \alpha)(x_t - p_t) - (1 - \alpha)(p_{t-1} + \pi_{t-1} - p_t) \\
&= (1 - \alpha)(x_t - p_t) + (1 - \alpha)(\pi_t - \pi_{t-1}).
\end{aligned}
\tag{7.69}
$$

Thus,

$$x_t - p_t = \frac{1 - \alpha}{\alpha}(\pi_t - \pi_{t-1}). \tag{7.70}$$

Equation (7.70) shows that to find the dynamics of inflation, we need to find $x_t - p_t$. That is, we need to determine how firms that review their prices set their relative prices in period $t$. As in the Calvo model, a firm wants to set its price to minimize the expected discounted sum of the squared differences between its optimal and actual prices during the period before it is next able to review its price. Suppose a firm sets a price of $x_t$ in period $t$ and that it does not have an opportunity to review its price before period $t + j$. Then, because of the lagged indexation, its price in $t + j$ (for $j \geq 1$) is $x_t + \sum_{\tau=0}^{j-1} \pi_{t+\tau}$. The profit-maximizing price in $t + j$ is $p_{t+j} + \phi y_{t+j}$, which equals $p_t + \sum_{\tau=1}^{j} \pi_{t+\tau} + \phi y_{t+j}$. Thus the difference between the profit-maximizing and actual prices in $t + j$, which we will denote $e_{t,t+j}$, is

$$e_{t,t+j} = (p_t - x_t) + (\pi_{t+j} - \pi_t) + \phi y_{t+j}. \tag{7.71}$$

Note that (7.71) holds for all $j \geq 0$. The discount factor is $\beta$, and the probability of nonadjustment each period is $1 - \alpha$. Thus, similarly to equation (7.56) in the Calvo model without indexation, the firm sets

$$x_t - p_t = [1 - \beta(1 - \alpha)] \sum_{j=0}^{\infty} \beta^j (1 - \alpha)^j [(E_t \pi_{t+j} - \pi_t) + \phi E_t y_{t+j}]. \tag{7.72}$$

As in the derivation of the new Keynesian Phillips curve, it is helpful to rewrite this expression in terms of period-$t$ variables and the expectation of

$x_{t+1} - p_{t+1}$. Equation (7.72) implies

$$x_{t+1} - p_{t+1}$$

(7.73)

$$= [1 - \beta(1 - \alpha)] \sum_{j=0}^{\infty} \beta^j (1 - \alpha)^j [(E_{t+1}\pi_{t+1+j} - \pi_{t+1}) + \phi E_{t+1}y_{t+1+j}].$$

Rewriting the $\pi_{t+1}$ term as $\pi_t + (\pi_{t+1} - \pi_t)$ and taking expectations as of $t$ (and using the law of iterated projections) gives us

$$E_t[x_{t+1} - p_{t+1}] = -E_t[\pi_{t+1} - \pi_t]$$

(7.74)

$$+ [1 - \beta(1 - \alpha)] \sum_{j=0}^{\infty} \beta^j (1 - \alpha)^j [(E_t\pi_{t+1+j} - \pi_t) + \phi E_t y_{t+1+j}].$$

We can therefore rewrite (7.72) as

$$x_t - p_t = [1 - \beta(1 - \alpha)]\phi y_t + \beta(1 - \alpha)\{E_t[x_{t+1} - p_{t+1}] + E_t[\pi_{t+1} - \pi_t]\}. \quad (7.75)$$

The final step is to use (7.70) applied to both periods $t$ and $t+1$: $x_t - p_t = [(1 - \alpha)/\alpha](\pi_t - \pi_{t-1})$, $E_t[x_{t+1} - p_{t+1}] = [(1 - \alpha)/\alpha](E_t[\pi_{t+1}] - \pi_t)$. Substituting these expressions into (7.75) and performing straightforward algebra yields

$$\pi_t = \frac{1}{1+\beta}\pi_{t-1} + \frac{\beta}{1+\beta}E_t\pi_{t+1} + \frac{1}{1+\beta}\frac{\alpha}{1-\alpha}[1 - \beta(1 - \alpha)]\phi y_t$$

(7.76)

$$\equiv \frac{1}{1+\beta}\pi_{t-1} + \frac{\beta}{1+\beta}E_t\pi_{t+1} + \chi y_t.$$

Equation (7.76) is the new *Keynesian Phillips curve with indexation*. It resembles the new Keynesian Phillips curve except that instead of a weight of $\beta$ on expected future inflation and no role for past inflation, there is a weight of $\beta/(1+\beta)$ on expected future inflation and a weight of $1/(1+\beta)$ on lagged inflation. If $\beta$ is close to 1, the weights are both close to one-half. An obvious generalization of (7.76) is

$$\pi_t = \gamma\pi_{t-1} + (1 - \gamma)E_t\pi_{t+1} + \chi y_t, \qquad 0 \leq \gamma \leq 1. \quad (7.77)$$

Equation (7.77) allows for any mix of weights on the two inflation terms.

Because they imply that past inflation has a direct impact on current inflation, and thus that there is inflation inertia, expressions like (7.76) and (7.77) often appear in modern dynamic stochastic general-equilibrium models with nominal rigidity.

## The Model's Implications for the Costs of Disinflation

The fact that equation (7.76) (or [7.77]) implies inflation inertia does not mean that the model can account for the apparent output costs of disinflation. To see this, consider the case of $\beta = 1$, so that (7.76) becomes $\pi_t = (\pi_{t-1}/2) + (E_t[\pi_{t+1}]/2) + \chi y_t$. Now suppose that there is a perfectly anticipated, gradual disinflation that occurs at a uniform rate: $\pi_t = \pi_0$ for $t \leq 0$; $\pi_t = 0$ for $t \geq T$; and $\pi_t = [(T - t)/T]\pi_0$ for $0 < t < T$. Because the disinflation proceeds linearly and is anticipated, $\pi_t$ equals the average of $\pi_{t-1}$ and $E_t[\pi_{t+1}]$ in all periods except $t = 0$ and $t = T$. In period 0, $\pi_0$ exceeds $(\pi_{t-1} + E_t[\pi_{t+1}])/2$, and in period $T$, it is less than $(\pi_{t-1} + E_t[\pi_{t+1}])/2$ by the same amount. Thus the disinflation is associated with above-normal output when it starts and an equal amount of below-normal output when it ends, and no departure of output from normal in between. That is, the model implies no systematic output cost of an anticipated disinflation.

One possible solution to this difficulty is to reintroduce the assumption that $\beta$ is less than 1. This results in more weight on $\pi_{t-1}$ and less on $E_t[\pi_{t+1}]$, and so creates output costs of disinflation. For reasonable values of $\beta$, however, this effect is small.

A second potential solution is to appeal to the generalization in equation (7.77) and to suppose that $\gamma > (1 - \gamma)$. But since (7.77) is not derived from microeconomic foundations, this comes at the cost of abandoning the initial goal of grounding our understanding of inflation dynamics in microeconomic behavior.

The final candidate solution is to argue that the prediction of no systematic output costs of an anticipated disinflation is reasonable. Recall that Ball's finding is that disinflations are generally associated with below-normal output. But recall also that the fact that disinflations are typically less than fully anticipated means that the output costs of actual disinflations tend to overstate the costs of perfectly anticipated disinflations. Perhaps the bias is sufficiently large that the average cost of an anticipated disinflation is zero.

The bottom line is that adding indexation to Calvo pricing introduces some inflation inertia. But whether that inertia is enough to explain actual inflation dynamics is not clear.

The other important limitation of the model is that its key microeconomic assumption appears unrealistic—we do not observe actual prices rising mechanically with lagged inflation. At the same time, however, it could be that price-setters behave in ways that cause their average prices to rise roughly with lagged inflation between the times that they seriously rethink their pricing policies in light of macroeconomic conditions, and that this average adjustment is masked by the fact that individual nominal prices are not continually adjusted.

## The Mankiw-Reis Model

Mankiw and Reis take a somewhat different approach to obtaining inflation inertia. Like Christiano, Eichenbaum, and Evans, they assume some adjustment of prices between the times that firms review their pricing policies. Their assumption, however, is that each time a firm reviews its price, it sets a *path* that the price will follow until the next review. That is, they reintroduce the idea from the Fischer model that prices are predetermined but not fixed.

Recall that a key result from our analysis in Section 7.2 is that with predetermined prices, a monetary shock ceases to have real effects once all price-setters have had an opportunity to respond. This is often taken to imply that predetermined prices cannot explain persistent real effects of monetary shocks. But recall also that when real rigidity is high, firms that do not change their prices have a disproportionate impact on the behavior of the aggregate economy. This raises the possibility that a small number of firms that are slow to change their price paths can cause monetary shocks to have important long-lasting effects with predetermined prices. This is the central idea of Mankiw and Reis's model (see also Devereux and Yetman, 2003).

Although the mechanics of the Mankiw–Reis model involve predetermined prices, their argument for predetermination differs from Fischer's. Fischer motivates his analysis in terms of labor contracts that specify a different wage for each period of the contract; prices are then determined as markups over wages. But such contracts do not appear sufficiently widespread to be a plausible source of substantial aggregate nominal rigidity. Mankiw and Reis appeal instead to what they call "sticky information." It is costly for price-setters to obtain and process information. Mankiw and Reis argue that as a result, they may choose not to continually update their prices, but to periodically choose a path for their prices that they follow until they next gather information and adjust their path.

Specifically, Mankiw and Reis begin with a model of predetermined prices like that of Section 7.2. Opportunities to adopt new price paths do not arise deterministically, as in the Fischer model, however. Instead, as in the Calvo and Christiano-Eichenbaum-Evans models, they follow a Poisson process. Paralleling those models, each period a fraction $\alpha$ of firms adopt a new piece path (where $0 < \alpha \leq 1$). And again $y_t = m_t - p_t$ and $p_t^* = p_t + \phi y_t$.

Our analysis of the Fischer model provides a strong indication of what the solution of the model will look like. Because a firm can set a different price for each period, the price it sets for a given period, period $t$, will depend only on information about $y_t$ and $p_t$. It follows that the aggregate price level, $p_t$ (and hence $y_t$), will depend only on information about $m_t$; information about $m$ in other periods will affect $y_t$ and $p_t$ only to the extent it conveys information about $m_t$. Further, if the value of $m_t$ were known arbitrarily far in advance, all firms would set their prices for $t$ equal to $m_t$, and so $y_t$ would be zero. Thus, departures of $y_t$ from zero will come only from information about $m_t$ revealed after some firms have set their prices for period $t$. And given the log-linear structure of the model, its solution will be log-linear.

Consider information about $m_t$ that arrives in period $t - i$ ($i \geq 0$); that is, consider $E_{t-i}m_t - E_{t-(i+1)}m_t$. If we let $a_i$ denote the fraction of $E_{t-i}m_t - E_{t-(i+1)}m_t$ that is passed into the aggregate price level, then the information about $m_t$ that arrives in period $t - i$ raises $p_t$ by $a_i(E_{t-i}m_t - E_{t-(i+1)}m_t)$ and raises $y_t$ by $(1 - a_i)(E_{t-i}m_t - E_{t-(i+1)}m_t)$. That is, $y_t$ will be given by an expression of the form

$$y_t = \sum_{i=0}^{\infty}(1 - a_i)(E_{t-i}m_t - E_{t-(i+1)}m_t). \tag{7.78}$$

To solve the model, we need to find the $a_i$'s. To do this, let $\lambda_i$ denote the fraction of firms that have an opportunity to change their price for period $t$ in response to information about $m_t$ that arrives in period $t - i$ (that is, in response to $E_{t-i}m_t - E_{t-(i+1)}m_t$). A firm does *not* have an opportunity to change its price for period $t$ in response to this information if it does not have an opportunity to set a new price path in any of periods $t - i$, $t - (i - 1), \ldots, t$. The probability of this occurring is $(1 - \alpha)^{i+1}$. Thus,

$$\lambda_i = 1 - (1 - \alpha)^{i+1}. \tag{7.79}$$

Because firms can set a different price for each period, the firms that adjust their prices are able to respond freely to the new information. We know that $p_t^* = (1 - \phi)p_t + \phi m_t$ and that the change in $p_t$ in response to the new information is $a_i(E_{t-i}m_t - E_{t-(i+1)}m_t)$. Thus, the firms that are able to respond raise their prices for period $t$ by $(1 - \phi)a_i(E_{t-i}m_t - E_{t-(i+1)}m_t) + \phi(E_{t-i}m_t - E_{t-(i+1)}m_t)$, or $[(1 - \phi)a_i + \phi](E_{t-i}m_t - E_{t-(i+1)}m_t)$. Since fraction $\lambda_i$ of firms are able to adjust their prices and the remaining firms cannot respond at all, the overall price level responds by $\lambda_i[(1 - \phi)a_i + \phi](E_{t-i}m_t - E_{t-(i+1)}m_t)$. Thus $a_i$ must satisfy

$$\lambda_i[(1 - \phi)a_i + \phi] = a_i. \tag{7.80}$$

Solving for $a_i$ yields

$$
\begin{aligned}
a_i &= \frac{\phi\lambda_i}{1 - (1 - \phi)\lambda_i} \\
&= \frac{\phi[1 - (1 - \alpha)^{i+1}]}{1 - (1 - \phi)[1 - (1 - \alpha)^{i+1}]},
\end{aligned}
\tag{7.81}
$$

where the second line uses (7.79) to substitute for $\lambda_i$. Finally, since $p_t + y_t = m_t$, we can write $p_t$ as

$$p_t = m_t - y_t. \tag{7.82}$$

## Implications

To understand the implications of the Mankiw–Reis model, it is helpful to start by examining the effects of a shift in the level of aggregate demand (as opposed to its growth rate).[19] Specifically, consider an unexpected, one-time, permanent increase in $m$ in period $t$ of amount $\Delta m$. The increase raises

---

[19] The reason for not considering this experiment for the Christiano-Eichenbaum-Evans model is that the model's implications concerning such a shift are complicated. See Problem 7.9.

$E_t m_{t+i} - E_{t-1} m_{t+i}$ by $\Delta m$ for all $i \geq 0$. Thus $p_{t+i}$ rises by $a_i \Delta m$ and $y_{t+i}$ rises by $(1 - a_i)\Delta m$.

Equation (7.80) implies that the $a_i$'s are increasing in $i$ and gradually approach 1. Thus the permanent increase in aggregate demand leads to a rise in output that gradually disappears, and to a gradual rise in the price level. If the degree of real rigidity is high, the output effects can be quite persistent even if price adjustment is frequent. Mankiw and Reis assume that a period corresponds to a quarter, and consider the case of $\lambda = 0.25$ and $\phi = 0.1$. These assumptions imply price adjustment on average every four periods and substantial real rigidity. For this case, $a_8 = 0.55$. Even though by period 8 firms have been able to adjust their price paths twice on average since the shock, there is a small fraction—7.5 percent—that have not been able to adjust at all. Because of the high degree of real rigidity, the result is that the price level has only adjusted slightly more than halfway to its long-run level.

Another implication concerns the time pattern of the response. Straight-forward differentiation of (7.81) shows that if $\phi < 1$, then $d^2 a_i / d\lambda_i^2 > 0$. That is, when there is real rigidity, the impact of a given change in the number of additional firms adjusting their prices is greater when more other firms are adjusting. Thus there are two competing effects on how the $a_i$'s vary with $i$. The fact that $d^2 a_i / d\lambda_i^2 > 0$ tends to make the $a_i$'s rise more rapidly as $i$ rises, but the fact that fewer additional firms are getting their first opportunity to respond to the shock as $i$ increases tends to make them rise less rapidly. For the parameter values that Mankiw and Reis consider, the $a_i$'s rise first at an increasing rate and then a decreasing one, with the greatest rate of increase occurring after about eight periods. That is, the peak effect of the demand expansion on inflation occurs with a lag.[20]

Now consider a disinflation. For concreteness, we start with the case of an immediate, unanticipated disinflation. In particular, assume that until date 0 all firms expect $m$ to follow the path $m_t = gt$ (where $g > 0$), but that the central bank stabilizes $m$ at 0 starting at date 0. Thus $m_t = 0$ for $t \geq 0$.

Because of the policy change, $E_0 m_t - E_{-1} m_t = -gt$ for all $t \geq 0$. This expression is always negative—that is, the actual money supply is always below what was expected by the firms that set their price paths before date 0. Since the $a_i$'s are always between 0 and 1, it follows that the disinflation lowers output. Specifically, equations (7.78) and (7.81) imply that the path of $y$ is given by

$$y_t = (1 - a_t)(-gt)$$

$$= -\frac{(1-\alpha)^{t+1}}{1 - (1-\phi)[1 - (1-\alpha)^{t+1}]} gt \qquad \text{for } t \geq 0.$$

(7.83)

---

[20] This is easier to see in a continuous-time version of the model (see Problem 7.11). In this case, equation (7.81) becomes $a(i) = \phi(1 - e^{-\alpha i})/[1 - (1-\phi)(1 - e^{-\alpha i})]$. The sign of $a'(i)$ is determined by the sign of $(1 - \phi)e^{-\alpha i} - \phi$. For Mankiw and Reis's parameter values, this is positive until $i \simeq 8.8$ and then negative.

The $(1 - a_t)$'s are falling over time, while $gt$ is rising. Initially the linear growth of the $gt$ term dominates, and so the output effect increases. Eventually, however, the fall in the $(1 - a_t)$'s dominates, and so the output effect decreases, and asymptotically it approaches zero. Thus the switch to a lower growth rate of aggregate demand produces a recession whose trough is reached with a lag. For the parameter values described above, the trough occurs after seven quarters.

For the first few periods after the policy shift, most firms still follow their old price paths. Moreover, the firms that are able to adjust do not change their prices for the first few periods very much, both because $m$ is not yet far below its old path and because (if $\phi < 1$) they do not want to deviate far from the prices charged by others. Thus initially inflation falls little. As time passes, however, these forces all act to create greater price adjustment, and so inflation falls. In the long run, output returns to normal and inflation equals the new growth rate of aggregate demand, which is zero. Thus, consistent with what we appear to observe, a shift to a disinflationary policy first produces a recession, and then a fall in inflation.

The polar extreme from a completely anticipated disinflation is one that is anticipated arbitrarily far in advance. The model immediately implies that such a disinflation is not associated with any departure of output from normal. If all firms know the value of $m_t$ for some period $t$ when they set their prices, then, regardless of what they expect about $m$ in any other period, they set $p_t = m_t$, and so we have $y_t = 0$.

For any disinflation, either instantaneous or gradual, that is not fully anticipated, there are output costs. The reason is simple: any disinflation involves a fall of aggregate demand below its prior path. Thus for sufficiently large values of $\tau$, $m_t$ is less than $E_{t-\tau}m_t$, and so the prices for period $t$ that are set in period $t - \tau$ are above $m_t$. As a result, the average value of prices, $p_t$, exceeds $m_t$, and thus $y_t$ (which equals $m_t - p_t$) is negative. Finally, recall that the $a_i$'s are increasing in $i$. Thus the further in advance a change in aggregate demand is anticipated, the smaller are its real effects.

At the same time, the model is not without difficulties. As with the Christiano-Eichenbaum-Evans model, its assumptions about price-setting do not match what we observe at the microeconomic level: many prices and wages are fixed for extended periods, and there is little evidence that many price-setters or wage-setters set price or wage paths of the sort that are central to the model. And some phenomena, such as the finding described in Section 6.10 that aggregate demand disturbances appear to have smaller and less persistent real effects in higher-inflation economies, seem hard to explain without fixed prices. It is possible that to fully capture the major features of fluctuations, our microeconomic model will need to incorporate important elements both of adjustments between formal reviews, as in the models of this section, and of fixed prices.

Another limitation of the Christiano–Eichenbaum–Evans and Mankiw–Reis models, like all models of pure time-dependence, is that the assumption of an exogenous and unchanging frequency of changes in firms' pricing plans is clearly too strong. The frequency of adjustment is surely the result of some type of optimizing calculation, not an exogenous parameter. Perhaps more importantly, it could change in response to policy changes, and this in turn could alter the effects of the policy changes. That is, a successful model may need to incorporate elements of both time-dependence and state-dependence.

This leaves us in an unsatisfactory position. It appears that any model of price behavior that does not include elements of both fixed prices and mechanical price adjustments, and elements of both time-dependence and state-dependence, will fail to capture important macroeconomic phenomena. Yet the hope that a single model could incorporate all these features and still be tractable seems far-fetched. The search for a single workhorse model of pricing behavior—or for a small number of workhorse models together with an understanding of when each is appropriate—continues.

# 7.8   The Canonical New Keynesian Model

The next step in constructing a complete model of fluctuations is to integrate a model of dynamic price adjustment into a larger model of the economy. Given the wide range of models of pricing behavior we have seen, it is not possible to single out one approach as the obvious starting point. Moreover, dynamic general-equilibrium models with the behavior of inflation built up from microeconomic foundations quickly become complicated. In this section, we therefore consider only an illustrative, relatively simple general-equilibrium model.

## Assumptions

The specific model we consider is the canonical three-equation new Keynesian model of Clarida, Galí, and Gertler (2000). The price-adjustment equation is the new Keynesian Phillips curve of Section 7.4. This treatment of price adjustment has two main strengths. The first is its strong microeconomic foundations: it comes directly from an assumption of infrequent adjustment of nominal prices. The other is its comparative simplicity: inflation depends only on expected future inflation and current output, with no role for past inflation or for more complicated dynamics. The aggregate-demand equation of the model is the new Keynesian IS curve of Sections 6.1 and 7.1. The final equation describes monetary policy. So far in this chapter, because our goal has been to shed light on the basic implications of various assumptions concerning price adjustment, we have considered only simple paths of the money supply (or aggregate demand). To build a model that is more

useful for analyzing actual macroeconomic fluctuations, however, we need
to assume that the central bank follows a rule for the interest rate along the
lines of Section 6.4. In particular, in keeping with the forward-looking character of the new Keynesian Phillips curve and the new Keynesian *IS* curve,
we assume the central bank follows a *forward-looking interest-rate rule,* adjusting the interest rate in response to changes in expected future inflation
and output.

The other ingredient of the model is its shocks: it includes serially correlated disturbances to all three equations. This allows us to analyze disturbances to private aggregate demand, price-setting behavior, and monetary
policy. Finally, for convenience, all the equations are linear and the constant
terms are set to zero. Thus the variables should be interpreted as differences
from their steady-state or trend values.

The three core equations are:

$$y_t = E_t[y_{t+1}] - \frac{1}{\theta}r_t + u_t^{IS}, \qquad \theta > 0, \tag{7.84}$$

$$\pi_t = \beta E_t[\pi_{t+1}] + \kappa y_t + u_t^{\pi}, \qquad 0 < \beta < 1, \qquad \kappa > 0, \tag{7.85}$$

$$r_t = \phi_\pi E_t[\pi_{t+1}] + \phi_y E_t[y_{t+1}] + u_t^{MP}, \qquad \phi_\pi > 0, \qquad \phi_y \geq 0. \tag{7.86}$$

Equation (7.84) is the new Keynesian *IS* curve, (7.85) is the new Keynesian
Phillips curve, and (7.86) is the forward-looking interest-rate rule. The shocks
follow independent AR-1 processes:

$$u_t^{IS} = \rho_{IS}u_{t-1}^{IS} + e_t^{IS}, \qquad -1 < \rho_{IS} < 1, \tag{7.87}$$

$$u_t^{\pi} = \rho_\pi u_{t-1}^{\pi} + e_t^{\pi}, \qquad -1 < \rho_\pi < 1, \tag{7.88}$$

$$u_t^{MP} = \rho_{MP}u_{t-1}^{MP} + e_t^{MP}, \qquad -1 < \rho_{MP} < 1, \tag{7.89}$$

where $e^{IS}, e^{\pi}$, and $e^{MP}$ are white-noise disturbances that are uncorrelated
with one another.

The model is obviously extremely stylized. To give just a few examples,
all behavior is forward-looking; the dynamics of inflation and aggregate demand are very simple; and the new Keynesian Phillips curve is assumed to
describe inflation dynamics despite its poor empirical performance. Nonetheless, because its core ingredients are so simple and have such appealing
microeconomic foundations, the model is a key reference point in modern
models of fluctuations. The model and variants of it are frequently used,
and it has been modified and extended in many ways.

Because of its forward-looking elements, for some parameter values the
model has sunspot solutions, like those we encountered in the model of
Section 6.4. Since we discussed such solutions there and will encounter them
again in our discussion of monetary policy in a model similar to this one in
Section 11.5, here we focus only on the fundamental, non-sunspot solution.

## The Case of White-Noise Disturbances

The first step in solving the model is to express output and inflation in terms of their expected future values and the disturbances. Applying straightforward algebra to (7.84)–(7.85) gives us

$$y_t = -\frac{\phi_\pi}{\theta} E_t[\pi_{t+1}] + \left(1 - \frac{\phi_y}{\theta}\right) E_t[y_{t+1}] + u_t^{IS} - \frac{1}{\theta} u_t^{MP}, \tag{7.90}$$

$$\pi_t = \left(\beta - \frac{\phi_\pi \kappa}{\theta}\right) E_t[\pi_{t+1}] + \left(1 - \frac{\phi_y}{\theta}\right) \kappa E_t[y_{t+1}] + \kappa u_t^{IS} + u_t^{\pi} - \frac{\kappa}{\theta} u_t^{MP}. \tag{7.91}$$

An important and instructive special case of the model occurs when there is no serial correlation in the disturbances (so $\rho_{IS} = \rho_\pi = \rho_{MP} = 0$). In this case, because of the absence of any backward-looking elements and any information about the future values of the disturbances, there is no force causing agents to expect the economy to depart from its steady state in the future. That is, the fundamental solution has $E_t[y_{t+1}]$ and $E_t[\pi_{t+1}]$ always equal to zero. To see this, note that with $E_t[y_{t+1}] = E_t[\pi_{t+1}] = 0$, equations (7.86), (7.90), and (7.91) simplify to

$$y_t = u_t^{IS} - \frac{1}{\theta} u_t^{MP}, \tag{7.92}$$

$$\pi_t = \kappa u_t^{IS} + u_t^{\pi} - \frac{\kappa}{\theta} u_t^{MP}, \tag{7.93}$$

$$r_t = u_t^{MP}. \tag{7.94}$$

If (7.92)–(7.94) describe the behavior of output, inflation, and the real interest rate, then, because we are considering the case where the $u$'s are white noise, the expectations of future output and inflation are always zero. (7.92)–(7.94) therefore represent the fundamental solution to the model in this case.

These expressions show the effects of the various shocks. A contractionary monetary-policy shock raises the real interest rate and lowers output and inflation. A positive shock to private aggregate demand raises output and inflation and has no impact on the real interest rate. And an unfavorable inflation shock raises inflation but has no other effects. These results are largely conventional. The $IS$ shock fails to affect the real interest rate because monetary policy is forward-looking, and so does not respond to the increases in current output and inflation. The fact that monetary policy is forward-looking is also the reason the inflation shock does not spill over to the other variables.

The key message of this case of the model, however, is that the model, like the baseline real-business-cycle model of Chapter 5, has no internal propagation mechanisms. Serial correlation in output, inflation, and the real interest rate can come only from serial correlation in the driving processes.

As a result, a major goal of extensions and variations of the model—such as those we will discuss in the next section—is to introduce forces that cause one-time shocks to trigger persistent changes in the macroeconomy.

## The General Case

A straightforward way to solve the model in the general case is to use the method of undetermined coefficients. Given the model's linear structure and absence of backward-looking behavior, it is reasonable to guess that the endogenous variables are linear functions of the disturbances. For output and inflation, we can write this as

$$y_t = a_{IS} u_t^{IS} + a_\pi u_t^\pi + a_{MP} u_t^{MP}, \tag{7.95}$$

$$\pi_t = b_{IS} u_t^{IS} + b_\pi u_t^\pi + b_{MP} u_t^{MP}. \tag{7.96}$$

This conjecture and the assumptions about the behavior of the disturbances in (7.87)–(7.89) determine $E_t[y_{t+1}]$ and $E_t[\pi_{t+1}]$: $E_t[y_{t+1}]$ equals $a_{IS} \rho_{IS} u_t^{IS} + a_\pi \rho_\pi u_t^\pi + a_{MP} \rho_{MP} u_t^{MP}$, and similarly for $E_t[\pi_{t+1}]$. We can then substitute these expressions and (7.95) and (7.96) into (7.90) and (7.91). This yields:

$$a_{IS} u_t^{IS} + a_\pi u_t^\pi + a_{MP} u_t^{MP} = -\frac{\phi_\pi}{\theta} \left( b_{IS} \rho_{IS} u_t^{IS} + b_\pi \rho_\pi u_t^\pi + b_{MP} \rho_{MP} u_t^{MP} \right)$$
$$+ \left( 1 - \frac{\phi_y}{\theta} \right) \left( a_{IS} \rho_{IS} u_t^{IS} + a_\pi \rho_\pi u_t^\pi + a_{MP} \rho_{MP} u_t^{MP} \right) + u_t^{IS} - \frac{1}{\theta} u_t^{MP}, \tag{7.97}$$

$$b_{IS} u_t^{IS} + b_\pi u_t^\pi + b_{MP} u_t^{MP} = \left( \beta - \frac{\phi_\pi \kappa}{\theta} \right) \left( b_{IS} \rho_{IS} u_t^{IS} + b_\pi \rho_\pi u_t^\pi + b_{MP} \rho_{MP} u_t^{MP} \right)$$
$$+ \left( 1 - \frac{\phi_y}{\theta} \right) \kappa \left( a_{IS} \rho_{IS} u_t^{IS} + a_\pi \rho_\pi u_t^\pi + a_{MP} \rho_{MP} u_t^{MP} \right) + \kappa u_t^{IS} + u_t^\pi - \frac{\kappa}{\theta} u_t^{MP}. \tag{7.98}$$

For the equations of the model to be satisfied when output and inflation are described by equations (7.95) and (7.96), the two sides of (7.97) must be equal for all values of $u_t^{IS}$, $u_t^\pi$, and $u_t^{MP}$. That is, the coefficients on $u_t^{IS}$ on the two sides must be equal, and similarly for the coefficients on $u_t^\pi$ and $u_t^{MP}$. This gives us three equations—one involving $a_{IS}$ and $b_{IS}$, one involving $a_\pi$ and $b_\pi$, and one involving $a_{MP}$ and $b_{MP}$. Equation (7.98) gives us three more equations. Once we have found the $a$'s and $b$'s, equations (7.95) and (7.96) tell us the behavior of output and inflation. We can then use (7.86) and the expressions for $E_t[\pi_{t+1}]$ and $E_t[y_{t+1}]$ to find the behavior of the real interest rate. Thus solving the model is just a matter of algebra.

Unfortunately, the equations determining the $a$'s and $b$'s are complicated, the algebra is tedious, and the resulting solutions for the $a$'s and $b$'s are complex and unintuitive. To get a sense of the model's implications, we will therefore assume values for the parameters and find their implications for how the economy responds to shocks. Specifically, following Galí (2008, Section 3.4.1), we interpret a time period as a quarter, and assume $\theta = 1$,

$\kappa = 0.1275$, $\beta = 0.99$, $\phi_\pi = 0.5$, and $\phi_y = 0.125$. For each of the disturbances, we will consider both the case of no serial correlation and a serial correlation coefficient of 0.5 to see how serial correlation affects the behavior of the economy.

Consider first a monetary-policy shock. With $\rho_{MP} = 0$, our parameter values and equations (7.92)–(7.94) imply that $y_t = -u_t^{MP}$, $\pi_t = -0.13u_t^{MP}$, and $r_t = u_t^{MP}$. With $\rho_{MP} = 0.5$, they imply that $y_t = -1.60u_t^{MP}$, $\pi_t = -0.40u_t^{MP}$, and $r_t = 0.80u_t^{MP}$. Intuitively, the fact that output and inflation will be below normal in later periods mutes the rise in the real interest rate. But because of the fall in future output, a larger fall in current output is needed for households to satisfy their Euler equation in response to the rise in the real rate. And both the greater fall in output and the decline in future inflation strengthen the response of inflation. As the economy returns to its steady state, the real rate is above normal and output is rising, consistent with the new Keynesian *IS* curve. And inflation is rising and output is below normal, consistent with the new Keynesian Phillips curve.

Next, consider an *IS* shock. When $\rho_{IS} = 0$, our parameter values imply $y_t = u_t^{IS}$, $\pi_t = 0.13u_t^{IS}$, and $r_t = 0$. When $\rho_{IS}$ rises to 0.5, we obtain $y_t = 1.60u_t^{IS}$, $\pi_t = 0.40u_t^{IS}$, and $r_t = 0.20u_t^{IS}$. Again, the impact of the shock on future output magnifies the output response via the new Keynesian *IS* curve. In addition, the increases in future inflation strengthen the inflation response through the new Keynesian Phillips curve. And with future output and inflation affected by the shock, the current real interest rate responds through the forward-looking interest-rate rule.

Finally, consider an inflation shock. As described above, in the absence of serial correlation, the shock is translated one-for-one into inflation and has no effect on output or the real interest rate. With $\rho_\pi = 0.5$, in contrast, $y_t = -0.80u_t^\pi$, $\pi_t = 1.78u_t^\pi$, and $r_t = 0.40u_t^\pi$. The persistence of the inflation shock increases the response of current inflation (through the forward-looking term of the new Keynesian Phillips curve) and raises the real interest rate (through the inflation term of the forward-looking interest-rate rule). The increase in the real rate reduces current output through the *IS* curve; and this effect is magnified by the fact that the curve is forward-looking.

# 7.9   Other Elements of Modern New Keynesian DSGE Models of Fluctuations

The model of Section 7.8 is a convenient illustrative model. But it is obviously far short of being rich enough to be useful for many applications. A policymaker wanting to forecast the path of the economy or evaluate the likely macroeconomic effects of some policy intervention would certainly need a considerably more complicated model.

A large and active literature is engaged in constructing and estimating more sophisticated quantitative DSGE models that, at their core, have important resemblances to the model of the previous section. The models do not lend themselves to analytic solutions or to transparency. But they are in widespread use not just in academia, but in central banks and other policymaking institutions. This section briefly discusses some of the most important modifications and extensions of the baseline model. Many of the changes come from the models of Christiano, Eichenbaum, and Evans (2005), Erceg, Henderson, and Levin (2000), and Smets and Wouters (2003).

## Aggregate Supply

The canonical new Keynesian model uses the new Keynesian Phillips curve to model the behavior of inflation. Richer models often extend this in two ways. First, recall that the evidence in favor of the distinctive predictions of the new Keynesian Phillips curve—notably its implication that an anticipated disinflation is associated with an output boom—is weak. Thus modern models often introduce inflation inertia. Because of its tractability, the usual approach is to posit a relationship along the lines suggested by the new Keynesian Phillips curve with indexation. Typically, the coefficients on lagged and expected future inflation are not constrained to equal $1/(1 + \beta)$ and $\beta/(1 + \beta)$, as in equation (7.76), but follow the more general set of possibilities allowed by equation (7.77).

Second, to better capture the behavior of prices and wages, the models often assume incomplete adjustment not just of goods prices, but also of wages. The most common approach is to assume Calvo wage adjustment (with an adjustment frequency potentially different from that for price changes). Under appropriate assumptions, the result is a new Keynesian Phillips curve for wage inflation:

$$\pi_t^w = \beta E_t\left[\pi_{t+1}^w\right] + \kappa_w y_t, \tag{7.99}$$

where $\pi^w$ is wage inflation. A natural alternative, paralleling the treatment of prices, is to assume indexation to lagged wage inflation between adjustments, leading to an equation for wage inflation analogous to the new Keynesian Phillips curve with indexation.

## Aggregate Demand

There are two major limitations of the new Keynesian *IS* curve. First, and most obviously, it leaves out investment, government purchases, and net exports. Virtually every model intended for practical use includes investment modeled as arising from the decisions of profit-maximizing firms. Government purchases are almost always included as well; they are generally modeled as exogenous. And there are numerous open-economy extensions. Examples include Obstfeld and Rogoff (2002); Corsetti and Pesenti (2005); Benigno and Benigno (2006); and Galí (2008, Chapter 7).

Second, the basic new Keynesian *IS* curve, even when it is extended to include other components of output, tends to imply large and rapid responses to shocks. To better match the data, the models therefore generally include ingredients that slow adjustment. With regard to consumption, the most common approach is to assume *habit formation.* That is, a consumer's utility is assumed to depend not just on the level of consumption, but also on its level relative to some reference amount, such as the consumer's or others' past consumption. Under appropriate assumptions, this slows the response of consumption to shocks. On the investment side, the most common way of slowing responses is to assume directly that there are costs of adjusting investment.

We will see in Chapter 8 that households' current income appears to have an important effect on their consumption, and we will see in Chapter 9 that firms' current cash flow may be important to their investment decisions. The new Keynesian *IS* curve, with or without the various modifications we have discussed, does not allow for these possibilities. To let current income affect the demand for goods, the usual approach is to assume that some fraction of consumption is determined by rule-of-thumb or liquidity-constrained households that devote all their current income to consumption.[21] This assumption can magnify the economy's responses to various disturbances and can introduce a role for shocks that shift the timing of income, which would otherwise not affect behavior.

## Credit-Market Imperfections

The crisis of 2008–2009 has made it clear that non-Walrasian features of credit markets have important macroeconomic consequences. Disruptions in credit markets can cause large swings in economic activity, and credit-market imperfections can have large effects on how other shocks affect the macroeconomy. As a result, introducing credit-market imperfections into new Keynesian DSGE models is an active area of research.

Three recent efforts in this area are those by Cúrdia and Woodford (2009), Gertler and Karadi (2009), and Christiano, Motto, and Rostagno (2009). In all three models, there is a financial sector that intermediates between saving and investment. Cúrdia and Woodford's model is conceptually the simplest.

---

[21] The models generally do not give current cash flow a role in investment. For some purposes, the assumption of rule-of-thumb consumers has similar implications, making it unnecessary to add this complication. In addition, some models that include credit-market imperfections, along the lines of the ones we will discuss in a moment, naturally imply an impact of cash flow on investment.

They assume a costly intermediation technology. The spread between borrowing and lending rates changes because of changes both in the marginal cost of intermediation and in intermediaries' markups. These fluctuations have an endogenous component, with changes in the quantity of intermediation changing its marginal cost, and an exogenous component, with shocks to both the intermediation technology and markups.

In Gertler and Karadi's model, the spread arises from constraints on the size of the intermediation sector. Intermediaries have limited capital. Because high leverage would create harmful incentives, the limited capital restricts intermediaries' ability to attract funds from savers. The result is that they effectively earn rents on their capital, charging more to borrowers than they pay to savers. Again, the spread moves both endogenously and exogenously. Various types of shocks affect intermediaries' capital, and so change their ability to attract funds and the spread. And shocks to the value of their capital directly affect their ability to attract funds, and so again affect the spread. Both endogenous and exogenous movements in the spread are propagated to the remainder of the economy.

Christiano, Motto, and Rostagno, building on their earlier work (Christiano, Motto, and Rostagno, 2003), focus on frictions in the relationship between intermediaries and borrowers. The limited capital of borrowers and the riskiness of their investments affect their ability to borrow and the interest rates they must pay. As a result, borrowing rates and the quantity of borrowing move endogenously in response to various types of disturbances. In addition, Christiano, Motto, and Rostagno assume that loan contracts are written in nominal terms (along the lines we discussed in Section 6.9), so that any disturbance that affects the price level affects borrowers' real indebtedness, which in turn affects the rest of the economy. And, as in the other models, there are exogenous disturbances to the factors governing spreads. Christiano, Motto, and Rostagno consider not only shocks to borrowers' net worth and to the riskiness of their projects, but also the arrival of news about the riskiness of future projects.

All three papers represent early efforts to incorporate financial-market imperfections and disruptions into larger models. Recent events leave no doubt that those imperfections and disruptions are important. But the question of how to best incorporate them in larger macroeconomic models is very much open.

## Policy

The policy assumptions of more sophisticated new Keynesian DSGE models of fluctuations depart from the simple interest-rate rule we considered in Section 7.8 in three main ways. The first, and most straightforward, is to consider other interest-rate rules. A seemingly infinite variety of interest-rate rules have been considered. The rules consider gradual adjustment, responses to current values or past values of variables instead of (or in addition to) their expected future values, responses to growth rates rather than levels of variables, and the possible inclusion of many variables other than output and inflation. A common strategy in this literature is to ask how some change in the rule, such as the addition of a new variable, affects macroeconomic outcomes, such as the variability of inflation and output.

The second, larger departure is to replace the assumption of a prespecified policy rule with the assumption that policymakers maximize some objective function. The objective function may be specified directly; for example, policymakers can be assumed to have a quadratic loss function over inflation and output. Alternatively, the function may be derived from microeconomic foundations; most commonly, policymakers' goal is assumed to be to maximize the expected utility of the representative household in the model. With this approach, it is necessary to specify a model rich enough that inflation affects welfare. Once the objective is in place (either by assumption or by derivation), policymakers' decisions come from maximizing that function.

A natural way to meld the approach based on interest-rate rules and the approach based on maximization is to ask how well various simple rules approximate optimal policy. There is a widespread view that policymakers would be reluctant to follow a complicated rule or the prescriptions of one particular model. Thus it is important to ask whether there are simple rules that perform relatively well across a range of models. We will investigate both modifications of simple interest-rate rules and the derivation of optimal policy further in Chapter 11, where we examine monetary policy in more depth.

The third way that recent models extend the analysis of policy is by considering policy instruments other than the short-term interest rate. One set of additional policy instruments are those associated with fiscal policy, notably government purchases, transfers, and various tax rates. And models that incorporate imperfections in credit markets naturally allow for consideration of various government interventions in those markets.

## Discussion

Assessments of this research program fall along a continuum between two extremes. Although few economists are at either extreme, they are useful reference points.

One extreme is that we are well on the way to having models of the macroeconomy that are sufficiently well grounded in microeconomic assumptions that their parameters can be thought of as structural (in the sense that they do not change when policies change), and that are sufficiently realistic that they can be used to obtain welfare-based recommendations about the conduct of policy. Advocates of this view can point to the facts that the models are built up from microeconomic foundations; that estimated versions of the models match some important features of fluctuations reasonably well; that many policymakers value the models enough to put weight on their predictions and recommendations; that there is microeconomic evidence for many of their assumptions; and that their sophistication is advancing rapidly.

The other extreme is that the models are ad hoc constructions that are sufficiently distant from reality that their policy recommendations are unreliable and their predictions likely to fail if the macroeconomic environment changes. Advocates of this view can point to two main facts. First, despite the models' complications, there is a great deal they leave out. For example, until the recent crisis, the models' treatment of credit-market imperfections was generally minimal. Second, the microeconomic case for some important features of the models is questionable. Most notably, the models include assumptions that generate inertia in decision making: inflation indexation in price adjustment, habit formation in consumption, and adjustment costs in investment. The inclusion of these features is mainly motivated not by microeconomic evidence, but by a desire to match macroeconomic facts. For example, at the microeconomic level we see nominal prices that are fixed for extended periods, not frequently adjusted to reflect recent inflation. Similarly, as we will see in Chapter 9, standard models of investment motivated by microeconomic evidence involve costs of adjusting the capital stock, not costs of adjusting investment. The need to introduce these features, in this view, suggests that the models have significant gaps.

Almost all macroeconomists agree that the models have important strengths and weaknesses, and thus that the truth lies between the two extremes. Nonetheless, where in that range the truth is matters for how macroeconomists should conduct their research. The closer it is to the first extreme, the greater the value of extending the models and of examining new phenomena by incorporating them into the models. The closer it is to the second extreme, the greater the value of working on new issues in narrower models and of postponing efforts to construct integrative models until our understanding of the component pieces is further advanced.

# Problems

**7.1. The Fischer model with unbalanced price-setting.** Suppose the economy is described by the model of Section 7.2, except that instead of half of firms setting their prices each period, fraction $f$ set their prices in odd periods and fraction $1 - f$ set their prices in even periods. Thus the price level is $f p_t^1 + (1-f) p_t^2$ if $t$ is even and $(1-f) p_t^1 + f p_t^2$ if $t$ is odd. Derive expressions analogous to (7.27) and (7.28) for $p_t$ and $y_t$ for even and odd periods.

**7.2. The instability of staggered price-setting.** Suppose the economy is described as in Problem 7.1, and assume for simplicity that $m$ is a random walk (so $m_t = m_{t-1} + u_t$, where $u$ is white noise and has a constant variance). Assume the profits a firm loses over two periods relative to always having $p_t = p_t^*$ is proportional to $(p_{it} - p_{it}^*)^2 + (p_{it+1} - p_{it+1}^*)^2$. If $f < 1/2$ and $\phi < 1$, is the expected value of this loss larger for the firms that set their prices in odd periods or for the firms that set their prices in even periods? In light of this, would you expect to see staggered price-setting if $\phi < 1$?

**7.3. Synchronized price-setting.** Consider the Taylor model. Suppose, however, that every other period all the firms set their prices for that period and the next. That is, in period $t$ prices are set for $t$ and $t + 1$; in $t + 1$, no prices are set; in $t + 2$, prices are set for $t + 2$ and $t + 3$; and so on. As in the Taylor model, prices are both predetermined and fixed, and firms set their prices according to (7.30). Finally, assume that $m$ follows a random walk.

(a) What is the representative firm's price in period $t$, $x_t$, as a function of $m_t$, $E_t m_{t+1}$, $p_t$, and $E_t p_{t+1}$?

(b) Use the fact that synchronization implies that $p_t$ and $p_{t+1}$ are both equal to $x_t$ to solve for $x_t$ in terms of $m_t$ and $E_t m_{t+1}$.

(c) What are $y_t$ and $y_{t+1}$? Does the central result of the Taylor model—that nominal disturbances continue to have real effects after all prices have been changed—still hold? Explain intuitively.

**7.4.** Consider the Taylor model with the money stock white noise rather than a random walk; that is, $m_t = \varepsilon_t$, where $\varepsilon_t$ is serially uncorrelated. Solve the model using the method of undetermined coefficients. (Hint: In the equation analogous to (7.33), is it still reasonable to impose $\lambda + \nu = 1$?)

**7.5.** Repeat Problem 7.4 using lag operators.

**7.6.** Consider the experiment described at the beginning of Section 7.4. Specifically, a Calvo economy is initially in long-run equilibrium with all prices equal to $m$, which we normalize to zero. In period 1, there is a one-time, permanent increase in $m$ to $m_1$.

Let us conjecture that the behavior of the price level for $t \geq 1$ is described by an expression of the form $p_t = (1 - \lambda^t) m_1$.

(a) Explain why this conjecture is or is not reasonable.

(b) Find $\lambda$ in terms of the primitive parameters of the model ($\alpha$, $\beta$, and $\phi$).

(c) How do increases in each of $\alpha$, $\beta$, and $\phi$ affect $\lambda$? Explain your answers intuitively.

**7.7. State-dependent pricing with both positive and negative inflation.** (Caplin and Leahy, 1991.) Consider an economy like that of the Caplin–Spulber model. Suppose, however, that $m$ can either rise or fall, and that firms therefore follow a simple two-sided $Ss$ policy: if $p_i - p_i^*(t)$ reaches either $S$ or $-S$, firm $i$ changes $p_i$ so that $p_i - p_i^*(t)$ equals 0. As in the Caplin–Spulber model, changes in $m$ are continuous.

Assume for simplicity that $p_i^*(t) = m(t)$. In addition, assume that $p_i - p_i^*(t)$ is initially distributed uniformly over some interval of width $S$; that is, $p_i - p_i^*(t)$ is distributed uniformly on $[X, X + S]$ for some $X$ between $-S$ and 0.

(a) Explain why, given these assumptions, $p_i - p_i^*(t)$ continues to be distributed uniformly over some interval of width $S$.

(b) Are there any values of $X$ for which an infinitesimal increase in $m$ of $dm$ raises average prices by less than $dm$? by more than $dm$? by exactly $dm$? Thus, what does this model imply about the real effects of monetary shocks?

**7.8.** (This follows Ball, 1994a.) Consider a continuous-time version of the Taylor model, so that $p(t) = (1/T) \int_{\tau=0}^{T} x(t - \tau) d\tau$, where $T$ is the interval between each individual's price changes and $x(t-\tau)$ is the price set by individuals who set their prices at time $t - \tau$. Assume that $\phi = 1$, so that $p_i^*(t) = m(t)$; thus $x(t) = (1/T) \int_{\tau=0}^{T} E_t m(t + \tau) d\tau$.

(a) Suppose that initially $m(t) = gt$ $(g > 0)$, and that $E_t m(t + \tau)$ is therefore $(t + \tau)g$. What are $x(t)$, $p(t)$, and $y(t) = m(t) - p(t)$?

(b) Suppose that at time 0 the government announces that it is steadily reducing money growth to zero over the next interval $T$ of time. Thus $m(t) = t[1 - (t/2T)]g$ for $0 < t < T$, and $m(t) = gT/2$ for $t \geq T$. The change is unexpected, so that prices set before $t = 0$ are as in part (a).

(i) Show that if $x(t) = gT/2$ for all $t > 0$, then $p(t) = m(t)$ for all $t > 0$, and thus that output is the same as it would be without the change in policy.

(ii) For $0 < t < T$, are the prices that firms set more than, less than, or equal to $gT/2$? What about for $T \leq t \leq 2T$? Given this, how does output during the period $(0,2T)$ compare with what it would be without the change in policy?

**7.9.** Consider the new Keynesian Phillips curve with indexation, equation (7.76), under the assumptions of perfect foresight and $\beta = 1$, together with our usual aggregate demand equation, $y_t = m_t - p_t$.

(a) Express $p_{t+1}$ in terms of its lagged values and $m_t$.

(b) Consider an anticipated, permanent, one-time increase in $m$: $m_t = 0$ for $t < 0$, $m_t = 1$ for $t \geq 0$. Sketch how you would find the resulting path of $p_t$. (Hint: Use the lag operator approach from Section 7.3.)

**7.10. The new Keynesian Phillips curve with partial indexation.** Consider the analysis of the new Keynesian Phillips curve with indexation in Section 7.7. Suppose, however, that the indexation is only partial. That is, if a firm does not have an opportunity to review its price in period $t$, its price in $t$ is the previous period's price plus $\gamma \pi_{t-1}$, $0 \leq \gamma \leq 1$. Find an expression for $\pi_t$ in terms of $\pi_{t-1}$, $E_t \pi_{t+1}$, $y_t$, and the parameters of the model. Check that your answer simplifies to the new Keynesian Phillips curve when $\gamma = 0$ and to the new Keynesian Phillips curve with indexation when $\gamma = 1$. (Hint: Start by showing that $[\alpha/(1 - \alpha)](x_t - p_t) = \pi_t - \gamma \pi_{t-1}$.)

**7.11.** Consider a continuous-time version of the Mankiw–Reis model. Opportunities to review pricing policies follow a Poisson process with arrival rate $\alpha > 0$. Thus the probability that a price path set at time $t$ is still being followed at time $t + i$ is $e^{-\alpha i}$. The other assumptions of the model are the same as before.

(a) Show that the expression analogous to (7.81) is $a(i) = \dfrac{\phi(1 - e^{-\alpha i})}{[1 - (1 - \phi)(1 - e^{-\alpha i})]}$.

(b) Consider the experiment of a permanent fall in the growth rate of aggregate demand discussed in Section 7.7. That is, until $t = 0$, all firms expect $m(t) = gt$ (where $g > 0$); thereafter, they expect $m(t) = 0$.

   (i) Find the expression analogous to (7.83).

   (ii) Find an expression for inflation, $\dot{p}(t)$, for $t \geq 0$. Is inflation ever negative during the transition to the new steady state?

   (iii) Suppose $\phi = 1$. When does output reach its lowest level? When does inflation reach its lowest level?

**7.12.** Consider the model of Section 7.8. Suppose, however, that monetary policy responds to current inflation and output: $r_t = \phi_\pi \pi_t + \phi_y y_t + u_t^{MP}$.

(a) For the case of white-noise disturbances, find expressions analogous to (7.92)–(7.94). What are the effects of an unfavorable inflation shock in this case?

(b) Describe how you would solve this model using the method of undetermined coefficients (but do not actually solve it).

# Chapter **8**
# CONSUMPTION

This chapter and the next investigate households' consumption choices and firms' investment decisions. Consumption and investment are important to both growth and fluctuations. With regard to growth, the division of society's resources between consumption and various types of investment—in physical capital, human capital, and research and development—is central to standards of living in the long run. That division is determined by the interaction of households' allocation of their incomes between consumption and saving given the rates of return and other constraints they face, and firms' investment demand given the interest rates and other constraints they face. With regard to fluctuations, consumption and investment make up the vast majority of the demand for goods. Thus to understand how such forces as government purchases, technology, and monetary policy affect aggregate output, we must understand how consumption and investment are determined.

There are two other reasons for studying consumption and investment. First, they introduce some important issues involving financial markets. Financial markets affect the macroeconomy mainly through their impact on consumption and investment. In addition, consumption and investment have important feedback effects on financial markets. We will investigate the interaction between financial markets and consumption and investment both in cases where financial markets function perfectly and in cases where they do not.

Second, much of the most insightful empirical work in macroeconomics in recent decades has been concerned with consumption and investment. These two chapters therefore have an unusually intensive empirical focus.

## 8.1 Consumption under Certainty: The Permanent-Income Hypothesis

### Assumptions

Although we have already examined aspects of individuals' consumption decisions in our investigations of the Ramsey and Diamond models in

Chapter 2 and of real-business-cycle theory in Chapter 5, here we start with a simple case. Consider an individual who lives for $T$ periods whose lifetime utility is

$$U = \sum_{t=1}^{T} u(C_t), \qquad u'(\bullet) > 0, \qquad u''(\bullet) < 0, \tag{8.1}$$

where $u(\bullet)$ is the instantaneous utility function and $C_t$ is consumption in period $t$. The individual has initial wealth of $A_0$ and labor incomes of $Y_1$, $Y_2, \ldots, Y_T$ in the $T$ periods of his or her life; the individual takes these as given. The individual can save or borrow at an exogenous interest rate, subject only to the constraint that any outstanding debt be repaid at the end of his or her life. For simplicity, this interest rate is set to 0.[1] Thus the individual's budget constraint is

$$\sum_{t=1}^{T} C_t \le A_0 + \sum_{t=1}^{T} Y_t. \tag{8.2}$$

## Behavior

Since the marginal utility of consumption is always positive, the individual satisfies the budget constraint with equality. The Lagrangian for his or her maximization problem is therefore

$$\mathcal{L} = \sum_{t=1}^{T} u(C_t) + \lambda \left( A_0 + \sum_{t=1}^{T} Y_t - \sum_{t=1}^{T} C_t \right). \tag{8.3}$$

The first-order condition for $C_t$ is

$$u'(C_t) = \lambda. \tag{8.4}$$

Since (8.4) holds in every period, the marginal utility of consumption is constant. And since the level of consumption uniquely determines its marginal utility, this means that consumption must be constant. Thus $C_1 = C_2 = \cdots = C_T$. Substituting this fact into the budget constraint yields

$$C_t = \frac{1}{T} \left( A_0 + \sum_{\tau=1}^{T} Y_\tau \right) \qquad \text{for all } t. \tag{8.5}$$

---

[1] Note that we have also assumed that the individual's discount rate is zero (see [8.1]). Assuming that the interest rate and the discount rate are equal but not necessarily zero would have almost no effect on the analysis in this section and the next. And assuming that they need not be equal would have only modest effects.

The term in parentheses is the individual's total lifetime resources. Thus (8.5) states that the individual divides his or her lifetime resources equally among each period of life.

## Implications

This analysis implies that the individual's consumption in a given period is determined not by income that period, but by income over his or her entire lifetime. In the terminology of Friedman (1957), the right-hand side of (8.5) is *permanent income,* and the difference between current and permanent income is *transitory income.* Equation (8.5) implies that consumption is determined by permanent income.

To see the importance of the distinction between permanent and transitory income, consider the effect of a windfall gain of amount $Z$ in the first period of life. Although this windfall raises current income by $Z$, it raises permanent income by only $Z/T$. Thus if the individual's horizon is fairly long, the windfall's impact on current consumption is small. One implication is that a temporary tax cut may have little impact on consumption.

Our analysis also implies that although the time pattern of income is not important to consumption, it is critical to saving. The individual's saving in period $t$ is the difference between income and consumption:

$$S_t = Y_t - C_t$$

$$= \left( Y_t - \frac{1}{T} \sum_{\tau=1}^{T} Y_\tau \right) - \frac{1}{T} A_0,$$

(8.6)

where the second line uses (8.5) to substitute for $C_t$. Thus saving is high when income is high relative to its average—that is, when transitory income is high. Similarly, when current income is less than permanent income, saving is negative. Thus the individual uses saving and borrowing to smooth the path of consumption. This is the key idea of the permanent-income hypothesis of Modigliani and Brumberg (1954) and Friedman (1957).

## What Is Saving?

At a more general level, the basic idea of the permanent-income hypothesis is a simple insight about saving: saving is future consumption. As long as an individual does not save just for the sake of saving, he or she saves to consume in the future. The saving may be used for conventional consumption later in life, or bequeathed to the individual's children for their consumption, or even used to erect monuments to the individual upon his or her death. But as long as the individual does not value saving in itself, the decision about the division of income between consumption and saving is driven by preferences between present and future consumption and information about future consumption prospects.

This observation suggests that many common statements about saving may be incorrect. For example, it is often asserted that poor individuals save a smaller fraction of their incomes than the wealthy do because their incomes are little above the level needed to provide a minimal standard of living. But this claim overlooks the fact that individuals who have trouble obtaining even a low standard of living today may also have trouble obtaining that standard in the future. Thus their saving is likely to be determined by the time pattern of their income, just as it is for the wealthy.

To take another example, consider the common assertion that individuals' concern about their consumption relative to others' tends to raise their consumption as they try to "keep up with the Joneses." Again, this claim fails to recognize what saving is: since saving represents future consumption, saving less implies consuming less in the future, and thus falling further behind the Joneses. Thus one can just as well argue that concern about relative consumption causes individuals to try to catch up with the Joneses in the future, and thus lowers rather than raises current consumption.[2]

## Empirical Application: Understanding Estimated Consumption Functions

The traditional Keynesian consumption function posits that consumption is determined by current disposable income. Keynes (1936) argued that "the amount of aggregate consumption mainly depends on the amount of aggregate income," and that this relationship "is a fairly stable function." He claimed further that "it is also obvious that a higher absolute level of income . . . will lead, as a rule, to a greater *proportion* of income being saved" (Keynes, 1936, pp. 96–97; emphasis in original).

The importance of the consumption function to Keynes's analysis of fluctuations led many researchers to estimate the relationship between consumption and current income. Contrary to Keynes's claims, these studies did not demonstrate a consistent, stable relationship. Across households at a point in time, the relationship is indeed of the type that Keynes postulated; an example of such a relationship is shown in Panel (a) of Figure 8.1. But within a country over time, aggregate consumption is essentially proportional to aggregate income; that is, one sees a relationship like that in

---

[2] For more on how individuals' concern about their consumption relative to others' affects saving once one recognizes that saving represents future consumption, see n. 14 below.

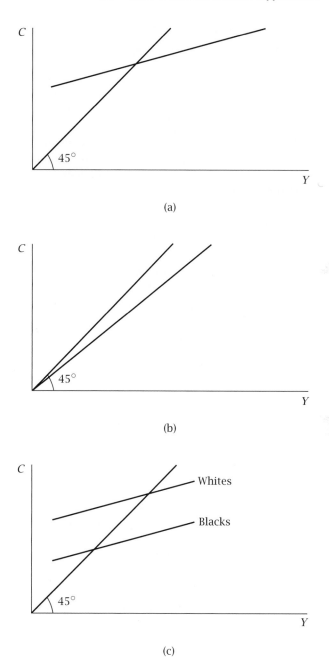

**FIGURE 8.1 Some different forms of the relationship between current income and consumption**

Panel (b) of the figure. Further, the cross-section consumption function differs across groups. For example, the slope of the estimated consumption function is similar for whites and blacks, but the intercept is higher for whites. This is shown in Panel (c) of the figure.

As Friedman (1957) demonstrates, the permanent-income hypothesis provides a straightforward explanation of all of these findings. Suppose consumption is in fact determined by permanent income: $C = Y^P$. Current income equals the sum of permanent and transitory income: $Y = Y^P + Y^T$. And since transitory income reflects departures of current income from permanent income, in most samples it has a mean near zero and is roughly uncorrelated with permanent income.

Now consider a regression of consumption on current income:

$$C_i = a + bY_i + e_i. \tag{8.7}$$

In a univariate regression, the estimated coefficient on the right-hand-side variable is the ratio of the covariance of the right-hand-side and left-hand-side variables to the variance of the right-hand-side variable. In this case, this implies

$$\begin{aligned}
\hat{b} &= \frac{\text{Cov}(Y,C)}{\text{Var}(Y)} \\
&= \frac{\text{Cov}(Y^P + Y^T, Y^P)}{\text{Var}(Y^P + Y^T)} \\
&= \frac{\text{Var}(Y^P)}{\text{Var}(Y^P) + \text{Var}(Y^T)}.
\end{aligned} \tag{8.8}$$

Here the second line uses the facts that current income equals the sum of permanent and transitory income and that consumption equals permanent income, and the last line uses the assumption that permanent and temporary income are uncorrelated. In addition, the estimated constant equals the mean of the left-hand-side variable minus the estimated slope coefficient times the mean of the right-hand-side variable. Thus,

$$\begin{aligned}
\hat{a} &= \overline{C} - \hat{b}\overline{Y} \\
&= \overline{Y}^P - \hat{b}(\overline{Y}^P + \overline{Y}^T) \\
&= (1 - \hat{b})\overline{Y}^P,
\end{aligned} \tag{8.9}$$

where the last line uses the assumption that the mean of transitory income is zero.

Thus the permanent-income hypothesis predicts that the key determinant of the slope of an estimated consumption function, $\hat{b}$, is the relative variation in permanent and transitory income. Intuitively, an increase in current income is associated with an increase in consumption only to the extent that it reflects an increase in permanent income. When the variation in permanent income is much greater than the variation in transitory income, almost all differences in current income reflect differences in permanent income; thus consumption rises nearly one-for-one with current income. But when the variation in permanent income is small relative to the variation in transitory income, little of the variation in current income comes from variation in permanent income, and so consumption rises little with current income.

This analysis can be used to understand the estimated consumption functions in Figure 8.1. Across households, much of the variation in income reflects such factors as unemployment and the fact that households are at different points in their life cycles. As a result, the estimated slope coefficient is substantially less than 1, and the estimated intercept is positive. Over time, in contrast, almost all the variation in aggregate income reflects long-run growth—that is, permanent increases in the economy's resources. Thus the estimated slope coefficient is close to 1, and the estimated intercept is close to zero.[3]

Now consider the differences between blacks and whites. The relative variances of permanent and transitory income are similar in the two groups, and so the estimates of $b$ are similar. But blacks' average incomes are lower than whites'; as a result, the estimate of $a$ for blacks is lower than the estimate for whites (see [8.9]).

To see the intuition for this result, consider a member of each group whose income equals the average income among whites. Since there are many more blacks with permanent incomes below this level than there are with permanent incomes above it, the black's permanent income is much more likely to be less than his or her current income than more. As a result, blacks with this current income have on average lower permanent income; thus on average they consume less than their income. For the white, in contrast, his or her permanent income is about as likely to be more than current income as it is to be less; as a result, whites with this current income on average have the same permanent income, and thus on average they consume their income. In sum, the permanent-income hypothesis attributes the different consumption patterns of blacks and whites to the different average incomes of the two groups, and not to any differences in tastes or culture.

---

[3] In this case, although consumption is approximately proportional to income, the constant of proportionality is less than 1; that is, consumption is on average less than permanent income. As Friedman describes, there are various ways of extending the basic theory to make it consistent with this result. One is to account for turnover among generations and long-run growth: if the young generally save and the old generally dissave, the fact that each generation is wealthier than the previous one implies that the young's saving is greater than the old's dissaving.

# 8.2   Consumption under Uncertainty: The Random-Walk Hypothesis

## Individual Behavior

We now extend our analysis to account for uncertainty. In particular, suppose there is uncertainty about the individual's labor income each period (the $Y_t$'s). Continue to assume that both the interest rate and the discount rate are zero. In addition, suppose that the instantaneous utility function, $u(\bullet)$, is quadratic. Thus the individual maximizes

$$E[U] = E\left[\sum_{t=1}^{T}\left(C_t - \frac{a}{2}C_t^2\right)\right], \qquad a > 0. \tag{8.10}$$

We will assume that the individual's wealth is such that consumption is always in the range where marginal utility is positive. As before, the individual must pay off any outstanding debts at the end of life. Thus the budget constraint is again given by equation (8.2), $\sum_{t=1}^{T} C_t \le A_0 + \sum_{t=1}^{T} Y_t$.

To describe the individual's behavior, we use our usual Euler equation approach. Specifically, suppose that the individual has chosen first-period consumption optimally given the information available, and suppose that he or she will choose consumption in each future period optimally given the information then available. Now consider a reduction in $C_1$ of $dC$ from the value the individual has chosen and an equal increase in consumption at some future date from the value he or she would have chosen. If the individual is optimizing, a marginal change of this type does not affect expected utility. Since the marginal utility of consumption in period 1 is $1 - aC_1$, the change has a utility cost of $(1 - aC_1)\,dC$. And since the marginal utility of period-$t$ consumption is $1 - aC_t$, the change has an expected utility benefit of $E_1[1 - aC_t]\,dC$, where $E_1[\bullet]$ denotes expectations conditional on the information available in period 1. Thus if the individual is optimizing,

$$1 - aC_1 = E_1[1 - aC_t], \qquad \text{for } t = 2, 3, \ldots, T. \tag{8.11}$$

Since $E_1[1 - aC_t]$ equals $1 - aE_1[C_t]$, this implies

$$C_1 = E_1[C_t], \qquad \text{for } t = 2, 3, \ldots, T. \tag{8.12}$$

The individual knows that his or her lifetime consumption will satisfy the budget constraint, (8.2), with equality. Thus the expectations of the two sides of the constraint must be equal:

$$\sum_{t=1}^{T} E_1[C_t] = A_0 + \sum_{t=1}^{T} E_1[Y_t]. \tag{8.13}$$

Equation (8.12) implies that the left-hand side of (8.13) is $TC_1$. Substituting this into (8.13) and dividing by $T$ yields

$$C_1 = \frac{1}{T}\left(A_0 + \sum_{t=1}^{T} E_1[Y_t]\right).\tag{8.14}$$

That is, the individual consumes $1/T$ of his or her expected lifetime resources.

## Implications

Equation (8.12) implies that the expectation as of period 1 of $C_2$ equals $C_1$. More generally, reasoning analogous to what we have just done implies that each period, expected next-period consumption equals current consumption. This implies that changes in consumption are unpredictable. By the definition of expectations, we can write

$$C_t = E_{t-1}[C_t] + e_t,\tag{8.15}$$

where $e_t$ is a variable whose expectation as of period $t - 1$ is zero. Thus, since $E_{t-1}[C_t] = C_{t-1}$, we have

$$C_t = C_{t-1} + e_t.\tag{8.16}$$

This is Hall's famous result that the permanent-income hypothesis implies that consumption follows a random walk (Hall, 1978).[4] The intuition for this result is straightforward: if consumption is expected to change, the individual can do a better job of smoothing consumption. Suppose, for example, that consumption is expected to rise. This means that the current marginal utility of consumption is greater than the expected future marginal utility of consumption, and thus that the individual is better off raising current consumption. Thus the individual adjusts his or her current consumption to the point where consumption is not expected to change.

In addition, our analysis can be used to find what determines the change in consumption, $e$. Consider for concreteness the change from period 1 to period 2. Reasoning parallel to that used to derive (8.14) implies that $C_2$

---

[4] Strictly speaking, the theory implies that consumption follows a *martingale* (a series whose changes are unpredictable) and not necessarily a random walk (a martingale whose changes are i.i.d.). The common practice, however, is to refer to martingales as random walks.

equals $1/(T-1)$ of the individual's expected remaining lifetime resources:

$$C_2 = \frac{1}{T-1}\left(A_1 + \sum_{t=2}^{T} E_2[Y_t]\right)$$

$$= \frac{1}{T-1}\left(A_0 + Y_1 - C_1 + \sum_{t=2}^{T} E_2[Y_t]\right), \tag{8.17}$$

where the second line uses the fact that $A_1 = A_0 + Y_1 - C_1$. We can rewrite the expectation as of period 2 of income over the remainder of life, $\sum_{t=2}^{T} E_2[Y_t]$, as the expectation of this quantity as of period 1, $\sum_{t=2}^{T} E_1[Y_t]$, plus the information learned between period 1 and period 2, $\sum_{t=2}^{T} E_2[Y_t] - \sum_{t=2}^{T} E_1[Y_t]$. Thus we can rewrite (8.17) as

$$C_2 = \frac{1}{T-1}\left[A_0 + Y_1 - C_1 + \sum_{t=2}^{T} E_1[Y_t] + \left(\sum_{t=2}^{T} E_2[Y_t] - \sum_{t=2}^{T} E_1[Y_t]\right)\right]. \tag{8.18}$$

From (8.14), $A_0 + Y_1 + \sum_{t=2}^{T} E_1[Y_t]$ equals $TC_1$. Thus (8.18) becomes

$$C_2 = \frac{1}{T-1}\left[TC_1 - C_1 + \left(\sum_{t=2}^{T} E_2[Y_t] - \sum_{t=2}^{T} E_1[Y_t]\right)\right]$$

$$= C_1 + \frac{1}{T-1}\left(\sum_{t=2}^{T} E_2[Y_t] - \sum_{t=2}^{T} E_1[Y_t]\right). \tag{8.19}$$

Equation (8.19) states that the change in consumption between period 1 and period 2 equals the change in the individual's estimate of his or her lifetime resources divided by the number of periods of life remaining.

Finally, note that the individual's behavior exhibits certainty equivalence: as (8.14) shows, the individual consumes the amount he or she would if his or her future incomes were certain to equal their means; that is, uncertainty about future income has no impact on consumption.

To see the intuition for this certainty-equivalence behavior, consider the Euler equation relating consumption in periods 1 and 2. With a general instantaneous utility function, this condition is

$$u'(C_1) = E_1[u'(C_2)]. \tag{8.20}$$

When utility is quadratic, marginal utility is linear. Thus the expected marginal utility of consumption is the same as the marginal utility of expected consumption. That is, since $E_1[1 - aC_2] = 1 - aE_1[C_2]$, for quadratic utility (8.20) is equivalent to

$$u'(C_1) = u'(E_1[C_2]). \tag{8.21}$$

This implies $C_1 = E_1[C_2]$.

This analysis shows that quadratic utility is the source of certainty-equivalence behavior: if utility is not quadratic, marginal utility is not linear, and so (8.21) does not follow from (8.20). We return to this point in Section 8.6.[5]

# 8.3   Empirical Application: Two Tests of the Random-Walk Hypothesis

Hall's random-walk result ran strongly counter to existing views about consumption.[6] The traditional view of consumption over the business cycle implies that when output declines, consumption declines but is expected to recover; thus it implies that there are predictable movements in consumption. Hall's extension of the permanent-income hypothesis, in contrast, predicts that when output declines unexpectedly, consumption declines only by the amount of the fall in permanent income; as a result, it is not expected to recover.

Because of this divergence in the predictions of the two views, a great deal of effort has been devoted to testing whether predictable changes in income produce predictable changes in consumption. The hypothesis that consumption responds to predictable income movements is referred to as *excess sensitivity* of consumption (Flavin, 1981).[7]

## Campbell and Mankiw's Test Using Aggregate Data

The random-walk hypothesis implies that the change in consumption is unpredictable; thus it implies that no information available at time $t - 1$ can be used to forecast the change in consumption from $t - 1$ to $t$. One approach

---

[5] Although the specific result that the change in consumption has a mean of zero and is unpredictable (equation [8.16]) depends on the assumption of quadratic utility (and on the assumption that the discount rate and the interest rate are equal), the result that departures of consumption growth from its average value are not predictable arises under more general assumptions. See Problem 8.5.

[6] Indeed, when Hall first presented the paper deriving and testing the random-walk result, one prominent macroeconomist told him that he must have been on drugs when he wrote the paper.

[7] The permanent-income hypothesis also makes predictions about how consumption responds to unexpected changes in income. In the model of Section 8.2, for example, the response to news is given by equation (8.19). The hypothesis that consumption responds less than the permanent-income hypothesis predicts to unexpected changes in income is referred to as *excess smoothness* of consumption. Since excess sensitivity concerns expected changes in income and excess smoothness concerns unexpected changes, it is possible for consumption to be excessively sensitive and excessively smooth at the same time. For more on excess smoothness, see Campbell and Deaton (1989); West (1988); Flavin (1993); and Problem 8.6.

to testing the random-walk hypothesis is therefore to regress the change in consumption on variables that are known at $t - 1$. If the random-walk hypothesis is correct, the coefficients on the variables should not differ systematically from zero.

This is the approach that Hall took in his original work. He was unable to reject the hypothesis that lagged values of either income or consumption cannot predict the change in consumption. He did find, however, that lagged stock-price movements have statistically significant predictive power for the change in consumption.

The disadvantage of this approach is that the results are hard to interpret. For example, Hall's result that lagged income does not have strong predictive power for consumption could arise not because predictable changes in income do not produce predictable changes in consumption, but because lagged values of income are of little use in predicting income movements. Similarly, it is hard to gauge the importance of the rejection of the random-walk prediction using stock-price data.

Campbell and Mankiw (1989) therefore use an instrumental-variables approach to test Hall's hypothesis against a specific alternative. The alternative they consider is that some fraction of consumers simply spend their current income, and the remainder behave according to Hall's theory. This alternative implies that the change in consumption from period $t - 1$ to period $t$ equals the change in income between $t - 1$ and $t$ for the first group of consumers, and equals the change in estimated permanent income between $t - 1$ and $t$ for the second group. Thus if we let $\lambda$ denote the fraction of consumption that is done by consumers in the first group, the change in aggregate consumption is

$$
\begin{aligned}
C_t - C_{t-1} &= \lambda(Y_t - Y_{t-1}) + (1 - \lambda)e_t \\
&\equiv \lambda Z_t + \nu_t,
\end{aligned}
\tag{8.22}
$$

where $e_t$ is the change in consumers' estimate of their permanent income from $t - 1$ to $t$.

$Z_t$ and $\nu_t$ are almost surely correlated. Times when income increases greatly are usually also times when households receive favorable news about their total lifetime incomes. But this means that the right-hand-side variable in (8.22) is positively correlated with the error term. Thus estimating (8.22) by OLS leads to estimates of $\lambda$ that are biased upward.

As described in Section 4.4, the solution to correlation between the right-hand-side variable and the error term is to use IV rather than OLS. The usual problem in using IV is finding valid instruments: it is often hard to find variables that one can be confident are uncorrelated with the residual. But in cases where the residual reflects new information between $t - 1$ and $t$, theory tells us that there are many candidate instruments: any variable that is known as of time $t - 1$ is uncorrelated with the residual. Campbell and Mankiw's specification therefore implies that there are many variables that can be used as instruments.

To carry out their test, Campbell and Mankiw measure consumption as real purchases of consumer nondurables and services per person, and income as real disposable income per person. The data are quarterly, and the sample period is 1953–1986. They consider various sets of instruments. They find that lagged changes in income have almost no predictive power for future changes. This suggests that Hall's failure to find predictive power of lagged income movements for consumption is not strong evidence against the traditional view of consumption. As a base case, they therefore use lagged values of the change in consumption as instruments. When three lags are used, the estimate of $\lambda$ is 0.42, with a standard error of 0.16; when five lags are used, the estimate is 0.52, with a standard error of 0.13. Other specifications yield similar results.

Thus Campbell and Mankiw's estimates suggest quantitatively large and statistically significant departures from the predictions of the random-walk model: consumption appears to increase by about fifty cents in response to an anticipated one-dollar increase in income, and the null hypothesis of no effect is strongly rejected. At the same time, the estimates of $\lambda$ are far below 1. Thus the results also suggest that the permanent-income hypothesis is important to understanding consumption.[8]

## Shea's Test Using Household Data

Testing the random-walk hypothesis with aggregate data has several disadvantages. Most obviously, the number of observations is small. In addition, it is difficult to find variables with much predictive power for changes in income; it is therefore hard to test the key prediction of the random-walk hypothesis that predictable changes in income are not associated with predictable changes in consumption. Finally, the theory concerns individuals' consumption, and additional assumptions are needed for the predictions of the model to apply to aggregate data. Entry and exit of households from

---

[8] In addition, the instrumental-variables approach has *overidentifying restrictions* that can be tested. If the lagged changes in consumption are valid instruments, they are uncorrelated with $v$. This implies that once we have extracted all the information in the instruments about income growth, they should have no additional predictive power for the left-hand-side variable: if they do, that means that they are correlated with $v$, and thus that they are not valid instruments. This implication can be tested by regressing the estimated residuals from (8.22) on the instruments and testing whether the instruments have any explanatory power. Specifically, one can show that under the null hypothesis of valid instruments, the $R^2$ of this regression times the number of observations is asymptotically distributed $\chi^2$ with degrees of freedom equal to the number of overidentifying restrictions—that is, the number of instruments minus the number of endogenous variables.

In Campbell and Mankiw's case, this $TR^2$ statistic is distributed $\chi^2_2$ when three lags of the change in consumption are used, and $\chi^2_4$ when five lags are used. The values of the test statistic in the two cases are only 1.83 and 2.94; these are only in the 59th and 43rd percentiles of the relevant $\chi^2$ distributions. Thus the hypothesis that the instruments are valid cannot be rejected.

the population, for example, can cause the predictions of the theory to fail in the aggregate even if they hold for each household individually.

Because of these considerations, many investigators have examined consumption behavior using data on individual households. Shea (1995) takes particular care to identify predictable changes in income. He focuses on households in the PSID with wage-earners covered by long-term union contracts. For these households, the wage increases and cost-of-living provisions in the contracts cause income growth to have an important predictable component.

Shea constructs a sample of 647 observations where the union contract provides clear information about the household's future earnings. A regression of actual real wage growth on the estimate constructed from the union contract and some control variables produces a coefficient on the constructed measure of 0.86, with a standard error of 0.20. Thus the union contract has important predictive power for changes in earnings.

Shea then regresses consumption growth on this measure of expected wage growth; the permanent-income hypothesis predicts that the coefficient should be 0.[9] The estimated coefficient is in fact 0.89, with a standard error of 0.46. Thus Shea also finds a quantitatively large (though only marginally statistically significant) departure from the random-walk prediction.

Recall that in our analysis in Sections 8.1 and 8.2, we assumed that households can borrow without limit as long as they eventually repay their debts. One reason that consumption might not follow a random walk is that this assumption might fail—that is, that households might face *liquidity constraints.* If households are unable to borrow and their current income is less than their permanent income, their consumption is determined by their current income. In this case, predictable changes in income produce predictable changes in consumption.

Shea tests for liquidity constraints in two ways. First, following Zeldes (1989) and others, he divides the households according to whether they have liquid assets. Households with liquid assets can smooth their consumption by running down these assets rather than by borrowing. Thus if liquidity constraints are the reason that predictable wage changes affect consumption growth, the prediction of the permanent-income hypothesis will fail only among the households with no assets. Shea finds, however, that the estimated effect of expected wage growth on consumption is essentially the same in the two groups.

Second, following Altonji and Siow (1987), Shea splits the low-wealth sample according to whether the expected change in the real wage is positive or

---

[9] An alternative would be to follow Campbell and Mankiw's approach and regress consumption growth on actual income growth by instrumental variables, using the constructed wage growth measure as an instrument. Given the almost one-for-one relationship between actual and constructed earnings growth, this approach would probably produce similar results.

negative. Individuals facing expected declines in income need to save rather than borrow to smooth their consumption. Thus if liquidity constraints are important, predictable wage increases produce predictable consumption increases, but predictable wage decreases do not produce predictable consumption decreases.

Shea's findings are the opposite of this. For the households with positive expected income growth, the estimated impact of the expected change in the real wage on consumption growth is 0.06 (with a standard error of 0.79); for the households with negative expected growth, the estimated effect is 2.24 (with a standard error of 0.95). Thus there is no evidence that liquidity constraints are the source of Shea's results.

## Discussion

Many other researchers have obtained findings similar to Campbell and Mankiw's and Shea's. For example, Parker (1999), Souleles (1999), Shapiro and Slemrod (2003), and Johnson, Parker, and Souleles (2006) identify features of government policy that cause predictable income movements. Parker focuses on the fact that workers do not pay social security taxes once their wage income for the year exceeds a certain level; Souleles examines income-tax refunds; and Shapiro and Slemrod and Johnson, Parker, and Souleles consider the distribution of tax rebates in 2001. All these authors find that the predictable changes in income resulting from the policies are associated with substantial predictable changes in consumption.

This pattern appears to break down, however, when the predictable movements in income are large and regular. Paxson (1993), Browning and Collado (2001), and Hsieh (2003) consider predictable income movements that are often 10 percent or more of a family's annual income. In Paxson's and Browning and Collado's cases, the movements stem from seasonal fluctuations in labor income; in Hsieh's case, they stem from the state of Alaska's annual payments to its residents from its oil royalties. In all three cases, the permanent-income hypothesis describes consumption behavior well.

Cyclical fluctuations in income are much smaller and much less obviously predictable than the movements considered by Paxson, Browning and Collado, and Hsieh. Thus the behavior of consumption over the business cycle seems more likely to resemble its behavior in response to the income movements considered by Shea and others than to resemble its behavior in response to the movements considered by Paxson and others. Certainly Campbell and Mankiw's findings are consistent with this view.

At the same time, it is possible that cyclical income fluctuations are different in some important way from the variations caused by contracts and the tax code; for example, they may be more salient to consumers. As a result, the behavior of consumption in response to aggregate income fluctuations could be closer to the predictions of the permanent-income hypothesis.

Unfortunately, it appears that only aggregate data can resolve the issue. And although those data point against the permanent-income hypothesis, they are far from decisive.

# 8.4   The Interest Rate and Saving

An important issue concerning consumption involves its response to rates of return. For example, many economists have argued that more favorable tax treatment of interest income would increase saving, and thus increase growth. But if consumption is relatively unresponsive to the rate of return, such policies would have little effect. Understanding the impact of rates of return on consumption is thus important.

## The Interest Rate and Consumption Growth

We begin by extending the analysis of consumption under certainty in Section 8.1 to allow for a nonzero interest rate. This largely repeats material in Section 2.2; for convenience, however, we quickly repeat that analysis here.

Once we allow for a nonzero interest rate, the individual's budget constraint is that the present value of lifetime consumption not exceed initial wealth plus the present value of lifetime labor income. For the case of a constant interest rate and a lifetime of $T$ periods, this constraint is

$$\sum_{t=1}^{T} \frac{1}{(1+r)^t} C_t \le A_0 + \sum_{t=1}^{T} \frac{1}{(1+r)^t} Y_t, \tag{8.23}$$

where $r$ is the interest rate and where all variables are discounted to period 0.

When we allow for a nonzero interest rate, it is also useful to allow for a nonzero discount rate. In addition, it simplifies the analysis to assume that the instantaneous utility function takes the constant-relative-risk-aversion form used in Chapter 2: $u(C_t) = C_t^{1-\theta}/(1-\theta)$, where $\theta$ is the coefficient of relative risk aversion (the inverse of the elasticity of substitution between consumption at different dates). Thus the utility function, (8.1), becomes

$$U = \sum_{t=1}^{T} \frac{1}{(1+\rho)^t} \frac{C_t^{1-\theta}}{1-\theta}, \tag{8.24}$$

where $\rho$ is the discount rate.

Now consider our usual experiment of a decrease in consumption in some period, period $t$, accompanied by an increase in consumption in the next period by $1+r$ times the amount of the decrease. Optimization requires that a marginal change of this type has no effect on lifetime utility. Since the marginal utilities of consumption in periods $t$ and $t+1$ are $C_t^{-\theta}/(1+\rho)^t$

and $C_{t+1}^{-\theta}/(1+\rho)^{t+1}$, this condition is

$$\frac{1}{(1+\rho)^t}C_t^{-\theta} = (1+r)\frac{1}{(1+\rho)^{t+1}}C_{t+1}^{-\theta}. \tag{8.25}$$

We can rearrange this condition to obtain

$$\frac{C_{t+1}}{C_t} = \left(\frac{1+r}{1+\rho}\right)^{1/\theta}. \tag{8.26}$$

This analysis implies that once we allow for the possibility that the real interest rate and the discount rate are not equal, consumption need not be a random walk: consumption is rising over time if $r$ exceeds $\rho$ and falling if $r$ is less than $\rho$. In addition, if there are variations in the real interest rate, there are variations in the predictable component of consumption growth. Hansen and Singleton (1983), Hall (1988b), Campbell and Mankiw (1989), and others therefore examine how much consumption growth responds to variations in the real interest rate. For the most part they find that it responds relatively little, which suggests that the intertemporal elasticity of substitution is low (that is, that $\theta$ is high).

## The Interest Rate and Saving in the Two-Period Case

Although an increase in the interest rate reduces the ratio of first-period to second-period consumption, it does not necessarily follow that the increase reduces first-period consumption and thereby raises saving. The complication is that the change in the interest rate has not only a substitution effect, but also an income effect. Specifically, if the individual is a net saver, the increase in the interest rate allows him or her to attain a higher path of consumption than before.

The qualitative issues can be seen in the case where the individual lives for only two periods. For this case, we can use the standard indifference-curve diagram shown in Figure 8.2. For simplicity, assume the individual has no initial wealth. Thus in $(C_1, C_2)$ space, the individual's budget constraint goes through the point $(Y_1, Y_2)$: the individual can choose to consume his or her income each period. The slope of the budget constraint is $-(1+r)$: giving up 1 unit of first-period consumption allows the individual to increase second-period consumption by $1+r$. When $r$ rises, the budget constraint continues to go through $(Y_1, Y_2)$ but becomes steeper; thus it pivots clockwise around $(Y_1, Y_2)$.

In Panel (a), the individual is initially at the point $(Y_1, Y_2)$; that is, saving is initially zero. In this case the increase in $r$ has no income effect—the individual's initial consumption bundle continues to be on the budget constraint. Thus first-period consumption necessarily falls, and so saving necessarily rises.

In Panel (b), $C_1$ is initially less than $Y_1$, and thus saving is positive. In this case the increase in $r$ has a positive income effect—the individual can

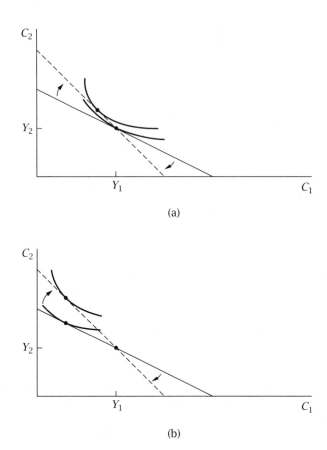

(a)

(b)

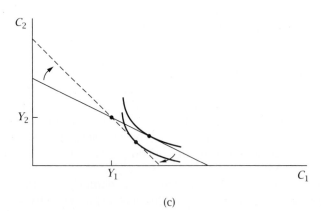

(c)

FIGURE 8.2   The interest rate and consumption choices in the two-period case

now afford strictly more than his or her initial bundle. The income effect acts to decrease saving, whereas the substitution effect acts to increase it. The overall effect is ambiguous; in the case shown in the figure, saving does not change.

Finally, in Panel (c) the individual is initially borrowing. In this case both the substitution and income effects reduce first-period consumption, and so saving necessarily rises.

Since the stock of wealth in the economy is positive, individuals are on average savers rather than borrowers. Thus the overall income effect of a rise in the interest rate is positive. An increase in the interest rate thus has two competing effects on overall saving, a positive one through the substitution effect and a negative one through the income effect.

## Complications

This discussion appears to imply that unless the elasticity of substitution between consumption in different periods is large, increases in the interest rate are unlikely to bring about substantial increases in saving. There are two reasons, however, that the importance of this conclusion is limited.

First, many of the changes we are interested in do not involve just changes in the interest rate. For tax policy, the relevant experiment is usually a change in composition between taxes on interest income and other taxes that leaves government revenue unchanged. As Problem 8.7 shows, such a change has only a substitution effect, and thus necessarily shifts consumption toward the future.

Second, and more subtly, if individuals have long horizons, small changes in saving can accumulate over time into large changes in wealth (Summers, 1981a). To see this, first consider an individual with an infinite horizon and constant labor income. Suppose that the interest rate equals the individual's discount rate. From (8.26), this means that the individual's consumption is constant. The budget constraint then implies that the individual consumes the sum of interest and labor incomes: any higher steady level of consumption implies violating the budget constraint, and any lower level implies failing to satisfy the constraint with equality. That is, the individual maintains his or her initial wealth level regardless of its value: the individual is willing to hold any amount of wealth if $r = \rho$. A similar analysis shows that if $r > \rho$, the individual's wealth grows without bound, and that if $r < \rho$, his or her wealth falls without bound. Thus the long-run supply of capital is perfectly elastic at $r = \rho$.

Summers shows that similar, though less extreme, results hold in the case of long but finite lifetimes. Suppose, for example, that $r$ is slightly larger than $\rho$, that the intertemporal elasticity of substitution is small, and that labor income is constant. The facts that $r$ exceeds $\rho$ and that the elasticity of substitution is small imply that consumption rises slowly over the individual's lifetime. But with a long lifetime, this means that consumption is much larger at the end of life than at the beginning. But since labor income is constant, this in turn implies that the individual gradually builds up considerable savings over the first part of his or her life and gradually decumulates them over the remainder. As a result, when horizons are finite but long, wealth holdings may be highly responsive to the interest rate in the long run even if the intertemporal elasticity of substitution is small.[10]

## 8.5   Consumption and Risky Assets

Individuals can invest in many assets, almost all of which have uncertain returns. Extending our analysis to account for multiple assets and risk raises some new issues concerning both household behavior and asset markets.

### The Conditions for Individual Optimization

Consider an individual reducing consumption in period $t$ by an infinitesimal amount and using the resulting saving to buy an asset, $i$, that produces a potentially uncertain stream of payoffs, $D^i_{t+1}, D^i_{t+2}, \ldots$. If the individual is optimizing, the marginal utility he or she forgoes from the reduced consumption in period $t$ must equal the expected sum of the discounted marginal utilities of the future consumption provided by the asset's payoffs. If we let $P^i_t$ denote the price of the asset, this condition is

$$u'(C_t)P^i_t = E_t\left[\sum_{k=1}^{\infty} \frac{1}{(1+\rho)^k} u'(C_{t+k})D^i_{t+k}\right] \qquad \text{for all } i. \qquad (8.27)$$

To see the implications (8.27), suppose the individual holds the asset for only one period, and define the return on the asset, $r^i_{t+1}$, by $r^i_{t+1} = \left(\frac{D^i_{t+1}}{P^i_t}\right) - 1$. (Note that here the payoff to the asset, $D^i_{t+1}$, includes not only any dividend payouts in period $t+1$, but also any proceeds from selling the asset.) Then (8.27) becomes

$$u'(C_t) = \frac{1}{1+\rho} E_t\left[\left(1 + r^i_{t+1}\right)u'(C_{t+1})\right] \qquad \text{for all } i. \qquad (8.28)$$

Since the expectation of the product of two variables equals the product of their expectations plus their covariance, we can rewrite this expression as

$$u'(C_t) = \frac{1}{1+\rho}\Big\{E_t\big[1 + r^i_{t+1}\big]E_t[u'(C_{t+1})] \\ + \text{Cov}_t\big(1 + r^i_{t+1}, u'(C_{t+1})\big)\Big\} \quad \text{for all } i, \qquad (8.29)$$

where $\text{Cov}_t(\bullet)$ is covariance conditional on information available at time $t$.

---

[10] Carroll (1997) shows, however, that the presence of uncertainty weakens this conclusion.

If we assume that utility is quadratic, $u(C) = C - aC^2/2$, then the marginal utility of consumption is $1 - aC$. Using this to substitute for the covariance term in (8.29), we obtain

$$u'(C_t) = \frac{1}{1+\rho} \left\{ E_t\left[1 + r_{t+1}^i\right] E_t[u'(C_{t+1})] - a\text{Cov}_t\left(1 + r_{t+1}^i, C_{t+1}\right) \right\}. \quad (8.30)$$

Equation (8.30) implies that in deciding whether to hold more of an asset, the individual is not concerned with how risky the asset is: the variance of the asset's return does not appear in (8.30). Intuitively, a marginal increase in holdings of an asset that is risky, but whose risk is not correlated with the overall risk the individual faces, does not increase the variance of the individual's consumption. Thus in evaluating that marginal decision, the individual considers only the asset's expected return.

Equation (8.30) implies that the aspect of riskiness that matters to the decision of whether to hold more of an asset is the relation between the asset's payoff and consumption. Suppose, for example, that the individual is given an opportunity to buy a new asset whose expected return equals the rate of return on a risk-free asset that the individual is already able to buy. If the payoff to the new asset is typically high when the marginal utility of consumption is high (that is, when consumption is low), buying one unit of the asset raises expected utility by more than buying one unit of the risk-free asset. Thus (since the individual was previously indifferent about buying more of the risk-free asset), the individual can raise his or her expected utility by buying the new asset. As the individual invests more in the asset, his or her consumption comes to depend more on the asset's payoff, and so the covariance between consumption and the asset's return becomes less negative. In the example we are considering, since the asset's expected return equals the risk-free rate, the individual invests in the asset until the covariance of its return with consumption reaches zero.

This discussion implies that hedging risks is crucial to optimal portfolio choices. A steelworker whose future labor income depends on the health of the U.S. steel industry should avoid—or better yet, sell short—assets whose returns are positively correlated with the fortunes of the steel industry, such as shares in U.S. steel companies. Instead the worker should invest in assets whose returns move inversely with the health of the U.S. steel industry, such as foreign steel companies or U.S. aluminum companies.

One implication of this analysis is that individuals should exhibit no particular tendency to hold shares of companies that operate in the individuals' own countries. In fact, because the analysis implies that individuals should avoid assets whose returns are correlated with other sources of risk to their consumption, it implies that their holdings should be skewed against domestic companies. For example, for plausible parameter values it predicts that the typical person in the United States should sell U.S. stocks short (Baxter and Jermann, 1997). In fact, however, individuals' portfolios are very heavily skewed toward domestic companies (French and Poterba, 1991). This pattern is known as *home bias.*

## The Consumption CAPM

This discussion takes assets' expected returns as given. But individuals' demands for assets determine these expected returns. If, for example, an asset's payoff is highly correlated with consumption, its price must be driven down to the point where its expected return is high for individuals to hold it.

To see the implications of this observation for asset prices, suppose that all individuals are the same, and return to the general first-order condition, (8.27). Solving this expression for $P_t^i$ yields

$$P_t^i = E_t \left[ \sum_{k=1}^{\infty} \frac{1}{(1+\rho)^k} \frac{u'(C_{t+k})}{u'(C_t)} D_{t+k}^i \right]. \tag{8.31}$$

The term $[1/(1+\rho)^k]u'(C_{t+k})/u'(C_t)$ shows how the consumer values future payoffs, and therefore how much he or she is willing to pay for various assets. It is referred to as the *pricing kernel* or *stochastic discount factor.* Similarly, we can find the implications of our analysis for expected returns by solving (8.30) for $E_t[1 + r_{t+1}^i]$:

$$E_t\left[1 + r_{t+1}^i\right] = \frac{1}{E_t[u'(C_{t+1})]} \left[(1+\rho)u'(C_t) + a\mathrm{Cov}_t\left(1 + r_{t+1}^i, C_{t+1}\right)\right]. \tag{8.32}$$

Equation (8.32) states that the higher the covariance of an asset's payoff with consumption, the higher its expected return must be.

We can simplify (8.32) by considering the return on a risk-free asset. If the payoff to an asset is certain, then the covariance of its payoff with consumption is zero. Thus the risk-free rate, $\bar{r}_{t+1}$, satisfies

$$1 + \bar{r}_{t+1} = \frac{(1+\rho)u'(C_t)}{E_t[u'(C_{t+1})]}. \tag{8.33}$$

Subtracting (8.33) from (8.32) gives

$$E_t\left[r_{t+1}^i\right] - \bar{r}_{t+1} = \frac{a\mathrm{Cov}_t\left(1 + r_{t+1}^i, C_{t+1}\right)}{E_t[u'(C_{t+1})]}. \tag{8.34}$$

Equation (8.34) states that the expected-return premium that an asset must offer relative to the risk-free rate is proportional to the covariance of its return with consumption.

This model of the determination of expected asset returns is known as the *consumption capital-asset pricing model,* or *consumption CAPM.* The coefficient from a regression of an asset's return on consumption growth is known as its *consumption beta*. Thus the central prediction of the consumption CAPM is that the premiums that assets offer are proportional to their consumption betas (Breeden, 1979; see also Merton, 1973, and Rubinstein, 1976).[11]

## Empirical Application: The Equity-Premium Puzzle

One of the most important implications of this analysis of assets' expected returns concerns the case where the risky asset is a broad portfolio of stocks. To see the issues involved, it is easiest to return to the Euler equation, (8.28), and to assume that individuals have constant-relative-risk-aversion utility rather than quadratic utility. With this assumption, the Euler equation becomes

$$C_t^{-\theta} = \frac{1}{1+\rho} E_t \left[ \left( 1 + r_{t+1}^i \right) C_{t+1}^{-\theta} \right], \tag{8.35}$$

where $\theta$ is the coefficient of relative risk aversion. If we divide both sides by $C_t^{-\theta}$ and multiply both sides by $1 + \rho$, this expression becomes

$$1 + \rho = E_t \left[ \left( 1 + r_{t+1}^i \right) \frac{C_{t+1}^{-\theta}}{C_t^{-\theta}} \right]. \tag{8.36}$$

Finally, it is convenient to let $g_{t+1}^c$ denote the growth rate of consumption from $t$ to $t+1$, $(C_{t+1}/C_t) - 1$, and to omit the time subscripts. Thus we have

$$E[(1 + r^i)(1 + g^c)^{-\theta}] = 1 + \rho. \tag{8.37}$$

To see the implications of (8.37), we take a second-order Taylor approximation of the left-hand side around $r = g = 0$. Computing the relevant derivatives yields

$$(1 + r)(1 + g)^{-\theta} \simeq 1 + r - \theta g - \theta gr + \tfrac{1}{2}\theta(\theta + 1)g^2. \tag{8.38}$$

Thus we can rewrite (8.37) as

$$E[r^i] - \theta E[g^c] - \theta\{E[r^i]E[g^c] + \text{Cov}(r^i, g^c)\}$$
$$+ \tfrac{1}{2}\theta(\theta + 1)\{(E[g^c])^2 + \text{Var}(g^c)\} \simeq \rho. \tag{8.39}$$

---

[11] The original CAPM assumes that investors are concerned with the mean and variance of the return on their portfolio rather than the mean and variance of consumption. That version of the model therefore focuses on *market betas*—that is, coefficients from regressions of assets' returns on the returns on the market portfolio—and predicts that expected-return premiums are proportional to market betas (Lintner, 1965, and Sharpe, 1964).

When the time period involved is short, the $E[r^i]E[g^c]$ and $(E[g^c])^2$ terms are small relative to the others.[12] Omitting these terms and solving the resulting expression for $E[r^i]$ yields

$$E[r^i] \simeq \rho + \theta E[g^c] + \theta \text{Cov}(r^i, g^c) - \tfrac{1}{2}\theta(\theta+1)\text{Var}(g^c). \qquad (8.40)$$

Equation (8.40) implies that the difference between the expected returns on two assets, $i$ and $j$, satisfies

$$\begin{aligned}
E[r^i] - E[r^j] &= \theta \text{Cov}(r^i, g^c) - \theta \text{Cov}(r^j, g^c) \\
&= \theta \text{Cov}(r^i - r^j, g^c).
\end{aligned} \qquad (8.41)$$

In a famous paper, Mehra and Prescott (1985) show that it is difficult to reconcile observed returns on stocks and bonds with equation (8.41). Mankiw and Zeldes (1991) report a simple calculation that shows the essence of the problem. For the United States during the period 1890–1979 (which is the sample that Mehra and Prescott consider), the difference between the average return on the stock market and the return on short-term government debt—the *equity premium*—is about 6 percentage points. Over the same period, the standard deviation of the growth of consumption (as measured by real purchases of nondurables and services) is 3.6 percentage points, and the standard deviation of the excess return on the market is 16.7 percentage points; the correlation between these two quantities is 0.40. These figures imply that the covariance of consumption growth and the excess return on the market is 0.40(0.036)(0.167), or 0.0024.

Equation (8.41) therefore implies that the coefficient of relative risk aversion needed to account for the equity premium is the solution to $0.06 = \theta(0.0024)$, or $\theta = 25$. This is an extraordinary level of risk aversion; it implies, for example, that individuals would rather accept a 17 percent reduction in consumption with certainty than risk a 50-50 chance of a 20 percent reduction. As Mehra and Prescott describe, other evidence suggests that risk aversion is much lower than this. Among other things, such a high degree of aversion to variations in consumption makes it puzzling that the average risk-free rate is close to zero despite the fact that consumption is growing over time.

Furthermore, the equity-premium puzzle has become more severe in the period since Mehra and Prescott identified it. From 1979 to 2008, the average equity premium is 7 percentage points, which is slightly higher than in Mehra and Prescott's sample period. More importantly, consumption growth has become more stable and less correlated with returns: the standard deviation of consumption growth over this period is 1.1 percentage points, the standard deviation of the excess market return is 14.2 percentage points, and the correlation between these two quantities is 0.33. These figures

---

[12] Indeed, for the continuous-time case, one can derive equation (8.40) without any approximations.

imply a coefficient of relative risk aversion of $0.07/[0.33(0.011)(0.142)]$, or about 140.

The large equity premium, particularly when coupled with the low risk-free rate, is thus difficult to reconcile with household optimization. This *equity-premium puzzle* has stimulated a large amount of research, and many explanations for it have been proposed. No clear resolution of the puzzle has been provided, however.[13]

# 8.6 Beyond the Permanent-Income Hypothesis

## Background: Buffer-Stock Saving

The permanent-income hypothesis provides appealing explanations of many important features of consumption. For example, it explains why temporary tax cuts appear to have much smaller effects than permanent ones, and it accounts for many features of the relationship between current income and consumption, such as those described in Section 8.1.

Yet there are also important features of consumption that appear inconsistent with the permanent-income hypothesis. For example, as described in Section 8.3, both macroeconomic and microeconomic evidence suggest that consumption often responds to predictable changes in income. And as we just saw, simple models of consumer optimization cannot account for the equity premium.

Indeed, the permanent-income hypothesis fails to explain some central features of consumption behavior. One of the hypothesis's key predictions is that there should be no relation between the expected growth of an individual's income over his or her lifetime and the expected growth of his or her consumption: consumption growth is determined by the real interest rate and the discount rate, not by the time pattern of income.

Carroll and Summers (1991) present extensive evidence that this prediction of the permanent-income hypothesis is incorrect. For example, individuals in countries where income growth is high typically have high rates of consumption growth over their lifetimes, and individuals in slowly growing countries typically have low rates of consumption growth. Similarly, typical

---

[13] Proposed explanations include incomplete markets and transactions costs (Mankiw, 1986; Mankiw and Zeldes, 1991; Heaton and Lucas, 1996; Luttmer, 1999; and Problem 8.11); habit formation (Constantinides, 1990; Campbell and Cochrane, 1999); nonexpected utility (Weil, 1989b; Epstein and Zin, 1991; Bekaert, Hodrick, and Marshall, 1997); concern about equity returns for reasons other than just their implications for consumption (Benartzi and Thaler, 1995; Barberis, Huang, and Santos, 2001); gradual adjustment of consumption (Gabaix and Laibson, 2001; Parker, 2001); and a small probability of a catastrophic decline in consumption and equity prices (Barro, 2006).

lifetime consumption patterns of individuals in different occupations tend to match typical lifetime income patterns in those occupations. Managers and professionals, for example, generally have earnings profiles that rise steeply until middle age and then level off; their consumption profiles follow a similar pattern.

More generally, most households have little wealth (see, for example, Wolff, 1998). Their consumption approximately tracks their income. As a result, as described in Section 8.3, their current income has a large role in determining their consumption. Nonetheless, these households have a small amount of saving that they use in the event of sharp falls in income or emergency spending needs. In the terminology of Deaton (1991), most households exhibit *buffer-stock* saving behavior. As a result, a small fraction of households hold the vast majority of wealth.

These failings of the permanent-income hypothesis have motivated a large amount of work on extensions or alternatives to the theory. Three ideas that have received particular attention are precautionary saving, liquidity constraints, and departures from full optimization. This section touches on some of the issues raised by these ideas.[14]

## Precautionary Saving

Recall that our derivation of the random-walk result in Section 8.2 was based on the assumption that utility is quadratic. Quadratic utility implies, however, that marginal utility reaches zero at some finite level of consumption and then becomes negative. It also implies that the utility cost of a given variance of consumption is independent of the level of consumption. This means that, since the marginal utility of consumption is declining, individuals have increasing absolute risk aversion: the amount of consumption they are willing to give up to avoid a given amount of uncertainty about the level of consumption rises as they become wealthier. These difficulties with quadratic utility suggest that marginal utility falls more slowly as consumption rises. That is, the third derivative of utility is almost certainly positive rather than zero.

To see the effects of a positive third derivative, assume that both the real interest rate and the discount rate are zero, and consider again the Euler equation relating consumption in consecutive periods, equation (8.20):

---

[14] Four extensions of the permanent-income hypothesis that we will not discuss are durability of consumption goods, habit formation, nonexpected utility, and complementarity between consumption and employment. For durability, see Mankiw (1982); Caballero (1990, 1993); Eberly (1994); and Problem 8.12. For habit formation, see Carroll, Overland, and Weil (1997); Dynan (2000); Fuhrer (2000); Canzoneri, Cumby, and Diba (2007); and Problem 8.13. For nonexpected utility, see Weil (1989b, 1990) and Epstein and Zin (1989, 1991). For complementarity, see Benhabib, Rogerson, and Wright (1991), Baxter and Jermann (1999), and Aguiar and Hurst (2005).

$u'(C_t) = E_t[u'(C_{t+1})]$. As described in Section 8.2, if utility is quadratic, marginal utility is linear, and so $E_t[u'(C_{t+1})]$ equals $u'(E_t[C_{t+1}])$. Thus in this case, the Euler equation reduces to $C_t = E_t[C_{t+1}]$. But if $u'''(\bullet)$ is positive, then $u'(C)$ is a convex function of $C$. In this case, $E_t[u'(C_{t+1})]$ exceeds $u'(E_t[C_{t+1}])$. But this means that if $C_t$ and $E_t[C_{t+1}]$ are equal, $E_t[u'(C_{t+1})]$ is greater than $u'(C_t)$, and so a marginal reduction in $C_t$ increases expected utility. Thus the combination of a positive third derivative of the utility function and uncertainty about future income reduces current consumption, and thus raises saving. This saving is known as *precautionary saving* (Leland, 1968).

Panel (a) of Figure 8.3 shows the impact of uncertainty and a positive third derivative of the utility function on the expected marginal utility of consumption. Since $u''(C)$ is negative, $u'(C)$ is decreasing in $C$. And since $u'''(C)$ is positive, $u'(C)$ declines less rapidly as $C$ rises. If consumption takes on only two possible values, $C_L$ and $C_H$, each with probability $\frac{1}{2}$, the expected marginal utility of consumption is the average of marginal utility at these two values. In terms of the diagram, this is shown by the midpoint of the line connecting $u'(C_L)$ and $u'(C_H)$. As the diagram shows, the fact that $u'(C)$ is convex implies that this quantity is larger than marginal utility at the average value of consumption, $(C_L + C_H)/2$.

Panel (b) depicts an increase in uncertainty. In particular, the low value of consumption, $C_L$, falls, and the high value, $C_H$, rises, with no change in their mean. When the high value of consumption rises, the fact that $u'''(C)$ is positive means that marginal utility falls relatively little; but when the low value falls, the positive third derivative magnifies the rise in marginal utility. As a result, the increase in uncertainty raises expected marginal utility for a given value of expected consumption. Thus the increase in uncertainty raises the incentive to save.

An important question, of course, is whether precautionary saving is quantitatively important. To address this issue, recall equation (8.40) from our analysis of the equity premium: $E[r^i] \simeq \rho + \theta E[g^c] + \theta \text{Cov}(r^i, g^c) - \frac{1}{2}\theta(\theta + 1)\text{Var}(g^c)$. If we consider a risk-free asset and assume $\bar{r} = \rho$ for simplicity, this expression becomes

$$\rho \simeq \rho + \theta E[g^c] - \tfrac{1}{2}\theta(\theta + 1)\text{Var}(g^c), \tag{8.42}$$

or

$$E[g^c] \simeq \tfrac{1}{2}(\theta + 1)\text{Var}(g^c). \tag{8.43}$$

Thus the impact of precautionary saving on expected consumption growth depends on the variance of consumption growth and the coefficient of relative risk aversion.[15] If both are substantial, precautionary saving can have a large effect on expected consumption growth. If the coefficient of relative risk aversion is 4 (which is toward the high end of values that are viewed

---

[15] For a general utility function, the $\theta + 1$ term is replaced by $-Cu'''(C)/u''(C)$. In analogy to the coefficient of relative risk aversion, $-Cu''(C)/u'(C)$, Kimball (1990) refers to $-Cu'''(C)/u''(C)$ as the coefficient of relative prudence.

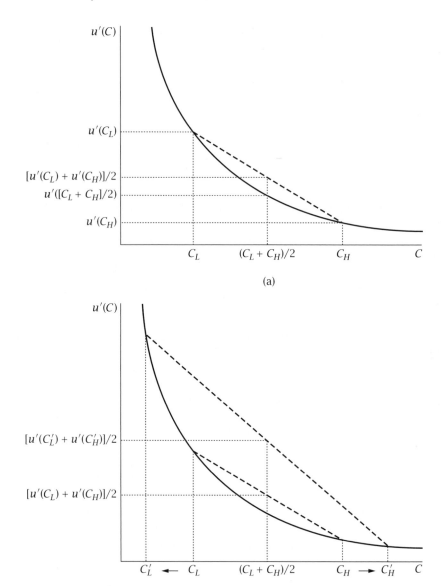

**FIGURE 8.3   The effects of a positive third derivative of the utility function on the expected marginal utility of consumption**

as plausible), and the standard deviation of households' uncertainty about their consumption 1 year ahead is 0.1 (which is consistent with the evidence in Dynan, 1993, and Carroll, 1992), (8.43) implies that precautionary saving raises expected consumption growth by $\frac{1}{2}(4 + 1)(0.1)^2$, or 2.5 percentage points.

This analysis implies that precautionary saving raises expected consumption growth; that is, it decreases current consumption and thus increases saving. But one of the basic features of household behavior we are trying to understand is that most households save very little. Carroll (1992, 1997) argues that the key to understanding this phenomenon is a combination of a precautionary motive for saving and a high discount rate. The high discount rate acts to decrease saving, offsetting the effect of the precautionary-saving motive.

This hypothesis does not, however, provide a reason for the two forces to approximately balance, so that savings are typically close to zero. Rather, this view implies that households that are particularly impatient, that have particularly steep paths of expected income, or that have particularly weak precautionary-saving motives will have consumption far in excess of income early in life. Explaining the fact that there are not many such households requires something further.[16]

## Liquidity Constraints

The permanent-income hypothesis assumes that individuals can borrow at the same interest rate at which they can save as long as they eventually repay their loans. Yet the interest rates that households pay on credit card debt, automobile loans, and other borrowing are often much higher than the rates they obtain on their savings. In addition, some individuals are unable to borrow more at any interest rate.

Liquidity constraints can raise saving in two ways. First, and most obviously, whenever a liquidity constraint is binding, it causes the individual to consume less than he or she otherwise would. Second, as Zeldes (1989) emphasizes, even if the constraints are not currently binding, the fact that they may bind in the future reduces current consumption. Suppose, for example, there is some chance of low income in the next period. If there are no liquidity constraints, and if income in fact turns out to be low, the individual can borrow to avoid a sharp fall in consumption. If there are liquidity constraints, however, the fall in income causes a large fall in consumption unless the individual has savings. Thus the presence of liquidity constraints causes individuals to save as insurance against the effects of future falls in income.

---

[16] Carroll points out that an extreme precautionary-saving motive can in fact account for the fact that there are not many such households. Suppose the marginal utility of consumption approaches infinity as consumption approaches some low level, $C_0$. Then households will make certain their consumption is always above this level. As a result, they will choose to limit their debt if there is *any* chance of their income path being only slightly above the level that would finance steady consumption at $C_0$. But plausible changes in assumptions (such as introducing income-support programs or assuming large but finite marginal utility at $C_0$) eliminate this result.

These points can be seen in a three-period model. To distinguish the effects of liquidity constraints from precautionary saving, assume that the instantaneous utility function is quadratic. In addition, continue to assume that the real interest rate and the discount rate are zero.

Begin by considering the individual's behavior in period 2. Let $A_t$ denote assets at the end of period $t$. Since the individual lives for only three periods, $C_3$ equals $A_2 + Y_3$, which in turn equals $A_1 + Y_2 + Y_3 - C_2$. The individual's expected utility over the last two periods of life as a function of his or her choice of $C_2$ is therefore

$$U = \left(C_2 - \tfrac{1}{2}aC_2^2\right) + E_2\left[(A_1 + Y_2 + Y_3 - C_2)\right.$$
$$\left. - \tfrac{1}{2}a(A_1 + Y_2 + Y_3 - C_2)^2\right]. \tag{8.44}$$

The derivative of this expression with respect to $C_2$ is

$$\frac{\partial U}{\partial C_2} = 1 - aC_2 - (1 - aE_2[A_1 + Y_2 + Y_3 - C_2])$$
$$= a(A_1 + Y_2 + E_2[Y_3] - 2C_2). \tag{8.45}$$

This expression is positive for $C_2 < (A_1 + Y_2 + E_2[Y_3])/2$, and negative thereafter. Thus, as we know from our earlier analysis, if the liquidity constraint does not bind, the individual chooses $C_2 = (A_1 + Y_2 + E_2[Y_3])/2$. But if it does bind, he or she sets consumption to the maximum attainable level, which is $A_1 + Y_2$. Thus,

$$C_2 = \min\left\{\frac{A_1 + Y_2 + E_2[Y_3]}{2}, A_1 + Y_2\right\}. \tag{8.46}$$

Thus the liquidity constraint reduces current consumption if it is binding.

Now consider the first period. If the liquidity constraint is not binding that period, the individual has the option of marginally raising $C_1$ and paying for this by reducing $C_2$. Thus if the individual's assets are not literally zero, the usual Euler equation holds. With the specific assumptions we are making, this means that $C_1$ equals the expectation of $C_2$.

But the fact that the Euler equation holds does not mean that the liquidity constraints do not affect consumption. Equation (8.46) implies that if the probability that the liquidity constraint will bind in the second period is strictly positive, the expectation of $C_2$ as of period 1 is strictly less than the expectation of $(A_1 + Y_2 + E_2[Y_3])/2$. $A_1$ is given by $A_0 + Y_1 - C_1$, and the law of iterated projections implies that $E_1[E_2[Y_3]]$ equals $E_1[Y_3]$. Thus,

$$C_1 < \frac{A_0 + Y_1 + E_1[Y_2] + E_1[Y_3] - C_1}{2}. \tag{8.47}$$

Adding $C_1/2$ to both sides of this expression and then dividing by $\tfrac{3}{2}$ yields

$$C_1 < \frac{A_0 + Y_1 + E_1[Y_2] + E_1[Y_3]}{3}. \tag{8.48}$$

Thus even when the liquidity constraint does not bind currently, the possibility that it will bind in the future reduces consumption.

Finally, if the value of $C_1$ that satisfies $C_1 = E_1[C_2]$ (given that $C_2$ is determined by [8.46]) is greater than the individual's period-1 resources, $A_0 + Y_1$, the first-period liquidity constraint is binding; in this case the individual consumes $A_0 + Y_1$.

Thus liquidity constraints alone, like precautionary saving alone, raise saving. Explaining why household wealth is often low on the basis of liquidity constraints therefore again requires appealing to a high discount rate. As before, the high discount rate tends to make households want to have high consumption. But with liquidity constraints, consumption cannot systematically exceed income early in life. Instead, households are constrained, and so their consumption follows their income.

The combination of liquidity constraints and impatience can also explain why households typically have some savings. When there are liquidity constraints, a household with no wealth faces asymmetric risks from increases and decreases in income even if its utility is quadratic. A large fall in income forces a corresponding fall in consumption, and thus a large rise in the marginal utility of consumption. In contrast, a large rise in income causes the household to save, and thus leads to only a moderate fall in marginal utility. This is precisely the reason that the possibility of future liquidity constraints lowers consumption. Researchers who have examined this issue quantitatively, however, generally find that this effect is not large enough to account for even the small savings we observe. Thus they typically introduce a precautionary-saving motive as well. The positive third derivative of the utility function increases consumers' desire to insure themselves against the fall in consumption that would result from a fall in income, and so increases the consumers' savings beyond what would come about from liquidity constraints and quadratic utility alone.[17]

## Empirical Application: Credit Limits and Borrowing

In the absence of liquidity constraints, an increase in the amount a particular lender is willing to lend will not affect consumption. But if there are binding liquidity constraints, such an increase will increase the consumption of households that are borrowing as much as they can. Moreover, by making it less likely that households will be up against their borrowing constraints in the future, the increase may raise the consumption of households that are not currently at their constraints.

---

[17] Gourinchas and Parker (2002) extend the analysis of impatience, liquidity constraints, and precautionary savings to the life cycle. Even a fairly impatient household wants to avoid a large drop in consumption at retirement. Gourinchas and Parker find that as a result, it appears that most households are mainly buffer-stock savers early in life but begin accumulating savings for retirement once they reach middle age.

Gross and Souleles (2002) test these predictions by examining the impact of changes in the credit limits on households' credit cards. Their basic regression takes the form:

$$\Delta B_{it} = b_0 \Delta L_{it} + b_1 \Delta L_{i,t-1} + \cdots + b_{12} \Delta L_{i,t-12} + a' X_{it} + e_{it}. \qquad (8.49)$$

Here $i$ indexes households and $t$ months, $B$ is interest-incurring credit-card debt, $L$ is the credit limit, and $X$ is a vector of control variables.

An obvious concern about equation (8.49) is that credit-card issuers might tend to raise credit limits when cardholders are more likely to borrow more. That is, there might be correlation between $e$, which captures other influences on borrowing, and the $\Delta L$ terms. Gross and Souleles take various approaches to dealing with this problem. For example, in most specifications they exclude cases where cardholders request increases in their borrowing limits. Their most compelling approach uses institutional features of how card issuers adjust credit limits that induce variation in $\Delta L$ that is almost certainly unrelated to variations in $e$. Most issuers are unlikely to raise a card's credit limit for a certain number of months after a previous increase, with different issuers doing this for different numbers of months. Gross and Souleles therefore introduce a set of dummy variables, $D^{jn}$, where $D^{jn}_{it}$ equals 1 if and only if household $i$'s card is from issuer $j$ and $i$'s credit limit was increased $n$ months before month $t$. They then estimate (8.49) by instrumental variables, using the $D^{jn}$'s as the instruments.

For Gross and Souleles's basic instrumental-variables specification, the sum of the estimated $b$'s in (8.49) is 0.111, with a standard error of 0.018. That is, a one-dollar increase in the credit limit is associated with an 11-cent increase in borrowing after 12 months. This estimate is highly robust to the estimation technique, control variables, and sample.[18]

Gross and Souleles then ask whether the increased borrowing is confined to households that are borrowing as much as they can. To do this, they split the sample by the utilization rate (the ratio of the credit-card balance to the credit limit) in month $t - 13$ (the month before the earliest $\Delta L$ term in [8.49]). For households with initial utilization rates above 90 percent, the sum of the $b$'s is very large: 0.452 (with a standard error of 0.125). Crucially, however, it remains clearly positive for households with lower utilization rates: 0.158 (with a standard error of 0.060) when the utilization rate is between 50 and 90 percent, and 0.068 (with a standard error of 0.018) when the utilization rate is less than 50 percent. Thus the data support not just the prediction of the theory that changes in liquidity constraints matter for households

---

[18] Gross and Souleles have data on borrowers' other credit-card debt; they find no evidence that the increased borrowing in response to the increases in credit limits lowers other credit-card debt. However, since they do not have complete data on households' balance sheets, they cannot rule out the possibility that the increased borrowing is associated with lower debt of other types or increased asset holdings. But they argue that since interest rates on credit-card debt are quite high, this effect is unlikely to be large.

that are currently constrained, but the more interesting prediction that they matter for households that are not currently constrained but may be in the future.

Gross and Souleles do uncover one important pattern that is at odds with the model, however. Using a separate data set, they find that it is common for households to have both interest-incurring credit-card debt and liquid assets. For example, one-third of households with positive interest-incurring credit-card debt have liquid assets worth more than one month's income. Given the large difference between the interest rates on credit-card debt and liquid assets, these households appear to be forgoing a virtually riskless opportunity to save money. Thus this behavior is puzzling not just for theories of liquidity constraints, but for virtually all theories.

## Departures from Complete Optimization

The assumption of costless optimization is a powerful modeling device, and it provides a good first approximation to how individuals respond to many changes. At the same time, it does not provide a perfect description of how people behave. There are well-documented cases in which individuals appear to depart consistently and systematically from the predictions of standard models of utility maximization, and in which those departures are quantitatively important (see, for example, Tversky and Kahneman, 1974, and Loewenstein and Thaler, 1989). This may be the case with choices between consumption and saving. The calculations involved are complex, the time periods are long, and there is a great deal of uncertainty that is difficult to quantify. So instead of attempting to be completely optimizing, individuals may follow rules of thumb in choosing their consumption (Shefrin and Thaler, 1988). Indeed, such rules of thumb may be the rational response to such factors as computation costs and fundamental uncertainty about how future after-tax income is determined. Examples of possible rules of thumb are that it is usually reasonable to spend one's current income and that assets should be dipped into only in exceptional circumstances. Relying on such rules may lead households to use saving and borrowing to smooth short-run income fluctuations; thus they will typically have some savings, and consumption will follow the predictions of the permanent-income hypothesis reasonably well at short horizons. But such behavior may also cause consumption to track income fairly closely over long horizons; thus savings will typically be small.

One specific departure from full optimization that has received considerable attention is time-inconsistent preferences (for example, Laibson, 1997). There is considerable evidence that individuals (and animals as well) are impatient at short horizons but patient at long horizons. This leads to time inconsistency. Consider, for example, choices concerning consumption over a two-week period. When the period is in the distant future—when it is a year away, for instance—individuals typically have little preference for consumption in the first week over consumption in the second. Thus they prefer roughly equal levels of consumption in the two weeks. When the two weeks arrive, however, individuals often want to depart from their earlier plans and have higher consumption in the first week.

Time inconsistency alone, like the other departures from the baseline model alone, cannot account for the puzzling features of consumption we are trying to understand. By itself, time inconsistency makes consumers act as though they are impatient: at each point in time, individuals value current consumption greatly relative to future consumption, and so their consumption is high (Barro, 1999). And time inconsistency alone provides no reason for consumption to approximately track income for a large number of households, so that their savings are close to zero. Other factors— liquidity constraints, the ability to save in illiquid forms (so that individuals can limit their future ability to indulge the strong preference they feel at each moment for current consumption), and perhaps a precautionary-saving motivation—appear needed for models with time inconsistency to fit the facts (Angeletos, Laibson, Repetto, Tobacman, and Weinberg, 2001).

## Conclusion

Two themes emerge from this discussion. First, no single factor can account for the main departures from the permanent-income hypothesis. Second, there is considerable agreement on the broad factors that must be present: a high degree of impatience (from either a high discount rate or time inconsistency with a perpetually high weight on current consumption); some force preventing consumption from running far ahead of income (either liquidity constraints or rules of thumb that stress the importance of avoiding debt); and a precautionary-saving motive.

# Problems

**8.1. Life-cycle saving.** (Modigliani and Brumberg, 1954.) Consider an individual who lives from 0 to $T$, and whose lifetime utility is given by $U = \int_{t=0}^{T} u(C(t))dt$, where $u'(\bullet) > 0, u''(\bullet) < 0$. The individual's income is $Y_0 + gt$ for $0 \le t < R$, and 0 for $R \le t \le T$. The retirement age, $R$, satisfies $0 < R < T$. The interest rate is zero, the individual has no initial wealth, and there is no uncertainty.

(a) What is the individual's lifetime budget constraint?

(b) What is the individual's utility-maximizing path of consumption, $C(t)$?

(c) What is the path of the individual's wealth as a function of $t$?

**8.2.** The average income of farmers is less than the average income of non-farmers, but fluctuates more from year to year. Given this, how does the permanent-income hypothesis predict that estimated consumption functions for farmers and nonfarmers differ?

8.3. **The time-averaging problem.** (Working, 1960.) Actual data give not consumption at a point in time, but average consumption over an extended period, such as a quarter. This problem asks you to examine the effects of this fact.

Suppose that consumption follows a random walk: $C_t = C_{t-1} + e_t$, where $e$ is white noise. Suppose, however, that the data provide average consumption over two-period intervals; that is, one observes $(C_t + C_{t+1})/2$, $(C_{t+2} + C_{t+3})/2$, and so on.

(a) Find an expression for the change in measured consumption from one two-period interval to the next in terms of the $e$'s.

(b) Is the change in measured consumption uncorrelated with the previous value of the change in measured consumption? In light of this, is measured consumption a random walk?

(c) Given your result in part (a), is the change in consumption from one two-period interval to the next necessarily uncorrelated with anything known as of the first of these two-period intervals? Is it necessarily uncorrelated with anything known as of the two-period interval immediately preceding the first of the two-period intervals?

(d) Suppose that measured consumption for a two-period interval is not the average over the interval, but consumption in the second of the two periods. That is, one observes $C_{t+1}$, $C_{t+3}$, and so on. In this case, is measured consumption a random walk?

8.4. In the model of Section 8.2, uncertainty about future income does not affect consumption. Does this mean that the uncertainty does not affect expected lifetime utility?

8.5. (This follows Hansen and Singleton, 1983.) Suppose instantaneous utility is of the constant-relative-risk-aversion form, $u(C_t) = C_t^{1-\theta}/(1-\theta)$, $\theta > 0$. Assume that the real interest rate, $r$, is constant but not necessarily equal to the discount rate, $\rho$.

(a) Find the Euler equation relating $C_t$ to expectations concerning $C_{t+1}$.

(b) Suppose that the log of income is distributed normally, and that as a result the log of $C_{t+1}$ is distributed normally; let $\sigma^2$ denote its variance conditional on information available at time $t$. Rewrite the expression in part (a) in terms of $\ln C_t$, $E_t[\ln C_{t+1}]$, $\sigma^2$, and the parameters $r$, $\rho$, and $\theta$. (Hint: If a variable $x$ is distributed normally with mean $\mu$ and variance $V$, $E[e^x] = e^\mu e^{V/2}$.)

(c) Show that if $r$ and $\sigma^2$ are constant over time, the result in part (b) implies that the log of consumption follows a random walk with drift: $\ln C_{t+1} = a + \ln C_t + u_{t+1}$, where $u$ is white noise.

(d) How do changes in each of $r$ and $\sigma^2$ affect expected consumption growth, $E_t[\ln C_{t+1} - \ln C_t]$? Interpret the effect of $\sigma^2$ on expected consumption growth in light of the discussion of precautionary saving in Section 8.6.

**8.6. A framework for investigating excess smoothness.** Suppose that $C_t$ equals $[r/(1 + r)]\{A_t + \sum_{s=0}^{\infty} E_t[Y_{t+s}]/(1 + r)^s\}$, and that $A_{t+1} = (1 + r)(A_t + Y_t - C_t)$.

(a) Show that these assumptions imply that $E_t[C_{t+1}] = C_t$ (and thus that consumption follows a random walk) and that $\sum_{s=0}^{\infty} E_t[C_{t+s}]/(1 + r)^s = A_t + \sum_{s=0}^{\infty} E_t[Y_{t+s}]/(1 + r)^s$.

(b) Suppose that $\Delta Y_t = \phi \Delta Y_{t-1} + u_t$, where $u$ is white noise. Suppose that $Y_t$ exceeds $E_{t-1}[Y_t]$ by 1 unit (that is, suppose $u_t = 1$). By how much does consumption increase?

(c) For the case of $\phi > 0$, which has a larger variance, the innovation in income, $u_t$, or the innovation in consumption, $C_t - E_{t-1}[C_t]$? Do consumers use saving and borrowing to smooth the path of consumption relative to income in this model? Explain.

**8.7.** Consider the two-period setup analyzed in Section 8.4. Suppose that the government initially raises revenue only by taxing interest income. Thus the individual's budget constraint is $C_1 + C_2/[1 + (1 - \tau)r] \le Y_1 + Y_2/[1 + (1 - \tau)r]$, where $\tau$ is the tax rate. The government's revenue is 0 in period 1 and $\tau r(Y_1 - C_1^0)$ in period 2, where $C_1^0$ is the individual's choice of $C_1$ given this tax rate. Now suppose the government eliminates the taxation of interest income and instead institutes lump-sum taxes of amounts $T_1$ and $T_2$ in the two periods; thus the individual's budget constraint is now $C_1 + C_2/(1+r) \le (Y_1 - T_1) + (Y_2 - T_2)/(1 + r)$. Assume that $Y_1$, $Y_2$, and $r$ are exogenous.

(a) What condition must the new taxes satisfy so that the change does not affect the present value of government revenues?

(b) If the new taxes satisfy the condition in part (a), is the old consumption bundle, $(C_1^0, C_2^0)$, not affordable, just affordable, or affordable with room to spare?

(c) If the new taxes satisfy the condition in part (a), does first-period consumption rise, fall, or stay the same?

**8.8.** Consider a stock that pays dividends of $D_t$ in period $t$ and whose price in period $t$ is $P_t$. Assume that consumers are risk-neutral and have a discount rate of $r$; thus they maximize $E[\sum_{t=0}^{\infty} C_t/(1 + r)^t]$.

(a) Show that equilibrium requires $P_t = E_t[(D_{t+1} + P_{t+1})/(1 + r)]$ (assume that if the stock is sold, this happens after that period's dividends have been paid).

(b) Assume that $\lim_{s \to \infty} E_t[P_{t+s}/(1 + r)^s] = 0$ (this is a *no-bubbles* condition; see the next problem). Iterate the expression in part (a) forward to derive an expression for $P_t$ in terms of expectations of future dividends.

**8.9. Bubbles.** Consider the setup of the previous problem without the assumption that $\lim_{s \to \infty} E_t[P_{t+s}/(1 + r)^s] = 0$.

(a) **Deterministic bubbles.** Suppose that $P_t$ equals the expression derived in part (b) of Problem 8.8 plus $(1 + r)^t b$, $b > 0$.

(i) Is consumers' first-order condition derived in part (a) of Problem 8.8 still satisfied?

(*ii*) Can *b* be negative? (Hint: Consider the strategy of never selling the stock.)

(*b*) **Bursting bubbles.** (Blanchard, 1979.) Suppose that $P_t$ equals the expression derived in part (*b*) of Problem 8.8 plus $q_t$, where $q_t$ equals $(1+r)q_{t-1}/\alpha$ with probability $\alpha$ and equals 0 with probability $1-\alpha$.

   (*i*) Is consumers' first-order condition derived in part (*a*) of Problem 8.8 still satisfied?

   (*ii*) If there is a bubble at time *t* (that is, if $q_t > 0$), what is the probability that the bubble has burst by time $t+s$ (that is, that $q_{t+s}=0$)? What is the limit of this probability as *s* approaches infinity?

(*c*) **Intrinsic bubbles.** (Froot and Obstfeld, 1991.) Suppose that dividends follow a random walk: $D_t = D_{t-1} + e_t$, where *e* is white noise.

   (*i*) In the absence of bubbles, what is the price of the stock in period *t*?

   (*ii*) Suppose that $P_t$ equals the expression derived in (*i*) plus $b_t$, where $b_t = (1+r)b_{t-1} + ce_t$, $c > 0$. Is consumers' first-order condition derived in part (*a*) of Problem 8.8 still satisfied? In what sense do stock prices overreact to changes in dividends?

**8.10.** **The Lucas asset-pricing model.** (Lucas, 1978.) Suppose the only assets in the economy are infinitely lived trees. Output equals the fruit of the trees, which is exogenous and cannot be stored; thus $C_t = Y_t$, where $Y_t$ is the exogenously determined output per person and $C_t$ is consumption per person. Assume that initially each consumer owns the same number of trees. Since all consumers are assumed to be the same, this means that, in equilibrium, the behavior of the price of trees must be such that, each period, the representative consumer does not want to either increase or decrease his or her holdings of trees.

Let $P_t$ denote the price of a tree in period *t* (assume that if the tree is sold, the sale occurs after the existing owner receives that period's output). Finally, assume that the representative consumer maximizes $E[\sum_{t=0}^{\infty} \ln C_t / (1+\rho)^t]$.

(*a*) Suppose the representative consumer reduces his or her consumption in period *t* by an infinitesimal amount, uses the resulting saving to increase his or her holdings of trees, and then sells these additional holdings in period $t+1$. Find the condition that $C_t$ and expectations involving $Y_{t+1}$, $P_{t+1}$, and $C_{t+1}$ must satisfy for this change not to affect expected utility. Solve this condition for $P_t$ in terms of $Y_t$ and expectations involving $Y_{t+1}$, $P_{t+1}$, and $C_{t+1}$.

(*b*) Assume that $\lim_{s\to\infty} E_t[(P_{t+s}/Y_{t+s})/(1+\rho)^s] = 0$. Given this assumption, iterate your answer to part (*a*) forward to solve for $P_t$. (Hint: Use the fact that $C_{t+s} = Y_{t+s}$ for all *s*.)

(*c*) Explain intuitively why an increase in expectations of future dividends does not affect the price of the asset.

(*d*) Does consumption follow a random walk in this model?

**8.11. The equity premium and the concentration of aggregate shocks.** (Mankiw, 1986.) Consider an economy with two possible states, each of which occurs with probability $\frac{1}{2}$. In the good state, each individual's consumption is 1. In the bad state, fraction $\lambda$ of the population consumes $1 - (\phi/\lambda)$ and the remainder consumes 1, where $0 < \phi < 1$ and $\phi \leq \lambda \leq 1$. $\phi$ measures the reduction in average consumption in the bad state, and $\lambda$ measures how broadly that reduction is shared.

Consider two assets, one that pays off 1 unit in the good state and one that pays off 1 unit in the bad state. Let $p$ denote the relative price of the bad-state asset to the good-state asset.

(a) Consider an individual whose initial holdings of the two assets are zero, and consider the experiment of the individual marginally reducing (that is, selling short) his or her holdings of the good-state asset and using the proceeds to purchase more of the bad-state asset. Derive the condition for this change not to affect the individual's expected utility.

(b) Since consumption in the two states is exogenous and individuals are ex ante identical, $p$ must adjust to the point where it is an equilibrium for individuals' holdings of both assets to be zero. Solve the condition derived in part (a) for this equilibrium value of $p$ in terms of $\phi$, $\lambda$, $U'(1)$, and $U'(1 - (\phi/\lambda))$.

(c) Find $\partial p/\partial \lambda$.

(d) Show that if utility is quadratic, $\partial p/\partial \lambda = 0$.

(e) Show that if $U'''(\bullet)$ is everywhere positive, $\partial p/\partial \lambda < 0$.

**8.12. Consumption of durable goods.** (Mankiw, 1982.) Suppose that, as in Section 8.2, the instantaneous utility function is quadratic and the interest rate and the discount rate are zero. Suppose, however, that goods are durable; specifically, $C_t = (1 - \delta)C_{t-1} + X_t$, where $X_t$ is purchases in period $t$ and $0 \leq \delta < 1$.

(a) Consider a marginal reduction in purchases in period $t$ of $dX_t$. Find values of $dX_{t+1}$ and $dX_{t+2}$ such that the combined changes in $X_t$, $X_{t+1}$, and $X_{t+2}$ leave the present value of spending unchanged (so $dX_t + dX_{t+1} + dX_{t+2} = 0$) and leave $C_{t+2}$ unchanged (so $(1 - \delta)^2 dX_t + (1 - \delta)dX_{t+1} + dX_{t+2} = 0$).

(b) What is the effect of the change in part (a) on $C_t$ and $C_{t+1}$? What is the effect on expected utility?

(c) What condition must $C_t$ and $E_t[C_{t+1}]$ satisfy for the change in part (a) not to affect expected utility? Does $C$ follow a random walk?

(d) Does $X$ follow a random walk? (Hint: Write $X_t - X_{t-1}$ in terms of $C_t - C_{t-1}$ and $C_{t-1} - C_{t-2}$.) Explain intuitively. If $\delta = 0$, what is the behavior of $X$?

**8.13. Habit formation and serial correlation in consumption growth.** Suppose that the utility of the representative consumer, individual $i$, is given by $\sum_{t=1}^{T}[1/(1 + \rho)^t](C_{it}/Z_{it})^{1-\theta}/(1 - \theta)$, $\rho > 0$, $\theta > 0$, where $Z_{it}$ is the "reference" level of consumption. Assume the interest rate is constant at some level, $r$, and that there is no uncertainty.

(a) **External habits.** Suppose $Z_{it} = C_{t-1}^{\phi}, 0 \le \phi \le 1$. Thus the reference level of consumption is determined by aggregate consumption, which individual $i$ takes as given.

   (i) Find the Euler equation for the experiment of reducing $C_{it}$ by $dC$ and increasing $C_{i,t+1}$ by $(1 + r)dC$. Express $C_{i,t+1}/C_{i,t}$ in terms of $C_t/C_{t-1}$ and $(1 + r)/(1 + \rho)$.

   (ii) In equilibrium, the consumption of the representative consumer must equal aggregate consumption: $C_{it} = C_t$ for all $t$. Use this fact to express current consumption growth, $\ln C_{t+1} - \ln C_t$, in terms of lagged consumption growth, $\ln C_t - \ln C_{t-1}$, and anything else that is relevant. If $\phi > 0$ and $\theta = 1$, does habit formation affect the behavior of consumption? What if $\phi > 0$ and $\theta > 1$? Explain your results intuitively.

(b) **Internal habits.** Suppose $Z_t = C_{i,t-1}$. Thus the reference level of consumption is determined by the individual's own level of past consumption (and the parameter $\phi$ is fixed at 1).

   (i) Find the Euler equation for the experiment considered in part (a) (i). (Note that $C_{it}$ affects utility in periods $t$ and $t + 1$, and $C_{i,t+1}$ affects utility in $t + 1$ and $t + 2$.)

   (ii) Let $g_t \equiv (C_t/C_{t-1}) - 1$ denote consumption growth from $t - 1$ to $t$. Assume that $\rho = r = 0$ and that consumption growth is close to zero (so that we can approximate expressions of the form $(C_t/C_{t-1})^{\gamma}$ with $1 + \gamma g_t$, and can ignore interaction terms). Using your results in (i), find an approximate expression for $g_{t+2} - g_{t+1}$ in terms of $g_{t+1} - g_t$ and anything else that is relevant. Explain your result intuitively.

**8.14. Precautionary saving with constant-absolute-risk-aversion utility.** Consider an individual who lives for two periods and has constant-absolute-risk-aversion utility, $U = -e^{-\gamma C_1} - e^{-\gamma C_2}, \gamma > 0$. The interest rate is zero and the individual has no initial wealth, so the individual's lifetime budget constraint is $C_1 + C_2 = Y_1 + Y_2$. $Y_1$ is certain, but $Y_2$ is normally distributed with mean $\bar{Y}_2$ and variance $\sigma^2$.

(a) With an instantaneous utility function $u(C) = -e^{-\gamma C}, \gamma > 0$, what is the sign of $U'''(C)$?

(b) What is the individual's expected lifetime utility as a function of $C_1$ and the exogenous parameters $Y_1$, $\bar{Y}_2$, $\sigma^2$, and $\gamma$? (Hint: See the hint in Problem 8.5, part (b).)

(c) Find an expression for $C_1$ in terms of $Y_1$, $\bar{Y}_2$, $\sigma^2$, and $\gamma$. What is $C_1$ if there is no uncertainty? How does an increase in uncertainty affect $C_1$?

**8.15. Time-inconsistent preferences.** Consider an individual who lives for three periods. In period 1, his or her objective function is $\ln c_1 + \delta \ln c_2 + \delta \ln c_3$, where $0 < \delta < 1$. In period 2, it is $\ln c_2 + \delta \ln c_3$. (Since the individual's period-3 choice problem is trivial, the period-3 objective function is irrelevant.) The individual has wealth of $W$ and faces a real interest rate of zero.

(*a*) Find the values of $c_1$, $c_2$, and $c_3$ under the following assumptions about how they are determined:

   (*i*) Commitment: The individual chooses $c_1$, $c_2$, and $c_3$ in period 1.

   (*ii*) No commitment, naivete: The individual chooses $c_1$ in period 1 to maximize the period-1 objective function, thinking he or she will also choose $c_2$ to maximize this objective function. In fact, however, the individual chooses $c_2$ to maximize the period-2 objective function.

   (*iii*) No commitment, sophistication: The individual chooses $c_1$ in period 1 to maximize the period-1 objective function, realizing that he or she will choose $c_2$ in period 2 to maximize the period-2 objective function.

(*b*)  (*i*) Use your answers to parts (*a*)(*i*) and (*a*)(*ii*) to explain in what sense the individuals' preferences are time-inconsistent.

   (*ii*) Explain intuitively why sophistication does not produce different behavior than naivete.

# Chapter 9
# INVESTMENT

This chapter investigates the demand for investment. As described at the beginning of Chapter 8, there are two main reasons for studying investment. First, the combination of firms' investment demand and households' saving supply determines how much of an economy's output is invested; as a result, investment demand is potentially important to the behavior of standards of living over the long run. Second, investment is highly volatile; thus investment demand may be important to short-run fluctuations.

Section 9.1 presents a baseline model of investment where firms face a perfectly elastic supply of capital goods and can adjust their capital stocks costlessly. We will see that this model, even though it is a natural one to consider, provides little insight into actual investment. It implies, for example, that discrete changes in the economic environment (such as discrete changes in interest rates) produce infinite rates of investment or disinvestment.

Sections 9.2 through 9.5 therefore develop and analyze the *q theory* model of investment. The model's key assumption is that firms face costs of adjusting their capital stocks. As a result, the model avoids the unreasonable implications of the baseline case and provides a useful framework for analyzing the effects that expectations and current conditions have on investment.

The remainder of the chapter examines extensions and empirical evidence. Sections 9.7 through 9.9 consider three issues that are omitted from the basic model: uncertainty, adjustment costs that take more complicated forms than the smooth adjustment costs of *q* theory, and financial-market imperfections. Sections 9.6 and 9.10 consider empirical evidence about the impact of the value of capital on investment and the importance of financial-market imperfections to investment decisions.

## 9.1 Investment and the Cost of Capital

### The Desired Capital Stock

Consider a firm that can rent capital at a price of $r_K$. The firm's profits at a point in time are given by $\pi(K, X_1, X_2, \ldots, X_n) - r_K K$, where $K$ is the amount of capital the firm rents and the $X$'s are variables that it takes as given. In the case of a perfectly competitive firm, for example, the $X$'s include the price of the firm's product and the costs of other inputs. $\pi(\bullet)$ is assumed to account for whatever optimization the firm can do on dimensions other than its choice of $K$. For a competitive firm, for example, $\pi(K,X_1,\ldots,X_n) - r_K K$ gives the firm's profits at the profit-maximizing choices of inputs other than capital given $K$ and the $X$'s. We assume that $\pi_K > 0$ and $\pi_{KK} < 0$, where subscripts denote partial derivatives.

The first-order condition for the profit-maximizing choice of $K$ is

$$\pi_K(K,X_1,\ldots,X_n) = r_K. \tag{9.1}$$

That is, the firm rents capital up to the point where its marginal revenue product equals its rental price.

Equation (9.1) implicitly defines the firm's desired capital stock as a function of $r_K$ and the $X$'s. We can differentiate this condition to find the impact of a change in one of these variables on the desired capital stock. Consider, for example, a change in the rental price of capital, $r_K$. By assumption, the $X$'s are exogenous; thus they do not change when $r_K$ changes. $K$, however, is chosen by the firm. Thus it adjusts so that (9.1) continues to hold. Differentiating both sides of (9.1) with respect to $r_K$ shows that this requires

$$\pi_{KK}(K,X_1,\ldots,X_n)\frac{\partial K(r_K,X_1,\ldots,X_n)}{\partial r_K} = 1. \tag{9.2}$$

Solving this expression for $\partial K/\partial r_K$ yields

$$\frac{\partial K(r_K,X_1,\ldots,X_n)}{\partial r_K} = \frac{1}{\pi_{KK}(K,X_1,\ldots,X_n)}. \tag{9.3}$$

Since $\pi_{KK}$ is negative, (9.3) implies that $K$ is decreasing in $r_K$. A similar analysis can be used to find the effects of changes in the $X$'s on $K$.

## The User Cost of Capital

Most capital is not rented but is owned by the firms that use it. Thus there is no clear empirical counterpart of $r_K$. This difficulty has given rise to a large literature on the *user cost of capital*.

Consider a firm that owns a unit of capital. Suppose the real market price of the capital at time $t$ is $p_K(t)$, and consider the firm's choice between selling the capital and continuing to use it. Keeping the capital has three costs to the firm. First, the firm forgoes the interest it would receive if it sold the capital and saved the proceeds. This has a real cost of $r(t)p_K(t)$ per unit time, where $r(t)$ is the real interest rate. Second, the capital is depreciating. This has a cost of $\delta p_K(t)$ per unit time, where $\delta$ is the depreciation rate. And third, the price of the capital may be changing. This increases the cost of using the capital if the price is falling (since the firm obtains less if it waits to sell the capital) and decreases the cost if the price is rising. This has a cost of $-\dot{p}_K(t)$ per unit time. Putting the three components together yields the user cost of capital:

$$r_K(t) = r(t)p_K(t) + \delta p_K(t) - \dot{p}_K(t)$$

$$= \left[ r(t) + \delta - \frac{\dot{p}_K(t)}{p_K(t)} \right] p_K(t). \tag{9.4}$$

This analysis ignores taxes. In practice, however, the tax treatments of investment and of capital income have large effects on the user cost of capital. To give an idea of these effects, consider an investment tax credit. Specifically, suppose the firm's income that is subject to the corporate income tax is reduced by fraction $f$ of its investment expenditures; for symmetry, suppose also that its taxable income is increased by fraction $f$ of any receipts from selling capital goods. Such an investment tax credit implies that the effective price of a unit of capital to the firm is $(1 - f\tau)p_K(t)$, where $\tau$ is the marginal corporate income tax rate. The user cost of capital is therefore

$$r_K(t) = \left[ r(t) + \delta - \frac{\dot{p}_K(t)}{p_K(t)} \right] (1 - f\tau) p_K(t). \tag{9.5}$$

Thus the investment tax credit reduces the user cost of capital, and hence increases firms' desired capital stocks. One can also investigate the effects of depreciation allowances, the tax treatment of interest, and many other features of the tax code on the user cost of capital and the desired capital stock.[1]

## Difficulties with the Baseline Model

This simple model of investment has at least two major failings as a description of actual behavior. The first concerns the impact of changes in the exogenous variables. Our model concerns firms' demand for capital, and it implies that firms' desired capital stocks are smooth functions of the exogenous variable. As a result, a discrete change in an exogenous variables leads to a discrete change in the desired capital stock. Suppose, for example, that the Federal Reserve reduces interest rates by a discrete amount. As the analysis above shows, this discretely reduces the cost of capital, $r_K$. This in turn means that the capital stock that satisfies (9.1) rises discretely.

The problem with this implication is that, since the rate of change of the capital stock equals investment minus depreciation, a discrete change in the capital stock requires an infinite rate of investment. For the economy as a whole, however, investment is limited by the economy's output; thus aggregate investment cannot be infinite.

The second problem with the model is that it does not identify any mechanism through which expectations affect investment demand. The model implies that firms equate the current marginal revenue product of capital

---

[1] The seminal paper is Hall and Jorgenson (1967). See also Problems 9.2 and 9.3.

with its current user cost, without regard to what they expect future marginal revenue products or user costs to be. Yet it is clear that in practice, expectations about demand and costs are central to investment decisions: firms expand their capital stocks when they expect their sales to be growing and the cost of capital to be low, and they contract them when they expect their sales to be falling and the cost of capital to be high.

Thus we need to modify the model if we are to obtain even a remotely reasonable picture of actual investment decisions. The standard theory that does this emphasizes the presence of costs to changing the capital stock. Those adjustment costs come in two forms, internal and external. *Internal adjustment costs* arise when firms face direct costs of changing their capital stocks (Eisner and Strotz, 1963; Lucas, 1967). Examples of such costs are the costs of installing the new capital and training workers to operate the new machines. Consider again a discrete cut in interest rates. If the adjustment costs approach infinity as the rate of change of the capital stock approaches infinity, the fall in interest rates causes investment to increase but not to become infinite. As a result, the capital stock moves gradually toward the new desired level.

*External adjustment costs* arise when each firm, as in our baseline model, faces a perfectly elastic supply of capital, but where the price of capital goods relative to other goods adjusts so that firms do not wish to invest or disinvest at infinite rates (Foley and Sidrauski, 1970). When the supply of capital is not perfectly elastic, a discrete change that increases firms' desired capital stocks bids up the price of capital goods. Under plausible assumptions, the result is that the rental price of capital does not change discontinuously but merely begins to adjust, and that again investment increases but does not become infinite.[2]

# 9.2   A Model of Investment with Adjustment Costs

We now turn to a model of investment with adjustment costs. For concreteness, the adjustment costs are assumed to be internal; it is straightforward, however, to reinterpret the model as one of external adjustment costs.[3] The model is known as the $q$ theory model of investment.

---

[2] As described in Section 7.9, some business-cycle models assume that there are costs of adjusting investment rather than costs of adjusting the capital stock (for example, Christiano, Eichenbaum, and Evans, 2005). Like the assumption of adjustment costs for capital, this assumption implies that investment is a smooth function of the exogenous variables and that expectations affect investment demand. We will focus on the more traditional assumption of capital adjustment costs, however, both because it is simpler and because it appears to better describe firm-level investment behavior (Eberly, Rebelo, and Vincent, 2009).

[3] See n. 10 and Problem 9.8. The model presented here is developed by Abel (1982), Hayashi (1982), and Summers (1981b).

## Assumptions

Consider an industry with $N$ identical firms. A representative firm's real profits at time $t$, neglecting any costs of acquiring and installing capital, are proportional to its capital stock, $\kappa(t)$, and decreasing in the industry-wide capital stock, $K(t)$; thus they take the form $\pi(K(t))\kappa(t)$, where $\pi'(\bullet) < 0$. The assumption that the firm's profits are proportional to its capital is appropriate if the production function has constant returns to scale, output markets are competitive, and the supply of all factors other than capital is perfectly elastic. Under these assumptions, if one firm has, for example, twice as much capital as another, it employs twice as much of all inputs; as a result, both its revenues and its costs are twice as high as the other's.[4] And the assumption that profits are decreasing in the industry's capital stock is appropriate if the demand curve for the industry's product is downward-sloping.

The key assumption of the model is that firms face costs of adjusting their capital stocks. The adjustment costs are a convex function of the rate of change of the firm's capital stock, $\dot{\kappa}$. Specifically, the adjustment costs, $C(\dot{\kappa})$, satisfy $C(0) = 0$, $C'(0) = 0$, and $C''(\bullet) > 0$. These assumptions imply that it is costly for a firm to increase or decrease its capital stock, and that the marginal adjustment cost is increasing in the size of the adjustment.

The purchase price of capital goods is constant and equal to 1; thus there are no external adjustment costs. Finally, for simplicity, the depreciation rate is assumed to be zero. It follows that $\dot{\kappa}(t) = I(t)$, where $I$ is the firm's investment.

These assumptions imply that the firm's profits at a point in time are $\pi(K)\kappa - I - C(I)$. The firm maximizes the present value of these profits,

$$\Pi = \int_{t=0}^{\infty} e^{-rt} \left[ \pi(K(t))\kappa(t) - I(t) - C(I(t)) \right] dt, \tag{9.6}$$

where we assume for simplicity that the real interest rate is constant. Each firm takes the path of the industry-wide capital stock, $K$, as given, and chooses its investment over time to maximize $\Pi$ given this path.

## A Discrete-Time Version of the Firm's Problem

To solve the firm's maximization problem, we need to employ the *calculus of variations*. To understand this method, it is helpful to first consider a discrete-time version of the firm's problem.[5] In discrete time, the firm's

---

[4] Note that these assumptions imply that in the model of Section 9.1, $\pi(K, X_1, \ldots, X_n)$ takes the form $\tilde{\pi}(X_1, \ldots, X_n)K$, and so the assumption that $\pi_{KK} < 0$ fails. Thus in this case, in the absence of adjustment costs, the firm's demand for capital is not well defined: it is infinite if $\tilde{\pi}(X_1, \ldots, X_n) > 0$, zero if $\tilde{\pi}(X_1, \ldots, X_n) < 0$, and indeterminate if $\tilde{\pi}(X_1, \ldots, X_n) = 0$.

[5] For more thorough and formal introductions to the calculus of variations, see Kamien and Schwartz (1991), Obstfeld (1992), and Barro and Sala-i-Martin (2003, Appendix A.3).

objective function is

$$\tilde{\Pi} = \sum_{t=0}^{\infty} \frac{1}{(1+r)^t} [\pi(K_t)\kappa_t - I_t - C(I_t)]. \tag{9.7}$$

For comparability with the continuous-time case, it is helpful to assume that the firm's investment and its capital stock are related by $\kappa_t = \kappa_{t-1} + I_t$ for all $t$.[6] We can think of the firm as choosing its investment and capital stock each period subject to the constraint $\kappa_t = \kappa_{t-1} + I_t$ for each $t$. Since there are infinitely many periods, there are infinitely many constraints.

The Lagrangian for the firm's maximization problem is

$$\mathcal{L} = \sum_{t=0}^{\infty} \frac{1}{(1+r)^t} [\pi(K_t)\kappa_t - I_t - C(I_t)] + \sum_{t=0}^{\infty} \lambda_t (\kappa_{t-1} + I_t - \kappa_t). \tag{9.8}$$

$\lambda_t$ is the Lagrange multiplier associated with the constraint relating $\kappa_t$ and $\kappa_{t-1}$. It therefore gives the marginal value of relaxing the constraint; that is, it gives the marginal impact of an exogenous increase in $\kappa_t$ on the lifetime value of the firm's profits discounted to time 0. This discussion implies that if we define $q_t = (1+r)^t \lambda_t$, then $q_t$ shows the value to the firm of an additional unit of capital at time $t$ in time-$t$ dollars. With this definition, we can rewrite the Lagrangian as

$$\mathcal{L}' = \sum_{t=0}^{\infty} \frac{1}{(1+r)^t} [\pi(K_t)\kappa_t - I_t - C(I_t) + q_t(\kappa_{t-1} + I_t - \kappa_t)]. \tag{9.9}$$

The first-order condition for the firm's investment in period $t$ is therefore

$$\frac{1}{(1+r)^t} [-1 - C'(I_t) + q_t] = 0, \tag{9.10}$$

which is equivalent to

$$1 + C'(I_t) = q_t. \tag{9.11}$$

To interpret this condition, observe that the cost of acquiring a unit of capital equals the purchase price (which is fixed at 1) plus the marginal adjustment cost. Thus (9.11) states that the firm invests to the point where the cost of acquiring capital equals the value of the capital.

Now consider the first-order condition for capital in period $t$. The term for period $t$ in the Lagrangian, (9.9), involves both $\kappa_t$ and $\kappa_{t-1}$. Thus the capital stock in period $t$, $\kappa_t$, appears in both the term for period $t$ and the

---

[6] The more standard assumption is $\kappa_t = \kappa_{t-1} + I_{t-1}$. However, this formulation imposes a one-period delay between investment and the resulting increase in capital that has no analogue in the continuous-time case.

term for period $t + 1$. The first-order condition for $\kappa_t$ is therefore

$$\frac{1}{(1+r)^t}[\pi(K_t) - q_t] + \frac{1}{(1+r)^{t+1}}q_{t+1} = 0. \tag{9.12}$$

Multiplying this expression by $(1 + r)^{t+1}$ and rearranging yields

$$(1+r)\pi(K_t) = (1+r)q_t - q_{t+1}. \tag{9.13}$$

If we define $\Delta q_t = q_{t+1} - q_t$, we can rewrite the right-hand side of (9.13) as $rq_t - \Delta q_t$. Thus we have

$$\pi(K_t) = \frac{1}{1+r}(rq_t - \Delta q_t). \tag{9.14}$$

The left-hand side of (9.14) is the marginal revenue product of capital, and the right-hand side is the opportunity cost of a unit of capital. Intuitively, owning a unit of capital for a period requires forgoing $rq_t$ of real interest and involves offsetting capital gains of $\Delta q_t$ (see [9.4] with the depreciation rate assumed to be zero; in addition, there is a factor of $1/(1 + r)$ that will disappear in the continuous-time case). For the firm to be optimizing, the returns to capital must equal this opportunity cost. This is what is stated by (9.14). This condition is thus analogous to the condition in the model without adjustment costs that the firm rents capital to the point where its marginal revenue product equals its rental price.

A second way of interpreting (9.14) is as a consistency requirement concerning how the firm values capital over time. To see this interpretation, rearrange (9.14) (or [9.13]) as

$$q_t = \pi(K_t) + \frac{1}{1+r}q_{t+1}. \tag{9.15}$$

By definition, $q_t$ is the value the firm attaches to a unit of capital in period $t$ measured in period-$t$ dollars, and $q_{t+1}$ is the value the firm will attach to a unit of capital in period $t + 1$ measured in period-$(t + 1)$ dollars. If $q_t$ does not equal the amount the capital contributes to the firm's objective function this period, $\pi(K_t)$, plus the value the firm will attach to the capital next period measured in this period's dollars, $q_{t+1}/(1 + r)$, its valuations in the two periods are inconsistent.

Conditions (9.11) and (9.15) are not enough to completely characterize profit-maximizing behavior, however. The problem is that although (9.15) requires the $q$'s to be consistent over time, it does not require them to actually equal the amount that an additional unit of capital contributes to the firm's objective function. To see this, suppose the firm has an additional unit of capital in period 0 that it holds forever. Since the additional unit of capital raises profits in period $t$ by $\pi(K_t)$, we can write the amount the capital contributes to the firm's objective function as

$$MB = \lim_{T \to \infty} \left[ \sum_{t=0}^{T-1} \frac{1}{(1+r)^t} \pi(K_t) \right]. \tag{9.16}$$

Now note that equation (9.15) implies that $q_0$ can be written as

$$q_0 = \pi(K_0) + \frac{1}{1+r} q_1$$

$$= \pi(K_0) + \frac{1}{1+r} \left[ \pi(K_1) + \frac{1}{1+r} q_2 \right] \tag{9.17}$$

$$= \dots$$

$$= \lim_{T \to \infty} \left\{ \left[ \sum_{t=0}^{T-1} \frac{1}{(1+r)^t} \pi(K_t) \right] + \frac{1}{(1+r)^T} q_T \right\},$$

where the first line uses (9.15) for $t = 0$, and the second uses it for $t = 1$.

Comparison of (9.16) and (9.17) shows that $q_0$ equals the contribution of an additional unit of capital to the firm's objective function if and only if

$$\lim_{T \to \infty} \frac{1}{(1+r)^T} q_T = 0. \tag{9.18}$$

If (9.18) fails, then marginally raising investment in period 0 (which, by [9.11], has a marginal cost of $q_0$) and holding the additional capital forever (which has a marginal benefit of $MB$) has a nonzero impact on the firm's profits, which would mean that the firm is not maximizing profits. Equation (9.18) is therefore necessary for profit maximization. This condition is known as the *transversality condition*.

An alternative version of the transversality condition is

$$\lim_{T \to \infty} \frac{1}{(1+r)^T} q_T \kappa_T = 0. \tag{9.19}$$

Intuitively, this version of the condition states that it cannot be optimal to hold valuable capital forever. In the model we are considering, $\dot{\kappa}$ and $q$ are linked through (9.11), and so $\kappa$ diverges if and only if $q$ does. One can show that as a result, (9.19) holds if and only if (9.18) does. Thus we can use either condition.

## The Continuous-Time Case

We can now consider the case when time is continuous. The firm's profit-maximizing behavior in this case is characterized by three conditions that are analogous to the three conditions that characterize its behavior in discrete time: (9.11), (9.14), and (9.19). Indeed, the optimality conditions for continuous time can be derived by considering the discrete-time problem where the time periods are separated by intervals of length $\Delta t$ and then taking the limit as $\Delta t$ approaches zero. We will not use this method, however. Instead we will simply describe how to find the optimality conditions, and justify them as necessary by way of analogy to the discrete-time case.

The firm's problem is now to maximize the continuous-time objective function, (9.6), rather than the discrete-time objective function, (9.7). The first step in analyzing this problem is to set up the *current-value Hamiltonian:*

$$H(\kappa(t), I(t)) = \pi(K(t))\kappa(t) - I(t) - C(I(t)) + q(t)I(t). \qquad (9.20)$$

This expression is analogous to the period-$t$ term in the Lagrangian for the discrete-time case with the term in the change in the capital stock omitted (see [9.9]). There is some standard terminology associated with this type of problem. The variable that can be controlled freely ($I$) is the *control variable;* the variable whose value at any time is determined by past decisions ($\kappa$) is the *state variable;* and the shadow value of the state variable ($q$) is the *costate variable.*

The first condition characterizing the optimum is that the derivative of the Hamiltonian with respect to the control variable at each point in time is zero. This is analogous to the condition in the discrete-time problem that the derivative of the Lagrangian with respect to $I$ for each $t$ is zero. For our problem, this condition is

$$1 + C'(I(t)) = q(t). \qquad (9.21)$$

This condition is analogous to (9.11) in the discrete-time case.

The second condition is that the derivative of the Hamiltonian with respect to the state variable equals the discount rate times the costate variable minus the derivative of the costate variable with respect to time. In our case, this condition is

$$\pi(K(t)) = rq(t) - \dot{q}(t). \qquad (9.22)$$

This condition is analogous to (9.14) in the discrete-time problem.

The final condition is the continuous-time version of the transversality condition. This condition is that the limit of the product of the discounted costate variable and the state variable is zero. In our model, this condition is

$$\lim_{t \to \infty} e^{-rt} q(t)\kappa(t) = 0. \qquad (9.23)$$

Equations (9.21), (9.22), and (9.23) characterize the firm's behavior.[7]

---

[7] An alternative approach is to formulate the *present-value Hamiltonian,* $\tilde{H}(\kappa(t), I(t)) = e^{-rt}[\pi(K(t))\kappa(t) - I(t) - C(I(t))] + \lambda(t)I(t)$. This is analogous to using the Lagrangian (9.8) rather than (9.9). With this formulation, (9.22) is replaced by $e^{-rt}\pi(K(t)) = -\dot{\lambda}(t)$, and (9.23) is replaced by $\lim_{t \to \infty} \lambda(t)\kappa(t) = 0$.

# 9.3 Tobin's *q*

Our analysis of the firm's maximization problem implies that *q* summarizes all information about the future that is relevant to a firm's investment decision. *q* shows how an additional dollar of capital affects the present value of profits. Thus the firm wants to increase its capital stock if *q* is high and reduce it if *q* is low; the firm does not need to know anything about the future other than the information that is summarized in *q* in order to make this decision (see [9.21]).

From our analysis of the discrete-time case, we know that *q* is the present discounted value of the future marginal revenue products of a unit of capital. In the continuous-time case, we can therefore express *q* as

$$q(t) = \int_{\tau=t}^{\infty} e^{-r(\tau-t)} \pi(K(\tau)) \, d\tau. \tag{9.24}$$

There is another interpretation of *q*. A unit increase in the firm's capital stock increases the present value of the firm's profits by *q*, and thus raises the value of the firm by *q*. Thus *q* is the market value of a unit of capital. If there is a market for shares in firms, for example, the total value of a firm with one more unit of capital than another firm exceeds the value of the other by *q*. And since we have assumed that the purchase price of capital is fixed at 1, *q* is also the ratio of the market value of a unit of capital to its replacement cost. Thus equation (9.21) states that a firm increases its capital stock if the market value of capital exceeds the cost of acquiring it, and that it decreases its capital stock if the market value of the capital is less than the cost of acquiring it.

The ratio of the market value to the replacement cost of capital is known as *Tobin's q* (Tobin, 1969); it is because of this terminology that we used *q* to denote the value of capital in the previous section. Our analysis implies that what is relevant to investment is *marginal q*—the ratio of the market value of a marginal unit of capital to its replacement cost. Marginal *q* is likely to be harder to measure than *average q*—the ratio of the total value of the firm to the replacement cost of its total capital stock. Thus it is important to know how marginal *q* and average *q* are related.

One can show that in our model, marginal *q* is less than average *q*. The reason is that when we assumed that adjustment costs depend only on $\dot{\kappa}$, we implicitly assumed diminishing returns to scale in adjustment costs. Our assumptions imply, for example, that it is more than twice as costly for a firm with 20 units of capital to add 2 more than it is for a firm with 10 units to add 1 more. Because of this assumption of diminishing returns, firms' lifetime profits, Π, rise less than proportionally with their capital stocks, and so marginal *q* is less than average *q*.

One can also show that if the model is modified to have constant returns in the adjustment costs, average *q* and marginal *q* are equal

(Hayashi, 1982).[8] The source of this result is that the constant returns in the costs of adjustment imply that $q$ determines the growth rate of a firm's capital stock. As a result, all firms choose the same growth rate of their capital stocks. Thus if, for example, one firm initially has twice as much capital as another and if both firms optimize, the larger firm will have twice as much capital as the other at every future date. In addition, profits are linear in a firm's capital stock. This implies that the present value of a firm's profits— the value of $\Pi$ when it chooses the path of its capital stock optimally—is proportional to its initial capital stock. Thus average $q$ and marginal $q$ are equal.

In other models, there are potentially more significant reasons than the degree of returns to scale in adjustment costs that average $q$ may differ from marginal $q$. For example, if a firm faces a downward-sloping demand curve for its product, doubling its capital stock is likely to less than double the present value of its profits; thus marginal $q$ is less than average $q$. If the firm owns a large amount of outmoded capital, on the other hand, its marginal $q$ may exceed its average $q$.

## 9.4 Analyzing the Model

We will analyze the model using a phase diagram similar to the one we used in Chapter 2 to analyze the Ramsey model. The two variables we will focus on are the aggregate quantity of capital, $K$, and its value, $q$. As with $k$ and $c$ in the Ramsey model, the initial value of one of these variables is given, but the other must be determined: the quantity of capital is something that the industry inherits from the past, but its price adjusts freely in the market.

Recall from the beginning of Section 9.2 that there are $N$ identical firms. Equation (9.21) states that each firm invests to the point where the purchase price of capital plus the marginal adjustment cost equals the value of capital: $1 + C'(I) = q$. Since $q$ is the same for all firms, all firms choose the same value of $I$. Thus the rate of change of the aggregate capital stock, $\dot{K}$, is given by the number of firms times the value of $I$ that satisfies (9.21). That is,

$$\dot{K}(t) = f(q(t)), \qquad f(1) = 0, \qquad f'(\bullet) > 0, \qquad (9.25)$$

where $f(q) \equiv NC'^{-1}(q-1)$. Since $C'(I)$ is increasing in $I$, $f(q)$ is increasing in $q$. And since $C'(0)$ equals zero, $f(1)$ is zero. Equation (9.25) therefore implies

---

[8] Constant returns can be introduced by assuming that the adjustment costs take the form $C(\dot{\kappa}/\kappa)\kappa$, with $C(\bullet)$ having the same properties as before. With this assumption, doubling both $\dot{\kappa}$ and $\kappa$ doubles the adjustment costs. Changing our model in this way implies that $\kappa$ affects profits not only directly, but also through its impact on adjustment costs for a given level of investment. As a result, it complicates the analysis. The basic messages are the same, however. See Problem 9.9.

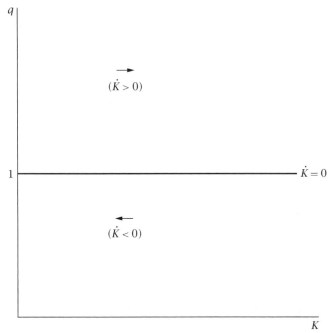

**FIGURE 9.1   The dynamics of the capital stock**

that $\dot{K}$ is positive when $q$ exceeds 1, negative when $q$ is less than 1, and zero when $q$ equals 1. This information is summarized in Figure 9.1.

Equation (9.22) states that the marginal revenue product of capital equals its user cost, $rq - \dot{q}$. Rewriting this as an equation for $\dot{q}$ yields

$$\dot{q}(t) = rq(t) - \pi(K(t)). \qquad (9.26)$$

This expression implies that $q$ is constant when $rq = \pi(K)$, or $q = \pi(K)/r$. Since $\pi(K)$ is decreasing in $K$, the set of points satisfying this condition is downward-sloping in $(K,q)$ space. In addition, (9.26) implies that $\dot{q}$ is increasing in $K$; thus $\dot{q}$ is positive to the right of the $\dot{q} = 0$ locus and negative to the left. This information is summarized in Figure 9.2.

## The Phase Diagram

Figure 9.3 combines the information in Figures 9.1 and 9.2. The diagram shows how $K$ and $q$ must behave to satisfy (9.25) and (9.26) at every point in time given their initial values. Suppose, for example, that $K$ and $q$ begin at Point A. Then, since $q$ is more than 1, firms increase their capital stocks; thus $\dot{K}$ is positive. And since $K$ is high and profits are therefore low, $q$ can

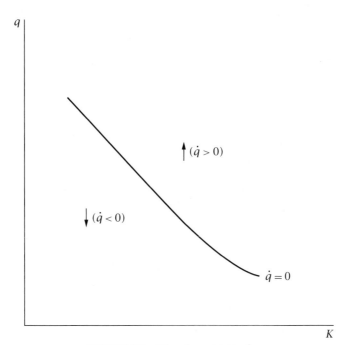

**FIGURE 9.2 The dynamics of *q***

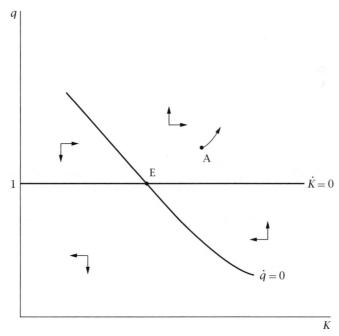

**FIGURE 9.3 The phase diagram**

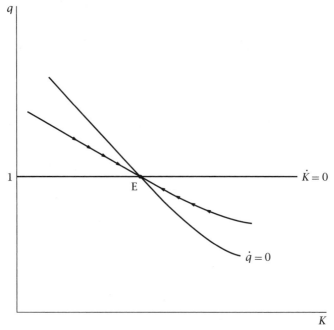

**FIGURE 9.4   The saddle path**

be high only if it is expected to rise; thus $\dot{q}$ is also positive. Thus $K$ and $q$ move up and to the right in the diagram.

As in the Ramsey model, the initial level of the capital stock is given. But the level of the other variable—consumption in the Ramsey model, the market value of capital in this model—is free to adjust. Thus its initial level must be determined. As in the Ramsey model, for a given level of $K$ there is a unique level of $q$ that produces a stable path. Specifically, there is a unique level of $q$ such that $K$ and $q$ converge to the point where they are stable (Point E in the diagram). If $q$ starts below this level, the industry eventually crosses into the region where both $K$ and $q$ are falling, and they then continue to fall indefinitely. Similarly, if $q$ starts too high, the industry eventually moves into the region where both $K$ and $q$ are rising and remains there. One can show that the transversality condition fails for these paths.[9] This means that firms are not maximizing profits on these paths, and thus that they are not equilibria.

Thus the unique equilibrium, given the initial value of $K$, is for $q$ to equal the value that puts the industry on the saddle path, and for $K$ and $q$ to then move along this saddle path to E. This saddle path is shown in Figure 9.4.

---

[9] See Abel (1982) and Hayashi (1982) for formal demonstrations of this result.

The long-run equilibrium, Point E, is characterized by $q = 1$ (which implies $\dot{K} = 0$) and $\dot{q} = 0$. The fact that $q$ equals 1 means that the market and replacement values of capital are equal; thus firms have no incentive to increase or decrease their capital stocks. And from (9.22), for $\dot{q}$ to equal 0 when $q$ is 1, the marginal revenue product of capital must equal $r$. This means that the profits from holding a unit of capital just offset the forgone interest, and thus that investors are content to hold capital without the prospect of either capital gains or losses.[10]

# 9.5 Implications

The model developed in the previous section can be used to address many issues. This section examines its implications for the effects of changes in output, interest rates, and tax policies.

## The Effects of Output Movements

An increase in aggregate output raises the demand for the industry's product, and thus raises profits for a given capital stock. Thus the natural way to model an increase in aggregate output is as an upward shift of the $\pi(\bullet)$ function.

For concreteness, assume that the industry is initially in long-run equilibrium, and that there is an unanticipated, permanent upward shift of the $\pi(\bullet)$ function. The effects of this change are shown in Figure 9.5. The upward shift of the $\pi(\bullet)$ function shifts the $\dot{q} = 0$ locus up: since profits are higher for a given capital stock, smaller capital gains are needed for investors to be willing to hold shares in firms (see [9.26]). From our analysis of phase diagrams in Chapter 2, we know what the effects of this change are. $q$ jumps immediately to the point on the new saddle path for the given capital stock; $K$ and $q$ then move down that path to the new long-run equilibrium at Point E'. Since the rate of change of the capital stock is an increasing function of $q$, this implies that $\dot{K}$ jumps at the time of the change and then gradually returns to zero. Thus a permanent increase in output leads to a temporary increase in investment.

The intuition behind these responses is straightforward. The increase in output raises the demand for the industry's product. Since the capital stock

---

[10] It is straightforward to modify the model to be one of external rather than internal adjustment costs. The key change is to replace the adjustment cost function with a supply curve for new capital goods, $\dot{K} = g(p_K)$, where $g'(\bullet) > 0$ and where $p_K$ is the relative price of capital. With this change, the market value of firms always equals the replacement cost of their capital stocks; the role played by $q$ in the model with internal adjustment costs is played instead by the relative price of capital. See Foley and Sidrauski (1970) and Problem 9.8.

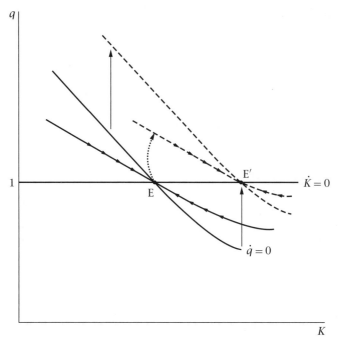

**FIGURE 9.5   The effects of a permanent increase in output**

cannot adjust instantly, existing capital in the industry earns rents, and so its market value rises. The higher market value of capital attracts investment, and so the capital stock begins to rise. As it does so, the industry's output rises, and thus the relative price of its product declines; thus profits and the value of capital fall. The process continues until the value of the capital returns to normal, at which point there are no incentives for further investment.

Now consider an increase in output that is known to be temporary. Specifically, the industry begins in long-run equilibrium. There is then an unexpected upward shift of the profit function; when this happens, it is known that the function will return to its initial position at some later time, $T$.

The key insight needed to find the effects of this change is that there cannot be an anticipated jump in $q$. If, for example, there is an anticipated downward jump in $q$, the owners of shares in firms will suffer capital losses at an infinite rate with certainty at that moment. But that means that no one will hold shares at that moment.

Thus at time $T$, $K$ and $q$ must be on the saddle path leading back to the initial long-run equilibrium: if they were not, $q$ would have to jump for the industry to get back to its long-run equilibrium. Between the time of the upward shift of the profit function and $T$, the dynamics of $K$ and $q$ are determined by the temporarily high profit function. Finally, the initial

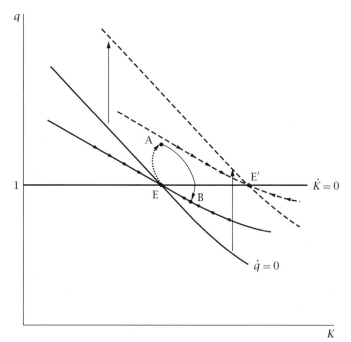

**FIGURE 9.6    The effects of a temporary increase in output**

value of $K$ is given, but (since the upward shift of the profit function is unexpected) $q$ can change discretely at the time of the initial shock.

Together, these facts tell us how the industry responds. At the time of the change, $q$ jumps to the point such that, with the dynamics of $K$ and $q$ given by the new profit function, they reach the old saddle path at exactly time $T$. This is shown in Figure 9.6. $q$ jumps from Point E to Point A at the time of the shock. $q$ and $K$ then move gradually to Point B, arriving there at time $T$. Finally, they then move up the old saddle path to E.

This analysis has several implications. First, the temporary increase in output raises investment: since output is higher for a period, firms increase their capital stocks to take advantage of this. Second, comparing Figure 9.6 with Figure 9.5 shows that $q$ rises less than it does if the increase in output is permanent; thus, since $q$ determines investment, investment responds less. Intuitively, since it is costly to reverse increases in capital, firms respond less to a rise in profits when they know they will reverse the increases. And third, Figure 9.6 shows that the path of $K$ and $q$ crosses the $\dot{K} = 0$ line before it reaches the old saddle path—that is, before time $T$. Thus the capital stock begins to decline before output returns to normal. To understand this intuitively, consider the time just before time $T$. The profit function is just about to return to its initial level; thus firms are about to want to have smaller capital stocks. And since it is costly to adjust the capital stock and since there is only a brief period of high profits left, there is a benefit and almost no cost to beginning the reduction immediately.

These results imply that it is not just current output but its entire path over time that affects investment. The comparison of permanent and temporary output movements shows that investment is higher when output is expected to be higher in the future than when it is not. Thus expectations of high output in the future raise current demand. In addition, as the example of a permanent increase in output shows, investment is higher when output has recently risen than when it has been high for an extended period. This impact of the change in output on the level of investment demand is known as the *accelerator*.

## The Effects of Interest-Rate Movements

Recall that the equation of motion for $q$ is $\dot{q} = rq - \pi(K)$ (equation [9.26]). Thus interest-rate movements, like shifts of the profit function, affect investment through their impact on the equation for $\dot{q}$. Their effects are therefore similar to the effects of output movements. A permanent decline in the interest rate, for example, shifts the $\dot{q} = 0$ locus up. In addition, since $r$ multiplies $q$ in the equation for $\dot{q}$, the decline makes the locus steeper. This is shown in Figure 9.7.

The figure can be used to analyze the effects of permanent and temporary changes in the interest rate along the lines of our analysis of the effects of permanent and temporary output movements. A permanent fall in the interest rate, for example, causes $q$ to jump to the point on the new saddle path (Point A in the diagram). $K$ and $q$ then move down to the new long-run equilibrium (Point E′). Thus the permanent decline in the interest rate produces a temporary boom in investment as the industry moves to a permanently higher capital stock.

Thus, just as with output, both past and expected future interest rates affect investment. The interest rate in our model, $r$, is the instantaneous rate of return; thus it corresponds to the short-term interest rate. One implication of this analysis is that the short-term rate does not reflect all the information about interest rates that is relevant for investment. As we will see in greater detail in Section 11.2, long-term interest rates are likely to reflect expectations of future short-term rates. If long-term rates are less than short-term rates, for example, it is likely that investors are expecting short-term rates to fall; if not, they are better off buying a series of short-term bonds than buying a long-term bond, and so no one is willing to hold long-term bonds. Thus, since our model implies that increases in expected future short-term rates reduce investment, it implies that, for a given level of current short-term rates, investment is lower when long-term rates are higher. Thus the model supports the standard view that long-term interest rates are important to investment.

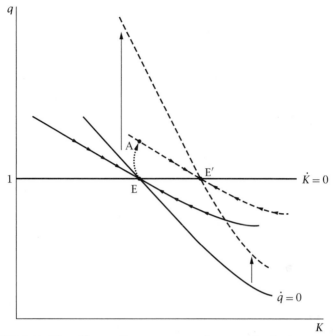

**FIGURE 9.7** **The effects of a permanent decrease in the interest rate**

## The Effects of Taxes: An Example

A temporary investment tax credit is often proposed as a way to stimulate aggregate demand during recessions. The argument is that an investment tax credit that is known to be temporary gives firms a strong incentive to invest while the credit is in effect. Our model can be used to investigate this argument.

For simplicity, assume that the investment tax credit takes the form of a direct rebate to the firm of fraction $\theta$ of the price of capital, and assume that the rebate applies to the purchase price but not to the adjustment costs. When there is a credit of this form, the firm invests as long as the value of the capital plus the rebate exceeds the capital's cost. Thus the first-order condition for current investment, (9.21), becomes

$$q(t) + \theta(t) = 1 + C'(I(t)), \tag{9.27}$$

where $\theta(t)$ is the credit at time $t$. The equation for $\dot{q}$, (9.26), is unchanged.

Equation (9.27) implies that the capital stock is constant when $q + \theta = 1$. An investment tax credit of $\theta$ therefore shifts the $\dot{K} = 0$ locus down by $\theta$; this is shown in Figure 9.8. If the credit is permanent, $q$ jumps down to the new saddle path at the time it is announced. Intuitively, because the credit

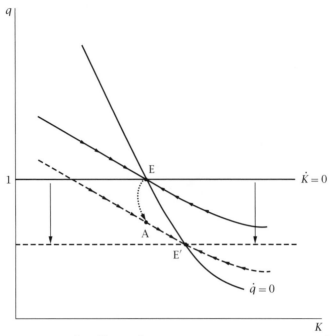

**FIGURE 9.8   The effects of a permanent investment tax credit**

increases investment, it means that the industry's profits (neglecting the credit) will be lower, and thus that existing capital is less valuable. $K$ and $q$ then move along the saddle path to the new long-run equilibrium, which involves higher $K$ and lower $q$.

Now consider a temporary credit. From our earlier analysis of a temporary change in output, we know that the announcement of the credit causes $q$ to fall to a point where the dynamics of $K$ and $q$, given the credit, bring them to the old saddle path just as the credit expires. They then move up that saddle path back to the initial long-run equilibrium.

This is shown in Figure 9.9. As the figure shows, $q$ does not fall all the way to its value on the new saddle path; thus the temporary credit reduces $q$ by less than a comparable permanent credit does. The reason is that, because the temporary credit does not lead to a permanent increase in the capital stock, it causes a smaller reduction in the value of existing capital. Now recall that the change in the capital stock, $\dot{K}$, depends on $q + \theta$ (see [9.27]). $q$ is higher under the temporary credit than under the permanent one; thus, just as the informal argument suggests, the temporary credit has a larger effect on investment than the permanent credit does. Finally, note that the figure shows that under the temporary credit, $q$ is rising in the later part of the period that the credit is in effect. Thus, after a point, the temporary credit leads to a growing investment boom as firms try to invest just before

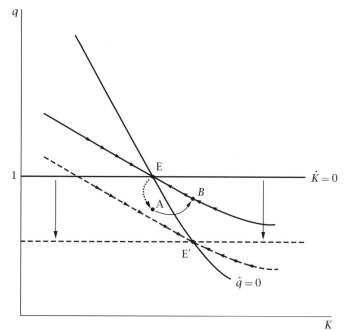

**FIGURE 9.9   The effects of a temporary investment tax credit**

the credit goes out of effect. Under the permanent credit, in contrast, the rate of change of the capital stock declines steadily as the industry moves toward its new long-run equilibrium.

# 9.6   Empirical Application: $q$ and Investment

## Summers's Test

One of the central predictions of our model of investment is that investment is increasing in $q$. This suggests the possibility of examining the relationship between investment and $q$ empirically. Summers (1981b) carries out such an investigation. He considers the version of the theory described in Section 9.3 where there are constant returns in the adjustment costs. To obtain an equation he can estimate, he assumes that the adjustment costs are quadratic in investment. Together, these assumptions imply:

$$C(I(t),\kappa(t)) = \frac{1}{2}a\left[\frac{I(t)}{\kappa(t)}\right]^2 \kappa(t), \qquad a > 0, \tag{9.28}$$

where the $\kappa(t)$ terms are included so that there are constant returns.

Recall that the condition relating investment to $q$ is that the cost of acquiring capital (the fixed purchase price of 1 plus the marginal adjustment cost) equals the value of capital: $1 + C'(I(t)) = q(t)$ (equation [9.21]). With the assumption about adjustment costs in (9.28), this condition is

$$1 + a\frac{I(t)}{\kappa(t)} = q(t), \tag{9.29}$$

which implies

$$\frac{I(t)}{\kappa(t)} = \frac{1}{a}[q(t) - 1]. \tag{9.30}$$

Based on this analysis, Summers estimates various regressions of the form

$$\frac{I_t}{K_t} = c + b[q_t - 1] + e_t. \tag{9.31}$$

He uses annual data for the United States for 1931–1978, and estimates most of his regressions by ordinary least squares. His measure of $q$ accounts for various features of the tax code that affect investment incentives.

Summers's central finding is that the coefficient on $q$ is very small. Equivalently, the implied value of $a$ is very large. In his baseline specification, the coefficient on $q$ is 0.031 (with a standard error of 0.005), which implies a value of $a$ of 32. This suggests that the adjustment costs associated with a value of $I/K$ of 0.2—a high but not exceptional figure—are equal to 65 percent of the value of the firm's capital stock (see [9.28]). When Summers embeds this estimate in a larger model, he finds that the capital stock takes 10 years to move halfway to its new steady-state value in response to a shock.

Two leading candidate explanations of these implausible results are measurement error and simultaneity. Measuring marginal $q$ (which is what the theory implies is relevant for investment) is extremely difficult; it requires estimating both the market value and the replacement cost of capital, accounting for a variety of subtle features of the tax code, and adjusting for a range of factors that could cause average and marginal $q$ to differ. To the extent that the variation in measured $q$ on the right-hand side of (9.31) is the result of measurement error, it is presumably unrelated to variation in investment. As a result, it biases estimates of the responsiveness of investment to $q$ toward zero.[11]

---

[11] Section 1.7 presents a formal model of the effects of measurement error in the context of investigations of cross-country income convergence. If one employs that model here (so that the true relationship is $I_t/K_t = c + bq_t^* + e_t$ and $\hat{q}_t = q_t^* + u_t$, where $q^*$ is actual $q$, $\hat{q}$ is measured $q$, and $e$ and $u$ are mean-zero disturbances uncorrelated with each other and with $q^*$), one can show that the estimate of $b$ from a regression of $I/K$ on $q - 1$ is biased toward zero.

To think about simultaneity, consider what happens when $e$ in (9.31)—which captures other forces affecting desired investment—is high. Increased investment demand is likely to raise interest rates. But recall that $q$ is the present discounted value of the future marginal revenue products of capital (equation [9.24]). Thus higher interest rates reduce $q$. This means that there is likely to be negative correlation between the right-hand-side variable and the residual, and thus that the coefficient on the right-hand-side variable is likely to be biased down.

## Cummins, Hassett, and Hubbard's Test

One way to address the problems of measurement error and simultaneity that may cause Summers's test to yield biased estimates is to find cases where most of the variation in measured $q$ comes from variations in actual $q$ that are not driven by changes in desired investment. Cummins, Hassett, and Hubbard (1994) argue that major U.S. tax reforms provide this type of variation. The tax reforms of 1962, 1971, 1982, and 1986 had very different effects on the tax benefits of different types of investment. Because the compositions of industries' capital stocks differ greatly, the result was that the reforms' effects on the after-tax cost of capital differed greatly across industries. Cummins, Hassett, and Hubbard argue that these differential impacts are so large that measurement error is likely to be small relative to the true variation in $q$ caused by the reforms. They also argue that the differential impacts were not a response to differences in investment demand across the industries, and thus that simultaneity is not a major concern.

Motivated by these considerations, Cummins, Hassett, and Hubbard (loosely speaking) run cross-industry regressions in the tax-reform years of investment rates, not on $q$, but only on the component of the change in $q$ (defined as the ratio of the market value of capital to its after-tax cost) that is due to the tax reforms. When they do this, a typical estimate of the coefficient on $q$ is 0.5 and is fairly precisely estimated. Thus $a$ is estimated to be around 2, which implies that the adjustment costs associated with $I/K = 0.2$ are about 4 percent of the value of the firm's capital stock—a much more plausible figure than the one obtained by Summers.

There are at least two limitations to this finding. First, it is not clear whether the cross-industry results carry over to aggregate investment. One potential problem is that forces that affect aggregate investment demand are likely to affect the price of investment goods; differential effects of tax reform on different industries, in contrast, seem much less likely to cause differential changes in the prices of different investment goods. That is, external adjustment costs may be more important for aggregate than for cross-section variations in investment. And indeed, Goolsbee (1998) finds evidence of substantial rises in the price of investment goods in response to tax incentives for investment.

Second, we will see in Section 9.10 that the funds that firms have available for investment appear to affect their investment decisions for a given $q$. But industries whose marginal cost of capital is reduced the most by tax reforms are likely to also be the ones whose tax payments are reduced the most by the reforms, and who will thus have the largest increases in the funds they have available for investment. Thus there may be positive correlation between Cummins, Hassett, and Hubbard's measure and the residual, and thus upward bias in their estimates.

## 9.7   The Effects of Uncertainty

Our analysis so far assumes that firms are certain about future profitability, interest rates, and tax policies. In practice, they face uncertainty about all of these. This section therefore introduces some of the issues raised by uncertainty.

### Uncertainty about Future Profitability

We begin with the case where there is no uncertainty about the path of the interest rate; for simplicity it is assumed to be constant. Thus the uncertainty concerns only future profitability. In the case, the value of 1 unit of capital is given by

$$q(t) = \int_{\tau=t}^{\infty} e^{-r(\tau-t)} E_t[\pi(K(\tau))] \, d\tau \tag{9.32}$$

(see [9.24]).

This expression can be used to find how $q$ is expected to evolve over time. Since (9.32) holds at all times, it implies that the expectation as of time $t$ of $q$ at some later time, $t + \Delta t$, is given by

$$E_t[q(t + \Delta t)] = E_t\left[\int_{\tau=t+\Delta t}^{\infty} e^{-r[\tau-(t+\Delta t)]} E_{t+\Delta t}[\pi(K(\tau))] \, d\tau\right]$$

$$= \int_{\tau=t+\Delta t}^{\infty} e^{-r[\tau-(t+\Delta t)]} E_t[\pi(K(\tau))] \, d\tau, \tag{9.33}$$

where the second line uses the fact that the law of iterated projections implies that $E_t[E_{t+\Delta t}[\pi(K(\tau))]]$ is just $E_t[\pi(K(\tau))]$. Differentiating (9.33) with respect to $\Delta t$ and evaluating the resulting expression at $\Delta t = 0$ gives us

$$E_t[\dot{q}(t)] = rq(t) - \pi(K(t)). \tag{9.34}$$

Except for the presence of the expectations term, this expression is identical to the equation for $\dot{q}$ in the model with certainty (see [9.26]).

As before, each firm invests to the point where the cost of acquiring new capital equals the market value of capital. Thus equation (9.25), $\dot{K}(t) = f(q(t))$, continues to hold.

Our analysis so far appears to imply that uncertainty has no effect on investment: firms invest as long as the value of new capital exceeds the cost of acquiring it, and the value of that capital depends only on its expected payoffs. But this analysis neglects the fact that it is not quite correct to assume that there is exogenous uncertainty about the future values of $\pi(K)$. Since the path of $K$ is determined within the model, what can be taken as exogenous is uncertainty about the position of the $\pi(\bullet)$ function; the combination of that uncertainty and firms' behavior then determines uncertainty about the values of $\pi(K)$.

In one natural baseline case, this subtlety proves to be unimportant: if $\pi(\bullet)$ is linear and $C(\bullet)$ is quadratic and if the uncertainty concerns the intercept of the $\pi(\bullet)$ function, then the uncertainty does not affect investment. That is, one can show that in this case, investment at any time is the same as it is if the future values of the intercept of the $\pi(\bullet)$ function are certain to equal their expected values (see Problems 9.10 and 9.11).

## An Example

Even in our baseline case, news about future profitability and the resolution of uncertainty about future profitability affect investment by affecting expectations of the mean of the intercept of the $\pi(\bullet)$ function. To see this, suppose that $\pi(\bullet)$ is linear and $C(\bullet)$ is quadratic, and that initially the $\pi(\bullet)$ function is constant and the industry is in long-run equilibrium. At some date, which we normalize to time 0, it becomes known that the government is considering a change in the tax code that would raise the intercept of the $\pi(\bullet)$ function. The proposal will be voted on at time $T$, and it has a 50 percent chance of passing. There is no other source of uncertainty.

The effects of this development are shown in Figure 9.10. The figure shows the $\dot{K} = 0$ locus and the $\dot{q} = 0$ loci and the saddle paths with the initial $\pi(\bullet)$ function and the potential new, higher function. Given our assumptions, all these loci are straight lines (see Problem 9.10). Initially, $K$ and $q$ are at Point E. After the proposal is voted on, they will move along the appropriate saddle path to the relevant long-run equilibrium (Point E′ if the proposal is passed, E if it is defeated). There cannot be an expected capital gain or loss at the time the proposal is voted on. Thus, since the proposal has a 50 percent chance of passing, $q$ must be midway vertically between the two saddle paths at the time of the vote; that is, it must be on the dotted line in the figure. Finally, before the vote the dynamics of $K$ and $q$ are given by (9.34) and (9.25) with the initial $\pi(\bullet)$ function and no uncertainty about $\dot{q}$.

Thus at the time it becomes known that the government is considering the proposal, $q$ jumps up to the point such that the dynamics of $K$ and $q$

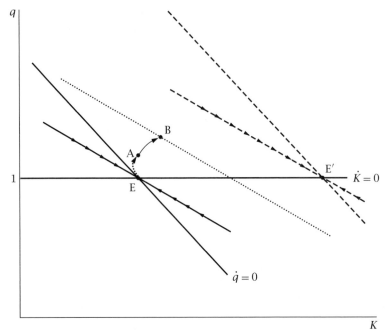

**FIGURE 9.10   The effects of uncertainty about future tax policy when adjustment costs are symmetric**

carry them to the dotted line at time *T*. *q* then jumps up or down depending on the outcome of the vote, and *K* and *q* then converge to the relevant long-run equilibrium.

## Irreversible Investment

If $\pi(\bullet)$ is not linear or $C(\bullet)$ is not quadratic, uncertainty about the $\pi(\bullet)$ function can affect expectations of future values of $\pi(K)$, and thus can affect current investment. Suppose, for example, that it is more costly for firms to reduce their capital stocks than to increase them. Then if $\pi(\bullet)$ shifts up, the industry-wide capital stock will rise rapidly, and so the increase in $\pi(K)$ will be brief; but if $\pi(\bullet)$ shifts down, *K* will fall only slowly, and so the decrease in $\pi(K)$ will be long-lasting. Thus with asymmetry in adjustment costs, uncertainty about the position of the profit function reduces expectations of future profitability, and thus reduces investment.

This type of asymmetry in adjustment costs means that investment is somewhat *irreversible:* it is easier to increase the capital stock than to reverse the increase. In the phase diagram, irreversibility causes the saddle path to be curved. If *K* exceeds its long-run equilibrium value, it falls only slowly; thus profits are depressed for an extended period, and so *q* is much

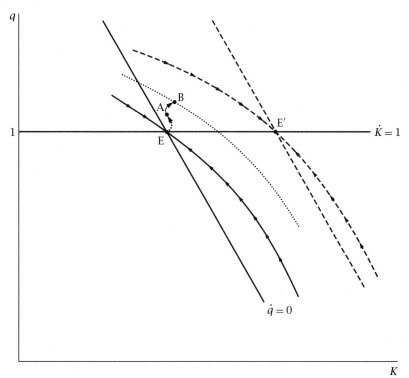

**FIGURE 9.11** **The effects of uncertainty about future tax policy when adjustment costs are asymmetric**

less than 1. If $K$ is less than its long-run equilibrium value, on the other hand, it rises rapidly, and so $q$ is only slightly more than 1.

To see the effects of irreversibility, consider our previous example, but now with the assumption that the costs of adjusting the capital stock are asymmetric. This situation is analyzed in Figure 9.11. As before, at the time the proposal is voted on, $q$ must be midway vertically between the two saddle paths, and again the dynamics of $K$ and $q$ before the vote are given by (9.34) and (9.25) with the initial $\pi(\bullet)$ function and no uncertainty about $\dot{q}$.

Thus, as before, when it becomes known that the government is considering the proposal, $q$ jumps up to the point such that the dynamics of $K$ and $q$ carry them to the dashed line at time $T$. As the figure shows, however, the asymmetry of the adjustment costs causes this jump to be smaller than it is under symmetric costs. The fact that it is costly to reduce capital holdings means that if firms build up large capital stocks before the vote and the proposal is then defeated, the fact that it is hard to reverse the increase causes $q$ to be quite low. This acts to reduce the value of capital before the vote, and thus reduces investment. Intuitively, when investment is irreversible, there is an *option value* to waiting rather than investing. If a firm does not invest, it retains the possibility of keeping its capital stock low; if it invests, on the other hand, it commits itself to a high capital stock.

## Uncertainty about Discount Factors

Firms are uncertain not only about what their future profits will be, but also about how those payoffs will be valued. To see the effects of this uncertainty, suppose the firm is owned by a representative consumer. As we saw in Section 8.5, the consumer values future payoffs not according to a constant interest rate, but according to the marginal utility of consumption. The discounted marginal utility of consumption at time $\tau$, relative to the marginal utility of consumption at $t$, is $e^{-\rho(\tau-t)}u'(C(\tau))/u'(C(t))$, where $\rho$ is the consumer's discount rate, $u(\bullet)$ is the instantaneous utility function, and $C$ is consumption (see equation [8.31]). Thus our expression for the value of a unit of capital, (9.32), becomes

$$q(t) = \int_{\tau=t}^{\infty} e^{-\rho(\tau-t)} E_t \left[ \frac{u'(C(\tau))}{u'(C(t))} \pi(K(\tau)) \right] d\tau. \tag{9.35}$$

As Craine (1989) emphasizes, (9.35) implies that the impact of a project's riskiness on investment in the project depends on the same considerations that determine the impact of assets' riskiness on their values in the consumption CAPM. Idiosyncratic risk—that is, randomness in $\pi(K)$ that is uncorrelated with $u'(C)$—has no impact on the market value of capital, and thus no impact on investment. But uncertainty that is positively correlated with aggregate risk—that is, positive correlation of $\pi(K)$ and $C$, and thus negative correlation of $\pi(K)$ and $u'(C)$—lowers the value of capital and hence reduces investment. And uncertainty that is negatively correlated with aggregate risk raises investment.

# 9.8   Kinked and Fixed Adjustment Costs

The previous section considers a simple form of partial irreversibility of investment. Realistically, however, adjustment costs are almost certainly more complicated than just being asymmetric around $I = 0$. One possibility is that the marginal cost of both the first unit of investment and the first unit of disinvestment are strictly positive. This could arise if there are transaction costs associated with both buying and selling capital. In this case, $C(I)$ is kinked at $I = 0$. An even larger departure from smooth adjustment costs arises if there is a fixed cost to undertaking any nonzero amount of investment. In this case, $C(I)$ is not just kinked at $I = 0$, but discontinuous.

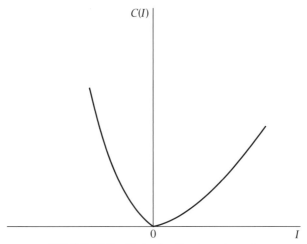

FIGURE 9.12   Kinked adjustment costs

## Kinked Costs

A kinked adjustment-cost function is shown in Figure 9.12. In the case shown, the adjustment cost for the first unit of positive investment, which we will denote $c^+$, is less than the adjustment cost for the first unit of disinvestment, $c^-$.

It is straightforward to modify our phase-diagram analysis to incorporate kinked adjustment costs. To do this, start by noting that firms neither invest nor disinvest when $1 - c^- \leq q(t) \leq 1 + c^+$ (Abel and Eberly, 1994). Thus there is a range of values of $q$ for which $\dot{K} = 0$. In terms of the phase diagram, this means that the $\dot{K} = 0$ line at $q = 1$ in the model with smooth adjustment costs is replaced by the area from $q = 1 - c^-$ to $q = 1 + c^+$. This is shown in Figure 9.13.

Recall that equation (9.26) for $\dot{q}$, $\dot{q}(t) = rq(t) - \pi(K(t))$, is simply a consistency requirement for how firms value capital over time. Thus assuming a more complicated form for adjustment costs does not change this condition. The $\dot{q} = 0$ locus is therefore the same as before; this is also shown in Figure 9.13.

Let $K_1$ denote the value of $K$ where the $\dot{q} = 0$ locus crosses into the $\dot{K} = 0$ region, and $K_2$ the level of $K$ where it leaves. If the initial value of $K$, $K(0)$, is less than $K_1$, then $q(0)$ exceeds $1 + c^+$. There is positive investment, and the economy moves down the saddle path until $K = K_1$ and $q = 1 + c^+$; this is Point $E^+$ in the diagram. Similarly, if $K(0)$ exceeds $K_2$, there is disinvestment, and the economy converges to Point $E^-$. And if $K(0)$ is between $K_1$ and $K_2$, there is neither investment nor disinvestment, and $K$ remains constant at $K(0)$. Thus the long-run equilibria are the points on the $\dot{q} = 0$ locus from $E^+$ to $E^-$.

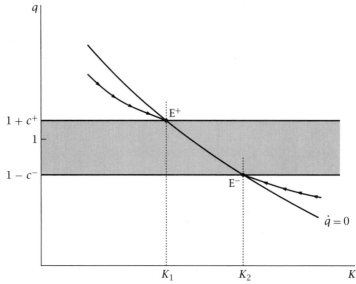

**FIGURE 9.13   The phase diagram with kinked adjustment costs**

Finally, the fact that $\dot{q}$ is zero when $K = K_1$ or $K = K_2$ allows us to characterize $K_1$ and $K_2$ in terms of the profit function. The expression for $\dot{q}$, $\dot{q}(t) = rq(t) - \pi(K(t))$, implies that when $\dot{q}$ is zero, $q$ equals $\pi(K)/r$. Thus $K_1$ satisfies $\pi(K_1)/r = 1 + c^+$, and $K_2$ satisfies $\pi(K_2)/r = 1 - c^-$. Similarly, the fact that $\dot{q} = 0$ when $K$ is between $K_1$ and $K_2$ implies that if $K(0)$ is in this range, $q$ equals $\pi(K(0))/r$.

## Fixed Costs

If there is a fixed cost to any nonzero quantity of investment, the adjustment-cost function is discontinuous. One might expect this to make the model very difficult to analyze: with a fixed cost, a small change in a firm's environment can cause a discrete change in its behavior. It turns out, however, that in a natural baseline case fixed costs do not greatly complicate the analysis of aggregate investment. Specifically, we will focus on the case where there are constant returns to scale in the adjustment costs. This assumption implies that the division of the aggregate capital stock among firms is irrelevant, and thus that we do not have to keep track of each firm's capital.

When there are fixed costs, adjustment costs per unit of investment are nonmonotonic in investment. The fixed costs act to make this ratio decreasing in investment at low positive levels of investment. But the remaining component of adjustment costs (which we assume continue to satisfy

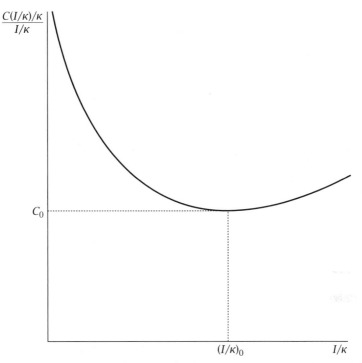

**FIGURE 9.14   Adjustment costs per unit of investment in the presence of fixed costs**

$C'(I) > 0$ for $I > 0$, $C'(I) < 0$ for $I < 0$, and $C''(I) > 0$) act to make this ratio increasing at high positive levels of investment.

Suppose, for example, that adjustment costs consist of a fixed cost and a quadratic component:

$$\frac{C(I,\kappa)}{\kappa} = \begin{cases} F + \dfrac{1}{2}a\left(\dfrac{I}{\kappa}\right)^2 & \text{if } I \neq 0 \\ 0 & \text{if } I = 0, \end{cases} \tag{9.36}$$

where $F > 0, a > 0$. (As in equation [9.28], the $\kappa$ terms ensure constant returns to scale. Doubling $I$ and $\kappa$ leaves $C(I,\kappa)/\kappa$ unchanged, and so doubles $C(I,\kappa)$.) Equation (9.36) implies that adjustment costs per unit of investment (both expressed relative to the firm's capital stock) are

$$\frac{C(I,\kappa)/\kappa}{I/\kappa} = \frac{F}{I/\kappa} + \frac{1}{2}a\left(\frac{I}{\kappa}\right) \qquad \text{if } I \neq 0. \tag{9.37}$$

As Figure 9.14 shows, this ratio is first decreasing and then increasing in the investment rate, $I/\kappa$.

A firm's value is linear in its investment: each unit of investment the firm undertakes at time $t$ raises its value by $q(t)$. As a result, the firm never chooses a level of investment in the range where $[C(I,\kappa)/\kappa]/(I/\kappa)$ is decreasing. If a quantity of investment in that range is profitable (in the sense that the increase in the firm's value, $q(t)I(t)$, is greater than the purchase costs of the capital plus the adjustment costs), a slightly higher level of investment is even more profitable. Thus, each firm acts as if it has a minimum investment rate (the level $(I/\kappa)_0$ in the diagram) and a minimum cost per unit of investment ($C_0$ in the diagram).

Recall, however, that there are many firms. As a result, for the economy as a whole there is no minimum level of investment. There can be aggregate investment at a rate less than $(I/\kappa)_0$ at a cost per unit of investment of $C_0$; all that is needed is for some firms to invest at rate $(I/\kappa)_0$. Thus the aggregate economy does not behave as though there are fixed adjustment costs. Instead, it behaves as though the first unit of investment has strictly positive adjustment costs and the adjustment costs per unit of investment are constant over some range. And the same is true of disinvestment. The aggregate implications of fixed adjustment costs in this case are therefore similar to those of kinked costs.

Fixed costs (and kinked costs) have potentially more interesting implications when firms are heterogeneous and there is uncertainty. There is a substantial literature investigating the microeconomic and macroeconomic effects of irreversibility, fixed costs, and uncertainty both theoretically and empirically. One important departure from the models we have been analyzing is the inclusion of imperfect competition and other forces that make a firm's profits concave rather than linear in its capital stock. This makes the composition of investment among firms no longer irrelevant, and thus eliminates the simple force in the model we have been considering that makes fixed costs unimportant to aggregate investment. Nonetheless, many (though not all) analyses find that investment behavior at the macroeconomic level in the presence of fixed adjustment costs at the microeconomic level is similar to its behavior with smooth adjustment costs.[12]

# 9.9  Financial-Market Imperfections

## Introduction

When firms and investors are equally well informed, financial markets function efficiently. Investments are valued according to their expected payoffs and riskiness. As a result, they are undertaken if their value exceeds the cost of acquiring and installing the necessary capital. These are the assumptions underlying our analysis so far. In particular, we have assumed that firms make investments if they raise the present value of profits evaluated using

---

[12] For more on these issues, see Caballero, Engel, and Haltiwanger (1995); Thomas (2002); Veracierto (2002); Cooper and Haltiwanger (2006); Gourio and Kashyap (2007); Bachmann, Caballero, and Engel (2008); and House (2008).

the prevailing economy-wide interest rate. Thus we have implicitly assumed that firms can borrow at that interest rate.

In practice, however, firms are much better informed than potential outside investors about their investment projects. Outside financing must ultimately come from individuals. These individuals usually have little contact with the firm and little expertise concerning the firm's activities. In addition, their stakes in the firm are usually low enough that their incentive to acquire relevant information is small.

Because of these problems, institutions such as banks, mutual funds, and bond-rating agencies that specialize in acquiring and transmitting information play central roles in financial markets. But even they are much less informed than the firms or individuals in whom they are investing their funds. The issuer of a credit card, for example, is usually much less informed than the holder of the card about the holder's financial circumstances and spending habits. In addition, the existence of intermediaries between the ultimate investors and firms means that there is a two-level problem of asymmetric information: there is asymmetric information not just between the intermediaries and the firms, but also between the individuals and the intermediaries (Diamond, 1984).

Asymmetric information creates *agency problems* between investors and firms. Some of the risk in the payoff to investment is usually borne by the investors rather than by the firm; this occurs, for example, in any situation where there is a possibility that the firm may go bankrupt. When this is the case, the firm can change its behavior to take advantage of its superior information. It can only borrow if it knows that its project is particularly risky, for example, or it can choose a high-risk strategy over a low-risk one even if this reduces expected returns. Thus asymmetric information can distort investment choices away from the most efficient projects. In addition, the presence of asymmetric information can lead the investors to expend resources monitoring the firms' activities; thus again it imposes costs.

This section presents a simple model of asymmetric information and the resulting agency problems, and discusses some of their effects. We will find that when there is asymmetric information, investment depends on more than just interest rates and profitability; such factors as investors' ability to monitor firms and firms' ability to finance their investment using internal funds also matter. We will also see that asymmetric information changes how interest rates and profitability affect investment.

## Assumptions

An entrepreneur has the opportunity to undertake a project that requires 1 unit of resources. The entrepreneur has wealth of $W$, which is less than 1. Thus he or she must obtain $1 - W$ units of outside financing to undertake the project. If the project is undertaken, it has an expected output of $\gamma$, which is positive. $\gamma$ is heterogeneous across entrepreneurs and is publicly observable. Actual output can differ from expected output, however; specifically, the actual output of a project with an expected output of $\gamma$ is distributed uniformly on $[0, 2\gamma]$. Since the entrepreneur's wealth is all invested in the project, his or her payment to the outside investors cannot exceed the project's output. This limit on the amount that the entrepreneur can pay to outside investors means that the investors must bear some of the project's risk.

If the entrepreneur does not undertake the project, he or she can invest at the risk-free interest rate, $r$. The entrepreneur is risk-neutral; thus he or she undertakes the project if the difference between $\gamma$ and the expected payments to the outside investors is greater than $(1 + r)W$.

The outside investors, like the entrepreneur, are risk-neutral and can invest their wealth at the risk-free rate. In addition, the outside investors are competitive. Thus in equilibrium their expected rate of return on any financing they provide to entrepreneurs must be $r$.

The key assumption of the model is that entrepreneurs are better informed than outside investors about their projects' actual output. Specifically, an entrepreneur observes his or her output costlessly; an outside investor, however, must pay a cost $c$ to observe output. $c$ is assumed to be positive; for convenience, it is also assumed to be less than expected output, $\gamma$.

This type of asymmetric information is known as *costly state verification* (Townsend, 1979). We focus on this type of asymmetric information between entrepreneurs and investors not because it is the most important type in practice, but because it is relatively straightforward to analyze. Other types of information asymmetries, such as asymmetric information about the riskiness of projects or entrepreneurs' actions, have broadly similar effects.

## The Equilibrium under Symmetric Information

In the absence of the cost of observing the project's output, the equilibrium is straightforward. Entrepreneurs whose projects have an expected payoff that exceeds $1 + r$ obtain financing and undertake their projects; entrepreneurs whose projects have an expected output less than $1 + r$ do not. For the projects that are undertaken, the contract between the entrepreneur and the outside investors provides the investors with expected payments of $(1 - W)(1 + r)$. There are many contracts that do this. One example is a contract that gives to investors the fraction $(1 - W)(1 + r)/\gamma$ of whatever output turns out to be. Since expected output is $\gamma$, this yields an expected payment of $(1 - W)(1 + r)$. The entrepreneur's expected income is then $\gamma - (1 - W)(1 + r)$, which equals $W(1 + r) + \gamma - (1 + r)$. Since $\gamma$ exceeds $1 + r$ by assumption, this is greater than $W(1 + r)$. Thus the entrepreneur is made better off by undertaking the project.

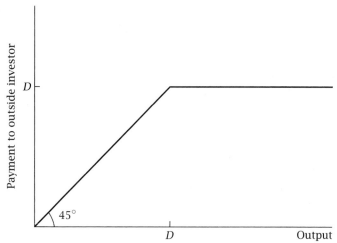

**FIGURE 9.15 The form of the optimal payment function**

## The Form of the Contract under Asymmetric Information

Now consider the case where it is costly for outside investors to observe a project's output. In addition, assume that each outsider's wealth is greater than $1 - W$. Thus we can focus on the case where, in equilibrium, each project has only a single outside investor. This allows us to avoid dealing with the complications that arise when there is more than one outside investor who may want to observe a project's output.

Since outside investors are risk-neutral and competitive, an entrepreneur's expected payment to the investor must equal $(1 + r)(1 - W)$ plus the investor's expected spending on verifying output. The entrepreneur's expected income equals the project's expected output, which is exogenous, minus the expected payment to the investor. Thus the optimal contract is the one that minimizes the fraction of the time that the investor verifies output while providing the outside investor with the required rate of return.

Given our assumptions, the contract that accomplishes this takes a simple form. If the payoff to the project exceeds some critical level $D$, then the entrepreneur pays the investor $D$ and the investor does not verify output. But if the payoff is less than $D$, the investor pays the verification cost and takes all of output. Thus the contract is a debt contract. The entrepreneur borrows $1 - W$ and promises to pay back $D$ if that is possible. If the entrepreneur's output exceeds the amount that is due, he or she pays off the loan and keeps the surplus. And if the entrepreneur cannot make the required payment, all of his or her resources go to the lender. This payment function is shown in Figure 9.15.

The argument that the optimal contract takes this form has several steps. First, when the investor does not verify output, the payment cannot depend on actual output. To see this, suppose that the payment is supposed to be $Q_1$ when output is $Y_1$ and $Q_2$ when output is $Y_2$, with $Q_2 > Q_1$, and that the investor does not verify output in either of these cases. Since the investor does not know output, when output is $Y_2$ the entrepreneur pretends that it is $Y_1$, and therefore pays $Q_1$. Thus the contract cannot make the payment when output is $Y_2$ exceed the payment when it is $Y_1$.

Second, and similarly, the payment with verification can never exceed the payment without verification, $D$; otherwise the entrepreneur always pretends that output is not equal to the values of output that yield a payment greater than $D$. In addition, the payment with verification cannot equal $D$; otherwise it is possible to reduce expected expenditures on verification by not verifying whenever the entrepreneur pays $D$.

Third, the payment is $D$ whenever output exceeds $D$. To see this, note that if the payment is ever less than $D$ when output is greater than $D$, it is possible to increase the investor's expected receipts and reduce expected verification costs by changing the payment to $D$ for these levels of output; as a result, it is possible to construct a more efficient contract.

Fourth, the entrepreneur cannot pay $D$ if output is less than $D$. Thus in these cases the investor must verify output.

Finally, if the payment is less than all of output when output is less than $D$, increasing the payment in these situations raises the investor's expected receipts without changing expected verification costs. But this means that it is possible to reduce $D$, and thus to save on verification costs.

Together, these facts imply that the optimal contract is a debt contract.[13]

## The Equilibrium Value of $D$

The next step of the analysis is to determine what value of $D$ is specified in the contract. Investors are risk-neutral and competitive, and the risk-free interest rate is $r$. Thus the expected payments to the investor, minus his or her expected spending on verification, must equal $1 + r$ times the amount of the loan, $1 - W$. To find the equilibrium value of $D$, we must therefore

---

[13] For formal proofs, see Townsend (1979) and Gale and Hellwig (1985). This analysis neglects two subtleties. First, it assumes that verification must be a deterministic function of the state. One can show, however, that a contract that makes verification a random function of the entrepreneur's announcement of output can improve on the contract shown in Figure 9.15 (Bernanke and Gertler, 1989). Second, the analysis assumes that the investor can commit to verification if the entrepreneur announces that output is less than $D$. For any announced level of output less than $D$, the investor prefers to receive that amount without verifying than with verifying. But if the investor can decide ex post not to verify, the entrepreneur has an incentive to announce low output. Thus the contract is not *renegotiation-proof*. For simplicity, we neglect these complications.

determine how the investor's expected receipts net of verification costs vary with $D$, and then find the value of $D$ that provides the investor with the required expected net receipts.

To find the investor's expected net receipts, suppose first that $D$ is less than the project's maximum possible output, $2\gamma$. In this case, actual output can be either more or less than $D$. If output is more than $D$, the investor does not pay the verification cost and receives $D$. Since output is distributed uniformly on $[0,2\gamma]$, the probability of this occurring is $(2\gamma - D)/(2\gamma)$. If output is less than $D$, the investor pays the verification cost and receives all of output. The assumption that output is distributed uniformly implies that the probability of this occurring is $D/(2\gamma)$, and that average output conditional on this event is $D/2$.

If $D$ exceeds $2\gamma$, on the other hand, then output is always less than $D$. Thus in this case the investor always pays the verification cost and receives all of output. In this case the expected payment is $\gamma$.

Thus the investor's expected receipts minus verification costs are

$$
R(D) = \begin{cases} \dfrac{2\gamma - D}{2\gamma}D + \dfrac{D}{2\gamma}\left(\dfrac{D}{2} - c\right) & \text{if } D \le 2\gamma \\[2ex] \gamma - c & \text{if } D > 2\gamma. \end{cases} \tag{9.38}
$$

Equation (9.38) implies that when $D$ is less than $2\gamma$, $R'(D)$ equals $1 - [c/(2\gamma)] - [D/(2\gamma)]$. Thus $R$ increases until $D = 2\gamma - c$ and then decreases. The reason that raising $D$ above $2\gamma - c$ lowers the investor's expected net revenues is that when the investor verifies output, the net amount he or she receives is always less than $2\gamma - c$. Thus setting $D = 2\gamma - c$ and accepting $2\gamma - c$ without verification when output exceeds $2\gamma - c$ makes the investor better off than setting $D > 2\gamma - c$.

Equation (9.38) implies that when $D = 2\gamma - c$, the investor's expected net revenues are $R(2\gamma - c) = [(2\gamma - c)/(2\gamma)]^2\gamma \equiv R^{\text{MAX}}$. Thus the maximum expected net revenues equal expected output when $c$ is zero, but are less than this when $c$ is greater than zero. Finally, $R$ declines to $\gamma - c$ at $D = 2\gamma$; thereafter further increases in $D$ do not affect $R(D)$. The $R(D)$ function is plotted in Figure 9.16.

Figure 9.17 shows three possible values of the investor's required net revenues, $(1+r)(1-W)$. If the required net revenues equal $V_1$—more generally, if they are less than $\gamma - c$—there is a unique value of $D$ that yields the investor the required net revenues. The contract therefore specifies this value of $D$. For the case when the required payment equals $V_1$, the equilibrium value of $D$ is given by $D_1$ in the figure.

If the required net revenues exceed $R^{\text{MAX}}$—if they equal $V_3$, for example—there is no value of $D$ that yields the necessary revenues for the investor. Thus in this situation there is *credit rationing:* investors refuse to lend to the entrepreneur at any interest rate.

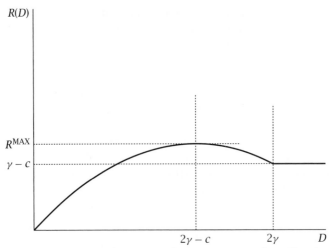

**FIGURE 9.16    The investor's expected revenues net of verification costs**

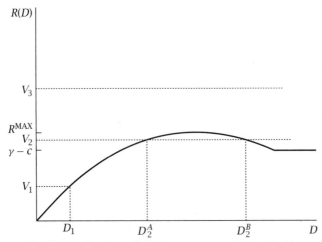

**FIGURE 9.17    The determination of the entrepreneur's required payment to the investor**

Finally, if the required net revenues are between $\gamma - c$ and $R^{\mathrm{MAX}}$, there are two possible values of $D$. For example, the figure shows that a $D$ of either $D_2^A$ or $D_2^B$ yields $R(D) = V_2$. The higher of these two $D$'s ($D_2^B$ in the figure) is not a competitive equilibrium, however: if an investor is making a loan to an entrepreneur with a required payment of $D_2^B$, other investors can profitably lend on more favorable terms. Thus competition drives $D$ down to $D_2^A$. The equilibrium value of $D$ is thus the smaller solution to $R(D) = (1 + r)(1 - W)$.

Expression (9.38) implies that this solution is[14]

$$D^* = 2\gamma - c - \sqrt{(2\gamma - c)^2 - 4\gamma(1 + r)(1 - W)}$$
$$\text{for } (1 + r)(1 - W) \le R^{\text{MAX}}.$$

(9.39)

## Equilibrium Investment

The final step of the analysis is to determine when the entrepreneur undertakes the project. Clearly a necessary condition is that he or she can obtain financing at some interest rate. But this is not sufficient: some entrepreneurs who can obtain financing may be better off investing in the safe asset.

An entrepreneur who invests in the safe asset obtains $(1 + r)W$. If the entrepreneur instead undertakes the project, his or her expected receipts are expected output, $\gamma$, minus expected payments to the outside investor. If the entrepreneur can obtain financing, the expected payments to the investor are the opportunity cost of the investor's funds, $(1 + r)(1 - W)$, plus the investor's expected spending on verification costs. Thus to determine when a project is undertaken, we need to determine these expected verification costs.

These can be found from equation (9.39). The investor verifies when output is less than $D^*$, which occurs with probability $D^*/(2\gamma)$. Thus expected verification costs are

$$A = \frac{D^*}{2\gamma}c$$

$$= \left[\frac{2\gamma - c}{2\gamma} - \sqrt{\left(\frac{2\gamma - c}{2\gamma}\right)^2 - \frac{(1 + r)(1 - W)}{\gamma}}\right]c.$$

(9.40)

Straightforward differentiation shows that $A$ is increasing in $c$ and $r$ and decreasing in $\gamma$ and $W$. We can therefore write

$$A = A(c, r, W, \gamma), \qquad A_c > 0, \qquad A_r > 0, \qquad A_W < 0, \qquad A_\gamma < 0. \quad (9.41)$$

The entrepreneur's expected payments to the investor are $(1+r)(1-W) + A(c, r, W, \gamma)$. Thus the project is undertaken if $(1 + r)(1 - W) \le R^{\text{MAX}}$ and if

$$\gamma - (1 + r)(1 - W) - A(c, r, W, \gamma) > (1 + r)W. \quad (9.42)$$

Although we have derived these results from a particular model of asymmetric information, the basic ideas are general. Suppose, for example, that there is asymmetric information about how much risk the entrepreneur is

---

[14] Note that the condition for the expression under the square root sign, $(2\gamma - c)^2 - 4\gamma(1+r)(1-W)$, to be negative is that $[(2\gamma - c)/(2\gamma)]^2\gamma < (1+r)(1-W)$—that is, that $R^{\text{MAX}}$ is less than required net revenues. Thus the case where the expression in (9.39) is not defined corresponds to the case where there is no value of $D$ at which investors are willing to lend.

taking. In such a situation, if the investor bears some of the cost of poor outcomes, the entrepreneur has an incentive to increase the riskiness of his or her activities beyond the point that maximizes the expected return to the project. Thus there is *moral hazard*. As a result, asymmetric information again reduces the total expected returns to the entrepreneur and the investor, just as it does in our model of costly state verification. Under plausible assumptions, these agency costs are decreasing in the amount of financing that the entrepreneur can provide ($W$), increasing in the amount that the investor must be paid for a given amount of financing ($r$), decreasing in the expected payoff to the project ($\gamma$), and increasing in the magnitude of the asymmetric information ($c$ when there is costly state verification, and the entrepreneur's ability to take high-risk actions when there is moral hazard).

Similarly, suppose that entrepreneurs are heterogeneous in terms of how risky their projects are, and that risk is not publicly observable—that is, suppose there is *adverse selection*. Then again there are agency costs of outside finance, and again those costs are determined by the same types of considerations as in our model. Thus the qualitative results of this model apply to many other models of asymmetric information in financial markets.

## Implications

This model has many implications. As the preceding discussion suggests, most of the major ones arise from financial-market imperfections in general rather than from our specific model. Here we discuss four of the most important.

First, the agency costs arising from asymmetric information raise the cost of external finance, and therefore discourage investment. Under symmetric information, investment occurs in our model if $\gamma > 1 + r$. But when there is asymmetric information, investment occurs only if $\gamma > 1 + r + A(c,r,W,\gamma)$. Thus the agency costs reduce investment at a given safe interest rate.

Second, because financial-market imperfections create agency costs that affect investment, they alter the impact of output and interest-rate movements on investment. Recall from Section 9.5 that when financial markets are perfect, output movements affect investment through their effect on future profitability. Financial-market imperfections create a second channel: because output movements affect firms' current profitability, they affect firms' ability to provide internal finance. In the context of our model, we can think of a fall in current output as lowering entrepreneurs' wealth, $W$; since a reduction in wealth increases agency costs, the fall in output reduces investment even if the profitability of investment projects (the distribution of the $\gamma$'s) is unchanged.

Similarly, interest-rate movements affect investment not only through the conventional channel, but also through their impact on agency costs: an increase in interest rates raises agency costs and thus discourages investment. Intuitively, an increase in $r$ raises the total amount the entrepreneur must pay the investor. This means that the probability that the investor is unable to make the required payment is higher, and thus that agency costs are higher. Specifically, since the investor's required net revenues are $(1 + r)(1 - W)$, an increase in $r$ of $\Delta r$ increases these required revenues by $(1 - W)\,\Delta r$. Thus it has the same effect on the required net revenues as a fall in $W$ of $[(1 - W)/(1 + r)]\,\Delta r$. As a result, as equation (9.40) shows, these two changes have the same effect on agency costs.

In addition, the model implies that the effects of changes in output and interest rates on investment do not all occur through their impact on entrepreneurs' decisions of whether to borrow at the prevailing interest rate. Instead some of the impact comes from changes in the set of entrepreneurs who are able to borrow.

The third implication of our analysis is that many variables that do not affect investment when capital markets are perfect matter when capital markets are imperfect. Entrepreneurs' wealth provides a simple example. Suppose that $\gamma$ and $W$ are heterogeneous across entrepreneurs. With perfect financial markets, whether a project is funded depends only on $\gamma$. Thus the projects that are undertaken are the most productive ones. This is shown in Panel (a) of Figure 9.18. With asymmetric information, in contrast, since $W$ affects the agency costs, whether a project is funded depends on both $\gamma$ and $W$. Thus a project with a lower expected payoff than another can be funded if the entrepreneur with the less productive project is wealthier. This is shown in Panel (b) of the figure.

The fact that financial-market imperfections cause entrepreneurs' wealth to affect investment implies that these imperfections can magnify the effects of shocks that occur outside the financial system. Declines in output arising from other sources act to reduce entrepreneurs' wealth. These reductions in wealth reduce investment, and thus increase the output declines (Bernanke and Gertler, 1989; Kiyotaki and Moore, 1997).

Two other examples of variables that affect investment only when capital markets are imperfect are average tax rates and idiosyncratic risk. If taxes are added to the model, the average rate (rather than just the marginal rate) affects investment through its impact on firms' ability to use internal finance. And risk, even if it is uncorrelated with consumption, affects investment through its impact on agency costs. Outside finance of a project whose payoff is certain, for example, involves no agency costs, since there is no possibility that the entrepreneur will be unable to repay the investor. But, as our model shows, outside finance of a risky project involves agency costs.

Fourth, and critically, our analysis implies that the financial system itself can be important to investment. The model implies that increases in $c$, the cost of verification, reduce investment. More generally, the existence of agency costs suggests that the efficiency of the financial system in processing information and monitoring borrowers is a potentially important determinant of investment.

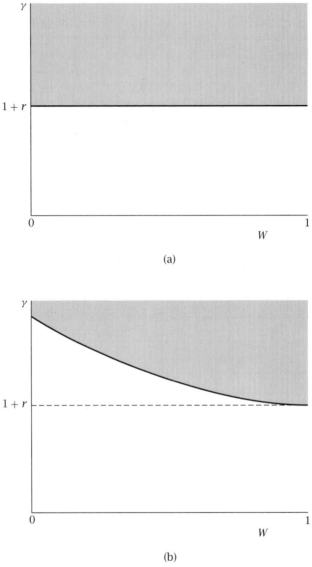

**FIGURE 9.18   The determination of the projects that are undertaken under symmetric and asymmetric information**

This observation has implications for both long-run growth and short-run fluctuations. With regard to long-run growth, McKinnon (1973) and others argue that the financial system has important effects on overall investment and on the quality of the investment projects undertaken, and thus on economies' growth over extended periods. Because the development of the financial system may be a by-product, rather than a cause, of growth, this argument is difficult to test. Nonetheless, there is at least suggestive evidence that financial development is important to growth (for example, Levine and Zervos, 1998, Rajan and Zingales, 1998, and Jayaratne and Strahan, 1996).

With regard to short-run fluctuations, our analysis implies that disruptions to the financial system can affect investment, and thus aggregate output. Recall that the transformation of saving into investment is often done via financial intermediaries, creating a two-level asymmetric information problem. This creates a potentially large propagation mechanism for shocks. Suppose some development—for example, the crash of the stock market in 1929 and the contraction of the economy in 1930, or the fall in house prices in 2007 and 2008—lowers borrowers' wealth. This not only reduces their ability to borrow and invest; it also weakens the position of financial intermediaries, and so reduces their ability to obtain funds from ultimate wealthholders. This reduces their lending, further depressing investment and output. This amplification can be compounded by links among intermediaries. In the extreme, some intermediaries fail. If they have specialized knowledge about particular borrowers, those borrowers' investment collapses. The end result can be catastrophic. Precisely these type of financial amplification mechanisms were at work in the Great Depression (Bernanke, 1983b), and they were central to the crisis that began in 2007—an issue we will return to in the Epilogue.

# 9.10 Empirical Application: Cash Flow and Investment

## Fazzari, Hubbard, and Petersen's Test

Theories of financial-market imperfections imply that internal finance is less costly than external finance. They therefore imply that all else equal, firms with higher profits invest more.

A naive way to test this prediction is to regress investment on measures of the cost of capital and on *cash flow*—loosely speaking, current revenues minus expenses and taxes. Such regressions can use either firm-level data at a point in time or aggregate data over time. In either form, they typically find a strong link between cash flow and investment.

There is a problem with this test, however. The regression does not control for the future profitability of capital, and cash flow is likely to be correlated with future profitability. We saw in Section 9.5, for example, that our model of investment without financial-market imperfections predicts that a rise in output that is not immediately reversed raises investment. The reason is not that higher current output reduces firms' need to rely on outside finance, but that higher future output means that capital is more valuable.

A similar relationship is likely to hold across firms at a point in time: firms with high cash flow probably have successful products or low costs, and thus have incentives to expand output. Because of this potential correlation between cash flow and current profitability, the regression may show a relationship between cash flow and investment even if financial markets are perfect.

A large literature, begun by Fazzari, Hubbard, and Petersen (1988), addresses this problem by comparing the investment behavior of different types of firms. Fazzari, Hubbard, and Petersen's idea is to divide firms into those that are likely to face significant costs of obtaining outside funds and those that are not. There is likely to be an association between cash flow and investment among both types of firms even if financial-market imperfections are not important. But the theory that financial-market imperfections have large effects on investment predicts that the association will be stronger among the firms that face greater barriers to external finance. And unless the association between current cash flow and future profitability is stronger for the firms with less access to financial markets, the view that financial-market imperfections are not important predicts no difference in the cash flow–investment link for the two groups. Thus, Fazzari, Hubbard, and Petersen argue, the difference in the cash flow–investment relationship between the two groups can be used to test for the importance of financial-market imperfections to investment.

The specific way that Fazzari, Hubbard, and Petersen divide their firms is according to their dividend payments as a fraction of income. Firms that pay high dividends can finance additional investment by reducing their dividends. Firms that pay low dividends, in contrast, must rely on external finance.[15]

The basic regression is a pooled time series–cross section regression of investment as a fraction of firms' capital stock on the ratio of cash flow to the capital stock, an estimate of $q$, and dummy variables for each firm and each year. The regression is estimated separately for the two groups of firms. The sample consists of 422 relatively large U.S. firms over the period 1970–1984. Low-dividend firms are defined as those with ratios of dividends to income consistently under 10 percent, and high-dividend firms are defined as those with dividend-income ratios consistently over 20 percent (Fazzari, Hubbard, and Petersen also consider an intermediate-dividend group).

For the high-dividend firms, the coefficient on cash flow is 0.230, with a standard error of 0.010; for the low-dividend firms, it is 0.461, with a

---

[15] One complication to this argument is that it may be costly for high-dividend firms to reduce their dividends: there is evidence that reductions in dividends are interpreted by the stock market as a signal of lower future profitability, and that the reductions therefore lower the value of firms' shares. Thus it is possible that the test could fail to find differences between the two groups of firms not because financial-market imperfections are unimportant, but because they are important to both groups.

standard error of 0.027. The $t$-statistic for the hypothesis that the two co-efficients are equal is 12.1; thus the hypothesis is overwhelmingly rejected. The point estimates imply that low-dividend firms invest 23 cents more of each extra dollar of cash flow than the high-dividend firms do. Thus even if we interpret the estimate for the high-dividend firms as reflecting only the correlation between cash flow and future profitability, the results still suggest that financial-market imperfections have a large effect on investment by low-dividend firms.

Many authors have used variations on Fazzari, Hubbard, and Petersen's approach. A few examples are Lamont (1997), Rauh (2006), and Blalock, Gertler, and Levine (2008), all of whom find important effects of cash flow. Gertler and Gilchrist (1994) carry out a test that is in the same spirit as these but that focuses on the effects of monetary policy. They begin by arguing that small firms are likely to face larger barriers to outside finance than large firms do; for example, the fixed costs associated with issuing publicly traded bonds may be more important for small firms. They then compare the behavior of small and large firms' inventories and sales following moves to tighter monetary policy. Again the results support the importance of im-perfect financial markets. Small firms account for a highly disproportionate share of the declines in sales, inventories, and short-term debt following monetary tightening. Indeed, large firms' borrowing increases after a mon-etary tightening, whereas small firms' borrowing declines sharply.

## Kaplan and Zingales's Critique

The findings described above are representative of the results that have been obtained in this area. Indeed, for the most part the literature on financial-market imperfections is one of unusual empirical consensus. The bulk of the evidence suggests that cash flow and other determinants of access to in-ternal resources affect investment, and that they do so in ways that suggest that the relationship is the result of financial-market imperfections.

Kaplan and Zingales (1997), however, challenge this consensus both the-oretically and empirically. Theoretically, they argue that the premise of the empirical tests is flawed. They agree that for a firm that faces no barriers to external finance, cash flow does not affect investment. But they argue that among firms that face costs of outside finance, there is little reason to ex-pect the relationship between investment and cash flow to be stronger for those facing greater costs of external finance.

To make this argument, Kaplan and Zingales consider a firm that has a fixed amount of internal funds, $W$, with an opportunity cost of $\bar{r}$ per unit. External funds, $E$, have costs $C(E)$, where $C(\bullet)$ satisfies $C'(\bullet) > \bar{r}$ and $C''(\bullet) > 0$. The firm chooses the amount of investment, $I$, to solve

$$\max_I \; F(I) - \bar{r}W - C(I - W), \tag{9.43}$$

where $F(I)$ is the firm's value as a function of the amount of investment; $F(\bullet)$ satisfies $F'(\bullet) > 0$ and $F''(\bullet) < 0$. Under the assumption that the solution involves $I > W$, the first-order condition for $I$ is

$$F'(I) = C'(I - W). \tag{9.44}$$

Implicitly differentiating this condition with respect to $W$ yields

$$F''(I)\frac{dI}{dW} = C''(I - W)\left(\frac{dI}{dW} - 1\right). \tag{9.45}$$

Solving this equation for $dI/dW$ shows how investment responds to internal funds:

$$\frac{dI}{dW} = \frac{C''(I - W)}{C''(I - W) - F''(I)} > 0. \tag{9.46}$$

Thus, as Fazzari, Hubbard, and Petersen argue, investment is increasing in internal resources when firms face financial-market imperfections. Recall, however, that their test involves comparing the sensitivity of investment to cash flow across firms facing different degrees of financial-market constraints. Since firms with fewer internal funds are more affected by financial-market imperfections, one way to address this is to ask how $dI/dW$ varies with $W$.[16] Differentiating (9.46) with respect to $W$ yields

$$\frac{d^2I}{dW^2} = \left\{[C''(I - W) - F''(I)]C'''(I - W)\left(\frac{dI}{dW} - 1\right)\right.$$

$$\left. -C''(I - W)\left[C'''(I - W)\left(\frac{dI}{dW} - 1\right) - F'''(I)\frac{dI}{dW}\right]\right\}\bigg/ [C''(I - W) - F''(I)]^2. \tag{9.47}$$

Substituting for $dI/dW$ and simplifying yields

$$\frac{d^2I}{dW^2} = \frac{[C''(I - W)]^2 F'''(I) - [F''(I)]^2 C'''(I - W)}{[C''(I - W) - F''(I)]^3}. \tag{9.48}$$

Kaplan and Zingales argue that the theory that financial-market imperfections are important to investment makes no clear predictions about the signs of $F'''(\bullet)$ and $C'''(\bullet)$, and thus that the theory does not make strong predictions about differences in the sensitivity of investment to cash flow across different kinds of firms.

Fazzari, Hubbard, and Petersen (2000) respond, however, that the theory does in fact plausibly make predictions about third derivatives. Specifically, they argue that over a range, the marginal cost of external funds is likely to be low (so that $C'(I - W)$ is only slightly above $\bar{r}$) and rising slowly (so that $C''(I - W)$ is small). At some point, the firm starts to be severely constrained in its access to external funds; that is, $C'(I - W)$ changes from rising slowly

---

[16] An alternative is to assume $C = C(E, \alpha)$, where $\alpha$ indexes financial-market imperfections (so that $C_\alpha(\bullet) > 0$, $C_{\alpha E}(\bullet) > 0$), and to ask how $dI/dW$ varies with $\alpha$. This yields similar results.

to rising rapidly, which corresponds to $C'''(I - W) > 0$. This will tend to make $d^2I/dW^2$ negative—that is, it will tend to make investment less sensitive to cash flow when firms can finance more investment from internal funds.

Empirically, Kaplan and Zingales focus on Fazzari, Hubbard, and Petersen's low-dividend firms. They use qualitative statements from firms' annual reports and quantitative information on such variables as firms' liquid assets and debt conditions to classify each firm-year according to the extent of financial constraints. They find that even in this sample—which is where Fazzari, Hubbard, and Petersen argue financial constraints are most likely to be important—for most firms in most years, both the discussions of liquidity in the firms' annual reports and quantitative evidence from the firms' balance sheets provide little evidence of important financial-market constraints. They also find that within this sample, firms that appear to face the greatest financial-market constraints have the lowest estimated sensitivities of investment to cash flow. Thus, they argue that direct examination of financial constraints yields conclusions opposite to Fazzari, Hubbard, and Petersen's.

Fazzari, Hubbard, and Petersen (2000) make three major points in response. First, they argue that Kaplan and Zingales understate the amount of investment these firms need to finance, and that as a result they understate the fraction of time they need significant outside finance. Second, they argue that Kaplan and Zingales's results stem partly from an extreme and not particularly interesting case where greater financial constraints reduce the cash flow–investment link: a firm in severe financial distress may find that the marginal dollar of cash flow must be paid to creditors and cannot be used for investment. And third, they point out that inferring the extent of financial constraints from balance-sheet information is problematic. For example, low levels of debt can result from either the absence of a need to borrow or the inability to do so.

As this discussion makes clear, Kaplan and Zingales's work raises important issues concerning the impact of financial-market imperfections on investment. The debate on those issues is very much open. Since the interpretation of a large literature hinges on the outcome, this is an important area of research.

# Problems

**9.1.** Consider a firm that produces output using a Cobb–Douglas combination of capital and labor: $Y = K^\alpha L^{1-\alpha}$, $0 < \alpha < 1$. Suppose that the firm's price is fixed in the short run; thus it takes both the price of its product, $P$, and the quantity, $Y$, as given. Input markets are competitive; thus the firm takes the wage, $W$, and the rental price of capital, $r_K$, as given.

(a) What is the firm's choice of $L$ given $P$, $Y$, $W$, and $K$?

(b) Given this choice of $L$, what are profits as a function of $P$, $Y$, $W$, and $K$?

(c) Find the first-order condition for the profit-maximizing choice of $K$. Is the second-order condition satisfied?

(d) Solve the first-order condition in part (c) for $K$ as a function of $P$, $Y$, $W$, and $r_K$. How, if at all, do changes in each of these variables affect $K$?

9.2. Corporations in the United States are allowed to subtract depreciation allowances from their taxable income. The depreciation allowances are based on the purchase price of the capital; a corporation that buys a new capital good at time $t$ can deduct fraction $D(s)$ of the purchase price from its taxable income at time $t + s$. Depreciation allowances often take the form of *straight-line depreciation*: $D(s)$ equals $1/T$ for $s \in [0,T]$, and equals 0 for $s > T$, where $T$ is the *tax life* of the capital good.

(a) Assume straight-line depreciation. If the marginal corporate income tax rate is constant at $\tau$ and the interest rate is constant at $i$, by how much does purchasing a unit of capital at a price of $P_K$ reduce the present value of the firm's corporate tax liabilities as a function of $T$, $\tau$, $i$, and $P_K$? Thus, what is the after-tax price of the capital good to the firm?

(b) Suppose that $i = r + \pi$, and that $\pi$ increases with no change in $r$. How does this affect the after-tax price of the capital good to the firm?

9.3. The major feature of the tax code that affects the user cost of capital in the case of owner-occupied housing in the United States is that nominal interest payments are tax-deductible. Thus the after-tax real interest rate relevant to home ownership is $r - \tau i$, where $r$ is the pretax real interest rate, $i$ is the nominal interest rate, and $\tau$ is the marginal tax rate. In this case, how does an increase in inflation for a given $r$ affect the user cost of capital and the desired capital stock?

9.4. **Using the calculus of variations to solve the social planner's problem in the Ramsey model.** Consider the social planner's problem that we analyzed in Section 2.4: the planner wants to maximize $\int_{t=0}^{\infty} e^{-\beta t}[c(t)^{1-\theta}/(1-\theta)]dt$ subject to $\dot{k}(t) = f(k(t)) - c(t) - (n + g)k(t)$.

(a) What is the current-value Hamiltonian? What variables are the control variable, the state variable, and the costate variable?

(b) Find the three conditions that characterize optimal behavior analogous to equations (9.21), (9.22), and (9.23) in Section 9.2.

(c) Show that the first two conditions in part (b), together with the fact that $f'(k(t)) = r(t)$, imply the Euler equation (equation [9.20]).

(d) Let $\mu$ denote the costate variable. Show that $[\dot{\mu}(t)/\mu(t)] - \beta = (n + g) - r(t)$, and thus that $e^{-\beta t}\mu(t)$ is proportional to $e^{-R(t)}e^{(n+g)t}$. Show that this implies that the transversality condition in part (b) holds if and only if the budget constraint, equation (2.15), holds with equality.

9.5. **Using the calculus of variations to find the socially optimal allocation in the Romer model.** Consider the Romer model of Section 3.5. For simplicity, neglect the constraint that $L_A$ cannot be negative. Set up the problem of choosing the path of $L_A(t)$ to maximize the lifetime utility of the representative individual. What is the control variable? What is the state variable? What is the current value Hamiltonian? Find the conditions that characterize the optimum. Is there an allocation where $L_A(t)$ is constant that satisfies those conditions? If so, what is the constant value of $L_A$? If not, why not?

**9.6.** Consider the model of investment in Sections 9.2–9.5. Describe the effects of each of the following changes on the $\dot{K} = 0$ and $\dot{q} = 0$ loci, on $K$ and $q$ at the time of the change, and on their behavior over time. In each case, assume that $K$ and $q$ are initially at their long-run equilibrium values.

(a) A war destroys half of the capital stock.

(b) The government taxes returns from owning firms at rate $\tau$ (so that a firm's profits per unit of capital for a given aggregate capital stock are $(1 - \tau)\pi(K(t))$ rather than $\pi(K(t))$).

(c) The government taxes investment. Specifically, firms pay the government $\gamma$ for each unit of capital they acquire, and receive a subsidy of $\gamma$ for each unit of disinvestment.

**9.7.** Consider the model of investment in Sections 9.2–9.5. Suppose it becomes known at some date that there will be a one-time capital levy. Specifically, capital holders will be taxed an amount equal to fraction $f$ of the value of their capital holdings at some time in the future, time $T$. Assume the industry is initially in long-run equilibrium. What happens at the time of this news? How do $K$ and $q$ behave between the time of the news and the time the levy is imposed? What happens to $K$ and $q$ at the time of the levy? How do they behave thereafter? (Hint: Is $q$ anticipated to change discontinuously at the time of the levy?)

**9.8. A model of the housing market.** (Poterba, 1984.) Let $H$ denote the stock of housing, $I$ the rate of investment, $p_H$ the real price of housing, and $R$ the rent. Assume that $I$ is increasing in $p_H$, so that $I = I(p_H)$, with $I'(\bullet) > 0$, and that $\dot{H} = I - \delta H$. Assume also that the rent is a decreasing function of $H$: $R = R(H)$, $R'(\bullet) < 0$. Finally, assume that rental income plus capital gains must equal the exogenous required rate of return, $r$: $(R + \dot{p}_H)/p_H = r$.

(a) Sketch the set of points in $(H, p_H)$ space such that $\dot{H} = 0$. Sketch the set of points such that $\dot{p}_H = 0$.

(b) What are the dynamics of $H$ and $p_H$ in each region of the resulting diagram? Sketch the saddle path.

(c) Suppose the market is initially in long-run equilibrium, and that there is an unexpected permanent increase in $r$. What happens to $H$ and $p_H$ at the time of the change? How do $H$, $p_H$, $I$, and $R$ behave over time following the change?

(d) Suppose the market is initially in long-run equilibrium, and that it becomes known that there will be a permanent increase in $r$ time $T$ in the future. What happens to $H$ and $p_H$ at the time of the news? How do $H$, $p_H$, $I$, and $R$ behave between the time of the news and the time of the increase? What happens to them when the increase occurs? How do they behave after the increase

(e) Are adjustment costs internal or external in this model? Explain.

(f) Why is the $\dot{H} = 0$ locus not horizontal in this model?

**9.9.** Suppose that the costs of adjustment exhibit constant returns in $\dot{\kappa}$ and $\kappa$. Specifically, suppose they are given by $C(\dot{\kappa}/\kappa)\kappa$, where $C(0) = 0$, $C'(0) = 0$, $C''(\bullet) > 0$. In addition, suppose capital depreciates at rate $\delta$; thus $\dot{\kappa}(t) = I(t) - \delta\kappa(t)$. Consider the representative firm's maximization problem.

(a) What is the current-value Hamiltonian?

(b) Find the three conditions that characterize optimal behavior analogous to equations (9.21), (9.22), and (9.23) in Section 9.2.

(c) Show that the condition analogous to (9.21) implies that the growth rate of each firm's capital stock, and thus the growth rate of the aggregate capital stock, is determined by $q$. In $(K, q)$ space, what is the $\dot{K} = 0$ locus?

(d) Substitute your result in part (c) into the condition analogous to (9.22) to express $\dot{q}$ in terms of $K$ and $q$.

(e) In $(K, q)$ space, what is the slope of the $\dot{q} = 0$ locus at the point where $q = 1$?

**9.10.** Suppose that $\pi(K) = a - bK$ and $C(I) = \alpha I^2/2$.

(a) What is the $\dot{q} = 0$ locus? What is the long-run equilibrium value of $K$?

(b) What is the slope of the saddle path? (Hint: Use the approach in Section 2.6.)

**9.11.** Consider the model of investment under uncertainty with a constant interest rate in Section 9.7. Suppose that, as in Problem 9.10, $\pi(K) = a - bK$ and that $C(I) = \alpha I^2/2$. In addition, suppose that what is uncertain is future values of $a$. This problem asks you to show that it is an equilibrium for $q(t)$ and $K(t)$ to have the values at each point in time that they would if there were no uncertainty about the path of $a$. Specifically, let $\hat{q}(t + \tau, t)$ and $\hat{K}(t + \tau, t)$ be the paths $q$ and $K$ would take after time $t$ if $a(t + \tau)$ were certain to equal $E_t[a(t + \tau)]$ for all $\tau \geq 0$.

(a) Show that if $E_t[q(t + \tau)] = \hat{q}(t + \tau, t)$ for all $\tau \geq 0$, then $E_t[K(t + \tau)] = \hat{K}(t + \tau, t)$ for all $\tau \geq 0$.

(b) Use equation (9.32) to show that this implies that if $E_t[q(t+\tau)] = \hat{q}(t+\tau, t)$, then $q(t) = \hat{q}(t, t)$, and thus that $\dot{K}(t) = N[\hat{q}(t, t) - 1]/\alpha$, where $N$ is the number of firms.

**9.12.** Consider the model of investment with kinked adjustment costs in Section 9.8. Describe the effect of each of the following on the $\dot{q} = 0$ locus, on the area where $\dot{K} = 0$, on $q$ and $K$ at the time of the change, and on their behavior over time. In each case, assume $q$ and $K$ are initially at Point $E^+$ in Figure 9.13.

(a) There is a permanent upward shift of the $\pi(\bullet)$ function.

(b) There is a small permanent rise in the interest rate.

(c) The cost of the first unit of positive investment, $c^+$, rises.

(d) The cost of the first unit of positive investment, $c^+$, falls.

**9.13.** (This follows Bernanke, 1983a, and Dixit and Pindyck, 1994.) Consider a firm that is contemplating undertaking an investment with a cost of $I$. There are two periods. The investment will pay off $\pi_1$ in period 1 and $\pi_2$ in period 2.

$\pi_1$ is certain, but $\pi_2$ is uncertain. The firm maximizes expected profits and, for simplicity, the interest rate is zero.

(a) Suppose the firm's only choices are to undertake the investment in period 1 or not to undertake it at all. Under what condition will the firm undertake the investment?

(b) Suppose the firm also has the possibility of undertaking the investment in period 2, after the value of $\pi_2$ is known; in this case the investment pays off only $\pi_2$. Is it possible for the condition in (a) to be satisfied but for the firm's expected profits to be higher if it does not invest in period 1 than if it does invest?

(c) Define the cost of waiting as $\pi_1$, and define the benefit of waiting as $\text{Prob}(\pi_2 < I)E[I - \pi_2 \,|\, \pi_2 < I]$. Explain why these represent the cost and the benefit of waiting. Show that the difference in the firm's expected profits between not investing in period 1 and investing in period 1 equals the benefit of waiting minus the cost.

9.14. **The Modigliani–Miller theorem.** (Modigliani and Miller, 1958.) Consider the analysis of the effects of uncertainty about discount factors in Section 9.7. Suppose, however, that the firm finances its investment using a mix of equity and risk-free debt. Specifically, consider the financing of the marginal unit of capital. The firm issues quantity $b$ of bonds; each bond pays 1 unit of output with certainty at time $t + \tau$ for all $\tau \geq 0$. Equity holders are the residual claimant; thus they receive $\pi(K(t + \tau)) - b$ at $t + \tau$ for all $\tau \geq 0$.

(a) Let $P(t)$ denote the value of a unit of debt at $t$, and $V(t)$ the value of the equity in the marginal unit of capital. Find expressions analogous to (9.35) for $P(t)$ and $V(t)$.

(b) How, if at all, does the division of financing between bonds and equity affect the market value of the claims on the unit of capital, $P(t)b + V(t)$? Explain intuitively.

(c) More generally, suppose the firm finances the investment by issuing $n$ financial instruments. Let $d_i(t + \tau)$ denote the payoff to instrument $i$ at time $t + \tau$; the payoffs satisfy $d_1(t + \tau) + \cdots + d_n(t + \tau) = \pi(K(t + \tau))$, but are otherwise unrestricted. How, if at all, does the total value of the $n$ assets depend on how the total payoff is divided among the assets?

(d) Return to the case of debt and equity finance. Suppose, however, that the firm's profits are taxed at rate $\theta$, and that interest payments are tax-deductible. Thus the payoff to bond holders is the same as before, but the payoff to equity holders at time $t + \tau$ is $(1 - \theta)[\pi(K(t + \tau)) - b]$. Does the result in part (b) still hold? Explain.

# Chapter **10**
# UNEMPLOYMENT

## 10.1 Introduction: Theories of Unemployment

In almost any economy at almost any time, many individuals appear to be unemployed. That is, there are many people who are not working but who say they want to work in jobs like those held by individuals similar to them, at the wages those individuals are earning.

The possibility of unemployment is a central subject of macroeconomics. There are two basic issues. The first concerns the determinants of average unemployment over extended periods. The central questions here are whether this unemployment represents a genuine failure of markets to clear, and if so, what its causes and consequences are. There is a wide range of possible views. At one extreme is the position that unemployment is largely illusory, or the working out of unimportant frictions in the process of matching up workers and jobs. At the other extreme is the view that unemployment is the result of non-Walrasian features of the economy and that it largely represents a waste of resources.

The second issue concerns the cyclical behavior of the labor market. As described in Section 6.3, the real wage appears to be only moderately procyclical. This is consistent with the view that the labor market is Walrasian only if labor supply is quite elastic or if shifts in labor supply play an important role in employment fluctuations. But as we saw in Section 5.10, there is little support for the hypothesis of highly elastic labor supply. And it seems unlikely that shifts in labor supply are central to fluctuations. The remaining possibility is that the labor market is not Walrasian, and that its non-Walrasian features are central to its cyclical behavior. That possibility is the focus of this chapter.

The issue of why shifts in labor demand appear to lead to large movements in employment and only small movements in the real wage is important to all theories of fluctuations. For example, we saw in Chapter 6 that if the real wage is highly procyclical in response to demand shocks, it is essentially impossible for the small barriers to nominal adjustment to generate substantial nominal rigidity. In the face of a decline in aggregate demand, for example, if prices remain fixed the real wage must fall sharply; as a result, each firm has a huge incentive to cut its price and hire labor to produce additional output. If, however, there is some non-Walrasian feature of the labor market that causes the cost of labor to respond little to the overall level of economic activity, then there is some hope for theories of small frictions in nominal adjustment.

This chapter considers various ways in which the labor market may depart from a competitive, textbook market. We investigate both whether these departures can lead to substantial unemployment and whether they can have large effects on the cyclical behavior of employment and the real wage.

If there is unemployment in a Walrasian labor market, unemployed workers immediately bid the wage down until supply and demand are in balance. Theories of unemployment can therefore be classified according to their view of why this mechanism fails to operate. Concretely, consider an unemployed worker who offers to work for a firm for slightly less than the firm is currently paying, and who is otherwise identical to the firm's current workers. There are at least four possible responses the firm can make to this offer.

First, the firm can say that it does not want to reduce wages. Theories in which there is a cost as well as a benefit to the firm of paying lower wages are known as *efficiency-wage* theories. (The name comes from the idea that higher wages may raise the productivity, or efficiency, of labor.) These theories are the subject of Sections 10.2 through 10.4. Section 10.2 first discusses the possible ways that paying lower wages can harm a firm; it then analyzes a simple model where wages affect productivity but where the reason for that link is not explicitly specified. Section 10.3 considers an important generalization of that model. Finally, Section 10.4 presents a model formalizing one particular view of why paying higher wages can be beneficial. The central idea is that if firms cannot monitor their workers' effort perfectly, they may pay more than market-clearing wages to induce workers not to shirk.

The second possible response the firm can make is that it wishes to cut wages, but that an explicit or implicit agreement with its workers prevents it from doing so.[1] Theories in which bargaining and contracts affect the macroeconomics of the labor market are known as *contracting models*. These models are considered in Section 10.5.

The third way the firm can respond to the unemployed worker's offer is to say that it does not accept the premise that the unemployed worker is identical to the firm's current employees. That is, heterogeneity among workers and jobs may be an essential feature of the labor market. In this

---

[1] The firm can also be prevented from cutting wages by minimum-wage laws. In most settings, this is relevant only to low-skill workers; thus it does not appear to be central to the macroeconomics of unemployment.

view, to think of the market for labor as a single market, or even as a large number of interconnected markets, is to commit a fundamental error. Instead, according to this view, each worker and each job should be thought of as distinct; as a result, the process of matching up workers and jobs occurs not through markets but through a complex process of search. Models of this type are known as *search and matching models*. They are discussed in Sections 10.6 and 10.7.

Finally, the firm can accept the worker's offer. That is, it is possible that the market for labor is approximately Walrasian. In this view, measured unemployment consists largely of people who are moving between jobs, or who would like to work at wages higher than those they can in fact obtain. Since the focus of this chapter is on unemployment, we will not develop this idea here. Nonetheless, it is important to keep in mind that this is one view of the labor market.

# 10.2   A Generic Efficiency-Wage Model

## Potential Reasons for Efficiency Wages

The key assumption of efficiency-wage models is that there is a benefit as well as a cost to a firm of paying a higher wage. There are many reasons that this could be the case. Here we describe four of the most important.

First, and most simply, a higher wage can increase workers' food consumption, and thereby cause them to be better nourished and more productive. Obviously this possibility is not important in developed economies. Nonetheless, it provides a concrete example of an advantage of paying a higher wage. For that reason, it is often a useful reference point.

Second, a higher wage can increase workers' effort in situations where the firm cannot monitor them perfectly. In a Walrasian labor market, workers are indifferent about losing their jobs, since identical jobs are immediately available. Thus if the only way that firms can punish workers who exert low effort is by firing them, workers in such a labor market have no incentive to exert effort. But if a firm pays more than the market-clearing wage, its jobs are valuable. Thus its workers may choose to exert effort even if there is some chance they will not be caught if they shirk. This idea is developed in Section 10.4.

Third, paying a higher wage can improve workers' ability along dimensions the firm cannot observe. Specifically, if higher-ability workers have higher reservation wages, offering a higher wage raises the average quality of the applicant pool, and thus raises the average ability of the workers the firm hires (Weiss, 1980).[2]

---

[2] When ability is observable, the firm can pay higher wages to more able workers. Thus observable ability differences do not lead to any departures from the Walrasian case.

Finally, a high wage can build loyalty among workers and hence induce high effort; conversely, a low wage can cause anger and desire for revenge, and thereby lead to shirking or sabotage. Akerlof and Yellen (1990) present extensive evidence that workers' effort is affected by such forces as anger, jealousy, and gratitude. For example, they describe studies showing that workers who believe they are underpaid sometimes perform their work in ways that are harder for them in order to reduce their employers' profits.[3]

## Other Compensation Schemes

This discussion implicitly assumes that a firm's financial arrangements with its workers take the form of some wage per unit of time. An important question is whether there are more complicated ways for the firm to compensate its workers that allow it to obtain the benefits of a higher wage less expensively. The nutritional advantages of a higher wage, for example, can be obtained by compensating workers partly in kind (such as by feeding them at work). To give another example, firms can give workers an incentive to exert effort by requiring them to post a bond that they lose if they are caught shirking.

If there are cheaper ways for firms to obtain the benefits of a higher wage, then these benefits lead not to a higher wage but just to complicated compensation policies. Whether the benefits can be obtained in such ways depends on the specific reason that a higher wage is advantageous. We will therefore not attempt a general treatment. The end of Section 10.4 discusses this issue in the context of efficiency-wage theories based on imperfect monitoring of workers' effort. In this section and the next, however, we simply assume that compensation takes the form of a conventional wage, and investigate the effects of efficiency wages under this assumption.

## Assumptions

We now turn to a model of efficiency wages. There is a large number, $N$, of identical competitive firms.[4] The representative firm seeks to maximize its profits, which are given by

$$\pi = Y - wL, \tag{10.1}$$

---

[3] See Problem 10.5 for a formalization of this idea. Three other potential advantages of a higher wage are that it can reduce turnover (and hence recruitment and training costs, if they are borne by the firm); that it can lower the likelihood that the workers will unionize; and that it can raise the utility of managers who have some ability to pursue objectives other than maximizing profits.

[4] We can think of the number of firms as being determined by the amount of capital in the economy, which is fixed in the short run.

where $Y$ is the firm's output, $w$ is the wage that it pays, and $L$ is the amount of labor it hires.

A firm's output depends on the number of workers it employs and on their effort. For simplicity, we neglect other inputs and assume that labor and effort enter the production function multiplicatively. Thus the representative firm's output is

$$Y = F(eL), \qquad F'(\bullet) > 0, \qquad F''(\bullet) < 0, \tag{10.2}$$

where $e$ denotes workers' effort. The crucial assumption of efficiency-wage models is that effort depends positively on the wage the firm pays. In this section we consider the simple case (due to Solow, 1979) where the wage is the only determinant of effort. Thus,

$$e = e(w), \qquad e'(\bullet) > 0. \tag{10.3}$$

Finally, there are $\overline{L}$ identical workers, each of whom supplies 1 unit of labor inelastically.

## Analyzing the Model

The problem facing the representative firm is

$$\max_{L,w} F(e(w)L) - wL. \tag{10.4}$$

If there are unemployed workers, the firm can choose the wage freely. If unemployment is zero, on the other hand, the firm must pay at least the wage paid by other firms.

When the firm is unconstrained, the first-order conditions for $L$ and $w$ are[5]

$$F'(e(w)L)e(w) - w = 0, \tag{10.5}$$

$$F'(e(w)L)Le'(w) - L = 0. \tag{10.6}$$

We can rewrite (10.5) as

$$F'(e(w)L) = \frac{w}{e(w)}. \tag{10.7}$$

Substituting (10.7) into (10.6) and dividing by $L$ yields

$$\frac{we'(w)}{e(w)} = 1. \tag{10.8}$$

Equation (10.8) states that at the optimum, the elasticity of effort with respect to the wage is 1. To understand this condition, note that output is a function of the quantity of effective labor, $eL$. The firm therefore wants to hire effective labor as cheaply as possible. When the firm hires a worker, it

---

[5] We assume that the second-order conditions are satisfied.

obtains $e(w)$ units of effective labor at a cost of $w$; thus the cost per unit of effective labor is $w/e(w)$. When the elasticity of $e$ with respect to $w$ is 1, a marginal change in $w$ has no effect on this ratio; thus this is the first-order condition for the problem of choosing $w$ to minimize the cost of effective labor. The wage satisfying (10.8) is known as the *efficiency wage*.

Figure 10.1 depicts the choice of $w$ graphically in $(w,e)$ space. The rays coming out from the origin are lines where the ratio of $e$ to $w$ is constant; the ratio is larger on the higher rays. Thus the firm wants to choose $w$ to attain as high a ray as possible. This occurs where the $e(w)$ function is just tangent to one of the rays—that is, where the elasticity of $e$ with respect to $w$ is 1. Panel (a) shows a case where effort is sufficiently responsive to the wage that over some range the firm prefers a higher wage. Panel (b) shows a case where the firm always prefers a lower wage.

Finally, equation (10.7) states that the firm hires workers until the marginal product of effective labor equals its cost. This is analogous to the condition in a standard labor-demand problem that the firm hires labor up to the point where the marginal product equals the wage.

Equations (10.7) and (10.8) describe the behavior of a single firm. Describing the economy-wide equilibrium is straightforward. Let $w^*$ and $L^*$ denote the values of $w$ and $L$ that satisfy (10.7) and (10.8). Since firms are identical, each firm chooses these same values of $w$ and $L$. Total labor demand is therefore $NL^*$. If labor supply, $\overline{L}$, exceeds this amount, firms are unconstrained in their choice of $w$. In this case the wage is $w^*$, employment is $NL^*$, and there is unemployment of amount $\overline{L} - NL^*$. If $NL^*$ exceeds $\overline{L}$, on the other hand, firms are constrained. In this case, the wage is bid up to the point where demand and supply are in balance, and there is no unemployment.

## Implications

This model shows how efficiency wages can give rise to unemployment. In addition, the model implies that the real wage is unresponsive to demand shifts. Suppose the demand for labor increases. Since the efficiency wage, $w^*$, is determined entirely by the properties of the effort function, $e(\bullet)$, there is no reason for firms to adjust their wages. Thus the model provides a candidate explanation of why shifts in labor demand lead to large movements in employment and small changes in the real wage. In addition, the fact that the real wage and effort do not change implies that the cost of a unit of effective labor does not change. As a result, in a model with price-setting firms, the incentive to adjust prices is small.

Unfortunately, these results are less promising than they appear. The difficulty is that they apply not just to the short run but to the long run: the model implies that as economic growth shifts the demand for labor outward, the real wage remains unchanged and unemployment trends downward. Eventually, unemployment reaches zero, at which point further increases in

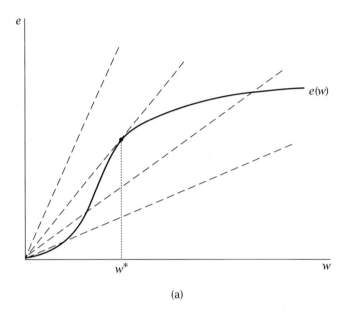

(a)

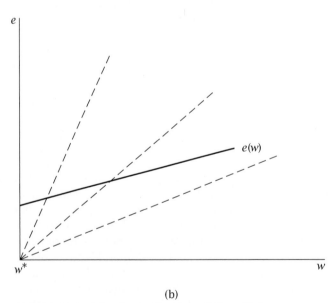

(b)

**FIGURE 10.1   The determination of the efficiency wage**

demand lead to increases in the real wage. In practice, however, we observe no clear trend in unemployment over extended periods. In other words, the basic fact about the labor market that we need to understand is not just that shifts in labor demand appear to have little impact on the real wage and fall mainly on employment in the short run; it is also that they fall almost entirely on the real wage in the long run. Our model does not explain this pattern.

## 10.3   A More General Version

### Introduction

With many of the potential sources of efficiency wages, the wage is unlikely to be the only determinant of effort. Suppose, for example, that the wage affects effort because firms cannot monitor workers perfectly and workers are concerned about the possibility of losing their jobs if the firm catches them shirking. In such a situation, the cost to a worker of being fired depends not just on the wage the job pays, but also on how easy it is to obtain other jobs and on the wages those jobs pay. Thus workers are likely to exert more effort at a given wage when unemployment is higher, and to exert less effort when the wage paid by other firms is higher. Similar arguments apply to situations where the wage affects effort because of unobserved ability or feelings of gratitude or anger.

Thus a natural generalization of the effort function, (10.3), is

$$e = e(w, w_a, u), \qquad e_1(\bullet) > 0, \qquad e_2(\bullet) < 0, \qquad e_3(\bullet) > 0, \qquad (10.9)$$

where $w_a$ is the wage paid by other firms and $u$ is the unemployment rate, and where subscripts denote partial derivatives.

Each firm is small relative to the economy, and therefore takes $w_a$ and $u$ as given. The representative firm's problem is the same as before, except that $w_a$ and $u$ now affect the effort function. The first-order conditions can therefore be rearranged to obtain

$$F'(e(w, w_a, u)L) = \frac{w}{e(w, w_a, u)}, \qquad (10.10)$$

$$\frac{we_1(w, w_a, u)}{e(w, w_a, u)} = 1. \qquad (10.11)$$

These conditions are analogous to (10.7) and (10.8) in the simpler version of the model.

Assume that the $e(\bullet)$ function is sufficiently well behaved that there is a unique optimal $w$ for a given $w_a$ and $u$. Given this assumption, equilibrium requires $w = w_a$; if not, each firm wants to pay a wage different from the prevailing wage. Let $w^*$ and $L^*$ denote the values of $w$ and $L$ satisfying (10.10)–(10.11) with $w = w_a$. As before, if $NL^*$ is less than $\bar{L}$, the equilibrium wage is $w^*$ and $\bar{L} - NL^*$ workers are unemployed. And if $NL^*$ exceeds $\bar{L}$, the wage is bid up and the labor market clears.

This extended version of the model has promise for accounting for both the absence of any trend in unemployment over the long run and the fact that shifts in labor demand appear to have large effects on unemployment in the short run. This is most easily seen by means of an example.

## Example

Following Summers (1988), suppose that effort is given by

$$
e = \begin{cases} \left( \dfrac{w - x}{x} \right)^{\beta} & \text{if } w > x \\[2mm] 0 & \text{otherwise,} \end{cases} \tag{10.12}
$$

$$
x = (1 - bu)w_a, \tag{10.13}
$$

where $0 < \beta < 1$ and $b > 0$. $x$ is a measure of labor-market conditions. If $b$ equals 1, $x$ is the wage paid at other firms multiplied by the fraction of workers who are employed. If $b$ is less than 1, workers put less weight on unemployment; this could occur if there are unemployment benefits or if workers value leisure. If $b$ is greater than 1, workers put more weight on unemployment; this might occur because workers who lose their jobs face unusually high chances of continued unemployment, or because of risk aversion. Finally, equation (10.12) states that for $w > x$, effort increases less than proportionately with $w - x$.

Differentiation of (10.12) shows that for this functional form, the condition that the elasticity of effort with respect to the wage equals 1 (equation [10.11]) is

$$
\beta \frac{w}{[(w - x)/x]^{\beta}} \left( \frac{w - x}{x} \right)^{\beta - 1} \frac{1}{x} = 1. \tag{10.14}
$$

Straightforward algebra can be used to simplify (10.14) to

$$
\begin{aligned}
w &= \frac{x}{1 - \beta} \\[2mm]
&= \frac{1 - bu}{1 - \beta} w_a.
\end{aligned} \tag{10.15}
$$

For small values of $\beta$, $1/(1 - \beta) \simeq 1 + \beta$. Thus (10.15) implies that when $\beta$ is small, the firm offers a premium of approximately fraction $\beta$ over the index of labor-market opportunities, $x$.

Equilibrium requires that the representative firm wants to pay the prevailing wage, or that $w = w_a$. Imposing this condition in (10.15) yields

$$(1 - \beta)w_a = (1 - bu)w_a. \tag{10.16}$$

For this condition to be satisfied, the unemployment rate must be given by

$$u = \frac{\beta}{b} \tag{10.17}$$
$$\equiv u_{EQ}.$$

As equation (10.15) shows, each firm wants to pay more than the prevailing wage if unemployment is less than $u_{EQ}$, and wants to pay less if unemployment is more than $u_{EQ}$. Thus equilibrium requires that $u = u_{EQ}$.

## Implications

This analysis has three important implications. First, (10.17) implies that equilibrium unemployment depends only on the parameters of the effort function; the production function is irrelevant. Thus an upward trend in the production function does not produce a trend in unemployment.

Second, relatively modest values of $\beta$—the elasticity of effort with respect to the premium firms pay over the index of labor-market conditions—can lead to nonnegligible unemployment. For example, either $\beta = 0.06$ and $b = 1$ or $\beta = 0.03$ and $b = 0.5$ imply that equilibrium unemployment is 6 percent. This result is not as strong as it may appear, however: while these parameter values imply a low elasticity of effort with respect to $(w - x)/x$, they also imply that workers exert no effort at all until the wage is quite high. For example, if $b$ is 0.5 and unemployment is at its equilibrium level of 6 percent, effort is zero until a firm's wage reaches 97 percent of the prevailing wage. In that sense, efficiency-wage forces are quite strong for these parameter values.

Third, firms' incentive to adjust wages or prices (or both) in response to changes in aggregate unemployment is likely to be small for reasonable cases. Suppose we embed this model of wages and effort in a model of price-setting firms along the lines of Chapter 6. Consider a situation where the economy is initially in equilibrium, so that $u = u_{EQ}$ and marginal revenue and marginal cost are equal for the representative firm. Now suppose that the money supply falls and firms do not change their nominal wages or prices; as a result, unemployment rises above $u_{EQ}$. We know from Chapter 6 that small barriers to wage and price adjustment can cause this to be an equilibrium only if the representative firm's incentive to adjust is small.

For concreteness, consider the incentive to adjust wages. Equation (10.15), $w = (1 - bu)w_a/(1 - \beta)$, shows that the cost-minimizing wage is decreasing in the unemployment rate. Thus the firm can reduce its costs, and hence raise its profits, by cutting its wage. The key issue is the size of the gain. Equation (10.12) for effort implies that if the firm leaves its wage equal to the prevailing wage, $w_a$, its cost per unit of effective labor, $w/e$, is

$$C_{\text{FIXED}} = \frac{w_a}{e(w_a, w_a, u)}$$

$$= \frac{w_a}{\left(\dfrac{w_a - x}{x}\right)^{\beta}}$$

$$= \frac{w_a}{\left[\dfrac{w_a - (1 - bu)w_a}{(1 - bu)w_a}\right]^{\beta}} \qquad (10.18)$$

$$= \left(\frac{1 - bu}{bu}\right)^{\beta} w_a.$$

If the firm changes its wage, on the other hand, it sets it according to (10.15), and thus chooses $w = x/(1 - \beta)$. In this case, the firm's cost per unit of effective labor is

$$C_{\text{ADJ}} = \frac{w}{\left(\dfrac{w - x}{x}\right)^{\beta}}$$

$$= \frac{x/(1 - \beta)}{\left\{\dfrac{[x/(1 - \beta)] - x}{x}\right\}^{\beta}} \qquad (10.19)$$

$$= \frac{x/(1 - \beta)}{[\beta/(1 - \beta)]^{\beta}}$$

$$= \frac{1}{\beta^{\beta}} \frac{1}{(1 - \beta)^{1-\beta}} (1 - bu)w_a.$$

Suppose that $\beta = 0.06$ and $b = 1$, so that $u_{\text{EQ}} = 6\%$. Suppose, however, that unemployment rises to 9 percent and that other firms do not change their wages. Equations (10.18) and (10.19) imply that this rise lowers $C_{\text{FIXED}}$ by 2.6 percent and $C_{\text{ADJ}}$ by 3.2 percent. Thus the firm can save only 0.6 percent of costs by cutting its wages. For $\beta = 0.03$ and $b = 0.5$, the declines in $C_{\text{FIXED}}$ and $C_{\text{ADJ}}$ are 1.3 percent and 1.5 percent; thus in this case the incentive to cut wages is even smaller.[6]

---

[6] One can also show that if firms do not change their wages, for reasonable cases their incentive to adjust their prices is also small. If wages are completely flexible, however, the incentive to adjust prices is not small. With $u$ greater than $u_{\text{EQ}}$, each firm wants to pay less than other firms are paying (see [10.15]). Thus if wages are completely flexible, they must fall to zero—or, if workers have a positive reservation wage, to the reservation wage. As a result, firms' labor costs are extremely low, and so their incentive to cut prices and increase output is high. Thus in the absence of any barriers to changing wages, small costs to changing prices are not enough to prevent price adjustment in this model.

In a competitive labor market, in contrast, the equilibrium wage falls by the percentage fall in employment divided by the elasticity of labor supply. For a 3 percent fall in employment and a labor supply elasticity of 0.2, for example, the equilibrium wage falls by 15 percent. And without endogenous effort, a 15 percent fall in wages translates directly into a 15 percent fall in costs. Firms therefore have an overwhelming incentive to cut wages and prices in this case.[7]

Thus efficiency wages have a potentially large impact on the incentive to adjust wages in the face of fluctuations in aggregate output. As a result, they have the potential to explain why shifts in labor demand mainly affect employment in the short run. Intuitively, in a competitive market firms are initially at a corner solution with respect to wages: firms pay the lowest possible wage at which they can hire workers. Thus wage reductions, if possible, are unambiguously beneficial. With efficiency wages, in contrast, firms are initially at an interior optimum where the marginal benefits and costs of wage cuts are equal.

# 10.4   The Shapiro–Stiglitz Model

One source of efficiency wages that has received a great deal of attention is the possibility that firms' limited monitoring abilities force them to provide their workers with an incentive to exert effort. This section presents a specific model, due to Shapiro and Stiglitz (1984), of this possibility.

Presenting a formal model of imperfect monitoring serves three purposes. First, it allows us to investigate whether this idea holds up under scrutiny. Second, it permits us to analyze additional questions. For example, only with a formal model can we ask whether government policies can improve welfare. Third, the mathematical tools the model employs are useful in other settings.

## Assumptions

The economy consists of a large number of workers, $\overline{L}$, and a large number of firms, $N$. Workers maximize their expected discounted utilities, and firms maximize their expected discounted profits. The model is set in continuous time. For simplicity, the analysis focuses on steady states.

---

[7] In fact, in a competitive labor market, an individual firm's incentive to reduce wages if other firms do not is even larger than the fall in the equilibrium wage. If other firms do not cut wages, some workers are unemployed. Thus the firm can hire workers at an arbitrarily small wage (or at workers' reservation wage).

Consider workers first. The representative worker's lifetime utility is

$$U = \int_{t=0}^{\infty} e^{-\rho t} u(t) dt, \qquad \rho > 0. \tag{10.20}$$

$u(t)$ is instantaneous utility at time $t$, and $\rho$ is the discount rate. Instantaneous utility is

$$u(t) = \begin{cases} w(t) - e(t) & \text{if employed} \\ 0 & \text{if unemployed.} \end{cases} \tag{10.21}$$

$w$ is the wage and $e$ is the worker's effort. There are only two possible effort levels, $e = 0$ and $e = \bar{e}$. Thus at any moment a worker must be in one of three states: employed and exerting effort (denoted $E$), employed and not exerting effort (denoted $S$, for shirking), or unemployed (denoted $U$).

A key ingredient of the model is its assumptions concerning workers' transitions among the three states. First, there is an exogenous rate at which jobs end. Specifically, if a worker begins working in a job at some time, $t_0$ (and if the worker exerts effort), the probability that the worker is still employed in the job at some later time, $t$, is

$$P(t) = e^{-b(t-t_0)}, \qquad b > 0. \tag{10.22}$$

(10.22) implies that $P(t+\tau)/P(t)$ equals $e^{-b\tau}$, and thus that it is independent of $t$: if a worker is employed at some time, the probability that he or she is still employed time $\tau$ later is $e^{-b\tau}$ regardless of how long the worker has already been employed. This assumption that job breakups follow a Poisson process simplifies the analysis greatly, because it implies that there is no need to keep track of how long workers have been in their jobs.

An equivalent way to describe the process of job breakup is to say that it occurs with probability $b$ per unit time, or to say that the *hazard rate* for job breakup is $b$. That is, the probability that an employed worker's job ends in the next $dt$ units of time approaches $bdt$ as $dt$ approaches zero. To see that our assumptions imply this, note that (10.22) implies $P'(t) = -bP(t)$.

The second assumption concerning workers' transitions between states is that firms' detection of workers who are shirking is also a Poisson process. Specifically, detection occurs with probability $q$ per unit time. $q$ is exogenous, and detection is independent of job breakups. Workers who are caught shirking are fired. Thus if a worker is employed but shirking, the probability that he or she is still employed time $\tau$ later is $e^{-q\tau}$ (the probability that the worker has not been caught and fired) times $e^{-b\tau}$ (the probability that the job has not ended exogenously).

Third, unemployed workers find employment at rate $a$ per unit time. Each worker takes $a$ as given. In the economy as a whole, however, $a$ is determined endogenously. When firms want to hire workers, they choose workers at random out of the pool of unemployed workers. Thus $a$ is determined by the rate at which firms are hiring (which is determined by the number of employed workers and the rate at which jobs end) and the number of unemployed workers. Because workers are identical, the probability of finding a job does not depend on how workers become unemployed or on how long they are unemployed.

Firms' behavior is straightforward. A firm's profits at $t$ are

$$\pi(t) = F(\bar{e}L(t)) - w(t)[L(t) + S(t)], \qquad F'(\bullet) > 0, \qquad F''(\bullet) < 0, \qquad (10.23)$$

where $L$ is the number of employees who are exerting effort and $S$ is the number who are shirking. The problem facing the firm is to set $w$ sufficiently high that its workers do not shirk, and to choose $L$. Because the firm's decisions at any date affect profits only at that date, there is no need to analyze the present value of profits: the firm chooses $w$ and $L$ at each moment to maximize the instantaneous flow of profits.

The final assumption of the model is $\bar{e}F'(\bar{e}\bar{L}/N) > \bar{e}$, or $F'(\bar{e}\bar{L}/N) > 1$. This condition states that if each firm hires $1/N$ of the labor force, the marginal product of labor exceeds the cost of exerting effort. Thus in the absence of imperfect monitoring, there is full employment.

## The Values of $E$, $U$, and $S$

Let $V_i$ denote the "value" of being in state $i$ (for $i = E$, $S$, and $U$). That is, $V_i$ is the expected value of discounted lifetime utility from the present moment forward of a worker who is in state $i$. Because transitions among states are Poisson processes, the $V_i$'s do not depend on how long the worker has been in the current state or on the worker's prior history. And because we are focusing on steady states, the $V_i$'s are constant over time.

To find $V_E$, $V_S$, and $V_U$, it is not necessary to analyze the various paths the worker may follow over the infinite future. Instead we can use *dynamic programming*. The central idea of dynamic programming is to look at only a brief interval of time and use the $V_i$'s themselves to summarize what occurs after the end of the interval.[8] Consider first a worker who is employed and exerting effort at time 0. Suppose temporarily that time is divided into intervals of length $\Delta t$, and that a worker who loses his or her job during one interval cannot begin to look for a new job until the beginning of the next interval. Let $V_E(\Delta t)$ and $V_U(\Delta t)$ denote the values of employment and unemployment as of the beginning of an interval under this assumption. In a moment we will let $\Delta t$ approach zero. When we do this, the constraint that a worker who loses his or her job during an interval cannot find a new job during the remainder of that interval becomes irrelevant. Thus $V_E(\Delta t)$ will approach $V_E$.

---

[8] If time is discrete rather than continuous, we look one period ahead. See Ljungqvist and Sargent (2004) for an introduction to dynamic programming.

If a worker is employed in a job paying a wage of $w$, $V_E(\Delta t)$ is given by

$$V_E(\Delta t) = \int_{t=0}^{\Delta t} e^{-bt} e^{-\rho t}(w - \bar{e})\, dt$$

$$+ e^{-\rho \Delta t}[e^{-b\Delta t} V_E(\Delta t) + (1 - e^{-b\Delta t}) V_U(\Delta t)]. \tag{10.24}$$

The first term of (10.24) reflects utility during the interval $(0, \Delta t)$. The probability that the worker is still employed at time $t$ is $e^{-bt}$. If the worker is employed, flow utility is $w - \bar{e}$. Discounting this back to time 0 yields an expected contribution to lifetime utility of $e^{-(\rho+b)t}(w - \bar{e})$.[9]

The second term of (10.24) reflects utility after $\Delta t$. At time $\Delta t$, the worker is employed with probability $e^{-b\Delta t}$ and unemployed with probability $1 - e^{-b\Delta t}$. Combining these probabilities with the $V$'s and discounting yields the second term.

If we compute the integral in (10.24), we can rewrite the equation as

$$V_E(\Delta t) = \frac{1}{\rho + b}\left(1 - e^{-(\rho+b)\Delta t}\right)(w - \bar{e})$$

$$+ e^{-\rho \Delta t}[e^{-b\Delta t} V_E(\Delta t) + (1 - e^{-b\Delta t}) V_U(\Delta t)]. \tag{10.25}$$

Solving this expression for $V_E(\Delta t)$ gives

$$V_E(\Delta t) = \frac{1}{\rho + b}(w - \bar{e}) + \frac{1}{1 - e^{-(\rho+b)\Delta t}} e^{-\rho \Delta t}(1 - e^{-b\Delta t}) V_U(\Delta t). \tag{10.26}$$

As described above, $V_E$ equals the limit of $V_E(\Delta t)$ as $\Delta t$ approaches zero. (Similarly, $V_U$ equals the limit of $V_U(\Delta t)$ as $t$ approaches zero.) To find this limit, we apply l'Hôpital's rule to (10.26). This yields

$$V_E = \frac{1}{\rho + b}[(w - \bar{e}) + bV_U]. \tag{10.27}$$

Equation (10.27) can also be derived intuitively. Think of an asset that pays dividends at rate $w - \bar{e}$ per unit time when the worker is employed and no dividends when the worker is unemployed. In addition, assume that the asset is being priced by risk-neutral investors with required rate of return $\rho$. Since the expected present value of lifetime dividends of this asset is the same as the worker's expected present value of lifetime utility, the asset's price must be $V_E$ when the worker is employed and $V_U$ when the worker is unemployed. For the asset to be held, it must provide an expected rate of return of $\rho$. That is, its dividends per unit time, plus any expected capital gains or losses per unit time, must equal $\rho V_E$. When the worker is employed, dividends per unit time are $w - \bar{e}$, and there is a probability $b$ per unit time

---

[9] Because of the steady-state assumption, if it is optimal for the worker to exert effort initially, it continues to be optimal. Thus we do not have to allow for the possibility of the worker beginning to shirk.

of a capital loss of $V_E - V_U$. Thus,

$$\rho V_E = (w - \bar{e}) - b(V_E - V_U). \tag{10.28}$$

Rearranging this expression yields (10.27).

If the worker is shirking, the "dividend" is $w$ per unit time, and the expected capital loss is $(b + q)(V_S - V_U)$ per unit time. Thus reasoning parallel to that used to derive (10.28) implies

$$\rho V_S = w - (b + q)(V_S - V_U). \tag{10.29}$$

Finally, if the worker is unemployed, the dividend is zero and the expected capital gain (assuming that firms pay sufficiently high wages that employed workers exert effort) is $a(V_E - V_U)$ per unit time.[10] Thus,

$$\rho V_U = a(V_E - V_U). \tag{10.30}$$

## The No-Shirking Condition

The firm must pay enough that $V_E \geq V_S$; otherwise its workers exert no effort and produce nothing. At the same time, since effort cannot exceed $\bar{e}$, there is no need to pay any excess over the minimum needed to induce effort. Thus the firm chooses $w$ so that $V_E$ just equals $V_S$:[11]

$$V_E = V_S. \tag{10.31}$$

This result tells us that the left-hand sides of (10.28) and (10.29) must be equal. Thus

$$(w - \bar{e}) - b(V_E - V_U) = w - (b + q)(V_E - V_U), \tag{10.32}$$

or

$$V_E - V_U = \frac{\bar{e}}{q}. \tag{10.33}$$

Equation (10.33) implies that firms set wages high enough that workers strictly prefer employment to unemployment. Thus workers obtain rents. The size of the premium is increasing in the cost of exerting effort, $\bar{e}$, and decreasing in firms' efficacy in detecting shirkers, $q$.

The next step is to find what the wage must be for the rent to employment to equal $\bar{e}/q$. Equations (10.28) and (10.30) imply

$$\rho(V_E - V_U) = (w - \bar{e}) - (a + b)(V_E - V_U). \tag{10.34}$$

---

[10] Equations (10.29) and (10.30) can also be derived by defining $V_U(\Delta t)$ and $V_S(\Delta t)$ and proceeding along the lines used to derive (10.27).

[11] Since all firms are the same, they choose the same wage.

It follows that for $V_E - V_U$ to equal $\bar{e}/q$, the wage must satisfy

$$w = \bar{e} + (a + b + \rho)\frac{\bar{e}}{q}. \tag{10.35}$$

Thus the wage needed to induce effort is increasing in the cost of effort ($\bar{e}$), the ease of finding jobs ($a$), the rate of job breakup ($b$), and the discount rate ($\rho$), and decreasing in the probability that shirkers are detected ($q$).

It turns out to be more convenient to express the wage needed to prevent shirking in terms of employment per firm, $L$, rather than the rate at which the unemployed find jobs, $a$. To substitute for $a$, we use the fact that, since the economy is in steady state, movements into and out of unemployment balance. The number of workers becoming unemployed per unit time is $N$ (the number of firms) times $L$ (the number of workers per firm) times $b$ (the rate of job breakup).[12] The number of unemployed workers finding jobs is $\bar{L} - NL$ times $a$. Equating these two quantities yields

$$a = \frac{NLb}{\bar{L} - NL}. \tag{10.36}$$

Equation (10.36) implies $a + b = \bar{L}b/(\bar{L} - NL)$. Substituting this into (10.35) yields

$$w = \bar{e} + \left(\rho + \frac{\bar{L}}{\bar{L} - NL}b\right)\frac{\bar{e}}{q}. \tag{10.37}$$

Equation (10.37) is the *no-shirking condition*. It shows, as a function of the level of employment, the wage that firms must pay to induce workers to exert effort. When more workers are employed, there are fewer unemployed workers and more workers leaving their jobs; thus it is easier for unemployed workers to find employment. The wage needed to deter shirking is therefore an increasing function of employment. At full employment, unemployed workers find work instantly, and so there is no cost to being fired and thus no wage that can deter shirking. The set of points in $(NL,w)$ space satisfying the no-shirking condition (NSC) is shown in Figure 10.2.

## Closing the Model

Firms hire workers up to the point where the marginal product of labor equals the wage. Equation (10.23) implies that when its workers are exerting effort, a firm's flow profits are $F(\bar{e}L) - wL$. Thus the condition for the marginal product of labor to equal the wage is

$$\bar{e}F'(\bar{e}L) = w. \tag{10.38}$$

---

[12] We are assuming that the economy is large enough that although the breakup of any individual job is random, aggregate breakups are not.

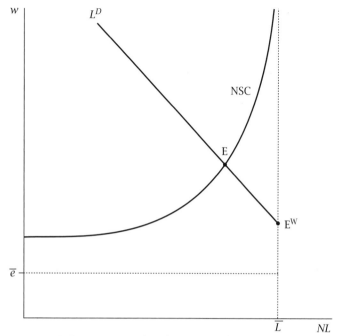

**FIGURE 10.2   The Shapiro–Stiglitz model**

The set of points satisfying (10.38) (which is simply a conventional labor demand curve) is also shown in Figure 10.2.

Labor supply is horizontal at $\bar{e}$ up to the number of workers, $\bar{L}$, and then vertical. In the absence of imperfect monitoring, equilibrium occurs at the intersection of labor demand and supply. Our assumption that the marginal product of labor at full employment exceeds the disutility of effort $(F'(\bar{e}\bar{L}/N) > 1)$ implies that this intersection occurs in the vertical part of the labor supply curve. The Walrasian equilibrium is shown as Point $E^W$ in the diagram.

With imperfect monitoring, equilibrium occurs at the intersection of the labor demand curve (equation [10.38]) and the no-shirking condition (equation [10.37]). This is shown as Point E in the diagram. At the equilibrium, there is unemployment. Unemployed workers strictly prefer to be employed at the prevailing wage and exert effort than to remain unemployed. Nonetheless, they cannot bid the wage down: firms know that if they hire additional workers at slightly less than the prevailing wage, the workers will prefer shirking to exerting effort. Thus the wage does not fall, and the unemployment remains.

Two examples may help to clarify the workings of the model. First, a rise in $q$—an increase in the probability per unit time that a shirker is detected—shifts the no-shirking locus down and does not affect the labor demand

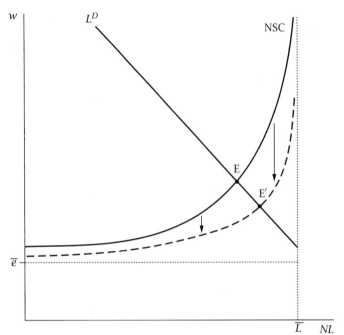

**FIGURE 10.3   The effects of a rise in $q$ in the Shapiro–Stiglitz model**

curve. This is shown in Figure 10.3. Thus the wage falls and employment rises. As $q$ approaches infinity, the probability that a shirker is detected in any finite length of time approaches 1. As a result, the no-shirking wage approaches $\bar{e}$ for any level of employment less than full employment. Thus the economy approaches the Walrasian equilibrium.

Second, if there is no turnover ($b = 0$), unemployed workers are never hired. As a result, the no-shirking wage is independent of the level of employment. From (10.37), the no-shirking wage in this case is $\bar{e} + \rho\bar{e}/q$. Intuitively, the gain from shirking relative to exerting effort is $\bar{e}$ per unit time. The cost is that there is probability $q$ per unit time of becoming permanently unemployed and thereby losing the discounted surplus from the job, which is $(w - \bar{e})/\rho$. Equating the cost and benefit gives $w = \bar{e} + \rho\bar{e}/q$. This case is shown in Figure 10.4.

## Implications

The model implies that there is equilibrium unemployment and suggests various factors that are likely to influence it. Thus the model has some promise as a candidate explanation of unemployment. Unfortunately, the model is so stylized that it is difficult to determine what level of unemployment it predicts.

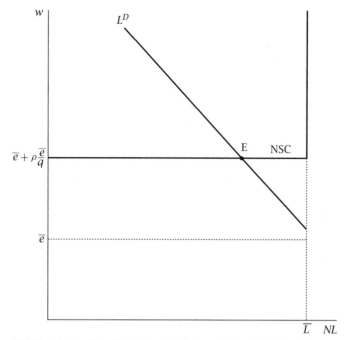

**FIGURE 10.4   The Shapiro–Stiglitz model without turnover**

With regard to short-run fluctuations, consider the impact of a fall in labor demand, shown in Figure 10.5. $w$ and $L$ move down along the no-shirking locus. Since labor supply is perfectly inelastic, employment necessarily responds more than it would without imperfect monitoring. Thus the model suggests one possible reason that wages may respond less to demand-driven output fluctuations than they would if workers were always on their labor supply curves.[13]

Unfortunately, however, this effect appears to be quantitatively small. When unemployment is lower, a worker who is fired can find a new job more easily, and so the wage needed to prevent shirking is higher; this is the reason the no-shirking locus slopes up. Attempts to calibrate the model suggest that the locus is quite steep at the levels of unemployment we observe. That is, the model implies that the impact of a shift in labor demand

---

[13] The simple model presented here has the same problem as the simple efficiency-wage model in Section 10.2: it implies that as technological progress continually shifts the labor demand curve up, unemployment trends down. One way to eliminate this prediction is to make the cost of exerting effort, $\bar{e}$, endogenous, and to structure the model so that $\bar{e}$ and output per worker grow at the same rate in the long run. This causes the NSC curve to shift up at the same rate as the labor demand curve in the long run, and thus eliminates the downward trend in unemployment.

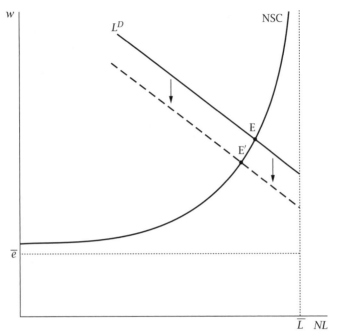

**FIGURE 10.5   The effects of a fall in labor demand in the Shapiro–Stiglitz model**

falls mainly on wages and relatively little on employment (Gomme, 1999; Alexopoulos, 2004).[14]

Finally, the model implies that the decentralized equilibrium is inefficient. To see this, note that the marginal product of labor at full employment, $\bar{e}F'(\bar{e}\bar{L}/N)$, exceeds the cost to workers of supplying effort, $\bar{e}$. Thus the first-best allocation is for everyone to be employed and exert effort. Of course, the government cannot bring this about simply by dictating that firms move down the labor demand curve until full employment is reached: this policy causes workers to shirk, and thus results in zero output. But Shapiro and Stiglitz note that wage subsidies financed by lump-sum taxes or profits taxes improve welfare. This policy shifts the labor demand curve up, and thus increases the wage and employment along the no-shirking locus. Since the value of the additional output exceeds the opportunity cost of producing it, overall welfare rises. How the gain is divided between workers and firms depends on how the wage subsidies are financed.

---

[14] In contrast to the simple analysis in the text, these authors analyze the dynamic effects of a shift in labor demand rather than comparing steady states with different levels of demand.

## Extensions

The basic model can be extended in many ways. Here we discuss four.

First, an important question about the labor market is why, given that unemployment appears so harmful to workers, employers rely on layoffs rather than work-sharing arrangements when they reduce the amount of labor they use. Shapiro and Stiglitz's model (modified so that the number of hours employees work can vary) suggests a possible answer. A reduction in hours lowers the surplus that employees are getting from their jobs. As a result, the wage that the firm has to pay to prevent shirking rises. Thus the firm may find layoffs preferable to work-sharing even though it subjects its workers to greater risk.

Second, Bulow and Summers (1986) extend the model to include a second type of job where effort can be monitored perfectly. Since there is no asymmetric information in this sector, the jobs provide no surplus and are not rationed. Under plausible assumptions, the absence of surplus results in high turnover. The jobs with imperfect monitoring continue to pay more than the market-clearing wage. Thus workers who obtain these jobs are reluctant to leave them. If the model is extended further to include groups of workers with different job attachments (different $b$'s), a higher wage is needed to induce effort from workers with less job attachment. As a result, firms with jobs that require monitoring are reluctant to hire workers with low job attachment, and so these workers are disproportionately employed in the low-wage, high-turnover sector. These predictions concerning wage levels, turnover, and occupational segregation fit the stylized facts about *primary* and *secondary* jobs identified by Doeringer and Piore (1971) in their theory of *dual labor markets*.

Third, Alexopoulos (2004) considers a variation on the model where shirkers, rather than being fired, receive a lower wage for some period. This change has a large impact on the model's implications for short-run fluctuations. The cost of forgoing a given amount of wage income does not depend on the prevailing unemployment rate. As a result, the no-shirking locus is flat, and the short-run impact of a shift in labor demand falls entirely on employment.

The final extension is more problematic for the theory. We have assumed that compensation takes the form of conventional wage payments. But, as suggested in the general discussion of potential sources of efficiency wages, more complicated compensation policies can dramatically change the effects of imperfect monitoring. Two examples of such compensation policies are *bonding* and *job selling*. Bonding occurs when firms require each new worker to post a bond that must be forfeited if he or she is caught shirking. By requiring sufficiently large bonds, the firm can induce workers not to shirk even at the market-clearing wage; that is, it can shift the no-shirking locus down until it coincides with the labor supply curve. Job selling occurs when firms require employees to pay a fee when they are hired. If firms are obtaining payments from new workers, their labor demand is higher for a given wage; thus the wage and employment rise as the economy moves up the no-shirking curve. If firms are able to require bonds or sell jobs, they will do so, and unemployment will be eliminated from the model.

Bonding, job selling, and the like may be limited by an absence of perfect capital markets (so that it is difficult for workers to post large bonds, or to pay large fees when they are hired). They may also be limited by workers' fears that the firm may falsely accuse them of shirking and claim the bonds, or dismiss them and keep the job fee. But, as Carmichael (1985) emphasizes, such considerations cannot eliminate these schemes entirely: if workers strictly prefer employment to unemployment, firms can raise their profits by, for example, charging marginally more for jobs. In such situations, jobs are not rationed, but go to those who are willing to pay the most for them. Thus even if these schemes are limited, they still eliminate unemployment. In short, the absence of job fees and performance bonds is a puzzle for the theory.

It is important to keep in mind that the Shapiro–Stiglitz model focuses on one particular source of efficiency wages. Neither its conclusions nor the difficulties it faces in explaining the absence of bonding and job selling are general. For example, suppose firms find high wages attractive because they improve the quality of job applicants on dimensions they cannot observe. Since the attractiveness of a job presumably depends on the overall compensation package, in this case firms have no incentive to adopt schemes such as job selling. Likewise, there is no reason to expect the implications of the Shapiro–Stiglitz model concerning the effects of a shift in labor demand to apply in this case.

As described in Section 10.8, workers' feelings of gratitude, anger, and fairness appear to be important to wage-setting. If these considerations are the reason that the labor market does not clear, again there is no reason to expect the Shapiro–Stiglitz model's implications concerning compensation schemes and the effects of shifts in labor demand to hold. In this case, theory provides little guidance. Generating predictions concerning the determinants of unemployment and the cyclical behavior of the labor market requires more detailed study of the determinants of workers' attitudes and their impact on productivity. Section 10.8 describes some preliminary attempts in this direction.

# 10.5   Contracting Models

The second departure from Walrasian assumptions about the labor market that we consider is the existence of long-term relationships between firms and workers. Firms do not hire workers afresh each period. Instead, many jobs involve long-term attachments and considerable firm-specific skills on the part of workers.

The possibility of long-term relationships implies that the wage does not have to adjust to clear the labor market each period. Workers are content to stay in their current jobs as long as the income streams they expect to obtain are preferable to their outside opportunities; because of their long-term relationships with their employers, their current wages may be relatively unimportant to this comparison. This section explores the consequences of this observation.

## A Baseline Model

Consider a firm dealing with a group of workers. The firm's profits are

$$\pi = AF(L) - wL, \qquad F'(\bullet) > 0, \qquad F''(\bullet) < 0, \qquad (10.39)$$

where $L$ is the quantity of labor the firm employs and $w$ is the wage. $A$ is a factor that shifts the profit function. It could reflect technology (so that a higher value means that the firm can produce more output from a given amount of labor), or economy-wide output (so that a higher value means that the firm can obtain a higher relative price for a given amount of output).

Instead of considering multiple periods, it is easier to consider a single period and assume that $A$ is random. Thus when workers decide whether to work for the firm, they consider the expected utility they obtain in the single period given the randomness in $A$, rather than the average utility they obtain over many periods as their income and hours vary in response to fluctuations in $A$.

The distribution of $A$ is discrete. There are $K$ possible values of $A$, indexed by $i$; $p_i$ denotes the probability that $A = A_i$. Thus the firm's expected profits are

$$E[\pi] = \sum_{i=1}^{K} p_i[A_i F(L_i) - w_i L_i], \qquad (10.40)$$

where $L_i$ and $w_i$ denote the quantity of labor and the wage if the realization of $A$ is $A_i$. The firm maximizes its expected profits; thus it is risk-neutral.

Each worker is assumed to work the same amount. The representative worker's utility is

$$u = U(C) - V(L), \quad U'(\bullet) > 0, \quad U''(\bullet) < 0, \quad V'(\bullet) > 0, \quad V''(\bullet) > 0, \quad (10.41)$$

where $U(\bullet)$ gives the utility from consumption and $V(\bullet)$ the disutility from working. Since $U''(\bullet)$ is negative, workers are risk-averse.[15]

Workers' consumption, $C$, is assumed to equal their labor income, $wL$.[16] That is, workers cannot purchase insurance against employment and wage fluctuations. In a more fully developed model, this might arise because workers are heterogeneous and have private information about their labor-market prospects. Here, however, the absence of outside insurance is simply assumed.

Equation (10.41) implies that the representative worker's expected utility is

$$E[u] = \sum_{i=1}^{K} p_i [U(C_i) - V(L_i)]. \tag{10.42}$$

There is some reservation level of expected utility, $u_0$, that workers must attain to be willing to work for the firm. There is no labor mobility once workers agree to a contract. Thus the only constraint on the contract involves the average level of utility it offers, not the level in any individual state.

## Implicit Contracts

One simple type of contract just specifies a wage and then lets the firm choose employment once $A$ is determined; many actual contracts at least appear to take this form. Under such a *wage contract,* unemployment and real wage rigidity arise immediately. A fall in labor demand, for example, causes the firm to reduce employment at the fixed real wage while labor supply does not shift, and thus creates unemployment (or, if all workers work the same amount, underemployment). And the cost of labor does not respond because, by assumption, the real wage is fixed.

But this is not a satisfactory explanation of unemployment and real wage rigidity. The difficulty is that this type of a contract is inefficient (Leontief, 1946). Since the wage is fixed and the firm chooses employment taking the wage as given, the marginal product of labor is independent of $A$. But since employment varies with $A$, the marginal disutility of working depends on

---

[15] Because the firm's owners can diversify away firm-specific risk by holding a broad portfolio, the assumption that the firm is risk-neutral is reasonable for firm-specific shocks. For aggregate shocks, however, the assumption that the firm is less risk-averse than the workers is harder to justify. Since the main goal of the theory is to explain the effects of aggregate shocks, this is a weak point of the model. One possibility is that the owners are wealthier than the workers and that risk aversion is declining in wealth.

[16] If there are $\overline{L}$ workers, the representative worker's hours and consumption are in fact $L/\overline{L}$ and $wL/\overline{L}$, and so utility takes the form $\tilde{U}(C/\overline{L}) - \tilde{V}(L/\overline{L})$. To eliminate $\overline{L}$, define $U(C) = \tilde{U}(C/\overline{L})$ and $V(L) = \tilde{V}(L/\overline{L})$.

A. Thus the marginal product of labor is generally not equal to the marginal disutility of work, and so it is possible to make both parties to the contract better off. And if labor supply is not very elastic, the inefficiency is large. When labor demand is low, for example, the marginal disutility of work is low, and so the firm and the workers could both be made better off if the workers worked slightly more.

To see how it is possible to improve on a wage contract, suppose the firm offers the workers a contract specifying the wage and hours for each possible realization of A. Since actual contracts do not explicitly specify employment and the wage as functions of the state, such contracts are known as *implicit contracts*.[17]

Recall that the firm must offer the workers at least some minimum level of expected utility, $u_0$, but is otherwise unconstrained. In addition, since $L_i$ and $w_i$ determine $C_i$, we can think of the firm's choice variables as $L$ and $C$ in each state rather than as $L$ and $w$. The Lagrangian for the firm's problem is therefore

$$\mathcal{L} = \sum_{i=1}^{K} p_i[A_i F(L_i) - C_i] + \lambda\left(\left\{\sum_{i=1}^{K} p_i[U(C_i) - V(L_i)]\right\} - u_0\right). \tag{10.43}$$

The first-order condition for $C_i$ is

$$-p_i + \lambda p_i U'(C_i) = 0, \tag{10.44}$$

or

$$U'(C_i) = \frac{1}{\lambda}. \tag{10.45}$$

Equation (10.45) implies that the marginal utility of consumption is constant across states, and thus that consumption is constant across states. Thus the risk-neutral firm fully insures the risk-averse workers.

The first-order condition for $L_i$ is

$$p_i A_i F'(L_i) = \lambda p_i V'(L_i). \tag{10.46}$$

Equation (10.45) implies $\lambda = 1/U'(C)$, where $C$ is the constant level of consumption. Substituting this fact into (10.46) and dividing both sides by $p_i$ yields

$$A_i F'(L_i) = \frac{V'(L_i)}{U'(C)}. \tag{10.47}$$

---

[17] The theory of implicit contracts is due to Azariadis (1975), Baily (1974), and Gordon (1974).

## Implications

Under efficient contracts, workers' real incomes are constant. In that sense, the model implies strong real wage rigidity. Indeed, because $L$ is higher when $A$ is higher, the model implies that the wage per hour is countercyclical. Unfortunately, however, this result does not help to account for the puzzle that shifts in labor demand appear to result in large changes in employment. The problem is that with long-term contracts, the wage is no longer playing an allocative role (Barro, 1977; Hall, 1980). That is, firms do not choose employment taking the wage as given. Rather, the level of employment as a function of the state is specified in the contract. And, from (10.47), this level is the level that equates the marginal product of labor with the marginal disutility of additional hours of work.

This discussion implies that the cost to the firm of varying the amount of labor it uses is likely to change greatly with its level of employment. Suppose the firm wants to increase employment marginally in state $i$. To do this, it must raise workers' compensation to make them no worse off than before. Since the expected utility cost to workers of the change is $p_i V'(L_i)$, $C$ must rise by $p_i V'(L_i)/U'(C)$. Thus the marginal cost to the firm of increasing employment in a given state is proportional to $V'(L_i)$. If labor supply is relatively inelastic, $V'(L_i)$ is sharply increasing in $L_i$, and so the cost of labor to the firm is much higher when employment is high than when it is low. Thus, for example, embedding this model of contracts in a model of price determination like that of Section 6.6 would not alter the result that relatively inelastic labor supply creates a strong incentive for firms to cut prices and increase employment in recessions, and to raise prices and reduce employment in booms.

In addition to failing to predict relatively acyclical labor costs, the model fails to predict unemployment: as emphasized above, the implicit contract equates the marginal product of labor and the marginal disutility of work. The model does, however, suggest a possible explanation for *apparent* unemployment. In the efficient contract, workers are not free to choose their labor supply given the wage. Instead, the wage and employment are simultaneously specified to yield optimal risk-sharing and allocative efficiency. When employment is low, the marginal disutility of work is low and the hourly wage, $C/L_i$, is high. Thus workers wish that they could work more at the wage the firm is paying. As a result, even though employment and the wage are chosen optimally, workers appear to be constrained in their labor supply.

## Insiders and Outsiders

One possible way of improving contracting models' ability to explain key features of labor markets is to relax the assumption that the firm is dealing with a fixed pool of workers. In reality, there are two groups of potential workers. The first group—the insiders—are workers who have some connection with the firm at the time of the bargaining, and whose interests are therefore taken into account in the contract. The second group—the outsiders—are workers who have no initial connection with the firm but who may be hired after the contract is set.

Oswald (1993) and Gottfries (1992), building on earlier work by Lindbeck and Snower (1986), Blanchard and Summers (1986), and Gregory (1986), argue that relationships between firms and insiders and outsiders have two features that are critical to how contracting affects the labor market. First, because of normal employment growth and turnover, most of the time the insiders are fully employed and the only hiring decision concerns how many outsiders to hire. This immediately implies that, just as in a conventional labor demand problem, but in sharp contrast to what happens in the basic implicit-contract model, employment is chosen to equate the marginal product of labor with the wage. To see this, note that if this condition fails, it is possible to increase the firm's profits with no change in the insiders' expected utility by changing the number of outsiders hired. Thus it cannot make sense for the insiders and the firm (who are the only ones involved in the original bargaining) to agree to such an arrangement.

The second feature of labor markets that Oswald and Gottfries emphasize is that the wages paid to the two types of workers cannot be set independently: in practice, the higher the wage that the firm pays to its existing employees, the more it must pay to its new hires. This implies that the insurance role of wages affects employment. Suppose, for example, that the insiders and the firm agree to keep the real wage fixed and so provide complete insurance to the insiders.[18] Then when the firm is hit by shocks, employment varies to keep the marginal product of labor equal to the constant real wage.

Because the wage is now playing both an insurance and an allocative role, in general the optimal contract does not make it independent of the state. Under natural assumptions, however, this actually strengthens the results: the optimal contract typically specifies a lower wage when the realization of $A$ is higher, and so further magnifies employment fluctuations. Intuitively, by lowering the wage in states where employment is high, the insiders and the firm reduce the amount of insurance the firm is providing but also lower the average amount spent hiring outsiders. The optimal contract involves a balancing of these two objectives, and thus a somewhat countercyclical wage.[19] Thus this model implies that the real wage is countercyclical and that it represents the true cost of labor to the firm.

---

[18] Recall that since the marginal hiring decisions involve outsiders, the amount the insiders work is independent of the state. Thus, in contrast to what happens in the basic implicit-contract model, here a constant wage makes the insiders' consumption constant.

[19] See Problem 10.8.

The crucial feature of the model is its assumption that the outsiders' and insiders' wages are linked. Without this link, the firm can hire outsiders at the prevailing economy-wide wage. With inelastic labor supply, that wage is low in recessions and high in booms, and so the marginal cost of labor to the firm is highly procyclical.

Unfortunately, the insider-outsider literature has not established that outsiders' and insiders' wages are linked. Gottfries argues that a link arises from the facts that the firm must be given some freedom to discharge insiders who are incompetent or shirking and that an excessive gap between insiders' and outsiders' wages would give the firm an incentive to take advantage of this freedom. Blanchard and Summers (1986) argue that the insiders are reluctant to allow the hiring of large numbers of outsiders at a low wage because they realize that, over time, such a policy would result in the outsiders controlling the bargaining process. But tying insiders' and outsiders' wages does not appear to be the best way of dealing with these problems. If the economy-wide wage is sometimes far below insiders', tying the insiders' and outsiders' wages is very costly. It appears that the firm and the insiders would therefore be better off if they instead agreed to some limitation on the firm's ability to hire outsiders, or if they charged new hires a fee (and let the fee vary with the gap between the insiders' wage and the economy-wide wage).

It is also possible that a link between insiders' and outsiders' wages could arise from workers' notions about fairness and the potential effects of the firm violating those notions, along the lines of the loyalty-based efficiency-wage models we discussed in Section 10.2. But in this case, it is not clear that the contracting and insider-outsider considerations would be important; the efficiency-wage forces alone might be enough to greatly change the labor market.

In short, we can conclude only that *if* a link between insiders' and outsiders' wages can be established, insider-outsider considerations may have important implications.

## Hysteresis and European Unemployment

One important extension of insider-outsider models involves dynamic settings. The previous discussion assumed that the insiders are always employed. But this assumption is likely to fail in some situations. Most importantly, if the insiders' bargaining power is sufficiently great, they will set the wage high enough to risk some unemployment: if the insiders are fully employed with certainty, there is a benefit but not a cost to them of raising the wage further. And variations in employment can give rise to dynamics in the number of insiders. Under many institutional arrangements, workers who become unemployed eventually lose a say in wage-setting; likewise, workers who are hired eventually gain a role in bargaining. Thus a fall in employment caused by a decline in labor demand is likely to reduce the number of insiders, and a rise in employment is likely to increase the number of insiders. This in turn affects future wage-setting and employment. When the number of insiders is smaller, they can afford to set a higher wage. Thus a one-time adverse shock to labor demand can lead to a persistent fall in employment. The extreme case where the effect is permanent is known as *hysteresis.*

The possibility of hysteresis has received considerable attention in the context of Europe. European unemployment fluctuated around very low levels in the 1950s and 1960s, rose fairly steadily to more than 10 percent from the mid-1970s to the mid-1980s, and has shown little tendency to decline since then. Thus there is no evidence of a stable natural rate that unemployment returns to after a shock. Blanchard and Summers (1986) argue that Europe in the 1970s and 1980s satisfied the conditions for insider-outsider considerations to produce hysteresis: workers had a great deal of power in wage-setting, there were large negative shocks, and the rules and institutions led to some extent to the disenfranchisement from the bargaining process of workers who lost their jobs.

Two possible sources of hysteresis other than insider-outsider considerations have also received considerable attention. One is deterioration of skills: workers who are unemployed do not acquire additional on-the-job training, and their existing human capital may decay or become obsolete. As a result, workers who lose their jobs when labor demand falls may have difficulty finding work when demand recovers, particularly if the downturn is extended. The second additional source of hysteresis operates through labor-force attachment. Workers who are unemployed for extended periods may adjust their standard of living to the lower level provided by income maintenance programs. In addition, a long period of high unemployment may reduce the social stigma of extended joblessness. Because of these effects, labor supply may be permanently lower when demand returns to normal.

Loosely speaking, views of European unemployment fall into two camps. One emphasizes not hysteresis, but shifts in the natural rate as a result of such features of European labor-market institutions as generous unemployment-insurance benefits. Since most of those features were in place well before the rise in unemployment, this view requires that institutions' effects operate with long lags. For example, because the social stigma of unemployment changes slowly, the impact of generous unemployment benefits on the natural rate may be felt only very gradually (see, for example, Lindbeck and Nyberg, 2006). The other view emphasizes hysteresis. In this view, the labor-market institutions converted what would have otherwise been short-lived increases in unemployment into very long-lasting ones through union wage-setting, skill deterioration, and loss of labor-force attachment.[20]

# 10.6    Search and Matching Models

The final departure of the labor market from Walrasian assumptions that we consider is the simple fact that workers and jobs are heterogeneous. In a frictionless labor market, firms are indifferent about losing their workers, since identical workers are costlessly available at the same wage; likewise, workers are indifferent about losing their jobs. These implications are obviously not accurate descriptions of actual labor markets.

When workers and jobs are highly heterogeneous, the labor market has little resemblance to a Walrasian market. Rather than meeting in centralized markets where employment and wages are determined by the intersections of supply and demand curves, workers and firms meet in a decentralized, one-on-one fashion, and engage in a costly process of trying to match up idiosyncratic preferences, skills, and needs. Since this process is not instantaneous, it results in some unemployment. In addition, it may have implications for how wages and employment respond to shocks.

This section presents a model of firm and worker heterogeneity and the matching process. Because modeling heterogeneity requires abandoning many of our usual tools, even a basic model is relatively complicated. As a result, the model here only introduces some of the issues involved. This class of models is known collectively as the *Mortensen–Pissarides model* (for example, Pissarides, 1985; Mortensen, 1986; Mortensen and Pissarides, 1994; Pissarides, 2000).

## Basic Assumptions

The model is set in continuous time. The economy consists of workers and jobs. There is a continuum of workers of mass 1. Each worker can be in one of two states: employed or unemployed. A worker who is employed produces an exogenous, constant amount $y$ per unit time and receives an endogenous and potentially time-varying wage $w(t)$ per unit time. A worker who is unemployed receives an exogenous, constant income of $b \geq 0$ per unit time (or, equivalently, receives utility from leisure that he or she values as much as income of $b$).

Workers are risk neutral. Thus a worker's utility per unit time is $w(t)$ if employed and $b$ if unemployed. Workers' discount rate is $r > 0$.

---

[20] For more on these issues, see Siebert (1997); Ljungqvist and Sargent (1998, 2006); Ball (1999a); Blanchard and Wolfers (2000); Prescott (2004); Rogerson (2008); and Alesina, Glaeser, and Sacerdote (2005).

A job can be either filled or vacant. If it is filled, there is output of $y$ per unit time and labor costs of $w(t)$ per unit time. If it is vacant, there is neither output nor labor costs. Any job, either filled or vacant, involves a constant, exogenous cost $c > 0$ per unit time of being maintained. Thus profits per unit time are $y - w(t) - c$ if a job is filled and $-c$ per unit time if it is vacant. $y$ is assumed to exceed $b + c$, so that a filled job produces positive value. Vacant jobs can be created freely (but must incur the flow maintenance cost once they are created). Thus the number of jobs is endogenous.

In the absence of search frictions, the equilibrium of the model is trivial. There is a mass 1 of jobs, all of which are filled. If there were fewer jobs, some workers would be unemployed, and so creating a job would be profitable. If there were more jobs, the unfilled jobs would be producing negative profits with no offsetting benefit, and so there would be exit. Workers earn their marginal product, $y - c$. If they earned more, profits would be negative; if they earned less, creating new jobs and bidding up the wage would be profitable. Thus all workers are employed and earn their marginal products. Shifts in labor demand—changes in $y$—lead to immediate changes in the wage and leave employment unchanged.

The central feature of the model, however, is that there are search frictions. That is, unemployed workers and vacant jobs cannot find each other costlessly. Instead, the stocks of unemployed workers and vacancies yield a flow of meetings between workers and firms. Let $E(t)$ and $U(t)$ denote the numbers of employed and unemployed workers at time $t$, and let $F(t)$ and $V(t)$ denote the numbers of filled and unfilled jobs. Then the number of meetings per unit time is

$$M(t) = M(U(t), V(t)), \qquad M_U > 0, M_V > 0. \tag{10.48}$$

This *matching function* proxies for the complicated process of employer recruitment, worker search, and mutual evaluation.

In addition to the flow of new matches, there is turnover in existing jobs. Paralleling the Shapiro–Stiglitz model, jobs end at an exogenous rate $\lambda$ per unit time. Thus if we assume that all meetings lead to hires, the dynamics of the number of employed workers are given by

$$\dot{E}(t) = M(U(t), V(t)) - \lambda E(t). \tag{10.49}$$

Because of the search frictions, the economy is not perfectly competitive. When an unemployed worker and a firm with a vacancy meet, the worker's alternative to accepting the position is to continue searching, which will lead, after a period of unemployment of random duration, to meeting another firm with a vacancy. Likewise, the firm's alternative to hiring the worker is to resume searching. Thus, collectively, the worker and the firm are strictly better off if the worker fills the position than if he or she does not. Equivalently, the worker's reservation wage is strictly less than his or her marginal revenue product.

One immediate implication is that either workers earn strictly more than their reservation wages or firms pay strictly less than the marginal revenue product of labor, or both. In standard versions of the model, as we will see, both inequalities are strict. Thus even though every agent is atomistic, standard competitive results fail.

Because a firm and a worker that meet are collectively better off if the firm hires the worker, they would be forgoing a mutually advantageous trade if the firm did not hire the worker. Thus the assumption that all meetings lead to hires is reasonable. But this does not uniquely determine the wage. The wage must be high enough that the worker wants to work in the job, and low enough that the firm wants to hire the worker. Because there is strictly positive surplus from the match, there is a range of wages that satisfy these requirements. Thus we need more structure to pin down the wage. The standard approach is to assume that the wage is determined by *Nash bargaining*. That is, there is some exogenous parameter, $\phi$, where $0 \leq \phi \leq 1$; the wage is determined by the condition that fraction $\phi$ of the surplus from forming the match goes to the worker and fraction $1 - \phi$ goes to the firm. The specifics of how this assumption allows us to pin down the wage will be clearer shortly, when we see how to specify the parties' surpluses from forming a match.

## The Matching Function

The properties of the matching function are crucial to the model. In principle, it need not have constant returns to scale. When it exhibits increasing returns, there are *thick-market effects*: increases in the resources devoted to search make the matching process operate more effectively, in the sense that it yields more output (matches) per unit of input (unemployment and vacancies). When the matching function has decreasing returns, there are *crowding* effects.

The prevailing view, however, is that in practice constant returns is a reasonable approximation. For a large economy, over the relevant range the thick-market and crowding effects may be relatively unimportant or may roughly balance. Empirical efforts to estimate the matching function have found no strong evidence of departures from constant returns (for example, Blanchard and Diamond, 1989).

The assumption of constant returns implies that a single number, the ratio of vacancies to unemployment, summarizes the tightness of the labor market. To see this, define $\theta(t) = V(t)/U(t)$, and note that constant returns imply

$$\begin{aligned} M(U(t),V(t)) &= U(t)M(1,V(t)/U(t)) \\ &\equiv U(t)m(\theta(t)), \end{aligned}$$

(10.50)

where $m(\theta) \equiv M(1,\theta)$. Then the *job-finding rate*—the probability per unit time that an unemployed worker finds a job—is

$$a(t) = \frac{M(U(t),V(t))}{U(t)} \tag{10.51}$$
$$= m(\theta(t)).$$

Similarly, the *vacancy-filling rate* is

$$\alpha(t) = \frac{M(U(t),V(t))}{V(t)} \tag{10.52}$$
$$= \frac{m(\theta(t))}{\theta(t)}.$$

Our assumptions that $M(U,V)$ exhibits constant returns and that it is increasing in both arguments imply that $m(\theta)$ is increasing in $\theta$, but that the increase is less than proportional. Thus when the labor market is tighter (that is, when $\theta$ is greater), the job-finding rate is higher and the vacancy-filling rate is lower.

When researchers want to assume a functional form for the matching function, they almost universally assume that it is Cobb-Douglas. We will take that approach here. Thus,

$$m(\theta) = k\theta^\gamma, \qquad k > 0, \qquad 0 < \gamma < 1. \tag{10.53}$$

## Equilibrium Conditions

As in the Shapiro–Stiglitz model, we use dynamic programming to describe the values of the various states. In contrast to how we analyzed that model, however, we will not impose the assumption that the economy is in steady state from the outset (although we will end up focusing on that case). Let $V_E(t)$ denote the value of being employed at time $t$. That is, $V_E(t)$ is the expected lifetime utility from time $t$ forward, discounted to time $t$, of a worker who is employed at $t$. $V_U(t)$, $V_F(t)$, and $V_V(t)$ are defined similarly.

Since we are not assuming that the economy is in steady state, the "return" on being employed consists of three terms: a "dividend" of $w(t)$ per unit time; the potential "capital gain" on being employed from the fact that the economy is not in steady state, $\dot{V}_E(t)$; and a probability $\lambda$ per unit time of a "capital loss" of $V_E(t) - V_U(t)$ as a result of becoming unemployed. Thus,

$$rV_E(t) = w(t) + \dot{V}_E(t) - \lambda[V_E(t) - V_U(t)]. \tag{10.54}$$

Similar reasoning implies

$$rV_U(t) = b + \dot{V}_U(t) + a(t)[V_E(t) - V_U(t)], \tag{10.55}$$
$$rV_F(t) = [y - w(t) - c] + \dot{V}_F(t) - \lambda[V_F(t) - V_V(t)], \tag{10.56}$$
$$rV_V(t) = -c + \dot{V}_V(t) + \alpha(t)[V_F(t) - V_V(t)]. \tag{10.57}$$

Four conditions complete the model. First, (10.49) and our assumptions about $M(\bullet)$ describe the evolution of the number of workers who are employed:

$$\dot{E}(t) = U(t)^{1-\gamma} V(t)^{\gamma} - \lambda E(t). \tag{10.58}$$

Second, recall our assumption of Nash bargaining. A worker's surplus from forming a match rather than continuing to work is $V_E(t) - V_U(t)$. Similarly, a firm's surplus from a match is $V_F(t) - V_V(t)$. Thus the Nash bargaining assumption implies

$$V_E(t) - V_U(t) = \frac{\phi}{1-\phi}[V_F(t) - V_V(t)]. \tag{10.59}$$

Third, since new vacancies can be created and eliminated freely,

$$V_V(t) = 0 \qquad \text{for all } t. \tag{10.60}$$

Finally, the initial level of employment, $E(0)$, is given. This completes the description of the model.

## Steady-State Equilibrium

Characterizing the full dynamic path of the economy starting from arbitrary initial conditions is complicated by the potentially time-varying paths of the $V$'s. We will therefore focus mainly on the steady state of the model. The assumption that the economy is in steady state implies that all the $\dot{V}(t)$'s and $\dot{E}(t)$ are zero and that $a(t)$ and $\alpha(t)$ are constant.

We solve the model by focusing on two variables, employment ($E$) and the value of a vacancy ($V_V$). We will first find the value of $V_V$ implied by a given level of employment, and then impose the free-entry condition that $V_V$ must be zero.

We begin by considering the determination of the wage and the value of a vacancy given $a$ and $\alpha$. Subtracting (10.55) from (10.54) (with the $\dot{V}(t)$ terms set to zero) and rearranging yields

$$V_E - V_U = \frac{w - b}{a + \lambda + r}. \tag{10.61}$$

Similarly, (10.56) and (10.57) imply

$$V_F - V_V = \frac{y - w}{\alpha + \lambda + r}. \tag{10.62}$$

Our Nash-bargaining assumption (equation [10.59]) implies that $V_E - V_U$ equals $\phi/(1 - \phi)$ times $V_F - V_V$. Thus (10.61) and (10.62) imply

$$\frac{w - b}{a + \lambda + r} = \frac{\phi}{1 - \phi} \frac{y - w}{\alpha + \lambda + r}. \tag{10.63}$$

Solving this condition for $w$ yields

$$w = b + \frac{(a + \lambda + r)\phi}{\phi a + (1 - \phi)\alpha + \lambda + r}(y - b). \tag{10.64}$$

To interpret (10.64), first consider the case when $a$ and $\alpha$ are equal. Then the wage is $b + \phi(y - b)$: fraction $\phi$ of the difference between output and the value of leisure goes to the worker, and fraction $1 - \phi$ goes to the firm. When $a$ exceeds $\alpha$, workers can find new jobs more rapidly than firms can find new employees, and so more of the output goes to the worker. When $\alpha$ exceeds $a$, the reverse occurs.

Recall that we want to focus on the value of a vacancy. Equation (10.57) states that $rV_V$ equals $-c + \alpha(V_F - V_V)$. Expression (10.62) for $V_F - V_V$ therefore gives us

$$rV_V = -c + \alpha\frac{y - w}{\alpha + \lambda + r}. \tag{10.65}$$

Substituting expression (10.64) for $w$ into this equation and performing straightforward algebra yields

$$rV_V = -c + \frac{(1 - \phi)\alpha}{\phi a + (1 - \phi)\alpha + \lambda + r}(y - b). \tag{10.66}$$

In this expression, $a$ and $\alpha$ are endogenous. Thus the next step is to express them in terms of $E$. In steady state, $\dot{E}(t)$ is zero, and so the number of new matches per unit time must equal the number of jobs that end per unit time, $\lambda E$ (equation [10.49]). Thus the job-finding rate, $a = M(U,V)/U$, is given by

$$a = \frac{\lambda E}{1 - E}, \tag{10.67}$$

where we use the fact that the mass of workers is 1, so that $E + U = 1$.

The vacancy-filling rate, $\alpha$, is $M(U,V)/V$ (equation [10.52]). We again know that in steady state, $M(U,V)$ equals $\lambda E$. To express $\alpha$ in terms of $E$, we therefore need to find the $V$ that implies $M(U,V) = \lambda E$ for a given $E$. Using the fact that $M(U,V) = kU^{1-\gamma}V^{\gamma}$, we can derive

$$V = k^{-1/\gamma}(\lambda E)^{1/\gamma}(1 - E)^{-(1-\gamma)/\gamma}, \tag{10.68}$$

$$\alpha = k^{1/\gamma}(\lambda E)^{(\gamma-1)/\gamma}(1 - E)^{(1-\gamma)/\gamma}. \tag{10.69}$$

For our purposes, the key features of (10.67) and (10.69) are that they imply that $a$ is increasing in $E$ and that $\alpha$ is decreasing. Thus (10.66) implies that $rV_V$ is a decreasing function of $E$. As $E$ approaches 1, $a$ approaches infinity and $\alpha$ approaches zero; hence $rV_V$ approaches $-c$. Similarly, as $E$ approaches zero, $a$ approaches zero and $\alpha$ approaches infinity. Thus in this case $rV_V$ approaches $y - (b + c)$, which we have assumed to be positive. This information is summarized in Figure 10.6.

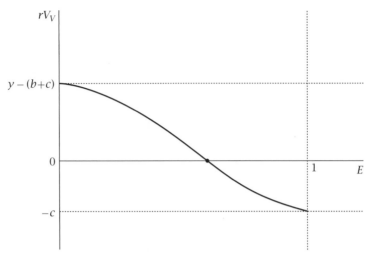

**FIGURE 10.6   The determination of equilibrium employment in the search and matching model**

The equilibrium level of employment is determined by the intersection of the $rV_V$ locus with the free-entry condition, which implies $rV_V = 0$. Imposing this condition on (10.66) yields

$$-c + \frac{(1 - \phi)\alpha(E)}{\phi a(E) + (1 - \phi)\alpha(E) + \lambda + r}(y - b) = 0. \qquad (10.70)$$

where the functions $a(E)$ and $\alpha(E)$ are given by (10.67) and (10.69). This expression implicitly defines $E$, and thus completes the solution of the model in the steady-state case.

## Extensions

This model can be extended in many directions. Here we discuss a few of the most important.[21]

One major set of extensions are ones that introduce greater heterogeneity. Although search and matching models are motivated by the enormous variety among workers and jobs, the model we have been considering assumes that both workers and jobs are homogeneous. A simple way to introduce heterogeneity and a reason for search and matching is to suppose that when a worker and a job meet, the worker's productivity, $y$, is not certain but is drawn from some distribution. This assumption implies that if the realized level of productivity is too low, the meeting does not lead to a match being formed but to continued search by both sides. Moreover, the

---

[21] Many of these extensions are surveyed by Rogerson, Shimer, and Wright (2005).

cut-off level of productivity is endogenous, so that the fraction of meetings that lead to jobs depends on the underlying parameters of the economy and may be time-varying. Similarly, if the worker's productivity in the job is subject to shocks, the break-up rate, which is exogenous and constant in the basic model, can be endogenized.

Another extension in the same spirit is to allow workers to continue searching even when they are employed and firms to continue searching even when their positions are filled. The result is that some of workers' transitions are directly from one job to another and that firms sometimes replace a worker with another.

Another important set of extensions involves making the process of search and information flow more sophisticated. In the basic model, search is completely random. But in practice, workers have some information about jobs, and they focus their search on the jobs that look most appealing. That is, to some extent search is not random but *directed*. Likewise, firms and workers generally do not bargain over compensation from scratch each time a worker is hired; many firms have wage policies that they are to some extent committed to. That is, to some extent wages are *posted*. Since one effect of posting wages is to affect workers' search, it is natural to combine the assumption that wages are posted with the assumption that search is directed. Such models are known as *competitive search models*.

# 10.7   Implications

## Unemployment

Search and matching models offer a straightforward explanation for average unemployment: it may be the result of continually matching workers and jobs in a complex and changing economy. Thus, much of observed unemployment may reflect what is traditionally known as *frictional* unemployment.

Labor markets are characterized by high rates of turnover. In U.S. manufacturing, for example, more than 3 percent of workers leave their jobs in a typical month. Moreover, many job changes are associated with wage increases, particularly for young workers (Topel and Ward, 1992); thus at least some of the turnover appears to be useful. In addition, there is high turnover of jobs themselves. In U.S. manufacturing, at least 10 percent of existing jobs disappear each year (Davis and Haltiwanger, 1990, 1992). These statistics suggest that a nonnegligible portion of unemployment is a largely inevitable result of the dynamics of the economy and the complexities of the labor market.

Unfortunately, it is difficult to go much beyond this general statement. Existing theoretical models and empirical evidence do not provide any clear way of discriminating between, for example, the hypothesis that search and matching considerations account for one-quarter of average unemployment and the hypothesis that they account for three-quarters. The importance of long-term unemployment in overall unemployment suggests, however, that at least some significant part of unemployment is not frictional. In the United States, although most workers who become unemployed remain so for less than a month, most of the workers who are unemployed at any time will have spells of unemployment that last more than 3 months; and nearly half will have spells that last more than 6 months (Clark and Summers, 1979). And in the European Community in the late 1980s, more than half of unemployed workers had been out of work for more than a year (Bean, 1994). It seems unlikely that search and matching considerations could be the source of most of this long-term unemployment.

A large recent literature moves away from such examinations of average rates of turnover and focuses on cyclical variations in turnover. From the firm side, this is often phrased in terms of the relative importance of changes in rates of *job creation* and *job destruction* to changes in unemployment. That is, this work asks to what extent increases in unemployment are the result of increases in the rate at which existing jobs disappear, and to what extent they are the result of decreases in the rate at which new jobs appear. From the worker side, the focus is on the relative importance of changes in the rates of inflows into and outflows from unemployment.

The two perspectives are not just mirror images of one another. For example, suppose the rate of job creation is constant over the business cycle and the rate of job destruction is countercyclical. Then on the worker side, both margins are cyclical: the rate of inflows rises in recessions because of the increase in the rate of job destruction, and the rate of outflow falls because of the increase in the number of unemployed workers and the constant rate of job creation.

One conclusion of this literature is that answering seemingly simple questions about the contributions of different margins to changes in unemployment is surprisingly hard. The details of the sample period, the precise measures used, and subtleties of the data can have large impacts on the results. To the extent that this work has reached firmer conclusions, it is that, from either the firm or the worker perspective, both margins are important to changes in overall unemployment.[22]

## The Impact of a Shift in Labor Demand

We now want to ask our usual question of whether the imperfection we are considering—in this case, the absence of a centralized market—affects

---

[22] A few contributions to this work are Blanchard and Diamond (1990); Foote (1998); Davis, Faberman, and Haltiwanger (2006); Shimer (2007); and Elsby, Michaels, and Solon (2009).

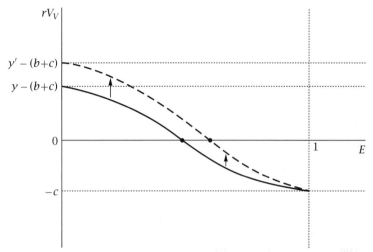

**FIGURE 10.7 The effects of a rise in labor demand in the search and matching model**

the cyclical behavior of the labor market. Specifically, we are interested in whether it causes a shift in labor demand to have a larger impact on employment and a smaller impact on the wage than it does in a Walrasian market.

Recall that we do not observe any long-run trend in unemployment. Thus a successful model of the labor market should imply that in response to long-run productivity growth, there is no change in unemployment. In this model, it is natural to model long-run productivity growth as increases of the same proportion in the output from a job ($y$), its nonlabor costs ($c$), and the income of the unemployed ($b$). From Figure 10.6 in the previous section, it is not immediately clear how such a change affects the point where the $rV_V$ line crosses the horizontal axis. Instead we must examine the equilibrium condition, (10.70). Inspecting this condition shows that if $y$, $b$, and $c$ change by the same proportion, the value of $E$ for which the condition holds does not change. Thus the model implies that long-run productivity growth does not affect employment. This means that $a$ and $\alpha$ do not change, and thus that the wage changes by the same proportion as $y$ (see [10.64]). In short, the model's long-run implications are reasonable.

We will model a cyclical change as a shift in $y$ with no change in $b$ and $c$. For concreteness, assume that $y$ rises, and continue to focus on steady states. From (10.70), this shifts the $rV_V$ locus up. Thus, as Figure 10.7 shows, employment rises. In a Walrasian market, in contrast, employment is unchanged at 1. Intuitively, in the absence of a frictionless market, workers are not costlessly available at the prevailing wage. The increase in $y$, with $b$ and $c$ fixed, raises the profits firms obtain when they find a worker relative to their costs of searching for one. Thus the number of firms—and hence employment—rises.

In addition, equation (10.68) implies that steady-state vacancies are $k^{-1/\gamma}(\lambda E)^{1/\gamma}(1-E)^{-(1-\gamma)/\gamma}$. Thus the rise in $y$ and the resulting increase in the number of firms increase vacancies. The model therefore implies a negative relation between unemployment and vacancies—a *Beveridge curve*.

The model does not imply substantial wage rigidity, however. From (10.67) and (10.69), the rise in $E$ causes $a$ to rise and $\alpha$ to fall: when unemployment is lower, workers can find jobs more rapidly than before, and firms cannot fill positions as easily. From (10.64), this implies that the wage rises more than proportionately with $y$.[23]

The employment effects of the shift in labor demand occur as a result of the creation of new vacancies. But the fact that the wage responds substantially to the shift in demand makes the incentives to create new vacancies small. Shimer (2005) shows that as a result, for reasonable parameter values search and matching models like the one considered here imply that shifts in labor demand have only small employment effects.

To address this difficulty, current research is examining wage rigidity in these models. There are two main issues. The first is the effects of wage rigidity. When wages respond less to an increase in labor demand, the profits from a filled job are larger, and so the rewards to creating a vacancy are greater. As a result, more vacancies are created, and the increase in demand has a larger impact on employment. Thus, it appears that the combination of search and matching considerations and wage rigidity may be important to the cyclical behavior of the labor market (Hall, 2005; Shimer, 2004).

The second, and more important, issue is whether there might be forces leading to wage rigidity in these settings. In the model we have been considering, there is a range of wages that yield surplus to both firms and workers. Thus, as Hall observes, there can be wage rigidity over some range without agents forgoing any profitable trades. This observation, however, does not imply that there is more likely to be wage rigidity than any other pattern of wage behavior that is consistent with the absence of unexploited profit opportunities. Moreover, the idea that wages are essentially indeterminate over some range seems implausible.

A promising variant on these ideas is related to the discussion of the curvature of firms' profit functions in Section 6.7. In a Walrasian labor market, a firm that fails to raise its wage in response to an increase in labor demand loses all its workers. In a search and matching environment, in contrast, failing to raise the wage has both a cost and a benefit. The firm will have more difficulty attracting and retaining workers than if it raised its wage, but the workers it retains will be cheaper. Thus the firm's profits are less sensitive to departures from the profit-maximizing wage. As a result, small barriers to wage adjustment might generate considerable wage rigidity.

---

[23] Since $w = y - c$ in the Walrasian market, the same result holds there. Thus it is not clear which case exhibits greater wage adjustment. Nonetheless, simply adding heterogeneity and matching does not appear to generate strong wage rigidity.

## Welfare

Because this economy is not Walrasian, firms' decisions concerning whether to enter have externalities both for workers and for other firms. Entry makes it easier for unemployed workers to find jobs, and increases their bargaining power when they do. But it also makes it harder for other firms to find workers, and decreases their bargaining power when they do. As a result, there is no presumption that equilibrium unemployment in this economy is efficient.

To illustrate the implications of search and matching models for welfare, consider the following static example (due to Rogerson, Shimer, and Wright, 2005). There are $U$ unemployed workers. If $V$ vacancies are created, the number of workers hired is $E = M(U,V) = kU^{1-\gamma}V^{\gamma}$. Each vacancy has a cost of $c$, and each employed worker produces $y$. Unemployed workers receive no income, and the wage is $w = \phi y$. Social welfare equals the sum of firms' profits and workers' utility, which equals $E(y - w) + Ew - Vc$, or $Ey - Vc$. (Note that in this static model, $V$ is the number of vacancies initially created, not the number left unfilled.)

Consider first the decentralized equilibrium. The value of a vacancy is the probability the position is filled, $M(U,V)/V$, times the firm's surplus from hiring a worker, $y - w$, minus the cost of creating the vacancy, $c$. Thus equilibrium occurs when

$$\frac{M(U,V)}{V}(y - w) - c = 0, \tag{10.71}$$

or

$$k\left(\frac{U}{V}\right)^{1-\gamma}(1 - \phi)y - c = 0. \tag{10.72}$$

The number of vacancies created is therefore given by

$$V^{EQ} = \left[\frac{k(1 - \phi)y}{c}\right]^{1/(1-\gamma)} U. \tag{10.73}$$

Now consider the optimal allocation. A social planner would choose $V$ to maximize $Ey - Vc$, or $kU^{1-\gamma}V^{\gamma}y - Vc$. The first-order condition is

$$\gamma kU^{1-\gamma}V^{\gamma-1}y - c = 0, \tag{10.74}$$

which implies

$$V^* = \left(\frac{k\gamma y}{c}\right)^{1/(1-\gamma)} U. \tag{10.75}$$

Comparison of (10.73) and (10.75) shows that the condition for the decentralized equilibrium to be efficient is that $\gamma = 1 - \phi$—that is, that the elasticity of matches with respect to vacancies equals the share of the match surplus that goes to the firm. If $\gamma < 1 - \phi$ (that is, if the elasticity of matches with respect to vacancies is less than the share of the surplus that goes to the firm), too many vacancies are created. If $\gamma > 1 - \phi$, too few are created.

This result—that the condition for the decentralized equilibrium to be efficient is that the elasticity of matches with respect to vacancies equals the share of the surplus that goes to the firm—holds in many other models, including the dynamic model we have been considering (Hosios, 1990).[24] To see the intuition behind it, note that creating a vacancy has a positive externality on the unemployed workers but a negative externality on other firms looking for workers. When $\gamma$ is larger, the positive externality is larger and the negative one is smaller. Thus for the decentralized equilibrium to be efficient when $\gamma$ is larger, the incentives to create vacancies must be larger; that is, $1 - \phi$ must be larger.

The result that the decentralized equilibrium need not be efficient is characteristic of economies where allocations are determined through one-on-one meetings rather than through centralized markets. In our model, there is only one endogenous decision—firms must decide whether to enter—and hence only one dimension along which the equilibrium can be inefficient. But in practice, participants in such markets have many choices. Workers can decide whether to enter the labor force, how intensively to look for jobs when they are unemployed, where to focus their search, whether to invest in job-specific or general skills when they are employed, whether to look for a different job while they are employed, and so on. Firms face a similar array of decisions. There is no guarantee that the decentralized economy produces an efficient outcome along any of these dimensions. Instead, agents' decisions are likely to have externalities through direct effects on other parties' surplus or through effects on the effectiveness of the matching process, or both.

This analysis implies that there is no reason to suppose that the natural rate of unemployment is optimal. This observation provides no guidance, however, concerning whether observed unemployment is inefficiently high, inefficiently low, or approximately efficient. Determining which of these cases is correct—and whether there are changes in policy that would lead to efficiency-enhancing changes in equilibrium unemployment—is an important open question.

# 10.8 Empirical Applications

## Contracting Effects on Employment

In our analysis of contracts in Section 10.5, we discussed two views of how employment can be determined when the wage is set by bargaining. In the first, a firm and its workers bargain only over the wage, and the firm chooses

---

[24] See Problem 10.17 for a demonstration in one special case of our dynamic model.

employment to equate the marginal product of labor with the agreed-upon wage. As we saw, this arrangement is inefficient. Thus the second view is that the bargaining determines how both employment and the wage depend on the conditions facing the firm. Since actual contracts do not spell out such arrangements, this view assumes that workers and the firm have some noncontractual understanding that the firm will not treat the cost of labor as being given by the wage. For example, workers are likely to agree to lower wages in future contracts if the firm chooses employment to equate the marginal product of labor with the opportunity cost of workers' time.

Which of these views is correct has important implications. If firms choose employment freely taking the wage as given, evidence that nominal wages are fixed for extended periods provides direct evidence that nominal disturbances have real effects. If the wage is unimportant to employment determination, on the other hand, nominal wage rigidity is unimportant to the effects of nominal shocks.

Bils (1991) proposes a way to test between the two views (see also Card, 1990). If employment is determined efficiently, then it equates the marginal product of labor and the marginal disutility of work at each date. Thus its behavior should not have any systematic relation to the times that firms and workers bargain.[25] A finding that movements in employment are related to the dates of contracts—for example, that employment rises unusually rapidly or slowly just after contracts are signed, or that it is more variable over the life of a contract than from one contract to the next—would therefore be evidence that it is not determined efficiently.

In addition, Bils shows that the alternative view that employment equates the marginal product of labor with the wage makes a specific prediction about how employment movements are likely to be related to the times of contracts. Consider Figure 10.8, which shows the marginal product of labor, the marginal disutility of labor, and a contract wage. In response to a negative shock to labor demand, a firm that views the cost of labor as being given by the contract wage reduces employment a great deal; in terms of the figure, it reduces employment from $L_A$ to $L_B$. The marginal product of labor now exceeds the opportunity cost of workers' time. Thus when the firm and the workers negotiate a new contract, they will make sure that employment is increased; in terms of the diagram, they will act to raise employment from $L_B$ to $L_C$. Thus if the wage determines employment (and if shocks to labor demand are the main source of employment fluctuations), changes in employment during contracts should be partly reversed when new contracts are signed.

To test between the predictions of these two views, Bils examines employment fluctuations in U.S. manufacturing industries. Specifically, he focuses on 12 industries that are highly unionized and where there are long-term

---

[25] This is not precisely correct if there are income effects on the marginal disutility of labor. Bils argues, however, that these effects are unlikely to be important to his test.

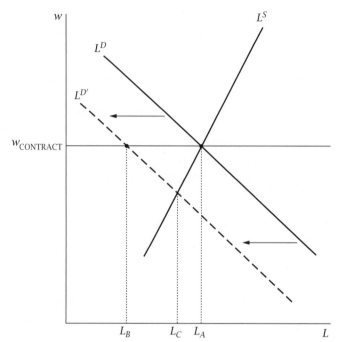

**FIGURE 10.8   Employment movements under wage contracts**

contracts that are signed at virtually the same time for the vast majority of workers in the industry. He estimates a regression of the form

$$\Delta \ln L_{i,t} = \alpha_i - \phi Z_{i,t} - \theta(\ln L_{i,t-1} - \ln L_{i,t-10}) + \Gamma D_{i,t} + \varepsilon_{i,t}. \qquad (10.76)$$

Here $i$ indexes industries, $L$ is employment, and $D_{i,t}$ is a dummy variable equal to 1 in quarters when a new contract goes into effect in industry $i$. The key variable is $Z_{i,t}$. If a new contract goes into effect in industry $i$ in quarter $t$ (that is, if $D_{i,t} = 1$), then $Z_{i,t}$ equals the change in log employment in the industry over the life of the previous contract; otherwise, $Z_{i,t}$ is zero. The parameter $\phi$ therefore measures the extent to which employment changes over the life of a contract are reversed when a new contract is signed. Bils includes $\ln L_{i,t-1} - \ln L_{i,t-10}$ to control for the possibility that employment changes are typically reversed even in the absence of new contracts; he chooses $t-10$ because the average contract in his sample lasts 10 quarters. Finally, $D_{i,t}$ allows for the possibility of unusual employment growth in the first quarter of a new contract.

Bils's estimates are $\phi = 0.198$ (with a standard error of 0.037), $\theta = 0.016$ (0.012), and $\Gamma = -0.0077$ (0.0045). Thus the results suggest highly significant and quantitatively large movements in employment related to the dates of new contracts: when a new contract is signed, on average 20 percent of the employment changes over the life of the previous contract are immediately reversed.

There is one puzzling feature of Bils's results, however. When a new contract is signed, the most natural way to undo an inefficient employment change during the previous contract is by adjusting the wage. In the case of the fall in labor demand shown in Figure 10.8, for example, the wage should be lowered when the new contract is signed. But Bils finds little relation between how the wage is set in a new contract and the change in employment over the life of the previous contract. In addition, when he looks across industries, he finds essentially no relation between the extent to which employment changes are reversed when a new contract is signed and the extent to which the wage is adjusted.

Bils suggests two possible explanations of this finding. One is that adjustments in compensation mainly take the form of changes to fringe benefits and other factors that are not captured by his wage measure. The second is that employment determination is more complex than either of the two views we have been considering.

## Interindustry Wage Differences

The basic idea of efficiency-wage models is that firms may pay wages above market-clearing levels. If there are reasons for firms to do this, those reasons are unlikely to be equally important everywhere in the economy. Motivated by this observation, Dickens and Katz (1987a) and Krueger and Summers (1988) investigate whether some industries pay systematically higher wages than others.

These authors begin by adding dummy variables for the industries that workers are employed in to conventional wage regressions. A typical specification is

$$\ln w_i = \alpha + \sum_{j=1}^{M} \beta_j X_{ij} + \sum_{k=1}^{N} \gamma_k D_{ik} + \varepsilon_i, \tag{10.77}$$

where $w_i$ is worker $i$'s wage, the $X_{ij}$'s are worker characteristics (such as age, education, occupation, and so on), and the $D_{ik}$'s are dummy variables for employment in different industries. In a competitive, frictionless labor market, wages depend only on workers' characteristics and not on what industry they are employed in. Thus if the $X$'s adequately capture workers' characteristics, the coefficients on the industry dummies will be zero.

Dickens and Katz's and Krueger and Summers's basic finding is that the estimated $\gamma_k$'s are large. Katz and Summers (1989), for example, consider U.S. workers in 1984. Since they consider a sample of more than 100,000 workers, it is not surprising that they find that most of the $\gamma$'s are highly significant. But they also find that they are quantitatively large. For example, the standard deviation of the estimated $\gamma$'s (weighted by the sizes of the industries) is 0.15, or 15 percent. Thus wages appear to differ considerably among industries.

Dickens and Katz and Krueger and Summers show that several possible explanations of these wage differences are contradicted by the data. The estimated differences are essentially the same when the sample is restricted to workers not covered by union contracts; thus they do not appear to be the result of union bargaining power. The differences are quite stable over time and across countries; thus they are unlikely to reflect transitory adjustments in the labor market (Krueger and Summers, 1987). When broader measures of compensation are used, the estimated differences typically become larger; thus the results do not appear to arise from differences in the mix of wage and nonwage compensation across industries. Finally, there is no evidence that working conditions are worse in the high-wage industries; thus the differences do not appear to be compensating differentials.

There is also some direct evidence that the differences represent genuine rents. Krueger and Summers (1988) and Akerlof, Rose, and Yellen (1988) find that workers in industries with higher estimated wage premiums quit much less often. Krueger and Summers also find that workers who move from one industry to another on average have their wages change by nearly as much as the difference between the estimated wage premiums for the two industries. And Gibbons and Katz (1992) consider workers who lose their jobs because the plants where they are working close. They find that the wage cuts the workers take when they accept new jobs are much higher when the jobs they lost were in higher-wage industries.

Two aspects of the results are more problematic for efficiency-wage theory, however. First, although many competitive explanations of the results are not supported at all by the data, there is one that cannot be readily dismissed. No wage equation can control for all relevant worker characteristics. Thus one possible explanation of the finding of apparent interindustry wage differences is that they reflect unmeasured differences in ability across workers in different industries rather than rents (Murphy and Topel, 1987b).

To understand this idea, imagine an econometrician studying wage differences among baseball leagues. If the econometrician could only control for the kinds of worker characteristics that studies of interindustry wage differences control for—age, experience, and so on—he or she would find that wages are systematically higher in some leagues than in others: major-league teams pay more than AAA minor-league teams, which pay more than AA minor-league teams, and so on. In addition, quit rates are much lower in the higher-wage leagues, and workers who move from lower-wage to higher-wage leagues experience large wage increases. But there is little doubt that large parts of the wage differences among baseball leagues reflect ability differences rather than rents. Just as an econometrician using Dickens and Katz's and Krueger and Summers's methods to study interleague wage differences in baseball would be led astray, perhaps econometricians studying interindustry wage differences have also been led astray.

Several pieces of evidence support this view. First, if some firms are paying more than the market-clearing wage, they face an excess supply of workers, and so they have some discretion to hire more able workers. Thus it would be surprising if at least some of the estimated wage differences did not reflect ability differences. Second, higher-wage industries have higher capital-labor ratios, which suggests that they need more skilled workers. Third, workers in higher-wage industries have higher measured ability (in terms of education, experience, and so on); thus it seems likely that they have higher unmeasured ability. Finally, the same patterns of interindustry earnings differences occur, although less strongly, among self-employed workers.

The hypothesis that estimated interindustry wage differences reflect unmeasured ability cannot easily account for all the findings about these differences, however. First, quantitative attempts to estimate how much of the differences can plausibly be due to unmeasured ability generally leave a substantial portion of the differences unaccounted for (see, for example, Katz and Summers, 1989). Second, the unmeasured-ability hypothesis cannot readily explain Gibbons and Katz's findings about the wage cuts of displaced workers. Third, the estimated wage premiums are higher in industries where profits are higher; this is not what the unmeasured-ability hypothesis naturally predicts. Finally, industries that pay higher wages generally do so in all occupations, from janitors to managers; it is not clear that unmeasured ability differences should be so strongly related across occupations. Thus, although the view that interindustry wage differences reflect unmeasured ability is troubling for rent-based explanations of those differences, it does not definitively refute them.

The second aspect of this literature's findings that is not easily accounted for by efficiency-wage theories concerns the characteristics of industries that pay high wages. As described above, higher-wage industries tend to have higher capital-labor ratios, more educated and experienced workers, and higher profits. In addition, they have larger establishments and larger fractions of male and of unionized workers (Dickens and Katz, 1987b). No single efficiency-wage theory predicts all these patterns. As a result, authors who believe that the estimated interindustry wage differences reflect rents tend to resort to complicated explanations of them. Dickens and Katz and Krueger and Summers, for example, appeal to a combination of efficiency-wage theories based on imperfect monitoring, efficiency-wage theories based on workers' perceptions of fairness, and worker power in wage determination.

In sum, the literature on interindustry wage differences has identified an interesting set of regularities that differ greatly from what simple theories of the labor market predict. The reasons for those regularities, however, have not been convincingly identified.

## Survey Evidence on Wage Rigidity

One of the main reasons we are interested in the labor market is that we would like to understand why falls in labor demand lead firms to reduce employment substantially and cut wages relatively little. This raises a natural question: Why not simply ask individuals responsible for firms' wage and employment policies why they do this?

Asking wage-setters the reasons for their behavior is not a panacea. Most importantly, they may not fully understand the factors underlying their decisions. They may have found successful policies through such means as trial and error, instruction from their predecessors, and observation of other firms' policies. Friedman and Savage (1948) give the analogy of an expert billiard player. Talking to the player is likely to be of little value in predicting how the player will shoot or in understanding the reasons for his or her choices. One would do better computing the optimal shots based on such considerations as the elasticity of the balls, the friction of the table surface, how spin affects the balls' bounces, and so on, even though these factors may not directly enter the player's thinking.

When wage-setters are not completely sure of the reasons for their decisions, small differences in how questions are phrased can be important. For example, economists use the phrases "shirk," "exert less effort," and "be less productive" more or less interchangeably to describe how workers may respond to a wage cut. But these phrases may have quite different connotations to wage-setters.

Despite these difficulties, surveys of wage-setters are potentially useful. If, for example, wage-setters disagree with a theory no matter how it is phrased and find its mechanisms implausible regardless of how they are described, we should be skeptical of the theory's relevance.

Examples of surveys of wage-setters include Blinder and Choi (1990), Campbell and Kamlani (1997), and Bewley (1999). Here we focus on Campbell and Kamlani's. These authors survey compensation managers at roughly 100 of the largest 1000 firms in the United States and at roughly 100 smaller U.S. firms. They ask the managers' views both about various theories of wage rigidity and about the mechanisms underlying the theories. Their central question asks the respondents their views concerning the importance of various possible reasons that "firms normally do not cut wages to the lowest level at which they can find the necessary number of qualified applicants during a recession."

The reason for not cutting wages in a recession that the survey participants view as clearly the most important is, "If your firm were to cut wages, your most productive workers might leave, whereas if you lay off workers, you can lay off the least productive workers." Campbell and Kamlani interpret the respondents' agreement with this statement as support for the importance of adverse selection. Unfortunately, however, this question serves mainly to illustrate the perils of surveys. The difficulty is that the phrasing of the statement presumes that firms know which workers are more productive. Adverse selection can arise, however, only from *unobservable* differences among workers. Thus it seems likely that compensation managers' strong agreement with the statement is due to other reasons.

Other surveys find much less support for the importance of adverse selection. For example, Blinder and Choi ask,

> There are two workers who are being considered for the same job. As far as you can tell, ... both workers are equally well qualified. One of the workers agrees to work for the wage you offer him. The other one says he needs more money to work for you. Based on this difference, do you think one of these workers is likely to be an inherently more productive worker?

All 18 respondents to Blinder and Choi's survey answer this question negatively. But this too is not decisive. For example, the reference to one worker being "inherently more productive" may be sufficiently strong that it biases the results against the adverse-selection hypothesis.

A hypothesis that fares better in surveys is that concern about quits is critical to wage-setting. The fact that the respondents to Campbell and Kamlani's survey agree strongly with the statement that wage cuts may cause highly productive workers to leave supports this view. The respondents also agree strongly with statements that an important reason not to cut wages is that cuts would increase quits and thereby raise recruitment and training costs and cause important losses of firm-specific human capital. Other surveys also find that firms' desire to avoid quits is important to their wage policies.

The impact of concern about quits on wage-setting is very much in the spirit of the Shapiro–Stiglitz model. There is an action under workers' control (shirking in the Shapiro–Stiglitz model, quitting here) that affects the firm. For some reason, the firm's compensation policy does not cause workers to internalize the action's impact on the firm. Thus the firm raises wages to discourage the action. In that sense, the survey evidence supports the Shapiro–Stiglitz model. If we take a narrow view of the model, however, the survey evidence is less favorable: respondents consistently express little sympathy for the idea that imperfect monitoring and effort on the job are important to their decisions about wages.

The other theme of surveys of wage-setters besides the importance of quits is the critical role of fairness considerations. The surveys consistently suggest that workers' morale and perceptions of whether they are being treated appropriately are crucial to their productivity. The surveys also suggest that workers have strong views about what actions by the firm are appropriate, and that as a result their sense of satisfaction is precarious.

The results are thus supportive of the fairness view of efficiency wages advocated by Akerlof and Yellen (1990) that we encountered in Section 10.2. They are also supportive of the key assumption of insider-outsider models that firms cannot set insiders' and outsiders' wages completely independently.

One important concern about this evidence is that if other forces cause a particular policy to be the equilibrium outcome, and therefore what normally occurs, that policy may come to be viewed as fair. That is, views concerning what is appropriate can be a reflection of the equilibrium outcome rather than an independent cause of it.

This effect may be the source of some of the apparent importance of fairness, but it seems unlikely to be the only one: concerns about fairness seem too strong to be just reflections of other forces. In addition, in some cases fairness considerations appear to push wage-setting in directions one would not otherwise expect. For example, there is evidence that individuals' views about what compensation policies are fair put some weight on equalizing compensation rather than equalizing compensation relative to marginal products. And there is evidence that firms in fact set wages so that they rise less than one-for-one with observable differences in workers' marginal products. Because of this, firms obtain greater surplus from their more productive workers. This provides a more plausible explanation than adverse selection for the survey respondents' strong agreement with Campbell and Kamlani's statement about the advantages of layoffs over wage cuts. To give another example of how fairness considerations appear to alter wage-setting in unusual ways, many researchers, beginning with Kahneman, Knetsch, and Thaler (1986), find that workers view reductions in real wages as highly objectionable if they result from cuts in nominal wages, but as not especially objectionable if they result from increases in nominal wages that are less than the inflation rate.

Finally, although Campbell and Kamlani focus on why firms do not cut wages in recessions, their results probably tell us more about why firms might pay more than market-clearing wages than about the cyclical behavior of wages. The reason is that they do not provide evidence concerning wage-setting in booms. For example, if concern about quits causes firms to pay more than they have to in recessions, it may do the same in booms. Indeed, concern about quits may have a bigger effect on wages in booms than in recessions.

# Problems

**10.1. Union wage premiums and efficiency wages.** (Summers, 1988.) Consider the efficiency-wage model analyzed in equations (10.12)–(10.17). Suppose, however, that fraction $f$ of workers belong to unions that are able to obtain a wage that exceeds the nonunion wage by proportion $\mu$. Thus, $w_u = (1+\mu)w_n$, where $w_u$ and $w_n$ denote wages in the union and nonunion sectors; and the average wage, $w_a$, is given by $fw_u + (1 - f)w_n$. Nonunion employers continue to set their wages freely; thus (by the same reasoning used to derive [10.15] in the text), $w_n = (1 - bu)w_a/(1 - \beta)$.

(a) Find the equilibrium unemployment rate in terms of $\beta$, $b$, $f$, and $\mu$.

(b) Suppose $\mu = f = 0.15$.

(i) What is the equilibrium unemployment rate if $\beta = 0.06$ and $b = 1$? By what proportion is the cost of effective labor higher in the union sector than in the nonunion sector?

(ii) Repeat part (i) for the case of $\beta = 0.03$ and $b = 0.5$.

**10.2. Efficiency wages and bargaining.** (Garino and Martin, 2000.) Summers (1988, p. 386) states, "In an efficiency wage environment, firms that are forced to pay their workers premium wages suffer only second-order losses. In almost any plausible bargaining framework, this makes it easier for workers to extract concessions." This problem asks you to investigate this claim.

Consider a firm with profits given by $\pi = [(eL)^\alpha/\alpha] - wL, 0 < \alpha < 1$, and a union with objective function $U = (w - x)L$, where $x$ is an index of its workers' outside opportunities. Assume that the firm and the union bargain over the wage, and that the firm then chooses $L$ taking $w$ as given.

(a) Suppose that $e$ is fixed at 1, so that efficiency-wage considerations are absent.

(i) What value of $L$ does the firm choose, given $w$? What is the resulting level of profits?

(ii) Suppose that the firm and the union choose $w$ to maximize $U^\gamma \pi^{1-\gamma}$, where $0 < \gamma < \alpha$ indexes the union's power in the bargaining. What level of $w$ do they choose?

(b) Suppose that $e$ is given by equation (10.12) in the text: $e = [(w - x)/x]^\beta$ for $w > x$, where $0 < \beta < 1$.

(i) What value of $L$ does the firm choose, given $w$? What is the resulting level of profits?

(ii) Suppose that the firm and the union choose $w$ to maximize $U^\gamma \pi^{1-\gamma}$, $0 < \gamma < \alpha$. What level of $w$ do they choose? (Hint: For the case of $\beta = 0$, your answer should simplify to your answer in part [a][ii].)

(iii) Is the proportional impact of workers' bargaining power on wages greater with efficiency wages than without, as Summers implies? Is it greater when efficiency-wage effects, $\beta$, are greater?

**10.3.** Describe how each of the following affect equilibrium employment and the wage in the Shapiro–Stiglitz model:

(a) An increase in workers' discount rate, $\rho$.

(b) An increase in the job breakup rate, $b$.

(c) A positive multiplicative shock to the production function (that is, suppose the production function is $AF(L)$, and consider an increase in $A$).

(d) An increase in the size of the labor force, $\overline{L}$.

**10.4.** Suppose that in the Shapiro–Stiglitz model, unemployed workers are hired according to how long they have been unemployed rather than at random; specifically, suppose that workers who have been unemployed the longest are hired first.

(a) Consider a steady state where there is no shirking. Derive an expression for how long it takes a worker who becomes unemployed to get a job as a function of $b$, $L$, $N$, and $\overline{L}$.

(b) Let $V_U$ be the value of being a worker who is newly unemployed. Derive an expression for $V_U$ as a function of the time it takes to get a job, workers' discount rate ($\rho$), and the value of being employed ($V_E$).

(c) Using your answers to parts (a) and (b), find the no-shirking condition for this version of the model.

(d) How, if at all, does the assumption that the longer-term unemployed get priority affect the equilibrium unemployment rate?

**10.5.** **The fair wage-effort hypothesis.** (Akerlof and Yellen, 1990.) Suppose there are a large number of firms, $N$, each with profits given by $F(eL) - wL$, $F'(\bullet) > 0$, $F''(\bullet) < 0$. $L$ is the number of workers the firm hires, $w$ is the wage it pays, and $e$ is workers' effort. Effort is given by $e = \min[w/w^*, 1]$, where $w^*$ is the "fair wage"; that is, if workers are paid less than the fair wage, they reduce their effort in proportion to the shortfall. Assume that there are $\overline{L}$ workers who are willing to work at any positive wage.

(a) If a firm can hire workers at any wage, what value (or range of values) of $w$ minimizes the cost per unit of effective labor, $w/e$? For the remainder of the problem, assume that if the firm is indifferent over a range of possible wages, it pays the highest value in this range.

(b) Suppose $w^*$ is given by $w^* = \overline{w} + a - bu$, where $u$ is the unemployment rate and $\overline{w}$ is the average wage paid by the firms in the economy. Assume $b > 0$ and $a/b < 1$.

(i) Given your answer to part (a) (and the assumption about what firms pay in cases of indifference), what wage does the representative firm pay if it can choose $w$ freely (taking $\overline{w}$ and $u$ as given)?

(ii) Under what conditions does the equilibrium involve positive unemployment and no constraints on firms' choice of $w$? (Hint: In this case, equilibrium requires that the representative firm, taking $\overline{w}$ as given, wishes to pay $\overline{w}$.) What is the unemployment rate in this case?

(iii) Under what conditions is there full employment?

(c) Suppose the representative firm's production function is modified to be $F(Ae_1 L_1 + e_2 L_2)$, $A > 1$, where $L_1$ and $L_2$ are the numbers of high-productivity and low-productivity workers the firm hires. Assume that $e_i = \min[w_i/w_i^*, 1]$, where $w_i^*$ is the fair wage for type-$i$ workers. $w_i^*$ is given by $w_i^* = [(\overline{w}_1 + \overline{w}_2)/2] - bu_i$, where $b > 0$, $\overline{w}_i$ is the average wage paid to workers of type $i$, and $u_i$ is their unemployment rate. Finally, assume there are $\overline{L}$ workers of each type.

(*i*) Explain why, given your answer to part (*a*) (and the assumption about what firms pay in cases of indifference), neither type of worker will be paid less than the fair wage for that type.

(*ii*) Explain why $w_1$ will exceed $w_2$ by a factor of $A$.

(*iii*) In equilibrium, is there unemployment among high-productivity workers? Explain. (Hint: If $u_1$ is positive, firms are unconstrained in their choice of $w_1$.)

(*iv*) In equilibrium, is there unemployment among low-productivity workers? Explain.

**10.6. Implicit contracts without variable hours.** Suppose that each worker must either work a fixed number of hours or be unemployed. Let $C_i^E$ denote the consumption of employed workers in state $i$ and $C_i^U$ the consumption of unemployed workers. The firm's profits in state $i$ are therefore $A_i F(L_i) - [C_i^E L_i + C_i^U (\overline{L} - L_i)]$, where $\overline{L}$ is the number of workers. Similarly, workers' expected utility in state $i$ is $(L_i/\overline{L})[U(C_i^E) - K] + [(\overline{L} - L_i)/\overline{L}]U(C_i^U)$, where $K > 0$ is the disutility of working.

(*a*) Set up the Lagrangian for the firm's problem of choosing the $L_i$'s, $C_i^E$'s, and $C_i^U$'s to maximize expected profits subject to the constraint that the representative worker's expected utility is $u_0$.[26]

(*b*) Find the first-order conditions for $L_i$, $C_i^E$, and $C_i^U$. How, if at all, do $C^E$ and $C^U$ depend on the state? What is the relation between $C_i^E$ and $C_i^U$?

(*c*) After $A$ is realized and some workers are chosen to work and others are chosen to be unemployed, which workers are better off?

**10.7. Implicit contracts under asymmetric information.** (Azariadis and Stiglitz, 1983.) Consider the model of Section 10.5. Suppose, however, that only the firm observes $A$. In addition, suppose there are only two possible values of $A$, $A_B$ and $A_G$ ($A_B < A_G$), each occurring with probability $\frac{1}{2}$.

We can think of the contract as specifying $w$ and $L$ as functions of the firm's announcement of the state, and as being subject to the restriction that it is never in the firm's interest to announce a state other than the actual one; formally, the contract must be *incentive-compatible*.

(*a*) Is the efficient contract under symmetric information derived in Section 10.5 incentive-compatible under asymmetric information? Specifically, if $A$ is $A_B$, is the firm better off claiming that $A$ is $A_G$ (so that $C$ and $L$ are given by $C_G$ and $L_G$) rather than that it is $A_B$? And if $A$ is $A_G$, is the firm better off claiming it is $A_B$ rather than $A_G$?

---

[26] For simplicity, neglect the constraint that $L$ cannot exceed $\overline{L}$. Accounting for this constraint, one would find that for $A_i$ above some critical level, $L_i$ would equal $\overline{L}$ rather than be determined by the condition derived in part (*b*).

(b) One can show that the constraint that the firm not prefer to claim that the state is bad when it is good is not binding, but that the constraint that it not prefer to claim that the state is good when it is bad is binding. Set up the Lagrangian for the firm's problem of choosing $C_G$, $C_B$, $L_G$, and $L_B$ subject to the constraints that workers' expected utility is $u_0$ and that the firm is indifferent about which state to announce when $A$ is $A_B$. Find the first-order conditions for $C_G$, $C_B$, $L_G$, and $L_B$.

(c) Show that the marginal product and the marginal disutility of labor are equated in the bad state—that is, that $A_B F'(L_B) = V'(L_B)/U'(C_B)$.

(d) Show that there is "overemployment" in the good state—that is, that $A_G F'(L_G) < V'(L_G)/U'(C_G)$.

(e) Is this model helpful in understanding the high level of average unemployment? Is it helpful in understanding the large size of employment fluctuations?

**10.8. An insider-outsider model.** Consider the following variant of the model in equations (10.39)–(10.42). The firm's profits are $\pi = AF(L_I + L_O) - w_I L_I - w_O L_O$, where $L_I$ and $L_O$ are the numbers of insiders and outsiders the firm hires, and $w_I$ and $w_O$ are their wages. $L_I$ always equals $\overline{L}_I$, and the insiders' utility in state $i$ is therefore simply $u_{Ii} = U(w_{Ii})$, where $U'(\bullet) > 0$ and $U''(\bullet) < 0$. We capture the idea that insiders' and outsiders' wages cannot be set independently by assuming that $w_{Oi}$ is given by $w_{Oi} = Rw_{Ii}$, where $0 < R \le 1$.

(a) Think of the firm's choice variables as $w_I$ and $L_O$ in each state, with $w_{Oi}$ given by $w_{Oi} = Rw_{Ii}$. Set up the Lagrangian analogous to (10.43) for the firm's problem of maximizing its expected profits subject to the constraint that the insiders' expected utility be $u_0$.

(b) What is the first-order condition for $L_{Oi}$? Does the firm choose employment so that the marginal product of labor and the real wage are equal in all states? (Assume there is always an interior solution for $L_{Oi}$.)

(c) What is the first-order condition for $w_{Ii}$? When $L_{Oi}$ is higher, is $w_{Ii}$ higher, lower, or unchanged? (Continue to assume that there is always an interior solution for $L_{Oi}$.)

**10.9. The Harris–Todaro model.** (Harris and Todaro, 1970.) Suppose there are two sectors. Jobs in the primary sector pay $w_p$; jobs in the secondary sector pay $w_s$. Each worker decides which sector to be in. All workers who choose the secondary sector obtain a job. But there are a fixed number, $N_p$, of primary-sector jobs. These jobs are allocated at random among workers who choose the primary sector. Primary-sector workers who do not get a job are unemployed, and receive an unemployment benefit of $b$. Workers are risk-neutral, and there is no disutility of working. Thus the expected utility of a primary-sector worker is $qw_p + (1 - q)b$, where $q$ is the probability of a primary-sector worker getting a job. Assume that $b < w_s < w_p$, and that $N_p/\overline{N} < (w_s - b)/(w_p - b)$.

(a) What is equilibrium unemployment as a function of $w_p$, $w_s$, $N_p$, $b$, and the size of the labor force, $\overline{N}$?

(*b*) How does an increase in $N_p$ affect unemployment? Explain intuitively why, even though unemployment takes the form of workers waiting for primary-sector jobs, increasing the number of these jobs can increase unemployment.

(*c*) What are the effects of an increase in the level of unemployment benefits?

**10.10. Partial-equilibrium search.** Consider a worker searching for a job. Wages, $w$, have a probability density function across jobs, $f(w)$, that is known to the worker; let $F(w)$ be the associated cumulative distribution function. Each time the worker samples a job from this distribution, he or she incurs a cost of $C$, where $0 < C < E[w]$. When the worker samples a job, he or she can either accept it (in which case the process ends) or sample another job. The worker maximizes the expected value of $w - nC$, where $w$ is the wage paid in the job the worker eventually accepts and $n$ is the number of jobs the worker ends up sampling.

Let $V$ denote the expected value of $w - n'C$ of a worker who has just rejected a job, where $n'$ is the number of jobs the worker will sample from that point on.

(*a*) Explain why the worker accepts a job offering $\hat{w}$ if $\hat{w} > V$, and rejects it if $\hat{w} < V$. (A search problem where the worker accepts a job if and only if it pays above some cutoff level is said to exhibit the *reservation-wage property*.)

(*b*) Explain why $V$ satisfies $V = F(V)V + \int_{w=V}^{\infty} wf(w)\,dw - C$.

(*c*) Show that an increase in $C$ reduces $V$.

(*d*) In this model, does a searcher ever want to accept a job that he or she has previously rejected?

**10.11.** In the setup described in Problem 10.10, suppose that $w$ is distributed uniformly on $[\mu - a, \mu + a]$ and that $C < \mu$.

(*a*) Find $V$ in terms of $\mu$, $a$, and $C$.

(*b*) How does an increase in $a$ affect $V$? Explain intuitively.

**10.12.** Describe how each of the following affects steady-state employment in the Mortensen–Pissarides model of Section 10.6:

(*a*) An increase in the job breakup rate, $\lambda$.

(*b*) An increase in the interest rate, $r$.

(*c*) An increase in the effectiveness of matching, $k$.

(*d*) An increase in income when unemployed, $b$.

(*e*) An increase in workers' bargaining power, $\phi$.

**10.13.** Consider the steady state of the Mortensen-Pissarides model of Section 10.6.

(*a*) Suppose that $\phi = 0$. What is the wage? What does the equilibrium condition (10.70) simplify to?

(b) Suppose that $\phi = 1$. What is the wage? What does the equilibrium condition (10.70) simplify to? Is there any value of $E$ for which it is satisfied? What is the steady state of the model in this case?

**10.14.** Consider the model of Section 10.6. Suppose the economy is initially in equilibrium, and that $y$ then falls permanently. Suppose, however, that entry and exit are ruled out; thus the total number of jobs, $F + V$, remains constant. How do unemployment and vacancies behave over time in response to the fall in $y$?

**10.15.** Consider the model of Section 10.6.

(a) Use equations (10.65) and (10.69), together with the fact that $V_V = 0$ in equilibrium, to find an expression for $E$ as a function of the wage and exogenous parameters of the model.

(b) Show that the impact of a rise in $y$ on $E$ is greater if $w$ remains fixed than if it adjusts so that $V_E - V_U$ remains equal to $V_F - V_V$.

**10.16.** Consider the static search and matching model analyzed in equations (10.71)–(10.75). Suppose, however, that the matching function, $M(\bullet)$, is not assumed to be Cobb–Douglas or to have constant returns. Is the condition for the decentralized equilibrium to be efficient still that the elasticity of matches with respect to vacancies, $VM_V(U,V)/M(U,V)$, equals the share of surplus going to the firm, $1 - \phi$? (Assume that $M(\bullet)$ is smooth and well-behaved, and that $V^{EQ}$ and $V^*$ are strictly positive.)

**10.17. The efficiency of the decentralized equilibrium in a search economy.** Consider the steady state of the model of Section 10.6. Let the discount rate, $r$, approach zero, and assume that the firms are owned by the households; thus welfare can be measured as the sum of utility and profits per unit time, which equals $yE - (F + V)c + bU$. Letting $N$ denote the total number of jobs, we can therefore write welfare as $W(N) = (y - b)E(N) + b - Nc$, where $E(N)$ gives equilibrium employment as a function of $N$.

(a) Use the matching function, (10.53), and the steady-state condition, $M(U,V) = \lambda E$, to derive an expression for the impact of a change in the number of jobs on employment, $E'(N)$, in terms of $E(N)$ and the parameters of the model.

(b) Substitute your result in part (a) into the expression for $W(N)$ to find $W'(N)$ in terms of $E(N)$ and the parameters of the model.

(c) Use (10.66) and the facts that $a = \lambda E/(1 - E)$ and $\alpha = \lambda E/V$ to find an expression for $c$ in terms of $N_{EQ}$, $E(N_{EQ})$, and $y$, where $N_{EQ}$ is the number of jobs in the decentralized equilibrium.

(d) Use your results in parts (b) and (c) to show that $W'(N_{EQ}) > 0$ if $\gamma > 1 - \phi$ and $W'(N_{EQ}) < 0$ if $\gamma < 1 - \phi$.

# Chapter 11

# INFLATION AND MONETARY POLICY

Our final two chapters are devoted to macroeconomic policy. This chapter considers monetary policy, and Chapter 12 considers fiscal policy. We will focus on two main aspects of policy. The first is its short-run conduct: we would like to know how policymakers should act in the face of the various disturbances that impinge on the economy. The second is its long-run performance. Monetary policy often causes high rates of inflation over extended periods, and fiscal policy often causes persistent high budget deficits. In many cases, these inflation rates and budget deficits appear to be higher than is socially optimal. That is, it appears that in at least some circumstances, there is *inflation bias* in monetary policy and *deficit bias* in fiscal policy.

Sections 11.1 and 11.2 begin our analysis of monetary policy by explaining why inflation is almost always the result of rapid growth of the money supply; they also investigate the effects of money growth on inflation, real balances, and interest rates. We then turn to stabilization policy. Section 11.3 considers the foundations of these policies by discussing what we know about the costs of inflation and output variability and about whether there are any significant potential benefits to stabilization. Sections 11.4 and 11.5 take as given that we understand these issues and analyze optimal stabilization policy in two baseline models—a backward-looking one in Section 11.4, and a forward-looking one in Section 11.5. Section 11.6 discusses some additional issues concerning the conduct of stabilization policy.

The final sections of the chapter discuss inflationary bias. Explanations of how such bias can arise fall into two main groups. The first emphasizes the output-inflation tradeoff. The fact that monetary policy has real effects can cause policymakers to want to increase the money supply in an effort to increase output. Theories of how this desire can lead to inflation that is on average too high are discussed in Section 11.7, and Section 11.8 examines some of the relevant evidence.

The second group of explanations of inflationary bias focuses on *seignorage*—the revenue the government gets from printing money. These

theories, which are more relevant to less developed countries than to industrialized ones, and which are at the heart of hyperinflations, are the subject
of Section 11.9.

# 11.1   Inflation, Money Growth, and Interest Rates

## Inflation and Money Growth

Inflation is an increase in the average price of goods and services in terms
of money. Thus to understand inflation, we need to examine the market for
money.

The model of Section 6.1 implies that the demand for real money balances
is decreasing in the nominal interest rate and increasing in real income. Thus
we can write the demand for real balances as $L(i,Y)$, $L_i < 0$, $L_Y > 0$, where
$i$ is the nominal interest rate and $Y$ is real income. With this specification,
the condition for equilibrium in the money market is

$$\frac{M}{P} = L(i,Y),  \tag{11.1}$$

where $M$ is the money stock and $P$ is the price level. This condition implies
that the price level is given by

$$P = \frac{M}{L(i,Y)}.  \tag{11.2}$$

Equation (11.2) suggests that there are many potential sources of inflation. The price level can rise as the result of increases in the money supply,
increases in interest rates, decreases in output, and decreases in money demand for a given $i$ and $Y$. Nonetheless, when it comes to understanding
inflation over the longer term, economists typically emphasize just one factor: growth of the money supply. The reason for this emphasis is that no
other factor is likely to lead to persistent increases in the price level. Long-
term declines in output are unlikely. The expected inflation component of
nominal interest rates reflects inflation itself, and the observed variation
in the real-interest-rate component is limited. Finally, there is no reason to
expect repeated large falls in money demand for a given $i$ and $Y$. The money
supply, in contrast, can grow at almost any rate, and we observe huge variations in money growth—from large and negative during some deflations to
immense and positive during hyperinflations.

It is possible to see these points quantitatively. Conventional estimates
of money demand suggest that the income elasticity of money demand is
about 1 and the interest elasticity is about $-0.2$ (see Goldfeld and Sichel,
1990, for example). Thus for the price level to double without a change in
the money supply, income must fall roughly in half or the interest rate must

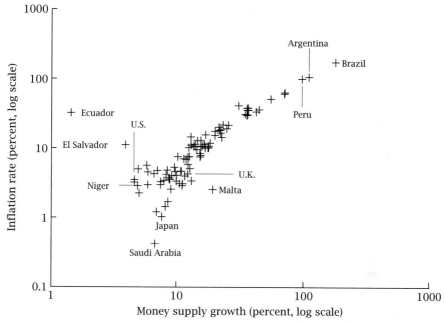

**FIGURE 11.1   Money growth and inflation**

rise by a factor of about 32. Alternatively, the demand for real balances at a given interest rate and income must fall in half. All these possibilities are essentially unheard of. In contrast, a doubling of the money supply, either over several years in a moderate inflation or over a few days at the height of a hyperinflation, is not uncommon.

Thus money growth plays a special role in determining inflation not because money affects prices more directly than other factors do, but because empirically money growth varies more than other determinants of inflation. Figure 11.1 provides powerful confirmation of the importance of money growth to inflation. The figure plots average inflation against average money growth for the period 1980–2006 for a sample of 97 countries. There is a clear and strong relationship between the two variables.

## Money Growth and Interest Rates

Since money growth is the main determinant of inflation, it is natural to examine its effects in greater detail. We begin with the case where prices are completely flexible; this is presumably a good description of the long run. As we know from our analysis of fluctuations, this assumption implies that the money supply does not affect real output or the real interest rate. For simplicity, we assume that these are constant at $\overline{Y}$ and $\overline{r}$, respectively.

By definition, the real interest rate is the difference between the nominal interest rate and expected inflation. That is, $r \equiv i - \pi^e$, or

$$i \equiv r + \pi^e. \tag{11.3}$$

Equation (11.3) is known as the *Fisher identity.*

Using (11.3) and our assumption that $r$ and $Y$ are constant, we can rewrite (11.2) as

$$P = \frac{M}{L(\bar{r} + \pi^e, \bar{Y})}. \tag{11.4}$$

Assume that initially $M$ and $P$ are growing together at some steady rate (so that $M/P$ is constant) and that $\pi^e$ equals actual inflation. Now suppose that at some time, time $t_0$, there is a permanent increase in money growth. The resulting path of the money stock is shown in the top panel of Figure 11.2. After the change, since $M$ is growing at a new steady rate and $r$ and $Y$ are constant by assumption, $M/P$ is constant. That is, (11.4) is satisfied with $P$ growing at the same rate as $M$ and with $\pi^e$ equal to the new rate of money growth.

But what happens at the time of the change? Since the price level rises faster after the change than before, expected inflation jumps up when the change occurs. Thus the nominal interest rate jumps up, and so the quantity of real balances demanded falls discontinuously. Since $M$ does not change discontinuously, it follows that $P$ must jump up at the time of the change. This information is summarized in the remaining panels of Figure 11.2.[1]

This analysis has two messages. First, the change in inflation resulting from the change in money growth is reflected one-for-one in the nominal interest rate. The hypothesis that inflation affects the nominal rate one-for-one is known as the *Fisher effect;* it follows from the Fisher identity and the assumption that inflation does not affect the real rate.

Second, a higher growth rate of the *nominal* money stock reduces the *real* money stock. The rise in money growth increases expected inflation, thereby increasing the nominal interest rate. This increase in the opportunity cost of holding money reduces the quantity of real balances that individuals want to hold. Thus equilibrium requires that $P$ rises more than $M$. That is, there must be a period when inflation exceeds the rate of money growth. In our model, this occurs at the moment that money growth increases. In models where prices are not completely flexible or individuals cannot adjust their real money holdings costlessly, it occurs over a longer period.

A corollary is that a reduction in inflation can be accompanied by a temporary period of unusually high money growth. Suppose that policymakers

---

[1] In addition to the path of $P$ described here, there may also be *bubble paths* that satisfy (11.4). Along these paths, $P$ rises at an increasing rate, thereby causing $\pi^e$ to be rising and the quantity of real balances demanded to be falling. See, for example, Problem 2.21 and Blanchard and Fischer (1989, Section 5.3).

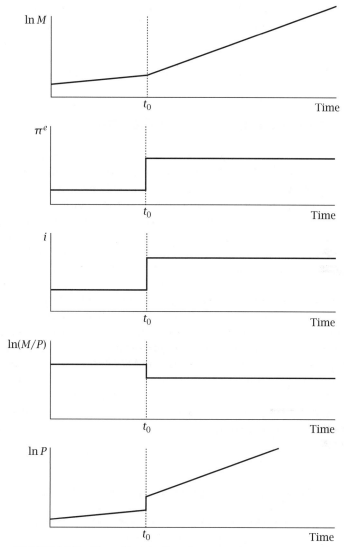

**FIGURE 11.2   The effects of an increase in money growth**

want to reduce inflation and that they do not want the price level to change discontinuously. What path of $M$ is needed to do this? The decline in inflation will reduce expected inflation, and thus lower the nominal interest rate and raise the quantity of real balances demanded. Writing the money market equilibrium condition as $M = PL(i,Y)$, it follows that—since $L(i,Y)$ increases discontinuously and $P$ does not jump—$M$ must jump up. Of course, to keep inflation low, the money stock must then grow slowly from this higher level.

Thus, the monetary policy that is consistent with a permanent drop in inflation is a sudden upward jump in the money supply, followed by low growth. And, in fact, the clearest examples of declines in inflation—the ends of hyperinflations—are accompanied by spurts of very high money growth that continue for a time after prices have stabilized (Sargent, 1982).[2]

## The Case of Incomplete Price Flexibility

In the preceding analysis, an increase in money growth increases nominal interest rates. In practice, however, the immediate effect of a monetary expansion is to lower short-term nominal rates. This negative effect of monetary expansions on nominal rates is known as the *liquidity effect.*

The conventional explanation of the liquidity effect is that monetary expansions reduce real rates. If prices are not completely flexible, an increase in the money stock raises output, which requires a decline in the real interest rate. In terms of the model of Section 6.1, a monetary expansion moves the economy down along the *IS* curve. If the decline in the real rate is large enough, it more than offsets the increase in expected inflation.[3]

If prices are fully flexible in the long run, then the real rate eventually returns to normal following a shift to higher money growth. Thus if the real-rate effect dominates the expected-inflation effect in the short run, the shift depresses the nominal rate in the short run but increases it in the long run. As Friedman (1968) pointed out, this appears to provide an accurate description of the effects of monetary policy in practice. The Federal Reserve's expansionary policies in the late 1960s, for example, lowered nominal rates for several years but, by generating inflation, raised them over the longer term.

# 11.2   Monetary Policy and the Term Structure of Interest Rates

In many situations, we are interested in the behavior not just of short-term interest rates, but also of long-term rates. To understand how monetary policy affects long-term rates, we must consider the relationship between short-term and long-term rates. The relationship among interest rates over different horizons is known as the *term structure of interest rates,* and the

---

[2] This analysis raises the question of why expected inflation falls when the money supply is exploding. We return to this issue in Section 11.9.

[3] See Problem 11.2. In addition, if inflation is completely unresponsive to monetary policy for any interval of time, then expectations of inflation over that interval do not rise. Thus in this case short-term nominal rates necessarily fall.

standard theory of that relationship is known as the *expectations theory of the term structure*. This section describes this theory and considers its implications for the effects of monetary policy.

## The Expectations Theory of the Term Structure

Consider the problem of an investor deciding how to invest a dollar over the next $n$ periods, and assume for simplicity that there is no uncertainty about future interest rates. Suppose first the investor puts the dollar in an $n$-period *zero-coupon* bond—that is, a bond whose entire payoff comes after $n$ periods. If the bond has a continuously compounded return of $i_t^n$ per period, the investor has $\exp(ni_t^n)$ dollars after $n$ periods. Now consider what happens if he or she puts the dollar into a sequence of 1-period bonds paying continuously compounded rates of return of $i_t^1, i_{t+1}^1, \ldots, i_{t+n-1}^1$ over the $n$ periods. In this case, he or she ends up with $\exp(i_t^1 + i_{t+1}^1 + \cdots + i_{t+n-1}^1)$ dollars.

Equilibrium requires that investors are willing to hold both 1-period and $n$-period bonds. Thus the returns on the investor's two strategies must be the same. This requires

$$i_t^n = \frac{i_t^1 + i_{t+1}^1 + \cdots + i_{t+n-1}^1}{n}. \tag{11.5}$$

That is, the interest rate on the long-term bond must equal the average of the interest rates on short-term bonds over its lifetime.

In this example, since there is no uncertainty, rationality alone implies that the term structure is determined by the path that short-term interest rates will take. With uncertainty, under plausible assumptions expectations concerning future short-term rates continue to play an important role in the determination of the term structure. A typical formulation is

$$i_t^n = \frac{i_t^1 + E_t i_{t+1}^1 + \cdots + E_t i_{t+n-1}^1}{n} + \theta_{nt}, \tag{11.6}$$

where $E_t$ denotes expectations as of period $t$. With uncertainty, the strategies of buying a single $n$-period bond and a sequence of 1-period bonds generally involve different risks. Thus rationality does not imply that the expected returns on the two strategies must be equal. This is reflected by the inclusion of $\theta$, the *term premium* to holding the long-term bond, in (11.6).

The expectations theory of the term structure is the hypothesis that changes in the term structure are determined by changes in expectations of future interest rates (rather than by changes in the term premium). Typically, the expectations are assumed to be rational.

As described at the end of Section 11.1, even if prices are not completely flexible, a permanent increase in money growth eventually increases the short-term nominal interest rate permanently. Thus even if short-term rates fall for some period, (11.6) implies that interest rates for sufficiently long maturities (that is, for sufficiently large $n$) are likely to rise immediately. Thus our analysis implies that a monetary expansion is likely to reduce short-term rates but increase long-term ones.

## Empirical Application: The Term Structure and Changes in the Federal Reserve's Funds-Rate Target

The Federal Reserve typically has a target level of a specific interest rate, the Federal funds rate, and implements monetary policy through discrete changes in its target. The Federal funds rate is the interest rate that banks charge one another on one-day loans of reserves; thus it is a very short-term rate. Cook and Hahn (1989) investigate the impact of changes in the target level of the funds rate on interest rates on bonds of different maturities.

Cook and Hahn focus on the period 1974–1979, which was a time when the Federal Reserve was targeting the funds rate closely. During this period, the Federal Reserve did not announce its target level of the funds rate. Instead, market participants had to infer the target from the Federal Reserve's open-market operations. Cook and Hahn therefore begin by compiling a record of the changes in the target over this period. They examine both the records of the Federal Reserve Bank of New York (which implemented the changes) and the reports of the changes in *The Wall Street Journal.* They find that despite the absence of announcements, the *Journal*'s reports are almost always correct. Thus it is reasonable to think of the changes in the target reported by the *Journal* as publicly observed.

As Cook and Hahn describe, the actual Federal funds rate moves closely with the Federal Reserve's target. Moreover, it is highly implausible that the Federal Reserve is changing the target in response to factors that would have moved the funds rate in the absence of the policy changes. For example, it is unlikely that, absent the Federal Reserve's actions, the funds rate would move by discrete amounts. In addition, there is often a lag of several days between the Federal Reserve's decision to change the target and the actual change. Thus arguing that the Federal Reserve is responding to forces that would have moved the funds rate in any event requires arguing that the Federal Reserve has advance knowledge of those forces.

The close link between the actual funds rate and the Federal Reserve's target thus provides strong evidence that monetary policy affects short-term interest rates. As Cook and Hahn describe, earlier investigations of this issue mainly regressed changes in interest rates over periods of a month or a quarter on changes in the money supply over those periods; the regressions produced no clear evidence of the Federal Reserve's ability to influence interest rates. The reason appears to be that the regressions are complicated by the same types of issues that complicate the money-output regressions discussed in Section 5.9: the money supply is not determined solely by the Federal Reserve, the Federal Reserve adjusts policy in response to information about the economy, and so on.

Cook and Hahn then examine the impact of changes in the Federal Reserve's target on longer-term interest rates. Specifically, they estimate regressions of the form

$$\Delta R_t^i = b_1^i + b_2^i \Delta FF_t + u_t^i, \tag{11.7}$$

where $\Delta R_t^i$ is the change in the nominal interest rate on a bond of maturity $i$ on day $t$, and $\Delta FF_t$ is the change in the target Federal funds rate on that day.

Cook and Hahn find, contrary to the predictions of the analysis in the first part of this section, that increases in the funds-rate target raise nominal interest rates at all horizons. An increase in the target of 100 basis points (that is, 1 percentage point) is associated with increases in the 3-month interest rate of 55 basis points (with a standard error of 6.8 basis points), in the 1-year rate of 50 basis points (5.2), in the 5-year rate of 21 basis points (3.2), and in the 20-year rate of 10 basis points (1.8).

Kuttner (2001) extends this work to later data. A key difference between the period studied by Cook and Hahn and the more recent period is that there has been a Federal-funds futures market since 1989. Under plausible assumptions, the main determinant of rates in the futures market is market participants' expectations about the path of the funds rate. Kuttner therefore uses data from the futures market to decompose changes in the Federal Reserve's target into the portions that were anticipated by market participants and the portions that were unanticipated.

Since long-term rates incorporate expectations of future short-term rates, movements in the funds rate that are anticipated should not affect long-term rates. Consistent with this, Kuttner finds that for the period since 1989, there is no evidence that anticipated changes in the target have any impact on interest rates on bonds with maturities ranging from 3 months to 30 years. Unanticipated changes, in contrast, have very large and highly significant effects. As in the 1970s, increases in the funds-rate target are associated with increases in nominal rates at all horizons. Indeed, the effects are larger than those that Cook and Hahn find for changes in the overall target rate in the 1970s. A likely explanation is that the moves in the 1970s were partially anticipated.

The idea that contractionary monetary policy should immediately lower long-term nominal interest rates is intuitive: contractionary policy is likely to raise real interest rates only briefly and to lower inflation over the longer term. Yet, as Cook and Hahn's and Kuttner's results show, the evidence does not support this prediction.

One possible explanation of this anomaly is that the Federal Reserve often changes policy on the basis of information that it has concerning future inflation that market participants do not have. As a result, when market participants observe a shift to tighter monetary policy, they do not infer that the Federal Reserve is tougher on inflation than they had previously believed. Rather, they infer that there is unfavorable information about inflation that they were previously not aware of.

C. Romer and D. Romer (2000) test this explanation by examining the inflation forecasts made by commercial forecasts and the Federal Reserve. Because the Federal Reserve's forecasts are made public only after 5 years, the forecasts provide a potential record of information that was known to the Federal Reserve but not to market participants. Romer and Romer ask whether individuals who know the commercial forecast could improve their forecasts if they also had access to the Federal Reserve's. Specifically, they estimate regressions of the form

$$\pi_t = a + b_C \hat{\pi}_t^C + b_F \hat{\pi}_t^F + e_t, \tag{11.8}$$

where $\pi_t$ is actual inflation and $\hat{\pi}_t^C$ and $\hat{\pi}_t^F$ are the commercial and Federal Reserve forecasts of $\pi_t$. Their main interest is in $b_F$, the coefficient on the Federal Reserve forecast.

For most specifications, the estimates of $b_F$ are close to 1 and overwhelmingly statistically significant. In addition, the estimates of $b_C$ are generally near 0 and highly insignificant. These results suggest that the Federal Reserve has useful information about inflation. Indeed, they suggest that the optimal forecasting strategy of someone with access to both forecasts would be to discard the commercial forecast and adopt the Federal Reserve's.

For the Federal Reserve's additional information to explain the increases in long-term rates in response to contractionary policy moves, the moves must reveal some of the Federal Reserve's information. Romer and Romer therefore consider the problem of a market participant trying to infer the Federal Reserve's forecast. To do this, they estimate regressions of the form

$$\hat{\pi}_t^F = \alpha + \beta \Delta FF_t + \gamma \hat{\pi}_t^C + \varepsilon_t, \tag{11.9}$$

where $\Delta FF$ is the change in the Federal-funds-rate target. A typical estimate of $\beta$ is around 0.25: a rise in the funds-rate target of 1 percentage point suggests that the Federal Reserve's inflation forecast is about $\frac{1}{4}$ percentage points higher than one would expect given the commercial forecast. In light of the results about the value of the Federal Reserve forecasts in predicting inflation, this suggests that the rise should increase market participants' expectations of inflation by about this amount; this is more than enough to account for Cook and Hahn's findings. Unfortunately, the estimates of $\beta$ are not very precise: typically the two-standard-error confidence interval ranges from less than 0 to above 0.5. Thus, although Romer and Romer's results are consistent with the information-revelation explanation of policy actions' impact on long-term interest rates, they do not provide decisive evidence for it.[4]

# 11.3 The Microeconomic Foundations of Stabilization Policy

We now turn to stabilization policy—that is, how policymakers should use their ability to influence the behavior of inflation and output. Discussions of stabilization policy often start from an assumption that policymakers' goal should be to keep inflation low and stable and to minimize departures of output from some smooth trend. Presumably, however, their ultimate goal should be to maximize welfare. How inflation and output affect welfare is not obvious. Thus the appropriate place to start the analysis of stabilization policy is by considering the welfare effects of inflation and output fluctuations. We begin with inflation, and then turn to output.

## The Costs of Inflation

Understanding the costs of inflation is a significant challenge. In many models, steady inflation just adds an equal amount to the growth rate of all prices and wages and to nominal interest rates on all assets. As a result, it has few easily identifiable costs.

The cost of inflation that is easiest to identify arises from the fact that, since the nominal return on high-powered money is fixed at zero, higher inflation causes people to exert more effort to reduce their holdings of high-powered money. For example, they make smaller and more frequent conversions of interest-bearing assets into currency. Since high-powered money is essentially costless to produce, these efforts have no social benefit, and so they represent a cost of inflation. They could be eliminated if inflation were chosen so that the nominal interest rate—and hence the opportunity cost

---

[4] The most recent work in this area takes advantage of another institutional development since the period studied by Cook and Hahn. Since 1997, the United States has issued not just conventional nominal bonds, whose payoffs are fixed in dollar terms, but also inflation-indexed bonds; in addition, the United Kingdom has issued inflation-indexed bonds since 1981. By logic like that underlying equation (11.6), the interest rate on an $n$-period inflation-indexed bond reflects expected one-period real interest rates over the $n$ periods and a term premium. If changes in term premia are small, one can therefore study the impact of unexpected changes in the funds-rate target and other developments not just on nominal rates, but on real rates and expected inflation separately. Examples of such analyses include Gürkaynak, Sack, and Swanson (2005), Gürkaynak, Levin, and Swanson (2008), and Beechey and Wright (2009).

of holding money—was zero. Since real interest rates are typically modestly positive, this requires slight deflation.[5]

A second readily identifiable cost of inflation comes from the fact that individual prices are not adjusted continuously. As a result, even steady inflation causes variations in relative prices as different firms adjust their prices at different times. These relative-price variations have no counterpart in social costs and benefits, and so cause misallocations. Likewise, the resources that firms devote to changing their prices to keep up with inflation represent costs of inflation. Under natural assumptions about the distribution of relative-price shocks, spurious movements in relative prices and the resources devoted to price adjustment are minimized with zero inflation.

The last cost of inflation that can be identified easily is that it distorts the tax system (see, for example, Feldstein, 1997). In most countries, income from capital gains and interest, and deductions for interest expenses and depreciation, are computed in nominal terms. As a result, inflation can have large effects on incentives for investment and saving. In the United States, the net effect of inflation through these various channels is to raise the effective tax rate on capital income substantially. In addition, inflation can significantly alter the relative attractiveness of different kinds of investment. For example, since the services from owner-occupied housing are generally not taxed and the income generated by ordinary business capital is, even without inflation the tax system encourages investment in owner-occupied housing relative to business capital. The fact that mortgage interest payments are deductible from income causes inflation to exacerbate this distortion.

Unfortunately, none of these costs can explain the strong aversion to inflation among policymakers and the public. The *shoe-leather* costs associated with more frequent conversions of interest-bearing assets into high-powered money are surely small for almost all inflation rates observed in practice. Even if the price level is doubling each month, money is losing value only at a rate of a few percent per day. Thus even in this case individuals will not incur extreme costs to reduce their money holdings. Similarly, because the costs of price adjustment and indexation are almost certainly small, both the costs of adjusting prices to keep up with inflation and the direct distortions caused by inflation-induced relative price variability are likely to be small. Finally, although the costs of inflation through tax distortions may be large, these costs are quite specific and can be overcome through indexation of the tax system. Yet the dislike of inflation seems much deeper.

Economists have therefore devoted considerable effort to investigating whether inflation might have important costs through less straightforward channels. Those costs could arise from steady, anticipated inflation, or from a link between the level of inflation and its variability.

In the case of steady inflation, there are three leading candidates for large costs of inflation. The first involves the inflation-induced relative-price

---

[5] See, for example, Tolley (1957) and Friedman (1969).

variability described above. Okun (1975) and Carlton (1982) argue informally that although this variability has only small effects on relatively Walrasian markets, it can significantly disrupt markets where buyers and sellers form long-term relationships. For example, it can make it harder for potential customers to decide whether to enter a long-term relationship, or for the parties to a long-term relationship to check the fairness of the price they are trading at by comparing it with other prices. Formal models suggest that inflation can have complicated effects on market structure, long-term relationships, and efficiency (for example, Bénabou, 1992, and Tommasi, 1994). This literature has not reached any consensus about the effects of inflation, but it does suggest some ways that inflation may have substantial costs.

Second, individuals and firms may have trouble accounting for inflation (Modigliani and Cohn, 1979; Hall, 1984). Ten percent annual inflation causes the price level to rise by a factor of 45 in 40 years; even 3 percent inflation causes it to triple over that period. As a result, inflation can cause households and firms, which typically do their financial planning in nominal terms, to make large errors in saving for their retirement, in assessing the real burdens of mortgages, or in making long-term investments.

Third, steady inflation may be costly not because of any real effects, but simply because people dislike it. People relate to their economic environment in terms of dollar values. They may therefore find large changes in dollar prices and wages disturbing even if the changes have no consequences for their real incomes. In Okun's (1975) analogy, a switch to a policy of reducing the length of the mile by a fixed amount each year might have few effects on real decisions, but might nonetheless cause considerable unhappiness. And indeed, Shiller (1997) reports survey evidence suggesting that people intensely dislike inflation for reasons other than the economic effects catalogued above. Since the ultimate goal of policy is presumably the public's well-being, such effects of inflation represent genuine costs.[6]

The other possible sources of large costs of inflation stem from its potential impact on inflation variability. Inflation is more variable and less predictable when it is higher (see, for example, Okun, 1971, Taylor, 1981, and Ball and Cecchetti, 1990). Okun, Ball and Cecchetti, and others argue that the association arises through the effect of inflation on policy. When inflation is low, there is a consensus that it should be kept low, and so inflation is steady and predictable. When inflation is moderate or high, however, there is disagreement about the importance of reducing it; indeed, the costs of

---

[6] Of course, it is also possible that the public's aversion to steady inflation represents neither some deep understanding of its effects that has eluded economists nor an intense dislike of inflation for its own sake, but a misapprehension. For example, Katona (1976) argues that the public perceives how inflation affects prices but not wages. Thus when it rises, individuals attribute only the faster growth of prices to the increase, and so incorrectly conclude that the change has reduced their standard of living. If Katona's argument is correct, it is wrong to infer from the public's dislike of inflation that it in fact reduces their well-being.

slightly greater inflation may appear small. As a result, inflation is variable and difficult to predict.

If this argument is correct, the relationship between the mean and the variance of inflation represents a true effect of the mean on the variance. This implies three potentially important additional costs of inflation. First, since many assets are denominated in nominal terms, unanticipated changes in inflation redistribute wealth. Thus greater inflation variability increases uncertainty and lowers welfare. Second, with debts denominated in nominal terms, increased uncertainty about inflation may make firms and individuals reluctant to undertake investment projects, especially long-term ones.[7] And finally, highly variable inflation (or even high average inflation alone) can also discourage long-term investment because firms and individuals view it as a symptom of a government that is functioning badly, and that may therefore resort to confiscatory taxation or other policies that are highly detrimental to capital-holders.

Empirically, there is a negative association between inflation and investment, and between inflation and growth (Fischer, 1993; Cukierman, Kalaitzidakis, Summers, and Webb, 1993; Bruno and Easterly, 1998). But we know little about whether these relationships are causal, and it is not difficult to think of reasons that the associations might not represent true effects of inflation. As a result, this evidence is of limited value in determining the costs of inflation.

## Potential Benefits of Inflation

Inflation can have benefits as well as costs. Two potential benefits are especially important. First, as Tobin (1972) observes, inflation can "grease the wheels" of the labor market. That is, if it is particularly hard for firms to cut nominal wages, real wages can make needed adjustments to sector-specific shocks more rapidly when inflation is higher. Empirically, we observe a substantial spike in the distribution of nominal wage changes at zero and relatively few nominal wage cuts. Two unsettled questions, however, are whether this results in substantial misallocation and whether the resistance to nominal wage cuts depends strongly on the average inflation rate.[8]

Second, as described in Section 11.6, a higher average rate of inflation makes it less likely that monetary policy will be constrained by the zero lower bound on nominal interest rates. For example, if the financial crisis that began in 2007 had taken place in an environment of higher average

---

[7] If these costs of inflation variability are large, however, there may be large incentives for individuals and firms to write contracts in real rather than nominal terms, or to create markets that allow them to insure against inflation risk. Thus a complete account of large costs of inflation through these channels must explain the absence of these institutions.

[8] For more on these issues, see Akerlof, Dickens, and Perry, 1996; Card and Hyslop, 1997; Bewley, 1999; and Elsby, 2009.

inflation, and thus higher nominal interest rates, central banks would have had more room to cut rates. The resulting stimulus would almost certainly have mitigated the downturn, perhaps substantially (Williams, 2009).

The bottom line is that research has not yet yielded any firm conclusions about the costs and benefits of inflation and the optimal rate of inflation. Thus economists and policymakers must rely on their judgment in weighing the different considerations. Loosely speaking, they fall into two groups. One group views inflation as pernicious, and believes that policy should focus on eliminating inflation and pay virtually no attention to other considerations. Members of this group generally believe that policy should aim for zero inflation or moderate deflation. The other group concludes that extremely low inflation is of little benefit, or perhaps even harmful, and believes that policy should aim to keep average inflation low to moderate but should keep other objectives in mind. The opinions of members of this group about the level of inflation that policy should aim for generally range from a few percent to close to about 5 percent.

## What Should Stabilization Policy Try to Accomplish on the Output Side?

We now turn to policymakers' concerns about real output, unemployment, and employment. It may seem obvious that policymakers should try to mitigate recessions and booms. In fact, however, the subject is considerably more complicated.

One important consideration is that not all output fluctuations are undesirable. Over the medium run, significant parts of output movements surely reflect not aggregate demand shocks and sticky prices, but changes in the growth rate of the economy's productive capacity. There is no reason for monetary and fiscal policy to try to prevent those movements. And even shorter-run fluctuations may be due to changes in the terms of trade, technology, and other forces that would affect output under completely flexible prices. Since Walrasian outcomes are Pareto efficient, it seems hard to make a strong case that policymakers should try to prevent output movements that would otherwise result from these forces.

The power of monetary policy comes from the fact that prices are not completely flexible. It is therefore tempting to say that policy should try to minimize departures of output from its flexible-price level. But this is not quite right either: not all movements in the flexible-price level of output are desirable. If an output movement is inefficient (for example, because of changes in firms' market power that result in changes in markups), monetary policy can improve welfare by mitigating it. In short, the correct statement is that policymakers should try to minimize fluctuations of output not around its trend, nor around its flexible-price level, but around its Walrasian level.

A second important consideration is that it is not obvious that there are significant potential benefits to this type of stabilization. Because monetary policy can have a powerful effect on average inflation, the potential benefits on the inflation side of conducting policy well rather than badly are clearly large. But in many models, stabilization policy has little or no influence on average output. Thus even though distortions presumably cause output to be systematically less than its Walrasian level, there may be little scope for stabilization policy to raise welfare by increasing average output. Its main potential welfare impact on the output side may be through reducing the variance of the gap between Walrasian and actual output. And it is not clear that this benefit is large.

To see this more formally, consider two baseline views of aggregate supply. The first is the Lucas supply curve,

$$y_t = y_t^n + b(\pi_t - \pi_t^e) + u_t, \tag{11.10}$$

where $y^n$ denotes the flexible-price (or *natural*) level of output. The other is the accelerationist Phillips curve,

$$\pi_t = \pi_{t-1} + \lambda(y_t - y_t^n) + v_t. \tag{11.11}$$

In addition, suppose that social welfare is a function of inflation and output, and suppose for the moment that it is linear in output—an assumption we will return to shortly. Thus we have,

$$W_t = -c[y_t^* - y_t] - f(\pi_t), \qquad c > 0. \tag{11.12}$$

Here $W$ gives the impact of output and inflation on welfare relative to the Walrasian outcome, and $y^*$ is the Walrasian level of output. Assume $f(\bullet)$ satisfies $f''(\bullet) > 0$, $\lim_{\pi \to -\infty} f'(\bullet) = -\infty$, $\lim_{\pi \to \infty} f'(\bullet) = \infty$, so that there is a well-defined optimal rate of inflation and that letting inflation grow or fall without bound is prohibitively costly.

Under either of these assumptions about aggregate supply, policy will not affect average output. Expression (11.10) implies that $y_t - y_t^n$ can differ systematically from zero only if $\pi_t$ differs systematically from $\pi_t^e$, which requires systematically irrational expectations. And expression (11.11) implies that $y_t - y_t^n$ can differ systematically from zero only if inflation rises or falls without bound, which we have assumed to be catastrophic. And with social welfare linear in $y$, there is no benefit to reducing the variability of output. Thus in this baseline case, regardless of how much policymakers care about output (that is, regardless of $c$), policymakers should try to keep inflation as close as possible to its optimal level and pay no attention to output.

## Is There a Case for Stabilization Policy?

The preceding argument that stabilization policy can have few benefits through its impact on output appears to have an obvious flaw. Individuals are risk-averse, and aggregate fluctuations cause consumption to vary. Thus social welfare is clearly not linear in aggregate economic activity. In a famous paper, however, Lucas (1987) shows that in a representative-agent setting, the potential welfare gain from stabilizing consumption around its mean is small. That is, he suggests that social welfare is not sufficiently nonlinear in output for there to be a significant gain from stabilization. His argument is straightforward. Suppose utility takes the constant-relative-risk-aversion form,

$$U(C) = \frac{C^{1-\theta}}{1-\theta}, \qquad \theta > 0, \tag{11.13}$$

where $\theta$ is the coefficient of relative risk aversion (see Section 2.1). Since $U''(C) = -\theta C^{-\theta-1}$, a second-order Taylor expansion of $U(\bullet)$ around the mean of consumption implies

$$E[U(C)] \simeq \frac{\bar{C}^{1-\theta}}{1-\theta} - \frac{\theta}{2}\bar{C}^{-\theta-1}\sigma_C^2, \tag{11.14}$$

where $\bar{C}$ and $\sigma_C^2$ are the mean and variance of consumption. Thus eliminating consumption variability would raise expected utility by approximately $(\theta/2)\bar{C}^{-\theta-1}\sigma_C^2$. Similarly, doubling consumption variability would lower welfare by approximately that amount.

To translate this into units that can be interpreted, note that the marginal utility of consumption at $\bar{C}$ is $\bar{C}^{-\theta}$. Thus setting $\sigma_C^2$ to zero would raise expected utility by approximately as much as would raising average consumption by $(\theta/2)\bar{C}^{-\theta-1}\sigma_C^2/\bar{C}^{-\theta} = (\theta/2)\bar{C}^{-1}\sigma_C^2$. As a fraction of average consumption, this equals $(\theta/2)\bar{C}^{-1}\sigma_C^2/\bar{C}$, or $(\theta/2)(\sigma_C/\bar{C})^2$.

Lucas argues that a generous estimate of the standard deviation of consumption due to short-run fluctuations is 1.5 percent of its mean, and that a generous estimate of the coefficient of relative risk aversion is 5. Thus, he concludes, an optimistic figure for the maximum possible welfare gain from more successful stabilization policy is equivalent to $(5/2)(0.015)^2$, or 0.06 percent, of average consumption—a very small amount.

This analysis assumes that there is a representative agent. But actual recessions do not reduce everyone's consumption by a small amount; instead, they reduce the consumption of a small fraction of the population by a large amount. Thus recessions' welfare costs are larger than they would be in a representative-agent setting. Atkeson and Phelan (1994) show, however, that accounting for the dispersion of consumption decreases rather than increases the potential gain from stabilization. Indeed, in the extreme their analysis suggests that there could be no gain at all from stabilizing output. Suppose that individuals have one level of consumption, $C_E$, when they are employed, and another level, $C_U$, when they are unemployed, and suppose that $C_E$ and $C_U$ do not depend on the state of the economy. In this case, social welfare is linear in aggregate consumption: average utility from consumption is $uU(C_U) + (1-u)U(C_E)$, where $u$ is the fraction of individuals who are unemployed. Since $C_U$ and $C_E$ are constant by assumption, changes in aggregate consumption take the form of changes in $u$, which affect average utility linearly. Intuitively, in this case stabilizing unemployment around its mean has no effect on the variance of individuals' consumption; individuals have consumption $C_E$ fraction $1 - E[u]$ of the time, and $C_U$ fraction $E[u]$ of the time.

This analysis suggests that stabilization policy has only modest potential benefits. If this is right, episodes like Great Depression and the financial crisis that began in 2007 are counterbalanced by periods of above-normal output with roughly offsetting welfare benefits. Thus, although we surely would have preferred a smoother path of output, the overall costs of departing from that path are small.

There are four main reasons that this view may be missing something important. The first two concern asymmetries in the welfare effects of recessions and booms. First, individuals might be much more risk-averse than Lucas's calculation assumes. Recall from Section 8.5 that stocks earn much higher average returns than bonds. One candidate explanation is that individuals dislike risk so much that they require a substantial premium to accept the moderate risk of holding stocks (for example, Kandel and Stambaugh, 1991, and Campbell and Cochrane, 1999). If this is right, the welfare costs of the variability associated with short-run fluctuations could be large.

Second, stabilization policy might have substantial benefits not by stabilizing consumption, but by stabilizing hours of work. Hours are much more cyclically variable than consumption; and if labor supply is relatively inelastic, utility may be much more sharply curved in hours than in consumption. Ball and D. Romer (1990) find that as a result, it is possible that the cost of fluctuations through variability of hours is substantial. Intuitively, the utility benefit of the additional leisure during periods of below-normal output may not nearly offset the utility cost of the reduced consumption, whereas the disutility from the additional hours during booms may nearly offset the benefit of the higher consumption.

The third possibility has to do with investment and the path of the economy's flexible-price level of output. A common informal view is that macroeconomic stability promotes investment of all types, from conventional physical-capital investment to research and development. If so, stabilization policy could raise income substantially over the long run.[9]

Finally, and perhaps most importantly, stabilization policy could have significant benefits if the specifications of inflation dynamics in (11.10) and (11.11) are missing something important. For example, although the conventional finding is that a linear specification provides an adequate descrip-

---

[9] Attempts to formalize this argument must confront two difficulties: the net effect of uncertainty on investment is complicated and not necessarily negative, and the risk that individual firms and entrepreneurs face from aggregate economic fluctuations is small compared with the risk they face from other sources.

tion of the data over the relevant range (see, for example, Ball and Mankiw, 1995, and Gordon, 1997), some work provides evidence of important non-linearities (Clark, Laxton, and Rose, 1996; Debelle and Laxton, 1997; Laxton, Rose, and Tambakis, 1999). These papers suggest that inflation may be less responsive to shortfalls of output from its natural rate than to output exceeding the natural rate. If this is right, periods of below-normal output are not matched by comparable periods of above-normal output, and so stabilization policy affects average output.

These arguments suggest that there may be an important role for stabilization policy after all. If social welfare or aggregate supply is substantially nonlinear in output, there may be large benefits to preventing fluctuations in aggregate demand.

## Concluding Comments

This discussion shows that our understanding of the costs of inflation and of output fluctuations is very limited. We know relatively little about such basic issues as what the main costs of inflation are, what level of inflation is best to aim for, and whether there are substantial benefits to stabilizing output. It is not feasible to wait until these issues are resolved before addressing questions concerning how stabilization policy should be conducted: those questions arise continually, and policymakers have no choice but to make decisions about them. The standard approach in modeling stabilization policy is therefore to tentatively assume that we understand the appropriate objective function. Typically it is assumed to be a simple function of a small number of variables, such as inflation and output. With regard to inflation, the most common approach is to assume that the optimal rate of inflation is zero (on the grounds that this is where distortionary relative-price movements and the costs of price adjustment are minimized), and that the costs of departing from this level are quadratic. With regard to output, the most common approach is to assume quadratic costs of departures from the Walrasian level. But it is important to remember that these assumptions are only shortcuts, and that our understanding of how policy should be conducted is likely to change substantially as our understanding of the microeconomic foundations of the goals of policy evolves.

# 11.4   Optimal Monetary Policy in a Simple Backward-Looking Model

We now turn from general discussions of what the goals of stabilization policy should be to models that yield precise statements concerning how policy should be conducted. This section considers a natural baseline model where private behavior is backward-looking, and Section 11.5 considers a baseline model where private behavior is forward-looking. In both models, in keeping with the comments at the end of the previous section, policymakers' objective function is assumed rather than derived. Thus the models are only illustrative. Nonetheless, they show how one can derive prescriptions about policy from formal models and show the types of considerations that govern optimal policy.

## Assumptions

The model is a variant of the model considered by Svensson (1997) and Ball (1999b). The economy is described by two equations, one characterizing aggregate demand and the other characterizing aggregate supply. In the spirit of traditional Keynesian models, the model omits any forward-looking elements of private behavior. This makes it comparatively transparent and easy to solve. The main difference from textbook Keynesian formulations is the inclusion of lags. The aggregate-demand equation states that output depends negatively on the previous period's real interest rate. The aggregate-supply equation states that the change in inflation depends positively on the previous period's output. Because of this lag structure, a change in the real interest rate has no effect on output until the following period and no effect on inflation until the period after that. This captures the conventional wisdom that policy works with a lag and that it affects output more rapidly than it affects inflation. In addition, there are disturbances to both aggregate demand and aggregate supply.

Specifically, let $y_t^n$ and $y_t^*$ denote the economy's flexible-price and Walrasian levels of output, both in logs; the rest of the notation is standard. Then the model is

$$y_t = -\beta r_{t-1} + u_t^{IS}, \qquad \beta > 0, \tag{11.15}$$

$$\pi_t = \pi_{t-1} + \alpha \left( y_{t-1} - y_{t-1}^n \right), \qquad \alpha > 0, \tag{11.16}$$

$$u_t^{IS} = \rho_{IS} u_{t-1}^{IS} + \varepsilon_t^{IS}, \qquad -1 < \rho_{IS} < 1, \tag{11.17}$$

$$y_t^n = \rho_Y y_{t-1}^n + \varepsilon_t^Y, \qquad 0 < \rho_Y < 1, \tag{11.18}$$

$$y_t^* - y_t^n = \Delta, \qquad \Delta \geq 0. \tag{11.19}$$

The first equation is a traditional $IS$ curve, with the constant term normalized to zero for convenience and with a lagged response to the interest rate. Here $r_{t-1}$ is the real interest rate, $i_{t-1} - E_{t-1}[\pi_t]$. The second equation is an accelerationist Phillips curve, with the change in inflation determined by the gap between the actual and flexible-price levels of output. The next two equations describe the behavior of the two driving processes—shocks to the $IS$ curve and to the flexible-price level of output. $\varepsilon^{IS}$ and $\varepsilon^Y$ are assumed to be independent white-noise processes.[10] The final equation states that there may be a constant gap between the Walrasian and flexible-price levels of output.

The central bank chooses $r_t$ after observing $u_t^{IS}$ and $y_t^n$. It dislikes both departures of output from the Walrasian level and departures of inflation from its preferred level. Specifically, it minimizes $E[(y - y^*)^2] + \lambda E[\pi^2]$, where $\lambda$ is a positive parameter showing the relative weight it puts on inflation and where the most preferred level of inflation is normalized to zero for simplicity. Without loss of generality, the analysis considers only rules for the real interest rate that are linear in variables describing the state of the economy.[11]

## Analyzing the Model

To solve the model, the first step is to define the output gap, $\tilde{y}$, as $y - y^n$, and to rewrite (11.15) and (11.16) as

$$\tilde{y}_t = -\beta r_{t-1} + u_t^{IS} - y_t^n, \tag{11.20}$$

$$\pi_t = \pi_{t-1} + \alpha \tilde{y}_{t-1}. \tag{11.21}$$

The second step is to note that the central bank's choice of $r_t$ has no impact on $\tilde{y}_t$, $\pi_t$, or $\pi_{t+1}$. Its first impact is on $\tilde{y}_{t+1}$, and it is only through $\tilde{y}_{t+1}$ that it affects inflation and output in subsequent periods. Thus one can think of policy as a rule not for $r_t$, but for the expectation as of period $t$ of $\tilde{y}$ in period $t + 1$. That is, for the moment we will think of the central bank as choosing $-\beta r_t + \rho_{IS} u_t^{IS} - \rho_Y y_t^n = E_t[\tilde{y}_{t+1}]$ (see [11.20] applied to period $t + 1$).

Now note that the paths of inflation and output beginning in period $t+1$ are determined by $E_t[\tilde{y}_{t+1}]$ (which is determined by the central bank's policy in $t$), $\pi_{t+1}$ (which is known at $t$ and is unaffected by the central bank's actions in period $t$), and future shocks. Because of this, the optimal policy will make $E_t[\tilde{y}_{t+1}]$ a function of $\pi_{t+1}$. Further, the aggregate supply equation, (11.21), implies that the average value of $\tilde{y}$ must be zero for inflation to be bounded. Thus it is reasonable to guess (and one can show formally) that when $\pi_{t+1}$ is zero, the central bank sets $E_t[\tilde{y}_{t+1}]$ to zero. Given the assumption of linearity, this means that the optimal policy takes the form

$$E_t \tilde{y}_{t+1} = -q\pi_{t+1}, \tag{11.22}$$

where the value of $q$ is to be determined.

---

[10] Adding an $\varepsilon_t^\pi$ term to (11.16) as a third type of shock has no effect on the messages of the model. See Problem 11.7.

[11] A more formal approach is not to assume linearity and to assume that the central bank minimizes the expected discounted sum of terms of the form $(y_t - y^*)^2 + \lambda \pi_t^2$, and to let the discount rate approach zero. As Svensson shows, this approach yields the rule derived below.

To find $q$, we need to find $E[(y - y^*)^2] + \lambda E[\pi^2]$ as a function of $q$. To do this, note that equation (11.20) implies

$$\tilde{y}_t = E_{t-1}\tilde{y}_t + \varepsilon_t^{IS} - \varepsilon_t^Y$$
$$= -q\pi_t + \varepsilon_t^{IS} - \varepsilon_t^Y, \tag{11.23}$$

where the second line uses (11.22) lagged one period. Equation (11.21) therefore implies

$$\pi_{t+1} = \pi_t + \alpha\tilde{y}_t$$
$$= (1 - \alpha q)\pi_t + \alpha\varepsilon_t^{IS} - \alpha\varepsilon_t^Y. \tag{11.24}$$

Given the linear structure of the model and the assumption of i.i.d. disturbances, in the long run the distribution of $\pi_t$ will be constant over time and independent of the economy's initial conditions. That is, in the long run $E[\pi_t^2]$ and $E[\pi_{t+1}^2]$ are equal. We can therefore solve (11.24) for $E[\pi^2]$. This yields

$$E[\pi^2] = \frac{\alpha^2}{1 - (1 - \alpha q)^2}\left(\sigma_Y^2 + \sigma_{IS}^2\right)$$
$$= \frac{\alpha^2}{\alpha q(2 - \alpha q)}\left(\sigma_Y^2 + \sigma_{IS}^2\right), \tag{11.25}$$

where $\sigma_Y^2$ and $\sigma_{IS}^2$ are the variances of $\varepsilon^Y$ and $\varepsilon^{IS}$.

To find $E[(y - y^*)^2]$, first note that $y - y^*$ equals $(y - y^n) - (y^* - y^n)$, which (by the definition of $\tilde{y}$ and [11.19]) equals $\tilde{y} - \Delta$. We can therefore use (11.23) to obtain:

$$E[(y - y^*)^2] = \Delta^2 + q^2 E[\pi^2] + \sigma_Y^2 + \sigma_{IS}^2. \tag{11.26}$$

Finding the optimal $q$ is now just a matter of algebra. Expressions (11.25) and (11.26) tell us the value of the central bank's loss function, $E[(y-y^*)^2] + \lambda E[\pi^2]$, as a function of $q$. The first-order condition for $q$ turns out to be a quadratic. One of the solutions is negative. Since a negative $q$ causes the variances of $y$ and $\pi$ to be infinite, we can rule out this solution. The remaining solution is

$$q^* = \frac{-\lambda\alpha + \sqrt{\alpha^2\lambda^2 + 4\lambda}}{2}. \tag{11.27}$$

## Discussion

The central bank's policy is described by $E_t[\tilde{y}_{t+1}] = -q^*\pi_{t+1}$ (see [11.22]). To interpret expression (11.27) for $q^*$, it is helpful to consider its implications for how $q^*$ varies with $\lambda$, the weight the central bank places on inflation stabilization. (11.27) implies that as $\lambda$ approaches zero, $q^*$ approaches zero: the central bank always conducts policy so that $E_t[\tilde{y}_{t+1}]$ is zero. Thus output is white noise around zero. The aggregate supply equation, (11.16), then implies that inflation is a random walk.

Equation (11.27) implies that as $\lambda$ rises, $q^*$ rises: as the central bank places more weight on inflation stabilization, it induces departures of output from its natural rate to bring inflation back to its optimal level after a departure. One can show that as $\lambda$ approaches infinity, $q^*$ approaches $1/\alpha$. This corresponds to a policy of bringing inflation back to zero as rapidly as possible after a shock. With $q^*$ equal to $1/\alpha$, $E_t[\tilde{y}_{t+1}]$ equals $-(1/\alpha)\pi_{t+1}$. The aggregate supply equation, (11.16), then implies that $E_t[\pi_{t+2}]$ equals zero. Note that as $\lambda$ approaches infinity, the variance of output does not approach infinity (see [11.26] with $q = 1/\alpha$): even if the central bank cares only about inflation, it wants to keep output close to its natural rate to prevent large movements in inflation.

As, Svensson and Ball point out, the optimal policy can be interpreted as a type of *inflation targeting*. To see this, note that equation (11.24) applied to $\pi_{t+2}$ implies that $E_t[\pi_{t+2}]$ equals $(1 - \alpha q)\pi_{t+1}$. Since $q$ is between 0 and $1/\alpha$, $1 - \alpha q$ is between 0 and 1. Thus the class of optimal policies consists of rules for the behavior of expected inflation of the form

$$E_t[\pi_{t+2}] = \phi\pi_{t+1}, \tag{11.28}$$

with $\phi$ between 0 and 1. Thus all optimal policies can be described in terms of a rule purely for the expected behavior of inflation. In the extreme case of $\lambda = \infty$ (that is, a central bank that cares only about inflation), $q$ equals $1/\alpha$, and so $\phi$ equals 0. In this case, $E_t[\pi_{t+2}]$ is always 0: the central bank always tries to achieve its inflation target as quickly as possible.[12] A central bank behaving this way is said to be a *strict* inflation targeter.

For all finite, strictly positive values of $\lambda$, $\phi$ is strictly between 0 and 1, and policies take the form of *flexible* inflation targeting. Specifically, the optimal policies take the form of trying to bring inflation back to the most preferred level (which we have normalized to zero) after a disturbance has pushed it away. Where the policies differ is in the speed that they do this with: the more the central bank cares about inflation (that is, the greater is $\lambda$), the faster it undoes changes in inflation (that is, the lower is $\phi$).

To see what the central bank's policy rule implies concerning interest rates, start by defining the *natural rate of interest, $r_t^n$,* to be the interest rate that causes output to equal its flexible-price level. Specifically, since $r_t$ affects $y_{t+1}$, $r_t^n$ is the value of $r_t$ that yields $y_{t+1} = y_{t+1}^n$. From (11.15) or

---

[12] Recall that the central bank's actions in $t$ do not affect $\pi_t$ or $\pi_{t+1}$.

(11.20), this interest rate is given by

$$r_t^n = -\frac{1}{\beta}\left(y_{t+1}^n - u_{t+1}^{IS}\right).$$ (11.29)

With this definition, we can rewrite (11.20) as

$$\tilde{y}_t = -\beta\left(r_{t-1} - r_{t-1}^n\right).$$ (11.30)

It follows that

$$E_t[\tilde{y}_{t+1}] = -\beta\left(r_t - E_t[r_t^n]\right).$$ (11.31)

(The reason that $E_t[r_t^n]$ rather than $r_t^n$ appears in this expression is that $r_t^n$ depends on $u_{t+1}^{IS}$ and $y_{t+1}^n$, which are not known at $t$.) Now recall that the central bank chooses $r_t$ so that $E_t[\tilde{y}_{t+1}]$ equals $-q\pi_{t+1}$, and that $\pi_{t+1}$ equals $\pi_t + \alpha\tilde{y}_t$. Substituting these facts into (11.31) gives us

$$-q[\pi_t + \alpha\tilde{y}_t] = -\beta\left(r_t - E_t[r_t^n]\right),$$ (11.32)

or

$$r_t = E_t[r_t^n] + \frac{q}{\beta}\pi_t + \frac{\alpha q}{\beta}\tilde{y}_t.$$ (11.33)

Thus optimal policy can be described as an *interest-rate rule:* the central bank sets the real interest rate equal to its estimate of the equilibrium or natural real rate plus a linear function of output and inflation.

This analysis implies that not all interest-rate rules are optimal. In particular, equation (11.33) places four restrictions on the rule (other than linearity, which follows naturally from the linearity of the model and the quadratic objective function). First, the real interest rate should be adjusted one-for-one with fluctuations in the equilibrium real rate. Since fluctuations in actual output relative to its equilibrium level are undesirable in their own right and lead to changes in inflation, the central bank wants to avoid them. Second, since $q^*$ ranges from zero to $1/\alpha$ as $\lambda$ ranges from zero to infinity, the coefficient on inflation must be between zero and $1/\alpha\beta$ and the coefficient on the output gap must be between zero and $1/\beta$. The reason the coefficients cannot be negative is that it cannot make sense to exacerbate fluctuations in inflation. The reason they cannot be too large is that there is a cost but no benefit to responding to fluctuations so aggressively that $E_t[\pi_{t+2}]$ has the opposite sign from $\pi_{t+1}$.

The final restriction that (11.33) places on the interest-rate rule is a relation between the two coefficients. Specifically, (11.33) implies that the coefficient on $y$ equals $\alpha$ times the coefficient on $\pi$. Thus when the coefficient on $\pi$ is higher, the coefficient on $y$ must be higher. The intuition is that if, for example, the central bank cares a great deal about inflation, it should respond aggressively to movements in both output and inflation to keep inflation under control; responding to one but not the other is inefficient.

# 11.5  Optimal Monetary Policy in a Simple Forward-Looking Model

The model of Section 11.4 is very traditional: the demand for goods depends on the lagged real interest rate, with no role for expectations about future income, and inflation depends on lagged inflation and the lagged output gap, with no role for expected inflation. Expectations matter only through the impact of expected inflation on the nominal interest rate the central bank must choose to achieve a given real rate. Although the model yields valuable insights, it is important to ask what happens if we introduce forward-looking elements into the demand for goods and the dynamics of inflation. In this section, we therefore go to the opposite extreme from the model of the previous section and consider a model that is almost entirely forward-looking. As we will see, this changes our earlier conclusions dramatically and raises important new issues.

## Assumptions

The two key equations of the model are the new Keynesian *IS* curve and the new Keynesian Phillips curve of the canonical three-equation new Keynesian model we examined in Section 7.8. Specifically, we assume

$$y_t = E_t[y_{t+1}] - \frac{1}{\theta}(i_t - E_t[\pi_{t+1}]) + u_t^{IS}, \qquad \theta > 0, \qquad (11.34)$$

$$\pi_t = \beta E_t[\pi_{t+1}] + \kappa(y_t - y_t^n), \qquad 0 < \beta < 1, \quad \kappa > 0 \qquad (11.35)$$

(see [7.84] and [7.85]). As in the previous section, $y^n$ is the flexible-price level of output. And as in that section, the behavior of the driving processes is given by $u_t^{IS} = \rho_{IS}u_{t-1}^{IS} + \varepsilon_t^{IS}$, $y_t^n = \rho_Y y_{t-1}^n + \varepsilon_t^Y$, where $\rho_{IS}$ and $\rho_Y$ are between $-1$ and 1 and where $\varepsilon^{IS}$ and $\varepsilon^Y$ are independent, white-noise processes (see [11.17] and [11.18]).

For the moment, we assume that the central bank's goal on the output side is to minimize departures of output from its flexible-price level, $y^n$, rather than from its Walrasian level, $y^*$. Below we discuss what happens if its goal is to minimize departures of output from its Walrasian level. On the inflation side, we again assume it wants to minimize departures of inflation from its optimal level, which we normalize to zero as before.

## The "Divine Coincidence"

The structure of the model and our assumptions about the central bank's objective function imply that optimal policy takes a simple form. The new

Keynesian Phillips curve implies that for $\pi_t$ to differ from zero, either $E_t[\pi_{t+1}]$ or $y_t - y_t^n$ (or both) must differ from zero. But this means that there is no conflict between output stabilization and inflation stabilization: if the central bank does its best to keep $y_t - y_t^n$ and $E_t[\pi_{t+1}]$ equal to zero, it will be doing as well as possible at keeping $\pi_t$ equal to zero.

To see this more formally, suppose the central bank conducts policy so that $E_t[\pi_{t+1}] = 0$. Then (11.34) and (11.35) become

$$y_t = E_t[y_{t+1}] - \frac{1}{\theta} i_t + u_t^{IS}, \tag{11.36}$$

$$\pi_t = \kappa \left( y_t - y_t^n \right). \tag{11.37}$$

If the central bank chooses $i_t$ so that $y_t = y_t^n$, it achieves not only its output objective, but (by [11.37]) its inflation objective as well. This result, which is due to Goodfriend and King (1997), is referred to by Blanchard and Galí (2007) as the *divine coincidence.*

To see the intuition behind the divine coincidence, consider a rise in $y_t^n$. This could be the result of a favorable technology shock, for example. The shock naturally makes firms want to produce more at a given level of prices. Thus if the central bank takes no action to change inflation, actual output rises along with the flexible-price level of output, just as the central bank wants.

Another way to describe the intuition is to say that it stems from the lack of backward-looking behavior in price-setting. If some disturbance were to push the economy away from its flexible-price equilibrium, there would be no force keeping it away. As a result, there would be no need for the central bank to manipulate inflation (or expected inflation) to move the economy back to the flexible-price equilibrium.

## Implementing the Optimal Policy

This discussion makes it seem that carrying out optimal policy is trivial. The central bank wants to achieve $y = y^n$ and $\pi = 0$ each period; it therefore wants (11.34) to hold with $y_t = y_t^n$, $E_t[y_{t+1}] = E_t[y_{t+1}^n]$, and $E_t[\pi_{t+1}] = 0$. Imposing these conditions on (11.34) and solving for $i_t$ yields

$$\begin{aligned} i_t &= \theta\{(E_t[y_{t+1}^n] - y_t^n) + u_t^{IS}\} \\ &= r_t^n. \end{aligned} \tag{11.38}$$

As in the model of Section 11.4, $r^n$, the economy's natural rate of interest, is the real interest rate that would prevail with flexible prices. Here it is given by the expression in (11.38). Thus the policy prescription is that the central bank should set the nominal interest rate equal to the natural interest rate.[13]

Unfortunately, as emphasized by Clarida, Galí, and Gertler (2000) and Galí (2008, Section 4.3), things are not so simple. Recall from Section 6.4 that forward-looking models are prone to sunspot equilibria—that is, to equilibria with self-fulfilling beliefs. This problem arises if the central bank follows (11.38). Although the desired outcome of $\pi_t = 0$ and $y_t = y_t^n$ for all $t$ is one equilibrium, there are also equilibria with spontaneous, self-fulfilling departures of actual and expected inflation from zero. Specifically, suppose inflation and output jump up and that agents expect them to return gradually to normal. With the nominal interest rate equal to the natural interest rate, the increase in expected inflation lowers the real rate. This means that declining output is needed for the new Keynesian $IS$ equation to be satisfied, which is what we assumed. And with inflation above expected inflation, the new Keynesian Phillips curve requires above-normal output, which is also what we assumed. As a result, for an appropriate speed of return to normal and an appropriate relationship between the output and inflation movements, the beliefs can be self-fulfilling.

The way for the central bank to avoid this problem that has received the most attention is for it to follow an interest-rate rule that coincides with (11.38) when $E_t[\pi_{t+1}] = 0$ and $E_t[y_{t+1}] = E_t[y_{t+1}^n]$, but that differs in other cases in a way that eliminates the sunspot equilibria. Since it is $E_t[\pi_{t+1}]$ and $E_t[y_{t+1}]$ that affect behavior, a natural way to do this is to make the interest rate a function of those two variables. Specifically, define $\tilde{y} = y - y^n$ as before, and consider a rule of the form

$$i_t = r_t^n + \phi_\pi E_t[\pi_{t+1}] + \phi_y(E_t[\tilde{y}_{t+1}])  \tag{11.39}$$

(see [7.86]). When $E_t[\pi_{t+1}] = 0$ and $E_t[\tilde{y}_{t+1}] = 0$, this rule immediately simplifies to (11.38). To see intuitively how appropriate coefficient values can rule out sunspot equilibria, suppose that $\phi_y = 0$ and that $\phi_\pi$ is greater than one. Then a self-fulfilling rise in inflation would require a rise in the real interest rate, and so require households to expect $y$ to be rising over time for the new Keynesian $IS$ equation to be satisfied. But this means that we cannot have the type of self-fulfilling expectations that can occur when the central just sets $i_t = r_t^n$. In other words, the threat to raise the interest rate in response to increases in expected inflation prevents any increases from occurring, and so never needs to be carried out.

We touched on the issue of when there can and cannot be self-fulfilling equilibria in models like this one in Section 6.4. To understand the issue

---

[13] The model, like the previous one, neglects the fact that the nominal interest rate cannot be negative; this constraint is discussed in the next section. Taken literally, the model implies that the nominal rate fluctuates symmetrically around zero, which suggests that the constraint is very important. With a positive inflation target and positive average output growth, however, the mean nominal rate would be positive.

more formally, suppose for a moment that we have a model with a single variable, $x_t$, that takes the form

$$x_t = AE_t x_{t+1}, \tag{11.40}$$

and that the possible values of $x$ are bounded. One solution of (11.40) is simply $x_t = 0$ for all $t$. Under what conditions is this the only solution? For a spontaneous change in $x$ in period $t$ to some $\bar{x} \neq 0$ to be consistent with (11.40), we would need $\bar{x} = AE_t x_{t+1}$, which in turn would require $E_t x_{t+1} = AE_t x_{t+2}$ and so on. Thus we would need $E_t x_{t+1} = \bar{x}/A$, $E_t x_{t+2} = \bar{x}/A^2$, and so on. If $|A| < 1$, this requires that agents expect $x$ to explode, which cannot occur. If $|A| \geq 1$, on the other hand, such expectations are possible. Thus in this simple example, the condition to rule out sunspot equilibria is that $|A|$ be less than 1.

In the case where $x$ is a vector rather than a single variable, the condition is analogous: multiple equilibria are ruled out if the eigenvalues of the matrix relating $x_t$ and $E_t x_{t+1}$ are less than 1 in absolute value, or *inside the unit circle*.[14]

To see how this works in practice, assume that there are no shocks, and consider again the interest-rate rule in (11.39) with $\phi_y = 0$. Substituting this rule (and the fact that $r_t^n = 0$ for all $t$ in the absence of shocks) into (11.34) and (11.35) allows us to rewrite the system as

$$\begin{bmatrix} \tilde{y}_t \\ \pi_t \end{bmatrix} = A \begin{bmatrix} E_t \tilde{y}_{t+1} \\ E_t \pi_{t+1} \end{bmatrix}, \qquad A = \begin{bmatrix} 1 & \frac{1-\phi_\pi}{\theta} \\ \kappa & \beta + \kappa \frac{1-\phi_\pi}{\theta} \end{bmatrix}. \tag{11.41}$$

The eigenvalues of $A$ are given by

$$\gamma = \frac{1 + \beta + \alpha \pm \sqrt{(1 + \beta + \alpha)^2 - 4\beta}}{2}, \tag{11.42}$$

where $\alpha \equiv \kappa(1 - \phi_\pi)/\theta$. When $\phi_\pi \leq 1$, the positive solution is greater than or equal to 1, and so the system has multiple equilibria. When the value of $\phi_\pi$ becomes larger than 1, multiple equilibria are ruled out. One can also show that for sufficiently large values of $\phi_\pi$, multiple equilibria reappear. Specifically, when $\kappa(1 - \phi_\pi)/\theta < -2(1 + \beta)$, the negative solution of (11.42) is less than $-1$, and so there can be self-fulfilling oscillatory fluctuations in inflation and output. As Galí (2008, Section 4.3.1.3) explains, however, for reasonable values of the other parameters, the value of $\phi_\pi$ needed for this to occur is extremely high.

An obvious variation on (11.39) is for the central bank to adopt a rule that responds to the current values of inflation and the output gap:

$$i_t = r_t^n + \phi_\pi \pi_t + \phi_y \tilde{y}_t. \tag{11.43}$$

---

[14] The name comes from the fact that values less than 1 in absolute value are inside the circle of radius 1 centered at the origin of the complex plane.

Again, for appropriate choices of coefficient values, the rule eliminates sunspot equilibria, and so actual interest rates never depart from the simple rule $i_t = r_t^n$. When $\phi_y = 0$, for example, this occurs when $\phi_\pi > 1$ (Galí, Section 4.3.1.2).

## Breaking the Divine Coincidence

The finding that there is no tradeoff between the central bank's inflation and output objectives is surprising and runs counter to the beliefs of most central bankers. Why might there not be a divine coincidence in practice? One possibility is that the backward-looking considerations that lead to a tradeoff in the model of Section 11.4 are important. But the divine coincidence can also fail in forward-looking models.

One reason that there might not be a coincidence between the two objectives that has attracted considerable attention is the possibility of variation over time in the gap between optimal and flexible-price output. Recall that so far in this section, we have assumed that on the output side, the central bank's goal is to keep actual output, $y$, as close as possible to flexible-price output, $y^n$. But recall also that the discussion in Section 11.3 suggests that the appropriate goal is to keep output as close as possible to Walrasian output, $y^*$.

Introducing the possibility of gaps between $y^n$ and $y^*$ raises several issues. To begin with, because of market imperfections and distortionary taxes, $y^*$ is almost surely larger than $y^n$. This creates an incentive for policymakers to choose an average level of inflation above their most preferred level of zero. Recall the new Keynesian Phillips curve: $\pi_t = \beta E_t[\pi_{t+1}] + \kappa(y_t - y_t^n)$. Since $\beta$ is less than 1, this relationahip implies a long-run output-inflation tradeoff. If inflation is steady at some level $\pi$, $y - y^n$ is steady at $(1 - \beta)\pi$. Thus by choosing an average inflation rate that is positive, policymakers can raise average output, and so bring it closer to the socially optimal level.

This discussion shows that if the central bank makes a one-time choice of average inflation, it has an incentive to choose a rate greater than zero. If it chooses policy each period, there is another complication. The central bank would like to achieve output above $y^n$ and zero inflation. The new Keynesian Phillips curve implies that if it could somehow induce agents to expect negative inflation and then surprise them by producing zero inflation, it could achieve both objectives. The central bank cannot consistently do this, since this would require that agents be systematically fooled. But the fact that the inflation rate the central bank would like agents to expect differs from the rate it would like to deliver after expectations are formed means that there is *dynamic inconsistency* in optimal monetary policy. This dynamic inconsistency is the subject of Section 11.7.

Neither of these complications affects our original motive for introducing the possibility of gaps between $y^*$ and $y^n$, which was to break the divine coincidence in how policy should respond to shocks. To focus solely on that issue, suppose that $y^* - y^n$ is subject to white-noise disturbances but has a mean of zero. This assumption eliminates the central bank's desire to pursue systematic inflation.

To check whether the divine coincidence holds in this environment, recall that when the central bank conducts policy so that $E_t[\pi_{t+1}] = 0$ and $E_t[y_{t+1}] = E_t[y_{t+1}^n] = E_t[y_t^*]$, we have $y_t = E_t[y_{t+1}^n] - (i_t/\theta) + u_t^{IS}$, $\pi_t = \kappa(y_t - y_t^n)$ (see [11.34]-[11.35]). To achieve its output objective, the central bank should choose $i_t$ so that the first expression holds with $y_t = y_t^*$. But to achieve its inflation objective, it should choose $i_t$ so that $y_t = y_t^n$. Thus there is a conflict between the two objectives—the divine coincidence fails.

In characterizing the exact form that optimal policy takes, the issue of dynamic inconsistency arises again, even though $y^* - y^n$ is on average zero. Suppose $y^* - y^n$ is temporarily high, so the central bank is especially interested in raising output. One approach would be for it to keep $E_t[\pi_{t+1}]$ equal to zero but allow $y_t$ to exceed $y_t^n$, and so come closer to its output objective at some cost to its inflation objective. But potentially even better would be to persuade private agents to expect $\pi_{t+1}$ to be negative. For an appropriate value of $E_t[\pi_{t+1}]$, the central bank could achieve both its objectives perfectly in period $t$. When period $t + 1$ arrived, however, the central bank would not want to actually produce a negative value of $\pi_{t+1}$, since at that point this would have no benefit. That is, its policy is again not dynamically consistent.

This discussion shows that even in this very simple model, optimal policy once the divine coincidence fails is complicated. The usual approach at this point is to assume that the central bank can commit to a rule for its policy choices, so that trying to depart systematically from what it has led agents to expect is not feasible. Even then, however, additional issues arise. These issues, along with other reasons for the divine coincidence to fail, are discussed by Clarida, Galí, and Gertler (1999); Woodford (2003, Chapters 7–8); Galí (2008, Chapter 5); and Blanchard and Galí (2007).

# 11.6   Additional Issues in the Conduct of Monetary Policy

The previous two sections investigate monetary policy in highly stylized models. Although the models are helpful for analyzing many issues, there is also a great deal they leave out. This section therefore discusses some other issues concerning the conduct of monetary policy.

## Interest-Rate Rules

Many traditional prescriptions for monetary policy focus on the money stock. For example, Friedman (1960) and others famously argue that the central bank should follow a *k-percent rule*. That is, they argue that monetary policymakers should aim to keep the money stock growing steadily at an annual rate of *k* percent (where *k* is some small number, such as 2 or 3), and otherwise forgo attempts to stabilize the economy.

Despite many economists' impassioned advocacy of money-stock rules, central banks have only rarely given the behavior of the money stock more than a minor role in policy. The measures of the money stock that the central bank can control tightly, such as high-powered money, are not closely linked to aggregate demand. And the measures of the money stock that are often closely linked with aggregate demand, such as *M*2, are difficult for the central bank to control. Further, in many countries the relationship between all measures of the money stock and aggregate demand has broken down in recent decades, weakening the case for money-stock rules even more.

Because of these difficulties, modern central banks almost universally conduct policy not by trying to achieve some target growth rate for the money stock, but by adjusting the short-term nominal interest rate in response to various disturbances. (In the background, of course, what allows them to do this is their control over the money supply.) This is the approach we took in the previous two sections: although the policies we considered there could be described in terms of their implications for the money supply, we focused on their implications for interest rates.

A key fact about conducting policy in terms of interest rates is that interest-rate policies, in contrast to money-supply policies, cannot be passive. Suppose, for example, the central bank keeps the nominal interest rate constant. With backward-looking behavior, this leads to instability. A disturbance to aggregate demand that pushes output above its natural rate causes inflation to rise. With the nominal interest rate fixed, this reduces the real interest rate, which raises output further, which causes inflation to rise even faster, and so on (Friedman, 1968). And with forward-looking behavior, keeping the nominal interest rate constant leads to indeterminacy.

Taylor (1993) and Bryant, Hooper, and Mann (1993) therefore argue that we should think about the conduct of monetary policy in terms of *rules* for the short-term nominal interest rate. That is, we should neither think of the central bank as choosing a path for the nominal rate that is unresponsive to economic conditions (which leads to instability or indeterminacy), nor think of it as adjusting the nominal rate on an ad hoc basis (which does not give us a way of analyzing its behavior or agents' expectations). Instead, we should think of the central bank as following a policy of adjusting the nominal rate in a predictable way to economic developments. Although no rule will fully capture what any central bank does, interest-rate rules may provide a reasonable approximation to actual central bank behavior and can be analyzed formally. This is the approach we took in the previous sections.

Probably the most famous interest-rate rule is the one proposed by Taylor. His rule has two elements. The first is for the nominal interest rate to rise more than one-for-one with inflation, so that the real rate increases when inflation rises. The second is for the interest rate to rise when output is above normal and fall when output is below normal. Taylor's proposed rule is linear in inflation and in the percentage departure of output from its natural rate. That is, his rule takes the form

$$i_t = a + \phi_\pi \pi_t + \phi_y \left( \ln Y_t - \ln Y_t^n \right), \qquad \phi_\pi > 0, \quad \phi_y > 0. \tag{11.44}$$

If we let $r_t^n$ denote the real interest rate that prevails when $Y_t = Y_t^n$ and if we assume that it is constant over time, (11.44) is equivalent to

$$i_t = r^n + \phi_\pi (\pi_t - \pi^*) + \phi_y \left( \ln Y_t - \ln Y_t^n \right), \tag{11.45}$$

where $\pi^* = (r^n - a)/\phi_\pi$. This way of presenting the rule says that the central bank should raise the real interest rate above its long-run equilibrium level in response to inflation exceeding its target and to output exceeding its natural rate. Interest-rate rules of the form in (11.44) and (11.45) are known as *Taylor rules*.

Taylor argues that a rule like (11.45) with $\phi_\pi = 1.5$, $\phi_y = 0.5$, and $r^n = \pi^* = 2\%$ provides a good description of U.S. monetary policy in the period since the Federal Reserve shifted to a clear policy of trying to adjust interest rates to keep inflation low and the economy fairly stable. Specifically, the interest rate predicted by the rule tracks the actual interest rate well starting around 1985. He also argues that this rule with these parameter values is likely to lead to relatively good macroeconomic outcomes.

## Some Issues in the Design of Interest-Rate Rules

Recent research has devoted a great deal of attention to trying to construct interest-rate rules that are likely to produce desirable outcomes. Central banks show little interest in actually committing themselves to a rule, or even in mechanically following the dictates of a rule. Thus research in this area has focused on the question of whether there are prescriptions for how interest rates should be adjusted that can provide valuable guidelines for policymakers.

This research for the most part presumes that central banks can commit to following an interest-rate rule even if they would sometimes want to depart from the rule ex post. That is, the work generally assumes that central banks have found some way of overcoming the types of dynamic-inconsistency problems that we encountered in the previous section and that we will examine further in Section 11.7.

The previous two sections provide simple examples of analyses of interest-rate rules. There, we posited objective functions for the central bank and models of the economy, found optimal policy, and showed how it could be characterized as an interest-rate rule. Much of the research in this area follows this approach. Other papers do not derive optimal policy but consider the relative performance of different interest-rate rules. And other papers are less formal. For example, one can ask how the policy of a particular central bank over some period would have differed from its actual policy if it had followed some rule, and then try to assess whether that would have led to better outcomes.

Research on interest-rate rules has tackled a wide range of questions. Many of them revolve around measurement issues. Taylor assumed that the equilibrium real interest rate is constant and known; that the other variables that enter the rule (inflation, output, and the natural rate of output) are known with certainty; and that the appropriate inflation measure is inflation from four quarters ago to the current quarter and the appropriate measure of the output gap is its current value. These assumptions raise at least four issues.

First, the equilibrium or natural real interest rate presumably varies over time. The logic of Taylor's argument (as well as of the formal models in Sections 11.4 and 11.5) suggests that policymakers should move actual rates one-for-one with movements in the natural interest rate, and thus that the constant $r^n$ in (11.45) should be replaced with the time-varying $r_t^n$.

Second, none of the variables in the rule are known with certainty. The fact that current inflation and output are not known exactly when the central bank sets the interest rate turns out to be relatively unimportant. For example, research has found that using the previous quarter's values has little impact on the rule's performance. A more serious issue is that at any time there is considerable uncertainty about the equilibrium real interest rate and the natural rate of output. For example, Staiger, Stock, and Watson (1997) show that a 95 percent confidence interval for the natural rate of unemployment is probably at least 2 percentage points wide. As a result, it is often hard for policymakers to tell whether output is above or below its natural rate. Thus $r_t^n$ and $Y_t^n$ need to be replaced with the current estimates of those variables.

Third, the issue of estimating $r^n$ and $Y^n$ is closely related to the issue of what values the coefficients on inflation, $\phi_\pi$ and $\phi_y$, should take. The usual finding is that *if* there were no measurement issues, larger coefficient values than those proposed by Taylor, particularly for $\phi_y$, are appropriate. The intuition is that inflation appears to respond to the output gap with a lag. As a result, responding aggressively to departures of output from its natural rate, perhaps with values of $\phi_y$ as high as 2, is desirable. However, the substantial measurement error in estimates of $Y^n$ makes this strategy dangerous. Once measurement error is accounted for, values closer to those proposed by Taylor appear appropriate (though, as we discuss below, measurement error also suggests that it may be desirable to change the form of the rule).[15]

Finally, it is not at all clear that policy should be reacting to current and past values of inflation and the output gap, since they are largely or entirely unaffected by current policy decisions. An obvious alternative is a *forward-looking interest-rate rule,* along the lines of what we considered in Section 11.5. For example, Clarida, Galí, and Gertler (2000) consider rules of the form

$$i_t = r_t^n + \phi_\pi (E_t[\pi_{t+k}] - \pi^*) + \phi_y E_t[\ln Y_{t+k} - \ln Y_{t+k}^n], \qquad k > 0. \quad (11.46)$$

Here, policy responds to information about the future values of the variables that the central bank is concerned with. The most common values of $k$ to consider are 1 quarter, which has the advantage of simplicity, and 4 quarters, which corresponds more closely to a horizon at which monetary policy is likely to have a significant impact.[16]

Many other issues about interest-rate rules concern whether additional variables should be included in the rule. The three types of additional variables that have received the most attention are the exchange rate, lagged interest rates, and measures of asset prices. An appreciation of the exchange rate, like a rise in the interest rate, dampens economic activity. Thus it lowers the interest rate needed to generate a given level of aggregate demand. One might therefore want to modify (11.45) to

$$i_t = r^n + \phi_\pi (\pi_t - \pi^*) + \phi_y (\ln Y_t - \ln Y_t^n) + \phi_e e_t, \qquad (11.47)$$

where $e$ is the real exchange rate (that is, the price of foreign goods in terms of domestic goods). Moving the exchange-rate term over to the right-hand side of this expression gives

$$i_t - \phi_e e_t = r^n + \phi_\pi (\pi_t - \pi^*) + \phi_y (\ln Y_t - \ln Y_t^n). \qquad (11.48)$$

The left-hand side of (11.48) is referred to as a *monetary conditions index.* It is a linear combination of the real exchange rate and the real interest rate. If the coefficient on the exchange rate, $\phi_e$, is chosen properly, the index shows the overall impact of the exchange rate and the interest rate on aggregate demand. Thus (11.48) is a rule for the monetary conditions index as a function of inflation and output.

Including the lagged interest rate may be desirable for three reasons. First, it can cause a given change in the interest rate to have a larger impact on the economy: agents will realize that, for example, a rise in rates implies that rates will remain high for an extended period. Second, by increasing the impact of a given change in the interest rate, it can reduce interest-rate volatility, which may be desirable for its own sake. And third, it can make

---

[15] See, for example, Rudebusch (2001) and Orphanides (2003a).

[16] For more on the use of forecasts in policymaking, see Bernanke and Woodford (1997) and many of the papers in Taylor (1999).

the rule more robust to errors in estimating the natural rates of interest and output. For example, the extreme case of a coefficient on the lagged interest rate of 1 corresponds to a prescription to keep raising the real interest rate when inflation is above target. Such a rule would presumably be certain to bring inflation back to its target level eventually (see, for example, Levin, Wieland, and Williams, 2003, and Orphanides and Williams, 2002). Because of these advantages, in some models the optimal policy does not just put a positive weight on the past interest rate, but raises the current rate more than one-for-one with the past rate. Rotemberg and Woodford (1999b) call such policies *super-inertial*.

The potential disadvantage of including the lagged interest rate is simple: having policy affected by a variable that is not of direct concern to policymakers may produce inefficient outcomes in terms of the variables that policymakers care about. In particular, putting a large weight on the lagged interest rate slows the response of policy to other variables, and so may lead to unnecessary macroeconomic volatility. A potential concrete example of this is the Federal Reserve's behavior in 2004 through 2006, when it raised its interest-rate target by $\frac{1}{4}$ of a percentage point at each of 17 consecutive meetings; this may have considerably delayed its response to economic developments relative to what it would have done had it put little weight on interest-rate smoothing.

Most analyses suggest that policy should react to asset prices only to the extent they provide information about the natural rate of interest and future movements in inflation and the output gap (see, for example, Bernanke and Gertler, 2001). In this view, asset prices might contain information that is valuable in forming the expectations that go into a forward-looking rule such as (11.46) and in estimating the natural rate of interest, but they should not enter the rule directly. The logic behind this conclusion is that because asset prices are not sticky, asset-price inflation, unlike goods-price inflation, does not lead to spurious relative-price variability or to wasteful spending on costs of adjusting prices.

Even if asset prices should not enter the interest-rate rule directly, this does not mean they are unimportant. One set of asset prices that may be particularly important is interest-rate spreads. The gaps between other interest rates and the short-term rate for lending between banks (which is the interest rate that interest-rate rules usually focus on) can vary substantially. And it is often those other interest rates that are relevant for households' and firms' spending decisions. Thus when spreads are higher, then, all else equal, the real short-term interbank interest rate that would lead output to equal its flexible-price level is lower. The logic behind interest-rate rules such as (11.46) therefore strongly suggests that interest-rate spreads should affect central banks' decisions. More formal analyses lead to the same conclusion (for example, Cúrdia and Woodford, 2009).

The argument that asset prices should not enter the central bank's rule breaks down if asset prices depart from the values that are warranted by fundamentals and if policymakers can identify those departures. Because such departures would lead to inefficient allocations of resources, it would be appropriate for policymakers concerned about social welfare to try to counteract them (Cecchetti, Genberg, and Wadhwani, 2003). The difficulty, of course, is that determining whether, for example, a large rise in asset prices is due to some type of irrationality or to new information about fundamentals or a changing willingness to accept risk is extremely challenging. As a result, most observers continue to believe that asset prices should have at most only a very small direct influence on policy.

## Empirical Application: Estimating Interest-Rate Rules

Not surprisingly, many authors have tried to estimate central banks' interest-rate rules. Two prominent efforts are those by Taylor (1999b), who estimates interest-rate rules similar to (11.45) over various periods in U.S. history back to 1879, and Clarida, Galí, and Gertler (2000), who estimate forward-looking rules like (11.46) over various periods of postwar U.S. history. Here we examine Clarida, Galí, and Gertler's procedure.

Clarida, Galí, and Gertler begin with an equation similar to (11.39) or (11.46) for the Federal Reserve's preferred Federal funds rate:

$$i_t^* = r^n + \phi_\pi(E_t[\pi_{t+k}] - \pi^*) + \phi_y E_t[y_{t+k} - y_{t+k}^n], \qquad k > 0. \tag{11.49}$$

where $y \equiv \ln Y$. The authors assume, however, that there is interest-rate smoothing, so that the Federal Reserve moves to its preferred rate only gradually:

$$i_t = \rho i_{t-1} + (1 - \rho)i_t^*, \qquad 0 \le \rho < 1. \tag{11.50}$$

Equations (11.49) and (11.50) imply:

$$\begin{aligned} i_t &= \rho i_{t-1} + (1 - \rho)r^n - (1 - \rho)\phi_\pi\pi^* \\ &\quad + (1 - \rho)\phi_\pi E_t[\pi_{t+k}] + (1 - \rho)\phi_y E_t[y_{t+k} - y_{t+k}^n] \\ &\equiv a + \rho i_{t-1} + b_\pi E_t[\pi_{t+k}] + b_y E_t[y_{t+k} - y_{t+k}^n]. \end{aligned} \tag{11.51}$$

To address the fact that we do not observe $E_t[\pi_{t+k}]$ and $E_t[y_{t+k} - y_{t+k}^n]$, Clarida, Galí, and Gertler use a procedure like the one we saw in tests of the permanent-income hypothesis is Section 8.3: they replace the expectational variables with their realized values minus the expectational errors, and then move the terms involving the expectational errors to the residual. This gives us

$$\begin{aligned} i_t &= a + \rho i_{t-1} + b_\pi \pi_{t+k} + b_y(y_{t+k} - y_{t+k}^n) - b_\pi(\pi_{t+k} - E_t[\pi_{t+k}]) \\ &\quad - b_y\{(y_{t+k} - y_{t+k}^n) - E_t[y_{t+k} - y_{t+k}^n]\} \\ &\equiv a + \rho i_{t-1} + b_\pi \pi_{t+k} + b_y(y_{t+k} - y_{t+k}^n) + e_t. \end{aligned} \tag{11.52}$$

Because $e_t$ depends only on differences between realized values and expectations, its expectation as of time $t$ is zero. We can therefore estimate (11.52) by instrumental variables, using variables known at time $t$ as instruments. Under Clarida, Galí, and Gertler's assumptions, the result will be consistent estimates of the parameters of the underlying rule, (11.51). This is the essence of what Clarida, Galí, and Gertler do. In their baseline specification, they set $k = 1$ (with time measured in quarters), measure the output gap using the estimates constructed by the Congressional Budget Office, and use lagged values of a range of macroeconomic variables as instruments. They focus on two periods: the "pre-Volcker" period, 1960Q1–1979Q2, and the "Volcker-Greenspan" period, 1979Q3–1996Q4.

For the pre-Volcker period, the estimated parameters (with standard errors in parentheses) are $\pi^* = 4.24$ (1.09), $\phi_\pi = 0.83$ (0.07), $\phi_y = 0.27$ (0.08), and $\rho = 0.68$ (0.05). For the Volcker-Greenspan period, they are $\pi^* = 3.58$ (0.50), $\phi_\pi = 2.15$ (0.40), $\phi_y = 0.93$ (0.42), and $\rho = 0.79$ (0.04).[17] The most striking feature of these results is the small value of $\phi_\pi$ in the first period, which implies that the Federal Reserve on average cut the real interest rate when inflation rose. Such a policy leads to explosive inflation or deflation in backward-looking models, and to sunspot equilibria in forward-looking ones. Clarida, Galí, and Gertler argue that this can account for the high inflation of the 1970s.

One limitation of Clarida, Galí, and Gertler's approach is that it does not include any reason for (11.52) not to hold perfectly other than expectational errors. That is, the Federal Reserve is assumed to follow the rule in equation (11.51) exactly. If the Federal Reserve departs from (11.51), Clarida, Galí, and Gertler's estimates may be biased. Suppose, for example, there is some variation in its inflation target over time. Then the error term in (11.52) also includes the term $-b_\pi(\pi_t^* - \overline{\pi}^*)$ (where $\overline{\pi}^*$ is the average inflation target). Thus, since actual and target inflation are almost certainly positively correlated, and since $b_\pi$ (which equals $(1 - \rho)\phi_\pi$) is almost certainly positive, there is negative correlation between inflation and the error term. As a result, there is downward bias in the estimate of $b_\pi$, and thus in the estimate of $\phi_\pi$. Other sources of departure from (11.51) (such as variation in $r^n$) are also likely to lead to biased estimates. As in many other applications, the facts that many factors may contribute to the residual and that it is difficult to find good instruments once we recognize the existence of nonexpectational terms in the residual make estimating the underlying parameters extremely challenging.

The finding of this literature that is robust, and that has been confirmed by many authors in addition to Clarida, Galí, and Gertler, is that for a given inflation rate and output gap, the Federal Reserve chose a much lower real

---

[17] All the parameters other than $\pi^*$ can be inferred directly from the estimates of (11.52). Inferring $\pi^*$ requires an estimate of $r^n$. Clarida, Galí, and Gertler assume that $r^n$ in each of their two sample periods is equal to the average real interest rate in that period.

interest rate in the 1960s and, especially, the 1970s than it did in the 1980s and 1990s (Taylor, 1999b; Orphanides, 2003b; C. Romer and D. Romer, 2002). In most models, a policy that implies lower real rates under a given set of macroeconomic conditions leads to higher average inflation. In that sense, the results of examinations of the Federal Reserve's interest-rate policies suggest a likely source of the high inflation of the 1970s. The deeper question that this leaves open is why the Federal Reserve followed low-interest-rate policies in this period. We will return to that question in Section 11.8.

## The Zero Lower Bound on the Nominal Interest Rate

Our discussion so far has presumed that the central bank can set the interest rate according to the interest-rate rule that it chooses. But if the rule prescribes a negative nominal interest rate, it cannot. Because high-powered money earns a nominal return of zero, there is no reason for anyone to buy an asset offering a negative nominal return. Thus the nominal rate cannot fall below zero.

The zero lower bound on the nominal interest rate was long thought to be mainly of historical and theoretical interest, relevant to the Great Depression but unlikely to be important to modern economies. Recent events have proven that view wrong. Nominal interest rates on short-term government debt in Japan have been virtually zero since the late 1990s. The Federal Reserve lowered the short-term nominal rate not far from zero in 2003. And most importantly, the economic and financial crisis that began in 2007 led most major central banks to lower their nominal interest-rate target to near zero. In the cases of Japan and of the recent crisis, it is reasonably clear that the zero lower bound was a binding constraint on monetary policy. For example, conventional interest-rate rules implied that the appropriate target level of the Federal funds rate in 2009 in the absence of the zero lower bound was negative 4 percent or lower (Rudebusch, 2009). Thus, the issue of how—if at all—policy can increase aggregate demand when the nominal interest rate is close to zero is important.

Various ways to stimulate an economy with a zero nominal rate have been suggested. One obvious possibility is to use fiscal policy. But as described in Section 12.4, there are cases where expansionary fiscal policy does not raise aggregate demand. And stimulative fiscal policy (at least in its standard forms) requires increasing the budget deficit, which has disadvantages— particularly in economies with severe long-run budget problems. Thus the possibility of using fiscal policy does not make the issue of whether monetary policy can be used irrelevant.

One way to try to use monetary policy to stimulate the economy when the short-term nominal rate is zero is to conduct conventional open-market operations. Although these operations cannot lower the nominal rate, they may be able to lower the real rate. Money growth is a crucial determinant of inflation in the long run. Thus expanding the money supply may generate expectations of inflation, and so reduce real interest rates. C. Romer (1992) presents evidence that the rapid money growth in the United States starting in 1933 raised inflationary expectations, stimulated interest-sensitive sectors of the economy, and fueled the recovery from the Great Depression.

The issue of whether monetary expansion with a zero nominal rate raises expected inflation is complicated, however. With a nominal rate of zero, at the margin agents do not value the liquidity services provided by money (since otherwise they would not be willing to hold zero-interest bonds). Thus when the central bank expands the money stock by purchasing bonds, individuals can just hold the additional money in place of the bonds. Thus it is not clear why expected inflation should rise.

Krugman (1998) and Eggertsson and Woodford (2003) show that the issue hinges on how the expansion affects expectations concerning what the money stock will be once the nominal rate becomes positive again. If the expansion raises expectations of those future money stocks, it should raise expectations of the price level in those periods, and so increase expected inflation today. But if the expansion does not affect expectations of those money stocks, there is no reason for it to raise expected inflation.

For the Depression, when the Federal Reserve did not have a clear view concerning the long-term path it wanted the money stock or the price level to follow, it is plausible that the large monetary expansion increased expectations of later money stocks substantially. But in modern economies, where central banks generally have reasonably clear explicit or implicit long-run inflation targets, agents may reasonably believe that the central bank will largely undo the increase in the money stock as soon as it starts to have an important effect on aggregate demand. As a result, expected inflation may not rise, and the open-market purchase may have little effect.

One way for the central bank to deal with the fact that expected inflation is crucial to the amount of stimulus it can provide by lowering the nominal rate to zero is to raise its inflation target. If agents expect sufficiently high inflation, the real interest rate at a zero nominal rate will be low enough to bring about recovery. Krugman (1998), for example, proposes that the Bank of Japan adopt a permanently higher target for inflation. However, Eggertsson and Woodford observe that the target needed to generate a sufficiently low real rate when the nominal rate is zero may be above the rate that would be optimal on other grounds. They argue that in this case, the central bank can do better by announcing that its policy is to aim for high inflation not at all times, but only after times when the nominal rate has fallen to zero. One step in the direction of the policy proposed by Eggertsson and Woodford is to adopt a target *price-level path*. A downturn that causes the central bank to lower the nominal rate to zero is likely to push inflation below the central bank's target. If the central bank has a policy of offsetting shortfalls from its target through later periods of above-normal inflation, the fall in inflation naturally generates an increase in expected inflation. There is no reason, however, that the resulting amount of expected inflation will generally be optimal. Thus the optimal policy is usually more complicated (Eggertsson and Woodford, 2003).

Another possible way for the central bank to provide stimulus in the face of the zero lower bound is to purchase assets other than short-term government debt in its open-market operations. For example, it can purchase long-term government debt or corporate debt, both of which are likely to offer positive nominal returns even when the interest rate on short-term government debt is zero. It is useful to think about such transactions as conventional open-market operations followed by exchanges of short-term zero-interest government debt for the alternative asset.[18] The potential additional benefit of this type of open-market operation comes from the second step. If investors are risk-neutral, with the positive nominal returns on the alternative asset reflecting default risk or expectations of positive future short-term interest rates, the exchange of short-term government debt for the alternative asset will have no effect on the asset's return. But in the realistic case where the demand for the alternative asset is downward-sloping, the exchange will reduce the interest rate on the alternative asset at least somewhat.

One specific type of unconventional open-market operation that has attracted considerable attention is exchange-market intervention. By purchasing foreign currency or other foreign assets, the central bank can presumably cause the domestic currency to depreciate. For example, temporarily pegging the exchange rate at a level that is highly depreciated relative to the current level should be straightforward. If the central bank announces that it is willing to buy foreign currency at a high price, it will face a large supply of foreign currency. But since it can print domestic currency, it will have no difficulty carrying out the promised trades. And exchange-rate depreciation will stimulate the economy.[19]

A final way that policy can attempt to stimulate the economy is by direct intervention in credit markets. In 2008 and 2009, the Federal Reserve and other central banks took actions aimed at the markets for specific types of credit, supporting commercial-paper issuance, mortgage lending, and so on. Such actions are clearly most likely to be effective when the particular markets they are aimed at have been disrupted, and their effectiveness

---

[18] Similarly, it is often argued that a money-financed tax cut is certain to stimulate an economy facing the zero nominal bound. But such a tax cut is a combination of a conventional tax cut and a conventional open-market operation. If neither component stimulates the economy, then (barring interaction effects, which seem unlikely to be important) the combination will be ineffective as well.

[19] Svensson (2001) offers a concrete proposal for how to use exchange-rate policy in a situation where the nominal rate is zero.

even then is unknown. Thus they do not provide a general solution to the constraints created by the zero lower bound.

This menu of possible policies at the zero lower bound requires a specialized vocabulary. Because the issues are so new, the terminology is still evolving. One usage is to refer to conventional open-market operations at the zero lower bound as *quantitative easing*; open-market operations that involve buying assets other than short-term government debt as *asset purchases*; interventions in credit markets as *credit policy*; and policies aimed at expectations of future inflation or interest rates as *expectations management*.

Five years ago,[20] there was considerable disagreement about the importance of the zero lower bound. One group viewed it as a powerful constraint on monetary policy, and felt that the possibility of an economy being trapped in a situation of low aggregate demand, with monetary policy powerless to help, was a serious concern. A situation where the nominal interest rate is zero and monetary policy is powerless is known as a *liquidity trap*. The other group stressed the many tools available to the central bank other than control over the short-term nominal rate, especially its ability to provide essentially unlimited amounts of money at zero cost. This clearly gives it the ability to create inflation in the long run, and hence almost surely implies an ability to create expected inflation.

The crisis that began in 2007 has largely settled the debate. Regardless of whether central banks *could* have used other tools to provide the stimulus to aggregate demand that would have been provided by further reductions in the nominal rate had the zero lower bound not been binding, the fact is that they did not. As a result, it is clear that the bound had very large effects. If unconstrained central banks had been faced with the prospects of a rapid output decline followed by years of high unemployment, all accompanied by inflation at or below their targets, there is no doubt they would have cut their interest-rate targets sharply, with the result that outcomes would have been substantially different. For example, Williams (2009) estimates that relative to the likely path of GDP even after accounting for the fiscal stimulus that was adopted and the various unconventional monetary actions that were taken, removing the zero lower bound would have resulted in GDP in the United States being on average about 3 percent higher over the period 2009–2012, for a cumulative output gain of about $1.7 trillion.

A final issue raised by this discussion is whether policy should be conducted differently in the future. If the crisis was a one-time event that we are unlikely to see anything like again, policy can proceed as before. If it was the preventable result of regulatory and other policy failures, the first-best solution is to correct those failures. But if we are likely to see other severe contractions in the future, then in the absence of any changes, the zero lower bound is likely to have large output costs again. Thus the question

---

[20] For example, at the time of the writing of the third edition of this book.

of how to avoid those costs—by raising the target inflation rate, adopting some type of price-level-path targeting, or in some other way—would be important. For example, Williams finds that in an environment of large shocks, an inflation target of about 4 percent may be needed to keep the zero lower bound from having large costs.

# 11.7   The Dynamic Inconsistency of Low-Inflation Monetary Policy

The previous three sections are devoted mainly to optimal monetary policy, analyzing how policy should be conducted in various environments. But actual policy often appears to be far from optimal. For example, monetary policymakers' failure to respond to shocks was an important source of the Great Depression; rapid money growth led to high inflation in many industrialized countries in the 1970s, and has often led to high inflation in other times and places; and explosive money growth results in hyperinflation. Our analysis so far provides no explanation of such policy failures.

Departures from optimal policy do not appear to be random. Episodes when money growth and inflation are too high seem far more common than episodes when they are too low. As a result, there is considerable interest in possible sources of inflationary bias in monetary policy.

For the major industrialized countries, where government revenue from money creation does not appear important, the underlying source of any inflationary bias is almost certainly the existence of an output-inflation tradeoff. Policymakers may increase the money supply to try to push output above its normal level. Or, if they are faced with inflation that they believe is too high, they may be reluctant to undergo a recession to reduce it.

Any theory of how an output-inflation tradeoff can lead to inflation must confront the fact that there is no significant tradeoff in the long run.[21] Since average inflation has little effect on average output, it might seem that the existence of a short-run tradeoff is largely irrelevant to the determination of average inflation. Consider, for example, two monetary policies that differ only because money growth is lower by a constant amount in every situation under one policy than the other. If the public is aware of the difference, there is no reason for output to behave differently under the low-inflation policy than under the high-inflation one.

In a famous paper, however, Kydland and Prescott (1977) show that the inability of policymakers to commit themselves to such a low-inflation policy can give rise to excessive inflation despite the absence of an

---

[21] As noted in Section 11.5, the new Keynesian Phillips curve implies a slight long-run tradeoff. When the discount factor is close to 1, however, the impact of average inflation on average output is small.

important long-run tradeoff. Kydland and Prescott's basic observation is that if expected inflation is low, so that the marginal cost of additional inflation is low, policymakers will pursue expansionary policies to push output temporarily above its normal level. But the public's knowledge that policymakers have this incentive means that they will not in fact expect low inflation. The end result is that policymakers' ability to pursue discretionary policy results in inflation without any increase in output. This section presents a simple model that formalizes this idea.

## Assumptions

Kydland and Prescott's argument requires three key ingredients: monetary changes have real effects, expectations concerning inflation affect output behavior, and the economy's flexible-price level of output is less than the socially optimal level. To model the first two ingredients as simply as possible (and to keep close to the spirit of Kydland and Prescott's original analysis), we assume that aggregate supply is given by the Lucas supply curve (see equations [6.24] and [6.84]):

$$y = y^n + b(\pi - \pi^e), \qquad b > 0, \tag{11.53}$$

where $y$ is the log of output and $y^n$ is the log of its flexible-price level. Other models with a role for expectations, such as the new Keynesian Phillips curve and various hybrid Phillips curves with a mix of backward-looking and forward-looking elements, would have broadly similar implications. To model the third ingredient, we assume that $y^n$ is less than Walrasian output, $y^*$.

Kydland and Prescott also assume that inflation above some level is costly, and that the marginal cost of inflation increases as inflation rises. A simple way to capture these assumptions is to make social welfare quadratic in both output and inflation. Thus the policymaker minimizes

$$L = \tfrac{1}{2}(y - y^*)^2 + \tfrac{1}{2}a(\pi - \pi^*)^2, \qquad y^* > y^n, \qquad a > 0. \tag{11.54}$$

The parameter $a$ reflects the relative importance of output and inflation in social welfare.

Finally, the policymaker can influence aggregate demand. Since there is no uncertainty, we can think of the policymaker as choosing inflation directly, subject to the constraint that inflation and output are related by the aggregate supply curve, (11.53).

## Analyzing the Model

To see the model's implications, consider two ways that monetary policy and expected inflation could be determined. In the first, the policymaker makes a binding commitment about what inflation will be before expected inflation is determined. Since the commitment is binding, expected inflation equals actual inflation, and so (by [11.53]) output equals its natural rate. Thus the policymaker's problem is to choose $\pi$ to minimize $(y^n - y^*)^2/2 + a(\pi - \pi^*)^2/2$. The solution is simply $\pi = \pi^*$.

In the second situation, the policymaker chooses inflation taking expectations of inflation as given. This could occur either if expected inflation is determined before actual inflation is, or if $\pi$ and $\pi^e$ are determined simultaneously. Substituting (11.53) into (11.54) implies that the policymaker's problem is

$$\min_{\pi} \tfrac{1}{2}[y^n + b(\pi - \pi^e) - y^*]^2 + \tfrac{1}{2}a(\pi - \pi^*)^2. \tag{11.55}$$

The first-order condition is

$$[y^n + b(\pi - \pi^e) - y^*]b + a(\pi - \pi^*) = 0. \tag{11.56}$$

Solving (11.56) for $\pi$ yields

$$\pi = \frac{b^2\pi^e + a\pi^* + b(y^* - y^n)}{a + b^2}$$

$$= \pi^* + \frac{b}{a + b^2}(y^* - y^n) + \frac{b^2}{a + b^2}(\pi^e - \pi^*). \tag{11.57}$$

Figure 11.3 plots the policymaker's choice of $\pi$ as a function of $\pi^e$. The relationship is upward-sloping with a slope less than 1. The figure and equation (11.57) show the policymaker's incentive to pursue expansionary policy. If the public expects the policymaker to choose the optimal rate of inflation, $\pi^*$, then the marginal cost of slightly higher inflation is zero, and the marginal benefit of the resulting higher output is positive. Thus in this situation the policymaker chooses an inflation rate greater than $\pi^*$.

Since there is no uncertainty, equilibrium requires that expected and actual inflation are equal. As Figure 11.3 shows, there is a unique inflation rate for which this is true. If we impose $\pi = \pi^e$ in (11.57) and then solve for this inflation rate, we obtain

$$\pi^e = \pi^* + \frac{b}{a}(y^* - y^n)$$

$$\equiv \pi^{EQ}. \tag{11.58}$$

If expected inflation exceeds this level, then actual inflation is less than individuals expect, and thus the economy is not in equilibrium. Similarly, if $\pi^e$ is less than $\pi^{EQ}$, then $\pi$ exceeds $\pi^e$.

Thus the only equilibrium is for $\pi$ and $\pi^e$ to equal $\pi^{EQ}$, and for $y$ to therefore equal $y^n$. Intuitively, expected inflation rises to the point where the policymaker, taking $\pi^e$ as given, chooses to set $\pi$ equal to $\pi^e$. In short,

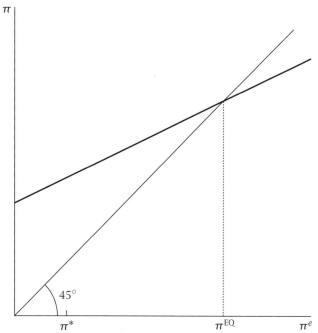

**FIGURE 11.3   The determination of inflation in the absence of commitment**

all that the policymaker's discretion does is to increase inflation without affecting output.[22]

## Discussion

The reason that the ability to choose inflation after expected inflation is determined makes the policymaker worse off is that the policy of announcing that inflation will be $\pi^*$, and then producing that inflation rate after expected inflation is determined, is not dynamically consistent. If the policymaker announces that inflation will equal $\pi^*$ and the public forms its expectations accordingly, the policymaker will deviate from the policy once expectations are formed. The public's knowledge that the policymaker will do this causes it to expect inflation greater than $\pi^*$. This expected inflation worsens the menu of choices that the policymaker faces.

---

[22] None of these results depend on the use of specific functional forms. With general functional forms, the equilibrium is for expected and actual inflation to rise to the point where the marginal cost of inflation just balances its marginal benefit through higher output. Thus output equals its natural rate and inflation is above the optimal level. The equilibrium if the policymaker can make a binding commitment is still for inflation to equal its optimal level and output to equal its natural rate.

To see that it is the knowledge that the policymaker has discretion, rather than the discretion itself, that is the source of the problem, consider what happens if the public believes the policymaker can commit but he or she in fact has discretion. In this case, the policymaker can announce that inflation will equal $\pi^*$ and thereby cause expected inflation to equal $\pi^*$. But the policymaker can then set inflation according to (11.57). Since (11.57) is the solution to the problem of minimizing the social loss function given expected inflation, this "reneging" on the commitment raises social welfare.

Dynamic inconsistency arises in many other situations. In the context of monetary policy, we already encountered it in the model of Section 11.5. There, policymakers would like to manipulate expectations of inflation to change the economy's response to shocks, but then not produce the inflation that agents expect. More important additional cases of dynamic inconsistency arise in contexts other than monetary policy. Policymakers choosing how to tax capital may want to encourage capital accumulation by adopting a low tax rate. Once the capital has been accumulated, however, taxing it is nondistortionary; thus it is optimal for policymakers to tax it at high rates.[23] To give another example, policymakers who want individuals to obey a law may want to promise that violators will be punished harshly. Once individuals have decided whether to comply, however, there is a cost and no benefit to punishing violators.

## Addressing the Dynamic-Inconsistency Problem

This analysis shows that discretionary monetary policy can give rise to inefficiently high inflation. This naturally raises the question of what can be done to avoid, or at least mitigate, this possibility.

One approach, of course, is to have monetary policy determined by rules rather than discretion. It is important to emphasize, however, that the rules must be binding. Suppose policymakers just announce that they are going to determine monetary policy according to some procedure, such as making the money stock grow at a constant rate or following some formula to choose their target nominal interest rate. If the public believes this announcement and therefore expects low inflation, policymakers can raise social welfare by departing from the announced policy and choosing a higher rate of money growth. Thus the public will not believe the announcement.

---

[23] A corollary of this observation is that low-inflation policy can be dynamically inconsistent not because of an output-inflation tradeoff, but because of government debt. Since government debt is generally denominated in nominal terms, unanticipated inflation is a lump-sum tax on debtholders. As a result, even if monetary shocks do not have real effects, a policy of setting $\pi = \pi^*$ is not dynamically consistent as long as the government has nominally denominated debt (Calvo, 1978b).

Only if the monetary authority relinquishes the ability to determine monetary policy does a rule solve the problem.

There are two problems, however, with using binding rules to overcome the dynamic-inconsistency problem. One is normative, the other positive. The normative problem is that rules cannot account for completely unexpected circumstances. There is no difficulty in constructing a rule that makes monetary policy respond to normal economic developments. But sometimes there are events that could not plausibly have been expected. In recent decades, for example, the United States experienced a collapse of the relationships between economic activity and many standard measures of the money stock, an almost unprecedented one-day crash in the stock market that caused a severe liquidity crisis, the aftershocks of various international crises, a major terrorist attack, and a financial collapse unlike any since the Great Depression. It is inconceivable that a rule would have anticipated all these possibilities.

The positive problem with binding rules as the solution to the dynamic-inconsistency problem is that we observe low rates of inflation in many situations (such as the United States in the 1950s and in recent years, and Germany over most of the postwar period) where policy is not made according to fixed rules. Thus there must be ways of alleviating the dynamic-inconsistency problem that do not involve binding commitments.

Because of considerations like these, there has been considerable interest in other ways of dealing with dynamic inconsistency. The two approaches that have received the most attention are reputation and delegation.[24]

The basic idea behind using reputation to deal with the dynamic-inconsistency problem is that the public is unsure about policymakers' characteristics and learns something about those characteristics by observing inflation. For example, the public may not know policymakers' preferences between output and inflation or their beliefs about the output-inflation tradeoff, or how costly it is to them to not follow through on their announcements about future policy. In such situations, policymakers' behavior conveys information about their characteristics, and thus affects the public's expectations of inflation in subsequent periods. Since policymakers face a

---

[24] Two other possibilities are punishment equilibria and incentive contracts. Punishment equilibria (which are often described as models of reputation, but which differ fundamentally from the models discussed below) arise in infinite-horizon models. These models typically have multiple equilibria, including ones where inflation stays below the one-time discretionary level (that is, below $\pi^{EQ}$). Low inflation is sustained by beliefs that if policymakers were to choose high inflation, the public would "punish" them by expecting high inflation in subsequent periods; the punishments are structured so that the expectations of high inflation would in fact be rational if that situation ever arose. See, for example, Barro and Gordon (1983) and Problems 11.16–11.18. Incentive contracts are arrangements in which the central banker is penalized (either financially or through loss of prestige) for inflation. In simple models, the appropriate choice of penalties produces the optimal policy (Persson and Tabellini, 1993; Walsh, 1995). The empirical relevance of such contracts is not clear, however.

more favorable menu of output-inflation choices when expected inflation is lower, this gives them an incentive to pursue low-inflation policies. This idea is developed formally by Backus and Driffill (1985) and Barro (1986) and in Problem 11.13.

The idea that concern about their reputations causes policymakers to pursue less expansionary policies seems not only theoretically appealing, but also realistic. Central bankers appear to be very concerned with establishing reputations as being tough on inflation and as being credible. If the public were certain of policymakers' preferences and beliefs, there would be no reason for this. Only if the public is uncertain and if expectations matter is this concern appropriate.

The basic idea behind the use of delegation to overcome dynamic inconsistency is that the output-inflation tradeoff is more favorable if monetary policy is controlled by individuals who are known to particularly dislike inflation (Rogoff, 1985). A straightforward extension of the model we have been considering shows how this can address the dynamic-inconsistency problem. Suppose that the output-inflation relationship and social welfare continue to be given by (11.53) and (11.54); thus $y = y^n + b(\pi - \pi^e)$ and $L = [(y - y^*)^2/2] + [a(\pi - \pi^*)^2/2]$. Suppose, however, that monetary policy is determined by an individual whose objective function is

$$L' = \tfrac{1}{2}(y - y^*)^2 + \tfrac{1}{2}a'(\pi - \pi^*)^2, \qquad y^* > y^n, \qquad a' > 0. \qquad (11.59)$$

$a'$ may differ from $a$, the weight that society as a whole places on inflation. Solving the policymaker's maximization problem along the lines of (11.55) implies that his or her choice of $\pi$, given $\pi^e$, is given by (11.57) with $a'$ in place of $a$. Thus,

$$\pi = \pi^* + \frac{b}{a' + b^2}(y^* - y^n) + \frac{b^2}{a' + b^2}(\pi^e - \pi^*). \qquad (11.60)$$

Figure 11.4 shows the effects of delegating policy to someone with a value of $a'$ greater than $a$. Because the policymaker puts more weight on inflation than before, he or she chooses a lower value of inflation for a given level of expected inflation (at least over the range where $\pi^e \geq \pi^*$); in addition, his or her response function is flatter.

As before, the public knows how inflation is determined. Thus equilibrium again requires that expected and actual inflation are equal. As a result, when we solve for expected inflation, we find that it is given by (11.58) with $a'$ in place of $a$:

$$\pi^{EQ} = \pi^* + \frac{b}{a'}(y^* - y^n). \qquad (11.61)$$

The equilibrium is for both actual and expected inflation to be given by (11.61), and for output to equal its natural rate.

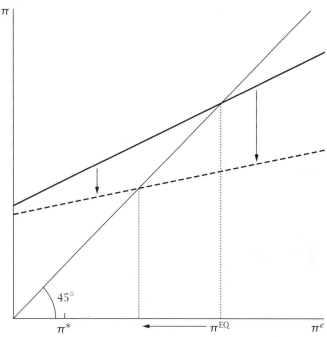

**FIGURE 11.4 The effect of delegation to a conservative policymaker on equilibrium inflation**

Now consider social welfare, which is higher when $(y - y^*)^2/2 + a(\pi - \pi^*)^2/2$ is lower. Output is equal to $y^n$ regardless of $a'$. But when $a'$ is higher, $\pi$ is closer to $\pi^*$. Thus when $a'$ is higher, social welfare is higher. Intuitively, when monetary policy is controlled by someone who cares strongly about inflation, the public realizes that the policymaker has little desire to pursue expansionary policy; the result is that expected inflation is low.

Rogoff extends this analysis to the case where the economy is affected by shocks. Under plausible assumptions, a policymaker whose preferences between output and inflation differ from society's does not respond optimally to shocks. Thus in choosing monetary policymakers, there is a trade-off: choosing policymakers with a stronger dislike of inflation produces a better performance in terms of average inflation, but a worse one in terms of responses to disturbances. As a result, there is some optimal level of "conservatism" for central bankers.[25]

Again, the idea that societies can address the dynamic-inconsistency problem by letting individuals who particularly dislike inflation control monetary policy appears realistic. In many countries, monetary policy is determined by independent central banks rather than by the central government.

---

[25] This idea is developed in Problem 11.14.

And the central government often seeks out individuals who are known to be particularly averse to inflation to run those banks. The result is that those who control monetary policy are often known for being more concerned about inflation than society as a whole, and only rarely for being less concerned.

# 11.8   Empirical Applications

## Central-Bank Independence and Inflation

Theories that attribute inflation to the dynamic inconsistency of low-inflation monetary policy are difficult to test. The theories suggest that inflation is related to such variables as the costs of inflation, policymakers' ability to commit, their ability to establish reputations, and the extent to which policy is delegated to individuals who particularly dislike inflation. All of these are hard to measure.

One variable that has received considerable attention is the independence of the central bank. Alesina (1988) argues that central-bank independence provides a measure of the delegation of policymaking to conservative policymakers. Intuitively, the greater the independence of the central bank, the greater the government's ability to delegate policy to individuals who especially dislike inflation. Empirically, central-bank independence is generally measured by qualitative indexes based on such factors as how the bank's governor and board are appointed and dismissed, whether there are government representatives on the board, and the government's ability to veto or directly control the bank's decisions.

Investigations of the relation between these measures of independence and inflation find that among industrialized countries, independence and inflation are strongly negatively related (Alesina, 1988; Grilli, Masciandaro, and Tabellini, 1991; Cukierman, Webb, and Neyapti, 1992). Figure 11.5 is representative of the results.

There are four limitations to this finding, however. First, it is not clear that theories of dynamic inconsistency and delegation predict that greater central-bank independence will produce lower inflation. The argument that they make this prediction implicitly assumes that the preferences of central bankers and government officials do not vary systematically with central-bank independence. But the delegation hypothesis implies that they will. Suppose, for example, that monetary policy depends on the central bank's and the government's preferences, with the weight on the bank's preferences increasing in its independence. Then when the bank is less independent, government officials should compensate by appointing more inflation-averse individuals to the bank. Similarly, when the government is less able to delegate policy to the bank, voters should elect more inflation-averse

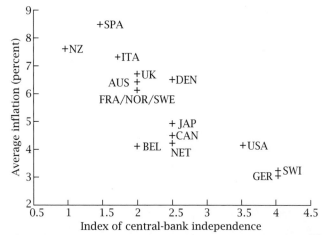

**FIGURE 11.5   Central-bank independence and inflation**[26]

governments. These effects will mitigate, and might even offset, the effects of reduced central-bank independence.

Second, the fact that there is a negative relation between central-bank independence and inflation does not mean that the independence is the source of the low inflation. As Posen (1993) observes, countries whose citizens are particularly averse to inflation are likely to try to insulate their central banks from political pressure. For example, it is widely believed that Germans especially dislike inflation, perhaps because of the hyperinflation that Germany experienced after World War I. And the institutions governing Germany's central bank appear to have been created largely because of this desire to avoid inflation. Thus some of Germany's low inflation is almost surely the result of the general aversion to inflation, rather than of the independence of its central bank.

Third, the empirical relationship is not in fact as strong as this discussion suggests. To begin with, there is no clear relationship between legal measures of central-bank independence and average inflation among nonindustrialized countries (Cukierman, Webb, and Neyapti, 1992; Campillo and Miron, 1997). Further, the usual measures of independence appear to be biased in favor of finding a link between independence and low inflation. For example, the measures put some weight on whether the bank's charter gives low inflation as its principal goal (Pollard, 1993).

---

[26] Figure 11.5, from "Central Bank Independence and Macroeconomic Performance" by Alberto Alesina and Lawrence H. Summers, *Journal of Money, Credit, and Banking*, Vol. 25, No. 2 (May 1993), is reprinted by permission. Copyright 1993 by the Ohio State University Press. All rights reserved.

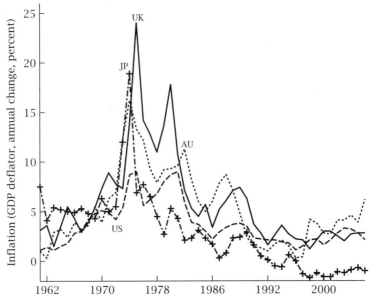

**FIGURE 11.6   Inflation in the United States, the United Kingdom, Australia, and Japan, 1961–2008**

Finally, even if independence is the source of the low inflation, the mechanism linking the two may not involve dynamic inconsistency. We will see another possibility in the next application.

## The Great Inflation

Most industrialized countries experienced high inflation in the 1970s. Figure 11.6 plots inflation in four countries—the United States, the United Kingdom, Australia, and Japan—since 1960. Two facts stand out. First, there was considerable heterogeneity across countries. In just these four countries, the peak level of inflation varied from less than 10 percent in the United States to almost 25 percent in the United Kingdom. In the United States, inflation rose gradually through the mid-1970s, fluctuated irregularly, and then fell sharply in the early 1980s; but in Australia, it rose sharply in the early 1970s and then fell gradually and irregularly for two decades. Second, despite the variety, all these countries—and many more—experienced much higher inflation in the 1970s than they did before or after. This period of high inflation is often referred to as the *Great Inflation*.

Understanding the Great Inflation is an important challenge in the study of macroeconomic policy. Unfortunately, its causes are far from fully understood. Thus we can do little better than to describe some of the leading candidates.

In light of the analysis in Section 11.7, one candidate is the dynamic inconsistency of low-inflation policy. Indeed, the high inflation of the 1970s was an important motivation for Kydland and Prescott's analysis. But this explanation faces an obvious challenge. Theories of dynamic inconsistency imply that high inflation is the result of optimizing behavior by the relevant players given the institutions. Thus they predict that in the absence of changes to those institutions, high inflation will remain. This is not what we observe. In the United States, for example, policymakers reduced inflation from about 10 percent at the end of the 1970s to under 5 percent just a few years later, and maintained the lower inflation, without any significant changes in the institutions or rules governing policy. Similarly, in countries such as New Zealand and the United Kingdom, reforms to increase central-bank independence followed rather than preceded major reductions in inflation.

To explain the Great Inflation, then, models of dynamic inconsistency need to appeal to changes in the forces that drive inflation in the models, such as the gap between equilibrium and optimal output and the slope of the output-inflation relationship. It is true that, at least in the United States, the natural rate of unemployment was unusually high in the 1970s, suggesting that $y^* - y^n$ may have been unusually high as well. Yet it seems unlikely that such changes can explain the magnitude and pervasiveness of the rise and fall in inflation.

A variation on the dynamic-inconsistency explanation is proposed by Sargent (1999) and Cho, Williams, and Sargent (2002). Their basic idea is that policymakers do not know the true structure of the economy, but must infer it from the dynamics of output and inflation. Even if the economy is in fact described by the Kydland–Prescott model, policymakers may sometimes infer that there is no output-inflation tradeoff, and thus that there is no cost to pursuing low-inflation policies. Policymakers' attempts at learning can therefore lead to recurring bouts of high and low inflation. Whether this account fits with actual experience is unclear, however. For example, it implies that policymakers during the Great Inflation believed that there was a short-run output-inflation tradeoff while their predecessors and successors did not. There does not appear to be any strong evidence for this view.

Before Kydland and Prescott's work, the conventional explanation of the Great Inflation was that it was due to a series of unfavorable supply shocks that pushed inflation higher, coupled with backward-looking inflation dynamics that translated those shocks into a higher embedded inflation (for example, Blinder, 1979). This explanation must confront at least two problems, however. First, there were important increases in inflation in the late 1960s and in parts of the 1970s that were not clearly associated with supply shocks (DeLong, 1997). Second, there have been large supply shocks since the 1970s, but they did not lead to renewed high inflation.[27]

---

[27] See Blinder and Rudd (2008) for a recent attempt to resuscitate the supply-shock view.

Another traditional explanation is that the high inflation was the result of political pressure on policymakers (for example, Weise, 2009). Again, however, this view has trouble explaining the timing. Recall that many countries were able to bring inflation down with no major changes in the institutions of monetary policy. Thus to explain why high inflation was particularly a phenomenon of the 1970s, this view must explain why politicians particularly pressured monetary policymakers in the 1970s or why monetary policymakers were particularly susceptible to such pressures in this period.

A fascinating theory of the Great Inflation is proposed by Orphanides (2003b). He considers applying the basic Taylor rule with Taylor's coefficients to the data on inflation and output and estimates of the natural rate of output that were available to policymakers in the 1970s. He finds that the resulting series for the interest rate corresponds fairly well with the actual series. In this view, the inflation of the 1970s was due not to policy being fundamentally different from what it is today, but only to the incorrect information about the economy's normal level of output (coupled with a failure of policymakers to recognize this possibility, and thus an overly high weight on the estimated output gap in determining policy).

Orphanides's explanation may be too simple, however. Policymakers in the 1970s often did not think about the economy using a natural-rate framework with a conventional view of the behavior of inflation. As a result, the measures from the 1970s that Orphanides interprets as estimates of the natural rate may have been intended as estimates of something more like the economy's maximum capacity. For example, Primiceri (2006) concludes from estimating a learning model that if 1970s policymakers had been confident that the natural-rate hypothesis was correct, their estimates of the natural rate of output would have been substantially below those they reported at the time.

This discussion of different frameworks for understanding the economy leads to the final candidate explanation of the Great Inflation: it may have resulted from beliefs on the part of policymakers about the economy that implied that it was appropriate to pursue inflationary policies (DeLong, 1997; Mayer, 1999; C. Romer and D. Romer, 2002; Nelson, 2005; Primiceri, 2006). At various times in the 1960s and 1970s, many economists and policymakers thought that there was a permanent output-inflation trade-off; that it was possible to have low unemployment and low inflation indefinitely; that tight monetary policy was of minimal value in lowering inflation; and that the costs of moderate inflation were low. To give one example, Samuelson and Solow (1960) described a downward-sloping Phillips curve as showing "the menu of choices between different degrees of unemployment and price stability," and went on to conclude, "To achieve the nonperfectionist's goal of high enough output to give us no more than

3 percent unemployment, the price index might have to rise by as much as 4 to 5 percent per year."[28]

This explanation must confront two major challenges. First, although one can bring various types of qualitative and quantitative evidence to bear on it, it is hard to subject it to definitive tests. Second, it can at best only partially address where the beliefs came from. For example, Primiceri is able to account for some of the changes in beliefs as endogenous responses to macroeconomic developments. But he takes the set of possible beliefs that policymakers could have adopted as given, and so leaves an important part of the Great Inflation unexplained.

# 11.9  Seignorage and Inflation

Inflation sometimes reaches extraordinarily high levels. The most extreme cases are *hyperinflations*, which are traditionally defined as periods when inflation exceeds 50 percent per month. The first modern hyperinflations took place in the aftermaths of World War I and World War II. Hyperinflations then disappeared for over a third of a century. But in the past 30 years, there have been hyperinflations in various parts of Latin America, many of the countries of the former Soviet Union, and several war-torn countries. The all-time record inflation took place in Hungary between August 1945 and July 1946. During this period, the price level rose by a factor of approximately $10^{27}$. In the peak month of the inflation, prices on average tripled daily. The hyperinflation in Zimbabwe in 2007–2009 was almost as large, with prices at times doubling daily. And many countries experience high inflation that falls short of hyperinflation: there are many cases where inflation was between 100 and 1000 percent per year for extended periods.

The existence of an output-inflation tradeoff cannot plausibly lead to hyperinflations, or even to very high rates of inflation that fall short of hyperinflation. By the time inflation reaches triple digits, the costs of inflation are almost surely large, and the real effects of monetary changes are almost surely small. No reasonable policymaker would choose to subject an economy to such large costs out of a desire to obtain such modest output gains.

The underlying cause of most, if not all, episodes of high inflation and hyperinflation is government's need to obtain seignorage—that is, revenue

---

[28] This view provides an alternative explanation of the link between central-bank independence and low inflation. Individuals who specialize in monetary policy are likely to be more knowledgeable about its effects. They are therefore likely to have more accurate estimates of the benefits and costs of expansionary policy. If incomplete knowledge of those costs and benefits leads to inflationary bias, increasing specialists' role in determining policy is likely to reduce that bias.

from printing money (Bresciani-Turroni, 1937; Cagan, 1956). Wars, falls in export prices, tax evasion, and political stalemate frequently leave governments with large budget deficits. And often investors do not have enough confidence that the government will honor its debts to be willing to buy its bonds. Thus the government's only choice is to resort to seignorage.[29]

This section therefore investigates the interactions among seignorage needs, money growth, and inflation. We begin by considering a situation where seignorage needs are sustainable, and see how this can lead to high inflation. We then consider what happens when seignorage needs are unsustainable, and see how that can lead to hyperinflation.

## The Inflation Rate and Seignorage

As in Section 11.1, assume that real money demand depends negatively on the nominal interest rate and positively on real income (see equation [11.1]):

$$\frac{M}{P} = L(i, Y)$$

$$= L(r + \pi^e, Y), \qquad L_i < 0, \qquad L_Y > 0. \tag{11.62}$$

Since we are interested in the government's revenue from money creation, $M$ should be interpreted as high-powered money (that is, currency and reserves issued by the government). Thus $L(\bullet)$ is the demand for high-powered money.

For the moment we focus on steady states. It is therefore reasonable to assume that output and the real interest rate are unaffected by the rate of money growth, and that actual inflation and expected inflation are equal. If we neglect output growth for simplicity, then in steady state the quantity of real balances is constant. This implies that inflation equals the rate of money growth. Thus we can rewrite (11.62) as

$$\frac{M}{P} = L(\bar{r} + g_M, \bar{Y}), \tag{11.63}$$

where $\bar{r}$ and $\bar{Y}$ are the real interest rate and output and where $g_M$ is the rate of money growth, $\dot{M}/M$.

The quantity of real purchases per unit time that the government finances from money creation equals the increase in the nominal money stock per

---

[29] An important question is how the political process leads to situations that require such large amounts of seignorage. The puzzle is that given the apparent high costs of the resulting inflation, there appear to be alternatives that all parties prefer. This issue is addressed in Section 12.7.

unit time divided by the price level:

$$S = \frac{\dot{M}}{P}$$

$$= \frac{\dot{M}}{M}\frac{M}{P} \qquad (11.64)$$

$$= g_M\frac{M}{P}.$$

Equation (11.64) shows that in steady state, real seignorage equals the growth rate of the money stock times the quantity of real balances. The growth rate of money is equal to the rate at which nominal money holdings lose real value, $\pi$. Thus, loosely speaking, seignorage equals the "tax rate" on real balances, $\pi$, times the amount being taxed, $M/P$. For this reason, seignorage revenues are often referred to as *inflation-tax* revenues.[30]

Substituting (11.63) into (11.64) yields

$$S = g_M L(\bar{r} + g_M, \overline{Y}). \qquad (11.65)$$

Equation (11.65) shows that an increase in $g_M$ increases seignorage by raising the rate at which real money holdings are taxed, but decreases it by reducing the tax base. Formally,

$$\frac{dS}{dg_M} = L(\bar{r} + g_M, \overline{Y}) + g_M L_1(\bar{r} + g_M, \overline{Y}), \qquad (11.66)$$

where $L_1(\bullet)$ denotes the derivative of $L(\bullet)$ with respect to its first argument.

The first term of (11.66) is positive and the second is negative. The second term approaches zero as $g_M$ approaches zero (unless $L_1(\bar{r} + g_M, \overline{Y})$ approaches minus infinity as $g_M$ approaches zero). Since $L(\bar{r}, \overline{Y})$ is strictly positive, it follows that $dS/dg_M$ is positive for sufficiently low values of $g_M$: at low tax rates, seignorage is increasing in the tax rate. It is plausible, however, that as $g_M$ becomes large, the second term eventually dominates; that is, it is reasonable to suppose that when the tax rate becomes extreme, further increases in the rate reduce revenue. The resulting "inflation-tax Laffer curve" is shown in Figure 11.7.

As a concrete example of the relation between inflation and steady-state seignorage, consider the money-demand function proposed by Cagan (1956). Cagan suggests that a good description of money demand, particularly at high inflation, is given by

$$\ln \frac{M}{P} = a - bi + \ln Y, \qquad b > 0. \qquad (11.67)$$

---

[30] Phelps (1973) shows that it is more natural to think of the tax rate on money balances as the nominal interest rate, since the nominal rate is the difference between the cost to agents of holding money (which is the nominal rate itself) and the cost to the government of producing it (which is essentially zero). In our framework, where the real rate is fixed and the nominal rate therefore moves one-for-one with inflation, this distinction is not important.

**FIGURE 11.7   The inflation-tax Laffer curve**

Converting (11.67) from logs to levels and substituting the resulting expression into (11.65) yields

$$S = g_M e^a \bar{Y} e^{-b(\bar{r}+g_M)}$$
$$= C g_M e^{-b g_M},$$

(11.68)

where $C \equiv e^a \bar{Y} e^{-b\bar{r}}$. The impact of a change in money growth on seignorage is therefore given by

$$\frac{dS}{dg_M} = C e^{-b g_M} - b C g_M e^{-b g_M}$$
$$= (1 - b g_M) C e^{-b g_M}.$$

(11.69)

This expression is positive for $g_M < 1/b$ and negative thereafter.

Cagan's estimates suggest that $b$ is between $\frac{1}{3}$ and $\frac{1}{2}$. This implies that the peak of the inflation-tax Laffer curve occurs when $g_M$ is between 2 and 3. This corresponds to a continuously compounded rate of money growth of 200 to 300 percent per year, which implies an increase in the money stock by a factor of between $e^2 \simeq 7.4$ and $e^3 \simeq 20$ per year. Cagan, Sachs and Larrain (1993), and others suggest that for most countries, seignorage at the peak of the Laffer curve is about 10 percent of GDP.

Now consider a government that has some amount of real purchases, $G$, that it needs to finance with seignorage. Assume that $G$ is less than the maximum feasible amount of seignorage, denoted $S^{\text{MAX}}$. Then, as Figure 11.8 shows, there are two rates of money growth that can finance the

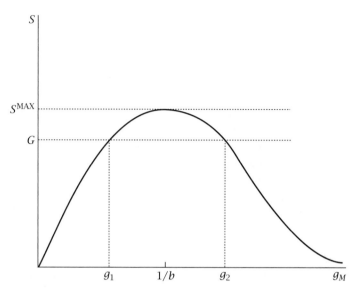

**FIGURE 11.8   How seignorage needs determine inflation**

purchases.[31] With one, inflation is low and real balances are high; with the other, inflation is high and real balances are low. The high-inflation equilibrium has peculiar comparative-statics properties; for example, a decrease in the government's seignorage needs raises inflation. Since we do not appear to observe such situations in practice, we focus on the low-inflation equilibrium. Thus the rate of money growth—and hence the rate of inflation—is given by $g_1$.

This analysis provides an explanation of high inflation: it stems from governments' need for seignorage. Suppose, for example, that $b = \frac{1}{3}$ and that seignorage at the peak of the Laffer curve, $S^{\text{MAX}}$, is 10 percent of GDP. Since seignorage is maximized when $g_M = 1/b$, (11.68) implies that $S^{\text{MAX}}$ is $Ce^{-1}/b$. Thus for $S^{\text{MAX}}$ to equal 10 percent of GDP when $b$ is $\frac{1}{3}$, $C$ must be about 9 percent of GDP. Straightforward calculations then show that raising 2 percent of GDP from seignorage requires $g_M \simeq 0.24$, raising 5 percent requires $g_M \simeq 0.70$, and raising 8 percent requires $g_M \simeq 1.42$. Thus moderate seignorage needs give rise to substantial inflation, and large seignorage needs produce high inflation.

---

[31] Figure 11.8 implicitly assumes that the seignorage needs are independent of the inflation rate. This assumption omits an important effect of inflation: because taxes are usually specified in nominal terms and collected with a lag, an increase in inflation typically reduces real tax revenues. As a result, seignorage needs are likely to be greater at higher inflation rates. This *Tanzi* (or *Olivera-Tanzi*) effect does not require any basic change in our analysis; we only have to replace the horizontal line at $G$ with an upward-sloping line. But the effect can be quantitatively significant, and is therefore important to understanding high inflation in practice.

## Seignorage and Hyperinflation

This analysis seems to imply that even governments' need for seignorage cannot account for hyperinflations: if seignorage revenue is maximized at inflation rates of several hundred percent, why do governments ever let inflation go higher? The answer is that the preceding analysis holds only in steady state. If the public does not immediately adjust its money holdings or its expectations of inflation to changes in the economic environment, then in the short run seignorage is always increasing in money growth, and the government can obtain more seignorage than the maximum sustainable amount, $S^{MAX}$. Thus hyperinflations arise when the government's seignorage needs exceed $S^{MAX}$ (Cagan, 1956).

Gradual adjustment of money holdings and gradual adjustment of expected inflation have similar implications for the dynamics of inflation. We focus on the case of gradual adjustment of money holdings. Specifically, assume that individuals' desired money holdings are given by the Cagan money-demand function, (11.67). In addition, continue to assume that the real interest rate and output are fixed at $\overline{r}$ and $\overline{Y}$: although both variables are likely to change somewhat over time, the effects of those variations are likely to be small relative to the effects of changes in inflation.

With these assumptions, desired real money holdings are

$$m^*(t) = Ce^{-b\pi(t)}. \tag{11.70}$$

The key assumption of the model is that actual money holdings adjust gradually toward desired holdings. Specifically, our assumption is

$$\frac{d\ln m(t)}{dt} = \beta[\ln m^*(t) - \ln m(t)], \tag{11.71}$$

or

$$\frac{\dot{m}(t)}{m(t)} = \beta[\ln C - b\pi(t) - \ln m(t)], \tag{11.72}$$

where we have used (11.70) to substitute for $\ln m^*(t)$. The idea behind this assumption of gradual adjustment is that it is difficult for individuals to adjust their money holdings; for example, they may have made arrangements to make certain types of purchases using money. As a result, they adjust their money holdings toward the desired level only gradually. The specific functional form is chosen for convenience. Finally, $\beta$ is assumed to be positive but less than $1/b$—that is, adjustment is assumed not to be too rapid.[32]

---

[32] The assumption that the change in real money holdings depends only on the current values of $m^*$ and $m$ implies that individuals are not forward-looking. A more appealing assumption, along the lines of the $q$ model of investment in Chapter 9, is that individuals consider the entire future path of inflation in deciding how to adjust their money holdings. This assumption complicates the analysis greatly without changing the implications for most of the issues we are interested in.

As before, seignorage equals $\dot{M}/P$, or $(\dot{M}/M)(M/P)$. Thus

$$S(t) = g_M(t)m(t). \tag{11.73}$$

Suppose that this economy is initially in steady state with the government's seignorage needs, $G$, less than $S^{\text{MAX}}$, and that $G$ then increases to a value greater than $S^{\text{MAX}}$. If adjustment is instantaneous, there is no equilibrium with positive money holdings. Since $S^{\text{MAX}}$ is the maximum amount of seignorage the government can obtain when individuals have adjusted their real money holdings to their desired level, the government cannot obtain more than this with instantaneous adjustment. As a result, the only possibility is for money to immediately become worthless and for the government to be unable to obtain the seignorage it needs.

With gradual adjustment, on the other hand, the government can obtain the needed seignorage through increasing money growth and inflation. With rising inflation, real money holdings are falling. But because the adjustment is not immediate, the real money stock exceeds $Ce^{-b\pi}$. As a result (as long as the adjustment is not too rapid), the government is able to obtain more than $S^{\text{MAX}}$. But with the real money stock falling, the required rate of money growth is rising. The result is explosive inflation.

To see the dynamics of the economy formally, it is easiest to focus on the dynamics of the real money stock, $m$. Since $m$ equals $M/P$, its growth rate, $\dot{m}/m$, equals the growth rate of nominal money, $g_M$, minus the rate of inflation, $\pi$; thus, $g_M$ equals $\dot{m}/m$ plus $\pi$. In addition, by assumption $S(t)$ is constant and equal to $G$. Using these facts, we can rewrite (11.73) as

$$G = \left[ \frac{\dot{m}(t)}{m(t)} + \pi(t) \right] m(t). \tag{11.74}$$

Equations (11.72) and (11.74) are two equations in $\dot{m}/m$ and $\pi$. At a point in time, $m(t)$ is given, and everything else in the equations is exogenous and constant. Solving the two equations for $\dot{m}/m$ yields

$$\frac{\dot{m}(t)}{m(t)} = \frac{\beta}{1-b\beta} \frac{b}{m(t)} \left[ \frac{\ln C - \ln m(t)}{b} m(t) - G \right]. \tag{11.75}$$

Our assumption that $G$ is greater than $S^{\text{MAX}}$ implies that the expression in brackets is negative for all values of $m$. To see this, note first that the rate of inflation needed to make desired money holdings equal $m$ is the solution to $Ce^{-b\pi} = m$; taking logs and rearranging the resulting expression shows that this inflation rate is $(\ln C - \ln m)/b$. Next, recall that if real money holdings are steady, seignorage is $\pi m$; thus the sustainable level of seignorage associated with real money balances of $m$ is $[(\ln C - \ln m)/b]m$. Finally, recall that $S^{\text{MAX}}$ is defined as the maximum sustainable level of seignorage. Thus the assumption that $S^{\text{MAX}}$ is less than $G$ implies that $[(\ln C - \ln m)/b]m$ is less than $G$ for all values of $m$. But this means that the expression in brackets in (11.75) is negative.

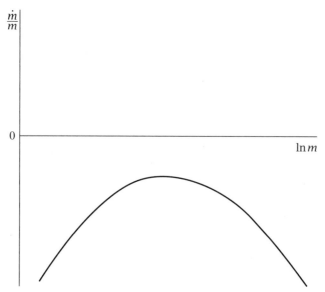

**FIGURE 11.9   The dynamics of the real money stock when seignorage needs are unsustainable**

Thus, since $b\beta$ is less than 1, the right-hand side of (11.75) is everywhere negative: regardless of where it starts, the real money stock continually falls. The associated phase diagram is shown in Figure 11.9.[33] With the real money stock continually falling, money growth must be continually rising for the government to obtain the seignorage it needs (see [11.73]). In short, the government can obtain seignorage greater than $S^{MAX}$, but only at the cost of explosive inflation.

This analysis can also be used to understand the dynamics of the real money stock and inflation under gradual adjustment of money holdings when $G$ is less than $S^{MAX}$. Consider the situation depicted in Figure 11.8. Sustainable seignorage, $\pi m^*$, equals $G$ if inflation is either $g_1$ or $g_2$; it is greater than $G$ if inflation is between $g_1$ and $g_2$; and it is less than $G$ otherwise. The resulting dynamics of the real money stock implied by (11.75) for this case are shown in Figure 11.10. The steady state with the higher real money stock (and thus with the lower inflation rate) is stable, and the steady state with the lower money stock is unstable.[34]

---

[33] By differentiating (11.75) twice, one can show that $d^2(\dot{m}/m)/(d\ln m)^2 < 0$, and thus that the phase diagram has the shape shown.

[34] Recall that this analysis depends on the assumption that $\beta < 1/b$. If this assumption fails, the denominator of (11.75) is negative. The stability and dynamics of the model are peculiar in this case. If $G < S^{MAX}$, the high-inflation equilibrium is stable and the low-inflation

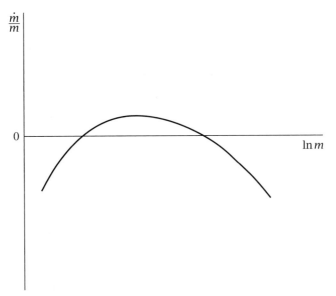

**FIGURE 11.10** **The dynamics of the real money stock when seignorage needs are sustainable**

This analysis of the relation between seignorage and inflation explains many of the main characteristics of high inflations and hyperinflations. Most basically, the analysis explains the puzzling fact that inflation often reaches extremely high levels. The analysis also explains why inflation can reach some level—empirically, in the triple-digit range—without becoming explosive, but that beyond this level it degenerates into hyperinflation. In addition, the model explains the central role of fiscal problems in causing high inflations and hyperinflations, and of fiscal reforms in ending them (Sargent, 1982).

Finally, the central role of seignorage in hyperinflations explains how the hyperinflations can end before money growth stabilizes. As described

---

equilibrium is unstable; if $G > S^{\mathrm{MAX}}$, $\dot{m} > 0$ everywhere, and thus there is explosive deflation. And with $G$ in either range, an increase in $G$ leads to a downward jump in inflation.

One interpretation of these results is that it is only because parameter values happen to fall in a particular range that we do not observe such unusual outcomes in practice. A more appealing interpretation, however, is that these results suggest that the model omits important features of actual economies. For example, if there is gradual adjustment of both real money holdings and expected inflation, then the stability and dynamics of the model are reasonable regardless of the adjustment speeds. More importantly, Ball (1993) and Cardoso (1991) argue that the assumption that $Y$ is fixed at $\overline{Y}$ omits crucial features of the dynamics of high inflations (though not necessarily of hyperinflations). Ball and Cardoso develop models that combine seignorage-driven monetary policy with the assumption that aggregate demand policies can reduce inflation only by temporarily depressing real output. They show that with this assumption, only the low-inflation steady state is stable. They then use their models to analyze various aspects of high-inflation economies.

in Section 11.1, the increased demand for real money balances after hyperinflations end is satisfied by continued rapid growth of the nominal money stock rather than by declines in the price level. But this leaves the question of why the public expects low inflation when there is still rapid money growth. The answer is that the hyperinflations end when fiscal and monetary reforms eliminate either the deficit or the government's ability to use seignorage to finance it, or both. At the end of the German hyperinflation of 1922–1923, for example, Germany's World War I reparations were reduced, and the existing central bank was replaced by a new institution with much greater independence. Because of reforms like these, the public knows that the burst of money growth is only temporary (Sargent, 1982).[35]

# Problems

**11.1.** Consider a discrete-time version of the analysis of money growth, inflation, and real balances in Section 11.1. Suppose that money demand is given by $m_t - p_t = c - b(E_t p_{t+1} - p_t)$, where $m$ and $p$ are the logs of the money stock and the price level, and where we are implicitly assuming that output and the real interest rate are constant (see [11.67]).

    (a) Solve for $p_t$ in terms of $m_t$ and $E_t p_{t+1}$.

    (b) Use the law of iterated projections to express $E_t p_{t+1}$ in terms of $E_t m_{t+1}$ and $E_t p_{t+2}$.

    (c) Iterate this process forward to express $p_t$ in terms of $m_t$, $E_t m_{t+1}$, $E_t m_{t+2}, \ldots$. (Assume that $\lim_{i \to \infty} E_t[\{b/(1 + b)\}^i p_{t+i}] = 0$. This is a no-bubbles condition analogous to the one in Problem 8.8.)

    (d) Explain intuitively why an increase in $E_t m_{t+i}$ for any $i > 0$ raises $p_t$.

    (e) Suppose expected money growth is constant, so $E_t m_{t+i} = m_t + gi$. Solve for $p_t$ in terms of $m_t$ and $g$. How does an increase in $g$ affect $p_t$?

**11.2.** Consider a discrete-time model where prices are completely unresponsive to unanticipated monetary shocks for one period and completely flexible thereafter. Suppose the IS equation is $y = c - ar$ and that the condition for equilibrium in the money market is $m - p = b + hy - ki$. Here $y$, $m$, and $p$ are the logs of output, the money supply, and the price level; $r$ is the real interest rate; $i$ is the nominal interest rate; and $a$, $h$, and $k$ are positive parameters.

    Assume that initially $m$ is constant at some level, which we normalize to zero, and that $y$ is constant at its flexible-price level, which we also normalize to zero. Now suppose that in some period—period 1 for simplicity—the

---

[35] To incorporate the effects of the knowledge that the money growth is temporary into our formal analysis, we would have to let the change in real money holdings at a given time depend not just on current holdings and current inflation, but on current holdings and the entire expected path of inflation. See n. 32.

monetary authority shifts unexpectedly to a policy of increasing $m$ by some amount $g > 0$ each period.

(a) What are $r$, $\pi^e$, $i$, and $p$ before the change in policy?

(b) Once prices have fully adjusted, $\pi^e = g$. Use this fact to find $r$, $i$, and $p$ in period 2.

(c) In period 1, what are $i$, $r$, $p$, and the expectation of inflation from period 1 to period 2, $E_1[p_2] - p_1$?

(d) What determines whether the short-run effect of the monetary expansion is to raise or lower the nominal interest rate?

**11.3.** Assume, as in Problem 11.2, that prices are completely unresponsive to unanticipated monetary shocks for one period and completely flexible thereafter. Assume also that $y = c - ar$ and $m - p = b + hy - ki$ hold each period. Suppose, however, that the money supply follows a random walk: $m_t = m_{t-1} + u_t$, where $u_t$ is a mean-zero, serially uncorrelated disturbance.

(a) Let $E_t$ denote expectations as of period $t$. Explain why, for any $t$, $E_t[E_{t+1}[p_{t+2}] - p_{t+1}] = 0$, and thus why $E_t m_{t+1} - E_t p_{t+1} = b + h\bar{y} - k\bar{r}$, where $\bar{y}$ and $\bar{r}$ are the flexible-price levels of $y$ and $r$.

(b) Use the result in part (a) to solve for $y_t$, $p_t$, $i_t$, and $r_t$ in terms of $m_{t-1}$ and $u_t$.

(c) Does the Fisher effect hold in this economy? That is, are changes in expected inflation reflected one-for-one in the nominal interest rate?

**11.4.** Suppose you want to test the hypothesis that the real interest rate is constant, so that all changes in the nominal interest rate reflect changes in expected inflation. Thus your hypothesis is $i_t = r + E_t \pi_{t+1}$.

(a) Consider a regression of $i_t$ on a constant and $\pi_{t+1}$. Does the hypothesis that the real interest rate is constant make a general prediction about the coefficient on $\pi_{t+1}$? Explain. (Hint: For a univariate OLS regression, the coefficient on the right-hand-side variable equals the covariance between the right-hand-side and left-hand-side variables divided by the variance of the right-hand-side variable.)

(b) Consider a regression of $\pi_{t+1}$ on a constant and $i_t$. Does the hypothesis that the real interest rate is constant make a general prediction about the coefficient on $i_t$? Explain.

(c) Some argue that the hypothesis that the real interest rate is constant implies that nominal interest rates move one-for-one with actual inflation in the long run—that is, that the hypothesis implies that in a regression of $i$ on a constant and the current and many lagged values of $\pi$, the sum of the coefficients on the inflation variables will be 1. Is this claim correct? (Hint: Suppose that the behavior of actual inflation is given by $\pi_t = \rho \pi_{t-1} + e_t$, where $e$ is white noise.)

**11.5.** **Policy rules, rational expectations, and regime changes.** (See Lucas, 1976, and Sargent, 1983.) Suppose that aggregate supply is given by the Lucas supply curve, $y_t = \bar{y} + b(\pi_t - \pi_t^e)$, $b > 0$, and suppose that monetary policy is determined by $m_t = m_{t-1} + a + \varepsilon_t$, where $\varepsilon$ is a white-noise disturbance. Assume that private agents do not know the current values of $m_t$ or $\varepsilon_t$; thus $\pi_t^e$ is the expectation of $p_t - p_{t-1}$ given $m_{t-1}, \varepsilon_{t-1}, y_{t-1}$, and $p_{t-1}$. Finally, assume that aggregate demand is given by $y_t = m_t - p_t$.

(a) Find $y_t$ in terms of $m_{t-1}$, $m_t$, and any other variables or parameters that are relevant.

(b) Are $m_{t-1}$ and $m_t$ all one needs to know about monetary policy to find $y_t$? Explain intuitively.

(c) Suppose that monetary policy is initially determined as above, with $a > 0$, and that the monetary authority then announces that it is switching to a new regime where $a$ is 0. Suppose that private agents believe that the probability that the announcement is true is $\rho$. What is $y_t$ in terms of $m_{t-1}$, $m_t$, $\rho$, $\bar{y}$, $b$, and the initial value of $a$?

(d) Using these results, describe how an examination of the money-output relationship might be used to measure the credibility of announcements of regime changes.

11.6. **Regime changes and the term structure of interest rates.** (See Mankiw and Miron, 1986.) Consider an economy where money is neutral. Specifically, assume that $\pi_t = \Delta m_t$ and that $r$ is constant at zero. Suppose that the money supply is given by $\Delta m_t = k \Delta m_{t-1} + \varepsilon_t$, where $\varepsilon$ is a white-noise disturbance.

(a) Assume that the rational-expectations theory of the term structure of interest rates holds (see [11.6]). Specifically, assume that the two-period interest rate is given by $i_t^2 = (i_t^1 + E_t i_{t+1}^1)/2$. $i_t^1$ denotes the nominal interest rate from $t$ to $t+1$; thus, by the Fisher identity, it equals $r_t + E_t[p_{t+1}] - p_t$.

  (i) What is $i_t^1$ as a function of $\Delta m_t$ and $k$? (Assume that $\Delta m_t$ is known at time $t$.)

  (ii) What is $E_t i_{t+1}^1$ as a function of $\Delta m_t$ and $k$?

  (iii) What is the relation between $i_t^2$ and $i_t^1$; that is, what is $i_t^2$ as a function of $i_t^1$ and $k$?

  (iv) How would a change in $k$ affect the relation between $i_t^2$ and $i_t^1$? Explain intuitively.

(b) Suppose that the two-period rate includes a time-varying term premium: $i_t^2 = (i_t^1 + E_t i_{t+1}^1)/2 + \theta_t$, where $\theta$ is a white-noise disturbance that is independent of $\varepsilon$. Consider the OLS regression $i_{t+1}^1 - i_t^1 = a + b(i_t^2 - i_t^1) + e_{t+1}$.

  (i) Under the rational-expectations theory of the term structure (with $\theta_t = 0$ for all $t$), what value would one expect for $b$? (Hint: For a univariate OLS regression, the coefficient on the right-hand-side variable equals the covariance between the right-hand-side and left-hand-side variables divided by the variance of the right-hand-side variable.)

  (ii) Now suppose that $\theta$ has variance $\sigma_\theta^2$. What value would one expect for $b$?

    (*iii*) How do changes in $k$ affect your answer to part (*ii*)? What happens to $b$ as $k$ approaches 1?

**11.7.** Consider the model of Section 11.4. Suppose, however, the aggregate supply equation, (11.16), is $\pi_t = \pi_{t-1} + \alpha(y_{t-1} - y_{t-1}^n) + \varepsilon_t^\pi$, where $\varepsilon^\pi$ is a white-noise shock that is independent of $\varepsilon^{IS}$ and $\varepsilon^Y$. How, if at all, does this change to the model change expression (11.27) for $q^*$?

**11.8.** Consider the system given by (11.41).

    (*a*) What does the system simplify to when $\phi_\pi = 1$? What are the eigenvalues of the system in this case? Suppose we look for self-fulfilling movements in $\tilde{y}$ and $\pi$ of the form $\pi_t = \lambda^t Z$, $\tilde{y}_t = c\lambda^t Z$, $|\lambda| \leq 1$. When $\phi_\pi = 1$, for what values of $\lambda$ and $c$ does such a solution satisfy (11.41)? Thus, what form do the self-fulfilling movements in inflation and output take?

    (*b*) Suppose $\phi_\pi$ is slightly (that is, infinitesimally) greater than 1. Are both eigenvalues inside the unit circle? What if $\phi_\pi$ is slightly less than 1?

    (*c*) Suppose $\kappa(1 - \phi_\pi)/\theta = -2(1 + \beta)$. What does the system simplify to in this case? What are the eigenvalues of the system in this case? Suppose we look for self-fulfilling movements in $\tilde{y}$ and $\pi$ of the form $\pi_t = \lambda^t Z$, $\tilde{y}_t = c\lambda^t Z$, $|\lambda| \leq 1$. When $\kappa(1 - \phi_\pi)/\theta = -2(1 + \beta)$, for what values of $\lambda$ and $c$ does such a solution satisfy (11.41)? Thus, what form do the self-fulfilling movements in inflation and output take?

**11.9. Money versus interest-rate targeting.** (Poole, 1970.) Suppose the economy is described by linear *IS* and money-market equilibrium equations that are subject to disturbances: $y = c - ai + \varepsilon_1$, $m - p = hy - ki + \varepsilon_2$, where $\varepsilon_1$ and $\varepsilon_2$ are independent, mean-zero shocks with variances $\sigma_1^2$ and $\sigma_2^2$, and where $a$, $h$, and $k$ are positive. Policymakers want to stabilize output, but they cannot observe $y$ or the shocks, $\varepsilon_1$ and $\varepsilon_2$. Assume for simplicity that $p$ is fixed.

    (*a*) Suppose the policymaker fixes $i$ at some level $\bar{i}$. What is the variance of $y$?

    (*b*) Suppose the policymaker fixes $m$ at some level $\bar{m}$. What is the variance of $y$?

    (*c*) If there are only monetary shocks (so $\sigma_1^2 = 0$), does money targeting or interest-rate targeting lead to a lower variance of $y$?

    (*d*) If there are only *IS* shocks (so $\sigma_2^2 = 0$), does money or interest-rate targeting lead to a lower variance of $y$?

    (*e*) Explain your results in parts (*c*) and (*d*) intuitively.

    (*f*) When there are only *IS* shocks, is there a policy that produces a variance of $y$ that is lower than either money or interest-rate targeting? If so, what policy minimizes the variance of $y$? If not, why not? (Hint: Consider the money-market equilibrium condition, $m - p = hy - ki$.)

**11.10. Uncertainty and policy.** (Brainard, 1967.) Suppose output is given by $y = x + (k + \varepsilon_k)z + u$, where $z$ is some policy instrument controlled by the government and $k$ is the expected value of the multiplier for that instrument. $\varepsilon_k$ and $u$ are independent, mean-zero disturbances that are unknown when the policymaker chooses $z$, and that have variances $\sigma_k^2$ and $\sigma_u^2$. Finally, $x$ is a disturbance that is known when $z$ is chosen. The policymaker wants to minimize $E[(y - y^*)^2]$.

(a) Find $E[(y - y^*)^2]$ as a function of $x$, $k$, $y^*$, $\sigma_k^2$, and $\sigma_u^2$.

(b) Find the first-order condition for $z$, and solve for $z$.

(c) How, if at all, does $\sigma_u^2$ affect how policy should respond to shocks (that is, to the realized value of $x$)? Thus, how does uncertainty about the state of the economy affect the case for "fine-tuning"?

(d) How, if at all, does $\sigma_k^2$ affect how policy should respond to shocks (that is, to the realized value of $x$)? Thus, how does uncertainty about the effects of policy affect the case for "fine-tuning"?

**11.11.** **The importance of using rather than saving your ammunition in the presence of the zero lower bound.** Suppose inflation is described by the accelerationist Phillips curve, $\dot{\pi}(t) = \lambda y(t), \lambda > 0$, and that output is determined by a simple $IS$ curve, $y(t) = -b[i(t) - \pi(t)]$, $b > 0$, Initially, the central bank is setting the nominal interest rate at a strictly positive level: $i(0) > 0$. Assume $-b[i(0) - \pi(0)] < 0 < b\pi(0)$.

(a) Suppose the central bank keeps $i$ constant at $i(0)$. Sketch the behavior of inflation and output over time.

(b) Suppose the central bank keeps $i$ constant at $i(0)$ until some time when $b\pi(t) < 0$, and then permanently reduces $i$ to zero. Sketch the behavior of inflation and output over time.

(c) Suppose the central bank permanently reduces $i$ to zero at $t = 0$. Sketch the behavior of inflation and output over time.

(d) Explain your results intuitively.

**11.12.** (Fischer and Summers, 1989.) Suppose inflation is determined as in Section 11.7. Suppose the government is able to reduce the costs of inflation; that is, suppose it reduces the parameter $a$ in equation (11.54). Is society made better or worse off by this change? Explain intuitively.

**11.13.** **A model of reputation and monetary policy.** (This follows Backus and Driffill, 1985, and Barro, 1986.) Suppose a policymaker is in office for two periods. Output is given by (11.53) each period. There are two possible types of policymaker, type 1 and type 2. A type-1 policymaker, which occurs with probability $p$, maximizes social welfare, which for simplicity is given by $(y_1 - a\pi_1^2/2) + (y_2 - a\pi_2^2/2)$, $a > 0$. A type-2 policymaker, which occurs with probability $1 - p$, cares only about inflation, and so sets inflation to zero in both periods. Assume $0 < p < \frac{1}{2}$.

(a) What value of $\pi_2$ will a type-1 policymaker choose?

(b) Consider a possible equilibrium where a type-1 policymaker always chooses $\pi_1 \neq 0$. In this situation, what is $\pi_2^e$ if $\pi_1 \neq 0$? What value of $\pi_1$ does a type-1 policymaker choose? What is the resulting level of social welfare over the two periods?

(c) Consider a possible equilibrium where a type-1 policymaker always chooses $\pi_1 = 0$. In this situation, what is $\pi_2^e$ if $\pi_1 = 0$? What is the resulting level of social welfare over the two periods?

(d) In light of your answers to (b) and (c), what is the equilibrium? In what sense, if any, does concern about reputation lower average inflation in this environment?

(e) In qualitative terms, what form do you think the equilibrium would take if $\frac{1}{2} < p < 1$? Why?

**11.14. The tradeoff between low average inflation and flexibility in response to shocks with delegation of control over monetary policy.** (Rogoff, 1985.) Suppose that output is given by $y = y^n + b(\pi - \pi^e)$, and that the social welfare function is $\gamma y - a\pi^2/2$, where $\gamma$ is a random variable with mean $\overline{\gamma}$ and variance $\sigma_\gamma^2$. $\pi^e$ is determined before $\gamma$ is observed; the policymaker, however, chooses $\pi$ after $\gamma$ is known. Suppose policy is made by someone whose objective function is $c\gamma y - a\pi^2/2$.

(a) What is the policymaker's choice of $\pi$ given $\pi^e$, $\gamma$, and $c$?

(b) What is $\pi^e$?

(c) What is the expected value of the true social welfare function, $\gamma y - a\pi^2/2$?

(d) What value of $c$ maximizes expected social welfare? Interpret your result.

**11.15.** In the model of delegation analyzed in Section 11.7, suppose that the policymaker's preferences are believed to be described by (11.59), with $a' > a$, when $\pi^e$ is determined. Is social welfare higher if these are actually the policymaker's preferences, or if the policymaker's preferences in fact match the social welfare function, (11.54)?

**11.16. Solving the dynamic-inconsistency problem through punishment.** (Barro and Gordon, 1983.) Consider a policymaker whose objective function is $\sum_{t=0}^{\infty} \beta^t(y_t - a\pi_t^2/2)$, where $a > 0$ and $0 < \beta < 1$. $y_t$ is determined by the Lucas supply curve, (11.53), each period. Expected inflation is determined as follows. If $\pi$ has equaled $\hat{\pi}$ (where $\hat{\pi}$ is a parameter) in all previous periods, then $\pi^e = \hat{\pi}$. If $\pi$ ever differs from $\hat{\pi}$, then $\pi^e = b/a$ in all later periods.

(a) What is the equilibrium of the model in all subsequent periods if $\pi$ ever differs from $\hat{\pi}$?

(b) Suppose $\pi$ has always been equal to $\hat{\pi}$, so $\pi^e = \hat{\pi}$. If the monetary authority chooses to depart from $\pi = \hat{\pi}$, what value of $\pi$ does it choose? What level of its lifetime objective function does it attain under this strategy? If the monetary authority continues to choose $\pi = \hat{\pi}$ every period, what level of its lifetime objective function does it attain?

(c) For what values of $\hat{\pi}$ does the monetary authority choose $\pi = \hat{\pi}$? Are there values of $a$, $b$, and $\beta$ such that if $\hat{\pi} = 0$, the monetary authority chooses $\pi = 0$?

**11.17. Other equilibria in the Barro–Gordon model.** Consider the situation described in Problem 11.16. Find the parameter values (if any) for which each of the following is an equilibrium:

(a) **One-period punishment.** $\pi_t^e$ equals $\hat{\pi}$ if $\pi_{t-1} = \pi_{t-1}^e$ and equals $b/a$ otherwise; $\pi = \hat{\pi}$ each period.

(b) **Severe punishment.** (Abreu, 1988, and Rogoff, 1987.) $\pi_t^e$ equals $\hat{\pi}$ if $\pi_{t-1} = \pi_{t-1}^e$, equals $\pi_0 > b/a$ if $\pi_{t-1}^e = \hat{\pi}$ and $\pi_{t-1} \neq \hat{\pi}$, and equals $b/a$ otherwise; $\pi = \hat{\pi}$ each period.

(c) **Repeated discretionary equilibrium.** $\pi = \pi^e = b/a$ each period.

**11.18.** Consider the situation analyzed in Problem 11.16, but assume that there is only some finite number of periods rather than an infinite number. What is the unique equilibrium? (Hint: Reason backward from the last period.)

**11.19. The political business cycle.** (Nordhaus, 1975.) Suppose the relationship between unemployment and inflation is described by $\pi_t = \pi_{t-1} - \alpha(u_t - \bar{u}) + \varepsilon_t^S$, $\alpha > 0$, where the $\varepsilon_t^S$'s are i.i.d., mean-zero disturbances with cumulative distribution function $F(\bullet)$. Consider a politician who takes office in period 1, taking $\pi_0$ as given, and who faces reelection at the end of period 2. The politician has complete control over $u_1$ and $u_2$, subject only to the limitations that there are minimum and maximum feasible levels of unemployment, $u_L$ and $u_H$. The politician is evaluated based on $u_2$ and $\pi_2$; specifically, he or she is reelected if and only if $\pi_2 + \beta u_2 < K$, where $\beta > 0$ and $K$ are exogenous parameters. If the politician wants to maximize the chances of reelection, what value of $u_1$ does he or she choose?

**11.20. Rational political business cycles.** (Alesina and Sachs, 1988.) Suppose the relationship between output and inflation is given by $y_t = \bar{y} + b(\pi_t - E_{t-1}\pi_t)$, where $b > 0$ and where $E_{t-1}$ denotes the expectation as of period $t - 1$. Suppose there are two types of politicians, "liberals" and "conservatives." Liberals maximize $a_L y_t - \pi_t^2/2$ each period, and conservatives maximize $a_C y_t - \pi_t^2/2$, where $a_L > a_C > 0$. Elected leaders stay in office for two periods. In period 0, it is not known who the leader in period 1 will be; it will be a liberal with probability $p$ and a conservative with probability $1 - p$. In period 1, the identity of the period-2 leader is known.

(a) Given $E_{t-1}\pi_t$, what value of $y_t$ will a liberal leader choose? What value will a conservative leader choose?

(b) What is $E_0\pi_1$? If a liberal is elected, what are $\pi_1$ and $Y_1$? If a conservative is elected, what are $\pi_1$ and $y_1$?

(c) If a liberal is elected, what are $\pi_2$ and $y_2$? If a conservative is elected, what are $\pi_2$ and $y_2$?

**11.21. Growth and seignorage, and an alternative explanation of the inflation-growth relationship.** (Friedman, 1971.) Suppose that money demand is given by $\ln(M/P) = a - bi + \ln Y$, and that $Y$ is growing at rate $g_Y$. What rate of inflation leads to the highest path of seignorage?

**11.22.** (Cagan, 1956.) Suppose that instead of adjusting their real money holdings gradually toward the desired level, individuals adjust their expectation of inflation gradually toward actual inflation. Thus equations (11.70) and (11.71) are replaced by $m(t) = C\exp(-b\pi^e(t))$ and $\dot{\pi}^e(t) = \beta[\pi(t) - \pi^e(t)], 0 < \beta < 1/b$.

(a) Follow steps analogous to the derivation of (11.75) to find an expression for $\dot{\pi}^e(t)$ as a function of $\pi(t)$.

(b) Sketch the resulting phase diagram for the case of $G > S^{\text{MAX}}$. What are the dynamics of $\pi^e$ and $m$?

(c) Sketch the phase diagram for the case of $G < S^{\text{MAX}}$.

# Chapter 12
# BUDGET DEFICITS AND FISCAL POLICY

The U.S. federal government has run large budget deficits since the early 1980s, interrupted only by a brief period of surpluses in the late 1990s. Furthermore, there is likely to be a sharp rise in the number of retirees relative to the number of workers in coming decades. In the absence of policy changes, the resulting increases in social security and health care spending are likely to lead to deficits that consistently exceed 10 percent of GDP within a few decades (Congressional Budget Office, 2009). Many other industrialized countries have run persistently large budget deficits in recent decades and face similar long-term budgetary challenges.

These large and persistent budget deficits have generated considerable concern. There is a widespread perception that they reduce growth, and that they could lead to a crisis of some type if they go on too long or become too large.

This chapter studies the sources and effects of budget deficits. Section 12.1 begins by describing the budget constraint a government faces and some accounting issues involving the budget; it also describes some of the specifics of the long-term fiscal outlook in the United States. Section 12.2 lays out a baseline model where the government's choice of whether to finance its purchases through taxes or borrowing has no impact on the economy. Section 12.3 discusses various reasons that this result of *Ricardian equivalence* may fail.

The next several sections consider the sources of budget deficits in settings where Ricardian equivalence fails. Section 12.4 presents the *tax-smoothing* model of deficits. The model's basic idea is that since taxes distort individuals' choices and since those distortions rise more than proportionally with the tax rate, steady moderate tax rates are preferable to alternating periods of high and low tax rates. As we will see, this theory provides an appealing explanation for such phenomena as governments' reliance on deficits to finance wars.

Tax-smoothing does not appear to account for large persistent deficits or for the pursuit of fiscal policies that are unlikely to be sustainable. The presentation therefore turns to the possibility that there is a systematic tendency for the political process to produce excessive deficits. Section 12.5 provides an introduction to the economic analysis of politics. Section 12.6 then presents a model where conflict over the composition of government spending can lead to excessive deficits, and Section 12.7 considers a model where excessive deficits can result from conflict over how the burden of reducing a deficit is to be divided among different groups.

Finally, Section 12.8 presents some empirical evidence about the sources of deficits, Section 12.9 discusses the costs of deficits, and Section 12.10 presents a simple model of debt crises.

For the most part, the chapter does not address the short-run impact of fiscal policy on the economy and the potential role of fiscal policy in stabilization. Until the recent crisis, there was considerable agreement that, largely because of the political barriers to the timely and sound use of fiscal policy, it was generally best to leave short-run stabilization to monetary policy. With the enormous economic downturn and the binding of the zero-lower-bound constraint on nominal interest rates for many central banks, however, there has been renewed interest in the use of fiscal tools for short-run stabilization. For example, almost every major advanced country employed discretionary fiscal stimulus in 2008 and 2009.

Much of the discussion of stabilization policy in Chapter 11, such as the analyses of the costs of inflation, whether there are substantial benefits to stabilization, and the possibility of dynamic inconsistency of optimal policy because of the importance of inflation expectations, carries over to fiscal policy. One important issue that is specific to fiscal policy concerns the possibility that reductions in taxes or increases in government purchases could fail to stimulate aggregate demand, or even be contractionary. We will touch on ways this could occur in Sections 12.2 and 12.4.

Finally, there is a rapidly growing literature investigating the short-run macroeconomic effects of fiscal policy empirically. Examples include Blanchard and Perotti (2002); Ramey (2009); C. Romer and D. Romer (2009a); Fisher (2009); Hall (2009); and Barro and Redlick (2009). The general consensus of this work is that fiscal policy normally operates in the expected direction: reductions in taxes and increases in government purchases raise output in the short run. However, once one turns to more specific issues, such as the magnitude and timing of the effects, their channels, and whether they depend strongly on the state of the economy, the work is still in its early stages.

# 12.1   The Government Budget Constraint

## The Basic Budget Constraint

To discuss fiscal policy, we need to know what the government can and cannot do. Thus we need to understand the government's budget constraint. A household's budget constraint is that the present value of its consumption must be less than or equal to its initial wealth plus the present value of its labor income. The government's budget constraint is analogous: the present value of its purchases of goods and services must be less than or equal to its initial wealth plus the present value of its tax receipts (net of transfer payments). To express this constraint, let $G(t)$ and $T(t)$ denote the government's real purchases and taxes at time $t$, and $D(0)$ its initial real debt outstanding. As in Section 2.2, let $R(t)$ denote $\int_{\tau=0}^{t} r(\tau)d\tau$, where $r(\tau)$ is the real interest rate at time $\tau$. Thus the value of a unit of output at time $t$ discounted back to time 0 is $e^{-R(t)}$. With this notation, the government's budget constraint is

$$\int_{t=0}^{\infty} e^{-R(t)} G(t)\, dt \le -D(0) + \int_{t=0}^{\infty} e^{-R(t)} T(t)\, dt. \qquad (12.1)$$

Note that because $D(0)$ represents debt rather than wealth, it enters negatively into the budget constraint.

The government's budget constraint does not prevent it from staying permanently in debt, or even from always increasing the amount of its debt. Recall that the household's budget constraint in the Ramsey model implies that the limit of the present value of its wealth cannot be negative (see Section 2.2). Similarly, the restriction the budget constraint places on the government is that the limit of the present value of its debt cannot be positive. That is, one can show that (12.1) is equivalent to

$$\lim_{s \to \infty} e^{-R(s)} D(s) \le 0. \qquad (12.2)$$

The derivation of (12.2) from (12.1) follows steps analogous to the derivation of (2.10) from (2.6).

If the real interest rate is always positive, a positive but constant value of $D$—so the government never pays off its debt—satisfies the budget constraint. Likewise, a policy where $D$ is always growing satisfies the budget constraint if the growth rate of $D$ is less than the real interest rate.

The simplest definition of the budget deficit is that it is the rate of change of the stock of debt. The rate of change in the stock of real debt equals the difference between the government's purchases and revenues, plus the real interest on its debt. That is,

$$\dot{D}(t) = [G(t) - T(t)] + r(t)D(t), \qquad (12.3)$$

where again $r(t)$ is the real interest rate at $t$.

The term in brackets on the right-hand side of (12.3) is referred to as the *primary deficit.* Considering the primary rather than the total deficit is often a better way of gauging how fiscal policy at a given time is contributing to the government's budget constraint. For example, we can rewrite the government budget constraint, (12.1), as

$$\int_{t=0}^{\infty} e^{-R(t)}[T(t) - G(t)]dt \geq D(0). \tag{12.4}$$

Expressed this way, the budget constraint states that the government must run primary surpluses large enough in present value to offset its initial debt.

## Some Measurement Issues

The government budget constraint involves the present values of the entire paths of purchases and revenues, and not the deficit at a point in time. As a result, conventional measures of either the primary or total deficit can be misleading about how fiscal actions are contributing to the budget constraint. Here we consider three examples.

The first example is inflation's effect on the measured deficit. The change in nominal debt outstanding—that is, the conventionally measured budget deficit—equals the difference between nominal purchases and revenues, plus the nominal interest on the debt. If we let $B$ denote the nominal debt, the nominal deficit is thus

$$\dot{B}(t) = P(t)[G(t) - T(t)] + i(t)P(t)D(t), \tag{12.5}$$

where $P$ is the price level and $i$ is the nominal interest rate. When inflation rises, the nominal interest rate rises for a given real rate. Thus interest payments and the deficit increase. Yet the higher interest payments are just offsetting the fact that the higher inflation is eroding the real value of debt. Nothing involving the behavior of the real stock of debt, and thus nothing involving the government's budget constraint, is affected.

To see this formally, we use the fact that, by definition, the nominal interest rate equals the real rate plus inflation.[1] This allows us to rewrite our expression for the nominal deficit as

$$\dot{B}(t) = P(t)[G(t) - T(t)] + [r(t) + \pi(t)]P(t)D(t)$$
$$= P(t)[\dot{D}(t) + \pi(t)D(t)], \tag{12.6}$$

---

[1] For simplicity, we assume there is no uncertainty, so there is no need to distinguish between expected and actual inflation.

where the second line uses equation (12.3) for the rate of change in real debt outstanding. Dividing both sides of (12.6) by the price level yields

$$\frac{\dot{B}(t)}{P(t)} = \dot{D}(t) + \pi(t)D(t). \tag{12.7}$$

That is, as long as the stock of debt is positive, higher inflation raises the conventional measure of the deficit even when it is deflated by the price level.

The second example is the sale of an asset. If the government sells an asset, it increases current revenue and thus reduces the current deficit. But it also forgoes the revenue the asset would have generated in the future. In the natural case where the value of the asset equals the present value of the revenue it will produce, the sale has no effect on the present value of the government's revenue. Thus the sale affects the current deficit but does not affect the budget constraint.

Our third example is an unfunded liability. An unfunded liability is a government commitment to incur expenses in the future that is made without provision for corresponding revenues. In contrast to an asset sale, an unfunded liability affects the budget constraint without affecting the current deficit. If the government sells an asset, the set of policies that satisfy the budget constraint is unchanged. If it incurs an unfunded liability, on the other hand, satisfying the budget constraint requires higher future taxes or lower future purchases.

The lack of a close relationship between the deficit and the budget constraint implies that the government can satisfy legislative or constitutional rules restricting the deficit without substantive changes. Asset sales and switches from conventional spending programs to unfunded liabilities are just two of the devices it can use to satisfy requirements about the measured deficit without any genuine changes in policies. Others include "off-budget" spending, mandates concerning private-sector spending, unrealistic forecasts, and shifts of spending among different fiscal years.

Despite this fact, the empirical evidence concerning the effects of deficit restrictions, though not clear-cut, suggests that they have genuine effects on government behavior.[2] If this is correct, it suggests that it is costly for governments to use devices that reduce measured deficits without substantive changes.

## Ponzi Games

The fact that the government's budget constraint involves the paths of purchases and revenues over the infinite future introduces another complication: there are cases where the government does not have to satisfy the

---

[2] Much of the evidence comes from the examination of U.S. states. See, for example, Poterba (1994).

constraint. An agent's budget constraint is not exogenous, but is determined by the transactions other agents are willing to make. If the economy consists of a finite number of individuals who have not reached satiation, the government does indeed have to satisfy (12.1). If the present value of the government's purchases exceeds the present value of its revenues, the limit of the present value of its debt is strictly positive (see [12.1] and [12.2]). And if there are a finite number of agents, at least one agent must be holding a strictly positive fraction of this debt. This means that the limit of the present value of the agent's wealth is strictly positive; that is, the present value of the agent's spending is strictly less than the present value of his or her after-tax income. This cannot be an equilibrium, because that agent can obtain higher utility by increasing his or her spending.

If there are infinitely many agents, however, this argument does not apply. Even if the present value of each agent's spending equals the present value of his or her after-tax income, the present value of the private sector's total spending may be less than the present value of its total after-tax income. To see this, consider the Diamond overlapping-generations model of Chapter 2. In that model, each individual saves early in life and dissaves late in life. As a result, at any time some individuals have saved and not yet dissaved. Thus the present value of private-sector income up to any date exceeds the present value of private-sector spending up to that date. If this difference does not approach zero, the government can take advantage of this by running a Ponzi scheme. That is, it can issue debt at some date and roll it over forever.

The specific condition that must be satisfied for the government to be able to run a Ponzi scheme in the Diamond model is that the equilibrium is dynamically inefficient, so that the real interest rate is less than the growth rate of the economy. Consider what happens in such a situation if the government issues a small amount of debt at time 0 and tries to roll it over indefinitely. That is, each period, when the previous period's debt comes due, the government just issues new debt to pay the principal and interest on the old debt. With this policy, the value of the debt outstanding grows at the real interest rate. Since the growth rate of the economy exceeds the real interest rate, the ratio of the value of the debt to the size of the economy is continually falling. Thus there is no reason the government cannot follow this policy. Yet the policy does not satisfy the conventional budget constraint: because the government is rolling the debt over forever, the value of the debt discounted to time 0 is constant, and so does not approach zero.

One implication is that debt issuance is a possible solution to dynamic inefficiency. By getting individuals to hold some of their savings in the form of government debt rather than capital, the government can reduce the capital stock from its inefficiently high level.

The possibility of a government Ponzi scheme is largely a theoretical curiosity, however. In the realistic case where the economy is not dynamically inefficient, Ponzi games are not feasible, and the government must satisfy the traditional present-value budget constraint.[3]

## Empirical Application: Is U.S. Fiscal Policy on a Sustainable Path?

The U.S. federal government has run large measured budget deficits over most of the past three decades. In addition, it has large pension and medical-care programs for the elderly, which it operates largely on a pay-as-you-go basis. In large part because of the impending retirement of the baby-boom generation, this means that it has an enormous quantity of unfunded liabilities. Because of these factors, there is significant concern about the United States's long-term fiscal prospects.

One way to assess the long-term fiscal situation is to ask whether it appears that if current policies were continued, the government would satisfy its budget constraint. A finding that the constraint would probably not be satisfied would suggest that changes in spending or taxes are likely to be needed.

Auerbach (1997) proposes a measure of the size of the expected fiscal imbalance. The first step is to project the paths of purchases, revenues, income, and interest rates under current policy. Auerbach's measure is then the answer to the following question: By what constant fraction of GDP would taxes have to be increased (or purchases decreased) for the budget constraint to be satisfied if the projections proved to be correct? That is, Auerbach's measure, $\Delta$, is the solution to

$$\int_{t=0}^{\infty} e^{-R^{\mathrm{PROJ}}(t)} \left[ \frac{T^{\mathrm{PROJ}}(t) - G^{\mathrm{PROJ}}(t)}{Y^{\mathrm{PROJ}}(t)} + \Delta \right] Y^{\mathrm{PROJ}}(t) = D(0). \qquad (12.8)$$

A larger value of $\Delta$ implies that larger adjustments in fiscal policy are likely to be needed.[4]

Auerbach and Gale (2009) apply this framework to U.S. fiscal policy. One problem in applying the framework is that it is not clear how one should

---

[3] The situation is more complicated under uncertainty. In an uncertain economy, the realized rate of return on government debt is sometimes less than the economy's growth rate even when the economy is not dynamically inefficient. As a result, an attempt to issue debt and roll it over forever has a positive probability of succeeding. See Bohn (1995), Ball, Elmendorf, and Mankiw (1998), and Blanchard and Weil (2001).

[4] Changing revenues or purchases would almost certainly affect the paths of $Y$ and $R$. For example, higher taxes might raise output and lower interest rates by increasing investment, or lower output through incentive effects. As a result, even in the absence of uncertainty, changing revenues or purchases at each point in time by fraction $\Delta$ of GDP would probably not bring the budget constraint exactly into balance. Nonetheless, $\Delta$ provides a useful summary of the magnitude of the imbalance under current policy.

define "current" policy. For example, all the tax cuts passed in 2001 and 2003 were officially scheduled to expire at the end of 2010. Yet this is not because Congress or the President actually wanted the cuts to expire completely, but only because some technical features of the budget process made the cuts easier to adopt with this feature. Thus it might be more useful to analyze the case where they do not expire. To give another example, a significant part of spending each year is allocated in that year's budget; any projection must make assumptions about this "discretionary" spending.

Auerbach and Gale begin with the assumptions and projections used by the Congressional Budget Office. They then modify those assumptions by assuming that the 2001 and 2003 tax cuts will not be allowed to expire on incomes less than $250,000 per year; that discretionary spending will remain approximately constant as a share of GDP (rather than constant in real terms); that the Alternative Minimum Tax (a feature of the tax code originally designed to prevent a small number of high-income taxpayers from greatly reducing their taxes) will be modified so that it does not affect an increasing number of taxpayers over time; and in several additional, less important ways. With these assumptions, they obtain an estimate of $\Delta$ of a stunning 9 percent. For comparison, in 2007, before the recession, federal revenues were about 19 percent of GDP. That is, Auerbach and Gale's point estimate is that current policies are extraordinarily far from satisfying the government budget constraint.

There are two main sources of this result. One is demographics. The first members of the baby boom are now about 65; over the next several decades, the ratio of working-age adults to individuals over 65 is likely to fall roughly in half. The other factor is technological progress in medicine. Technological advances have led to the development of many extremely valuable procedures and drugs. The result has been greatly increased medical spending, much of which is paid for by the government (particularly in the case of the elderly). Because of these developments, under current law federal spending on Social Security, Medicare, and Medicaid is projected to rise from about 10 percent of GDP today to almost 20 percent by 2060.

To make matters worse, Auerbach and Gale's estimates probably understate the extent of the expected fiscal imbalance. The government demographic projections underlying their calculations appear to understate the likely improvement in longevity among the elderly. The projections assume a sharp slowing of the increase in life expectancy, even though countries with life expectancies well above the United States's show no signs of such a slowing (Lee and Skinner, 1999). The assumptions about technological progress in medicine are also quite conservative.

In short, the best available evidence suggests that extremely large adjustments will be needed for the government to satisfy its budget constraint. The possible forms of the adjustments are spending reductions, tax increases, and implicit or explicit reneging on government debt through hyperinflation or default.[5]

An obvious issue is how much confidence one should have in these estimates. On the one hand, the estimates of the needed adjustments are based on projections over very long horizons; thus one might think they are very uncertain. On the other hand, the forces driving the estimates—demographics and technological progress in medicine—are simple and highly persistent; thus one might think we can estimate the size of the necessary adjustments fairly precisely.

It turns out that the first intuition is correct. Both the demographic changes and long-run growth in demography-adjusted medical spending are very uncertain. For example, Lee and Skinner (1999) estimate that the 95 percent confidence interval for the ratio of working-age adults to individuals over 65 in 2070 is [1.5, 4.0]. Even more importantly, trend productivity growth is quite uncertain and has enormous implications for the long-run fiscal outlook. For example, the combination of the productivity-growth rebound and unexpectedly high tax revenues for a given level of GDP caused estimates of the long-run fiscal imbalance to fall rapidly in the second half of the 1990s despite only small changes in policy. Although a confidence interval has not been estimated formally, it appears that it would not be surprising if the actual adjustments that are needed differ from our current estimates of $\Delta$ by 5 percentage points or more.

The fact that there is great uncertainty about the needed adjustments is not an argument for inaction, however. The needed adjustments could turn out to be either much smaller or much larger than our point estimate. The results from Section 8.6 about the impact of uncertainty on optimal consumption are helpful in thinking about how uncertainty affects optimal policy. If the costs of fiscal adjustment are quadratic in the size of the adjustment, uncertainty does not affect the expected benefits of, for example, an action that would reduce the government's debt today. And if the costs are more sharply curved than in the quadratic case, uncertainty raises the expected benefits of such an action.

# 12.2   The Ricardian Equivalence Result

We now turn to the effects of the government's choice between taxes and bonds. A natural starting point is the Ramsey–Cass–Koopmans model of Chapter 2 with lump-sum taxation, since that model avoids all complications involving market imperfections and heterogeneous households.

---

[5] The forces underlying the fiscal imbalance in the United States are present in most industrialized countries. As a result, most of those countries face long-term fiscal problems similar to those in the United States.

When there are taxes, the representative household's budget constraint is that the present value of its consumption cannot exceed its initial wealth plus the present value of its after-tax labor income. And with no uncertainty or market imperfections, there is no reason for the interest rate the household faces at each point in time to differ from the one the government faces. Thus the household's budget constraint is

$$\int_{t=0}^{\infty} e^{-R(t)} C(t)\, dt \leq K(0) + D(0) + \int_{t=0}^{\infty} e^{-R(t)}[W(t) - T(t)]\, dt. \qquad (12.9)$$

Here $C(t)$ is consumption at $t$, $W(t)$ is labor income, and $T(t)$ is taxes; $K(0)$ and $D(0)$ are the quantities of capital and government bonds at time 0.[6]

Breaking the integral on the right-hand side of (12.9) in two gives us

$$\int_{t=0}^{\infty} e^{-R(t)} C(t)\, dt$$
$$\leq K(0) + D(0) + \int_{t=0}^{\infty} e^{-R(t)} W(t)\, dt - \int_{t=0}^{\infty} e^{-R(t)} T(t)\, dt. \qquad (12.10)$$

It is reasonable to assume that the government satisfies its budget constraint, (12.1), with equality. If it did not, its wealth would be growing forever, which does not seem realistic.[7] With that assumption, (12.1) implies that the present value of taxes, $\int_{t=0}^{\infty} e^{-R(t)} T(t)\, dt$, equals initial debt, $D(0)$, plus the present value of government purchases, $\int_{t=0}^{\infty} e^{-R(t)} G(t)\, dt$. Substituting this fact into (12.10) gives us

$$\int_{t=0}^{\infty} e^{-R(t)} C(t)\, dt \leq K(0) + \int_{t=0}^{\infty} e^{-R(t)} W(t)\, dt - \int_{t=0}^{\infty} e^{-R(t)} G(t)\, dt. \qquad (12.11)$$

Equation (12.11) shows that we can express households' budget constraint in terms of the present value of government purchases without reference to the division of the financing of those purchases at any point in time between taxes and bonds. In addition, it is reasonable to assume that taxes do not enter directly into households' preferences; this is true in any model where utility depends only on such conventional economic goods as consumption, leisure, and so on. Since the path of taxes does not enter either households' budget constraint or their preferences, it does not

---

[6] In writing the representative household's budget constraint in this way, we are implicitly normalizing the number of households to 1. With $H$ households, all the terms in (12.9) must be divided by $H$: the representative household's consumption at $t$ is $1/H$ of total consumption, its initial wealth is $1/H$ of $K(0) + D(0)$, and so on. Multiplying both sides by $H$ then yields (12.9).

[7] Moreover, if the government attempts such a policy, an equilibrium may not exist if its debt is denominated in real terms. See, for example, Aiyagari and Gertler (1985) and Woodford (1995).

affect consumption. Likewise, it is government purchases, not taxes, that affect capital accumulation, since investment equals output minus the sum of consumption and government purchases. Thus we have a key result: only the quantity of government purchases, not the division of the financing of those purchases between taxes and bonds, affects the economy.

The result of the irrelevance of the government's financing decisions is the famous Ricardian equivalence between debt and taxes.[8] The logic of the result is simple. To see it clearly, think of the government giving some amount $D$ of bonds to each household at some date $t_1$ and planning to retire this debt at a later date $t_2$; this requires that each household be taxed amount $e^{R(t_2)-R(t_1)}D$ at $t_2$. Such a policy has two effects on the representative household. First, the household has acquired an asset—the bond—that has present value as of $t_1$ of $D$. Second, it has acquired a liability—the future tax obligation—that also has present value as of $t_1$ of $D$. Thus the bond does not represent "net wealth" to the household, and it therefore does not affect the household's consumption behavior. In effect, the household simply saves the bond and the interest the bond is accumulating until $t_2$, at which point it uses the bond and interest to pay the taxes the government is levying to retire the bond.

Traditional economic models, and many informal discussions, assume that a shift from tax to bond finance increases consumption. Traditional analyses of consumption often model consumption as depending just on current disposable income, $Y - T$. With this assumption, a bond-financed tax cut raises consumption. The Ricardian and traditional views of consumption have very different implications for many policy issues. For example, the United States cut taxes in 2008 and 2009. In the traditional view (which motivated the actions), the cuts are increasing consumption. But the Ricardian view implies that they are not. To give another example, the traditional view implies that the United States's sustained budget deficits over the past several decades increased consumption, and thus reduced capital accumulation and growth. But the Ricardian view implies that they had no effect on consumption or capital accumulation.

# 12.3   Ricardian Equivalence in Practice

An enormous amount of research has been devoted to trying to determine how much truth there is to Ricardian equivalence. There are, of course, many reasons that Ricardian equivalence does not hold exactly. The important question, however, is whether there are large departures from it.

---

[8] The name comes from the fact that this idea was first proposed (though ultimately rejected) by David Ricardo. See O'Driscoll (1977).

## The Entry of New Households into the Economy

One reason that Ricardian equivalence is likely not to be exactly correct is that there is turnover in the population. When new individuals are entering the economy, some of the future tax burden associated with a bond issue is borne by individuals who are not alive when the bond is issued. As a result, the bond represents net wealth to those who are currently living, and thus affects their behavior. This possibility is illustrated by the Diamond overlapping-generations model.

There are two difficulties with this objection to Ricardian equivalence. First, a series of individuals with finite lifetimes may behave as if they are a single household. In particular, if individuals care about the welfare of their descendants, and if that concern is sufficiently strong that they make positive bequests, the government's financing decisions may again be irrelevant. This result, like the basic Ricardian equivalence result, follows from the logic of budget constraints. Consider the example of a bond issue today repaid by a tax levied several generations in the future. It is possible for the consumption of all the generations involved to remain unchanged. All that is needed is for each generation, beginning with the one alive at the time of the bond issue, to increase its bequest by the size of the bond issue plus the accumulated interest; the generation living at the time of the tax increase can then use those funds to pay the tax levied to retire the bond.

Although this discussion shows that individuals can keep their consumption paths unchanged in response to the bond issue, it does not establish whether they do. The bond issue does provide each generation involved (other than the last) with some possibilities it did not have before. Because government purchases are unchanged, the bond issue is associated with a cut in current taxes. The bond issue therefore increases the lifetime resources available to the individuals then alive. But the fact that the individuals are already planning to leave positive bequests means that they are at an interior optimum in choosing between their own consumption and that of their descendants. Thus they do not change their behavior. Only if the requirement that bequests not be negative is a binding constraint—that is, only if bequests are zero—does the bond issue affect consumption. Since we have assumed that this is not the case, the individuals do not change their consumption; instead they pass the bond and the accumulated interest on to the next generation. Those individuals, for the same reason, do the same, and the process continues until the generation that has to retire the debt uses its additional inheritance to do so.

The result that intergenerational links can cause a series of individuals with finite lifetimes to behave as if they are a household with an infinite horizon is due to Barro (1974). It was this insight that started the debate on Ricardian equivalence, and it has led to a large literature on the reasons for

bequests and transfers among generations, their extent, and their implications for Ricardian equivalence and many other issues.[9]

The second difficulty with the argument that finite lifetimes cause Ricardian equivalence to fail is more prosaic. As a practical matter, lifetimes are
long enough that if the only reason that governments' financing decisions
matter is because lifetimes are finite, Ricardian equivalence is a good approximation (Poterba and Summers, 1987). For realistic cases, large parts
of the present value of the taxes associated with bond issues are levied
during the lifetimes of the individuals alive at the time of the issue. For example, Poterba and Summers calculate that most of the burden of retiring
the United States's World War II debt was borne by people who were already
of working age at the time of the war, and they find that similar results hold
for other wartime debt issues. Thus even in the absence of intergenerational
links, bonds represent only a small amount of net wealth.

Further, the fact that lifetimes are long means that an increase in wealth
has only a modest impact on consumption. For example, if individuals
spread out the spending of an unexpected wealth increase equally over the
remainder of their lives, an individual with 30 years left to live increases
consumption spending in response to a one-dollar increase in wealth only
by about three cents.[10] Thus it appears that if Ricardian equivalence fails
in a quantitatively important way, it must be for some reason other than an
absence of intergenerational links.

## Ricardian Equivalence and the Permanent-Income Hypothesis

The issue of whether Ricardian equivalence is a good approximation is
closely connected with the issue of whether the permanent-income hypothesis provides a good description of consumption behavior. In the permanent-
income model, only a household's lifetime budget constraint affects its
behavior; the time path of its after-tax income does not matter. A bond
issue today repaid by future taxes affects the path of after-tax income without changing the lifetime budget constraint. Thus if the permanent-income
hypothesis describes consumption behavior well, Ricardian equivalence is
likely to be a good approximation. But significant departures from the
permanent-income hypothesis can lead to significant departures from
Ricardian equivalence.

We saw in Chapter 8 that the permanent-income hypothesis fails in important ways: most households have little wealth, and predictable changes

---

[9] For a few examples, see Bernheim, Shleifer, and Summers (1985); Bernheim and Bagwell (1988); Wilhelm (1996); and Altonji, Hayashi, and Kotlikoff (1997).

[10] Of course, this is not exactly what an optimizing individual would do. See, for example, Problem 2.5.

in after-tax income lead to predictable changes in consumption. This suggests that Ricardian equivalence may fail in a quantitatively important way as well: if current disposable income has a significant impact on consumption for a given lifetime budget constraint, a tax cut accompanied by an offsetting future tax increase is likely to have a significant impact on consumption.

Exactly how failures of the permanent-income hypothesis can lead to failures of Ricardian equivalence depends on the sources of the failures. Here we consider two possibilities. The first is liquidity constraints. When the government issues a bond to a household to be repaid by higher taxes on the household at a later date, it is in effect borrowing on the household's behalf. If the household already had the option of borrowing at the same interest rate as the government, the policy has no effect on its opportunities, and thus no effect on its behavior. But suppose the household faces a higher interest rate for borrowing than the government does. If the household would borrow at the government interest rate and increase its consumption if that were possible, it will respond to the government's borrowing on its behalf by raising its consumption.[11]

Second, recall from Section 8.6 that a precautionary-saving motive can lead to failure of the permanent-income hypothesis, and that the combination of precautionary saving and a high discount rate can help account for buffer-stock saving and the large role of current disposable income in consumption choices. Suppose that these forces are important to consumption, and consider our standard example of a bond issue to be repaid by higher taxes in the future. If taxes were lump-sum, the bond issue would have no impact on the household's budget constraint. That is, the present value of the household's lifetime after-tax income in every state of the world would be unchanged. As a result, the bond issue would not affect consumption.

Since taxes are a function of income, however, in practice the situation is very different. The bond issue causes the household's future tax liabilities to be only slightly higher if its income turns out to be low. That is, the combination of the tax cut today and the higher future taxes raises the present value of the household's lifetime after-tax income in the event that

---

[11] This discussion treats liquidity constraints as exogenous. But when the government issues bonds today to be repaid by future taxes, households' future liabilities are increased. If lenders do not change the amounts and terms on which they are willing to lend, the chances that their loans will be repaid therefore fall. Thus rational lenders respond to the bond issue by reducing the amounts they lend. Indeed, if taxes are lump-sum, there are cases where the amount that households can borrow falls one-for-one with government bond issues, so that Ricardian equivalence holds even in the presence of liquidity constraints (Yotsuzuka, 1987). In the more realistic case when taxes are a function of income, however, bond issues have little impact on the amounts households can borrow, and so liquidity constraints cause Ricardian equivalence to fail. Intuitively, when a borrower fails to repay a loan, it is usually because his or her income turned out to be low. But if taxes are a function of income, this is precisely the case when the borrower's share of the tax liability associated with a bond issue is small.

its future income is low, and reduces it in the event that its future income is high. As a result, the household has little incentive to increase its saving. Instead it can indulge its high discount rate and increase its consumption, knowing that its tax liabilities will be high only if its income is high (Barsky, Mankiw, and Zeldes, 1986).

This discussion suggests that there is little reason to expect Ricardian equivalence to provide a good first approximation in practice. The Ricardian equivalence result rests on the permanent-income hypothesis, and the permanent-income hypothesis fails in quantitatively important ways. Nonetheless, because it is so simple and logical, Ricardian equivalence (like the permanent-income hypothesis) is a valuable theoretical baseline.

# 12.4   Tax-Smoothing

We now turn to the question of what determines the deficit. This section develops a model, due to Barro (1979), in which deficits are chosen optimally. Sections 12.5 through 12.7 consider reasons that deficits might be inefficiently high.

Barro focuses on the government's desire to minimize the distortions associated with obtaining revenue. The distortions created by taxes are likely to increase more than proportionally with the amount of revenue raised. In standard models, for example, a tax has no distortion costs to first order. Thus for low taxes, the distortion costs are approximately proportional to the square of the amount of revenue raised. When distortions rise more than proportionally with taxes, they are on average higher under a policy of variable taxes than under one with steady taxes at the same average level. Thus the desire to minimize distortions provides a reason for the government to smooth the path of taxes over time.

To investigate the implications of this observation, Barro considers an environment where the distortions associated with taxes are the only departure from Ricardian equivalence.[12] The government's problem is then similar to the problem facing a household in the permanent-income hypothesis. In the permanent-income hypothesis, the household wants to maximize its discounted lifetime utility subject to the constraint that the present value of its lifetime spending not exceed some level. Because there is diminishing marginal utility of consumption, the household chooses a smooth path for consumption. Here, the government wants to minimize the present value of distortions from raising revenue subject to the constraint that the present

---

[12] Alternatively, one can consider a setting where there are other departures from Ricardian equivalence but where the government can offset the other effects of its choice between bond and tax finance. For example, it can use monetary policy to offset any impact on overall economic activity, and tax incentives to offset any impact on the division of output between consumption and investment.

value of its revenues not be less than some level. Because there are increasing marginal distortion costs of raising revenue, the government chooses a smooth path for taxes. Our analysis of tax-smoothing will therefore parallel our analysis of the permanent-income hypothesis in Sections 8.1 and 8.2. As in those sections, we will first assume that there is certainty and then consider the case of uncertainty.

## Tax-Smoothing under Certainty

Consider a discrete-time economy. The paths of output ($Y$), government purchases ($G$), and the real interest rate ($r$) are exogenously given and certain. For simplicity, the real interest rate is constant. There is some initial stock of outstanding government debt, $D_0$. The government wants to choose the path of taxes ($T$) to satisfy its budget constraint while minimizing the present value of the costs of the distortions that the taxes create.[13] Following Barro, we will not model the sources of those distortion costs. Instead, we just assume that the distortion costs from raising amount $T_t$ are given by

$$C_t = Y_t f\left(\frac{T_t}{Y_t}\right), \qquad f(0) = 0, \qquad f'(0) = 0, \qquad f''(\bullet) > 0, \qquad (12.12)$$

where $C_t$ is the cost of the distortions in period $t$. This formulation implies that distortions relative to output are a function of taxes relative to output, and that they rise more than proportionally with taxes relative to output. These implications seem reasonable.

The government's problem is to choose the path of taxes to minimize the present value of the distortion costs subject to the requirement that it satisfy its overall budget constraint. Formally, this problem is

$$\min_{T_0, T_1, \dots} \sum_{t=0}^{\infty} \frac{1}{(1+r)^t} Y_t f\left(\frac{T_t}{Y_t}\right) \qquad \text{subject to}$$

$$\sum_{t=0}^{\infty} \frac{1}{(1+r)^t} T_t = D_0 + \sum_{t=0}^{\infty} \frac{1}{(1+r)^t} G_t. \qquad (12.13)$$

One can solve the government's problem either by setting up the Lagrangian and proceeding in the standard way, or by using perturbation arguments to find the Euler equation. We will use the second approach. Specifically, consider the government reducing taxes in period $t$ by a small amount $\Delta T$ and increasing taxes in the next period by $(1+r)\Delta T$, with taxes in all other

---

[13] For most of the models in this chapter, it is easiest to define $G$ as government purchases and $T$ as taxes net of transfers. Raising taxes to finance transfers involves distortions, however. Thus for this model, $G$ should be thought of as purchases plus transfers and $T$ as gross taxes. For consistency with the other models in the chapter, however, the presentation here neglects transfers and refers to $G$ as government purchases.

periods unchanged. This change does not affect the present value of its revenues. Thus if the government was initially satisfying its budget constraint, it continues to satisfy it after the change. And if the government's initial policy was optimal, the marginal impact of the change on its objective function must be zero. That is, the marginal benefit and marginal cost of the change must be equal.

The benefit of the change is that it reduces distortions in period $t$. Specifically, equation (12.13) implies that the marginal reduction in the present value of distortions, MB, is

$$\text{MB} = \frac{1}{(1+r)^t} Y_t f'\left(\frac{T_t}{Y_t}\right)\frac{1}{Y_t}\Delta T$$

$$= \frac{1}{(1+r)^t} f'\left(\frac{T_t}{Y_t}\right)\Delta T.$$

(12.14)

The cost of the change is that it increases distortion in $t+1$. From (12.13) and the fact that taxes in period $t+1$ rise by $(1+r)\Delta T$, the marginal increase in the present value of distortions, MC, is

$$\text{MC} = \frac{1}{(1+r)^{t+1}} Y_{t+1} f'\left(\frac{T_{t+1}}{Y_{t+1}}\right)\frac{1}{Y_{t+1}}(1+r)\Delta T$$

$$= \frac{1}{(1+r)^t} f'\left(\frac{T_{t+1}}{Y_{t+1}}\right)\Delta T.$$

(12.15)

Comparing (12.14) and (12.15) shows that the condition for the marginal benefit and marginal cost to be equal is

$$f'\left(\frac{T_t}{Y_t}\right) = f'\left(\frac{T_{t+1}}{Y_{t+1}}\right).$$

(12.16)

This requires

$$\frac{T_t}{Y_t} = \frac{T_{t+1}}{Y_{t+1}}.$$

(12.17)

That is, taxes as a share of output—the tax rate—must be constant. As described above, the intuition is that with increasing marginal distortion costs from higher taxes, smooth taxes minimize distortion costs. More precisely, because the marginal distortion cost per unit of revenue raised is increasing in the tax rate, a smooth tax rate minimizes distortion costs.[14]

---

[14] To find the level of the tax rate, one needs to combine the government's budget constraint in (12.13) with the fact that the tax rate is constant. This calculation shows that the tax rate equals the ratio of the present value of the revenue the government must raise to the present value of output.

## Tax-Smoothing under Uncertainty

Extending the analysis to allow for uncertainty about the path of government purchases is straightforward. The government's new problem is to minimize the expected present value of the distortions from raising revenue. Its budget constraint is the same as before: the present value of tax revenues must equal initial debt plus the present value of purchases.

We can analyze this problem using a perturbation argument like the one we used for the case of certainty. Consider the government reducing taxes in period $t$ by a small amount $\Delta T$ from the value it was planning to choose given its information available at that time. To continue to satisfy its budget constraint, it increases taxes in period $t + 1$ by $(1 + r) \Delta T$ from whatever value it would have chosen given its information in that period. If the government is optimizing, this change does not affect the expected present value of distortions. Reasoning like that we used to derive expression (12.16) shows that this condition is

$$f'\left(\frac{T_t}{Y_t}\right) = E_t\left[f'\left(\frac{T_{t+1}}{Y_{t+1}}\right)\right], \tag{12.18}$$

where $E_t[\bullet]$ denotes expectations given the information available in period $t$. This condition states that there cannot be predictable changes in the marginal distortion costs of obtaining revenue.

In the case where the distortion costs, $f(\bullet)$, are quadratic, equation (12.18) can be simplified. When $f(\bullet)$ is quadratic, $f'(\bullet)$ is linear. Thus, $E_t[f'(T_{t+1}/Y_{t+1})]$ equals $f'(E_t[T_{t+1}/Y_{t+1}])$. Equation (12.18) becomes

$$f'\left(\frac{T_t}{Y_t}\right) = f'\left(E_t\left[\frac{T_{t+1}}{Y_{t+1}}\right]\right), \tag{12.19}$$

which requires

$$\frac{T_t}{Y_t} = E_t\left[\frac{T_{t+1}}{Y_{t+1}}\right]. \tag{12.20}$$

This equation states that there cannot be predictable changes in the tax rate. That is, the tax rate follows a random walk.

## Implications

Our motive for studying tax-smoothing was to examine its implications for the behavior of deficits. The model implies that if government purchases as a share of output are a random walk, there will be no deficits: when purchases are a random walk, a balanced-budget policy causes the tax rate to follow a random walk. Thus the model implies that deficits and surpluses arise when the ratio of government purchases to output is expected to change.

The most obvious potential sources of predictable movements in the purchases-to-output ratio are wars and recessions. Military purchases are usually temporarily high during wars. Similarly, government purchases are roughly acyclical, and are thus likely to be temporarily high relative to output in recessions.[15] That is, wars and recessions are times when the expected future ratio of government purchases to output is less than the current ratio. Consistent with the tax-smoothing model, we observe that governments usually run deficits during these times. The literature testing the tax-smoothing model formally finds that the response of deficits to temporary military purchases and cyclical fluctuations is generally consistent with the model's qualitative predictions. Some tests find, however, that the model's specific quantitative predictions are rejected by the data.[16]

## Extensions

The basic analysis of tax-smoothing can be extended in many ways. Here we consider three.

First, Lucas and Stokey (1983) observe that the same logic that suggests that governments should smooth taxes suggests that they should issue contingent debt. Expected distortions are lower if government debt has a low real payoff when there is a positive shock to government purchases and a high real payoff when there is a negative shock. With fully contingent debt, the government can equalize tax rates across all possible states, and so the tax rate never changes (Bohn, 1990). This strong implication is obviously incorrect. But Bohn (1988) notes that the government can make the real payoff on its debt somewhat contingent on shocks to its purchases by issuing nominal debt and then following policies that produce high inflation in response to positive shocks to purchases and low inflation in response to negative shocks. Thus the desire to reduce distortions provides a candidate explanation of governments' use of nominal debt.

Second, the analysis can be extended to include capital accumulation. If the government can commit to its policies, a policy of no capital taxation is likely to be optimal or nearly so. Both capital taxes and labor-income taxes distort individuals' labor-leisure choice, since both reduce the overall

---

[15] Also, recall that the relevant variable for the model is in fact not government purchases, but purchases plus transfer payments (see n. 13). Transfers are generally countercyclical, and thus also likely to be temporarily high relative to output in recessions.

[16] Two early papers testing the tax-smoothing model are Barro's original paper (Barro, 1979) and Sahasakul (1986). For more recent tests, see Huang and Lin (1993) and Ghosh (1995), both of which build on the analysis of consumption and saving in Campbell (1987).

attractiveness of working. But the capital income tax also distorts individuals' intertemporal choices.[17]

Ex post, a tax on existing capital is not distortionary, and thus is desirable from the standpoint of minimizing distortions. As a result, a policy of no or low capital taxation is not dynamically consistent (Kydland and Prescott, 1977). That is, if the government cannot make binding commitments about future tax policies, it will not be able to follow a policy of no capital taxation. The prediction of optimal tax models with commitment that capital taxes are close to zero is clearly false. Whether this reflects imperfect commitment or something else is not known.

Third, the model of tax-smoothing we have been considering takes the path of government purchases as exogenous. But purchases are likely to be affected by their costs and benefits. A bond issue accompanied by a tax cut increases the revenue the government must raise in the future, and therefore implies that future tax rates must be higher. Thus the marginal cost of financing a given path of government purchases is higher. When the government is choosing its purchases by trading off the costs and benefits, it will respond to this change with a mix of higher taxes and lower purchases. The lower government purchases increase households' lifetime resources, and therefore increase their consumption. Thus recognizing that taxes are distortionary suggests another reason for there to be departures from Ricardian equivalence (Bohn, 1992).

## Expansionary Fiscal Contractions?

Under the assumptions that give rise to Ricardian equivalence, a tax cut raises expectations of the present value of future tax payments by exactly the amount of the cut. Households' lifetime resources are therefore unaffected, and so their consumption does not change. In the case of endogenous government purchases that we have just discussed, a tax cut raises expectations of future tax payments by less than the amount of the cut, and so consumption rises. This role of expectations raises the possibility that there are situations where an increase in taxes or a reduction in government purchases raises the overall demand for goods and services. Suppose, for example, that for some reason a small tax increase signals that there will be large reductions in future government purchases—and thus large future tax cuts. Then households will respond to the tax increase by raising their estimates of their lifetime resources; as a result, they may raise their consumption. Similarly, a small reduction in current government purchases could signal large future reductions, and therefore cause consumption to rise by more than the fall in government purchases.

---

[17] See Chari and Kehoe (1999) and Golosov, Kocherlakota, and Tsyvinski (2003) for more on optimal taxation when there is capital.

Surprisingly, these possibilities appear to be not just theoretical. Giavazzi and Pagano (1990) provide evidence that fiscal reform packages in Denmark and Ireland in the 1980s caused consumption booms, and they argue that effects operating through expectations were the reason. Similarly, Alesina and Perotti (1997) present evidence that deficit reductions coming from cuts in government employment and transfers are much more likely to be maintained than reductions coming from tax increases, and that, consistent with the importance of expectations, the first type of deficit reduction is often expansionary while the second type usually is not. The United States's deficit reduction policies in 1993 may be another example of an expansionary fiscal contraction; similarly, the tax cuts enacted in 2001 may have had a depressing effect on economic activity.

Work on the possibility of expansionary fiscal contractions has emphasized two channels other than households' beliefs about their lifetime tax liabilities through which expectations can cause fiscal tightenings to raise aggregate demand. The first is through interest rates. Since reductions in government purchases reduce interest rates, expectations of lower future purchases reduce expectations of future interest rates. Similarly, if Ricardian equivalence fails, expectations of higher future taxes reduce expectations of future interest rates. And, as described in Section 9.5, expectations of lower future interest rates raise current investment. They also raise the present value of households' lifetime after-tax incomes, and thus raise current consumption.

The second channel is through the supply side. Lower future taxes imply lower future distortions, and thus higher future income. Further, we will see in Sections 12.9 and 12.10 that a sufficiently high level of government debt can lead to a fiscal crisis, with a range of harmful effects on the economy. Fiscal contractions can lower estimates of the likelihood of a crisis, and thus again raise estimates of future income. And higher estimates of future income are likely to raise current consumption and investment (Bertola and Drazen, 1993; Perotti, 1999).

# 12.5   Political-Economy Theories of Budget Deficits

The tax-smoothing hypothesis provides a candidate explanation of variations in budget deficits over time, but not of a systematic tendency toward high deficits. In light of many countries' persistent deficits in the 1980s and 1990s and the evidence that many countries' current fiscal policies are far from sustainable, a great deal of research has been devoted to possible sources of *deficit bias* in fiscal policy. That is, this work asks whether there are forces that tend to cause fiscal policy to produce deficits that are on average inefficiently high.

Most of this work falls under the heading of *new political economy*. This is the field devoted to applying economic tools to politics. In this line of work, politicians are viewed not as benevolent social planners, but as individuals who maximize their objective functions given the constraints they face and the information they have. Likewise, voters are viewed as neither the idealized citizens of high-school civics classes nor the mechanical actors of much of political science, but as rational economic agents.

One strand of new political economy uses economic tools to understand issues that have traditionally been in the domain of political science, such as the behavior of political candidates and voters. A second strand—and the one we will focus on—is concerned with the importance of political forces for traditional economic issues. Probably the most important question tackled by this work is how the political process can produce inefficient outcomes. Even casual observation suggests that governments are sources of enormous inefficiencies. Officials enrich themselves at a cost to society that vastly exceeds the wealth they accumulate; regulators influence markets using highly distortionary price controls and command-and-control regulations rather than taxes and subsidies; legislatures and officials dole out innumerable favors to individuals and small groups, thereby causing large amounts of resources to be devoted to rent-seeking; high and persistent inflation and budget deficits are common; and so on. But a basic message of economics is that when there are large inefficiencies, there are large incentives to eliminate them. Thus the apparent existence of large inefficiencies resulting from the political process is an important puzzle.

Work in new political economy has proposed several candidate explanations for inefficient political outcomes. Although excessive deficits are surely not the largest inefficiency produced by the political process, many of those candidate explanations have been applied to deficit bias. Indeed, some were developed in that context. Thus we will examine work on possible political sources of deficit bias both for what it tells us about deficits and as a way of providing an introduction to new political economy.

One potential source of inefficient policies is that politicians and voters may not know what the optimal policies are. Individuals have heterogeneous understandings of economics and of the impacts of alternative policies. The fact that some individuals are less well informed than others can cause them to support policies that the best available evidence suggests are inefficient. For example, one reason that support for protectionist policies is so widespread is probably that comparative advantage is a sufficiently subtle idea that many people do not understand it.

Some features of policy are difficult to understand unless we recognize that voters' and policymakers' knowledge is incomplete. New ideas can influence policy only if the ideas were not already universally known. Similarly, passionate debates about the effects that alternative policies would have make sense only if individuals' knowledge is heterogeneous.[18]

Buchanan and Wagner (1977) argue that incomplete knowledge is an important source of deficit bias. The benefits of high purchases and low taxes are direct and evident, while the costs—the lower future purchases and higher future taxes that are needed to satisfy the government's budget constraint—are indirect and less obvious. If individuals do not recognize the extent of the costs, there will be a tendency toward excessive deficits. Buchanan and Wagner develop this idea, and argue that the history of views about deficits can explain why limited understanding of deficits' costs did not produce a systematic pattern of high deficits until the 1970s.

Although limited knowledge may be an important source of excessive deficits, it is not the only one. In some situations, there are policies that would clearly make almost everyone considerably better off. Perhaps the most obvious examples are hyperinflations. A hyperinflation's costs are large and obvious. Thus it is reasonably clear that a general tax increase or spending reduction that eliminated the need for seignorage, and thereby allowed the government to end the hyperinflation, would make the vast majority of the population better off. Yet hyperinflations often go on for months or years before fiscal policy is changed.

Most work in new political economy does not focus on limited knowledge. This may be because of cases like hyperinflations that are almost surely not due to limited knowledge. Or it may be because models of limited knowledge are not well developed and therefore lack an accepted framework that can be applied to new situations, or because it is difficult to derive specific empirical predictions from the models.

The bulk of work in new political economy focuses instead on the possibility that strategic interactions can cause the political process to produce outcomes that are known to be inefficient. That is, this work considers the possibility that the structure of the policymaking process and of the economy causes each participant's pursuit of his or her objective to produce inefficiency. The model of the dynamic inconsistency of low-inflation monetary policy we considered in Section 11.7 is an example of such a model. In that model, policymakers' inability to commit to low inflation, coupled with their incentive to inflate once expected inflation has been determined, leads to inefficient inflation.

In the case of fiscal policy, researchers have suggested two main ways that strategic interactions can produce inefficient deficits. First, an elected

---

[18] It is through ideas that economists' activities as researchers, teachers, and policy advisers affect policy. If observed outcomes, even highly undesirable ones, were the equilibria of interactions of individuals who were fully informed about the consequences of alternative policies, we could hope to observe and understand those outcomes but not to change them. But the participants do not know all there is to know about policies' consequences. As a result, by learning more about them through our research and providing information about them through our teaching and advising, economists can sometimes change outcomes.

leader may accumulate an inefficient amount of debt to restrain his or her successor's spending (Persson and Svensson, 1989; Tabellini and Alesina, 1990). A desire to restrain future spending is often cited in current debates over U.S. fiscal policy, for example.[19]

Second, disagreement about how to divide the burden of reducing the deficit can cause delay in fiscal reform as each group tries to get others to bear a disproportionate share (Alesina and Drazen, 1991). This mechanism is almost surely relevant to hyperinflations.[20]

Sections 12.6 and 12.7 present specific models that illustrate these potential sources of deficit bias. We will see that both models have serious limitations; neither one shows unambiguously that the mechanism it considers gives rise to deficit bias. Thus the purpose of considering the models is not to settle the issue of the sources of deficits. Rather, it is to show what is needed for these forces to produce deficit bias, and to introduce some general issues concerning political-economy models.[21]

# 12.6   Strategic Debt Accumulation

This section investigates a specific mechanism through which strategic considerations can produce inefficiently high deficits. The key idea is that current policymakers realize that future policy may be determined by individuals whose views they disagree with. In particular, it may be determined by individuals who prefer to expend resources in ways the current policymakers view as undesirable. This can cause current policymakers to want to restrain future policymakers' spending. If high levels of government debt reduce government spending, this provides current policymakers with a reason to accumulate debt.

---

[19] At least in the case of the United States, however, there is little evidence that tax reductions and debt accumulation have a substantial effect on future spending. See C. Romer and D. Romer (2009b).

[20] Another way that strategic interactions can lead to inefficient deficits is through signaling. Voters are likely to have better information about the taxes they pay and the government services they receive than about the government's overall fiscal position. If politicians differ in their ability to provide government services cheaply, this gives them an incentive to choose high spending and low taxes to try to signal that they are especially able (Rogoff, 1990).

[21] By focusing on deficit bias, the presentation omits some potential sources of inefficient political outcomes that have been proposed. For example, Shleifer and Vishny (1992, 1993, 1994) suggest reasons that politicians' pursuit of their self-interest and strategic interactions might give rise to rationing, corruption, and inefficient public employment; Coate and Morris (1995) argue that signaling considerations may explain why politicians often use inefficient pork-barrel spending rather than straightforward transfers to enrich their friends and allies; and Acemoglu and Robinson (2000, 2002) argue that inefficiency is likely to persist in situations where eliminating it would reduce the political power of individuals who are benefiting from the existing system.

This general idea has been formalized in two ways. Persson and Svensson (1989) consider disagreement about the *level* of government spending: conservative policymakers prefer low spending, and liberal policymakers prefer high spending. Persson and Svensson show that if the conservative policymakers' preference for low spending is strong enough, it causes them to run deficits.[22]

Persson and Svensson's model does not provide a candidate explanation of a general tendency toward deficits. In their model, the same forces that can make conservative policymakers run deficits can cause liberal ones to run surpluses. Tabellini and Alesina (1990) therefore consider disagreement about the *composition* of government spending. Their basic idea is that if each type of policymaker believes that the type of spending the other would undertake is undesirable, both types may have an incentive to accumulate debt.

This section presents Tabellini and Alesina's model and investigates its implications. One advantage of this model is that it goes further than most political-economy models in building the analysis of political behavior from microeconomic foundations. In many political-economy models, political parties' preferences and probabilities of being in power are exogenous. But in Tabellini and Alesina's analysis, electoral outcomes are derived from assumptions about the preferences and behavior of individual voters. As a result, their model illustrates some of the microeconomic issues that arise in modeling political behavior.

## Economic Assumptions

The economy lasts for two periods, 1 and 2. The real interest rate is exogenous and equal to zero. Government spending is devoted to two types of public goods, denoted $M$ and $N$. For concreteness, we will refer to them as military and nonmilitary goods.

The period-1 policymaker chooses the period-1 levels of the two goods, $M_1$ and $N_1$, and how much debt, $D$, to issue. The period-2 policymaker chooses $M_2$ and $N_2$, and must repay any debt issued in the first period.

For the amount of debt issued in the first period to affect what happens in the second, Ricardian equivalence must fail. The literature on strategic debt accumulation has emphasized two sources of failure. In Persson and Svensson's model, the source is the distortionary impact of taxation that is the focus of Barro's analysis of tax-smoothing. A higher level of debt means that the taxes associated with a given level of government purchases are greater. But if taxes are distortionary and the distortions have increasing marginal cost, this means that the marginal cost of a given level of

---

[22] Problem 12.10 develops this idea. It also investigates the possibility that the disagreement can cause conservative policymakers to run surpluses rather than deficits.

government purchases is greater when the level of debt is greater. As described in Section 12.4, this in turn implies that an optimizing policymaker will choose a lower level of purchases.

The second reason that debt can affect second-period policy is by affecting the economy's wealth. If the issue of debt in period 1 reduces wealth in period 2, it tends to reduce period-2 government purchases. The most plausible way for debt issue to reduce wealth is by increasing consumption. But modeling such an effect through liquidity constraints, a precautionary-saving motive, or some other mechanism is likely to be complicated. Tabellini and Alesina therefore take a shortcut. They assume that private consumption is absent, and that debt represents borrowing from abroad that directly increases period-1 government purchases and reduces the resources available in period 2.

Specifically, the economy's period-1 budget constraint is

$$M_1 + N_1 = W + D, \tag{12.21}$$

where $W$ is the economy's endowment each period and $D$ is the amount of debt the policymaker issues. Since the interest rate is fixed at zero, the period-2 constraint is

$$M_2 + N_2 = W - D. \tag{12.22}$$

The $M$'s and $N$'s are required to be nonnegative. Thus $D$ must satisfy $-W \le D \le W$.

A key assumption of the model is that individuals' preferences over the two types of public goods are heterogeneous. Specifically, individual $i$'s objective function is

$$V_i = E\left[\sum_{t=1}^{2} \alpha_i U(M_t) + (1 - \alpha_i)U(N_t)\right], \tag{12.23}$$

$$0 \le \alpha_i \le 1, \qquad U'(\bullet) > 0, \qquad U''(\bullet) < 0,$$

where $\alpha_i$ is the weight that individual $i$ puts on military relative to nonmilitary goods. That is, all individuals get nonnegative utility from both types of goods, but the relative contributions of the two types to utility differ across individuals.

The model's assumptions imply that debt issue is never desirable. Since the real interest rate equals the discount rate and each individual has diminishing marginal utility, smooth paths of $M$ and $N$ are optimal for all individuals. Debt issue causes spending in period 1 to exceed spending in period 2, and thus violates this requirement. Likewise, saving (that is, a negative value of $D$) is also inefficient.

## Political Assumptions

For the period-1 policymaker to have any possible interest in constraining the period-2 policymaker's behavior, there must be some chance that the second policymaker's preferences will differ from the first's. To allow for this possibility, Tabellini and Alesina assume that individuals' preferences are fixed, but that their participation in the political process is random. This makes the period-1 policymaker uncertain about what preferences the period-2 policymaker will have.

To describe the specifics of Tabellini and Alesina's assumptions about how the policymakers' preferences are determined, it is easiest to begin with the second period. Given the choice of military purchases, $M_2$, nonmilitary purchases are determined by the period-2 budget constraint: $N_2 = (W - D) - M_2$. Thus there is effectively only a single choice variable in period 2, $M_2$. Individual $i$'s utility in period 2 as a function of $M_2$ is

$$V_i^2(M_2) = \alpha_i U(M_2) + (1 - \alpha_i)U([W - D] - M_2). \tag{12.24}$$

Since $U''(\bullet)$ is negative, $V_i^{2\prime\prime}(\bullet)$ is also negative. This means that the individual's preferences over $M_2$ are *single-peaked*. The individual has some most preferred value of $M_2$, $M_{2i}^*$. For any two values of $M_2$ on the same side of $M_{2i}^*$, the individual prefers the one closer to $M_{2i}^*$. If $M_2^A < M_2^B < M_{2i}^*$, for example, the individual prefers $M_2^B$ to $M_2^A$. Figure 12.1 shows two examples of single-peaked preferences. In Panel (a), the individual's most preferred value is in the interior of the range of feasible values of $M_2$, $[0, W - D]$. In Panel (b), it is at an extreme.

The facts that there is only a single choice variable and that preferences are single-peaked means that the *median-voter theorem* applies to this situation. This theorem states that when the choice variable is a scalar and preferences are single-peaked, the median of voters' most preferred values of the choice variable wins a two-way contest against any other value of the choice variable. To understand why this occurs, let $M_2^{*\mathrm{MED}}$ denote the median value of $M_{2i}^*$ among period-2 voters. Now consider a referendum in which voters are asked to choose between $M_2^{*\mathrm{MED}}$ and some other value of $M_2$, $M_2^0$. For concreteness, suppose $M_2^0$ is greater than $M_2^{*\mathrm{MED}}$. Since $M_2^{*\mathrm{MED}}$ is the median value of $M_{2i}^*$, a majority of voters' $M_{2i}^*$'s are less than or equal to $M_2^{*\mathrm{MED}}$. And since preferences are single-peaked, all these voters prefer $M_2^{*\mathrm{MED}}$ to $M_2^0$. A similar analysis applies to the case when $M_2^0$ is less than $M_2^{*\mathrm{MED}}$.

Appealing to the median-voter theorem, Tabellini and Alesina assume that the political process leads to $M_2^{*\mathrm{MED}}$ being chosen as the value of $M_2$. Since $M_2^*$ is a monotonic function of $\alpha$—a voter with a higher value of $\alpha$ prefers a higher value of $M_2$—this is equivalent to assuming that $M_2$ is determined by the preferences of the individual with the median value of $\alpha$ among period-2 voters.

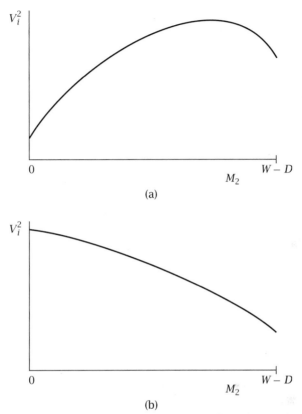

**FIGURE 12.1   Single-peaked preferences**

Tabellini and Alesina do not explicitly model the process through which the political process produces this result. Their idea, which is reasonable, is that the logic of the median-voter theorem suggests that $M_2^{*\mathrm{MED}}$ is a more plausible outcome than any other value of $M_2$. One specific mechanism that would lead to $M_2^{*\mathrm{MED}}$ being chosen is the one outlined by Downs (1957). Suppose that there are two candidates for office, that their objective is to maximize their chances of being elected, and that they can make commitments about the policies they will follow if elected. Suppose also that the distribution of the preferences of the individuals who will vote in period 2 is known before the election takes place. With these assumptions, the only Nash equilibrium is for both candidates to announce that they will choose $M_2 = M_2^{*\mathrm{MED}}$ if elected.

Little would be gained by explicitly modeling the randomness in voter participation and how it induces randomness in voters' median value of $M_2^*$. For example, these features of the model could easily be derived from assumptions about random costs of voting. Tabellini and Alesina therefore take the distribution of the $\alpha$ of the median voter in period 2, $\alpha_2^{\text{MED}}$, as exogenous.

Now consider the determination of policy in period 1. There are two complications relative to period 2. First, the set of policy choices is two-dimensional rather than one-dimensional. Specifically, we can think of the period-1 policymaker as choosing $M_1$ and $D$, with $N_1$ determined by the requirement that $M_1 + N_1 = W + D$. Second, in determining their preferences over $M_1$ and $D$, individuals must take into account their uncertainty about the period-2 policymaker's preferences. Tabellini and Alesina show, however, that a generalization of the median-voter theorem implies that the combination of $M_1$ and $D$ preferred by the individual with the median value of $\alpha$ among period-1 voters wins a two-way contest against any other combination. They therefore assume that policy in period 1 is determined by the individual with the median $\alpha$ among period-1 voters.

This completes the description of the model. Although we have described a general version, we will confine our analysis of the model to two specific cases that together show its main messages. In the first, the only values of $\alpha$ in the population are 0 and 1. In the second, the values of $\alpha$ are strictly between 0 and 1, and $U(\bullet)$ is logarithmic.

## Extreme Preferences

We begin with the case where the only types of individuals are ones who would like to spend all resources on military goods and ones who would like to spend all resources on nonmilitary goods. That is, there are only two values of $\alpha$ in the population, 0 and 1.

To solve a dynamic model with a fixed number of periods like this one, it is usually easiest to start with the last period and work backward. Thus we start with the second period. The period-2 median voter's choice problem is trivial: he or she devotes all the available resources to the purpose he or she prefers. Thus if $\alpha_2^{\text{MED}} = 1$ (that is, if the majority of the period-2 voters have $\alpha = 1$), $M_2 = W - D$ and $N_2 = 0$. And if $\alpha_2^{\text{MED}} = 0$, $M_2 = 0$ and $N_2 = W - D$. Let $\pi$ denote the probability that $\alpha_2^{\text{MED}} = 1$.

Now consider the first period. Suppose first that the period-1 median voter has $\alpha = 1$. Since nonmilitary goods give him or her no utility, he or she purchases only military goods. Thus $M_1 = W + D$ and $N_1 = 0$. The only question concerns the policymaker's choice of $D$. His or her expected utility as a function of $D$ is

$$U(W + D) + \pi U(W - D) + (1 - \pi)U(0). \tag{12.25}$$

The first term reflects the policymaker's utility from setting $M_1 = W + D$. The remaining two terms show the policymaker's expected period-2 utility. With probability $\pi$, policy in period 2 is determined by an individual with

$\alpha = 1$. In this case, $M_2 = W - D$, and so the period-1 policymaker obtains utility $U(W - D)$. With probability $1 - \pi$, policy is determined by someone with $\alpha = 0$. In this case $M_2 = 0$, and so the period-1 policymaker obtains utility $U(0)$.

Equation (12.25) implies that the first-order condition for the period-1 policymaker's choice of $D$ is

$$U'(W + D) - \pi U'(W - D) = 0. \qquad (12.26)$$

We can rearrange this as

$$\frac{U'(W + D)}{U'(W - D)} = \pi. \qquad (12.27)$$

This equation implies that if there is some chance that the period-2 policymaker will not share the period-1 policymaker's preferences (that is, if $\pi < 1$), $U'(W + D)$ must be less than $U'(W - D)$. Since $U''(\bullet)$ is negative, this means that $D$ must be positive. And when $\pi$ is smaller, the required gap between $U'(W + D)$ and $U'(W - D)$ is greater, and so $D$ is larger. That is, $D$ is decreasing in $\pi$.[23]

The analysis of the case where the median voter in period 1 has $\alpha = 0$ is very similar. In this case, $M_1 = 0$ and $N_1 = W + D$, and the first-order condition for $D$ implies

$$\frac{U'(W + D)}{U'(W - D)} = 1 - \pi. \qquad (12.28)$$

Here, it is the possibility of the period-2 median voter having $\alpha = 1$ that causes the period-1 policymaker to choose a positive deficit. When this probability is higher (that is, when $1 - \pi$ is lower), the deficit is higher.

## Discussion

This analysis shows that as long as $\pi$ is strictly between 0 and 1, both types of potential period-1 policymaker run a deficit. Further, the deficit is increasing in the probability of a change in preferences from the period-1 policymaker to the period-2 policymaker.

The intuition for these results is straightforward. There is a positive probability that the period-2 policymaker will devote the economy's resources to an activity that, in the view of the period-1 policymaker, simply wastes resources. The period-1 policymaker would therefore like to transfer resources from period 2 to period 1, where he or she can devote

---

[23] This discussion implicitly assumes an interior solution. Recall that $D$ cannot exceed $W$. If $U'(2W) - \pi U'(0)$ is positive, the period-1 policymaker sets $D = W$ (see [12.26]). Thus in this case the economy's entire second-period endowment is used to pay off debt. One implication is that if $\pi$ is sufficiently low that $U'(2W) - \pi U'(0)$ is positive, further reductions in $\pi$ do not affect $D$.

them to the activity he or she views as useful. Borrowing provides a way of doing this.

Thus, disagreement over the composition of government spending can give rise to inefficient budget deficits. One way to describe the inefficiency is to note that if the period-1 policymaker and potential period-2 policymakers can make binding agreements about their policies, they will agree to a deficit of zero: since any policy with a nonzero deficit is Pareto-inefficient, a binding agreement among all relevant players always produces no deficit. Thus one reason that deficits arise in the model is that individuals are assumed to be unable to make commitments about how they will behave if they are able to set policy in period 2.

Underlying policymakers' inability to make binding agreements about their behavior is individuals' inability to make binding commitments about their voting behavior. Suppose that the period-1 policymaker and a potential period-2 policymaker who prefer different types of purchases are able to make a legally enforceable agreement about what each will do if he or she is the period-2 policymaker. If they make such an agreement, neither will be chosen as the period-2 policymaker: the median period-2 voter will prefer an individual who shares his or her tastes and has not made any commitments to devote resources to both types of goods in period 2.

The assumption that voters cannot make commitments about their behavior is reasonable. In the economy described by the model, however, there are other mechanisms that would prevent the inefficiency. For example, the election of the period-2 policymaker could occur before the period-1 policymaker chooses $D$, and the two policymakers could be permitted to make a binding agreement. Or there could be a constitutional restriction on deficits.[24] But it seems likely that extending the model to incorporate shocks to the relative value of spending in different periods and of military and nonmilitary spending would cause such mechanisms to have disadvantages of their own.

It is also worth noting that Tabellini and Alesina's model does not address some of the basic issues that arise in almost any attempt to use economic tools to model politics. Here we mention two. The first, and more important, is why individuals participate in the political process at all. As many authors have observed, it is hard to understand broad political participation on the basis of conventional economic considerations. Most individuals' personal stake in political outcomes is no more than moderate. And if many individuals participate, each one's chance of affecting the outcome is extremely small. A typical voter's chance of changing the outcome of a U.S. presidential election, for example, is almost surely well below one in a million. This means that minuscule costs of participation are enough to keep broad participation from being an equilibrium (Olson, 1965; see also Ledyard, 1984, and Palfrey and Rosenthal, 1985).

---

[24] See Problem 12.8 for an analysis of deficit restrictions in the model.

The usual way of addressing this issue is simply to assume that individuals participate (as in Tabellini and Alesina's model), or to assume that they get utility from participation. This is a reasonable modeling strategy: it does not make sense to insist that we have a full understanding of the sources of political participation before we model the impact of that participation. At the same time, an understanding of why people participate may change the analysis of how they participate. For example, suppose a major reason for participation is that people get utility from being civic-minded, or from expressing their like or dislike of candidates' positions or actions even if those expressions have only a trivial chance of affecting the outcome (P. Romer, 1996). If such nonstandard considerations are important to people's decision to participate, they may also be important to their behavior conditional on participating. That is, the assumption that people who participate support the outcome that maximizes their conventionally defined self-interest may be wrong. Yet this is a basic assumption of Tabellini and Alesina's model (where people vote for the outcome that maximizes their conventionally defined utility), and of most other economic models of politics.[25]

The second issue is more specific to Tabellini and Alesina's model. In their model, individuals' preferences are fixed, and who is chosen as the policymaker may change between the two periods because participation may change. In practice, however, changes in individuals' preferences are important to changes in policymakers. In the United States, for example, the main reason for the election-to-election swings in the relative performances of the Democratic and Republican parties is not variation in participation, but variation in swing voters' opinions. In analyzing the consequences of changes in policymakers, it matters whether the changes stem from changes in participation or changes in preferences. Suppose, for example, the period-1 policymaker believes that the period-2 policymaker's preferences may differ from his or her own because of new information about the relative merits of the two types of purchases. Then the period-1 policymaker has no reason to restrain the period-2 policymaker's spending. Indeed, the period-1 policymaker may want to transfer resources from period 1 to period 2 so that more spending can be based on the new information.

## Logarithmic Utility

We now turn to the second case of Tabellini and Alesina's model that we will consider. Its key feature is that preferences are such that all potential policymakers devote resources to both military and nonmilitary goods. To see the issues clearly, we consider the case where the utility function $U(\bullet)$ is logarithmic. And to ensure that policymakers always devote resources to

---

[25] Green and Shapiro (1994) provide a strong critique of economic models of voting behavior.

both types of goods, we assume the median voters' $\alpha$'s are always strictly between 0 and 1.

As before, we begin by considering the second period. The problem of the period-2 median voter is to allocate the available resources, $W - D$, between military and nonmilitary goods to maximize his or her utility. Formally, the problem is

$$\max_{M_2} \alpha_2^{\text{MED}} \ln M_2 + \left(1 - \alpha_2^{\text{MED}}\right) \ln([W - D] - M_2), \tag{12.29}$$

where $\alpha_2^{\text{MED}}$ is the period-2 median voter's $\alpha$. Solving this problem yields the usual result that with logarithmic preferences, spending on each good is proportional to its weight in the utility function:

$$M_2 = \alpha_2^{\text{MED}}(W - D), \tag{12.30}$$

$$N_2 = (1 - \alpha_2^{\text{MED}})(W - D). \tag{12.31}$$

Now consider period 1. Our main interest is in the period-1 policymaker's choice of $D$. To find this, it turns out that we do not need to solve the policymaker's full maximization problem. Instead, it is enough to consider the utility the policymaker obtains from the period-2 policymaker's choices for a given value of $D$ and a given realization of $\alpha_2^{\text{MED}}$. Let $V_1^2(D,\alpha_2^{\text{MED}})$ denote this utility. It is given by

$$V_1^2\left(D,\alpha_2^{\text{MED}}\right) = \alpha_1^{\text{MED}} \ln\left[\alpha_2^{\text{MED}}(W - D)\right] \\ + \left(1 - \alpha_1^{\text{MED}}\right) \ln\left[\left(1 - \alpha_2^{\text{MED}}\right)(W - D)\right], \tag{12.32}$$

where we have used (12.30) and (12.31) to express $M_2$ and $N_2$ in terms of $\alpha_2^{\text{MED}}$ and $D$, and where $\alpha_1^{\text{MED}}$ is the period-1 policymaker's $\alpha$. Note that the values of $M_2$ and $N_2$ depend on the period-2 policymaker's preferences ($\alpha_2^{\text{MED}}$), but the weights assigned to them in the period-1 policymaker's utility depend on that policymaker's preferences ($\alpha_1^{\text{MED}}$).

Expanding expression (12.32) and simplifying gives us

$$V_1^2\left(D,\alpha_2^{\text{MED}}\right) = \alpha_1^{\text{MED}} \ln\left(\alpha_2^{\text{MED}}\right) + \alpha_1^{\text{MED}} \ln(W - D) + \left(1 - \alpha_1^{\text{MED}}\right) \ln\left(1 - \alpha_2^{\text{MED}}\right) \\ + \left(1 - \alpha_1^{\text{MED}}\right) \ln(W - D) \tag{12.33}$$

$$= \alpha_1^{\text{MED}} \ln\left(\alpha_2^{\text{MED}}\right) + \left(1 - \alpha_1^{\text{MED}}\right) \ln\left(1 - \alpha_2^{\text{MED}}\right) + \ln(W - D).$$

Equation (12.33) shows us that the period-2 policymaker's preferences affect the *level* of utility the period-1 policymaker obtains from what happens in period 2, but not the impact of $D$ on that utility. Since the realization of $\alpha_2^{\text{MED}}$ does not affect the impact of $D$ on the period-1 policymaker's utility from what will happen in period 2, it cannot affect his or her utility-maximizing choice of $D$. That is, the period-1 policymaker's choice of $D$ must be independent of the distribution of $\alpha_2^{\text{MED}}$. Since the choice of $D$ is the same for all distributions of $\alpha_2^{\text{MED}}$, we can just look at the case when $\alpha_2^{\text{MED}}$ will equal $\alpha_1^{\text{MED}}$ with certainty. But we know that in that case, the period-1 policymaker chooses $D = 0$. In short, with logarithmic preferences, there is no deficit bias in Tabellini and Alesina's model.

The intuition for this result is that when all potential policymakers devote resources to both types of goods, there is a disadvantage as well as an advantage to the period-1 policymaker to running a deficit. To understand this, consider what happens if the period-1 policymaker has a high value of $\alpha$ and the period-2 policymaker has a low one. The advantage of a deficit to the period-1 policymaker is that, as before, he or she devotes a large fraction of the resources transferred from period 2 to period 1 to a use that he or she considers more desirable than the main use the period-2 policymaker would put those resources to. That is, the period-1 policymaker devotes most of the resources transferred from period 2 to period 1 to military goods. The disadvantage is that the period-2 policymaker would have devoted some of those resources to military purchases in period 2. Crucially, because the low value of the period-2 policymaker's $\alpha$ causes period-2 military purchases to be low, the marginal utility of those additional military purchases to the period-1 policymaker is high. In the case of logarithmic utility, this advantage and disadvantage of a deficit just balance, and so the period-1 policymaker runs a balanced budget. In the general case, the overall effect can go either way. For example, in the case where the utility function $U(\bullet)$ is more sharply curved than logarithmic, the period-1 policymaker runs a surplus.

This analysis shows that with logarithmic preferences, disagreement over the composition of purchases does not produce deficit bias. Such preferences are a common case to consider. In the case of individuals' preferences concerning government purchases of different kinds of goods, however, we have little idea whether they are a reasonable approximation. As a result, it is difficult to gauge the likely magnitude of the potential deficit bias stemming from the mechanism identified by Tabellini and Alesina.

# 12.7 Delayed Stabilization

We now turn to the second source of inefficient deficits emphasized in work in new political economy. The basic idea is that when no single individual or interest group controls policy at a given time, interactions among policymakers can produce inefficient deficits. Specifically, inefficient deficits can persist because each policymaker or interest group delays agreeing to fiscal reform in the hope that others will bear a larger portion of the burden.

There are many cases that appear to fit this general idea. Hyperinflations are the clearest example. Given the enormous disruptions hyperinflations create, there is little doubt that there are policies that would make most people considerably better off. Yet reform is often delayed as interest groups

struggle over how to divide the burden of the reform. In the hyperinflations after World War I, the struggles were largely over whether higher taxes
should be levied on capital or labor. In modern hyperinflations, the struggles
are typically over whether the budget deficit will be closed by broad-based
tax increases or by reductions in government employment and subsidies.

Another example is U.S. fiscal policy in the 1980s and early 1990s. In this
period, there was general consensus among policymakers that the budget
deficit should be lower. Indeed, there was probably broad agreement that
deficit reduction through a mix of broad spending cuts and tax increases
was preferable to the status quo. But there was disagreement over the best
way to reduce the deficit. As a result, policymakers were unable to agree on
any specific set of measures.

The idea that conflict over how the burden of reform will be divided can
cause deficits to persist is due to Alesina and Drazen (1991). Their basic idea
is that each party in the bargaining may choose to delay to try to get a better
deal for itself. By accepting a continuation of the current situation rather
than agreeing to immediate reform, a group signals that it is costly for it
to accept reform. As a result, choosing to delay may improve the group's
expected outcome at the cost of worsening the overall economic situation.
The end result can be delayed stabilization even though there are policies
that are known to make everyone better off.

There is a natural analogy with labor strikes. Ex post, strikes are inefficient: both sides would have been better off if they had agreed to the
eventual settlement without a strike. Yet strikes occur. A leading proposed
explanation is that each side is uncertain of the other's situation, and that
there is no way for them to convey information to one another costlessly.
For example, a statement by management that a proposed settlement would
almost surely bankrupt the firm is not credible: if such a statement would
get management a better deal, management may make the statement even
if it is false. But if management chooses to suffer a strike rather than accept
the proposed settlement, this demonstrates that it views the settlement as
very costly (for example, Hayes, 1984).

In their model, Alesina and Drazen assume that a fiscal reform must be
undertaken, and that the burden of the reform will be distributed asymmet-
rically between two interest groups. Each group delays agreeing to accept
the larger share of the burden in the hope that the other will. The less costly
it is for a group to accept the larger share, the sooner it decides that the
benefits of conceding outweigh the benefits of continued delay. Formally,
Alesina and Drazen consider a *war of attrition*.

We will analyze a version of the variant of Alesina and Drazen's model
developed by Hsieh (2000). Instead of considering a war of attrition, Hsieh
considers a bargaining model based on the models used to analyze strikes.
One advantage of this approach is that it makes the asymmetry of the burden of reform the outcome of a bargaining process rather than exogenous. A
second advantage is that it is simpler than Alesina and Drazen's approach.

## Assumptions

There are two groups, which we will refer to as capitalists and workers. The two groups must decide whether to reform fiscal policy and, if so, how to divide the burden of reform. If there is no reform, both groups receive a payoff of zero. If there is reform, capitalists receive pretax income of $R$ and workers receive pretax income of $W > 0$. However, reform requires that taxes of amount $T$ be levied. $T$ is assumed to satisfy $0 < T < W$. We let $X$ denote the amount of taxes paid by capitalists. Thus after-tax incomes under reform are $R - X$ for capitalists and $(W - T) + X$ for workers.

A central assumption of the model is that $R$ is random and that its realization is known only to the capitalists. Specifically, it is distributed uniformly on some interval $[A, B]$, where $B \geq A \geq 0$. Together with our earlier assumptions, the assumption that $R$ cannot be less than $A$ implies that any choice of $X$ between 0 and $A$ necessarily makes both groups better off than without reform.

We consider a very simple model of the bargaining between the two groups. Workers make a proposal concerning $X$ to the capitalists. If the capitalists accept the proposal, fiscal policy is reformed. If they reject it, there is no reform. Both capitalists and workers seek to maximize their expected after-tax incomes.[26]

## Analyzing the Model

If the capitalists accept the workers' proposal, their payoff is $R - X$. If they reject it, their payoff is 0. They therefore accept when $R - X > 0$. Thus the probability that the proposal is accepted is the probability that $R$ is greater than $X$. Since $R$ is distributed uniformly on $[A, B]$, this probability is

$$P(X) = \begin{cases} 1 & \text{if } X \leq A \\ \dfrac{B - X}{B - A} & \text{if } A < X < B \\ 0 & \text{if } X \geq B. \end{cases} \tag{12.34}$$

The workers receive $(W - T) + X$ if their proposal is accepted and zero if it is rejected. Their expected payoff, which we denote $V(X)$, therefore equals

---

[26] There are many possible extensions of the bargaining model. In particular, it is natural to consider the possibility that rejection of a proposal delays reform, and therefore imposes costs on both sides, but leaves opportunities for additional proposals. In Hsieh's model, for example, there are two potential rounds of proposals. In many models of strikes, there are infinitely many potential rounds.

$P(X)[(W - T) + X]$. Using expression (12.34) for $P(X)$, this is

$$V(X) = \begin{cases} (W - T) + X & \text{if } X \leq A \\ \dfrac{(B - X)[(W - T) + X]}{B - A} & \text{if } A < X < B \\ 0 & \text{if } X \geq B. \end{cases} \qquad (12.35)$$

The workers will clearly not make a proposal that will be rejected for sure. Such a proposal has an expected payoff of zero, and there are other proposals that have positive expected payoffs. For example, since $W - T$ is positive by assumption, a proposal of $X = 0$—so the workers bear the entire burden of the reform—has a strictly positive payoff. One can also see that there is a cost but no benefit to the workers to reducing their proposed value of $X$ below the lowest level that they know will be accepted for sure.

Thus there are two possibilities. First, the workers may choose a value of $X$ in the interior of $[A,B]$, so that the probability of the capitalists accepting the proposal is strictly between 0 and 1. Second, the workers may make the least generous proposal that they know will be accepted for sure. Since the capitalists' payoff is $R - X$ and the lowest possible value of $R$ is $A$, this corresponds to a proposal of $X = A$.

To analyze workers' behavior formally, we use equation (12.35) to find the derivative of $V(X)$ with respect to $X$ for $A < X < B$. This yields

$$V'(X) = \frac{[B - (W - T)] - 2X}{B - A} \qquad \text{if } A < X < B. \qquad (12.36)$$

Note that $V''(X)$ is negative over this whole range. Thus if $V'(X)$ is negative at $X = A$, it is negative for all values of $X$ between $A$ and $B$. In this case, the workers propose $X = A$; that is, they make a proposal that they know will be accepted. Inspection of (12.36) shows that this occurs when $[B - (W - T)] - 2A$ is negative.

The alternative is for $V'(X)$ to be positive at $X = A$. In this case, the optimum is interior to the interval $[A, B]$, and is defined by the condition $V'(X) = 0$. From (12.36), this occurs when $[B - (W - T)] - 2X = 0$. Thus we have

$$X^* = \begin{cases} A & \text{if } [B - (W - T)] - 2A \leq 0 \\ \dfrac{B - (W - T)}{2} & \text{if } [B - (W - T)] - 2A > 0. \end{cases} \qquad (12.37)$$

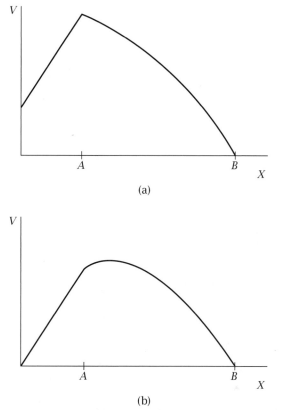

(a)

(b)

**FIGURE 12.2   Workers' expected payoff as a function of their proposal**

Equation (12.34) implies that the equilibrium probability that the proposal is accepted is

$$P(X^*) = \begin{cases} 1 & \text{if } [B - (W - T)] - 2A \leq 0 \\ \dfrac{B + (W - T)}{2(B - A)} & \text{if } [B - (W - T)] - 2A > 0. \end{cases} \quad (12.38)$$

Figure 12.2 shows the two possibilities for how workers' expected payoff, $V$, varies with their proposal, $X$. The expected payoff always rises one-for-one with $X$ over the range where the proposal is accepted for sure (that is, until $X = A$). And when $X \geq B$, the workers' proposal is rejected for sure, and so their expected payoff is 0. Panel (a) of the figure shows a case where the expected payoff is decreasing over the entire range $[A, B]$, so that the workers propose $X = A$. Panel (b) shows a case where the expected payoff is first increasing and then decreasing over the range $[A, B]$, so that the workers make a proposal strictly within this range.

## Discussion

The model's key implication is that $P(X^*)$ can be less than 1: the two sides can fail to agree on a reform package even though there are packages that both sides know are certain to make them both better off. The workers can offer to pay $T - A$ themselves and to have the capitalists pay $A$, in which case there is reform for sure and both sides are better off than without reform. But if the condition $[B - (W - T)] - 2A > 0$ holds, the workers make a less generous proposal, and thereby run a risk of no agreement being reached. Their motive in doing this is to improve their expected outcome at the expense of the capitalists'.

A necessary condition for the possibility of an inefficient outcome is that the workers do not know how much reform matters to capitalists (that is, that they do not know the value of $R$). To see this, consider what happens as $B - A$, the difference between the highest and lowest possible values of $R$, approaches zero. The condition for workers to make a proposal that is less than certain of being accepted is $[B - (W - T)] - 2A > 0$, or $(B - A) - [(W - T) + A] > 0$. Since $(W - T) + A$ is positive by assumption, this condition fails if $B - A$ is small enough. In this case, the workers propose $X = A$—the highest value of $X$ they are certain the capitalists will accept—and there is reform for sure.[27]

This analysis of delayed stabilization captures the fact that there are situations where policies persist despite the existence of alternatives that appear superior for the relevant parties. At the same time, the model has two important limitations. The first is that it assumes that there are only two types of individuals. Most individuals are not just capitalists or just workers, but receive both capital and labor income. Thus it may not be reasonable to assume that there is bargaining between exogenous groups with strongly opposed interests rather than, for example, a political process that converges quickly to the preferences of the median voter.

The second problem is that this analysis does not actually identify a source of deficit bias. It identifies a source of delay in policy changes of any type. Thus it identifies a reason for excessive deficits, once they arise, to persist. But it identifies an equally strong reason for excessive surpluses to persist if they arise. By itself, it provides no reason for us to expect deficits to be excessive on average.

One possibility is that other considerations cause the average level of deficits to be excessive, and that the considerations identified by Alesina and Drazen cause inertia in departures of the deficit from its average level. In such a situation, inertia in response to a shock that moves the deficit above its usual level is very socially costly, since the deficit is too high to

---

[27] One implication of this discussion is that as $B - A$ approaches zero, all the surplus from the reform accrues to the workers. This is an artifact of the assumption that they are able to make a take-it-or-leave-it proposal to the capitalists.

start with. Inertia in response to a shock that moves the deficit below its average level, on the other hand, is desirable (and therefore attracts less attention), since the deficit has moved closer to its optimal level.[28]

Finally, Alesina and Drazen's analysis has implications for the role of crises in spurring reform. An old and appealing idea is that a crisis—specifically, a situation where continuation of the status quo would be very harmful—can actually be beneficial by bringing about reforms that would not occur otherwise. In a model like Alesina and Drazen's or Hsieh's, increasing the cost of failing to reform may make the parties alter their behavior in ways that make reform more likely. Whether this effect is strong enough to make the overall effect of a crisis beneficial is not obvious. This issue is investigated by Drazen and Grilli (1993) and by Hsieh, and in Problem 12.12. It turns out that there are indeed cases where a crisis improves expected welfare.

A corollary of this observation is that well-intentioned foreign aid to ease the suffering caused by a crisis can be counterproductive. Aid that increases the incentives for reform, on the other hand, may be more desirable. This idea is investigated by Hsieh and in Problem 12.13.

# 12.8 Empirical Application: Politics and Deficits in Industrialized Countries

Political-economy theories of fiscal policy suggest that political institutions and outcomes may be important to budget deficits. Beginning with Roubini and Sachs (1989) and Grilli, Masciandaro, and Tabellini (1991), various researchers have therefore examined the relationship between political variables and deficits. Papers in this area generally do not try to derive sharp predictions from political-economy theories and test them formally. Rather, they try to identify broad patterns or stylized facts in the data and relate them informally to different views of the sources of deficits.

## Preliminary Findings

There is considerable variation in the behavior of deficits. In some countries, such as Belgium and Italy, debt-to-GDP ratios rose steadily for extended

---

[28] U.S. fiscal policy in 1999–2000 appears to have fit this pattern. A series of favorable shocks had produced projected surpluses. Although the best available projections suggested that increases in the surpluses were needed for fiscal policy to be sustainable, there was widespread support among policymakers for policy changes that would reduce the surpluses. Disagreement about the specifics of those changes made reaching an agreement difficult, and so no significant policy changes were made until the 2000 election changed the balance of political power. Thus there appears to have been persistence of the departure of the deficit away from a high level.

periods to very high levels. In others, such as Australia and Finland, debt-to-GDP ratios have been consistently low. And other countries display more complicated patterns. In addition, debt-to-GDP ratios were falling in most countries until the early 1970s, generally rising from then until the mid-1990s, and generally falling since then until the recent crisis.

This diversity of behavior is modest evidence in favor of political-economy models of deficits. For example, it is hard to believe that economic fundamentals are so different between Belgium and the Netherlands as to warrant a gap of 50 percentage points in their debt-to-GDP ratios. If purely economic forces cannot account for variations in deficits, other forces must be at work. Political forces are one candidate.

Further, Roubini and Sachs (1989) show that the behavior of deficits appears to depart in an important way from tax-smoothing. They consider 15 OECD countries over the period 1960–1986. In every country they consider, the tax-to-GDP ratio had an upward trend, and in most cases the trend was quantitatively and statistically significant. This is what one would expect with deficit bias. The government sets taxes too low relative to what tax-smoothing requires, and as a result starts to accumulate debt. As the debt mounts, the government must raise taxes to satisfy its budget constraint. With continuing deficit bias, the tax rate is always below the value that would be expected to satisfy the budget constraint if it were kept constant, and so there are repeated tax increases. Thus the finding of an upward trend in tax rates also supports political-economy models.

## Weak Governments and Budget Deficits

We now turn to results that specifically concern political factors. The central finding of this literature, due to Roubini and Sachs, is that there are systematic differences in the political characteristics of countries that ran large deficits in the decade after the first oil price shocks in 1973 and countries that did not. Countries in the first group had governments that were short-lived and often took the form of multiparty coalitions, while countries in the second group had longer-lived, stronger governments. To test the strength of this pattern, Roubini and Sachs regress the deficit as a share of GDP on a set of economic variables and a political variable measuring how weak the government is. Specifically, their political variable measures the extent to which policy is not controlled by a single party; it ranges from 0 for a presidential or one-party-majority government to 3 for a minority government. Roubini and Sachs's regression takes the form

$$D_{it} = a + b\,\text{WEAK}_{it} + c'X_{it} + e_{it}. \tag{12.39}$$

$D_{it}$ is the budget deficit in country $i$ in year $t$ as a share of GDP, $\text{WEAK}_{it}$ is the political variable, and $X_{it}$ is a vector of other variables. The resulting estimate of $b$ is 0.4, with a standard error of 0.14. That is, the point estimate suggests that a change in the political variable from 0 to 3 is associated with an increase in the deficit-to-GDP ratio of 1.2 percentage points, which is substantial.

The theory that is most suggestive of the importance of weak governments is Alesina and Drazen's: their model implies that inefficiency arises because no single interest group or party is setting policy. But recall that the model does not imply that weak governments cause high deficits; rather, it implies that weak governments cause persistence of existing deficits or surpluses. This prediction can be tested by including an interaction term between the political variable and the lagged deficit in the regression. That is, one can modify equation (12.39) to

$$D_{it} = a + b_1 \text{WEAK}_{it} + b_2 D_{i,t-1} + b_3 D_{i,t-1} \text{WEAK}_{it} + c' X_{it} + e_{it}. \qquad (12.40)$$

With this specification, the persistence of the deficit from one year to the next, $\partial D_{it}/\partial D_{i,t-1}$, is $b_2 + b_3 \text{WEAK}_{it}$. Persistence is $b_2$ under the strongest governments ($\text{WEAK}_{it} = 0$) and $b_2 + 3b_3$ under the weakest ($\text{WEAK}_{it} = 3$). Thus Alesina and Drazen's model predicts $b_3 > 0$.

In estimating a regression with an interaction term, it is almost always important to also include the interacted variables individually. This is done by the inclusion of $b_1 \text{WEAK}_{it}$ and $b_2 D_{i,t-1}$ in (12.40). If $b_2 D_{i,t-1}$ is excluded, for example, the persistence of the deficit is $b_3 \text{WEAK}_{it}$. Thus the specification without $b_2 D_{i,t-1}$ forces persistence to equal zero when $\text{WEAK}_{it}$ equals zero. This is not a reasonable restriction to impose. Further, imposing it can bias the estimate of the main parameter of interest, $b_3$. For example, suppose that deficits are persistent but that their persistence does not vary with the strength of the government. Thus the truth is $b_2 > 0$ and $b_3 = 0$. In a regression without $b_2 D_{i,t-1}$, the best fit to the data is obtained with a positive value of $\hat{b}_3$, since this at least allows the regression to fit the fact that deficits are persistent under weak governments. Thus in this case the exclusion of $b_2 D_{i,t-1}$ biases the estimate of $b_3$ up. A similar analysis shows that one should include the $b_1 \text{WEAK}_{it}$ term as well.[29]

When Roubini and Sachs estimate equation (12.40), they obtain an estimate of $b_2$ of 0.66 (with a standard error of 0.07) and an estimate of $b_3$ of 0.03 (with a standard error of 0.03). Thus the null hypothesis that the strength of the government has no effect on the persistence of deficits cannot be rejected. More importantly, the point estimate implies that deficits are only slightly more persistent under the weakest governments than under the strongest (0.75 versus 0.66). Thus the results provide little support for a key prediction of Alesina and Drazen's model.

---

[29] Note also that when a variable enters a regression both directly and via an interaction term, the coefficient on the variable is no longer the correct measure of its estimated average impact on the dependent variable. In (12.40), for example, the average effect of WEAK on $D$ is not $b_1$, but $b_1 + b_3 \overline{D}_{i,t-1}$, where $\overline{D}_{i,t-1}$ is the average value of $D_{i,t-1}$. Because of this, the point estimate and confidence interval for $b_1 + b_3 \overline{D}_{i,t-1}$ are likely to be of much greater interest than those for $b_1$.

## Is the Relationship Causal?

One concern about the finding that weaker governments run larger deficits is the usual one about statistical relationships: the finding may not reflect an impact of government weakness on deficits. Specifically, unfavorable economic and budgetary shocks that we are not able to control for in the regression can lead to both deficits and weak governments.

Two pieces of evidence suggest that this potential problem is not the main source of the correlation between deficits and weak government. First, Grilli, Masciandaro, and Tabellini (1991) find that there is a strong correlation between countries' deficits and whether they have proportional-representation systems. Countries did not adopt proportional representation in response to unfavorable shocks. And countries with proportional representation have on average weaker governments.

Second, Roubini and Sachs present a *case study* of France around the time of the founding of the Fifth Republic to attempt to determine whether weak government leads to high deficits. A case study is a detailed examination of what in a formal statistical analysis would be just a single data point or a handful of data points. Some case studies consist of little more than descriptions of the behavior of various variables, and are therefore less useful than statistical analysis of those variables. But well-executed case studies can serve two more constructive purposes. First, they can provide ideas for research. In situations where one does not yet have a hypothesis to test, detailed examination of an episode may suggest possibilities. Second, a case study can help to untangle the problems of omitted-variable bias and reverse causation that plague statistical work.

Roubini and Sachs's case study is of the second type. From 1946 to 1958, France had a proportional-representation system, divided and unstable governments, and high deficits. A presidential system was adopted in 1958–1959. After its adoption and de Gaulle's accession to the presidency, deficits fell rapidly and then remained low.

This bare-bones description adds nothing to statistical work. But Roubini and Sachs present several pieces of evidence that suggest that the political variables had large effects on deficits. First, there were no unfavorable shocks large enough to explain the large deficits of the 1950s on the basis of factors other than the political system. France did have unusually large military expenditures in this period because of its involvements in Vietnam and Algeria, but the expenditures were too small to account for a large part of the deficits. Second, there were enormous difficulties in agreeing on budgets in this period. Third, getting a budget passed often required adding large amounts of spending on patronage and local projects. And finally, de Gaulle used his powers under the new constitution to adopt a range of deficit-cutting measures that had failed under the old system or had been viewed as politically impossible. Thus, Roubini and Sachs's additional evidence strongly suggests that the conjunction of weak government and high deficits in the Fourth Republic and of strong government and low deficits in the Fifth Republic reflects an impact of political strength and stability on budgetary outcomes.

## Other Findings

The literature has identified two other interesting relationships between political variables and deficits. First, Grilli, Masciandaro, and Tabellini find that average deficits are higher when governments are less durable. Specifically, they find that deficits are much more strongly associated with the frequency of changes in the executive than with the frequency of major changes in government. Roubini and Sachs's case study of France suggests, however, that this association may not be causal. At least in France in the 1950s, changes in governments were often the *result* of failures to agree on a budget. Thus here the additional evidence provided by a case study does not support a causal interpretation of a regression coefficient, but casts doubt on it.

Second, some work examines the relation between the institutions of budget-making and deficits. Much of this work views deficits as the result of a *common-pool* problem in government spending. Suppose that government spending is determined by several players, each of whom has particular influence over spending that benefits an interest group that the player is especially concerned about (such as the members of his or her legislative district). In effect, each player gets to choose how much of the economy's overall tax base (the common pool) to exploit to finance spending that particularly benefits him or her. The result is inefficiently high spending (Weingast, Shepsle, and Johnsen, 1981; see also Problem 12.15).

This account has several limitations as a model of deficits. First, it is not clear why the relatively small number of major participants in the budgetary process do not find some way of agreeing on an outcome that avoids this inefficiency. Second, spending that benefits narrow interests does not appear to be large enough for the common-pool problem to produce significant bias. And third, in its basic form the model predicts spending bias rather than deficit bias.[30]

Despite these concerns, several papers examine the relationship between budgetary institutions and deficits (for example, von Hagen and Harden, 1995, and Baqir, 2002). von Hagen and Harden construct an index of the extent to which countries' budgetary institutions are hierarchical and transparent. By *hierarchical*, they mean institutions that give the prime minister or finance minister a large role in the process. By *transparent*, they mean institutions that make the official budget more informative about what actual taxes and purchases will be. Neither hierarchy nor transparency provides a clear-cut test of the importance of the common-pool problem.

---

[30] On this last point, see Chari and Cole (1993), Velasco (1999), and Problem 12.16.

Hierarchical institutions can reduce deficits for the same reasons as strong governments in Alesina and Drazen's model rather than by mitigating the common-pool problem. And transparency appears more likely to counter deficit bias stemming from signaling or imperfect understanding than from the common-pool problem.

von Hagen and Harden find a strong correlation between their index and fiscal outcomes among a sample of 12 European countries. For example, the three countries with the lowest values of the index had average deficit-to-GDP ratios in the 1980s over 10 percent, and average debt-to-GDP ratios of about 100 percent. The three highest-ranked countries had average deficit-to-GDP ratios less than 2 percent and average debt-to-GDP ratios of about 40 percent.

## Conclusion

This line of work has established two main results. First, countries' political characteristics affect their deficits. Second, the political characteristics that appear to matter most are ones that Alesina and Drazen's model suggests lead to delay, such as divided government and division of power in budget-making. The macroeconomic evidence does not support the idea that deficits result from the deliberate decisions of one set of policymakers to leave large debts to their successors to restrain their spending, as in Tabellini and Alesina's model. We do not see large deficits in countries like the United Kingdom, where parties with very different ideologies alternate having strong control of policy. Instead we see them in countries like Belgium and Italy, where there is a succession of coalition and minority governments.[31] This suggests that it is important to understand how division of power can lead to deficits. In particular, we would like to know whether a variation on Alesina and Drazen's analysis accounts for the link between divided government and deficits, or whether there is some other factor at work.

# 12.9   The Costs of Deficits

Much of this chapter discusses forces that can give rise to excessive deficits. But it says little about the nature and size of the costs of excessive deficits. This section provides an introduction to this issue.

The costs of deficits, like the costs of inflation, are poorly understood. The reasons are quite different, however. In the case of inflation, the difficulty is that the popular perception is that inflation is very costly, but economists have difficulty identifying channels through which it is likely to

---

[31] Pettersson-Lidbom (2001), however, finds evidence from local governments of the effects predicted by Tabellini and Alesina's model and by Persson and Svensson (1989).

have important effects. In the case of deficits, it is not hard to find reasons that they can have significant effects. The difficulty is that the effects are complicated. As a result, it is hard to do welfare analysis in which one can have much confidence.

The first part of this section considers the effects of sustainable deficit policies. The second part discusses the effects of embarking on a policy that cannot be sustained, focusing especially on what can happen if the unsustainable policy ends with a crisis or "hard landing." Section 12.10 presents a simple model of how a crisis can come about.

## The Effects of Sustainable Deficits

The most obvious cost of excessive deficits is that they involve a departure from tax-smoothing. If the tax rate is below the level needed for the government's budget constraint to be satisfied in expectation, then the expected future tax rate exceeds the current tax rate. This means that the expected discounted value of the distortion costs from raising revenue is unnecessarily high.

Unless the marginal distortion costs of raising revenue rise sharply with the amount of revenue raised, however, the costs of a moderate period of modestly excessive deficits through this channel are probably small. But this does not mean that departures from tax-smoothing are never important. Some projections suggest that if no changes are made in U.S. fiscal policy over the next few decades, satisfying the government budget constraint solely through tax increases would require average tax rates well over 50 percent. The distortion costs from such a policy would surely be substantial. To give another example, Cooley and Ohanian (1997) argue that Britain's heavy reliance on taxes rather than debt to finance its purchases during World War II—which corresponded to a policy of inefficiently *low* deficits relative to tax-smoothing—had large welfare costs.[32]

Deficits are likely to have larger welfare effects as a result of failures of Ricardian equivalence. Deficits almost surely raise aggregate consumption, and thus lower the economy's future wealth. Unfortunately, obtaining estimates of the resulting welfare effects is very difficult, for three reasons. First, simply obtaining estimates of deficits' impact on the paths of such variables as consumption, capital, foreign asset holdings, and so on requires estimates of the magnitude of departures from Ricardian equivalence. Here we do not have a precise figure. Nonetheless, one can make a rough estimate and proceed. For example, Bernheim (1987) argues that a reasonable estimate is that private saving offsets about half the decline in government saving that results from a switch from tax to deficit finance.

---

[32] However, some of the costs they estimate come from high taxes on capital income rather than departures from tax-smoothing.

Second, the welfare effects depend not just on the magnitude of the departures from Ricardian equivalence, but also on the reasons for the departures. For example, suppose Ricardian equivalence fails because of liquidity constraints. This means that the marginal utility of current consumption is high relative to that of future consumption, and thus that there is a large benefit to greater current consumption. In this case, running a higher deficit than is consistent with tax-smoothing can raise welfare (Hubbard and Judd, 1986). Or suppose Ricardian equivalence fails because consumption is determined partly by rules of thumb. In this case, we cannot use households' consumption choices to infer their preferences. This leaves us with no clear way of evaluating the desirability of alternative paths of consumption.

The third difficulty is that deficits have distributional effects. Since some of the taxes needed to repay new debt fall on future generations, deficits redistribute from future generations to the current one. In addition, to the extent that deficits reduce the capital stock, they depress wages and raise real interest rates, and thus redistribute from workers to capitalists. The fact that deficits do not create Pareto improvements or Pareto worsenings does not imply that one should have no opinion about their merits. For example, most individuals (including most economists) believe that a policy that benefits many people but involves small costs to a few is desirable, even if the losers are never compensated. In the case of the redistribution from workers to capitalists, the fact that workers are generally poorer than capitalists may be a reason to find the redistribution undesirable. The redistribution from future generations to the current one is more complicated. On one hand, future generations are likely to be better off than the current one; this is likely to make us view the redistribution more favorably. On the other hand, the common view that saving is too low implicitly takes the view that rates of return are high enough to make redistribution from those currently alive to future generations desirable; this suggests that the redistribution from future generations to the current one may be undesirable. For all these reasons, the welfare effects of sustainable deficits are difficult to evaluate.

## The Effects of Unsustainable Deficits

Countries often embark on paths for fiscal policy that cannot be sustained. For example, they often pursue policies involving an ever-rising ratio of debt to GDP. By definition, an unsustainable policy cannot continue indefinitely. Thus the fact that the government is following such a policy does not imply that it needs to take deliberate actions to change course. This idea was expressed by Herbert Stein in what is now known as Stein's law: "If something cannot go on forever, it will stop." The difficulty, however, is that stopping may be sudden and unexpected. Policy is unsustainable when the government is trying to behave in a way that violates its budget constraint. In such a situation, at some point outside developments force it to abandon this attempt. And as we will see in the next section, the forced change is likely to take the form of a crisis rather than a smooth transition. Typically, the crisis involves a sharp contraction in fiscal policy, a large decline in aggregate demand, major repercussions in capital and foreign-exchange markets, and perhaps default on the government's debt.

The possibility of a fiscal crisis creates additional costs to deficits. It is important to note, however, that government default is not in itself a cost. The default is a transfer from bondholders to taxpayers. Typically this means that it is a transfer from wealthier to poorer individuals. Further, to the extent the debt is held by foreigners, the default is a transfer from foreigners to domestic residents. From the point of view of the domestic residents, this is an advantage to default. Finally, default reduces the amount of revenue the government must raise in the future. Since raising revenue involves distortions, this means that default does not just cause transfers, but also improves efficiency.

Nonetheless, there are costs to crises. Some of the most important arise because a crisis is likely to increase the price of foreign goods greatly. When a country's budget deficit falls sharply, its capital and financial account surplus is likely to fall sharply as well. That is, the economy is likely to move from a situation where foreigners are buying large quantities of the country's assets to one where they are buying few or none. But this means that the trade balance must swing sharply toward surplus. For this to happen, there must be a large depreciation of the real exchange rate. In the Mexican crisis of 1994–1995, for example, the value of the Mexican peso fell roughly in half. And in the East Asian crisis of 1997–1998, the values of many of the affected currencies fell by considerably more.

Such real depreciation reduces welfare through several channels. Because it corresponds to a rise in the real price of foreign goods, it lowers welfare directly. Further, it tends to raise output in export and import-competing sectors and reduce it elsewhere. That is, it is a sectoral shock that induces a reallocation of labor and other inputs among sectors. Since reallocation is not instantaneous, the result is a temporary rise in unemployment and other unused resources. Finally, the depreciation is likely to increase inflation. Because workers purchase some foreign goods, the depreciation raises the cost of living and thus creates upward pressure on wages. In addition, because some inputs are imported, the depreciation raises firms' costs. In the terminology of Section 6.4, real depreciation is an unfavorable supply shock.

Some other major costs of fiscal crises stem from the fact that they disrupt capital markets. Government default, plummeting asset prices, and falling output are likely to bankrupt many firms and financial intermediaries. In addition, because firms' and intermediaries' debts are often denominated in foreign currencies, real depreciation directly worsens their financial situations and thus further increases bankruptcies. The bankruptcies cause a loss of information and long-term relationships that help direct capital and other resources to their most productive uses. And even when firms and intermediaries are not bankrupted by the crisis, the worsening of their financial positions magnifies the effects of financial-market imperfections.

One effect of these financial-market disruptions is that investment is lower. This effect, however, can be offset by expansionary (or less contractionary) monetary policy. But another effect is that for a given amount of investment, the average quality of projects is lower, since the financial system now allocates capital less effectively. Similarly, output is lower for a given level of employment, since many firms with profitable production opportunities are unable to produce because of bankruptcy or an inability to obtain loans to pay their wages and purchase inputs. Bernanke (1983b) argues that such financial-market disruptions played a large role in the Great Depression. And they appear to have been important in more recent fiscal crises as well. In Indonesia in 1998, for example, a large majority of firms were at least technically bankrupt, although many continued to function in some form.

At the microeconomic level, crises can cause large redistributions with severe consequences. For example, suppose a government that is borrowing to pay for pensions and medical care for the elderly faces a sudden default that makes it unable to do any further borrowing. One result is likely to be a sudden drop in the standards of living of the elderly, along with those whose wealth holdings were concentrated in government debt.

Fiscal crises can have other costs as well. Since fiscal crises are unexpected, trying to follow an unsustainable policy increases uncertainty. Default and other failures to repay its debts can reduce a government's ability to borrow in the future.[33] Finally, a crisis can lead to harmful policies, such as broad trade restrictions, hyperinflation, and very high tax rates on capital.

One way to summarize the macroeconomic effects of a fiscal crisis is to note that it typically leads to a sharp fall in output followed by only a gradual recovery. This summary, however, overstates the costs of embarking on unsustainable fiscal policy, for two reasons. First, unsustainable fiscal policy is usually not the only source of a crisis; thus it is not appropriate to attribute the crisis's full costs to fiscal policy. Second, there may be benefits to the policy before the crisis. For example, it may lead to real appreciation, with benefits that are the converse of the costs of real depreciation, and to a period of high output. Nonetheless, the costs of an attempt to pursue unsustainable fiscal policy that ends in a crisis are almost surely substantial.

# 12.10   A Model of Debt Crises

We now turn to a simple model of a government attempting to issue debt. We focus on the questions of what can cause investors to be unwilling to

---

[33] Because there is no authority analogous to domestic courts to force borrowers to repay, there are some important issues specifically related to international borrowing. See Obstfeld and Rogoff (1996, Chapter 6) for an introduction.

buy the debt at any interest rate, and of whether such a crisis is likely to occur unexpectedly.[34]

## Assumptions

Consider a government that has quantity $D$ of debt coming due. It has no funds immediately available, and so wants to roll the debt over (that is, to issue $D$ of new debt to pay off the debt coming due). It will be obtaining tax revenues the following period, and so wants investors to hold the debt for one period.

The government offers an *interest factor* of $R$; that is, it offers a real interest rate of $R - 1$. Let $T$ denote tax revenues the following period. $T$ is random, and its cumulative distribution function, $F(\bullet)$, is continuous. If $T$ exceeds the amount due on the debt in that period, $RD$, the government pays the debtholders. If $T$ is less than $RD$, the government defaults. Default corresponds to a debt crisis.

Two simplifying assumptions make the model tractable. First, default is all-or-nothing: if the government cannot pay $RD$, it repudiates the debt entirely. Second, investors are risk-neutral, and the risk-free interest factor, $\bar{R}$, is independent of $R$ and $D$. These assumptions do not appear critical to the model's main messages.

## Analyzing the Model

Equilibrium is described by two equations in the probability of default, denoted $\pi$, and the interest factor on government debt, $R$. Since investors are risk-neutral, the expected payoff from holding government debt must equal the risk-free payoff, $\bar{R}$. Government debt pays $R$ with probability $1 - \pi$ and 0 with probability $\pi$. Thus equilibrium requires

$$(1 - \pi)R = \bar{R}. \tag{12.41}$$

For comparison with the second equilibrium condition, it is useful to rearrange this condition as an expression for $\pi$ as a function of $R$. This yields

$$\pi = \frac{R - \bar{R}}{R}. \tag{12.42}$$

The locus of points satisfying (12.42) is plotted in $(R,\pi)$ space in Figure 12.3. When the government is certain to repay (that is, when $\pi = 0$), $R$ equals $\bar{R}$. As the probability of default rises, the interest factor the government must

---

[34] See Calvo (1988) and Cole and Kehoe (2000) for examples of richer models of debt crises.

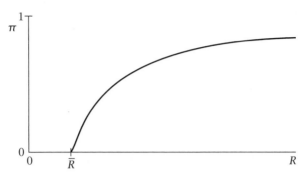

**FIGURE 12.3    The condition for investors to be willing to hold government debt**

offer rises; thus the locus is upward-sloping. Finally, $R$ approaches infinity as the probability of default approaches 1.

The other equilibrium condition comes from the fact that whether the government defaults is determined by its available revenues relative to the amount due bondholders. Specifically, the government defaults if and only if $T$ is less than $RD$. Thus the probability of default is the probability that $T$ is less than $RD$. Since $T$'s distribution function is $F(\bullet)$, we can write this condition as

$$\pi = F(RD). \tag{12.43}$$

The set of points satisfying (12.43) is plotted in Figure 12.4. If there are minimum and maximum possible values of $T$, $\underline{T}$ and $\overline{T}$, the probability of default is 0 for $R < \underline{T}/D$ and 1 for $R > \overline{T}/D$. And if the density function of $T$ is bell-shaped, the distribution function has an $S$ shape like that shown in the figure.

Equilibrium occurs at a point where both (12.42) and (12.43) are satisfied. At such a point, the interest factor on government debt makes investors willing to purchase the debt given the probability of default, and the probability of default is the probability that tax revenues are insufficient to pay off the debt given the interest factor. In addition to any equilibria satisfying these two conditions, however, there is always an equilibrium where investors are certain the government will not pay off the debt the following period and are therefore unwilling to purchase the debt at any interest factor. If investors refuse to purchase the debt at any interest factor, the probability of default is 1; and if the probability of default is 1, investors refuse to purchase the debt at any interest factor. Loosely speaking, this equilibrium corresponds to the point $R = \infty$, $\pi = 1$ in the diagram.[35]

---

[35] It is straightforward to extend the analysis to the case where default is not all-or-nothing. For example, suppose that when revenue is less than $RD$, the government pays all of it to debtholders. To analyze the model in this case, define $\pi$ as the expected fraction of

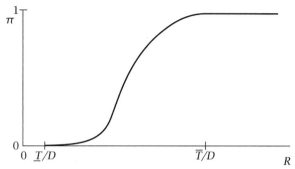

**FIGURE 12.4   The probability of default as a function of the interest factor**

## Implications

The model has at least four interesting implications. The first is that there is a simple force tending to create multiple equilibria in the probability of default. The higher the probability of default, the higher the interest factor investors demand; but the higher the interest factor investors demand, the higher the probability of default. In terms of the diagram, the fact that the curves showing the equilibrium conditions are both upward-sloping means that they can have multiple intersections.

Figure 12.5 shows one possibility. In this case, there are three equilibria. At Point A, the probability of default is low and the interest factor on government debt is only slightly above the safe interest factor. At Point B, there is a substantial chance of default and the interest factor on the debt is well above the safe factor. Finally, there is the equilibrium where default is certain and investors refuse to purchase the government's debt at any interest factor.[36]

the amount due to investors, $RD$, that they do not receive. With this definition, the condition for investors to be willing to hold government debt, $(1 - \pi)R = \overline{R}$, is the same as before, and so equation (12.42) holds as before. The expression for the expected fraction of the amount due to investors that they do not receive as a function of the interest factor the government offers is now more complicated than (12.43). It still has the same basic shape in $(R, \pi)$ space, however: it is 0 for $R$ sufficiently small, upward-sloping, and approaches 1 as $R$ approaches infinity. Because this change in assumptions does not change one curve at all and does not change the other's main features, the model's main messages are unaffected.

[36] One natural question is whether the government can avoid the multiplicity by issuing its debt at the lowest equilibrium interest rate. The answer depends on how investors form their expectations of the probability of default. One possibility is that they tentatively assume that the government can successfully issue debt at the interest factor it is offering; they then purchase the debt if the expected return given this assumption at least equals the risk-free return. In this case, the government can issue debt at the lowest interest factor where the two curves intersect. But this is not the only possibility. For example, suppose each investor believes that others believe the government will default for sure, and that others are therefore unwilling to purchase the debt at any interest factor. Then no investor purchases the debt, and so the beliefs prove correct.

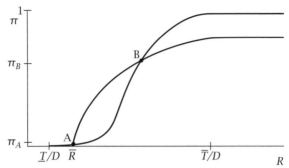

**FIGURE 12.5   The determination of the interest factor and the probability of default**

Under plausible dynamics, the equilibrium at B is unstable and the other two are stable. Suppose, for example, investors believe the probability of default is slightly below $\pi_B$. Then at the interest factor needed to induce them to buy the debt given this belief, the actual probability of default is less than what they conjecture. It is plausible that their estimate of the probability of default therefore falls, and that this process continues until the equilibrium at Point A is reached. A similar argument suggests that if investors conjecture that the probability of default exceeds $\pi_B$, the economy converges to the equilibrium where investors will not hold the debt at any interest factor. Thus there are two stable equilibria. In one, the interest factor and the probability of default are low. In the other, the government cannot get investors to purchase its debt at any interest factor, and so it defaults immediately on its outstanding debt. In short, there can be a self-fulfilling element to default.

The second implication is that large differences in fundamentals are not needed for large differences in outcomes. One reason for this is the multiplicity just described: two economies can have the same fundamentals, but one can be in the equilibrium with low $R$ and low $\pi$ and the other in the equilibrium where investors refuse to buy the debt at any interest factor. A more interesting source of large differences stems from differences in the set of equilibria. Suppose the two curves have the form shown in Figure 12.5, and suppose an economy is in the equilibrium with low $R$ and low $\pi$ at Point A. A rise in $\bar{R}$ shifts the $\pi = (R - \bar{R})/R$ curve to the right. Similarly, a rise in $D$ shifts the $\pi = F(RD)$ curve to the left. For small enough changes, $\pi$ and $R$ change smoothly in response to either of these developments. Figure 12.6, for example, shows the effects of a moderate change in $\bar{R}$ from $\bar{R}_0$ to $\bar{R}_1$. The equilibrium with low $R$ and low $\pi$ changes smoothly from A to A'. But now suppose $\bar{R}$ rises further. If $\bar{R}$ becomes sufficiently large—if it rises to $\bar{R}_2$, for example—the two curves no longer intersect. In this situation, the only equilibrium is the one where investors will not buy the debt. Thus two economies can have similar fundamentals, but in one there is an equilibrium where the government can issue debt at a low interest rate while in

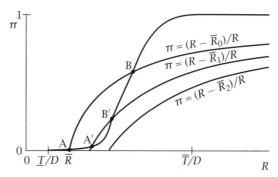

**FIGURE 12.6   The effects of increases in the safe interest factor**

the other the only equilibrium is for the government to be unable to issue debt at any interest rate.

Third, the model suggests that default, when it occurs, may always be quite unexpected. That is, it may be that for realistic cases, there is never an equilibrium value of $\pi$ that is substantial but strictly less than 1. If there is little uncertainty about $T$, the revenue the government can obtain to pay off the debt, the $\pi = F(RD)$ locus has sharp bends near $\pi = 0$ and $\pi = 1$ like those in Figure 12.6. Since the $\pi = (R - \bar{R})/R$ locus does not bend sharply, in this case the switch to the situation where default is the only equilibrium occurs at a low value of $\pi$. That is, there may never be a situation where investors believe the probability of default is substantial but strictly less than 1. As a result, defaults are always a surprise.

The final implication is the most straightforward. Default depends not only on self-fulfilling beliefs, but also on fundamentals. In particular, an increase in the amount the government wants to borrow, an increase in the safe interest factor, and a downward shift in the distribution of potential revenue all make default more likely. Each of these developments shifts either the $\pi = (R - \bar{R})/R$ locus down or the $\pi = F(RD)$ locus up. As a result, each development increases $\pi$ at any stable equilibrium. In addition, each development can move the economy to a situation where the only equilibrium is the one where there is no interest factor at which investors will hold the debt. Thus one message of the model is that high debt, a high required rate of return, and low future revenues all make default more likely.

## Multiple Periods

A version of the model with multiple periods raises some interesting additional issues. For instance, suppose the government wants to issue debt for two periods. The government inherits a stock of debt in period 0, $D_0$. Let $R_1$ denote the interest factor it pays from period 0 to period 1, and $R_2$ the interest factor from period 1 to period 2. For simplicity, the government receives tax revenue only in period 2. Thus it pays off the debt in period 2 if and only if its available revenues, $T$, exceed the amount due, $R_1 R_2 D_0$. Finally, since the multiperiod version does not provide important additional insights into the possibility of multiple equilibria, assume that the equilibrium with the lowest $\pi$ (and hence the lowest $R$) is selected when there is more than one equilibrium.

The most interesting new issues raised by the multiperiod model concern the importance of investors' beliefs, their beliefs about other investors' beliefs, and so on. The question of when investors can have heterogeneous beliefs in equilibrium is difficult and important. For this discussion, however, we simply assume that heterogeneous beliefs are possible. Consider an investor in period 0. In the one-period case with the issue of multiple equilibria assumed away, the investor's beliefs about others' beliefs are irrelevant to his or her behavior. The investor holds the debt if the interest factor times his or her estimate of the probability that tax revenues will be sufficient to pay off the debt is greater than or equal to the safe interest factor. But in the two-period case, the investor's willingness to hold the debt depends not only on $R_1$ and the distribution of $T$, but also on what $R_2$ will be. This in turn depends on what other investors will believe as of period 1 about the distribution of $T$. Suppose, for example, that for some $R_1$, the investor's own beliefs about $F(\bullet)$ imply that if the government offered an $R_2$ only slightly above the safe factor, the probability of default would be low, so that it would be sensible to hold the debt. Suppose, however, he or she believes that others' beliefs will make them unwilling to hold the debt from period 1 to period 2 at any interest factor. Then the investor believes the government will default in period 1. He or she therefore does not purchase the debt in period 0 despite the fact that his or her own beliefs about fundamentals suggest that the government's policy is reasonable.

Even a belief that there is a small chance that in period 1 others' beliefs will make them unwilling to hold the debt at any interest rate can matter. Such a belief increases the $R_1$ that investors require to buy the debt in period 0. This raises the amount of debt the government has to roll over in period 1, which reduces the chances that it will be able to do so, which raises $R_1$ further, and so on. The end result is that the government may not be able to sell its debt in period 0.

With more periods, even more complicated beliefs can matter. For example, if there are three periods rather than two, an investor in period 0 may be unwilling to purchase the debt because he or she believes that in period 1 others may think that in period 2 investors may believe that there is no interest factor that makes it worthwhile for them to hold the debt.

This discussion implies that it is rational for investors to be concerned about others' beliefs about governments' solvency, about others' beliefs about others' beliefs, and so on. Those beliefs affect the government's ability to service its debt and thus the expected return from holding debt. An additional implication is that a change in the debt market, or even a crisis, can be caused by information not about fundamentals, but about beliefs about fundamentals, or about beliefs about beliefs about fundamentals.

# Problems

**12.1. The stability of fiscal policy.** (Blinder and Solow, 1973.) By definition, the budget deficit equals the rate of change of the amount of debt outstanding: $\delta(t) \equiv \dot{D}(t)$. Define $d(t)$ to be the ratio of debt to output: $d(t) = D(t)/Y(t)$. Assume that $Y(t)$ grows at a constant rate $g > 0$.

   (a) Suppose that the deficit-to-output ratio is constant: $\delta(t)/Y(t) = a$, where $a > 0$.

    (i) Find an expression for $\dot{d}(t)$ in terms of $a$, $g$, and $d(t)$.

    (ii) Sketch $\dot{d}(t)$ as a function of $d(t)$. Is this system stable?

   (b) Suppose that the ratio of the primary deficit to output is constant and equal to $a > 0$. Thus the total deficit at $t$, $\delta(t)$, is given by $\delta(t) = aY(t) + r(t)D(t)$, where $r(t)$ is the interest rate at $t$. Assume that $r$ is an increasing function of the debt-to-output ratio: $r(t) = r(d(t))$, where $r'(\bullet) > 0$, $r''(\bullet) > 0$, $\lim_{d \to -\infty} r(d) < g$, $\lim_{d \to \infty} r(d) > g$.

    (i) Find an expression for $\dot{d}(t)$ in terms of $a$, $g$, and $d(t)$.

    (ii) Sketch $\dot{d}(t)$ as a function of $d(t)$. In the case where $a$ is sufficiently small that $\dot{d}$ is negative for some values of $d$, what are the stability properties of the system? What about the case where $a$ is sufficiently large that $\dot{d}$ is positive for all values of $d$?

**12.2. Precautionary saving, non-lump-sum taxation, and Ricardian equivalence.** (Leland, 1968, and Barsky, Mankiw, and Zeldes, 1986.) Consider an individual who lives for two periods. The individual has no initial wealth and earns labor incomes of amounts $Y_1$ and $Y_2$ in the two periods. $Y_1$ is known, but $Y_2$ is random; assume for simplicity that $E[Y_2] = Y_1$. The government taxes income at rate $\tau_1$ in period 1 and $\tau_2$ in period 2. The individual can borrow and lend at a fixed interest rate, which for simplicity is assumed to be zero. Thus second-period consumption is $C_2 = (1 - \tau_1)Y_1 - C_1 + (1 - \tau_2)Y_2$. The individual chooses $C_1$ to maximize expected lifetime utility, $U(C_1) + E[U(C_2)]$.

   (a) Find the first-order condition for $C_1$.

   (b) Show that $E[C_2] = C_1$ if $Y_2$ is not random or if utility is quadratic.

   (c) Show that if $U'''(\bullet) > 0$ and $Y_2$ is random, $E[C_2] > C_1$.

   (d) Suppose that the government marginally lowers $\tau_1$ and raises $\tau_2$ by the same amount, so that its expected total revenue, $\tau_1 Y_1 + \tau_2 E[Y_2]$, is unchanged. Implicitly differentiate the first-order condition in part (a) to find an expression for how $C_1$ responds to this change.

   (e) Show that $C_1$ is unaffected by this change if $Y_2$ is not random or if utility is quadratic.

(f) Show that $C_1$ increases in response to this change if $U'''(\bullet) > 0$ and $Y_2$ is random.

12.3. Consider the Barro tax-smoothing model. Suppose that output, $Y$, and the real interest rate, $r$, are constant, and that the level of government debt outstanding at time 0 is zero. Suppose that there will be a temporary war from time 0 to time $\tau$. Thus $G(t)$ equals $G_H$ for $0 \le t \le \tau$, and equals $G_L$ thereafter, where $G_H > G_L$. What are the paths of taxes, $T(t)$, and government debt outstanding, $D(t)$?

12.4. Consider the Barro tax-smoothing model. Suppose there are two possible values of $G(t)$—$G_H$ and $G_L$—with $G_H > G_L$. Transitions between the two values follow Poisson processes (see Section 7.4). Specifically, if $G$ equals $G_H$, the probability per unit time that purchases fall to $G_L$ is $a$; if $G$ equals $G_L$, the probability per unit time that purchases rise to $G_H$ is $b$. Suppose also that output, $Y$, and the real interest rate, $r$, are constant and that distortion costs are quadratic.

(a) Derive expressions for taxes at a given time as a function of whether $G$ equals $G_H$ or $G_L$, the amount of debt outstanding, and the exogenous parameters. (Hint: Use dynamic programming, described in Section 10.4, to find an expression for the expected present value of the revenue the government must raise as a function of $G$, the amount of debt outstanding, and the exogenous parameters.)

(b) Discuss your results. What is the path of taxes during an interval when $G$ equals $G_H$? Why are taxes not constant during such an interval? What happens to taxes at a moment when $G$ falls to $G_L$? What is the path of taxes during an interval when $G$ equals $G_L$?

12.5. If the tax rate follows a random walk (and if the variance of its innovations is bounded from below by a strictly positive number), then with probability 1 it will eventually exceed 100 percent or be negative. Does this observation suggest that the tax-smoothing model with quadratic distortion costs is not useful as either a positive or normative model of fiscal policy, since it has an implication that is both clearly incorrect as a description of the world and clearly undesirable as a prescription for policy? Explain your answer briefly.

12.6. **The Condorcet paradox.** Suppose there are three voters, 1, 2, and 3, and three possible policies, A, B, and C. Voter 1's preference ordering is A, B, C; voter 2's is B, C, A; and voter 3's is C, A, B. Does any policy win a majority of votes in a two-way contest against each of the alternatives? Explain.

12.7. Consider the Tabellini–Alesina model in the case where $\alpha$ can only take on the values 0 and 1. Suppose that there is some initial level of debt, $D_0$. How, if at all, does $D_0$ affect the deficit in period 1?

12.8. Consider the Tabellini–Alesina model in the case where $\alpha$ can only take on the values 0 and 1. Suppose that the amount of debt to be issued, $D$, is determined before the preferences of the period-1 median voter are known. Specifically, voters vote on $D$ at a time when the probabilities that $\alpha_1^{\text{MED}} = 1$ and that $\alpha_2^{\text{MED}} = 1$ are equal. Let $\pi$ denote this common value. Assume that the draws of the two median voters are independent.

(a) What is the expected utility of an individual with $\alpha = 1$ as a function of $D$, $\pi$, and $W$?

(b) What is the first-order condition for this individual's most preferred value of $D$? What is the associated value of $D$?

(c) What is the most preferred value of $D$ of an individual with $\alpha = 0$?

(d) Given these results, if voters vote on $D$ before the period-1 median voter is known, what value of $D$ does the median voter prefer?

(e) Explain briefly how, if at all, the question analyzed in part (d) differs from the question of whether individuals will support a balanced-budget requirement if it is proposed before the preferences of the period-1 median voter are known.

12.9. Consider the Tabellini–Alesina model in the case where $\alpha$ can only take on the values 0 and 1. Suppose, however, that there are 3 periods. The period-1 median voter sets policy in periods 1 and 2, but in period 3 a new median voter sets policy. Assume that the period-1 median voter's $\alpha$ is 1, and that the probability that the period-3 median voter's $\alpha$ is 1 is $\pi$.

(a) Does $M_1 = M_2$?

(b) Suppose that after choosing purchases in period 1, the period-1 median voter learns that the probability that the period-3 median voter's $\alpha$ will be 1 is not $\pi$ but $\pi'$, where $\pi' < \pi$. How does this news affect his or her choice of purchases in period 2?

12.10. **The Persson-Svensson model.** (Persson and Svensson, 1989.) Suppose there are two periods. Government policy will be controlled by different policy-makers in the two periods. The objective function of the period-$t$ policymaker is $U + \alpha_t[V(G_1) + V(G_2)]$, where $U$ is citizens' utility from their private consumption; $\alpha_t$ is the weight that the period-$t$ policymaker puts on public consumption; $G_t$ is public consumption in period $t$; and $V(\bullet)$ satisfies $V'(\bullet) > 0$, $V''(\bullet) < 0$. Private utility, $U$, is given by $U = W - C(T_1) - C(T_2)$, where $W$ is the endowment; $T_t$ is taxes in period $t$; and $C(\bullet)$, the cost of raising revenue, satisfies $C'(\bullet) \geq 1$, $C''(\bullet) > 0$. All government debt must be paid off at the end of period 2. This implies $T_2 = G_2 + D$, where $D = G_1 - T_1$ is the amount of government debt issued in period 1 and where the interest rate is assumed to equal zero.

(a) Find the first-order condition for the period-2 policymaker's choice of $G_2$ given $D$. (Note: Throughout, assume that the solutions to the policy-makers' maximization problems are interior.)

(b) How does a change in $D$ affect $G_2$?

(c) Think of the period-1 policymaker as choosing $G_1$ and $D$. Find the first-order condition for his or her choice of $D$.

(d) Show that if $\alpha_1$ is less than $\alpha_2$, the equilibrium involves inefficiently low taxation in period 1 relative to tax-smoothing (that is, that it has $T_1 < T_2$). Explain intuitively why this occurs.

(e) Does the result in part (d) imply that if $\alpha_1$ is less than $\alpha_2$, the period-1 policymaker necessarily runs a deficit? Explain.

**12.11.** Consider the Alesina–Drazen model. Describe how, if at all, each of the following developments affects workers' proposal and the probability of reform:

(a) A fall in $T$.

(b) A rise in $B$.

(c) An equal rise in $A$ and $B$.

**12.12. Crises and reform.** Consider the model in Section 12.7. Suppose, however, that if there is no reform, workers and capitalists both receive payoffs of $-C$ rather than 0, where $C \geq 0$.

(a) Find expressions analogous to (12.37) and (12.38) for workers' proposal and the probability of reform.

(b) Define social welfare as the sum of the expected payoffs of workers and capitalists. Show that an increase in $C$ can raise this measure of social welfare.

**12.13. Conditionality and reform.** Consider the model in Section 12.7. Suppose an international agency offers to give the workers and capitalists each an amount $F > 0$ if they agree to reform. Use analysis like that in Problem 12.12 to show that this aid policy unambiguously raises the probability of reform and the social welfare measure defined in part (b) of that problem.

**12.14. Status-quo bias.** (Fernandez and Rodrik, 1991.) There are two possible policies, A and B. Each individual is either one unit of utility better off under Policy A or one unit worse off. Fraction $f$ of the population knows what its welfare would be under each policy. Of these individuals, fraction $\alpha$ are better off under Policy A and fraction $1 - \alpha$ are worse off. The remaining individuals in the population know only that fraction $\beta$ of them are better off under Policy A and fraction $1 - \beta$ are worse off.

A decision of whether to adopt the policy not currently in effect is made by majority vote. If the proposal passes, all individuals learn which policy makes them better off; a decision of whether to revert to the original policy is then made by majority vote. Each individual votes for the policy that gives him or her the higher expected utility. But if the proposal to revert to the original policy would be adopted in the event that the proposal to adopt the alternative policy passed, no one votes for the alternative policy. (This assumption can be justified by introducing a small cost of changing policies.)

(a) Find an expression for the fraction of the population that prefers Policy A (as a function of $f$, $\alpha$, and $\beta$) for the case where fraction $1 - f$ of the population knows only that fraction $\beta$ of them are better off under Policy A.

(b) Find the analogous expression for the case where all individuals know their welfare under both policies.

(c) Given your answers to parts (a) and (b), can there be cases when whichever policy is initially in effect is retained?

**12.15. The common-pool problem in government spending.** (Weingast, Shepsle, and Johnsen, 1981.) Suppose the economy consists of $M > 1$ congressional districts. The utility of the representative person living in district $i$ is $E + V(G_i) - C(T)$. $E$ is the endowment, $G_i$ is the level of a local public good in district $i$, and $T$ is taxes (which are assumed to be the same in all districts). Assume $V'(\bullet) > 0$, $V''(\bullet) < 0$, $C'(\bullet) > 0$, and $C''(\bullet) > 0$. The government budget constraint is $\sum_{i=1}^{M} G_i = MT$. The representative from each district dictates the values of $G$ in his or her district. Each representative maximizes the utility of the representative person living in his or her district.

(a) Find the first-order condition for the value of $G_j$ chosen by the representative from district $j$, given the values of $G_i$ chosen by the other representatives and the government budget constraint (which implies $T = (\sum_{i=1}^{M} G_i)/M$). (Note: Throughout, assume interior solutions.)

(b) Find the condition for the Nash equilibrium value of $G$. That is, find the condition for the value of $G$ such that if all other representatives choose that value for their $G_i$, a given representative wants to choose that value.

(c) Is the Nash equilibrium Pareto-efficient? Explain. What is the intuition for this result?

**12.16. Debt as a means of mitigating the common-pool problem.** (Chari and Cole, 1993.) Consider the same setup as in Problem 12.15. Suppose, however, that there is an initial level of debt, $D$. The government budget constraint is therefore $D + \sum_{i=1}^{M} G_i = MT$.

(a) How does an increase in $D$ affect the Nash equilibrium level of $G$?

(b) Explain intuitively why your results in part (a) and in Problem 12.15 suggest that in a two-period model in which the representatives choose $D$ after the first-period value of $G$ is determined, the representatives would choose $D > 0$.

(c) Do you think that in a two-period model where the representatives choose $D$ before the first-period value of $G$ is determined, the representatives would choose $D > 0$? Explain intuitively.

**12.17.** Consider the model of crises in Section 12.10, and suppose $T$ is distributed uniformly on some interval $[\mu - X, \mu + X]$, where $X > 0$ and $\mu - X \geq 0$. Describe how, if at all, each of the following developments affects the two curves in $(R, \pi)$ space that show the determination of $R$ and $\pi$:

(a) A rise in $\mu$.

(b) A fall in $X$.

# Epilogue
# THE FINANCIAL AND MACROECONOMIC CRISIS OF 2008 AND BEYOND

The period from the end of the Volcker disinflation in the mid-1980s to 2007 was one of unprecedented macroeconomic stability. The United States went through only two recessions in this period, both of them mild. The unemployment rate never exceeded 8 percent, and there were only five quarters in which real GDP fell.

There are three leading explanations of this *Great Moderation*. The first is simply good luck, in the form of smaller shocks hitting the economy (Stock and Watson, 2003). The second is changes in the structure of the economy, such as a larger role of services and improvements in inventory management (McConnell and Perez-Quiros, 2000; see also Ramey and Vine, 2004). The third is improved policy. When policymakers were unsure of the correct model of the economy and the costs of inflation, they repeatedly pursued policies that caused inflation to rise, then induced recessions to reduce it. With the triumph of the natural-rate hypothesis, general agreement on realistic estimates of the natural rate, and the emergence of a consensus that inflation should be kept low, this boom-bust cycle disappeared (C. Romer, 1999).

This period of stability ended dramatically in 2008—though whether the end was temporary or permanent is not yet known. House prices had been rising rapidly since the late 1990s. By 2003, both the level of real house prices and the ratio of the prices of existing houses to the costs of building new ones were above their previous postwar highs. Yet the rapid price increases continued for three more years. The increases were accompanied by—and perhaps fueled by—the growth of new types of mortgages, many of them issued on the basis of little or no documentation on the part of the borrower, and by a proliferation of new ways of repackaging and insuring the mortgages, often leaving it unclear who was bearing the risk of default.

House prices started falling in 2007, and the macroeconomy weakened soon thereafter. The decline in the value of housing-related assets reduced the net worth of many financial institutions and increased uncertainty about that net worth, and thereby put significant strains on credit markets. For example, spreads between interest rates on overnight loans between banks and interest rates on government debt rose sharply, and the Federal Reserve and other central banks judged it necessary to intervene directly in credit markets in various ways. But the initial downturn in the macroeconomy was mild. For example, as of August 2008, a common view was that the economy was probably in a recession but that any recession was likely to be even milder than the previous two.

In September 2008, however, Lehman Brothers, a major investment bank, declared bankruptcy. In the aftermath, financial markets suffered dramatic turmoil, and the recession changed from mild to severe. Equity prices fell by more than 25 percent in just 4 weeks; spreads between interest rates on conventional but slightly risky loans and those on the safest and most liquid assets skyrocketed; and many borrowers were unable to borrow at any interest rate. Real GDP suffered its largest two-quarter decline since 1957–1958; and from September 2008 to May 2009, employment fell by 3.8 percent and the unemployment rate rose by 3.2 percentage points. By most measures, the recession of 2007–2009 was the largest since World War II. Many other countries suffered similar downturns.

The initial part of the recovery has been slow. In addition, the prevailing view is that unemployment will remain above the natural rate and output will remain below its normal level for years, and that the events of 2008 and 2009 may have long-term effects on the normal levels of unemployment and output. And there is heated debate about what, if anything, policymakers should do to speed the recovery and reduce the long-term damage.

The events of the past few years were a profound shock not just to the macroeconomy, but also to the field of macroeconomics. Short-run aggregate fluctuations, which we thought we had largely tamed, have reemerged dramatically. Moreover, the nature of the recent recession is very different from that of other major postwar recessions. Financial-market disruptions appear to have been central, and tight monetary policy played little or no role.

Thus our models and analysis will surely change. But how is not clear. In many ways, macroeconomics today is in a position similar to where it stood in the early 1970s, when the emergence of the combination of high unemployment and high inflation challenged accepted views. Then, as now, one possibility was that the unexpected developments would lead only to straightforward modifications of the existing framework. But another possibility—and the one that in fact occurred—was that the developments would lead to large and unexpected changes in the field.

Obviously, we can never predict fundamental changes in macroeconomics before they occur. All we can do is identify some of the key issues that the crisis raises for the field and some possible directions of research.

Several of the central issues involve financial markets. One important message of the crisis is the vulnerability of financial markets to runs. Many financial institutions issue short-term debt to finance long-term investments. The extreme is a traditional bank, which issues demand deposits and holds a variety of long-term assets, such as 30-year mortgages. Why financial institutions engage in such *maturity transformation*, and why their short-term contracts take such simple forms (such as noncontingent debt payable on demand), are complicated questions. But given these arrangements, there is a strong force acting to create multiple equilibria: a debtholder is more likely to demand that the debt be repaid or refuse to roll it over if he or she believes that others will do the same. The recent crisis shows that this logic applies not just to a traditional bank, as in the classic Diamond–Dybvig model of bank runs (Diamond and Dybvig, 1983). It also applies to a financial institution financing itself through collateralized overnight loans (Gorton and Metrick, 2009) or through overlapping short-term debt contracts (He and Xiong, 2010).

Another message of the crisis concerning financial markets is that there are limits to the forces bringing asset prices in line with fundamentals. Our analysis of asset pricing in Section 8.5 generated strong predictions about how assets *should* be priced. But what happens if prices differ from those levels? For example, house prices before the crisis appear to have been above the levels warranted by likely payoffs in different states of the world; and the same is true of the prices of various assets whose payoffs were tied to the housing market, such as mortgage-backed securities. In the case of those securities, one difficulty was that credit-rating agencies focused on evaluating the probability of default, and not on the states in which default would occur (Coval, Jurek, and Stafford, 2009). And there is evidence that pricing errors may have switched signs once the crisis hit, with many risky assets selling at prices below what was warranted by fundamentals.

If an individual believes that an asset is mispriced, he or she has an incentive to trade in a way that will push prices back toward fundamentals. But mispricings of the types we have been discussing do not create *arbitrage* opportunities—that is, investment strategies that will be profitable with certainty. Instead, trades that move prices back toward fundamentals involve risks, both from changes in fundamentals and from exacerbations of the mispricings. Consider an investor contemplating buying apparently underpriced assets in the midst of the crisis. If the apparent panic were to intensify before subsiding, the investor might be forced to liquidate his or her position, and so incur a loss in precisely the situation where the economy was deteriorating further and the marginal utility of consumption was especially high. This risk limits the investor's demand for the underpriced asset, and so blunts the forces pushing prices toward fundamentals (DeLong, Shleifer, Summers, and Waldmann, 1990). If the specialized investors who attempt to profit from mispricing are financed by outside capital, their situation is even more difficult. Underpriced assets are typically ones whose recent returns have been low. As a result, specialized investors may find that the amount of funding they can obtain from nonexperts is lower when mispricing is greater (Shleifer and Vishny, 1997).

The crisis also shows clearly that financial-market imperfections are important not just to conventional firms, but also to financial firms. As discussed in Section 9.9, much of finance involves two levels of imperfections: one between the ultimate user of the capital and a financial intermediary, and another between the intermediary and the ultimate provider of capital. Most analyses of financial-market imperfections, including that in Section 9.9, ignore this fact and focus on asymmetric information between the ultimate users and the providers of their capital. But asymmetric information between the financial intermediaries and the ultimate providers appears to have been very important during the crisis. For example, many financial firms had extreme difficulty obtaining capital, and fears about the incentives facing firms close to bankruptcy appear to have been a major source of this difficulty.

Another issue involving financial markets raised by the crisis concerns the transmission of credit-market disruptions to the rest of the economy. The credit-market turmoil in the fall of 2008 was followed by a quick and rapid decline in economic activity. Some of the decline was clearly due to the direct effects of the disruptions. Firms that were unable to get credit canceled investment projects and cut back on inventories; households that could not get mortgages did not buy new homes; importers who could no longer obtain credit canceled orders; and households whose wealth had declined reduced their consumption. The microeconomics of these effects are shown by the model of investment in the presence of financial-market imperfections that we analyzed in Section 9.9. And the macroeconomic implications are investigated in the extensions of business-cycle models to incorporate financial-market imperfections that we discussed in Section 7.9.

Yet these analyses are incomplete in at least two very important ways. First, we know little about the magnitudes of the different channels. For example, we have little evidence concerning the importance of imperfections in the relationships between financial-market institutions and their suppliers of funds relative to that of imperfections in the relationships between these institutions and their borrowers. Likewise, we know little about whether it is effects on day-to-day lending, such as loans for payroll and inventory, or effects on the financing of larger projects, such as new homes and factories, that are especially important. Second, some of the impact of the disruptions appears to have operated not through their direct effects, but through more amorphous effects on the "confidence" of households and firms. Given the size of the downturn, determining the roles of these various factors and the channels through which they operated is an important task.

The crisis has also raised a range of issues less directly related to credit markets. It has made clear that the zero lower bound on nominal interest rates is a crucial constraint on monetary policy. As described in Section 11.6, there is little doubt that in the absence of the constraint, the Federal Reserve and many other central banks would have cut interest rates much more than they did, and that the downturn would have been less severe and the recovery much more rapid. Thus the crisis elevates the importance of issues related to the zero lower bound.

A more speculative view is that the crisis shows the importance of political-economy issues for understanding both the shocks that give rise to fluctuations and the policy responses that have important implications for their consequences. Many of the regulatory decisions before the crisis, as well as some of the microeconomic and macroeconomic policy actions during the crisis, seem difficult to understand with the traditional view of policymakers as knowledgeable and benevolent. To give one example, before the crisis hit, there were warning signs of overvalued asset prices and some highly questionable credit-market practices; yet policymakers did little in response.

This list of issues that the crisis raises for macroeconomics is far from complete. Others include the reasons for the flight to "liquidity" in response to financial turmoil, as well as the meaning and importance of the very concept of liquidity (for example, Holmstrom and Tirole, 1998); the central bank's role as a lender of last resort; how various fiscal actions affect the macroeconomy in the short run; the roles of foreign-currency reserves, exchange-rate regimes, and other factors in determining how a crisis is transmitted across countries; the seemingly puzzlingly small fall in inflation so far during the crisis, and what that indicates about the structure of the economy and competing theories of inflation; the magnitude and determinants of the long-term macroeconomic effects of financial crises; and much more. Indeed, one of the few silver linings of the crisis is that it makes today a particularly exciting, and particularly important, time for macroeconomics.

# REFERENCES

## A

**Abel, Andrew B. 1982.** "Dynamic Effects of Permanent and Temporary Tax Policies in a $q$ Model of Investment." *Journal of Monetary Economics* 9 (May): 353–373.

**Abel, Andrew B., and Eberly, Janice C. 1994.** "A Unified Model of Investment under Uncertainty." *American Economic Review* 84 (December): 1369–1384.

**Abel, Andrew B., Mankiw, N. Gregory, Summers, Lawrence H., and Zeckhauser, Richard J. 1989.** "Assessing Dynamic Efficiency: Theory and Evidence." *Review of Economic Studies* 56 (January): 1–20.

**Abraham, Katharine G., and Katz, Lawrence F. 1986.** "Cyclical Unemployment: Sectoral Shifts or Aggregate Disturbances?" *Journal of Political Economy* 94 (June): 507–522.

**Abramovitz, Moses. 1956.** "Resource and Output Trends in the United States since 1870." *American Economic Review* 46 (May): 5–23.

**Abreu, Dilip. 1988.** "On the Theory of Infinitely Repeated Games with Discounting." *Econometrica* 56 (March): 383–396.

**Acemoglu, Daron, Johnson, Simon, and Robinson, James A. 2001.** "The Colonial Origins of Comparative Development: An Empirical Investigation." *American Economic Review* 91 (December): 1369–1401.

**Acemoglu, Daron, Johnson, Simon, and Robinson, James A. 2002.** "Reversal of Fortune: Geography and Institutions in the Making of the Modern World Income Distribution." *Quarterly Journal of Economics* 117 (November): 1231–1294.

**Acemoglu, Daron, Johnson, Simon, and Robinson, James A. 2006.** "Reply to the Revised (May 2006) version of David Albouy's "The Colonial Origins of Comparative Development: An Investigation of the Settler Mortality Data." Unpublished paper, M.I.T. (September).

**Acemoglu, Daron, and Robinson, James A. 2000.** "Political Losers as a Barrier to Economic Development." *American Economic Review* 90 (May): 126–130.

**Acemoglu, Daron, and Robinson, James A. 2002.** "Economic Backwardness in Political Perspective." Unpublished paper, University of California, Berkeley (May).

**Aghion, Philippe, and Howitt, Peter. 1992.** "A Model of Growth through Creative Destruction." *Econometrica* 60 (March): 323–351.

**Aguiar, Mark, and Hurst, Erik. 2005.** "Consumption versus Expenditure." *Journal of Political Economy* 113 (October): 919–948.

**Aiyagari, S. Rao, Christiano, Lawrence J., and Eichenbaum, Martin. 1992.** "The Output, Employment, and Interest Rate Effects of Government Consumption." *Journal of Monetary Economics* 30 (October): 73–86.

**Aiyagari, S. Rao, and Gertler, Mark. 1985.** "The Backing of Government Bonds and Monetarism." *Journal of Monetary Economics* 16 (July): 19–44.

**Akerlof, George A., Dickens, William T., and Perry, George L. 1996.** "The Macroeconomics of Low Inflation." *Brookings Papers on Economic Activity,* no. 1, 1–76.

**Akerlof, George A., Rose, Andrew K., and Yellen, Janet L. 1988.** "Job Switching and Job Satisfaction in the U.S. Labor Market." *Brookings Papers on Economic Activity,* no. 2, 495–582.

**Akerlof, George A., and Yellen, Janet L. 1985.** "A Near-Rational Model of the Business Cycle, with Wage and Price Inertia." *Quarterly Journal of Economics* 100 (Supplement): 823–838.

**Akerlof, George A., and Yellen, Janet L. 1990.** "The Fair Wage-Effort Hypothesis and Unemployment." *Quarterly Journal of Economics* 105 (May): 255–283.

**Albouy, David. 2008.** "The Colonial Origins of Comparative Development: An Investigation of the Settler Mortality Data." National Bureau of Economic Research Working Paper No. 14130 (June).

**Alesina, Alberto. 1988.** "Macroeconomics and Politics." *NBER Macroeconomics Annual* 3: 13–52.

**Alesina, Alberto, Devleeschauwer, Arnaud, Easterly, William, Kurlat, Sergio, and Wacziarg, Romain. 2003.** "Fractionalization." *Journal of Economic Growth* 8 (June): 155–194.

**Alesina, Alberto, and Drazen, Allan. 1991.** "Why Are Stabilizations Delayed?" *American Economic Review* 81 (December): 1170–1188.

**Alesina, Alberto, Glaeser, Edward, and Sacerdote, Bruce. 2005.** "Work and Leisure in the United States and Europe: Why So Different?" *NBER Macroeconomics Annual* 20: 1–64.

**Alesina, Alberto, and Perotti, Roberto. 1997.** "Fiscal Adjustments in OECD Countries: Composition and Macroeconomic Effects." *IMF Staff Papers* 44 (June): 210–248.

**Alesina, Alberto, and Sachs, Jeffrey. 1988.** "Political Parties and the Business Cycle in the United States, 1948–1984." *Journal of Money, Credit, and Banking* 20 (February): 63–82.

**Alesina, Alberto, and Summers, Lawrence H. 1993.** "Central Bank Independence and Macroeconomic Performance." *Journal of Money, Credit, and Banking* 25 (May): 151–162.

**Alexopoulos, Michelle. 2004.** "Unemployment and the Business Cycle." *Journal of Monetary Economics* 51 (March): 277–298.

**Allais, Maurice. 1947.** *Économie et Intérêt.* Paris: Impremerie Nationale.

**Altonji, Joseph G. 1986.** "Intertemporal Substitution in Labor Supply: Evidence from Micro Data." *Journal of Political Economy* 94 (June, Part 2): S176–S215.

**Altonji, Joseph G., Hayashi, Fumio, and Kotlikoff, Laurence J. 1997.** "Parental Altruism and *Inter Vivos* Transfers: Theory and Evidence." *Journal of Political Economy* 105 (December): 1121–1166.

**Altonji, Joseph G., and Siow, Aloysius. 1987.** "Testing the Response of Consumption to Income Changes with (Noisy) Panel Data." *Quarterly Journal of Economics* 102 (May): 293–328.

**Andersen, Leonall C., and Jordan, Jerry L. 1968.** "Monetary and Fiscal Actions: A Test of Their Relative Importance in Economic Stabilization." Federal Reserve Bank of St. Louis *Review* 50 (November): 11–24.

**Angeletos, George-Marios, Laibson, David, Repetto, Andrea, Tobacman, Jeremy, and Weinberg, Stephen. 2001.** "The Hyperbolic Consumption Model: Calibration, Simulation, and Empirical Evaluation." *Journal of Economic Perspectives* 15 (Summer): 47-68.

**Arrow, Kenneth J. 1962.** "The Economic Implications of Learning by Doing." *Review of Economic Studies* 29 (June): 155-173.

**Atkeson, Andrew, and Phelan, Christopher. 1994.** "Reconsidering the Costs of Business Cycles with Incomplete Markets." *NBER Macroeconomics Annual* 9: 187-207.

**Auerbach, Alan J. 1997.** "Quantifying the Current U.S. Fiscal Imbalance." *National Tax Journal* 50 (September): 387-398.

**Auerbach, Alan J., and Gale, William G. 2009.** The Economic Crisis and the Fiscal Crisis: 2009 and Beyond. An Update." *Tax Notes* 125 (October 5): 101-130.

**Auerbach, Alan J., and Kotlikoff, Laurence J. 1987.** *Dynamic Fiscal Policy.* Cambridge: Cambridge University Press.

**Azariadis, Costas. 1975.** "Implicit Contracts and Underemployment Equilibria." *Journal of Political Economy* 83 (December): 1183-1202.

**Azariadis, Costas, and Stiglitz, Joseph E. 1983.** "Implicit Contracts and Fixed-Price Equilibria." *Quarterly Journal of Economics* 98 (Supplement): 1-22.

## B

**Bachmann, Ruediger, Caballero, Ricardo J., and Engel, Eduardo M. R. A. 2008.** "Aggregate Implications of Lumpy Investment: New Evidence and a DSGE Model." Unpublished paper (June).

**Backus, David, and Driffill, John. 1985.** "Inflation and Reputation." *American Economic Review* 75 (June): 530-538.

**Baily, Martin Neil. 1974.** "Wages and Employment under Uncertain Demand." *Review of Economic Studies* 41 (January): 37-50.

**Ball, Laurence. 1988.** "Is Equilibrium Indexation Efficient?" *Quarterly Journal of Economics* 103 (May): 299-311.

**Ball, Laurence. 1993.** "The Dynamics of High Inflation." National Bureau of Economic Research Working Paper No. 4578 (December).

**Ball, Laurence. 1994a.** "Credible Disinflation with Staggered Price-Setting." *American Economic Review* 84 (March): 282-289.

**Ball, Laurence. 1994b.** "What Determines the Sacrifice Ratio?" In N. Gregory Mankiw, ed., *Monetary Policy,* 155-182. Chicago: University of Chicago Press.

**Ball, Laurence. 1999a.** "Aggregate Demand and Long-Term Unemployment." *Brookings Papers on Economic Activity,* no. 2, 189-251.

**Ball, Laurence. 1999b.** "Efficient Rules for Monetary Policy." *International Finance* 2 (April): 63-83.

**Ball, Laurence, and Cecchetti, Stephen G. 1990.** "Inflation and Uncertainty at Short and Long Horizons." *Brookings Papers on Economic Activity,* no. 1, 215-254.

**Ball, Laurence, Elmendorf, Douglas W., and Mankiw, N. Gregory. 1998.** "The Deficit Gamble." *Journal of Money, Credit, and Banking* 30 (November): 699-720.

**Ball, Laurence, and Mankiw, N. Gregory. 1995.** "Relative-Price Changes as Aggregate Supply Shocks." *Quarterly Journal of Economics* 110 (February): 161-193.

**Ball, Laurence, Mankiw, N. Gregory, and Romer, David. 1988.** "The New Keynesian Economics and the Output-Inflation Tradeoff." *Brookings Papers on Economic Activity,* no. 1, 1-65.

Ball, Laurence, and Moffitt, Robert. 2001. "Productivity Growth and the Phillips Curve." In Alan B. Krueger and Robert M. Solow, eds., *The Roaring Nineties: Can Full Employment Be Sustained?* 61-91. New York: Russell Sage Foundation.

Ball, Laurence, and Romer, David. 1990. "Real Rigidities and the Non-Neutrality of Money." *Review of Economic Studies* 57 (April): 183-203.

Ball, Laurence, and Romer, David. 1991. "Sticky Prices as Coordination Failure." *American Economic Review* 81 (June): 539-552.

Baqir, Reza. 2002. "Districting and Government Overspending." *Journal of Political Economy* 110 (December): 1318-1354.

Barberis, Nicholas, Huang, Ming, and Santos, Tano. 2001. "Prospect Theory and Asset Prices." *Quarterly Journal of Economics* 116 (February): 1-53.

Barro, Robert J. 1972. "A Theory of Monopolistic Price Adjustment." *Review of Economic Studies* 34 (January): 17-26.

Barro, Robert J. 1974. "Are Government Bonds Net Wealth?" *Journal of Political Economy* 82 (November/December): 1095-1117.

Barro, Robert J. 1976. "Rational Expectations and the Role of Monetary Policy." *Journal of Monetary Economics* 2 (January): 1-32.

Barro, Robert J. 1977. "Long-Term Contracting, Sticky Prices, and Monetary Policy." *Journal of Monetary Economics* 3 (July): 305-316.

Barro, Robert J. 1979. "On the Determination of the Public Debt." *Journal of Political Economy* 87 (October): 940-971.

Barro, Robert J. 1986. "Reputation in a Model of Monetary Policy with Incomplete Information." *Journal of Monetary Economics* 17 (January): 3-20.

Barro, Robert J. 1987. "Government Spending, Interest Rates, Prices, and Budget Deficits in the United Kingdom, 1701-1918." *Journal of Monetary Economics* 20 (September): 221-247.

Barro, Robert J. 1999. "Ramsey Meets Laibson in the Neoclassical Growth Model." *Quarterly Journal of Economics* 114 (November): 1125-1152.

Barro, Robert J. 2006. "Rare Disasters and Asset Markets in the Twentieth Century." *Quarterly Journal of Economics* 121 (August): 823-866.

Barro, Robert J., and Gordon, David B. 1983. "Rules, Discretion and Reputation in a Model of Monetary Policy." *Journal of Monetary Economics* 12 (July): 101-121.

Barro, Robert J., Mankiw, N. Gregory, and Sala-i-Martin, Xavier. 1995. "Capital Mobility in Neoclassical Models of Growth." *American Economic Review* 85 (March): 103-115.

Barro, Robert J., and Redlick, Charles J. 2009. "Macroeconomic Effects from Government Purchases and Taxes." National Bureau of Economic Research Working Paper No. 15369 (September).

Barro, Robert J., and Sala-i-Martin, Xavier. 1991. "Convergence across States and Regions." *Brookings Papers on Economic Activity,* no. 1, 107-182.

Barro, Robert J., and Sala-i-Martin, Xavier. 1992. "Convergence." *Journal of Political Economy* 100 (April): 223-251.

Barro, Robert J., and Sala-i-Martin, Xavier. 2003. *Economic Growth,* 2d ed. Cambridge, MA: MIT Press.

Barsky, Robert B., Mankiw, N. Gregory, and Zeldes, Stephen P. 1986. "Ricardian Consumers with Keynesian Propensities." *American Economic Review* 76 (September): 676-691.

Barsky, Robert B., and Miron, Jeffrey A. 1989. "The Seasonal Cycle and the Business Cycle." *Journal of Political Economy* 97 (June): 503-534.

Barth, Marvin J., III, and Ramey, Valerie A. 2001. "The Cost Channel of Monetary Transmission." *NBER Macroeconomics Annual* 16: 199–240.

Basu, Susanto. 1995. "Intermediate Goods and Business Cycles: Implications for Productivity and Welfare." *American Economic Review* 85 (June): 512–531.

Basu, Susanto. 1996. "Procyclical Productivity: Increasing Returns or Cyclical Utilization?" *Quarterly Journal of Economics* 111 (August): 719–751.

Basu, Susanto, and Fernald, John G. 1995. "Are Apparent Productivity Spillovers a Figment of Specification Error?" *Journal of Monetary Economics* 36 (August): 165–188.

Basu, Susanto, and Fernald, John G. 1997. "Returns to Scale in U.S. Production: Estimates and Implications." *Journal of Political Economy* 105 (April): 249–283.

Basu, Susanto, Fernald, John G., and Kimball, Miles. 2006. "Are Technology Improvements Contractionary?" *American Economic Review* 96 (December): 1418–1448.

Basu, Susanto, Fernald, John G., Oulton, Nicholas, and Srinivasan, Sylaja. 2003. "The Case of the Missing Productivity Growth, or Does Information Technology Explain Why Productivity Accelerated in the United States but Not in the United Kingdom?" *NBER Macroeconomics Annual* 18: 9–63.

Basu, Susanto, and Weil, David N. 1999. "Appropriate Technology and Growth." *Quarterly Journal of Economics* 113 (November): 1025–1054.

Baumol, William J. 1952. "The Transactions Demand for Cash: An Inventory Theoretic Approach." *Quarterly Journal of Economics* 66 (November): 545–556.

Baumol, William. 1986. "Productivity Growth, Convergence, and Welfare." *American Economic Review* 76 (December): 1072–1085.

Baumol, William. 1990. "Entrepreneurship: Productive, Unproductive, and Destructive." *Journal of Political Economy* 98 (October, Part 1): 893–921.

Baxter, Marianne, and Crucini, Mario J. 1993. "Explaining Saving-Investment Correlations." *American Economic Review* 83 (June): 416–436.

Baxter, Marianne, and Jermann, Urban J. 1997. "The International Diversification Puzzle Is Worse Than You Think." *American Economic Review* 87 (March): 170–180.

Baxter, Marianne, and Jermann, Urban J. 1999. "Household Production and the Excess Sensitivity of Consumption to Current Income." *American Economic Review* 89 (September): 902–920.

Baxter, Marianne, and King, Robert G. 1993. "Fiscal Policy in General Equilibrium." *American Economic Review* 83 (June): 315–334.

Baxter, Marianne, and Stockman, Alan C. 1989. "Business Cycles and the Exchange-Rate Regime: Some International Evidence." *Journal of Monetary Economics* 23 (May): 377–400.

Bean, Charles R. 1994. "European Unemployment: A Survey." *Journal of Economic Literature* 32 (June): 573–619.

Beechey, Meredith J., and Wright, Jonathan H. 2009. "The High-Frequency Impact of News on Long-Term Yields and Forward Rates: Is It Real?" *Journal of Monetary Economics* 56 (May): 535–544.

Bekaert, Geert, Hodrick, Robert J., and Marshall, David A. 1997. "The Implications of First-Order Risk Aversion for Asset Market Risk Premiums." *Journal of Monetary Economics* 40 (September): 3–39.

Bénabou, Roland. 1992. "Inflation and Efficiency in Search Markets." *Review of Economic Studies* 59 (April): 299–329.

**Benartzi, Shlomo, and Thaler, Richard H. 1995.** "Myopic Loss Aversion and the Equity Premium Puzzle." *Quarterly Journal of Economics* 110 (February): 73-92.

**Benhabib, Jess, and Farmer, Roger E. A. 1999.** "Indeterminacy and Sunspots in Macroeconomics." In John B. Taylor and Michael Woodford, eds., *Handbook of Macroeconomics,* 387-448. Amsterdam: Elsevier.

**Benhabib, Jess, Rogerson, Richard, and Wright, Randall. 1991.** "Homework in Macroeconomics: Household Production and Aggregate Fluctuations." *Journal of Political Economy* 99 (December): 1166-1187.

**Benigno, Gianluca, and Benigno, Pierpaolo. 2006.** "Designing Targeting Rules for International Monetary Policy Cooperation." *Journal of Monetary Economics* 53 (April): 473-506.

**Bernanke, Ben S. 1983a.** "Irreversibility, Uncertainty, and Cyclical Investment." *Quarterly Journal of Economics* 98 (February): 85-106.

**Bernanke, Ben S. 1983b.** "Nonmonetary Effects of the Financial Crisis in the Propagation of the Great Depression." *American Economic Review* 73 (June): 257-276.

**Bernanke, Ben S. 1986.** "Alternative Explanations of the Money-Income Correlation." *Carnegie-Rochester Conference Series on Public Policy* 25 (Autumn): 49-99.

**Bernanke, Ben S., and Blinder, Alan S. 1992.** "The Federal Funds Rate and the Channels of Monetary Transmission." *American Economic Review* 82 (September): 901-921.

**Bernanke, Ben S., and Gertler, Mark. 1989.** "Agency Costs, Net Worth, and Business Fluctuations." *American Economic Review* 79 (March): 14-31.

**Bernanke, Ben S., and Gertler, Mark. 2001.** "How Should Central Bankers Respond to Asset Prices?" *American Economic Review* 91 (May): 253-257.

**Bernanke, Ben S., and Mihov, Ilian. 1998.** "Measuring Monetary Policy." *Quarterly Journal of Economics* 113 (August): 869-902.

**Bernanke, Ben S., and Parkinson, Martin L. 1991.** "Procyclical Labor Productivity and Competing Theories of the Business Cycle: Some Evidence from Interwar U.S. Manufacturing Industries." *Journal of Political Economy* 99 (June): 439-459.

**Bernanke, Ben S., and Woodford, Michael. 1997.** "Inflation Forecasts and Monetary Policy." *Journal of Money, Credit, and Banking* 29 (November, Part 2): 653-684.

**Bernheim, B. Douglas. 1987.** "Ricardian Equivalence: An Evaluation of Theory and Evidence." *NBER Macroeconomics Annual* 2: 263-304.

**Bernheim, B. Douglas, and Bagwell, Kyle. 1988.** "Is Everything Neutral?" *Journal of Political Economy* 96 (April): 308-338.

**Bernheim, B. Douglas, Shleifer, Andrei, and Summers, Lawrence H. 1985.** "The Strategic Bequest Motive." *Journal of Political Economy* 93 (December): 1045-1076.

**Bertola, Giuseppe, and Drazen, Allan. 1993.** "Trigger Points and Budget Cuts: Explaining the Effects of Fiscal Austerity." *American Economic Review* 83 (March): 11-26.

**Bewley, Truman F. 1999.** *Why Wages Don't Fall during a Recession.* Cambridge, MA: Harvard University Press.

**Bils, Mark J. 1985.** "Real Wages over the Business Cycle: Evidence from Panel Data." *Journal of Political Economy* 93 (August): 666-689.

**Bils, Mark J. 1987.** "The Cyclical Behavior of Marginal Cost and Price." *American Economic Review* 77 (December): 838-857.

**Bils, Mark J. 1991.** "Testing for Contracting Effects on Employment." *Quarterly Journal of Economics* 106 (November): 1129-1156.

**Bils, Mark J., and Klenow, Peter J. 1998.** "Using Consumer Theory to Test Competing Business Cycle Models." *Journal of Political Economy* 106 (April): 233-261.

**Bils, Mark J., and Klenow, Peter J. 2000.** "Does Schooling Cause Growth?" *American Economic Review* 90 (December): 1160-1183.

**Bils, Mark J., and Klenow, Peter J. 2004.** "Some Evidence on the Importance of Sticky Prices." *Journal of Political Economy* 112 (October): 947-985.

**Black, Fischer. 1974.** "Uniqueness of the Price Level in Monetary Growth Models with Rational Expectations." *Journal of Economic Theory* 7 (January): 53-65.

**Black, Fischer. 1982.** "General Equilibrium and Business Cycles." National Bureau of Economic Research Working Paper No. 950 (August).

**Blalock, Garrick, Gertler, Paul J., and Levine, David I. 2008.** "Financial Constraints on Investment in an Emerging Market Crisis." *Journal of Monetary Economics* 55 (April): 568-591.

**Blanchard, Olivier J. 1979.** "Speculative Bubbles, Crashes and Rational Expectations." *Economics Letters* 3: 387-389.

**Blanchard, Olivier J. 1985.** "Debts, Deficits, and Finite Horizons." *Journal of Political Economy* 93 (April): 223-247.

**Blanchard, Olivier J., and Diamond, Peter A. 1989.** "The Beveridge Curve." *Brookings Papers on Economic Activity,* no. 1, 1-76.

**Blanchard, Olivier J., and Diamond, Peter A. 1990.** "The Cyclical Behavior of the Gross Flows of U.S. Workers." *Brookings Papers on Economic Activity,* no. 2, 85-156.

**Blanchard, Olivier J., and Fischer, Stanley. 1989.** *Lectures on Macroeconomics.* Cambridge, MA: MIT Press.

**Blanchard, Olivier J., and Galí, Jordi. 2007.** "Real Wage Rigidities and the New Keynesian Model." *Journal of Money, Credit, and Banking* 39 (February): 35-65.

**Blanchard, Olivier J., and Kahn, Charles M. 1980.** "The Solution of Linear Difference Models under Rational Expectations." *Econometrica* 48 (July): 1305-1311.

**Blanchard, Olivier J., and Kiyotaki, Nobuhiro. 1987.** "Monopolistic Competition and the Effects of Aggregate Demand." *American Economic Review* 77 (September): 647-666.

**Blanchard, Olivier J., and Perotti, Roberto. 2002.** "An Empirical Characterization of the Dynamic Effects of Changes in Government Spending and Taxes on Output." *Quarterly Journal of Economics* 117 (November): 1329-1368.

**Blanchard, Olivier J., and Summers, Lawrence, H. 1986.** "Hysteresis and the European Unemployment Problem." *NBER Macroeconomics Annual* 1: 15-78.

**Blanchard, Olivier J., and Watson, Mark W. 1986.** "Are Business Cycles All Alike?" In Robert J. Gordon, ed., *The American Business Cycle: Continuity and Change,* 123-156. Chicago: University of Chicago Press.

**Blanchard, Olivier J., and Weil, Philippe. 2001.** "Dynamic Efficiency, the Riskless Rate, and Debt Ponzi Games under Uncertainty." *Advances in Macroeconomics* 1, no. 2, Article 3.

**Blanchard, Olivier J., and Wolfers, Justin. 2000.** "The Role of Shocks and Institutions in the Rise of European Unemployment: The Aggregate Evidence." *Economic Journal* 110 (March): C1-C33.

**Blank, Rebecca M. 1990.** "Why Are Wages Cyclical in the 1970s?" *Journal of Labor Economics* 8 (January, Part 1): 16-47.

Blinder, Alan S. 1979. *Economic Policy and the Great Stagflation.* New York: Academic Press.

Blinder, Alan S. 1998. *Asking about Prices: A New Approach to Understanding Price Stickiness.* New York: Russell Sage Foundation.

Blinder, Alan S., and Choi, Don H. 1990. "A Shred of Evidence on Theories of Wage Stickiness." *Quarterly Journal of Economics* 105 (November): 1003–1015.

Blinder, Alan S., and Rudd, Jeremy B. 2008. "The Supply-Shock Explanation of the Great Stagflation Revisited." National Bureau of Economic Research Working Paper No. 14563 (June).

Blinder, Alan S., and Solow, Robert M. 1973. "Does Fiscal Policy Matter?" *Journal of Public Economics* 2 (November): 318–337.

Bloom, David E., and Sachs, Jeffrey D. 1998. "Geography, Demography, and Economic Growth in Africa." *Brookings Papers on Economic Activity,* no. 2, 207–295.

Bloom, Nick, Sadun, Raffaella, and Van Reenan, John. 2008. "Americans Do I.T. Better: US Multinationals and the Productivity Miracle." Unpublished paper, Stanford University (April).

Blough, Stephen R. 1992. "The Relationship between Power and Level for Generic Unit Root Tests in Finite Samples." *Applied Econometrics* 7 (July–September): 295–308.

Bohn, Henning. 1988. "Why Do We Have Nominal Government Debt?" *Journal of Monetary Economics* 21 (January): 127–140.

Bohn, Henning. 1990. "Tax Smoothing with Financial Instruments." *American Economic Review* 80 (December): 1217–1230.

Bohn, Henning. 1992. "Endogenous Government Spending and Ricardian Equivalence." *Economic Journal* 102 (May): 588–597.

Bohn, Henning. 1995. "The Sustainability of Budget Deficits in a Stochastic Economy." *Journal of Money, Credit, and Banking* 27 (February): 257–271.

Borjas, George J. 1987. "Self-Selection and the Earnings of Immigrants." *American Economic Review* 77 (September): 531–553.

Boskin, Michael J., Dulberger, Ellen R., Gordon, Robert J., Griliches, Zvi, and Jorgenson, Dale. 1998. "Consumer Prices, the Consumer Price Index, and the Cost of Living." *Journal of Economic Perspectives* 12 (Winter): 3–26.

Brainard, William. 1967. "Uncertainty and the Effectiveness of Policy." *American Economic Review* 57 (May): 411–425.

Brander, James A., and Taylor, M. Scott. 1998. "The Simple Economics of Easter Island: A Ricardo-Malthus Model of Renewable Resource Use." *American Economic Review* 88 (March): 119–138.

Braun, R. Anton. 1994. "Tax Disturbances and Real Economic Activity in the Postwar United States." *Journal of Monetary Economics* 33 (June): 441–462.

Braun, Steven. 1984. "Productivity and the NIIRU (and Other Phillips Curve Issues)." Federal Reserve Board, Economic Activity Working Paper No. 34 (June).

Breeden, Douglas. 1979. "An Intertemporal Asset Pricing Model with Stochastic Consumption and Investment." *Journal of Financial Economics* 7 (September): 265–296.

Bresciani-Turroni, Constantino. 1937. *The Economics of Inflation: A Study of Currency Depreciation in Post-War Germany.* London: Allen and Unwin.

Bresnahan, Timothy F., Brynjolfsson, Erik, and Hitt, Lorin M. 2002. "Information Technology, Workplace Organization, and the Demand for Skilled Labor: Firm-Level Evidence." *Quarterly Journal of Economics* 117 (February): 339–376.

**Brock, William. 1975.** "A Simple Perfect Foresight Monetary Model." *Journal of Monetary Economics* 1 (April): 133–150.

**Browning, Martin, and Collado, M. Dolores. 2001.** "The Response of Expenditures to Anticipated Income Changes: Panel Data Estimates." *American Economic Review* 91 (June): 681–692.

**Bruno, Michael, and Easterly, William. 1998.** "Inflation Crises and Long-Run Growth." *Journal of Monetary Economics* 41 (February): 3–26.

**Bryant, John. 1983.** "A Simple Rational Expectations Keynes-Type Model." *Quarterly Journal of Economics* 98 (August): 525–528.

**Bryant, Ralph C., Hooper, Peter, and Mann, Catherine L., eds. 1993.** *Evaluating Policy Regimes: New Research in Empirical Macroeconomics.* Washington, DC: Brookings Institution Press.

**Buchanan, James M., and Wagner, Richard E. 1977.** *Democracy in Deficit: The Political Legacy of Lord Keynes.* New York: Academic Press.

**Bulow, Jeremy, and Summers, Lawrence H. 1986.** "A Theory of Dual Labor Markets with Applications to Industrial Policy, Discrimination, and Keynesian Unemployment." *Journal of Labor Economics* 4: 376–414.

**Burnside, Craig, Eichenbaum, Martin. 1996.** "Factor-Hoarding and the Propagation of Business-Cycle Shocks." *American Economic Review* 86 (December): 1154–1174.

**Burnside, Craig, Eichenbaum, Martin, and Rebelo, Sergio. 1993.** "Labor Hoarding and the Business Cycle." *Journal of Political Economy* 101 (April): 245–273.

**Burnside, Craig, Eichenbaum, Martin, and Rebelo, Sergio. 1995.** "Capital Utilization and Returns to Scale." *NBER Macroeconomics Annual* 10: 67–110.

## C

**Caballero, Ricardo J. 1990.** "Expenditure on Durable Goods: A Case for Slow Adjustment." *Quarterly Journal of Economics* 105 (August): 727–743.

**Caballero, Ricardo J. 1993.** "Durable Goods: An Explanation for Their Slow Adjustment." *Journal of Political Economy* 101 (April): 351–384.

**Caballero, Ricardo J., and Engel, Eduardo M. R. A. 1993.** "Heterogeneity and Output Fluctuations in a Dynamic Menu-Cost Economy." *Review of Economic Studies* 60 (January): 95–119.

**Caballero, Ricardo J., Engel, Eduardo M. R. A., and Haltiwanger, John C. 1995.** "Plant-Level Adjustment and Aggregate Investment Dynamics." *Brookings Papers on Economic Activity,* no. 2, 1–54.

**Caballero, Ricardo J., and Lyons, Richard K. 1992.** "External Effects in U.S. Procyclical Productivity." *Journal of Monetary Economics* 29 (April): 209–225.

**Cagan, Philip. 1956.** "The Monetary Dynamics of Hyperinflation." In Milton Friedman, ed., *Studies in the Quantity Theory of Money,* 25–117. Chicago: University of Chicago Press.

**Calvo, Guillermo. 1978a.** "On the Indeterminacy of Interest Rates and Wages with Perfect Foresight." *Journal of Economic Theory* 19 (December): 321–337.

**Calvo, Guillermo. 1978b.** "On the Time Consistency of Optimal Policy in a Monetary Economy." *Econometrica* 46 (November): 1411–1428.

**Calvo, Guillermo. 1983.** "Staggered Prices in a Utility-Maximizing Framework." *Journal of Monetary Economics* 12 (September): 383–398.

Calvo, Guillermo. 1988. "Servicing the Public Debt: The Role of Expectations." *American Economic Review* 78 (September): 647-661.

Calvo, Guillermo, and Végh, Carlos. 1999. "Inflation Stabilization and BOP Crises in Developing Countries." In John B. Taylor and Michael Woodford, eds., *Handbook of Macroeconomics,* 1531-1614. Amsterdam: Elsevier.

Campbell, Carl M., III, and Kamlani, Kunal S. 1997. "The Reasons for Wage Rigidity: Evidence from a Survey of Firms." *Quarterly Journal of Economics* 112 (August): 759-789.

Campbell, John Y. 1987. "Does Saving Anticipate Declining Labor Income? An Alternative Test of the Permanent Income Hypothesis." *Econometrica* 55 (November): 1249-1273.

Campbell, John Y. 1994. "Inspecting the Mechanism: An Analytical Approach to the Stochastic Growth Model." *Journal of Monetary Economics* 33 (June): 463-506.

Campbell, John Y., and Cochrane, John H. 1999. "By Force of Habit: A Consumption-Based Explanation of Aggregate Stock Market Behavior." *Journal of Political Economy* 107 (April): 205-251.

Campbell, John Y., and Deaton, Angus. 1989. "Why Is Consumption So Smooth?" *Review of Economic Studies* 56 (July): 357-374.

Campbell, John Y., and Mankiw, N. Gregory. 1989. "Consumption, Income, and Interest Rates: Reinterpreting the Time Series Evidence." *NBER Macroeconomics Annual* 4: 185-216.

Campbell, John Y., and Perron, Pierre. 1991. "Pitfalls and Opportunities: What Macroeconomists Should Know about Unit Roots." *NBER Macroeconomics Annual* 6: 141-201.

Campillo, Marta, and Miron, Jeffrey A. 1997. "Why Does Inflation Differ across Countries?" In Christina D. Romer and David H. Romer, eds., *Reducing Inflation: Motivation and Strategy,* 335-362 (Chicago: University of Chicago Press).

Canzoneri, Matthew B., Cumby, Robert E., and Diba, Behzad T. 2007. "Euler Equations and Money Market Interest Rates: A Challenge for Monetary Policy Models." *Journal of Monetary Economics* 54 (October): 1863-1881.

Caplin, Andrew S., and Leahy, John. 1991. "State-Dependent Pricing and the Dynamics of Money and Output." *Quarterly Journal of Economics* 106 (August): 683-708.

Caplin, Andrew S., and Spulber, Daniel F. 1987. "Menu Costs and the Neutrality of Money." *Quarterly Journal of Economics* 102 (November): 703-725.

Card, David. 1990. "Unexpected Inflation, Real Wages, and Employment Determination in Union Contracts." *American Economic Review* 80 (September): 669-688.

Card, David, and Hyslop, Dean. 1997. "Does Inflation 'Grease the Wheels of the Labor Market'?" In Christina D. Romer and David H. Romer, eds., *Reducing Inflation: Motivation and Strategy,* 71-114. Chicago: University of Chicago Press.

Cardoso, Eliana. 1991. "From Inertia to Megainflation: Brazil in the 1980s." In Michael Bruno et al., eds., *Lessons of Economic Stabilization and Its Aftermath,* 143-177. Cambridge, MA: MIT Press.

Carlton, Dennis W. 1982. "The Disruptive Effects of Inflation on the Organization of Markets." In Robert E. Hall, ed., *Inflation: Causes and Effects,* 139-152. Chicago: University of Chicago Press.

Carmichael, Lorne. 1985. "Can Unemployment Be Involuntary? Comment." *American Economic Review* 75 (December): 1213-1214.

Carroll, Christopher D. 1992. "The Buffer-Stock Theory of Saving: Some Macroeconomic Evidence." *Brookings Papers on Economic Activity,* no. 2, 61-156.

Carroll, Christopher D. 1997. "Buffer-Stock Saving and the Life Cycle/Permanent Income Hypothesis." *Quarterly Journal of Economics* 112 (February): 1-55.

Carroll, Christopher D., Overland, Jody, and Weil, David N. 1997. "Comparison Utility in a Growth Model." *Journal of Economic Growth* 2 (December): 339-367.

Carroll, Christopher D., and Summers, Lawrence H. 1991. "Consumption Growth Parallels Income Growth: Some New Evidence." In B. Douglas Bernheim and John B. Shoven, eds., *National Saving and Economic Performance,* 305-343. Chicago: University of Chicago Press.

Carvalho, Carlos. 2006. "Heterogeneity in Price Stickiness and the Real Effects of Monetary Shocks." *Frontiers of Macroeconomics* 2:1, Article 1.

Caselli, Francesco, and Feyrer, James. 2007. "The Marginal Product of Capital." *Quarterly Journal of Economics* 122 (May): 535-568.

Cass, David. 1965. "Optimum Growth in an Aggregative Model of Capital Accumulation." *Review of Economic Studies* 32 (July): 233-240.

Cecchetti, Stephen G., Genberg, Hans, and Wadhwani, Sushil. 2003. "Asset Prices in a Flexible Inflation Targeting Framework." In William Curt Hunter, George G. Kaufman, Michael Pomerleano, eds., *Asset Price Bubbles: The Implications for Monetary, Regulatory, and International Polices,* 427-444. Cambridge, MA: MIT Press.

Chang, Yongsung, Gomes, Joao F., and Schorfheide, Frank. 2002. "Learning-by-Doing as a Propagation Mechanism." *American Economic Review* 92 (December): 1498-1520.

Chari, V. V., and Cole, Harold. 1993. "Why Are Representative Democracies Fiscally Irresponsible?" Federal Reserve Bank of Minneapolis Research Department, Staff Report No. 163 (August).

Chari, V. V., and Kehoe, Patrick J. 1999. "Optimal Fiscal and Monetary Policy." In John B. Taylor and Michael Woodford, eds., *Handbook of Macroeconomics,* 1671-1745. Amsterdam: Elsevier.

Chevalier, Judith A., Kashyap, Anil K, and Rossi, Peter E. 2000. "Why Don't Prices Rise during Periods of Peak Demand? Evidence from Scanner Data." National Bureau of Economic Research Working Paper No. 7981 (October).

Chevalier, Judith A., Kashyap, Anil K, and Rossi, Peter E. 2003. "Why Don't Prices Rise during Periods of Peak Demand? Evidence from Scanner Data." *American Economic Review* 93 (March): 15-37.

Chevalier, Judith A., and Scharfstein, David S. 1996. "Capital-Market Imperfections and Countercyclical Markups: Theory and Evidence." *American Economic Review* 86 (September): 703-725.

Cho, Dongchul, and Graham, Stephen. 1996. "The Other Side of Conditional Convergence." *Economics Letters* 50 (February): 285-290.

Cho, In-Koo, Williams, Noah, and Sargent, Thomas J. 2002. "Escaping Nash Inflation." *Review of Economic Studies* 69 (January): 1-40.

Christiano, Lawrence J., and Eichenbaum, Martin. 1992. "Current Real-Business-Cycle Theories and Aggregate Labor-Market Fluctuations." *American Economic Review* 82 (June): 430-450.

Christiano, Lawrence J., Eichenbaum, Martin, and Evans, Charles. 1996. "The Effects of Monetary Policy Shocks: Evidence from the Flow of Funds." *Review of Economics and Statistics* 78 (February): 16-34.

Christiano, Lawrence J., Eichenbaum, Martin, and Evans, Charles. 1997. "Sticky Price and Limited Participation Models: A Comparison." *European Economic Review* 41 (June): 1201–1249.

Christiano, Lawrence J., Eichenbaum, Martin, and Evans, Charles. 2005. "Nominal Rigidities and the Dynamic Effects of a Shock to Monetary Policy." *Journal of Political Economy* 113 (February): 1–45.

Christiano, Lawrence J., and Harrison, Sharon G. 1999. "Chaos, Sunspots, and Automatic Stabilizers." *Journal of Monetary Economics* 44 (August): 3–31.

Christiano, Lawrence, Motto, Roberto, and Rostagno, Massimo. 2003 "The Great Depression and the Friedman-Schwartz Hypothesis." *Journal of Money, Credit, and Banking* 35 (December, Part 2): 1119–1198.

Christiano, Lawrence, Motto, Roberto, and Rostagno, Massimo. 2009. "Financial Factors in Economic Fluctuations." Unpublished paper (May).

Clarida, Richard, Galí, Jordi, and Gertler, Mark. 1999. "The Science of Monetary Policy: A New Keynesian Perspective." *Journal of Economic Literature* 37 (December): 1661–1707.

Clarida, Richard, Galí, Jordi, and Gertler, Mark. 2000. "Monetary Policy Rules and Macroeconomic Stability: Evidence and Some Theory." *Quarterly Journal of Economics* 115 (February): 147–180.

Clark, Gregory. 1987. "Why Isn't the Whole World Developed? Lessons from the Cotton Mills." *Journal of Economic History* 47 (March): 141–173.

Clark, Kim B., and Summers, Lawrence H. 1979. "Labor Market Dynamics and Unemployment: A Reconsideration." *Brookings Papers on Economic Activity,* no. 1, 13–60.

Clark, Peter, Laxton, Douglas, and Rose, David. 1996. "Asymmetry in the U.S. Output-Inflation Nexus." *IMF Staff Papers* 43 (March): 216–251.

Coate, Stephen, and Morris, Stephen. 1995. "On the Form of Transfers to Special Interests." *Journal of Political Economy* 103 (December): 1210–1235.

Cochrane, John H. 1998. "What Do the VARs Mean? Measuring the Output Effects of Monetary Policy." *Journal of Monetary Economics* 41 (April): 277–300.

Cogley, Timothy, and Nason, James M. 1995. "Output Dynamics in Real-Business-Cycle Models." *American Economic Review* 85 (June): 492–511.

Cole, Harold L., and Kehoe, Timothy J. 2000. "Self-Fulfilling Debt Crises." *Review of Economic Studies* 67 (January): 91–116.

Coleman, Thomas S. 1984. "Essays in Aggregate Labor Market Business Cycle Fluctuations." Ph.D. dissertation, University of Chicago.

Congressional Budget Office. 2009. *The Long-Term Budget Outlook* (June).

Constantinides, George M. 1990. "Habit Formation: A Resolution of the Equity Premium Puzzle." *Journal of Political Economy* 98 (June): 519–543.

Cook, Timothy, and Hahn, Thomas. 1989. "The Effect of Changes in the Federal Funds Rate Target on Market Interest Rates in the 1970s." *Journal of Monetary Economics* 24 (November): 331–351.

Cooley, Thomas F., and LeRoy, Stephen F. 1985. "Atheoretical Macroeconomics: A Critique." *Journal of Monetary Economics* 16 (November): 283–308.

Cooley, Thomas F., and Ohanian, Lee E. 1997. "Postwar British Economic Growth and the Legacy of Keynes." *Journal of Political Economy* 105 (June): 439–472.

Cooper, Russell W., and Haltiwanger, John. 1996. "Evidence on Macroeconomic Complementarities." *Review of Economics and Statistics* 103 (April): 1106–1117.

**Cooper, Russell W., and Haltiwanger, John. 2006.** "On the Nature of Capital Adjustment Costs." *Review of Economic Studies* 73 (July): 611-633.

**Cooper, Russell W., and John, Andrew. 1988.** "Coordinating Coordination Failures in Keynesian Models." *Quarterly Journal of Economics* 103 (August): 441-463.

**Cooper, Russell W., and Johri, Alok. 2002.** "Learning-by-Doing and Aggregate Fluctuations." *Journal of Monetary Economics* 49 (November): 1539-1566.

**Corsetti, Giancarlo, and Pesenti, Paolo. 2005.** "International Dimensions of Optimal Monetary Policy." *Journal of Monetary Economics* 52 (March): 281-305.

**Coval, Joshua, Jurek, Jakub, and Stafford, Erik. 2009.** "The Economics of Structured Finance." *Journal of Economic Perspectives* 23 (Winter): 3-25.

**Craine, Roger. 1989.** "Risky Business: The Allocation of Capital." *Journal of Monetary Economics* 23 (March): 201-218.

**Cukierman, Alex, Kalaitzidakis, Pantelis, Summers, Lawrence H., and Webb, Steven B. 1993.** "Central Bank Independence, Growth, Investment, and Real Rates." *Carnegie-Rochester Conference Series on Public Policy* 39 (December): 95-140.

**Cukierman, Alex, Webb, Steven B., and Neyapti, Bilin. 1992.** "Measuring the Independence of Central Banks and Its Effect on Policy Outcomes." *World Bank Economic Review* 6 (September): 353-398.

**Cummins, Jason G., Hassett, Kevin A., and Hubbard, R. Glenn. 1994.** "A Reconsideration of Investment Behavior Using Tax Reforms as Natural Experiments." *Brookings Papers on Economic Activity,* no. 2, 1-74.

**Cúrdia, Vasco, and Woodford, Michael. 2009.** "Credit Frictions and Optimal Monetary Policy." Unpublished paper (May).

# D

**Danthine, Jean-Pierre, and Donaldson, John B. 1990.** "Efficiency Wages and the Business Cycle Puzzle." *European Economic Review* (November): 1275-1301.

**Danziger, Leif. 1999.** "A Dynamic Economy with Costly Price Adjustments." *American Economic Review* 89 (September): 878-901.

**Davis, Joseph H. 2004.** "An Annual Index of U.S. Industrial Production, 1790-1915." *Quarterly Journal of Economics* 119 (November): 1177-1215.

**Davis, Steven J., Faberman, R. Jason, and Haltiwanger, John. 2006.** "The Flow Approach to Labor Markets: New Data Sources and Micro-Macro Links." *Journal of Economic Perspectives* 20 (Summer): 3-26.

**Davis, Steven J., and Haltiwanger, John. 1990.** "Gross Job Creation and Destruction: Microeconomic Evidence and Macroeconomic Implications." *NBER Macroeconomics Annual* 5: 123-168.

**Davis, Steven J., and Haltiwanger, John. 1992.** "Gross Job Creation, Gross Job Destruction, and Employment Reallocation." *Quarterly Journal of Economics* 107 (August): 819-863.

**Davis, Steven J., and Haltiwanger, John. 1999.** "On the Driving Forces behind Cyclical Movements in Employment and Job Reallocation." *American Economic Review* 89 (December): 1234-1258.

**Deaton, Angus. 1991.** "Saving and Liquidity Constraints." *Econometrica* 59 (September): 1221-1248.

**Deaton, Angus. 1992.** *Understanding Consumption.* Oxford: Oxford University Press.

**Debelle, Guy, and Laxton, Douglas. 1997.** "Is the Phillips Curve Really a Curve? Some Evidence for Canada, the United Kingdom, and the United States." *IMF Staff Papers* 44 (June): 249–282.

**DeLong, J. Bradford. 1988.** "Productivity Growth, Convergence, and Welfare: Comment." *American Economic Review* 78 (December): 1138–1154.

**DeLong, J. Bradford. 1997.** "America's Peacetime Inflation: The 1970s." In Christina D. Romer and David H. Romer, eds., *Reducing Inflation: Motivation and Strategy,* 247–276. Chicago: University of Chicago Press.

**DeLong, J. Bradford, and Shleifer, Andrei. 1993.** "Princes and Merchants." *Journal of Law and Economics* 36 (October): 671–702.

**DeLong, J. Bradford, Shleifer, Andrei, Summers, Lawrence H., and Waldmann, Robert J. 1990.** "Noise Trader Risk in Financial Markets." *Journal of Political Economy* 108 (August): 703–738.

**den Haan, Wouter J., Ramey, Garey, and Watson, Joel. 2000.** "Job Destruction and Propagation of Shocks." *American Economic Review* 90 (June): 482–498.

**Deschenes, Olivier, and Greenstone, Michael. 2007.** "The Economic Impacts of Climate Change: Evidence from Agricultural Output and Random Fluctuations in Weather." *American Economic Review* 97 (March): 354–385.

**Devereux, Michael B., and Yetman, James. 2003.** "Predetermined Prices and Persistent Effects of Money on Output." *Journal of Money, Credit, and Banking* 35 (October): 729–741.

**Diamond, Douglas W. 1984.** "Financial Intermediation and Delegated Monitoring." *Review of Economic Studies* 51 (July): 393–414.

**Diamond, Douglas W., and Dybvig, Philip H. 1983.** "Bank Runs, Deposit Insurance, and Liquidity." *Journal of Political Economy* 91 (June): 401–419.

**Diamond, Jared. 1997.** *Guns, Germs, and Steel: The Fates of Human Societies.* New York: W. W. Norton.

**Diamond, Peter A. 1965.** "National Debt in a Neoclassical Growth Model." *American Economic Review* 55 (December): 1126–1150.

**Diamond, Peter A. 1982.** "Aggregate Demand Management in Search Equilibrium." *Journal of Political Economy* 90 (October): 881–894.

**Dickens, William T., and Katz, Lawrence F. 1987a.** "Inter-Industry Wage Differences and Theories of Wage Determination." National Bureau of Economic Research Working Paper No. 2271 (July).

**Dickens, William T., and Katz, Lawrence F. 1987b.** "Inter-Industry Wage Differences and Industry Characteristics." In Kevin Lang and Jonathan S. Leonard, eds., *Unemployment and the Structure of Labor Markets,* 48–89. Oxford: Basil Blackwell.

**Dinopoulos, Elias, and Thompson, Peter. 1998.** "Schumpeterian Growth without Scale Effects." *Journal of Economic Growth* 3 (December): 313–335.

**Dixit, Avinash K., and Pindyck, Robert S. 1994.** *Investment under Uncertainty.* Princeton, NJ: Princeton University Press.

**Dixit, Avinash K., and Stiglitz, Joseph E. 1977.** "Monopolistic Competition and Optimum Product Diversity." *American Economic Review* 67 (June): 297–308.

**Doeringer, Peter B., and Piore, Michael J. 1971.** *Internal Labor Markets and Manpower Analysis.* Lexington, MA: D.C. Heath.

**Dotsey, Michael, King, Robert G., and Wolman, Alexander L. 1999.** "State-Dependent Pricing and the General Equilibrium Dynamics of Money and Output." *Quarterly Journal of Economics* 114 (May): 655–690.

**Downs, Anthony. 1957.** *An Economic Theory of Democracy.* New York: Harper and Row.

**Dowrick, Steve, and Nguyen, Duc-Tho. 1989.** "OECD Comparative Economic Growth 1950-85: Catch-up and Convergence." *American Economic Review* 79 (December): 1010-1030.

**Drazen, Allan, and Grilli, Vittorio. 1993.** "The Benefit of Crises for Economic Reform." *American Economic Review* 83 (June): 598-607.

**Dynan, Karen E. 1993.** "How Prudent Are Consumers?" *Journal of Political Economy* 101 (December): 1104-1113.

**Dynan, Karen E. 2000.** "Habit Formation in Consumer Preferences: Evidence from Panel Data." *American Economic Review* 90 (June): 391-406.

## E

**Easterly, William, and Levine, Ross. 1997.** "Africa's Growth Tragedy: Policies and Ethnic Divisions." *Quarterly Journal of Economics* 112 (November): 1203-1250.

**Easterly, William, and Levine, Ross. 2003.** "Tropics, Germs, and Crops: How Endowments Influence Economic Development." *Journal of Monetary Economics* 50 (January): 3-39.

**Eberly, Janice C. 1994.** "Adjustment of Consumers' Durables Stocks: Evidence from Automobile Purchases." *Journal of Political Economy* 102 (June): 403-436.

**Eberly, Janice C., Rebelo, Sergio, and Vincent, Nicolas. 2009.** "Investment and Value: A Neoclassical Benchmark." Unpublished paper (March).

**Eggertsson, Gauti, and Woodford, Michael. 2003.** "The Zero Bound on Interest Rates and Optimal Monetary Policy." *Brookings Papers on Economic Activity,* no. 1, 139-233.

**Eisner, Robert, and Strotz, Robert H. 1963.** "Determinants of Business Fixed Investment." In Commission on Money and Credit, *Impacts of Monetary Policy,* 59-337. Englewood Cliffs, NJ: Prentice-Hall.

**Elsby, Michael W. L. 2009.** "Evaluating the Economic Significance of Downward Nominal Wage Rigidity." *Journal of Monetary Economics* 56 (March): 154-169.

**Elsby, Michael W. L., Michaels, Ryan, and Solon, Gary. 2009.** "The Ins and Outs of Cyclical Unemployment." *American Economic Journal: Macroeconomics* 1 (January): 84-110.

**Engerman, Stanley L., and Sokoloff, Kenneth L. 2002.** "Factor Endowments, Inequality, and Paths of Development among New World Economies." National Bureau of Economic Research Working Paper No. 9259 (October).

**Epstein, Larry G., and Zin, Stanley E. 1989.** "Substitution, Risk Aversion, and the Temporal Behavior of Consumption and Asset Returns: A Theoretical Framework." *Econometrica* 46 (July): 937-969.

**Epstein, Larry G., and Zin, Stanley E. 1991.** "Substitution, Risk Aversion, and the Temporal Behavior of Consumption and Asset Returns: An Empirical Analysis." *Journal of Political Economy* 99 (April): 263-286.

**Erceg, Christopher J., Henderson, Dale W., and Levin, Andrew T. 2000.** "Optimal Monetary Policy with Staggered Wage and Price Contracts." *Journal of Monetary Economics* 46 (March): 281-313.

**Ethier, Wilfred J. 1982.** "National and International Returns to Scale in the Modern Theory of International Trade." *American Economic Review* 72 (June): 389-405.

# F

Fazzari, Steven M., Hubbard, R. Glenn, and Petersen, Bruce C. 1988. "Financing Constraints and Corporate Investment." *Brookings Papers on Economic Activity,* no. 1, 141-195.

Fazzari, Steven M., Hubbard, R. Glenn, and Petersen, Bruce C. 2000. "Investment-Cash Flow Sensitivities Are Useful: A Comment on Kaplan and Zingales." *Quarterly Journal of Economics* 115 (May): 695-705.

Feenstra, Robert C. 1986. "Functional Equivalence between Liquidity Costs and the Utility of Money." *Journal of Monetary Economics* 17 (March): 271-291.

Feldstein, Martin. 1997. "The Costs and Benefits of Going from Low Inflation to Price Stability." In Christina D. Romer and David H. Romer, eds., *Reducing Inflation: Motivation and Strategy,* 123-156. Chicago: University of Chicago Press.

Feldstein, Martin, and Horioka, Charles. 1980. "Domestic Saving and International Capital Flows." *Economic Journal* 90 (June): 314-329.

Fernald, John G. 2007. "Trend Breaks, Long-Run Restrictions, and Contractionary Technology Improvements." *Journal of Monetary Economics* 54 (November): 2467-2485.

Fernald, John, and Neiman, Brent. 2008. "Measuring the Miracle: Market Imperfections and Asia's Growth Experience." Unpublished paper, University of Chicago (December).

Fernandez, Raquel, and Rodrik, Dani. 1991. "Resistance to Reform: Status Quo Bias in the Presence of Individual-Specific Uncertainty." *American Economic Review* 71 (December): 1146-1155.

Fischer, Stanley. 1977. "Long-Term Contracts, Rational Expectations, and the Optimal Money Supply Rule." *Journal of Political Economy* 85 (February): 191-205.

Fischer, Stanley. 1993. "The Role of Macroeconomic Factors in Growth." *Journal of Monetary Economics* 32 (December): 485-512.

Fischer, Stanley, and Summers, Lawrence H. 1989. "Should Governments Learn to Live with Inflation?" *American Economic Review* 79 (May): 382-387.

Fisher, Irving. 1933. "The Debt-Deflation Theory of Great Depressions." *Econometrica* 1 (October): 337-357.

Fisher, Jonas D. M., and Peters, Ryan. 2009. "Using Stock Returns to Identify Government Spending Shocks." Federal Reserve Bank of Chicago Working Paper No. 2009-03 (August).

Flavin, Marjorie A. 1981. "The Adjustment of Consumption to Changing Expectations about Future Income." *Journal of Political Economy* 89 (October): 974-1009.

Flavin, Marjorie A. 1993. "The Excess Smoothness of Consumption: Identification and Estimation." *Review of Economic Studies* 60 (July): 651-666.

Foley, Duncan K., and Sidrauski, Miguel. 1970. "Portfolio Choice, Investment and Growth." *American Economic Review* 60 (March): 44-63.

Foote, Christopher L. 1998. "Trend Employment Growth and the Bunching of Job Creation and Destruction." *Quarterly Journal of Economics* 113 (August): 809-834.

Francis, Neville, and Ramey, Valerie A. 2005. "Is the Technology-Driven Real Business Cycle Hypothesis Dead? Shocks and Aggregate Fluctuations Revisited." *Journal of Monetary Economics,* 52 (November): 1379-1399.

Frankel, Jeffrey A. and Romer, David. 1999. "Does Trade Cause Growth?" *American Economic Review* 89 (June): 379-399.

French, Kenneth R., and Poterba, James M. 1991. "Investor Diversification and International Equity Markets." *American Economic Review* 81 (May): 222-226.

Friedman, Milton. 1953. "The Case for Flexible Exchange Rates." In *Essays in Positive Economics,* 153-203. Chicago: University of Chicago Press.

Friedman, Milton. 1957. *A Theory of the Consumption Function.* Princeton, NJ: Princeton University Press.

Friedman, Milton. 1960. *A Program for Monetary Stability.* New York: Fordham University Press.

Friedman, Milton. 1968. "The Role of Monetary Policy." *American Economic Review* 58 (March): 1-17.

Friedman, Milton. 1969. "The Optimum Quantity of Money." In *The Optimum Quantity of Money and Other Essays,* 1-50. Chicago: Aldine Publishing.

Friedman, Milton. 1971. "Government Revenue from Inflation." *Journal of Political Economy* 79 (July/August): 846-856.

Friedman, Milton, and Savage, L. J. 1948. "The Utility Analysis of Choices Involving Risk." *Journal of Political Economy* 56 (August): 279-304.

Friedman, Milton, and Schwartz, Anna J. 1963. *A Monetary History of the United States, 1867-1960.* Princeton, NJ: Princeton University Press.

Froot, Kenneth A., and Obstfeld, Maurice. 1991. "Intrinsic Bubbles: The Case of Stock Prices." *American Economic Review* 81 (December): 1189-1214.

Fuhrer, Jeffrey C. 2000. "Habit Formation in Consumption and Its Implications for Monetary-Policy Models." *American Economic Review* 90 (June): 367-390.

Fuhrer, Jeffrey C., and Moore, George R. 1995. "Inflation Persistence." *Quarterly Journal of Economics* 110 (February): 127-159.

# G

Gabaix, Xavier, and Laibson, David. 2001. "The 6D Bias and the Equity-Premium Puzzle." *NBER Macroeconomics Annual* 16: 257-312.

Gale, Douglas, and Hellwig, Martin. 1985. "Incentive-Compatible Debt Contracts I: The One-Period Problem." *Review of Economic Studies* 52 (October): 647-663.

Galí, Jordi. 1992. "How Well Does the IS-LM Model Fit Postwar U.S. Data?" *Quarterly Journal of Economics* 107 (May): 709-738.

Galí, Jordi. 2008. *Monetary Policy, Inflation, and the Business Cycle: An Introduction to the New Keynesian Framework.* Princeton, NJ: Princeton University Press.

Galí, Jordi, and Gertler, Mark. 1999. "Inflation Dynamics: A Structural Econometric Analysis." *Journal of Monetary Economics* 44 (October): 195-222.

Galí, Jordi, and Rabanal, Pau. 2004. "Technology Shocks and Aggregate Fluctuations: How Well Does the Real Business Cycle Model Fit Postwar U.S. Data?" *NBER Macroeconomics Annual* 19: 225-288.

Garino, Gaia, and Martin, Christopher. 2000. "Efficiency Wages and Union-Firm Bargaining." *Economics Letters* 69 (November): 181-185.

Geary, Patrick T., and Kennan, John. 1982. "The Employment-Real Wage Relationship: An International Study." *Journal of Political Economy* 90 (August): 854-871.

Genberg, Hans. 1978. "Purchasing Power Parity under Fixed and Flexible Exchange Rates." *Journal of International Economics* 8 (May): 247-276.

Gertler, Mark, and Gilchrist, Simon. 1994. "Monetary Policy, Business Cycles, and the Behavior of Small Manufacturing Firms." *Quarterly Journal of Economics* 109 (May): 309–340.

Gertler, Mark, and Karadi, Peter. 2009. "A Model of Unconventional Monetary Policy." Unpublished paper (April).

Ghosh, Atish R. 1995. "Intertemporal Tax-Smoothing and the Government Budget Surplus: Canada and the United States." *Journal of Money, Credit, and Banking* 27 (November, Part 1): 1033–1045.

Giavazzi, Francesco, and Pagano, Marco. 1990. "Can Severe Fiscal Contractions Be Expansionary? Tales of Two Small European Countries." *NBER Macroeconomics Annual* 5: 75–111.

Gibbons, Robert, and Katz, Lawrence. 1992. "Does Unmeasured Ability Explain Inter-Industry Wage Differentials?" *Review of Economic Studies* 59 (July): 515–535.

Glaeser, Edward L., La Porta, Rafael, Lopez-de-Silanes, Florencio, Shleifer, Andrei. 2004. "Do Institutions Cause Growth?" *Journal of Economic Growth* 9 (September): 271–303.

Goldfeld, Stephen M., and Sichel, Daniel E. 1990. "The Demand for Money." In Benjamin M. Friedman and Frank Hahn, eds., *Handbook of Monetary Economics*, vol. 1, 299–356. Amsterdam: Elsevier.

Gollin, Douglas. 2002. "Getting Income Shares Right." *Journal of Political Economy* 110 (April): 458–474.

Golosov, Mikhail, Kocherlakota, Narayana, and Tsyvinski, Aleh. 2003. "Optimal Indirect and Capital Taxation." *Review of Economic Studies* 70 (July): 569–587.

Golosov, Mikhail, and Lucas, Robert E., Jr. 2007. "Menu Costs and Phillips Curves." *Journal of Political Economy* 115 (April): 171–199.

Gomme, Paul. 1999. "Shirking, Unemployment and Aggregate Fluctuations." *International Economic Review* 40 (February): 3–21.

Goodfriend, Marvin, and King, Robert G. 1997. "The New Neoclassical Synthesis and the Role of Monetary Policy." *NBER Macroeconomics Annual* 12: 231–283.

Goolsbee, Austan. 1998. "Investment Tax Incentives, Prices, and the Supply of Capital Goods." *Quarterly Journal of Economics* 113 (February): 121–148.

Gopinath, Gita, and Rigobon, Roberto. 2008. "Sticky Borders." *Quarterly Journal of Economics* 123 (May): 531–575.

Gordon, David. 1974. "A Neoclassical Theory of Underemployment." *Economic Inquiry* 12 (December): 432–459.

Gordon, Robert J. 1997. "The Time-Varying NAIRU and Its Implications for Policy." *Journal of Economic Perspectives* 11 (Winter): 11–32.

Gorton, Gary B., and Metrick, Andrew. 2009. "Securitized Banking and the Run on Repo." National Bureau of Economic Research Working Paper No. 15223 (August).

Gottfries, Nils. 1992. "Insiders, Outsiders, and Nominal Wage Contracts." *Journal of Political Economy* 100 (April): 252–270.

Gourinchas, Pierre-Oliver, and Parker, Jonathan A. 2002. "Consumption over the Life Cycle." *Econometrica* 70 (January): 47–89.

Gourio, François, and Kashyap, Anil K. 2007. "Spikes: New Facts and a General Equilibrium Exploration." *Journal of Monetary Economics* 54 (September, Supplement): 1–22.

Green, Donald P., and Shapiro, Ian. 1994. *Pathologies of Rational Choice Theory: A Critique of Applications in Political Science.* New Haven, CT: Yale University Press.

**Greenwald, Bruce C., Stiglitz, Joseph E., and Weiss, Andrew. 1984.** "Informational Imperfections in Capital Markets and Macroeconomic Fluctuations." *American Economic Review* 74 (May): 194-199.

**Greenwood, Jeremy, and Hercowitz, Zvi. 1991.** "The Allocation of Capital and Time over the Business Cycle." *Journal of Political Economy* 99 (December): 1188-1214.

**Greenwood, Jeremy, Hercowitz, Zvi, and Huffman, Gregory W. 1988.** "Investment, Capacity Utilization, and the Real Business Cycle." *American Economic Review* 78 (June): 402-417.

**Greenwood, Jeremy, and Huffman, Gregory W. 1991.** "Tax Analysis in a Real-Business-Cycle Model: On Measuring Harberger Triangles and Okun Gaps." *Journal of Monetary Economics* 27 (April): 167-190.

**Gregory, R. G. 1986.** "Wages Policy and Unemployment in Australia." *Economica* 53 (Supplement): S53-S74.

**Grilli, Vittorio, Masciandaro, Donato, and Tabellini, Guido. 1991.** "Political and Monetary Institutions and Public Financial Policies in the Industrial Countries." *Economic Policy* 13 (October): 341-392.

**Gross, David B., and Souleles, Nicholas S. 2002.** "Do Liquidity Constraints and Interest Rates Matter for Consumer Behavior? Evidence from Credit Card Data." *Quarterly Journal of Economics* 117 (February): 149-185.

**Grossman, Gene M., and Helpman, Elhanan. 1991a.** *Innovation and Growth in the Global Economy.* Cambridge, MA: MIT Press.

**Grossman, Gene M., and Helpman, Elhanan. 1991b.** "Endogenous Product Cycles." *Economic Journal* 101 (September): 1214-1229.

**Gürkaynak, Refet S., Levin, Andrew T., and Swanson, Eric T. 2008.** "Does Inflation Targeting Anchor Long-Run Inflation Expectations? Evidence from Long-Term Bond Yields in the U.S., U.K., and Sweden." Unpublished paper (October). *Journal of the European Economic Association,* forthcoming.

**Gürkaynak, Refet S., Sack, Brian, and Swanson, Eric T. 2005.** "The Sensitivity of Long-Term Interest Rates to Economic News: Evidence and Implications for Macroeconomic Models." *American Economic Review* 95 (March): 425-436.

## H

**Haavelmo, Trygve. 1945.** "Multiplier Effects of a Balanced Budget." *Econometrica* 13 (October): 311-318.

**Hall, Robert E. 1978.** "Stochastic Implications of the Life Cycle-Permanent Income Hypothesis: Theory and Evidence." *Journal of Political Economy* 86 (December): 971-987.

**Hall, Robert E. 1980.** "Employment Fluctuations and Wage Rigidity." *Brookings Papers on Economic Activity,* no. 1, 91-123.

**Hall, Robert E. 1984.** "Monetary Strategy with an Elastic Price Standard." In *Price Stability and Public Policy,* 137-159. Kansas City: Federal Reserve Bank of Kansas City.

**Hall, Robert E. 1988a.** "The Relation between Price and Marginal Cost in U.S. Industry." *Journal of Political Economy* 96 (October): 921-947.

**Hall, Robert E. 1988b.** "Intertemporal Substitution in Consumption." *Journal of Political Economy* 96 (April): 339-357.

**Hall, Robert E. 2005.** "Employment Fluctuations with Equilibrium Wage Stickiness." *American Economic Review* 95 (March): 50-65.

**Hall, Robert E. 2009.** "By How Much Does GDP Rise If the Government Buys More Output?" *Brookings Papers on Economic Activity,* no. 2, 183-231.

**Hall, Robert E., and Jones, Charles I. 1999.** "Why Do Some Countries Produce So Much More Output per Worker than Others?" *Quarterly Journal of Economics* 114 (February): 83-116.

**Hall, Robert E., and Jorgenson, Dale W. 1967.** "Tax Policy and Investment Behavior." *American Economic Review* 57 (June): 391-414.

**Haltiwanger, John, and Waldman, Michael. 1989.** "Limited Rationality and Strategic Complements: The Implications for Macroeconomics." *Quarterly Journal of Economics* 104 (August): 463-483.

**Ham, John C., and Reilly, Kevin T. 2002.** "Testing Intertemporal Substitution, Implicit Contracts, and Hours Restrictions Models of the Labor Market Using Micro Data." *American Economic Review* 92 (September): 905-927.

**Hamilton, James. 1994.** *Time Series Analysis.* Princeton, NJ: Princeton University Press.

**Hansen, Gary D. 1985.** "Indivisible Labor and the Business Cycle." *Journal of Monetary Economics* 16 (November): 309-327.

**Hansen, Gary D., and Wright, Randall. 1992.** "The Labor Market in Real Business Cycle Theory." Federal Reserve Bank of Minneapolis *Quarterly Review* 16 (Spring): 2-12.

**Hansen, Lars Peter, and Singleton, Kenneth J. 1983.** "Stochastic Consumption, Risk Aversion, and the Temporal Behavior of Asset Returns." *Journal of Political Economy* 91 (April): 249-265.

**Hanson, Michael S. 2004.** "The 'Price Puzzle' Reconsidered." *Journal of Monetary Economics* 51 (October): 1385-1413.

**Harris, John R., and Todaro, Michael P. 1970.** "Migration, Unemployment and Development: A Two-Sector Analysis." *American Economic Review* 60 (March): 126-142.

**Hayashi, Fumio. 1982.** "Tobin's Marginal $q$ and Average $q$: A Neoclassical Interpretation." *Econometrica* 50 (January): 213-224.

**Hayes, Beth. 1984.** "Unions and Strikes with Asymmetric Information." *Journal of Labor Economics* 12 (January): 57-83.

**He, Zhiguo, and Xiong, Wei. 2010.** "Dynamic Debt Runs." Unpublished paper (February).

**Heaton, John, and Lucas, Deborah J. 1996.** "Evaluating the Effects of Incomplete Markets on Risk Sharing and Asset Pricing." *Journal of Political Economy* 104 (June): 443-487.

**Helliwell, John F. 1998.** *How Much Do National Borders Matter?* Washington, DC: Brookings Institution.

**Hendricks, Lutz. 2002.** "How Important Is Human Capital for Development? Evidence from Immigrant Earnings." *American Economic Review* 92 (March): 198-219.

**Hodrick, Robert J., and Prescott, Edward C. 1997.** "Postwar U.S. Business Cycles: An Empirical Investigation." *Journal of Money, Credit, and Banking* 29 (February): 1-16.

**Holmstrom, Bengt, and Tirole, Jean. 1998.** "Private and Public Supply of Liquidity." *Journal of Political Economy* 52 (March): 1-40.

**Hornstein, Andreas, and Krusell, Per. 1996.** "Can Technology Improvements Cause Productivity Slowdowns?" *NBER Macroeconomics Annual* 11: 209-259.

**Hosios, Arthur J, 1990.** "On the Efficiency of Matching and Related Models of Search and Unemployment." *Review of Economic Studies* 57 (April): 279–298.

**House, Christopher L. 2008.** "Fixed Costs and Long-Lived Investments." National Bureau of Economic Research Working Paper No. 14402 (October).

**Howitt, Peter. 1999.** "Steady Endogenous Growth with Population and R&D Inputs Growing." *Journal of Political Economy* 107 (August): 715–730.

**Hsieh, Chang-Tai. 2000.** "Bargaining over Reform." *European Economic Review* 44 (October): 1659–1676.

**Hsieh, Chang-Tai. 2002.** "What Explains the Industrial Revolution in East Asia? Evidence from the Factor Markets." *American Economic Review* 92 (June): 502–526.

**Hsieh, Chang-Tai. 2003.** "Do Consumers React to Anticipated Income Changes? Evidence from the Alaska Permanent Fund." *American Economic Review* 93 (March): 397–405.

**Hsieh, Chang-Tai, and Klenow, Peter J. 2007.** "Relative Prices and Relative Prosperity." *American Economic Review* (June): 562–585.

**Hsieh, Chang-Tai, and Klenow, Peter J. 2008.** "Misallocation and Manufacturing TFP in China and India." Unpublished paper, Stanford University (December). *Quarterly Journal of Economics*, forthcoming.

**Huang, Chao-Hsi, and Lin, Kenneth S. 1993.** "Deficits, Government Expenditures, and Tax Smoothing in the United States, 1929–1988." *Journal of Monetary Economics* 31 (June): 317–339.

**Huang, Kevin X. D., and Liu, Zheng. 2002.** "Staggered Price-Setting, Staggered Wage-Setting, and Business Cycle Persistence." *Journal of Monetary Economics* 49 (March): 405–433.

**Hubbard, R. Glenn, and Judd, Kenneth L. 1986.** "Liquidity Constraints, Fiscal Policy, and Consumption." *Brookings Papers on Economic Activity,* no. 1, 1–50.

## I

**Inada, Kenichi. 1964.** "Some Structural Characteristics of Turnpike Theorems." *Review of Economic Studies* 31 (January): 43–58.

## J

**Jayaratne, Jith, and Strahan, Philip E. 1996.** "The Finance-Growth Nexus: Evidence from Bank Branch Deregulation." *Quarterly Journal of Economics* 111 (August): 639–670.

**Johnson, David S., Parker, Jonathan A., and Souleles, Nicholas. 2006.** "Household Expenditure and the Income Tax Rebates of 2001." *American Economic Review* 96 (December): 1589–1610.

**Jones, Benjamin F., and Olken, Benjamin A. 2005.** *"Do Leaders Matter? National Leadership and Growth since World War II." Quarterly Journal of Economics* 120 (August): 835–864.

**Jones, Charles I. 1994.** "Economic Growth and the Relative Price of Capital." *Journal of Monetary Economics* 34 (December): 359–382.

**Jones, Charles I. 1995a.** "R&D-Based Models of Economic Growth." *Journal of Political Economy* 103 (August): 759–784.

**Jones, Charles I. 1995b.** "Time Series Tests of Endogenous Growth Models." *Quarterly Journal of Economics* 110 (May): 495–525.

Jones, Charles I. 1999. "Growth: With or without Scale Effects?" *American Economic Review* 89 (May): 139–144.

Jones, Charles I. 2002a. "Sources of U.S. Economic Growth in a World of Ideas." *American Economic Review* 92 (March): 220–239.

Jones, Charles I. 2002b. *Introduction to Economic Growth,* 2d ed. New York: W. W. Norton.


# K

Kahneman, Daniel, Knetsch, Jack L., and Thaler, Richard. 1986. "Fairness as a Constraint on Profit Seeking: Entitlements in the Market." *American Economic Review* 76 (September): 728–741.

Kamien, Morton I., and Schwartz, Nancy L. 1991. *Dynamic Optimization: The Calculus of Variations and Optimal Control in Economics and Management,* 2d ed. Amsterdam: Elsevier.

Kandel, Shmuel, and Stambaugh, Robert F. 1991. "Asset Returns and Intertemporal Preferences." *Journal of Monetary Economics* 27 (February): 39–71.

Kaplan, Steven N., and Zingales, Luigi. 1997. "Do Investment-Cash Flow Sensitivities Provide Useful Measures of Financing Constraints?" *Quarterly Journal of Economics* 112 (February): 169–215.

Kareken, John H., and Solow, Robert M. 1963. "Lags in Monetary Policy." In Commission on Money and Credit, *Stabilization Policy,* 14–96. Englewood Cliffs, NJ: Prentice-Hall.

Katona, George. 1976. "The Psychology of Inflation." In Richard T. Curtin, ed., *Surveys of Consumers, 1974–75,* 9–19. Ann Arbor, MI: Institute for Social Research, University of Michigan.

Katz, Lawrence F., and Summers, Lawrence H. 1989. "Industry Rents: Evidence and Implications." *Brookings Papers on Economic Activity,* Microeconomics, 209–275.

Kerr, William, and King, Robert G. 1996. "Limits on Interest Rate Rules in the IS Model." Federal Reserve Bank of Richmond *Economic Quarterly* 82 (Spring): 47–75.

Keynes, John Maynard. 1936. *The General Theory of Employment, Interest, and Money.* London: Macmillan.

Keynes, John Maynard. 1939. "Relative Movements of Real Wages and Output." *Economic Journal* 49 (March): 34–51.

Kiley, Michael T. 2000. "Endogenous Price Stickiness and Business Cycle Persistence." *Journal of Money, Credit, and Banking* 32 (February): 28–53.

Kimball, Miles S. 1990. "Precautionary Saving in the Small and the Large." *Econometrica* 58 (January): 53–73.

Kimball, Miles S. 1991. "The Quantitative Analytics of the Basic Real Business Cycle Model." Unpublished paper, University of Michigan (November).

Kimball, Miles S. 1995. "The Quantitative Analytics of the Basic Neomonetarist Model." *Journal of Money, Credit, and Banking* 27 (November, Part 2): 1241–1277.

King, Robert G., and Plosser, Charles I. 1984. "Money, Credit, and Prices in a Real Business Cycle." *American Economic Review* 64 (June): 363–380.

King, Robert G., and Plosser, Charles I., eds. 2005. "Theme Issue: The Econometrics of the New Keynesian Price Equation." *Journal of Monetary Economics* 52 (September).

Kiyotaki, Nobuhiro, and Moore, John. 1997. "Credit Cycles." *Journal of Political Economy* 105 (April): 211–248.

Klenow, Peter J., and Kryvtsov, Oleksiy. 2008. "State-Dependent or Price-Dependent Pricing: Does It Matter for Recent U.S. Inflation?" *Quarterly Journal of Economics* 123 (August): 863–904.

Klenow, Peter J., and Rodríguez-Clare, Andrés. 1997. "The Neoclassical Revival in Growth Economics: Has It Gone Too Far?" *NBER Macroeconomics Annual* 12: 73–103.

Klenow, Peter J., and Willis, Jonathan L. 2006. "Real Rigidities and Nominal Price Changes." Unpublished paper, Stanford University (March).

Knack, Stephen, and Keefer, Philip. 1995. "Institutions and Economic Performance: Cross-Country Tests Using Alternative Institutional Measures." *Economics and Politics* 7 (November): 207–227.

Knack, Stephen, and Keefer, Philip. 1997. "Does Social Capital Have an Economic Payoff? A Cross-Country Investigation." *Quarterly Journal of Economics* 112 (November): 1251–1288.

Koopmans, Tjalling C. 1965. "On the Concept of Optimal Economic Growth." In *The Economic Approach to Development Planning.* Amsterdam: Elsevier.

Kremer, Michael. 1993. "Population Growth and Technological Change: One Million B.C. to 1990." *Quarterly Journal of Economics* 108 (August): 681–716.

Krueger, Alan B., and Summers, Lawrence H. 1987. "Reflections on the Inter-Industry Wage Structure." In Kevin Lang and Jonathan S. Leonard, eds., *Unemployment and the Structure of Labor Markets,* 17–47. Oxford: Basil Blackwell.

Krueger, Alan B., and Summers, Lawrence H. 1988. "Efficiency Wages and the Interindustry Wage Structure." *Econometrica* 56 (March): 259–293.

Krueger, Anne O. 1974. "The Political Economy of the Rent-Seeking Society." *American Economic Review* 64 (June): 291–303.

Krueger, Anne O. 1993. "Virtuous and Vicious Circles in Economic Development." *American Economic Review* 83 (May): 351–355.

Krugman, Paul R. 1979. "A Model of Innovation, Technology Transfer, and the World Distribution of Income." *Journal of Political Economy* 87 (April): 253–266.

Krugman, Paul R. 1998. "It's Baaack: Japan's Slump and the Return of the Liquidity Trap." *Brookings Papers on Economic Activity,* no. 2, 137–205.

Krusell, Per, and Smith, Anthony A., Jr. 1998. "Income and Wealth Heterogeneity in the Macroeconomy." *Journal of Political Economy* 88 (October): 867–896.

Kuttner, Kenneth N. 2001. "Monetary Policy Surprises and Interest Rates: Evidence from the Fed Funds Futures Market." *Journal of Monetary Economics* 47 (June): 523–544.

Kydland, Finn E., and Prescott, Edward C. 1977. "Rules Rather than Discretion: The Inconsistency of Optimal Plans." *Journal of Political Economy* 85 (June): 473–492.

Kydland, Finn E., and Prescott, Edward C. 1982. "Time to Build and Aggregate Fluctuations." *Econometrica* 50 (November): 1345–1370.


## L

Lagakos, David. 2009. "Superstores or Mom and Pops? Technology Adoption and Productivity Differences in Retail Trade." Unpublished paper, Federal Reserve Bank of Minneapolis (January).

**Laibson, David. 1997.** "Golden Eggs and Hyperbolic Discounting." *Quarterly Journal of Economics* 112 (May): 443-477.

**Lamont, Owen. 1997.** "Cash Flow and Investment: Evidence from Internal Capital Markets." *Journal of Finance* 52 (March): 83-109.

**Landes, David S. 1998.** *The Wealth and Poverty of Nations: Why Are Some So Rich and Others So Poor?* New York: W.W. Norton.

**La Porta, Rafael, Lopez-de-Silanes, Florencio, Shleifer, Andrei, and Vishny, Robert W. 1997.** "Trust in Large Organizations." *American Economic Review* 87 (May): 333-338.

**Laxton, Douglas, Rose, David, and Tambakis, Demosthenes. 1999.** "The U.S. Phillips Curve: The Case for Asymmetry." *Journal of Economic Dynamics and Control* 23 (September): 1459-1485.

**Ledyard, John O. 1984.** "The Pure Theory of Large Two-Candidate Elections." *Public Choice* 44: 7-41.

**Lee, Ronald, and Skinner, Jonathan. 1999.** "Will Aging Baby Boomers Bust the Federal Budget?" *Journal of Economic Perspectives* 13 (Winter): 117-140.

**Leland, Hayne E. 1968.** "Saving and Uncertainty: The Precautionary Demand for Saving." *Quarterly Journal of Economics* 82 (August): 465-473.

**Leontief, Wassily. 1946.** "The Pure Theory of the Guaranteed Annual Wage Contract." *Journal of Political Economy* 54 (February): 76-79.

**Levin, Andrew, Wieland, Volker, and Williams, John C. 2003.** "The Performance of Forecast-Based Monetary Policy Rules under Model Uncertainty." *American Economic Review* 93 (June): 622-645.

**Levine, Ross, and Zervos, Sara. 1998.** "Stock Markets, Banks, and Economic Growth." *American Economic Review* 88 (June): 537-558.

**Levy, Daniel, Bergen, Mark, Dutta, Shantanu, and Venable, Robert. 1997.** "The Magnitude of Menu Costs: Direct Evidence from Large U.S. Supermarket Chains." *Quarterly Journal of Economics* 112 (August): 791-825.

**Li, Chol-Won. 2000.** "Endogenous vs. Semi-Endogenous Growth in a Two-R&D-Sector Model." *Economic Journal* 110 (March): C109-C122.

**Lilien, David M. 1982.** "Sectoral Shifts and Cyclical Unemployment." *Journal of Political Economy* 90 (August): 777-793.

**Lindbeck, Assar, and Nyberg, Sten. 2006.** "Raising Children to Work Hard: Altruism, Work Norms, and Social Insurance." *Quarterly Journal of Economics* 121 (November): 1473-1503.

**Lindbeck, Assar, and Snower, Dennis J. 1986.** "Wage Setting, Unemployment, and Insider-Outsider Relations." *American Economic Review* 76 (May): 235-239.

**Lintner, John. 1965.** "The Valuation of Risky Assets and the Selection of Risky Investments in Stock Portfolios and Capital Budgets." *Review of Economics and Statistics* 47 (February): 13-37.

**Ljungqvist, Lars, and Sargent, Thomas J. 1998.** "The European Unemployment Dilemma." *Journal of Political Economy* 108 (June): 514-550.

**Ljungqvist, Lars, and Sargent, Thomas J. 2004.** *Recursive Macroeconomic Theory*, 2d ed. Cambridge: MIT Press.

**Ljungqvist, Lars, and Sargent, Thomas J. 2006.** "Do Taxes Explain European Employment? Indivisible Labor, Human Capital, Lotteries, and Savings." *NBER Macroeconomics Annual* 21: 181-224.

**Loewenstein, George, and Thaler, Richard H. 1989.** "Anomalies: Intertemporal Choice." *Journal of Economic Perspectives* 3 (Fall): 181-193.

Long, John B., and Plosser, Charles I. 1983. "Real Business Cycles." *Journal of Political Economy* 91 (February): 39-69.

Lucas, Robert E., Jr. 1967. "Adjustment Costs and the Theory of Supply." *Journal of Political Economy* 75 (August): 321-334.

Lucas, Robert E., Jr. 1972. "Expectations and the Neutrality of Money." *Journal of Economic Theory* 4 (April): 103-124.

Lucas, Robert E., Jr. 1973. "Some International Evidence on Output-Inflation Trade-offs." *American Economic Review* 63 (June): 326-334.

Lucas, Robert E., Jr. 1976. "Econometric Policy Evaluation: A Critique." *Carnegie-Rochester Conference Series on Public Policy* 1: 19-46.

Lucas, Robert E., Jr. 1978. "Asset Prices in an Exchange Economy." *Econometrica* 46 (December): 1429-1445.

Lucas, Robert E., Jr. 1987. *Models of Business Cycles.* Oxford: Basil Blackwell.

Lucas, Robert E., Jr. 1988. "On the Mechanics of Economic Development." *Journal of Monetary Economics* 22 (July): 3-42.

Lucas, Robert E., Jr. 1990. "Why Doesn't Capital Flow from Rich to Poor Countries?" *American Economic Review* 80 (May): 92-96.

Lucas, Robert E., Jr., and Rapping, Leonard. 1969. "Real Wages, Employment and Inflation." *Journal of Political Economy* 77 (September/October): 721-754.

Lucas, Robert E., Jr., and Stokey, Nancy L. 1983. "Optimal Fiscal and Monetary Policy in an Economy without Capital." *Journal of Monetary Economics* 12 (July): 55-93.

Luttmer, Erzo G. J. 1999. "What Level of Fixed Costs Can Reconcile Consumption and Stock Returns?" *Journal of Political Economy* 107 (October): 969-997.


## M

MaCurdy, Thomas E. 1981. "An Empirical Model of Labor Supply in a Life-Cycle Setting." *Journal of Political Economy* 89 (December): 1059-1085.

Maddison, Angus. 1982. *Phases of Capitalist Development.* Oxford: Oxford University Press.

Maddison, Angus. 1995. *Monitoring the World Economy: 1820-1992.* Paris: Organization for Economic Cooperation and Development.

Maddison, Angus. 2006. *The World Economy.* Paris: OECD Development Centre.

Malthus, Thomas Robert. 1798. *An Essay on the Principle of Population, as It Affects the Future Improvement of Society.* London: J. Johnson.

Mankiw, N. Gregory. 1982. "Hall's Consumption Hypothesis and Durable Goods." *Journal of Monetary Economics* 10 (November): 417-425.

Mankiw, N. Gregory. 1985. "Small Menu Costs and Large Business Cycles: A Macroeconomic Model of Monopoly." *Quarterly Journal of Economics* 100 (May): 529-539.

Mankiw, N. Gregory. 1986. "The Equity Premium and the Concentration of Aggregate Shocks." *Journal of Financial Economics* 17 (September): 211-219.

Mankiw, N. Gregory. 1989. "Real Business Cycles: A New Keynesian Perspective." *Journal of Economic Perspectives* 3 (Summer): 79-90.

Mankiw, N. Gregory, and Miron, Jeffrey A. 1986. "The Changing Behavior of the Term Structure of Interest Rates." *Quarterly Journal of Economics* 101 (May): 211-228.

Mankiw, N. Gregory, and Reis, Ricardo. 2002. "Sticky Information versus Sticky Prices: A Proposal to Replace the New Keynesian Phillips Curve." *Quarterly Journal of Economics* 117 (November): 1295-1328.

Mankiw, N. Gregory, Romer, David, and Weil, David N. 1992. "A Contribution to the Empirics of Economic Growth." *Quarterly Journal of Economics* 107 (May): 407-437.

Mankiw, N. Gregory, and Zeldes, Stephen P. 1991. "The Consumption of Stockholders and Nonstockholders." *Journal of Financial Economics* 29 (March): 97-112.

Mauro, Paolo. 1995. "Corruption and Growth." *Quarterly Journal of Economics* 110 (August): 681-712.

Mayer, Thomas. 1999. *Monetary Policy and the Great Inflation in the United States: The Federal Reserve and the Failure of Macroeconomic Policy, 1965-1979.* Cheltenham, United Kingdom: Edward Elgar.

McCallum, Bennett T. 1989. "Real Business Cycle Models." In Robert J. Barro, ed., *Modern Business Cycle Theory,* 16-50. Cambridge, MA: Harvard University Press.

McCallum, Bennett T., and Nelson, Edward. 1999. "An Optimizing IS-LM Specification for Monetary Policy and Business Cycle Analysis." *Journal of Money, Credit, and Banking* 31 (August, Part 1): 296-316.

McConnell, Margaret M., and Perez-Quiros, Gabriel. 2000. "Output Fluctuations in the United States: What Has Changed Since the Early 1980's?" *American Economic Review* 90 (December): 1464-1476.

McGrattan, Ellen R. 1994. "The Macroeconomic Effects of Distortionary Taxation." *Journal of Monetary Economics* 33 (June): 573-601.

McKinnon, Ronald I. 1973. *Money and Capital in Economic Development.* Washington: The Brookings Institution.

Meese, Richard, and Rogoff, Kenneth. 1983. "Empirical Exchange Rate Models of the Seventies: Do They Fit Out of Sample?" *Journal of International Economics* 14 (February): 3-24.

Mehra, Rajnish, and Prescott, Edward C. 1985. "The Equity Premium: A Puzzle." *Journal of Monetary Economics* 15 (March): 145-161.

Mendelsohn, Robert, Nordhaus, William D., and Shaw, Daigee. 1994. "The Impact of Global Warming on Agriculture: A Ricardian Analysis." *American Economic Review* 84 (September): 753-771.

Merton, Robert C. 1973. "An Intertemporal Capital Asset Pricing Model." *Econometrica* 41 (September): 867-887.

Midrigan, Virgiliu. 2009. "Menu Costs, Multi-Product Firms and Aggregate Fluctuations." Unpublished paper, New York University (July).

Miron, Jeffrey A. 1996. *The Economics of Seasonal Cycles.* Cambridge, MA: MIT Press.

Modigliani, Franco, and Brumberg, Richard. 1954. "Utility Analysis and the Consumption Function: An Interpretation of Cross-Section Data." In Kenneth K. Kurihara, ed., *Post-Keynesian Economics,* 388-436. New Brunswick, NJ: Rutgers University Press.

Modigliani, Franco, and Cohn, Richard A. 1979. "Inflation and the Stock Market." *Financial Analysts Journal* 35 (March/April): 24-44.

Modigliani, Franco, and Miller, Merton H. 1958. "The Cost of Capital, Corporation Finance and the Theory of Investment." *American Economic Review* 48 (June): 261-297.

Morris, Stephen, and Shin, Hyun Song. 1998. "Unique Equilibrium in a Model of Self-Fulfilling Currency Attacks." *American Economic Review* 88 (June): 587–597.

Morris, Stephen, and Shin, Hyun Song. 2000. "Rethinking Multiple Equilibria in Macroeconomic Modeling." *NBER Macroeconomics Annual* 15: 139-161.

Mortensen, Dale T. 1986. "Job Search and Labor Market Analysis." In Orley Ashenfelter and Richard Layard, eds., *Handbook of Labor Economics,* vol. 2, 849-919. Amsterdam: Elsevier.

Mortensen, Dale T., and Pissarides, Christopher A. 1994. "Job Creation and Job Destruction in the Theory of Unemployment." *Review of Economic Studies* 61 (July): 397–415.

Murphy, Kevin M., Shleifer, Andrei, and Vishny, Robert W. 1991. "The Allocation of Talent: Implications for Growth." *Quarterly Journal of Economics* 106 (May): 503-530.

Murphy, Kevin M., and Topel, Robert H. 1987a. "The Evolution of Unemployment in the United States." *NBER Macroeconomics Annual* 2: 11-58.

Murphy, Kevin M., and Topel, Robert H. 1987b. "Unemployment, Risk, and Earnings: Testing for Equalizing Differences in the Labor Market." In Kevin Lang and Jonathan S. Leonard, eds., *Unemployment and the Structure of Labor Markets,* 103-140. Oxford: Basil Blackwell.

Mussa, Michael L. 1986. "Nominal Exchange Rate Regimes and the Behavior of Real Exchange Rates." *Carnegie-Rochester Conference Series on Public Policy* 25 (Autumn): 117-213.


# N

Nakamura, Emi, and Steinsson, Jón. 2008. "Five Facts about Prices: A Reevaluation of Menu Cost Models." *Quarterly Journal of Economics* 123 (November): 1415-1464.

Nekarda, Christopher J., and Ramey, Valerie A. 2009. "The Cyclical Behavior of the Price-Cost Markup." Unpublished paper, University of California, San Diego (September).

Nelson, Edward. 2005. "The Great Inflation of the 1970s: What Really Happened?" *Advances in Macroeconomics* 5:1, Article 3.

Nordhaus, William D. 1975. "The Political Business Cycle." *Review of Economic Studies* 42 (April): 169-190.

Nordhaus, William D. 1992. "Lethal Model 2: The Limits to Growth Revisited." *Brookings Papers on Economic Activity,* no. 2, 1-43.

Nordhaus, William D. 1997. "Do Real-Output and Real-Wage Measures Capture Reality? The History of Lighting Suggests Not." In Timothy F. Bresnahan and Robert J. Gordon, eds., *The Economics of New Goods,* 29-66. Chicago: University of Chicago Press.

Nordhaus, William D. 2008. *A Question of Balance: Weighing the Options on Global Warming Policies.* New Haven: Yale University Press.

North, Douglass C. 1981. *Structure and Change in Economic History.* New York: W. W. Norton.

Nunn, Nathan, and Puga, Diego. 2007. "Ruggedness: The Blessing of Bad Geography in Africa." Unpublished paper, Harvard University (March).

# O

Obstfeld, Maurice. 1992. "Dynamic Optimization in Continuous-Time Economic Models (A Guide for the Perplexed)." Unpublished paper, University of California, Berkeley (April). Available at http://elsa.berkeley.edu/~obstfeld/index.html.

Obstfeld, Maurice, and Rogoff, Kenneth. 1996. *Foundations of International Macroeconomics.* Cambridge, MA: MIT Press.

Obstfeld, Maurice, and Rogoff, Kenneth. 2002. "Global Implications of Self-Oriented National Monetary Rules." *Quarterly Journal of Economics* 117 (May): 503–535.

O'Driscoll, Gerald P., Jr. 1977. "The Ricardian Nonequivalence Theorem." *Journal of Political Economy* 85 (February): 207–210.

Okun, Arthur M. 1962. "Potential GNP: Its Measurement and Significance." In *Proceedings of the Business and Economics Statistics Section, American Statistical Association,* 98–103. Washington: American Statistical Association.

Okun, Arthur M. 1971. "The Mirage of Steady Inflation." *Brookings Papers on Economic Activity,* no. 2, 485–498.

Okun, Arthur M. 1975. "Inflation: Its Mechanics and Welfare Costs." *Brookings Papers on Economic Activity,* no. 2, 351–390.

Oliner, Stephen D., and Sichel, Daniel E. 2002. "Information Technology and Productivity: Where Are We Now and Where Are We Going?" Federal Reserve Bank of Atlanta *Economic Review* 87 (Third Quarter): 15–44.

Oliner, Stephen D., Sichel, Daniel E., and Stiroh, Kevin J. 2007. "Explaining a Productive Decade." *Brookings Papers on Economic Activity,* no. 1, 81–152.

Olson, Mancur, Jr. 1965. *The Logic of Collective Action.* Cambridge, MA: Harvard University Press.

Olson, Mancur, Jr. 1982. *The Rise and Decline of Nations.* New Haven, CT: Yale University Press.

Olson, Mancur, Jr. 1996. "Big Bills Left on the Sidewalk: Why Some Nations Are Rich, and Others Poor." *Journal of Economic Perspectives* 10 (Spring): 3–24.

Orphanides, Athanasios. 2003a. "Monetary Policy Evaluation with Noisy Information." *Journal of Monetary Economics* 50 (April): 605–631.

Orphanides, Athanasios. 2003b. "The Quest for Prosperity without Inflation." *Journal of Monetary Economics* 50 (April): 633–663.

Orphanides, Athanasios, and Williams, John C. 2002. "Robust Monetary Policy Rules with Unknown Natural Rates." *Brookings Papers on Economic Activity,* no. 2, 63–145.

Oswald, Andrew J. 1993. "Efficient Contracts Are on the Labour Demand Curve: Theory and Facts." *Labour Economics* 1 (June): 85–113.

# P

Palfrey, Thomas R., and Rosenthal, Howard. 1985. "Voter Participation and Strategic Uncertainty." *American Political Science Review* 79 (March): 62–78.

Parente, Stephen L., and Prescott, Edward C. 1999. "Monopoly Rights: A Barrier to Riches." *American Economic Review* 89 (December): 1216–1233.

Parker, Jonathan A., 1999. "The Response of Household Consumption to Predictable Changes in Social Security Taxes." *American Economic Review* 89 (September): 959–973.

**Parker, Jonathan A. 2001.** "The Consumption Risk of the Stock Market." *Brookings Papers on Economic Activity,* no. 2, 279–348.

**Parkin, Michael. 1986.** "The Output-Inflation Tradeoff When Prices Are Costly to Change." *Journal of Political Economy* 94 (February): 200–224.

**Paxson, Christina H. 1992.** "Consumption and Income Seasonality in Thailand." *Journal of Political Economy* 101 (February): 39–72.

**Peretto, Pietro F. 1998.** "Technological Change and Population Growth." *Journal of Economic Growth* 4 (December): 283–311.

**Perotti, Roberto. 1999.** "Fiscal Policy in Good Times and Bad." *Quarterly Journal of Economics* 114 (November): 1399–1436.

**Persson, Torsten, and Svensson, Lars E. O. 1989.** "Why a Stubborn Conservative Would Run a Deficit: Policy with Time-Inconsistent Preferences." *Quarterly Journal of Economics* 104 (May): 325–345.

**Persson, Torsten, and Tabellini, Guido. 1993.** "Designing Institutions for Monetary Stability." *Carnegie-Rochester Conference Series on Public Policy* 39 (December): 53–84.

**Pettersson-Lidbom, Per. 2001.** "An Empirical Investigation of the Strategic Use of Debt." *Journal of Political Economy* 109 (June): 570–583.

**Phelan, Christopher, and Trejos, Alberto. 2000.** "The Aggregate Effects of Sectoral Reallocations." *Journal of Monetary Economics* 45 (April): 249–268.

**Phelps, Edmund S. 1966a.** *Golden Rules of Economic Growth.* New York: W. W. Norton.

**Phelps, Edmund S. 1966b.** "Models of Technical Progress and the Golden Rule of Research." *Review of Economic Studies* 33 (April): 133–146.

**Phelps, Edmund S. 1968.** "Money-Wage Dynamics and Labor Market Equilibrium." *Journal of Political Economy* 76 (July/August, Part 2): 678–711.

**Phelps, Edmund S. 1970.** "Introduction." In Edmund S. Phelps et al., *Microeconomic Foundations of Employment and Inflation Theory.* New York: W. W. Norton.

**Phelps, Edmund S. 1973.** "Inflation in the Theory of Public Finance." *Swedish Journal of Economics* 75 (March): 67–82.

**Phelps, Edmund S., and Taylor, John B. 1977.** "Stabilizing Powers of Monetary Policy under Rational Expectations." *Journal of Political Economy* 85 (February): 163–190.

**Phillips, A. W. 1958.** "The Relationship between Unemployment and the Rate of Change of Money Wages in the United Kingdom, 1861–1957." *Economica* 25 (November): 283–299.

**Pissarides, Christopher A. 1985.** "Short-Run Dynamics of Unemployment, Vacancies, and Real Wages." *American Economic Review* 75 (September): 676–690.

**Pissarides, Christopher A. 2000.** *Equilibrium Unemployment Theory,* 2d ed. Cambridge, MA: MIT Press.

**Pollard, Patricia S. 1993.** "Central Bank Independence and Economic Performance." Federal Reserve Bank of St. Louis *Review* 75 (July/August): 21–36.

**Poole, William. 1970.** "Optimal Choice of Monetary Instruments in a Simple Stochastic Macro Model." *Quarterly Journal of Economics* 84 (May): 197–216.

**Posen, Adam S. 1993.** "Why Central Bank Independence Does Not Cause Low Inflation: There Is No Institutional Fix for Politics." *Finance and the International Economy* 7: 40–65.

**Posner, Richard A. 1975.** "The Social Costs of Monopoly and Regulation." *Journal of Political Economy* 83 (August): 807–827.

**Poterba, James M. 1984.** "Tax Subsidies to Owner-Occupied Housing: An Asset-Market Approach." *Quarterly Journal of Economics* 99 (November): 729-752.

**Poterba, James M. 1994.** "State Responses to Fiscal Crises: The Effects of Budgetary Institutions and Politics." *Journal of Political Economy* 102 (August): 799-821.

**Poterba, James M., and Summers, Lawrence H. 1987.** "Finite Lifetimes and the Effects of Budget Deficits on National Saving." *Journal of Monetary Economics* 20 (September): 369-391.

**Prescott, Edward C. 1986.** "Theory Ahead of Business-Cycle Measurement." *Carnegie-Rochester Conference Series on Public Policy* 25 (Autumn): 11-44.

**Prescott, Edward C. 2004.** "Why Do Americans Work So Much More than Europeans?" Federal Reserve Bank Minneapolis *Quarterly Review* 28 (July): 2-13.

**Primiceri, Giorgio E. 2006.** "Why Inflation Rose and Fell: Policy-Makers' Beliefs and U.S. Postwar Stabilization Policy." *Quarterly Journal of Economics* 121 (August): 867-901.

**Pritchett, Lant. 1997.** "Divergence, Big Time." *Journal of Economic Perspectives* 11 (Summer): 3-17.

**Pritchett, Lant. 2000.** "The Tyranny of Concepts: CUDIE (Cumulated, Depreciated, Investment Effort) is *Not* Capital." *Journal of Economic Growth* 5 (December): 361-384.

# R

**Rajan, Raghuram G., and Zingales, Luigi. 1998.** "Financial Dependence and Growth." *American Economic Review* 88 (June): 559-586.

**Ramey, Valerie A. 2009.** "Identifying Government Spending Shocks: It's All in the Timing." Unpublished paper, University of California, San Diego (October).

**Ramey, Valerie A., and Vine, Daniel J. 2004.** "Tracking the Source of the Decline in GDP Volatility: An Analysis of the Automobile Industry." Unpublished paper, University of California, San Diego (March).

**Ramsey, F. P. 1928.** "A Mathematical Theory of Saving." *Economic Journal* 38 (December): 543-559.

**Rauh, Joshua D. 2006.** "Investment and Financing Constraints: Evidence from the Funding of Corporate Pension Plans." *Journal of Finance* 61 (February): 33-71.

**Rebelo, Sergio. 1991.** "Long-Run Policy Analysis and Long-Run Growth." *Journal of Political Economy* 99 (June): 500-521.

**Rebelo, Sergio, and Végh, Carlos. 1995.** "Real Effects of Exchange-Rate-Based Stabilization: An Analysis of Competing Theories." *NBER Macroeconomics Annual* 10: 125-174.

**Roberts, John M. 1995.** "New Keynesian Economics and the Phillips Curve." *Journal of Money, Credit, and Banking* 27 (November, Part 1): 975-984.

**Rodrik, Dani, Subramanian, Arvind, and Trebbi, Francesco. 2004.** "Institutions Rule: The Primacy of Institutions over Geography and Integration in Economic Development." *Journal of Economic Growth* 9 (June): 131-165.

**Rogerson, Richard. 1988.** "Indivisible Labor, Lotteries and Equilibrium." *Journal of Monetary Economics* 21 (January): 3-16.

**Rogerson, Richard. 2008.** "Structural Transformation and the Deterioration of European Labor Market Outcomes." *Journal of Political Economy* 116 (April): 235-259.

**Rogerson, Richard, Shimer, Robert, and Wright, Randall. 2005.** "Search-Theoretic Models of the Labor Market: A Survey." *Journal of Economic Literature* 43 (December): 959–988.

**Rogerson, Richard, and Wright, Randall. 1988.** "Involuntary Unemployment in Economies with Efficient Risk Sharing." *Journal of Monetary Economics* 22 (November): 501–515.

**Rogoff, Kenneth. 1985.** "The Optimal Degree of Commitment to an Intermediate Monetary Target." *Quarterly Journal of Economics* 100 (November): 1169–1189.

**Rogoff, Kenneth. 1987.** "Reputational Constraints on Monetary Policy." *Carnegie-Rochester Conference Series on Public Policy* 26 (Spring): 141–182.

**Rogoff, Kenneth. 1990.** "Equilibrium Political Budget Cycles." *American Economic Review* 80 (March): 21–36.

**Romer, Christina D. 1986.** "Spurious Volatility in Historical Unemployment Data." *Journal of Political Economy* 94 (February): 1–37.

**Romer, Christina D. 1989.** "The Prewar Business Cycle Reconsidered: New Estimates of Gross National Product, 1869–1908." *Journal of Political Economy* 97 (February): 1–37.

**Romer, Christina D. 1992.** "What Ended the Great Depression?" *Journal of Economic History* 52 (December): 757–784.

**Romer, Christina D. 1999.** "Changes in Business Cycles: Evidence and Explanations." *Journal of Economic Perspectives* 13 (Spring): 23–44.

**Romer, Christina D., and Romer, David H. 1989.** "Does Monetary Policy Matter? A New Test in the Spirit of Friedman and Schwartz." *NBER Macroeconomics Annual* 4: 121–170.

**Romer, Christina D., and Romer, David H. 2000.** "Federal Reserve Information and the Behavior of Interest Rates." *American Economic Review* 90 (June): 429–457.

**Romer, Christina D., and Romer, David H. 2002.** "The Evolution of Economic Understanding and Postwar Stabilization Policy." In *Rethinking Stabilization Policy,* 11–78. Kansas City: Federal Reserve Bank of Kansas City.

**Romer, Christina D., and Romer, David H. 2004.** "A New Measure of Monetary Shocks: Derivation and Implications." *American Economic Review* 94 (September): 1055–1084.

**Romer, Christina D., and Romer, David H. 2009a.** "The Macroeconomic Effects of Tax Changes: Estimates Based on a New Measure of Fiscal Shocks." Unpublished paper, University of California, Berkeley (April). *American Economic Review,* forthcoming.

**Romer, Christina D., and Romer, David H. 2009b.** "Do Tax Cuts Starve the Beast? The Effect of Tax Changes on Government Spending." *Brookings Papers on Economic Activity,* no. 1, 139–200.

**Romer, David. 1993.** "The New Keynesian Synthesis." *Journal of Economic Perspectives* 7 (Winter): 5–22.

**Romer, Paul M. 1986.** "Increasing Returns and Long Run Growth." *Journal of Political Economy* 94 (October): 1002–1037.

**Romer, Paul M. 1990.** "Endogenous Technological Change." *Journal of Political Economy* 98 (October, Part 2): S71–S102.

**Romer, Paul M. 1996.** "Preferences, Promises, and the Politics of Entitlement." In Victor R. Fuchs, ed., *Individual and Social Responsibility: Child Care, Education,*

*Medical Care and Long-Term Care in America,* 195–220. Chicago: University of Chicago Press.

Rotemberg, Julio J. 1982. "Sticky Prices in the United States." *Journal of Political Economy* 90 (December): 1187–1211.

Rotemberg, Julio J. 1987. "The New Keynesian Microfoundations." *NBER Macroeconomics Annual* 2: 69–104.

Rotemberg, Julio J., and Woodford, Michael. 1996. "Real-Business-Cycle Models and Forecastable Movements in Output, Hours, and Consumption." *American Economic Review* 86 (March): 71–89.

Rotemberg, Julio J., and Woodford, Michael. 1999a. "The Cyclical Behavior of Prices and Costs." In John B. Taylor and Michael Woodford, eds., *Handbook of Macroeconomics,* 1052–1135. Amsterdam: Elsevier.

Rotemberg, Julio J., and Woodford, Michael. 1999b. "Interest-Rate Rules in an Estimated Sticky Price Model." In John B. Taylor, ed., *Monetary Policy Rules,* 57–119. Chicago: University of Chicago Press.

Roubini, Nouriel, and Sachs, Jeffrey D. 1989. "Political and Economic Determinants of Budget Deficits in the Industrial Democracies." *European Economic Review* 33 (May): 903–933.

Rubinstein, Mark. 1976. "The Valuation of Uncertain Income Streams and the Pricing of Options." *Bell Journal of Economics* 7 (Autumn): 407–425.

Rudd, Jeremy, and Whelan, Karl. 2005. "Does Labor's Share Drive Inflation?" *Journal of Money, Credit, and Banking* 37 (April): 297–312.

Rudd, Jeremy, and Whelan, Karl. 2006. "Can Rational Expectations Sticky-Price Models Explain Inflation Dynamics?" *American Economic Review* 96 (March): 303–320.

Rudebusch, Glenn D. 1998. "Do Measures of Monetary Policy in a VAR Make Sense?" *International Economic Review* 39 (November): 907–931.

Rudebusch, Glenn D. 2001. "Is the Fed Too Timid? Monetary Policy in an Uncertain World." *Review of Economics and Statistics* 83 (May): 203–217.

Rudebusch, Glenn D. 2009. "The Fed's Monetary Policy Response to the Current Crisis." *Federal Reserve Bank of San Francisco Economic Letter,* No. 2009-17 (May).

## S

Sachs, Jeffrey D. 2003. "Institutions Don't Rule: Direct Effects of Geography on Per Capita Income." National Bureau of Economic Research Working Paper No. 9490 (February).

Sachs, Jeffrey D., and Larrain, Felipe B. 1993. *Macroeconomics in the Global Economy.* Englewood Cliffs, NJ: Prentice-Hall.

Sachs, Jeffrey D., and Warner, Andrew. 1995. "Economic Reform and the Process of Global Integration." *Brookings Papers on Economic Activity,* no. 1, 1–95.

Sahasakul, Chaipat. 1986. "The U.S. Evidence on Optimal Taxation over Time." *Journal of Monetary Economics* 18 (November): 251–275.

Samuelson, Paul A. 1939. "Interaction between the Multiplier Analysis and the Principle of Acceleration." *Review of Economics and Statistics* 21 (May): 75–78.

Samuelson, Paul A. 1958. "An Exact Consumption-Loan Model of Interest with or without the Social Contrivance of Money." *Journal of Political Economy* 66 (December): 467–482.

Samuelson, Paul A., and Solow, Robert M. 1960. "Analytical Aspects of Anti-Inflation Policy." *American Economic Review* 50 (May): 177–194.

**Sargent, Thomas J. 1976.** "The Observational Equivalence of Natural and Unnatural Rate Theories of Macroeconomics." *Journal of Political Economy* 84 (June): 631–640.

**Sargent, Thomas J. 1982.** "The End of Four Big Inflations." In Robert E. Hall, ed., *Inflation, 41–98.* Chicago: University of Chicago Press.

**Sargent, Thomas J. 1983.** "Stopping Moderate Inflations: The Methods of Poincare and Thatcher." In Rudiger Dornbusch and Mario Henrique Simonsen, eds., *Inflation, Debt, and Indexation,* 54–96. Cambridge, MA: MIT Press.

**Sargent, Thomas J. 1987.** *Macroeconomic Theory,* 2d ed. Boston: Academic Press.

**Sargent, Thomas J. 1999.** *The Conquest of American Inflation.* Princeton, NJ: Princeton University Press.

**Sargent, Thomas J., and Wallace, Neil. 1975.** " 'Rational Expectations,' the Optimal Monetary Instrument, and the Optimal Money Supply Rule." *Journal of Political Economy* 83 (April): 241–254.

**Sato, K. 1966.** "On the Adjustment Time in Neo-Classical Growth Models." *Review of Economic Studies* 33 (July): 263–268.

**Sbordone, Argia M. 2002.** "Prices and Unit Labor Costs: A New Test of Price Stickiness." *Journal of Monetary Economics* 49 (March): 265–292.

**Schmitz, James A., Jr. 2005.** "What Determines Productivity? Lessons from the Dramatic Recovery of the U.S. and Canadian Iron Ore Industries Following Their Early 1980s Crisis." *Journal of Political Economy* 113 (June): 582–625.

**Shapiro, Carl, and Stiglitz, Joseph E. 1984.** "Equilibrium Unemployment as a Worker Discipline Device." *American Economic Review* 74 (June): 433–444.

**Shapiro, Matthew D., and Slemrod, Joel. 2003.** "Consumer Response to Tax Rebates." *American Economic Review* 93 (March): 381–396.

**Sharpe, William F. 1964.** "Capital Asset Prices: A Theory of Market Equilibrium under Conditions of Risk." *Journal of Finance* 19 (September): 425–442.

**Shea, John. 1995.** "Union Contracts and the Life-Cycle/Permanent-Income Hypothesis." *American Economic Review* 85 (March): 186–200.

**Shea, John. 1998.** "What Do Technology Shocks Do?" *NBER Macroeconomics Annual* 13: 275–310.

**Shefrin, Hersh M., and Thaler, Richard H. 1988.** "The Behavioral Life-Cycle Hypothesis." *Economic Inquiry* 26 (October): 609–643.

**Shell, Karl. 1966.** "Toward a Theory of Inventive Activity and Capital Accumulation." *American Economic Review* 56 (May): 62–68.

**Shell, Karl. 1967.** "A Model of Inventive Activity and Capital Accumulation." In Karl Shell, ed., *Essays on the Theory of Optimal Economic Growth,* 67–85. Cambridge, MA: MIT Press.

**Shell, Karl. 1971.** "Notes on the Economics of Infinity." *Journal of Political Economy* 79 (September–October): 1002–1011.

**Sheshinski, Eytan, and Weiss, Yoram. 1977.** "Inflation and Costs of Price Adjustment." *Review of Economic Studies* 44 (June): 287–303.

**Shiller, Robert J. 1997.** "Why Do People Dislike Inflation?" In Christina D. Romer and David H. Romer, eds., *Reducing Inflation: Motivation and Strategy,* 13–65. Chicago: University of Chicago Press.

**Shimer, Robert. 2004.** "The Consequences of Rigid Wages in Search Models." *Journal of the European Economic Association* 2 (April–May): 469–479.

**Shimer, Robert. 2005.** "The Cyclical Behavior of Equilibrium Unemployment and Vacancies." 2005. *American Economic Review* 95 (March): 25–49.

**Shimer, Robert. 2007.** "Reassessing the Ins and Outs of Unemployment." Unpublished paper, University of Chicago (October).

**Shleifer, Andrei, and Vishny, Robert W. 1992.** "Pervasive Shortages under Socialism." *Rand Journal of Economics* 23 (Summer): 237-246.

**Shleifer, Andrei, and Vishny, Robert W. 1993.** "Corruption." *Quarterly Journal of Economics* 108 (August): 599-617.

**Shleifer, Andrei, and Vishny, Robert W. 1994.** "Politicians and Firms." *Quarterly Journal of Economics* 109 (November): 995-1025.

**Shleifer, Andrei, and Vishny, Robert W. 1997.** "The Limits of Arbitrage." *Journal of Finance* 52 (March): 35-55.

**Sichel, Daniel E. 1993.** "Business Cycle Asymmetry: A Deeper Look." *Economic Inquiry* 31 (April): 224-236.

**Siebert, Horst. 1997.** "Labor Market Rigidities: At the Root of Unemployment in Europe." *Journal of Economic Perspectives* 11 (Summer): 37-54.

**Simon, Carl P., and Blume, Lawrence. 1994.** *Mathematics for Economists.* New York: W. W. Norton.

**Sims, Christopher A. 1980.** "Macroeconomics and Reality." *Econometrica* 48 (January): 1-48.

**Sims, Christopher A. 1986.** "Are Forecasting Models Usable for Policy Analysis?" Federal Reserve Bank of Minneapolis *Quarterly Review* 10 (Winter): 2-16.

**Sims, Christopher A. 1992.** "Interpreting the Macroeconomic Time Series Facts: The Effects of Monetary Policy." *European Economic Review* 36 (June): 975-1000.

**Smets, Frank, and Wouters, Raf. 2003.** "An Estimated Dynamic Stochastic General Equilibrium Model of the Euro Area." *Journal of the European Economic Association* 1 (September): 1123-1175.

**Smith, William T. 2006.** "A Closed Form Solution to the Ramsey Model." *Contributions to Macroeconomics* 6:1, Article 3.

**Solon, Gary, Barsky, Robert, and Parker, Jonathan A. 1994.** "Measuring the Cyclicality of Real Wages: How Important Is Composition Bias?" *Quarterly Journal of Economics* 109 (February): 1-25.

**Solow, Robert M. 1956.** "A Contribution to the Theory of Economic Growth." *Quarterly Journal of Economics* 70 (February): 65-94.

**Solow, Robert M. 1957.** "Technical Change and the Aggregate Production Function." *Review of Economics and Statistics* 39: 312-320.

**Solow, Robert M. 1960.** "Investment and Technical Progress." In Kenneth J. Arrow, Samuel Korbin, and Patrick Suppes, eds., *Mathematical Methods in the Social Sciences 1959,* 89-104. Stanford: Stanford University Press.

**Solow, Robert M. 1979.** "Another Possible Source of Wage Stickiness." *Journal of Macroeconomics* 1 (Winter): 79-82.

**Souleles, Nicholas S. 1999.** "The Response of Household Consumption to Income Tax Refunds." *American Economic Review* 89 (September): 947-958.

**Staiger, Douglas, and Stock, James H. 1997.** "Instrumental Variables Regression with Weak Instruments." *Econometrica* 65 (May): 557-586.

**Staiger, Douglas, Stock, James H., and Watson, Mark W. 1997.** "How Precise Are Estimates of the Natural Rate of Unemployment?" In Christina D. Romer and David H. Romer, eds., *Reducing Inflation: Motivation and Strategy,* 195-242. Chicago: University of Chicago Press.

**Stiglitz, Joseph E. 1979.** "Equilibrium in Product Markets with Imperfect Information." *American Economic Review* 69 (May): 339-345.

Stock, James H., and Watson, Mark W. 2003. "Has the Business Cycle Changed? Evidence and Explanations." In *Monetary Policy and Uncertainty: Adapting to a Changing Economy,* 9–56. Kansas City: Federal Reserve Bank of Kansas City.

Stockman, Alan C. 1983. "Real Exchange Rates under Alternative Nominal Exchange Rate Systems." *Journal of International Money and Finance* 2 (August): 147–166.

Stokey, Nancy L., and Lucas, Robert E., Jr., with Prescott, Edward C. 1989. *Recursive Methods in Economic Dynamics.* Cambridge, MA: Harvard University Press.

Summers, Lawrence H. 1981a. "Capital Taxation and Accumulation in a Life Cycle Growth Model." *American Economic Review* 71 (September): 533–544.

Summers, Lawrence H. 1981b. "Taxation and Corporate Investment: A *q*-Theory Approach." *Brookings Papers on Economic Activity,* no. 1, 67–127.

Summers, Lawrence H. 1988. "Relative Wages, Efficiency Wages, and Keynesian Unemployment." *American Economic Review* 78 (May): 383–388.

Svensson, Lars E. O. 1997. "Inflation Forecast Targeting: Implementing and Monitoring Inflation Targets." *European Economic Review* 41 (June): 1111–1146.

Svensson, Lars E. O. 2001. "The Zero Bound in an Open Economy: A Foolproof Way of Escaping from a Liquidity Trap." *Monetary and Economic Studies* 19 (February): 277–312.

Swan, T. W. 1956. "Economic Growth and Capital Accumulation." *Economic Record* 32 (November): 334–361.

## T

Tabellini, Guido, and Alesina, Alberto. 1990. "Voting on the Budget Deficit." *American Economic Review* 80 (March): 37–49.

Taylor, John B. 1979. "Staggered Wage Setting in a Macro Model." *American Economic Review* 69 (May): 108–113.

Taylor, John B. 1980. "Aggregate Dynamics and Staggered Contracts." *Journal of Political Economy* 88 (February): 1–23.

Taylor, John B. 1981. "On the Relation between the Variability of Inflation and the Average Inflation Rate." *Carnegie-Rochester Conference Series on Public Policy* 15 (Autumn): 57–86.

Taylor, John B. 1993. "Discretion versus Policy Rules in Practice." *Carnegie-Rochester Conference Series on Public Policy* 39 (December): 195–214.

Taylor, John B., ed. 1999a. *Monetary Policy Rules.* Chicago: University of Chicago Press.

Taylor, John B. 1999b. "A Historical Analysis of Monetary Policy Rules." In John B. Taylor, ed., *Monetary Policy Rules,* 319–341. Chicago: University of Chicago Press.

Thomas, Julia K. 2002. "Is Lumpy Investment Relevant for the Business Cycle?" *Journal of Political Economy* 110 (June): 508–534.

Tobin, James. 1956. "The Interest Elasticity of the Transactions Demand for Cash." *Review of Economics and Statistics* 38 (August): 241–247.

Tobin, James. 1969. "A General Equilibrium Approach to Monetary Theory." *Journal of Money, Credit, and Banking* 1 (February): 15–29.

Tobin, James. 1972. "Inflation and Unemployment." *American Economic Review* 62 (March): 1–18.

Tolley, George S. 1957. "Providing for the Growth of the Money Supply." *Journal of Political Economy* 65 (December): 465–485.

Tommasi, Mariano. 1994. "The Consequences of Price Instability on Search Markets: Toward Understanding the Effects of Inflation." *American Economic Review* 84 (December): 1385–1396.

Topel, Robert H., and Ward, Michael P. 1992. "Job Mobility and the Careers of Young Men." *Quarterly Journal of Economics* 107 (May): 439–479.

Townsend, Robert M. 1979. "Optimal Contracts and Competitive Markets with Costly State Verification." *Journal of Economic Theory* 21 (October): 265–293.

Tsiddon, Daniel. 1991. "On the Stubbornness of Sticky Prices." *International Economic Review* 32 (February): 69–75.

Tullock, Gordon. 1967. "The Welfare Costs of Tariffs, Monopolies, and Theft." *Western Economic Journal* 5 (June): 224–232.

Tversky, Amos, and Kahneman, Daniel. 1974. "Judgment under Uncertainty: Heuristics and Biases." *Science* 185 (September): 1124–1131.

## U

Uzawa, Hirofumi. 1965. "Optimum Technical Change in an Aggregative Model of Economic Growth." *International Economic Review* 6 (January): 12–31.

## V

Van Huyck, John B., Battalio, Raymond C., and Beil, Richard O. 1990. "Tacit Coordination Games, Strategic Uncertainty, and Coordination Failure." *American Economic Review* 80 (March): 234–248.

Velasco, Andrés. 1999. "A Model of Endogenous Fiscal Deficits and Delayed Fiscal Reforms." In James M. Poterba and Jürgen von Hagen, eds., *Fiscal Institutions and Fiscal Performance,* 37–57. Chicago: University of Chicago Press.

Velde, François R. 2008. "Chronicle of a Deflation Unforetold." Unpublished manuscript, Federal Reserve Bank of Chicago (August).

Veracierto, Marcelo L. 2002. "Plant-Level Irreversible Investment and Equilibrium Business Cycles." *American Economic Review* 92 (March): 181–197.

von Hagen, Jürgen, and Harden, Ian. 1995. "Budget Processes and Commitment to Fiscal Discipline." *European Economic Review* 39 (April): 771–779.

## W

Walsh, Carl E. 1995. "Optimal Contracts for Central Bankers." *American Economic Review* 85 (March): 150–167.

Warner, Elizabeth J., and Barsky, Robert B. 1995. "The Timing and Magnitude of Retail Store Markdowns: Evidence from Weekends and Holidays." *Quarterly Journal of Economics* 110 (May): 321–352.

Weber, Ernst Juerg. 2008. "The Role of the Real Interest Rate in U.S. Macroeconomic History." Unpublished paper, University of Western Australia (March).

Weil, Philippe. 1989a. "Overlapping Families of Infinitely-Lived Agents." *Journal of Public Economics* 38 (March): 183–198.

Weil, Philippe. 1989b. "The Equity Premium Puzzle and the Risk-Free Rate Puzzle." *Journal of Monetary Economics* 24 (November): 401–421.

Weil, Philippe. 1990. "Nonexpected Utility in Macroeconomics." *Quarterly Journal of Economics* 105 (February): 29–42.

**Weingast, Barry, Shepsle, Kenneth, and Johnsen, Christopher. 1981.** "The Political Economy of Benefits and Costs: A Neoclassical Approach to Distributive Politics." *Journal of Political Economy* 89 (August): 642-664.

**Weise, Charles. 2009.** "Political Constraints on Monetary Policy during the U.S. Great Inflation." Unpublished paper (October).

**Weiss, Andrew. 1980.** "Job Queues and Layoffs in Labor Markets with Flexible Wages." *Journal of Political Economy* 88 (June): 526-538.

**Weitzman, Martin L. 1974.** "Prices vs. Quantities." *Review of Economic Studies* 41 (October): 477-491.

**West, Kenneth D. 1988.** "The Insensitivity of Consumption to News about Income." *Journal of Monetary Economics* 21 (January): 17-33.

**Wilhelm, Mark O. 1996.** "Bequest Behavior and the Effect of Heirs' Earnings: Testing the Altruistic Model of Bequests." *American Economic Review* 86 (September): 874-892.

**Williams, John C. 2009.** "Heeding Daedalus: Optimal Inflation and the Zero Lower Bound." Unpublished paper (October). *Brookings Papers on Economic Activity*, forthcoming.

**Williamson, Stephen D. 2008.** "Monetary Policy and Distribution." *Journal of Monetary Economics* 55 (September): 1038-1053.

**Woglom, Geoffrey. 1982.** "Underemployment Equilibrium with Rational Expectations." *Quarterly Journal of Economics* 97 (February): 89-107.

**Wolff, Edward N. 1998.** "Recent Trends in the Size Distribution of Household Wealth." *Journal of Economic Perspectives* 12 (Summer): 131-150.

**Woodford, Michael. 1990.** "Learning to Believe in Sunspots." *Econometrica* 58 (March): 277-307.

**Woodford, Michael. 1995.** "Price-Level Determinacy without Control of a Monetary Aggregate." *Carnegie-Rochester Conference Series on Public Policy* 43 (December): 1-46.

**Woodford, Michael. 2003.** *Interest and Prices: Foundations of a Theory of Monetary Policy.* Princeton: Princeton University Press.

**Working, Holbrook. 1960.** "A Note on the Correlation of First Differences of Averages in a Random Chain." *Econometrica* 28 (October): 916-918.

# Y

**Yotsuzuka, Toshiki. 1987.** "Ricardian Equivalence in the Presence of Capital Market Imperfections." *Journal of Monetary Economics* 20 (September): 411-436.

**Young, Alwyn. 1995.** "The Tyranny of Numbers: Confronting the Statistical Reality of the East Asian Growth Experience." *Quarterly Journal of Economics* 110 (August): 641-680.

**Young, Alwyn. 1998.** "Alternative Estimates of Productivity Growth in the NIC's: A Comment on the Findings of Chang-Tai Hsieh." National Bureau of Economic Research Working Paper No. 6657 (July).

# Z

**Zeldes, Stephen P. 1989.** "Consumption and Liquidity Constraints: An Empirical Investigation." *Journal of Political Economy* 97 (April): 305-346.

# AUTHOR INDEX

# SUBJECT INDEX

C6
ROM: Adv
(A)